The Great American Mosaic

Volume 1
African American Experience

Volume 2
American Indian Experience

Volume 3
Asian American and Pacific Islander Experience

Volume 4
Latino American Experience

The Great American Mosaic

An Exploration of Diversity in Primary Documents

Gary Y. Okihiro, General Editor

Volume 4
Latino American Experience

Guadalupe Compeán, Volume Editor

GREENWOOD

AN IMPRINT OF ABC-CLIO, LLC
Santa Barbara, California • Denver, Colorado • Oxford, England

Every reasonable effort has been made to trace the owners of copyright materials in this book, but in some instances this has proven impossible. The editors and publisher will be glad to receive information leading to more complete acknowledgments in subsequent printings of the book and in the meantime extend their apologies for any omissions.

Library of Congress Cataloging-in-Publication Data

The great American mosaic: an exploration of diversity in primary documents/Gary Y. Okihiro, general editor.
volumes cm
Contents: Volume 1. African American Experience/Lionel C. Bascom, volume editor.
ISBN 978-1-61069-612-8 (hardback : acid-free paper)—ISBN
978-1-61069-613-5 (ebook) 1. Cultural pluralism—United States—History—Sources. 2. United States—Race relations—History—Sources. 3. United States—Ethnic relations—History—Sources. 4. Minorities—United States—History—Sources. 5. United States—History—Sources. I. Okihiro, Gary Y., 1945- II. Bascom, Lionel C.
E184.A1G826 2014
305.800973—dc23 2014007428

ISBN: 978-1-61069-612-8
EISBN: 978-1-61069-613-5

18 17 16 15 14 1 2 3 4 5

This book is also available on the World Wide Web as an eBook.
Visit www.abc-clio.com for details.

Greenwood
An Imprint of ABC-CLIO, LLC

ABC-CLIO, LLC
130 Cremona Drive, P.O. Box 1911
Santa Barbara, California 93116-1911

This book is printed on acid-free paper ♾
Manufactured in the United States of America

Contents

Volume 4: Latino American Experience

Colonies of New Spain (1500–1802)

Struggles for Independence (1803–1846)

Mexican-American War

Defining the U.S.-Mexico Border

Voices Mexicanas (1850s–1870s)

Concepts of Land (1848–1900)

Latinos and Independence Movements South of the Border (1848–1860)

Chicano Movement

Latinos (1980–2010)

Chicanas/Chicanos and Mexican Americans in Contemporary Society

General Introduction

Peoples of color—African Americans, Asian and Pacific Islander Americans, Latinas/Latinos, and Native Americans—were not always included within the American mosaic. In fact, throughout much of the nation's history, peoples of color were not members or citizens of these United States. In 1787, John Jay, a Founding Father and a leading designer of the nation-state, declared in "Concerning the Dangers from Foreign Force and Influence," essays that were part of *The Federalist* papers, that Americans are "one united people—a people descended from the same ancestors, speaking the same language, professing the same religion, attached to the same principles of government, very similar in their manners and customs."

Jay's "one united people" were Europeans, foreigners, who called themselves "persons" and "whites" in the new nation's Constitution, laws, and census. Those not included within that racialized, nationalized category or "the citizen race" in the words of U.S. Supreme Court chief justice Roger Taney in *Dred Scott v. Sandford* (1857), were of "another and different class of persons" and they represented "foreign dangers," threatening disunity and conflict. It is the experiences of those peoples that *The Great American Mosaic: An Exploration of Diversity in Primary Documents* covers in its four volumes. Volume 1 provides a collection of documents exploring the African American experience; Volume 2, the American Indian experience; Volume 3, the Asian American and Pacific Islander experience; and Volume 4, the Latino experience.

Standard narratives of the nation routinely excluded peoples of color. Only around the mid-20th century did U.S. history textbooks reflect more fully the nation's diversity, highlighting especially the presence of African Americans. Still, the architecture of American history remains white at its core; Native Americans, including American Indians and Pacific Islanders, formed the environment and background for white expansion and settlement, and African and Asian Americans and Latinas/Latinos played minor notes in an anthem devoted to the European nation.

Indeed, the nation, since the English invasion and colonization of America in the 17th century, systematically excluded peoples of color from the privileges and protections accorded Taney's "citizen race." "We, the people" of the U.S. Constitution was never intended to embrace nonwhites; that exclusion is the foundational premise upon which the nation was conceived. Conversely, the inclusion of peoples of color democratized the nation and was truly revolutionary. The American Revolution, by contrast, was not transformative in that the new nation was an extension of the original white settler colonialism that infringed upon these shores.

American Indians

To the invaders, American Indians were impediments to their freedom, especially embodied in the concept of "free" land. Conquest and expulsion were the means of American Indian alienation whereby English foreigners became natives on their sovereign estates, and the land's natives became aliens. The English-drawn border of 1763, despite its porous nature, was indicative of that demarcation, that segregation of "citizens" from "aliens."

The postcolonial nation acknowledged that arrangement in the Treaty of Greenville (1795), which recognized Indian sovereignty in territories not claimed by the United States. In *Worcester v. Georgia* (1832), the U.S. Supreme Court declared the Cherokee nation to be a "foreign state," a condition reaffirmed by Chief Justice Taney in his *Dred Scott* (1857) majority opinion. As Taney wrote, the United States signed treaties with American Indian nations, "under subjection to the white race," and, accordingly, in the United States whites were the "citizen race" and American Indians were "aliens."

That exclusion shifted with the white flood, which by the late 19th century had engulfed the entire continent from sea to shining sea. Following the final bloody wars of conquest waged mainly against Indians of the Great Plains, the U.S. census of 1890 declared in that year, which saw the massacre of Indian men, women, and children at Wounded Knee, that the entire continent had been filled (by whites). President Theodore Roosevelt called those lands, memorably, the "red wastes," and other men called them "virgin land." There were no more frontiers for manly probing and capture.

Conquest achieved, the Dawes Act (1887) sought to dissolve Indian nations and assimilate American Indians as individuals. Soon thereafter, the U.S. Supreme Court affirmed, in *Lone Wolf v. Hitchcock* (1903), the plenary powers of Congress over Indian nations because they constituted "domestic dependent nations." The assimilation continued with U.S. citizenship bestowed in 1924 on those born after that year, and, in 1940, on all American Indians.

Following a brief interlude during the New Deal of the 1930s, the attempt to absorb American Indians politically and culturally continued into the 1950s, when Dillon Myer, as chief of the Bureau of Indian Affairs, pursued the policy called appropriately "termination." Myer had experience with termination, having administered the concentration camps for Japanese Americans as the War Relocation Authority's director during World War II.

American Indians, thus, were at first excluded as "foreign" nations and peoples, and, after conquest, were assimilated and rendered domestic dependencies and dependents.

African Americans

Like American Indians, African Americans were "aliens" excluded from community membership. In 1669, a Virginia colony jury ruled that Anthony Johnson was "a Negroe and by consequence an alien." Race determined citizenship. The postcolonial nation and its founding

Constitution (1787) specified that African Americans were not "persons" but "three fifths of all other Persons" and thereby failed to qualify for full representation in the Congress.

In fact, as Chief Justice Taney held in *Dred Scott* (1857): "Negroes of the African race" and their descendants "are not included, and were not intended to be included, under the word 'citizens' in the Constitution, and can therefore claim none of the rights and privileges which that instrument provides for and secures to citizens of the United States." Moreover, Taney pointed out, from the republic's founding, the 1790 Naturalization Act limited citizenship to "free white persons," making clear the distinction between the "citizen race" or whites and "persons of color" or those "not included in the word citizens."

That separation dissolved with the Thirteenth (1865), Fourteenth (1868), and Fifteenth (1870) Amendments to the U.S. Constitution, which, respectively, ended slavery, extended citizenship to all persons born in the United States, and enfranchised men regardless of "race, color, or previous condition of servitude." In 1870, Congress extended to Africans the right of naturalization. African American citizens, although without full equality under Jim Crow, transformed the complexion of the "citizen race" and, thus, the nation. The change was a radical break with the past; it was, in fact, revolutionary.

Still, racial segregation was the primary instrument of the state to secure African American political and economic dependency, and Jim Crow, as was affirmed by *Plessy v. Ferguson* (1896), ruled the land until *Brown v. Board of Education* (1954), which integrated public schools. In *Plessy*, the U.S. Supreme Court ruled that racial segregation in private businesses, conducted under the doctrine of "separate but equal," fulfilled the Fourteenth Amendment's equal protection clause. States routinely denied African American men and, after 1920, women access to the ballot through property and literacy requirements from the end of Reconstruction in the 1870s to the Voting Rights Act of 1965.

Latinas/Latinos

Mexican Americans were a people made through conquest, much like American Indians. In the 1820s and 1830s, Americans, many of them owning slaves, settled in the Mexican province of Texas. These white Protestant settlers, never comfortable in a Catholic republic that sought to end slavery, shook off Mexican control in 1836. In 1845, the United States admitted Texas as a state, an action that helped precipitate the Mexican American War (1846–1848). Driven by Manifest Destiny, an expansionist doctrine that proclaimed the God-given right of the United States to expand across the North American continent, the U.S. government, after defeating Mexico, demanded the cession of almost half of Mexico's territory, land that later formed the entire states of California, Nevada, and Utah, as well as portions of Colorado, Wyoming, Arizona, and New Mexico. The Treaty of Guadalupe Hidalgo (1848), which ended the war, granted U.S. citizenship to Mexican residents of the ceded lands, and Mexicans were thus rendered "white" by treaty. At the same time, many Mexican Americans lost their farms and land, like American Indians, and were widely denied equality in employment, housing, and education on the basis of race, class, and culture.

Judicial decisions commonly cited the contradiction between Mexican whiteness by treaty and Mexicans as a mestizo and "mongrel" race by scientific and common opinion. Further, courts decided, in accordance with the one-drop rule, that is, one drop of nonwhite blood meant a person was considered nonwhite, that children of whites and nonwhites were "colored." This principle was applied in such cases as *In re Camille* (1880), involving a white father and American Indian mother, and *In re Young* (1912), involving a white father and Japanese mother. Still, as *In re Rodriguez* (1897), the courts were compelled to rule that Mexican Americans were white and thus citizens. At the same time, whiteness in theory disallowed Mexican American claims of racial discrimination in practice, such as the right to a trial of their peers, which, if granted, would end instances of all-Anglo juries ruling on Mexican Americans.

The state segregated Mexican American children in inferior schools on the basis of language and "migrant farming patterns," as was affirmed by a Texas court in *Independent School District v. Salvatierra* (1930). Mexicans emerged from the white race in the 1930 U.S. census and appeared as "Mexicans." The enumeration facilitated the expulsion to Mexico of about half a million Mexican and Mexican Americans from the United States during the Great Depression, when their labor was no longer required. That removal complemented the 1935 Filipino Repatriation Act, which offered Filipino Americans, like Mexican American migrant laborers, free passage to the Philippines.

Asian and Pacific Islander Americans

The 1790 Naturalization Act, which limited U.S. citizenship to "free white persons," excluded Pacific Islanders and Asians, like American Indians and African Americans, from the "citizen race." In the 1850s, California's supreme court chief judge Hugh Murray affirmed the distinction between "a free white citizen of this State" and American Indians, Africans, Pacific Islanders, and Asians, those "not of white blood," in Murray's words. Unlike Native Americans, including American Indians and Pacific Islanders, whose utility to the nation involved mainly their land, Asians were employed, like African and Mexican Americans, as laborers.

As persons "not of white blood," Pacific Islander and Asian men served as slaves and servants to whites; appealed to whites and antislavery societies for manumission; married American Indian, African American, and Mexican women; were counted in the U.S. census as colored and mulatto; fought in African American units in the Civil War; and were buried in colored cemeteries. Like Mexicans, Asians and Pacific Islanders served employers as migrant laborers, mainly in agriculture but also in mines and on railroads; formed unions irrespective of race; and married and produced bicultural children.

Unique among people of color in the United States was the persistent condition of Asians as "aliens ineligible to citizenship" under the 1790 Naturalization Act. Mexicans by treaty and African Americans and American Indians through law acquired U.S. citizenship, albeit absent its full rights and privileges. Unable to naturalize, Asians and Pacific Islanders gained U.S. citizenship by birth under the Fourteenth Amendment. Chinese acquired the right to naturalization in 1943, South Asians and Filipinos in 1946, and Japanese and Koreans not until 1952. Accordingly, the United States denied Asians naturalization rights for more than 160 years, from 1790 to 1952.

Tempering those acts of inclusion were immigration quotas imposed on Asians and Pacific Islanders. Starting in 1929, under the Johnson-Reed Immigrant Act (1924), Congress assigned an annual quota of 100 each to those immigrating from Australia and Melanesia, Bhutan, China, India, Iran, Iraq, Japan, Micronesia, Nepal, New Zealand, Oman, Sāmoa, and Thailand.

The law gave to Turkey, straddling Europe and Asia, a quota of 226. Likewise, the law assigned to African nations, from Egypt to South Africa, annual quotas of 100.

European countries, by contrast, which supplied the "citizen race," received quotas of 1,181 (Denmark), 2,377 (Norway), 3,153 (Netherlands), 5,802 (Italy), 17,853 (Irish Free State), 25,957 (Germany), and 65,721 (Great Britain and Northern Ireland). In force until 1965, the Johnson-Reed Act established the nation's first comprehensive, restrictive immigration policy. The act also served to define the nation, its citizens, and its peoples—called a race—by excluding those who were deemed unworthy or even dangerous. In that sense, immigration is a matter of national defense and homeland security.

Imperialism

Conquest did not end with the filling of the continent. The nation, in the late 19th century, extended its imperial reach overseas to the Caribbean and Pacific. Peoples indigenous to and settled upon those territories thereby became Americans, though not fully. After the Spanish-American War of 1898, Puerto Ricans and Filipinos, natives of unincorporated territories, followed divergent paths; Puerto Ricans became U.S. citizens in 1917, and Filipino nationals became Asian aliens in 1934. Contrarily, Hawaiians and Alaska's indigenous peoples, natives of incorporated territories, became U.S. citizens, whereas those in the unincorporated territories of Guam, where "America's day begins," are U.S. citizens while those in American Sāmoa are nationals.

American Mosaic

Founding Father John Jay's "one united people" diversified with the nation's expansion. European immigration during the late 19th century was unlike the usual flow from Great Britain and northern Europe. These new immigrants came from southern and eastern Europe and brought with them different religions, languages, and cultures. Nonetheless, most, through Americanization and assimilation, became members of the white, citizen race.

Peoples of color were not counted among that number at first, and when they became Americans and citizens, they transformed the nation and its peoples from a people descended from the same ancestors to an American mosaic. Racism and segregation, nonetheless, deferred dreams and attenuated the achievement of that revolution. As the documents in these four volumes testify, however, peoples of color are more than minor figures in the nation's narrative; they are central to it, and the documents collected in these volumes shed new light on that history, revealing a more complex, diverse, and troubled American past.

These documents expand upon the standard narratives of nation, which have, for the most part, excluded and marginalized peoples of color. They offer a fuller, more comprehensive understanding of these United States, and are of great consequence for all Americans. They are also important for peoples of color. As Frantz Fanon pointed out in his *The Wretched of the Earth* (1961), colonization denies a people their past, leading to "estrangement" from their history and culture. Freedom requires a recuperation of "the whole body of efforts made by a people in the sphere of thought to describe, justify, and praise the action through which that people has created itself and keeps itself in existence" (p. 233).

We, the people, and descendants of the nation's branching genealogy possess the ability and share the responsibility to shape a more inclusive, equitable, and democratic future.

Gary Y. Okihiro

Volume Introduction

Introduction: The Latino American Experience

Latino American Experience, volume 4 of *The Great Mosaic: An Exploration of Diversity in Primary Documents,* offers a balance of primary and secondary documents that shed light on relations between Latinos and other ethnic groups. As a group, Latinos include Mexican Americans, Puerto Ricans, Cuban Americans, Dominican Americans, and Central American immigrants. Although the primary focus of this volume is Latinos in the United States, contextual documents concerning events in Mexico, Puerto Rico, Cuba and the Caribbean, and Central and South America are included as well. Source types include letters, memoirs, speeches, articles, essays, interviews, treaties, government reports, testimony, oral histories, and other documents of historical importance. This volume contains documents that present the voices of whites and African Americans as well as of Latinos, of people both prominent and obscure, and of European Americans as well as of people outside the United States. The volume does not provide documents for each of the more than 20 Latin American nations equally, as it would if it were documenting the history of Latin America.

The Colonial Period

In the New World, the Spanish colonial period ran from the first voyage of Christopher Columbus in 1492 to the success of the colonial independence movements in Mexico and Central and South America in the early 19th century. During the period, Spain controlled not only the lands of the former Aztec empire in central Mexico but also territories to the north that today extend across northern Mexico and into the present-day American states of Texas, New Mexico, Arizona, Utah, Nevada, and California. Spain also controlled Central America, most of South America (except for Portuguese Brazil), and the Caribbean. Spanish language, culture, and religion, mixed with the thought and culture of the indigenous peoples the Spanish ruled, permeated these areas during the 400 years they were governed by the Spanish Crown. It was this blend of Spanish and indigenous cultures that Americans encountered when they began to expand across the North American continent in the early 19th century.

The documents covering this period provide views of the Aztec state as it existed at the time of the Spanish arrival in Tenochtitlan, the Aztec capital, in 1519, as well as descriptions of the establishment of Spanish rule in Mexico, Central America, and the American Southwest. Travelers' accounts from the 16th and 17th centuries provide the first lines of a continuous and evolving narrative of Latino history.

The 19th Century

The 19th century saw the formation of borders between the United States and Latin America. Slowly, the United States exceeded its borders, encroaching on the lands of Native Americans and then of neighboring nations. Slavery was the engine that drove U.S. expansion at a frantic pace. After the United States annexed the Louisiana Territory in 1803, the country looked south to what is today Mexico, and, in 1819, after it absorbed Florida into its borders, slave interests looked to Cuba.

By the 1820s, the religious notion of Manifest Destiny found expression in the Monroe Doctrine (1823), which essentially proclaimed that the Americas were for Americans. Slave interests moved into what is today Texas. Two wars were fought with Mexico (1836, 1846–1848); these conflicts, along with the Gadsden Purchase (1853), created 2,000 miles of border dividing the United States and Mexico. The Texas-Mexican War (1836) and the Mexican-American War (1846–1848) left indelible scars. Mexico lost half its land and great rivers like the Rio Grande, Colorado, and Gila. The Treaty of Guadalupe Hidalgo (1848) is one of the most important primary documents in the history of people of Mexican origin in the United States. This important treaty affected their property and civil rights, and this document collection explores the treaty.

Documents from the period after 1848 deal with European American and Mexican relations on the border. The largest mass of Spanish-speaking people was found along the 2,000-mile U.S.-Mexican border as people of Mexican origin crossed at will. Latinos other than Mexicans lived in the Southwest; however, they were generally assimilated into the Mexican community. Treaties, boundary commissions, and racism became important elements of this dialectic once the border was defined and incorporated people of Mexican and Indian extraction into the United States.

Newspapers were an important part of the Mexican experience, as was racial conflict. It has been estimated that at least 132 Spanish-language or bilingual newspapers were published in the southwestern United States between 1848 and 1900. In many ways, the documents in this collection show the other side—the English-language side. The Mexican voices include María Amparo Ruiz de Burton, the first Mexican woman to write novels in English.

The next Latino nationalities in contact with European Americans were Cubans and Puerto Ricans. The Cuban presence was felt by the 1850s in the aftermath of the Mexican-American War. Cuba is 90 miles south of Florida. Despite Cuba's proximity to the United States, the Cuban experience differed from the Mexican experience; it was a lot easier to walk across a line than to swim across a sea. Puerto Rico is a thousand miles from Florida, and distance definitely was a barrier to mass migration. These two Caribbean islands did not gain independence until the turn of the century. Nevertheless, they inherited the negative feelings European Americans had toward Mexicans and Spaniards.

Many European Americans—especially southerners—believed it was just a matter of time before the United States acquired these fertile islands off the coast of Florida that were run by what they considered corrupt Spaniards. In 1850, Cuba had a white population of 565,560; it also had 204,570 free Africans, and 436,400 African slaves. The Puerto Rican population was not as large as the Cuban population but was concentrated in a much smaller space. The fact that Central America is an isthmus containing the shortest point between the Atlantic and Pacific oceans, made it vital to the interests of the United States. Central American market resources, such as coffee and bananas, also attracted European American adventurers and investors who wanted to seize land for the United States. Because of trade between the two sides of the hemisphere, especially after the 1849 California Gold Rush, interest in an inter-ocean canal increased, and Cuba and then Puerto Rico became gateways to the isthmus of Central America.

Exiles such as José Martí spent two decades in the United States. He began his exile in this country full of hope for the independence of Cuba from Spain, but racism and political realities embittered him. The Cuban cigar industry began a presence in Key West, Florida, in 1831. By the 1880s, cigar makers were closely associated with the Cuban independence movement. During this period, Cuba overshadowed Puerto Rico, not because the latter did not have its share of intellectuals—as mentioned, its population numbers rivaled those of Cuba—but because of Puerto Rico's distance from the U.S. mainland.

The Spanish-American War to 1930

Many documents in this volume deal with the forging of an imperialist U.S. mentality—an attitude that would lead to Latin Americans labeling the United States the "Colossus of the North"—an image that was confirmed during the first three decades of the 20th century by U.S. treatment of the Caribbean and Central America. At the conclusion of the Spanish-American War in 1898, Puerto Ricans were forcefully annexed to the United States, and life for Puerto Ricans worsened under the U.S. occupation. The tenuousness of the relation reinforced Puerto Rican nationalism. The war transformed the Puerto Rican economy and accelerated the diaspora of Puerto Rican workers throughout the region and to parts of the United States. In some documents, readers will be introduced to Puerto Ricans who are not normally portrayed in texts. After the United States took over the Panama Canal project in 1904, President Theodore Roosevelt built a web that included the Caribbean and Central America within the "U.S. sphere of influence" and with a policy that called for defense of "America's" canal in Panama at all costs.

Throughout their history in the United States, Mexican Americans and Puerto Ricans fought for civil rights, and, as their populations grew, they won the entitlements and guarantees that all Latinos now have and enjoy under the law. One of the first court cases was brought by Ricardo Rodríguez, a native of Mexico who had lived in Texas for 10 years. He petitioned to become a naturalized U.S. citizen in 1897, but was denied. The catch-22 was that only white people could become citizens; Mexicans were not considered white, so they could not be citizens. The dilemma was resolved by blurring the racial status of Mexicans because the Treaty of Guadalupe Hidalgo, which ended the Mexican-American War in 1848, inferred that they were white—that is, the treaty made Mexicans neither Indians nor Asians because they could be citizens. Time and again the catch-22 was not resolved but short-circuited to the disadvantage of Latinos.

In the 1880s, the Mexican Central Railroad linked Mexico with the United States, facilitating and determining the movement of huge numbers of workers from Mexico's interior to build the American Southwest. Industrialization demanded large numbers of unskilled workers. This migration accelerated at the turn of the century, which also saw large waves of Mexicans pulled into the United States by the dramatic expansion of U.S. mines, farms, railroads, and cities. The U.S. economic expansion in Mexico accelerated the demise of small subsistence farms and uprooted thousands of small farmers and peasants.

The immigration history of other groups that came to the United States greatly affected the migration of Mexicans to the United States—the exclusion of the Chinese and then the limiting of European immigration created a demand for Mexican labor. The start of the Mexican Revolution in 1910 accelerated migration to the United States. Because of the proximity of Mexico, the populations on both sides of the border reacted to events north and south of the border. Hence, the Mexican Revolution played a huge role in the formation of stereotypes, such as the violent Mexican outlaw and the need for the Texas Rangers. Later, World War I acted as a key event in forming a Mexican American identity.

The formation of the Puerto Rican identity differed from that of the Mexican identity during the 1910s. Readers should not limit themselves to what is happening on the U.S. mainland but must also take into account the island of Puerto Rico, which is, after all, part of the United States. The Jones-Shafroth Act (1917) made Puerto Ricans citizens—consequently, they were eligible for the military draft.

During the 1920s, U.S. intervention in the Caribbean and Central America increased. The documents of this period provide a valuable context for future migration and understanding the Latino stereotype. Cuban exiles and workers had been trickling into the United States for some time. According to the 1910 Census, the number of Cubans in the United States was officially more than 15,000, and most Cubans were concentrated in Florida and New York.

During the 1920s, second-generation middle-class and labor organizations emerged among Mexican Americans. By this time, the profile of the group was shifting from rural to urban. Before this time, mutual aid societies were the most popular form of organization. As with Puerto Rican and other Latino nationalities, first-generation societies concentrated on homeland issues. The 1920s saw a transformation of these groups that formed second-generation associations to deal more with local issues and obtaining equality under the law than with concerns about the homeland. The link between population and power became more evident as more groups took to the courts to protect their civil rights.

Between 1910 and 1920, at least 219,000 Mexican immigrants entered the United States. (The actual figure was probably closer to one million.) This doubled the population of Mexican origin in Arizona, New Mexico, and Texas. In California, it quadrupled. The best estimate is that there were between 1.5 and 2 million people of Mexican origin in the United States by 1930. Some would say that the number was closer to 3 million. The growing Mexican presence produced an intense nativist reaction, and segregated schools jumped in number by at least 50 percent. This was all done under the guise of Americanization.

The immigration acts of 1921 and 1924 are cornerstones in the history of all Latinos, with the exception of Puerto Ricans, who were U.S. citizens as of 1917. The early 20th century began a period of social engineering when U.S. immigration policy was designed to maintain a nation that was not only white but also as northern European as possible. Mexicans were excluded from the quotas because they were crucial to U.S. agriculture, and Latin Americans were not subjected to immigration quotas because they simply lived too far away to come here in significant numbers. During this period, Mexican individuals and organizations filed successful desegregation suits.

Greater numbers meant more organizations, more people studying the group, more literacy, and more awareness. A significant number of Mexican Americans served during World War I; they returned home with a much different attitude toward their rights. The 1920s ended, almost symbolically, with the 1929 formation of the League of United Latin American Citizens, a middle-class, citizens-only organization that was the premier Mexican American civil rights organization of the time.

The Great Depression, World War II, and the 1950s

The next period covered in the documents is the Great Depression, which began in 1929 and lasted throughout most of the 1930s. The Depression devastated Puerto Rico, where the remaining small farmers were almost wiped out. But also important is that Pan American Airlines began its first flights to Miami, Florida, from the island—partially overcoming the 1,000-mile gap between Puerto Rico and the mainland. Meanwhile, Florida continued to house a large Cuban population, many of whom were Afro-Cubans. The cigar industry declined in the Great Depression, and an unsuccessful 1931 strike devastated the union. The decade accelerated a migration of Afro-Cubans back to Cuba and to the U.S. Northeast. Fifty percent of Florida's Afro-Cuban population left Florida in the 1930s. Job opportunities seemed better in Cuba or the North. Fifty percent of the Afro-Cuban community left Tampa between 1930 and 1940, leaving older members to try keeping the community together.

Militancy remained high in Puerto Rico as the needle workers, mostly women, struck for better wages. New Deal acts such as the National Recovery Administration bypassed the island, worsening an already dire economic situation. The decade also saw the rise of the Puerto Rican Nationalist Party as misery on the island grew. Throughout the Caribbean, sugar prices fell drastically, and workers were without a source of income. In turn, the lack of income increased political discontent. On March 21, 1937, at Ponce, Puerto Rico, some 100 demonstrators were wounded and 19 killed, including 17 men, a woman, and a seven-year-old girl. The documents on Puerto Rico from this era are key because they set the stage for the mass migration to the mainland that accelerated in 1945.

The Great Depression also had a huge impact on the segment of the U.S. population that was of Mexican origin. Between 600,000 and a million Mexicans were repatriated (deported) and targeted as scapegoats for economic problems during the Depression. The documents included in this volume encapsulate this period. What was life like for these people? Because of the size of the group, more interviews and oral histories were recorded than in previous years, and attention was paid to this group.

At this time, Mexicans were also migrating within the United States and beginning to live outside the Southwest. The Midwest had a sizable Mexican population in the 1930s. Chicago had as many as 25,000 Mexicans in 1930. However, as in every aspect of Mexican life, repatriation drives affected the Mexican community in the Midwest, which shrank to 16,000 by the end of the decade.

An estimated 400,000 Mexican Americans and 53,000 Puerto Ricans fought in World War II. The war was a turning point in the history of these people. They were greatly affected and changed by the experience. As in previous sections, the documents from the war years complement existing texts.

The war changed the worldviews of an entire generation. The war brought changes in Latino groups as well as to Mexican Americans. Many Latino soldiers returned to the home front only to encounter the same racial discrimination they had left before going to war. The Zoot Suit Riots in 1943 and the infamous Sleepy Lagoon murder trial the year before represent turning points in the cultural identities and historical experiences of Mexican Americans in the United States. In the case of Puerto Ricans, many had been transported to the mainland and taken across oceans to Africa, Europe, and Asia. The war brought an increased awareness of the strategic value of Puerto Rico and Latin America, as technological breakthroughs in aviation made travel cheaper and safer than before.

Many Puerto Ricans were brought over on labor contracts. Disillusionment gripped many Puerto Ricans, and some refused military service. Still, approximately 60,000 Puerto Ricans served in Korea in the early 1950s. Meanwhile, tensions built on the island as the Nationalists gained strength. The fact that poverty increased and the U.S. presence grew on the island solidified opposition. In 1950, Nationalists led an assault on Blair House in Washington, D.C., where President Harry Truman was being temporarily housed. Four years later, the Nationalists led an attack on Congress. They were labeled terrorists instead of nationalists. The surge in Puerto Rican nationalism accompanied the rise of nationalist, populist, and anticolonial movements throughout Latin America.

Fear of Soviet-Communist involvement in the hemisphere renewed calls for adherence to the Monroe Doctrine and saw increased U.S. support of right-wing dictatorships. Four years after the attack on Blair House, the Central Intelligence Agency (CIA) directed the overthrow of the constitutionally elected Guatemalan government. In 1958, the United States sent troops to Panama after flag protests erupted there. The decade ended with the success of Fidel Castro in Cuba and his triumphant march into Havana.

World War II brought changes for the 350,000 to 400,000 Mexican Americans who served in the armed forces. The war caused labor shortages and thus created opportunity for those who remained behind. Women were pressed into service in the labor force. Mexican Americans won 17 Medals of Honor during the war. Many returned from the frontlines determined to demand first-class citizenship and their rights as Americans. Cases such as the Sleepy Lagoon case (1942) increased awareness of racial injustices. New organizations such as the American G.I. Forum and the Community Service Organization evolved in response to inequality. They joined older Mexican American organizations in the courts.

After the war, more Mexican Americans also participated in the political process by registering to vote in their communities. The corresponding documents reflect on the growing concern over immigration and the role of the Mexican American community in protecting the rights of the foreign born. Mexican Americans closed out the 1950s a more aware and involved community.

The 1960s to the Present

The 1960s were driven by a global decline in colonialism, the baby boom, the African American civil rights movement, and the Vietnam War. There had been a surge in the Puerto Rican population on the mainland during the previous decades. After the triumph of Fidel

Castro in the Cuban Revolution, the number of Cubans, mostly in the Miami, Florida, area, increased dramatically. In 1959, the number of Cubans in the United States was estimated at 124,000. After this point, many of the wealthier Cubans fled the island to protect their assets. During the 1960s, about 215,000 Cubans moved to the United States.

Economic problems and political turmoil in the Dominican Republic also led to a vast migration of Dominicans to the United States. Throughout the century, the United States had sought stability in the region by supporting dictators. The United States worsened the situation in 1965 by invading the Dominican Republic and preventing constitutionally elected president Juan Bosch from taking office.

The 1960 census counted 892,513 Puerto Ricans in the mainland United States. Almost 72 percent, 642,622, lived in New York; 55,351 in New Jersey; and 36,081 in Illinois. The rest were scattered throughout the country. During the preceding decade, migration had quickened, with an average of 45,000 annually migrating to the United States. Migration slowed in the 1960s in response to temporary improvements and jobs created by Operation Bootstrap, which had been started in 1948 to industrialize the island. The annual migration of Puerto Ricans was cut by more than half. However, the natural increase offset this decrease.

The U.S. Cubans remained obsessed with what was happening in Cuba. Because the first wave of immigrants was an educated portion of the middle class, Cuban Americans acquired political power, whereas Puerto Ricans remained marginal. The Borinquen (as the island of Puerto Rico was called by the Taíno Indians native to the island) community was involved in protesting the Vietnam War and demanding civil rights for the community. There were still cries for self-determination for the island but the struggle for equality in the United States took some of the steam from that movement—although not entirely. For example, there was uproar about reports that mainland employers on the island used the mass sterilizations of Puerto Rican women as a hiring practice. Nationalism continued, mingling with the socialist ideas of the day.

In 1973, the CIA participated in the overthrow of Chilean president Salvador Allende. This act sent ripples throughout Latin America and led to the immigration of a small number of Chilean political refugees. Changes were also taking place in Central America that would influence the composition of the Latino community in the United States. Since the 1960s, the Catholic Church through *comunidades de base*, base communities, had been politicizing Central Americans. As they grew more militant, the military and local elites clamped down on the dissidents. In El Salvador, the military assassinated a Jesuit priest in 1977. The opposition grew, and, in 1979, rebels overthrew Nicaraguan dictator Anastasio Somoza, who moved to Miami, Florida.

In 1960, there were officially about 3.5 million U.S. residents of Mexican origin in the Southwest (actual numbers were surely much larger). The largest concentrations were in California and Texas, about 1.5 million Mexicans apiece. Fewer than 55 percent were native born, and their median age was 19.6 compared with 30.4 for European Americans. The median age had fallen by a year in both cases. Migration from Mexico quickened during the decade as Mexico's population from 1940 to 1970 increased by 250 percent—growing at an average of 3.4 percent per year from 1960 to 1970. Mexico's population zoomed from 27.4 million in 1950 to 37.1 million in 1960 and 51.2 million in 1970.

The period saw the rise of grassroots political and labor movements. Cesar Chavez and the United Farm Workers worked for economic and social justice in order to secure the right to unionize and empower migrant laborers through nonviolent principles. Chicano youth were nationalistic and wanted to end the exploitation of Mexicans in the United States. As a group, young Chicanos were exposed to civil rights violations and the horrors of the Vietnam War. Activist groups like the Black Berets and the Brown Berets were part of this formation that included Chicano students. Their rhetoric took on cultural symbols, and they reacted vigorously to racism. Aztlán, the legendary birthplace of the Aztecs, became a symbol to show that they were not foreigners in the United States but were native to the land and had ties to a culture that predated the original 13 colonies. They adopted the name Chicano, and increasingly militant tactics invigorated the social movements of the time by giving hope that their catch-22 dilemma could be resolved.

The 1960s brought a growing awareness of inequities as organizations evolved to take advantage of the recognition of Chicanos as an entitled group. Both Puerto Ricans and Mexican Americans were influenced by nationalism, socialism, and anticolonial theories. This brought about the question not only of equality of race but also of gender. For Chicanos, these events reached a climax at the Chicano Moratorium of 1970, after which three people involved in a peaceful rally were killed, including journalist Rubén Salazar. For Puerto Ricans, the 1970s witnessed Puerto Rican nationalist uprisings.

The 1970s also brought increased numbers of Mexican immigrants who did not accept the Chicano identity, in large part because it was not defined for them. Immigrants did not have the same historical memory or sense as the Mexican Americans or Chicanos had, and the schools substituted the illusion of inclusion for the reality that they were not Hispanics or Latinos. This development shifted the focus from the struggle, protections, and entitlements under the law won by the Mexican American and Chicano generations. Subtly, the illusion arose that the catch-22 dilemma could be solved for all Latinos through political brokers and more professionals.

Meanwhile, events south of the border increased immigration. The Immigration Act of 1965 brought large numbers of Asians and Middle Easterners to the country as its policy shifted from national origins to family preferences. In reality, Latin Americans were discriminated against because the United States had historically sold the myth that the peoples of the Americas were members of the same family. This part of the family was not subject to immigration quotas until 1965.

Shaken by the fall of U.S.-friendly Nicaraguan dictator Anastasio Somoza in 1979, the United States stepped up its involvement in Central America. The United States carried on a war to overthrow the leftist Sandinistas in Nicaragua in the 1980s and gave massive military aid to the right-wing governments of El Salvador, Guatemala, and Honduras, as well as continuing its economic boycott and political subversion of Cuba. Civil wars pushed millions of Central American Latinos north. The documents covering these topics appear in the section covering the 1980s, when more than a million Central Americans immigrated to the United States.

With the arrival of such large numbers of Central Americans and critical numbers of South Americans, identity became more problematic, and the hegemony of Mexicans, Puerto Ricans, and Cuban Americans was challenged. Even before this time, Mexicans had moved in substantial numbers to the Midwest and Northwest. In Chicago, they lived in close proximity to Puerto Ricans. More than a million Mexicans migrated to the United States in the 1970s; this migration did not slow down in the next two decades, when Mexican immigrants were joined by millions of other Latin Americans. For the first time, these groups shared a common space, which was one of the requisites for sharing a nationality. This development raised the question of a Latino identity, which will be resolved in the future through intellectual discourse and life experiences.

By the 1990s, the new Latino immigrants were forming their own distinct identities, although the so-called Latino populations became more diverse, spreading to the U.S. South and the East Coast. Mexican populations in New York City increased from around 62,000 in 1990 to more than 400,000, by many estimates, at the turn of the century. In New York, they share space with Puerto Ricans and other Latinos. Growth in numbers and lawsuits by the Mexican American Legal Defense and Educational Fund, as well as the Puerto Rican Legal Defense and Education Fund, has increased the number of Latino elected officials immeasurably.

In 2010, there were 50.5 million Latinos in the U.S. population: 63 percent were of Mexican origin, 13.5 percent were Central and South American, 9 percent were Puerto Rican, 6.3 percent were Cuban and Dominican, and the remaining 8.2 percent were of other Hispanic origins. Because many of these communities lived in close proximity, sharing the same economic class, intermarriage was taking place. In Los Angeles, for example, many college students are half Mexican and half Salvadoran. Both have large populations. Intermarriage is widespread among U.S.-born Mexican Americans. The 2010 census showed that almost half (48 percent) of Mexican American marriages involved a non-Mexican spouse. Census data also showed that intermarriage is a fundamental factor in whether or not the children of Mexican Americans retain their ethnic identification. With either two U.S.-born Mexicans or a U.S.-born Mexican and a Mexican immigrant, the child's Mexican identification is almost ensured. Other Latino groups follow a similar trend.

Guadalupe Compeán

Brief Guide to Primary Sources

Primary sources are original, direct, firsthand stories, personal experiences, testimony, and viewpoints that are created during the time period involved. They may include such forms as diaries, journals, letters, personal narratives, government records, graffiti, laws, court cases, plays, novels, poems, architectural plans, maps, memoirs, autobiographies, sound recordings, songs, advertisements, photographs, paintings, prints, speeches, and other material objects. The sources become the raw material that historians, or other scholars, use to create their works in book or article form. Secondary sources are interpretations, which are often made using myriad primary sources.

Primary sources provide readers with a wealth of firsthand information that gets them close to the actual experiences of the historical time period, people, and events. Firsthand material offers a window to a particular time and place, viewpoints, and eyewitness accounts that supplement information and facts typically provided in textbooks and other secondary sources. Primary sources offer readers the raw material of history that has not been analyzed and interpreted.

How to Read and Reflect on Primary Documents

Primary sources in written form, as illustrated by the document selections included in *The Great American Mosaic: An Exploration of Diversity in Primary Documents*, were produced at a particular historical moment and for a particular purpose. These volumes are intended to provide an outlet for the voices of people of color whose experiences and viewpoints are often overlooked or downplayed in the larger American history narrative. Some of these documents were written by an author conscious of a larger audience or with the expectation that they would be published; others were written for personal reasons without the expectation that others would read them. Some documents were intended to persuade, inform, or entertain. Note that documents are based on the particular viewpoints, experiences, and memories of the writer and can reflect selective memories, mistaken information, or deception. The reader is left to evaluate the relevance, reliability, and value of the information and to take into account the analysis and interpretations of secondary sources. The documents in *The Great American Mosaic* provide readers with a variety of firsthand content, ranging from creation myths to legislation to reflections on historical events that provide insights into the experiences of people of color in the United States.

What Questions Should You Ask as You Read?

- Who wrote or produced the document, and what do we know about him or her?
- When and where was the source written or produced, and how does it fit into the timeline of the events and period described?
- Where was the source written or produced? Does that material portray cultural, social, or religious values? What form did it take originally?
- Why was the source material written or produced? What was its creator's intention or purpose? What is the overall tone of the source material?
- Who was the intended audience? How was the document used, and how widely distributed or read was it?
- Overall, how do we evaluate the relevance, reliability, and value of the content? What might the author have left out, intentionally or not?

Bernal Díaz del Castillo, Description of a Tour through Tenochtitlán (1519)

Tenochtitlán, the capital city of the Aztec empire, clearly impressed the Spanish conquistadores, as the following document demonstrates. Throughout the eyewitness account of Bernal Díaz del Castillo, an excerpt of which is given below, the Aztec city is compared favorably with the great cities of Europe: "Those who had been at Rome and at Constantinople said, that for convenience, regularity, and population, they had never seen the like." The inhabitants likewise are given high praise. Although Díaz is complimentary in general to the Aztec civilization, he refers to the Aztec idols as "accursed," and he focuses on the altar stained with the blood of human sacrifices. Although the next generation of Spanish colonialists, especially the profiteering businessmen, would frequently look down on the indigenous, many of the original 16th-century conquistadores were simply impressed. Begun in the 1550s and completed around 1568, Díaz's True History of the Conquest of Mexico, *from which this excerpt was taken, was not published until 1632, almost 50 years after his death.*

The place where the artists principally resided was named Escapuzalco, and was at the distance of about a league from the city. Here were the shops and manufactories of all their gold and silver smiths, whose works in these metals, and in jewelry, when they were brought to Spain, surprised our ablest artists. Their painters we may also judge of by what we now see, for there are three Indians in Mexico, who are named Marcos de Aquino, Juan de la Cruz, and Crespillo, who, if they had lived with Apelles in ancient times, or were compared with Michaelangelo or Berruguete in modern times, would not be held inferior to them. Their fine manufactures of cotton and feathers, were principally brought from the province of Costitlan. The women of the family of the great Montezuma [II] also, of all ranks, were extremely ingenious in these works, and constantly employed; as was a certain description of females who lived together in the manner of nuns.

One part of the city was entirely occupied by Montezuma's dancers, of different kinds, some of whom bore a stick on their feet, others flew in the air, and some danced like those in Italy called by us Matachines. He had also a number of carpenters and handicraft men constantly in his employ. His gardens, which were of great extent, were irrigated by canals of running water, and shaded with every variety of trees. In them were baths of cut stone, pavilions for feasting or retirement, and theatres for shows, and for the dancers and singers; all which were kept in the most exact order, by a number of laborers constantly employed.

When we had been four days in Mexico, Cortes wished to take a view of the city, and in consequence sent to request the permission of his Majesty. Accordingly, Aquilar, Donna Marina, and a little page of our general's called Orteguilla, who already understood something of the language, went to the palace for that purpose. Montezuma was pleased immediately to accede, but being apprehensive that we might offer some insult to his temple, he determined to go thither in person, which he accordingly did, in the same form, and with the same retinue, as when he first came out to meet us, but that he was on this occasion preceded by two lords bearing scepters in their hands, which they carried on high, as a signal of the king's approach. Montezuma, in his litter, with a small rod in his hand, one half of which was gold, and the other half wood, and which he bore elevated like a rod of justice, for such it was, approached the temple, and there quitted his litter and mounted the steps, attended by a number of priests, and offering incense with many ceremonies to his war gods.

Cortes at the head of his cavalry, and the principal part of our soldiers under arms, marched to the grand square, attended by many noblemen of the court. When we arrived there, we were astonished at the crowds of people, and the regularity which prevailed, as well as at the vast quantities of merchandise, which those who attended us were assiduous in pointing out. Each kind had its particular place, which was distinguished by a sign. The articles consisted of gold, silver, jewels, feathers, mantles, chocolate, skins dressed and undressed, sandals, and other manufactures of the roots and fibres of nequen, and great numbers of male and female slaves, some of whom were fastened by the neck, in collars, to long poles. The meat market was stocked with fowls, game, and dogs. Vegetables, fruits, articles of food ready dressed, salt, bread, honey, and sweet pastry made in various ways were also sold here. Other places in the square were appointed to the sale of earthen ware, wooden household furniture such as tables and benches, firewood, paper, sweet canes filled with tobacco mixed with liquid amber, copper axes and working tools, and wooden vessels highly painted. Numbers of women sold fish, and little loaves made of a certain mud which they find in the lake, and which resembles cheese. The makers of stone blades were busily employed shaping them out of the rough material, and the merchants who dealt in gold, had the metal in grains as it came from the mines, in transparent tubes, so that they could be reckoned, and the gold was valued at so many mantles, or so many xiquipils of cocoa, according to the size of the quills. The entire square was enclosed in piazzas, under which great quantities of grain were stored, and where were also shops for various kinds of goods. I must apologize for adding, that boat loads of human ordure were on the borders of the adjoining canals, for the purpose of tanning leather, which they said could not be done without it. Some may laugh at this but I assert the fact is as I have stated it, and moreover, upon all the public roads, places for passengers to resort to, were built of canes, and thatch with straw or grass, in order to collect this material. The courts of justice, where three judges sat, occupied a part of the square, their under-officers going in the market, inspecting the merchandise.

From the square we proceeded to the great temple, but before we entered it we made a circuit through a number of large courts, the smallest of which appeared to me to contain more ground than the great square in Salamanca, with double enclosures built of lime and stone, and the courts paved with large white cut stone, very clean; or where not paved, they were plastered and polished. When we approached the gate of the great temple, to the flat summit of which the ascent was by a hundred and fourteen steps, and before we had mounted one of them, Montezuma sent down to us six priests, and two of his noblemen, to carry Cortes up, as they had done their sovereign, which he politely declined. When we had ascended to the summit of the temple, we observed on the platform as we passed, the large stones whereon were placed the victims who were to be sacrificed. Here was a great figure which resembled a dragon, and much blood fresh spilt. Montezuma came out from an adoratory in which his accursed idols were placed, attended by two priests, and addressing himself to Cortes, expressed his apprehension that he was fatigued; to which Cortes replied, that fatigue was unknown to us.

Montezuma then took him by the hand, and pointed out to him the different parts of the city, and its vicinity, all of which were commanded from that place. Here we had a clear prospect of the three causeways by which Mexico communicated with the land, and of the aqueduct of Chapultepeque, which supplied the city with the finest water. We were struck with the numbers of canoes, passing to and from the main land, loaded with provisions and merchandise, and we could now perceive, that in this great city, and all the others of that neighbourhood which were built in the water, the houses stood separate from each other, communicating only by small drawbridges, and by boats, and that they were built with terraced tops.

We observed also the temples and adoratories of the adjacent cities, built in the form of towers and fortresses, and others on the causeway, all white-washed, and wonderfully brilliant. The noise and bustle of the market-place below us could be heard almost a league off, and those who had been at Rome and at Constantinople said, that for convenience, regularity, and population, they had never seen the like.

Source: Díaz del Castillo, Bernal. *The True History of the Conquest of Mexico*. Translated by Maurice Keatinge. London: Harrap, 1927, 175–178.

Hernán Cortés, Letter to Charles I Describing Mexico (1520)

A Spanish explorer and adventurer, Hernán Cortés landed in Mexico in 1519 and promptly claimed the region for Spain. Over the next two years, he successfully conquered the native Aztecs and established a firm basis for Spanish colonial rule in Mesoamerica. Here is an excerpt of a letter he wrote to Spain's King Charles I in 1520, describing Mexico.

IN ORDER, most potent Sire, to convey to your Majesty a just conception of the great extent of this noble city of Temixtitlan, and of the many rare and wonderful objects it contains; of the government and dominions of Moctezuma, the sovereign: of the religious rights and customs that prevail, and the order that exists in this as well as the other cities appertaining to his realm: it would require the labor of many accomplished writers, and much time for the completion of the task. I shall not be able to relate an hundredth part of what could be told respecting these matters; but I will endeavor to describe, in the best manner in my power, what I have myself seen; and imperfectly as I may succeed in the attempt, I am fully aware that the account will appear so wonderful as to be deemed scarcely worthy of credit; since even we who have seen these things with our own eyes, are yet so amazed as to be unable to comprehend their reality. But your Majesty may be assured that if there is any fault in my relation, either in regard to the present subject, or to any other matters of which I shall give your Majesty an account, it will arise from too great brevity rather than extravagance or prolixity in the details; and it seems to me but just to my Prince and Sovereign to declare the truth in the clearest manner, without saying anything that would detract from it, or add to it.

Before I begin to describe this great city and the others already mentioned, it may be well for the better understanding of the subject to say something of the configuration of Mexico, in which they are situated, it being the principal seat of Moctezuma's power. This Province is in the form of a circle, surrounded on all sides by lofty and rugged mountains; its level surface comprises an area of about seventy leagues in circumference, including two lakes, that overspread nearly the whole valley, being navigated by boats more than fifty leagues round. One of these lakes contains fresh and the other, which is the larger of the two, salt water. On one side of the lakes, in the middle of the valley, a range of highlands divides them from one another, with the exception of a narrow strait which lies between the highlands and the lofty sierras. This strait is a bow-shot wide, and connects the two lakes; and by this means a trade is carried on between the cities and other settlements on the lakes in canoes without the necessity of traveling by land. As the salt lake rises and falls with its tides like the sea, during the time of high water it pours into the other lake with the rapidity of a powerful stream; and on the other hand, when the tide has ebbed, the water runs from the fresh into the salt lake.

This great city of Temixtitlan [Mexico] is situated in this salt lake, and from the main land to the denser parts of it, by whichever route one chooses to enter, the distance is two leagues. There are four avenues or entrances to the city, all of which are formed by artificial causeways, two spears' length in width. The city is as large as Seville or Cordova; its streets, I speak of the principal ones, are very wide and straight; some of these, and all the inferior ones, are half land and half water, and are navigated by canoes. All the streets at intervals have openings, through which the water flows, crossing from one street to another; and at these openings, some of which are very wide, there are also very wide bridges, composed of large pieces of timber, of great strength and well put together; on many of these bridges ten horses can go abreast. Foreseeing that if the inhabitants of the city should prove treacherous, they would possess great advantages from the manner in which the city is constructed, since by removing the bridges at the entrances, and abandoning the place, they could leave us to perish by famine without our being able to reach the main land, as soon as I had entered it, I made great haste to build four brigantines, which were soon finished, and were large enough to take ashore three hundred men and the horses, whenever it should become necessary.

This city has many public squares, in which are situated the markets and other places for buying and selling. There is one square twice as large as that of the city of Salamanca, surrounded by porticoes, where are daily assembled more than sixty thousand souls, engaged in buying and selling; and where are found all kinds of merchandise that the world affords, embracing the necessaries of life, as for instance articles of food, as well as jewels of gold and silver, lead, brass, copper, tin, precious stones, bones, shells, snails, and feathers. There are also exposed for sale wrought and unwrought stone, bricks burnt and unburnt, timber hewn and unhewn, of different sorts. There is a street for game, where every variety of birds in the country are sold, as fowls, partridges, quails, wild ducks, fly-catchers, widgeons, turtledoves, pigeons, reed-birds, parrots, sparrows, eagles, hawks, owls, and kestrels; they sell likewise the skins of some birds of prey, with their feathers, head, beak, and claws. There are also sold rabbits, hares, deer, and little dogs [i.e., the chihuahua], which are raised for eating. There is also an herb street, where may be obtained all sorts of roots and medicinal herbs that the country affords. There are apothecaries' shops, where prepared medicines, liquids, ointments, and plasters are sold; barbers' shops, where they wash and shave the head; and restaurateurs, that furnish food and drink at a certain price. There is also a class of men like those called in Castile porters, for carrying burdens. Wood and coal are seen in abundance, and braziers of earthenware for burning coals; mats of various kinds for beds, others of a lighter sort for seats, and for halls and bedrooms.

There are all kinds of green vegetables, especially onions, leeks, garlic, watercresses, nasturtium, borage, sorrel, artichokes, and golden thistle; fruits also of numerous descriptions, amongst which are cherries and plums, similar to those in Spain; honey and wax from bees, and from the stalks of maize, which are as sweet as the sugar-cane; honey is also extracted from the plant called maguey, which is superior to sweet or new wine; from the same plant they extract sugar and wine, which they also sell. Different kinds of cotton thread of all colors in skeins are exposed for sale in one quarter of the market, which has the appearance of the silk-market at Granada, although the former is supplied more abundantly. Painters' colors, as numerous as can be found in Spain, and as fine shades; deerskins dressed and undressed, dyed different colors; earthen-ware of a large size and excellent quality; large and small jars, jugs, pots, bricks, and endless variety of vessels, all made of fine clay, and all or most of them glazed and painted; maize or Indian corn, in the grain and in the form of bread, preferred in the grain for its flavor to that of the other islands and terra-firma; patés of birds and fish; great quantities of fish—fresh, salt, cooked and uncooked; the eggs of hens, geese, and of all the other birds I have mentioned, in great abundance, and cakes made of eggs; finally, everything that can be found throughout the whole country is sold in the markets, comprising articles so numerous that to avoid prolixity, and because their names are not retained in my memory, or are unknown to me, I shall not attempt to enumerate them.

Every kind of merchandise is sold in a particular street or quarter assigned to it exclusively, and thus the best order is preserved. They sell everything by number or measure; at least so far we have not observed them to sell anything by weight. There is a building in the great square that is used as an audience house, where ten or twelve persons, who are magistrates, sit and decide all controversies that arise in the market, and order delinquents to be punished. In the same square there are other persons who go constantly about among the people observing what is sold, and the measures used in selling; and they have been seen to break measures that were not true.

This great city contains a large number of temples, or houses, for their idols, very handsome edifices, which are situated in the different districts and the suburbs; in the principal ones religious persons of each particular sect are constantly residing, for whose use, besides the houses containing the idols, there are other convenient habitations. All these persons dress in black, and never cut or comb their hair from the time they enter the priesthood until they leave it; and all the sons of the principal inhabitants, both nobles and respectable citizens, are placed in the temples and wear the same dress from the age of seven or eight years until they are taken out to be married; which occurs more frequently with the first-born who inherit estates than with the others. The priests are debarred from female society, nor is any woman permitted to enter the religious houses. They also abstain from eating certain kinds of food, more at some seasons of the year than others.

Among these temples there is one which far surpasses all the rest, whose grandeur of architectural details no human tongue is able to describe; for within its precincts, surrounded by a lofty wall, there is room enough for a town of five hundred families. Around the interior of the enclosure there are handsome edifices, containing large halls and corridors, in which the religious persons attached to the temple reside. There are fully forty towers, which are lofty and well built, the largest of which has fifty steps leading to its main body, and is higher than the tower of the principal tower of the church at Seville. The stone and wood of which they are constructed are so well wrought in every part, that nothing could be better done, for the interior of the chapels containing the idols consists of curious imagery, wrought in stone, with plaster ceilings, and wood-work carved in relief, and painted with figures of monsters and other objects. All these towers are the burial places of the nobles, and every chapel in them is dedicated to a particular idol, to which they pay their devotions.

Three halls are in this grand temple, which contain the principal idols; these are of wonderful extent and height, and admirable workmanship, adorned with figures sculptured in stone and wood; leading from the halls are chapels with very small doors, to which the light is not admitted, nor are any persons except the priests, and not all of them. In these chapels are the images of idols, although, as I have before said, many of them are also found on the outside; the principal ones, in which the people have greatest faith and confidence, I precipitated from their pedestals, and cast them down the steps of the temple, purifying the chapels in which they had stood, as they were all polluted with human blood, shed ill the sacrifices. In the place of these I put images of Our Lady and the Saints, which excited not a little feeling in Moctezuma and the inhabitants, who at first remonstrated, declaring that if my proceedings were known throughout the country, the people would rise against me; for they believed that their idols bestowed on them all temporal good, and if they permitted them to be ill-treated, they would be angry and without their gifts, and by this means the people would be deprived of the fruits of the earth and perish with famine. I answered, through the interpreters, that they were deceived in expecting any favors from idols, the work of their own hands, formed of unclean things; and that they must learn there was but one God, the universal Lord of all, who had created the heavens and earth, and all things else, and had made them and us; that He was without beginning and immortal, and they were bound to adore and believe Him, and no other creature or thing.

I said everything to them I could to divert them from their idolatries, and draw them to a knowledge of God our Lord. Moctezuma replied, the others assenting to what he said, "That they had already informed me they were not the aborigines of the country, but that their ancestors had emigrated to it many years ago; and they fully believed that after so long an absence from their native land, they might have fallen into some errors; that I having more recently arrived must know better than themselves what they ought to believe; and that if I would instruct them in these matters, and make them understand the true faith, they would follow my directions, as being for the best." Afterwards, Moctezuma and many of the principal citizens remained with me until I had removed the idols, purified the chapels, and placed the images in them, manifesting apparent pleasure; and I forbade them sacrificing human beings to their idols as they had been accustomed to do; because, besides being abhorrent in the sight of God, your sacred Majesty had prohibited it by law, and commanded to put to death whoever should take the life of another. Thus, from that time, they refrained from the practice, and during the whole period of my abode in that city, they were never seen to kill or sacrifice a human being.

The figures of the idols in which these people believe surpass in stature a person of more than ordinary size; some of them are composed of a mass of seeds and leguminous plants, such as are used for food, ground and mixed together, and kneaded with the blood of human hearts taken from the breasts of living persons, from which a paste is formed in a sufficient quantity to form large statues. When these are completed they make them offerings of the hearts of other victims, which they sacrifice to them, and besmear their faces with the blood. For everything they have an idol, consecrated by the use of the nations that in ancient times honored the same gods. Thus they have an idol that they petition for victory in war; another for success in their labors; and so for everything in which they seek or desire prosperity, they have their idols, which they honor and serve.

This noble city contains many fine and magnificent houses; which may be accounted for from the fact, that all the nobility of the country, who are the vassals of Moctezuma, have houses in the city, in which they reside a certain part of the year; and besides, there are numerous wealthy citizens who also possess fine houses. All these persons, in addition to the large and spacious apartments for ordinary purposes, have others, both upper and lower, that contain conservatories of flowers. Along one of these causeways that lead into the city are laid two pipes, constructed of masonry, each of which is two paces in width, and about five feet in height. An abundant supply of excellent water, forming a volume equal in bulk to the human body, is conveyed by one of these pipes, and distributed about the city, where it is used by the inhabitants for drink and other purposes. The other pipe, in the meantime, is kept empty until the former requires to be cleansed, when the water is let into it and continues to be used till the cleaning is finished. As the water is necessarily carried over bridges on account of the salt water crossing its route, reservoirs resembling canals are constructed on the bridges, through which the fresh water is conveyed. These reservoirs are of the breadth of the body of an ox, and of the same length as the bridges. The whole city is thus served with water, which they carry in canoes through all the streets for sale, taking it from the aqueduct in the following manner: the canoes pass under the bridges on which the reservoirs are placed, when men stationed above fill them with water, for which service they are paid. At all the entrances of the city, and in those parts where the canoes are discharged, that is, where the greatest quantity of provisions is brought in, huts are erected, and persons stationed as guards, who receive a certain sum of everything that enters. I know not whether the sovereign receives this duty or the city, as I have not yet been informed; but I believe that it appertains to the sovereign, as in the markets of other provinces a tax is collected for the benefit of the cacique.

In all the markets and public places of this city are seen daily many laborers waiting for some one to hire them. The inhabitants of this city pay a greater regard to style in their mode of dress and politeness of manners than those of the other provinces and cities; since, as the Cacique Moctezuma has his residence in the capital, and all the nobility, his vassals, are in constant habit of meeting there, a general courtesy of demeanor necessarily prevails. But not to be prolix in describing what relates to the affairs of this great city, although it is with difficulty I refrain from proceeding, I will say no more than that the manners of the people, as shown in their intercourse with one another, are marked by as great an attention to the proprieties of life as in Spain, and good order is equally well observed; and considering that they are barbarous people, without the knowledge of God, having no intercourse with civilized nations, these traits of character are worthy of admiration.

In regard to the domestic appointments of Moctezuma, and the wonderful grandeur and state that he maintains, there is so much to be told, that I assure your Highness I know not where to begin my relation, so as to be able to finish any part of it. For, as I have already stated, what can be more wonderful than a barbarous monarch, as he is, should have every object found in his dominions imitated in gold, silver, precious stones, and feathers; the gold and silver being wrought so naturally as not to be surpassed by any smith in the world; the stone work executed with such perfection that it is difficult to conceive what instruments could have been used; and the feather work superior to the finest productions in wax or embroidery. The extent of Moctezuma's dominions has not been ascertained, since to whatever point he despatched his messengers, even two hundred leagues from his capital, his commands were obeyed, although some of his provinces were in the midst of countries with which he was at war. But as nearly as I have been able to learn, his territories are equal in extent to Spain itself, for he sent messengers to the inhabitants of a city called Cumatan (requiring them to become subjects of your Majesty), which is sixty leagues beyond that part of Putunchan watered by the river Grijalva, and two hundred and thirty leagues distant from the great city; and I sent some of our people a distance of one hundred and fifty leagues in the same direction.

All the principle chiefs of these provinces, especially those in the vicinity of the capital, reside, as I have already stated, the greater part of the year in that great city, and all or most of them have their oldest sons in the service of Moctezuma. There are fortified places in all the provinces, garrisoned with his own men, where are also stationed his governors and collectors of the rents and tribute, rendered him by every province; and an account is kept of what each is obliged to pay, as they have characters and figures made on paper that are used for this purpose. Each province renders a tribute of its own peculiar productions, so that the sovereign receives a great variety of articles from different quarters. No prince was ever more feared by his subjects, both in his presence and absence. He possessed out of the city as well as within numerous villas, each of which had its peculiar sources of amusement, and all were constructed in the best possible manner for the use of a great prince and lord. Within the city his palaces were so wonderful that it is hardly possible to describe their beauty and extent; I can only say that in Spain there is nothing equal to them.

There was one palace somewhat inferior to the rest, attached to which was a beautiful garden with balconies extending over it, supported by marble columns, and having a floor formed of jasper elegantly inlaid. There were apartments in this palace sufficient to lodge two princes of the highest rank with their retinues. There were likewise belonging to it ten pools of water, in which were kept the different species of water birds found in this country, of which there is a great variety, all of which are domesticated; for the sea birds there were pools of salt water, and for the river birds, of fresh water. The water is let off at certain times to keep it pure, and is replenished by means of pipes. Each specie of bird is supplied with the food natural to it, which it feeds upon when wild. Thus fish is given to the birds that usually eat it; worms, maize, and the finer seeds, to such as prefer them. And I assure your Highness, that to the birds accustomed to eat fish there is given the enormous quantity of ten arrobas every day, taken in the salt lake. The emperor has three hundred men whose sole employment is to take care of these birds; and there are others whose only business is to attend to the birds that are in bad health.

Over the polls for the birds there are corridors and galleries, to which Moctezuma resorts, and from which he can look out and amuse himself with the sight of them. There is an apartment in the same palace in which are men, women and children, whose faces, bodies, hair, eyebrows, and eyelashes are white from their birth. The emperor has another very beautiful palace, with a large courtyard, paved with handsome flags, in the style of a chess-board. There are also cages, about nine feet in height and six paces square, each of which was half covered with a roof of tiles, and the other half had over it a wooden grate, skillfully made. Every cage contained a bird of prey, of all the species found in Spain, from the kestrel to the eagle, and many unknown there. There was a great number of each kind; and in the covered part of the cages there was a perch, and another on the outside of the grating, the former of which the birds used in the night time, and when it rained; and the other enabled them to enjoy the sun and air. To all these birds fowls were daily given for food, and nothing else. There were in the same palace several large halls on the ground floor, filled with immense cages built of heavy pieces of timber, well put together, in all or most of which were kept lions, tigers, wolves, foxes, and a variety of animals of the cat kind, in great numbers, which were fed also on fowls. The care of these animals and birds was assigned to three hundred men. There was another palace that contained a number of men and women of monstrous size, and also dwarfs, and crooked and ill-formed persons, each of which had their separate apartments. These also had their respective keepers. As to the other remarkable things that the emperor had in his city for his amusement, I can only say that they were numerous and of various kinds.

He was served in the following manner: Every day as soon as it was light, six hundred nobles and men of rank were in attendance at the palace, who either sat, or walked about the halls and galleries, and passed their time in conversation, but without entering the apartment where his person was. The servants and attendants of these nobles remained in the court-yards, of which there were two or three of great extent, and in the adjoining street, which was also very spacious. They all remained in attendance from morning until night; and when his meals were served, the nobles were likewise served with equal profusion, and their servants and secretaries also had their allowance. Daily his larder and wine-cellar were open to all who wished to eat or drink. The meals were served by three or four hundred youths, who brought on an infinite variety of dishes; indeed, whenever he dined or supped, the table was loaded with every kind of flesh, fish, fruits, and vegetables that the country produced. As the climate is cold, they put a chafing-dish with live coals under every plate and dish, to keep them warm. The meals were served in a large hall, in which Moctezuma was accustomed to eat, and the dishes quite filled the room, which was covered with mats and kept very clean. He sat on a small cushion curiously wrought of leather. During the meals there were present, at a little distance from him, five or six elderly caciques, to whom he presented some of the food. And there was constantly in attendance one of the servants, who arranged and handed the dishes, and who received from others whatever was wanted for the supply of the table.

Both at the beginning and end of every meal, they furnished water for the hands; and the napkins used on these occasions were never used a second time; this was the case also with the plates and dishes, which were not brought again, but new ones in place of them; it was the same also with the chafing-dishes. He is also dressed every day in four different suits, entirely new, which he never wears a second time. None of the caciques who enter his palace have their feet covered, and when those for whom he sends enters his presence, they incline their heads and look down, bending their bodies; and when they address him, they do not look him in the face; this arises from excessive modesty and reverence. I am satisfied that it proceeds from respect, since certain caciques reproved the Spaniards for their boldness in addressing me, saying that it showed a want of becoming deference. Whenever Moctezuma appeared in public, which is seldom the case, all those who accompanied him, or whom he accidentally met in the streets, turned away without looking towards him, and others prostrated themselves until he had passed. One of the nobles always preceded him on these occasions, carrying three slender rods erect, which I suppose was to give notice of the approach of his person. And when they descended from the litters, he took one of them in his hand, and held it until he reached the place where he was going. So many and various were the ceremonies and customs observed by those in the service of Moctezuma, that more space than I can spare would be required for the details, as well as a better memory than I have to recollect them; since no sultan or other infidel lord, of whom any knowledge now exists; ever had so much ceremonial in his court.

Source: Thatcher, Oliver Joseph. *The Ideas That Have Influenced Civilization, in the Original Documents*. Vol. 5. Milwaukee, WI: Roberts-Manchester, 1901

Bernal Díaz del Castillo, Account of *La Noche Triste* ("The Sorrowful Night") (1520)

La Noche Triste, *Spanish for "the sorrowful night," refers to the escape of Hernán Cortés and his conquistador army from Tenochtitlán (modern-day Mexico City) on the night of June 30 to July 1, 1520, during the first battle between Spanish forces and Aztec warriors in the Aztec capital. The Spaniards and their indigenous allies had arrived as honored guests of the Aztec emperor Montezuma II in November 1519, but relations between the Aztecs and their guests quickly soured when Cortés took Montezuma as an unofficial hostage. Matters became much worse when Pedro de Alvarado slaughtered numerous Aztec nobles in the main temple during Cortés's absence. When Cortés returned to Tenochtitlán, open warfare erupted, resulting in the death of Montezuma at the hands of either the Spanish or the Aztecs themselves. Cortés's men, heavily outnumbered, attempted to flee the city, taking with them as much gold and booty as they could carry. Hundreds of Spanish and thousands of indigenous persons were killed. Because of the large death toll on both sides, July 1 is commemorated as La Noche Triste in Mexico.*

The following account of the battle comes from Bernal Díaz del Castillo (ca. 1492–1583), a conquistador who served with Cortés and fought during La Noche Triste. Although Díaz del Castillo was an eyewitness to the events, he did not begin to write his history until almost 50 years after the events occurred, so the accuracy of some of the smaller details in the account may be questioned, although the overall picture is confirmed by other surviving accounts. The account highlights several interesting aspects of the conflict. First, Díaz del Castillo highlights the Spanish reliance on technology and their attempts to gain technological superiority. The Spaniards' metal swords, muskets, and body armor gave them more destructive force and more protection in comparison with the Aztec warriors. As the passage recounts, the Spanish attempted to further these advantages by building movable bulwarks to provide cover and firing positions for up to 25 men each. Second, the choice of target—the main temple in Tenochtitlán—demonstrates the role of strategy in the Spanish campaign. In 16th-century Mesoamerican culture, temples served as the symbolic heart of a city and its people. Aztec paintings, for example, record a victory over a neighboring people by showing the enemy's temple broken and in flames. The Spanish attack on the temple of Tenochtitlán, the Aztec capital, therefore was an attack on the very heart of the Aztec Empire. The symbolic importance of the target demonstrates the understanding the Spanish conquistadores had of Mesoamerican culture and explains the fierce resistance the conquistadores met there. Generally outnumbered, the Spanish conquistadores concentrated on strategically important targets, such as Montezuma or the temple, instead of attempting to control the whole city or territory.

On this day we lost ten or twelve soldiers, and all of us who came back were severely wounded. From the period of our return we were occupied in making preparation for a general sally on the next day but one, with four military machines constructed of very strong timber, in the form of towers, and each capable of containing twenty five men under cover, with port holes for the artillery and also for the musquetiers and crossbow-men. This work occupied us for the space of one day, except that we were obliged likewise to repair the breaches made in our walls, and resist those who attempted to scale them in twenty different places at the same time. They continued their reviling language, saying that the voracious animals of their temples had now been kept two days fasting, in order to devour us at the period which was speedily approaching, when they were to sacrifice us to their gods; that our allies were to be put up in cages to fatten; and that they would soon repossess our ill acquired treasure. At other times they plaintively called to us to give them their king, and during the night we were constantly annoyed by showers of arrows, which they accompanied by shouts and whistlings.

At day break on the ensuing morning, after recommending ourselves to God, we sallied out with our turrets, which as well as I recollect were called burros or mantas, in other places where I have seen them, with some of our musquetry and cross-bows in front, and our cavalry occasionally charging. The enemy this day showed themselves more determined than ever, and we were equally resolved to force our way to the great temple, although it should cost the life of every man of us; we therefore advanced with our turrets in that direction. I will not detail the desperate battle which we had with the enemy in a very strong house, nor how their arrows wounded our horses, notwithstanding their armour, and if at any time the horsemen attempted to pursue the Mexicans, the latter threw themselves into the canals, and others sallied out upon our people and massacred them with large lances.

As to setting fire to the buildings, or tearing them down, it was utterly in vain to attempt; they all stood in the water, and only communicating by draw bridges, it was too dangerous to attempt to reach them by swimming, for they showered stones from their slings, and masses of cut stone taken from the buildings, upon our heads, from the terraces of the houses. Whenever we attempted to set fire to a house, it was an entire day before it took effect, and when it did, the flames could not spread to others, as they were separated from it by the water, and also because the roofs of them were terraced.

We at length arrived at the great temple, and immediately and instantly above four thousand Mexicans rushed up into it, without including in that number other bodies who occupied it before, and defended it against us with lances, stones, and darts. They thus prevented our ascending for some time, neither turrets, nor musquetry, nor cavalry availing, for although the latter body several times attempted to charge, the stone pavement of the courts of the temple was so smooth that the horses could not keep their feet, and fell. From the steps of the great temple they opposed us in front, and we were attacked by such numbers on both sides, that although our guns swept off ten or fifteen of them at each discharge, and that in each attack of our infantry we killed many with our swords, their numbers were such that we could not make any effectual impression, or ascend the steps. We were then forced to abandon our turrets, which the enemy had destroyed, and with great concert, making an effort without them, we forced our way up. Here Cortes shewed himself the man that he really was. What a desperate engagement we then had! Every man of us was covered with blood, and above forty dead upon the spot. It was God's will that we should at length reach the place where we had put up the image of our Lady, but when we came there it was not to be found, and it seems that Montezuma, actuated either by fear or by devotion, had caused it to be removed. We set fire to the building, and burned a part of the temple of the gods Huitzilopochtli and Tezcatepuco. Here our Tlascalan allies served us essentially. While thus engaged, some setting the temple on fire, others fighting, above three thousand noble Mexicans with their priests were about us, and attacking us, drove us down six and even ten of the steps, while others who were in the corridors, or within the side the railings and concavities of the great temple, shot such clouds of arrows at us that we could not maintain our ground, when thus attacked from every part. We therefore began our retreat, every man of us being wounded, and forty six left dead upon the spot. We were pursued with a violence and desperation which is not in my power to describe, nor in that of any one to form an idea of who did not see it. During all this time also other bodies of the Mexicans had been continually attacking our quarters, and endeavoring to set fire to them. In this battle, we made prisoners two of the principal priests. I have often seen this engagement represented in the paintings of the natives, both of Mexico and Tlascala, and our ascent into the great temple. In these our party is represented with many dead, and all wounded. The setting fire to the temple when so many warriors were defending it in the corridors, railings, and concavities, and other bodies of them on the plain ground, and filling the courts, and on the sides, and our turrets demolished, is considered by them as a most heroic action.

With great difficulty we reached our quarters, which we found the enemy almost in possession of, as they had beaten down a part of the walls; but they desisted in a great measure from their attacks on our arrival, still throwing in upon us however showers of arrows, darts, and stones. The night was employed by us in repairing the breaches, in dressing our wounds, burying our dead, and consulting upon our future measures. No gleam of hope could be now rationally formed by us, and we were utterly sunk in despair. Those who had come with Narvaez showered maledictions upon Cortes, nor did they forget Velasquez by whom they had been induced to quit their comfortable and peaceable habitations in the island of Cuba. It was determined to try if we could not procure from the enemy a cessation of hostilities, on condition of our quitting the city; but at day break they assembled round our quarters and attacked them with greater fury than ever, nor could our fire arms repel them, although they did considerable execution.

[Omitted here is a passage detailing the death of Montezuma when he was sent to try to broker a peace treaty.]

Orders were now given to make a portable bridge of very strong timber, to be thrown over the canals where the enemy had broken down the bridges, and for conveying, guarding, and placing this, were assigned one hundred and fifty of our soldiers and four hundred of the allies. The advanced guard was composed of Sandoval, Azevido el Pulido, F. de Lugo, D. de Ordas, A. de Tapia, and eight more captains of those who came with Narvaez, having under them one hundred picked soldiers, of the youngest and most active. The rear guard was composed of one hundred soldiers, mostly those of Narvaez, and many cavalry, under the command of Alvarado and Velasquez de Leon. The prisoners, with Donna Marina and Donna Luisa, were put under the care of thirty soldiers and three hundred Tlascalans; and Cortes, with A. de Avila, C. de Oli, Bernardino Vasquez de Tapia and other officers, with fifty soldiers, composed a reserve, to act wherever occasion should require.

By the time that all this was arranged night drew on. Cortes then ordered all the gold which was in his apartment to be brought to the great saloon, which being done, he desired the officers of his Majesty, A. de Avila and Gonzalo Mexia, to take his Majesty's due, in their charge, assigning to them for the conveyance of it eight lame or wounded horses, and upwards of eighty Tlascalans. Upon these were loaded as much as they could carry of the gold which had been run into large bars, and much more remained heaped up in the saloon. Cortes then called to his secretary Hernandez and other royal notaries and said, "Bear witness that I can be no longer responsible for this gold; here is to the value of above six hundred thousand crowns, I can secure no more than what is already packed; let every soldier take what he will, better so than that it should remain for those dogs of Mexicans." As soon as he had said this, many soldiers of those of Narvaez, and also some of ours fell to work, and loaded themselves with treasure. I never was avaricious, and now thought more of saving my life which was in much danger; however when the opportunity thus offered, I did not omit seizing out of a casket, four calchihuis, those precious stones so highly esteemed amongst the Indians; and although Cortes ordered the casket and its contents to be taken care of by his major domo, I luckily secured these jewels in time, and afterwards found them of infinite advantage as a resource against famine.

A little before midnight the detachment which took charge of the portable bridge set out upon its march, and arriving at the first canal or aperture of water, it was thrown across. The night was dark and misty, and it began to rain. The bridge being fixed, the baggage artillery, and some of the cavalry passed over it, as also the Tlascalans with the gold. Sandoval and those with him passed, also Cortes and his party after the first, and many other soldiers. At this moment the trumpets and shouts of the enemy were heard, and the alarm was given by them, crying out, "Taltelulco, Taltelulco, out with your canoes! The Teules are going, attack them at the bridges!" In an instant the enemy were upon us by land, and the lake and canals were covered with canoes. They immediately flew to the bridges, and fell on us there, so that they entirely intercepted our line of march. As misfortunes do not come single, it also rained so heavily that some of the horses were terrified, and growing restive fell into the water, and the bridge was broken in at the same time. The enemy attacked us here now with redoubled fury, and our soldiers making a stout resistance, the aperture of water was soon filled with the dead and dying men, and horses, and those who were struggling to escape, all heaped together, with artillery, packs, and bales of baggage, and those who carried them. Many were drowned here, and many put into the canoes and carried off for sacrifice. It was dreadful to hear the cries of the unfortunate sufferers, calling for assistance and invoking the Holy Virgin or St. Iago, while others who escaped by swimming, or by clambering upon the chests, bales of baggage, and dead bodies, earnestly begged for help to get up to the causeway. Many who, on their reaching the ground, thought themselves safe were there seized or knocked in the head with clubs.

Away went whatever regularity had been in the march at first; for Cortes and the captains and soldiers who were mounted clapt spurs to their horses and galloped off, along the causeway; nor can I blame them, for the cavalry could do nothing against the enemy, of any effect; for when they attacked them, the latter threw themselves into the water on each side of the causeway, and others from the houses with arrows, or on the ground with large lances, killed the horses. It is evident we could make no battle with them in the water, and without powder, and in the night, what else could we do than what we did; which was, to join in bodies of thirty or forty soldiers, and when the Indians closed upon us, to drive them off with a few cuts and thrusts of our swords, and then hurry on, to get over the causeway as soon as we could. As to waiting for one another, that would have lost us all; and had it happened in the day time, things would have been even worse with us. The escape of such as were fortunate enough to effect it, was owing to God's mercy, who gave us force to do so; for the very sight of the number of the enemy who surrounded us, and carried off our companions in their canoes to sacrifice, was terrible. About fifty of us, soldiers of Cortes, and some of those of Narvaez, went together in a body, by the causeway; every now and then parties of Indians came up, calling us Luilones, a term of reproach, and attempting to seize us, and we, when they came within our reach, facing about, repelling them with a few thrusts of our swords, and then hurrying on. Thus we proceeded, until we reached the firm ground near Tacuba, where Cortes, Sandoval, De Oli, Salcedo, Dominguez, Lares, and others of the cavalry, with such of the infantry soldiers as had crossed the bridge before it was destroyed, were already arrived. When we came near them, we heard the voices of Sandoval, De Oli, and De Morla, calling to Cortes who was riding at their head, that he should turn about, and assist those who were coming along the causeway, and who complained that he had abandoned them. Cortes replied that those who had escaped owed it to a miracle, and if they returned to the bridges all would lose their lives. Notwithstanding, he, with ten or twelve of the cavalry and some of the infantry who had escaped unhurt, countermarched and proceeded along the causeway; they had gone however but a very short distance when they met P. de Alvarado with his lance in his hand, badly wounded, and on foot, for his chestnut mare had been killed; he had with him three of our soldiers, and four of those of Narvaez, all badly wounded, and eight Tlascalans covered with blood. While Cortes proceeded along the causeway, we reposed in the enclosed courts hard by Tacuba. Messengers had already been sent out from the city of Mexico, to call the people of Tacuba, Ezcapuzalco, and Teneyuca together, in order to intercept us. In consequence they now began to surround and harass us with arrows, and stones, and to attack us with lances headed with the swords which had fallen into their hands on the preceding night. We made some attacks upon them, and defended ourselves as well as we could.

To revert to Cortes and his companions, when they learned from Alvarado that they were not to expect to see any more of our soldiers, the tears ran from their eyes, for Alvarado had with him in the rear guard, Velasquez de Leon, with above twenty more of the cavalry, and upwards of one hundred infantry. On enquiry Cortes was told that they were all dead, to the number of one hundred and fifty more. Alvarado also told them that after the horses had been killed, about eighty assembled in a body and passed the first aperture, upon the dead bodies and heaps of luggage; I do not perfectly recollect if he said that he passed upon the dead bodies, for we were more attentive to what he related to Cortes of the deaths of J. Velasquez and above two hundred more companions, those of Narvaez included, who were with him, and who were killed at that canal. He also said that at the other bridge God's mercy saved them, and that the whole of the causeway was full of the enemy.

Source: Díaz del Castillo, Bernal. *The True History of the Conquest of Mexico*. Translated by Maurice Keatinge. London: Harrap, 1927, 249–252, 256–260.

Fray Marcos de Niza, Reports of Cibola (1539)

Spanish suspicions that enormous wealth could be found in the unexplored areas north of Mexico were supposedly confirmed in August 1539 by reports brought back to Mexico City by Fray Marcos de Niza, who had been sent out to the region the previous March with one of Álvar Núñez Cabeza de Vaca's companions and a number of Indians. The small party made a reconnaissance trip through the Southwest, traveling into present-day New Mexico and Arizona, When the group was attacked by Zuni Indians, Niza hurriedly returned to Mexico City after glimpsing, though only from a distance, the city of Cíbola. At the capital, he rendered an account of the things he had seen and heard to the viceroy and other officials of New Spain. Niza embellished his narrative somewhat, repeating as true the rumors passed on to him by various Indians and other members of his party, but it is clear that he believed the Indians. It took only a little encouragement for his hearers to be persuaded. Based on Niza's tales, the ill-fated Coronado expedition scoured the whole territory in search of gold from 1540 to 1542. This selection reprints the opening paragraphs of Niza's Relación *of 1539, detailing the early reports of Cibola.*

With the aid and favor of the most holy Virgin Mary, our Lady, and of our seraphic father St. Francis, I, Fray Marcos de Niza, a professed religious of the order of St. Francis, in fulfillment of the instructions above given of the most illustrious lord Don Antonio de Mendoza, viceroy and governor for H[is]. M[ajesty]. of New Spain, left the town of San Miguel, in the province of Culiacan, on Friday, March 7th, 1539. I took with me as companion Friar Honoratus and also Stephen of Dorantes, a negro, and certain Indians, which the said Lord Viceroy bought for the purpose and set at liberty. They were delivered to me by Francisco de Coronado, governor of New Galicia, along with many other Indians from Petatlan and from the village of Cuchillo, situated about fifty leagues from the said town. All these came to the valley of Culiacan, manifesting great joy, because it had been certified to them that the Indians were free, the said governor having sent in advance to acquaint them of their freedom and to tell them that it was the desire and command of H. M. that they should not be enslaved nor made war upon nor badly treated.

With this company as stated, I took my way towards the town of Petatlan, receiving much hospitality and presents of food, roses and other such things; besides which, at all the stopping-places where there were no people, huts were constructed for me of mats and branches. In this town of Petatlan I stayed three days, because my companion Friar Honoratus fell sick. I found it advisable to leave him there and, conformably with the instructions given to me, I followed the way in which I was guided, though unworthy, by the Holy Ghost. There went with me Stephen Dorantes, the negro, some of the freed Indians and many people of that country. I was received everywhere I went with much hospitality and rejoicing and with triumphal arches. The inhabitants also gave me what food they had, which was little, because they said it had not rained for three years, and because the Indians of that territory think more of hiding than of growing crops, for fear of the Christians of the town of San Miguel, who up to that time were accustomed to make war upon and enslave them. On all this road, which would be about 25 or 30 leagues beyond Petatlan, I did not see anything worthy of being set down here, except that there came to me some Indians from the island visited by the Marquess of Valle, and who informed me that it was really an island and not, as some think, part of the mainland. I saw that they passed to and from the mainland on rafts and that the distance between the island and the mainland might be half a sea league, rather more or less. Likewise there came to see me Indians from another larger and more distant island, by whom I was told that there were thirty other small islands, inhabited, but with poor food excepting two, which they said had maize. These Indians wore suspended from their necks many shells of the kind which contain pearls; I showed them a pearl which I carried for sample and they told me that there were some in the islands, but I did not see any.

I took my way over a desert for four days and there went with me some Indians from the islands mentioned as well as from the villages which I left behind, and at the end of the desert I found some other Indians, who were astonished to see me, as they had no news of Christians, having no traffic with the people on the other side of the desert. These Indians made me very welcome, giving me plenty of food, and they endeavored to touch my clothes, calling me *Sayota*, which means in their language "man from heaven." I made them understand, the best I could by my interpreters, the content of my instructions, namely, the knowledge of Our Lord in heaven and of H. M. on earth. And always, by all the means that I could, I sought to learn about a country with numerous towns and a people of a higher culture than those I was encountering, but I had no news except that they told me that in the country beyond, four or five days' journey thence, where the chains of mountains ended, there was an extensive and level open tract, in which they told me there were many and very large towns inhabited by a people clothed with cotton. When I showed them some metals which I was carrying, in order to take account of the metals of the country, they took a piece of gold and told me that there were vessels of it among the people of the region and that they wear certain articles of that metal suspended from their noses and ears, and that they had some little blades of it, with which they scrape and relieve themselves of sweat. But as this tract lies inland and my intention was to stay near the coast, I determined to leave it till my return, because then I would be able to see it better. And so I marched three days through a country inhabited by the same people, by whom I was received in the same manner as by those I had already passed. I came to a medium-sized town named Vacapa, where they made me a great welcome and gave me much food, of which they had plenty, as the whole land is irrigated. From this town to the sea is forty leagues. As I found myself so far away from the sea, and as it was two days before Passion Sunday, I determined to stay there until Easter, to inform myself concerning the islands of which I said above that I had news. So I sent Indian messengers to the sea, by three ways, whom I charged to bring back to me people from the coast and from some of the islands, that I might inform myself concerning them. In another direction I sent Stephen Dorantes, the negro, whom I instructed to take the route towards the north for fifty or sixty leagues to see if by that way he might obtain an account of any important thing such as we were seeking. I agreed with him that if he had any news of a populous, rich and important country he should not continue further but should return in person or send me Indians with a certain signal which we arranged, namely, that if it were something of medium importance, he should send me a white cross of a hand's breadth, if it were something of great importance, he should send me one of two hands' breadth, while if it were bigger and better than New Spain, he should send me a great cross. And so the said negro Stephen departed from me on Passion Sunday after dinner, whilst I stayed in the town, which I say is called Vacapa.

In four day's time there came messengers from Stephen with a very great cross, as high as a man, and they told me on Stephen's behalf that I should immediately come and follow him, because he had met people who gave him an account of the greatest country in the world, and that he had Indians who had been there, of whom he sent me one. This man told me so many wonderful things about the country, that I forebore to believe them until I should have seen them or should have more certitude of the matter. He told me that it was thirty days' journey from where Stephen was staying to the first city of the country, which was named Cíbola. As it appears to me to be worth while to put in this paper what this Indian, whom Stephen sent me, said, concerning the country, I will do so. He asserted that in the first province there were seven very great cities, all under one lord, that the houses, constructed of stone and lime, were large, that the smallest were of one storey with a terrace above, that there were others of two and three storeys, whilst that of the lord had four, and all were joined under his rule. He said that the doorways of the principal houses were much ornamented with turquoises, of which there was a great abundance, and that the people of those cities went very well clothed. He told me many other particulars, not only of the seven cities but of other provinces beyond them, each one of which he said was much bigger than that of the seven cities.

Source: Moquin, Wayne, with Charles Van Doren, eds. *A Documentary History of the Mexican Americans*. New York: Praeger, 1971.

Juan Rodríguez Cabrillo, Excerpts from His Diary of a Voyage along the California Coast

(1542)

By 1533, the peninsula of Baja California had been discovered by the Spanish, and further interest in the northern reaches developed when Álvar Núñez Cabeza de Vaca told of his wanderings among the Indians from Florida to Texas and when Fray Marcos de Niza returned to Mexico with his news of the seven cities of Cíbola. In June 1542, a small expedition captained by Juan Rodríguez Cabrillo sailed from Puerto de Navidad in Mexico to explore the coast of California. His party sailed north along the coast in two small ships, stopping at many points to land and converse with the Indians of the region. They probably sailed farther north than the San Francisco Bay area but never sighted it. On the return trip, Cabrillo died of injuries received in a fall, but the ships, after numerous difficulties, finally made it back to Mexico on April 14, 1543, 10 months after their departure. A short portion of Cabrillo's diary of the voyage, covering the weeks from September 23 to October 17, 1542, is reprinted here.

On Saturday, the 23d of said month [September], they left said port of San Mateo and sailed along the coast until the Monday following, when they must have gone about eighteen leagues. They saw very beautiful valleys and groves, and country both level and rough, but no Indians were seen.

On the following Tuesday and Wednesday they sailed along the coast about eight leagues, passing by some three islands completely denuded of soil. One of them is larger than the others. It is about two leagues in circumference and affords shelter from the west winds. They are three leagues from the mainland, and are in thirty-four degrees. They called them Islas Desiertas (Desert Islands). This day great smokes were seen on the land. The country appears to be good and has large valleys, and in the interior there are high mountains.

On the following Thursday they went about six leagues along a coast running north-northwest, and discovered a port, closed and very good, which they named San Miguel [San Diego Bay]. It is in thirty-four and one-third degrees. Having cast anchor in it, they went ashore where there were people. Three of them waited, but all the rest fled. To these three they gave some presents and they said by signs that in the interior men like the Spaniards had passed. They gave signs of great fear. On the night of this day they went ashore from the ships to fish with a net, and it appears that here there were some Indians, and that they began to shoot at them with arrows and wounded three men.

Next day in the morning they went with the boat farther into the port, which is large, and brought two boys, who understood nothing but signs. They gave them both shirts and sent them away immediately.

Next day in the morning three adult Indians came to the ships and said by signs that in the interior men like us were travelling about, bearded, clothed, and armed like those of the ships. They made signs that they carried crossbows and swords; and they made gestures with the right arm as if they were throwing lances, and ran around as if they were on horseback. They made signs that they were killing many native Indians, and that for this reason they were afraid. These people are comely and large. They go about covered with skins of animals. While they were in this port a heavy storm occurred, but since the port is good they did not feel it at all. It was a violent storm from the west-southwest and the south-southwest. This is the first storm which they have experienced. They remained in this port until the following Tuesday. The people here called the Christians Guacamal.

On the following Tuesday, the 3d of the month of October, they departed from this port of San Miguel, and on Wednesday, Thursday, and Friday, they held their course a matter of eighteen leagues along the coast, where they saw many valleys and plains, and many smokes, and mountains in the interior. At nightfall they were near some islands which are some seven leagues from the mainland, but because the wind went down they could not reach them that night.

At daybreak on Saturday, the 7th of the month of October, they were at the islands which they named San Salvador [San Clemente] and La Vitoria [Santa Catalina]. They anchored at one of them and went ashore with the boat to see if there were people; and when the boat came near, a great number of Indians emerged from the bushes and grass, shouting, dancing, and making signs that they should land. As they saw that the women were fleeing from the boats they made signs that they should not be afraid. Immediately they were reassured, and laid their bows and arrows on the ground and launched in the water a good canoe which held eight or ten Indians, and came to the ships. They gave them beads and other articles, with which they were pleased, and then they returned. Afterward the Spaniards went ashore, and they, the Indian women, and all felt very secure. Here an old Indian made signs to them that men like the Spaniards, clothed and bearded, were going about on the mainland. They remained on this island only till midday.

On the following Sunday, the 8th of said month, they drew near to the mainland in a large bay which they called Bay of Los Fumos, (Bay of the Smokes)

[Santa Monica], because of the many smokes which they saw on it. Here they held a colloquy with some Indians whom they captured in a canoe, and who made signs that toward the north there were Spaniards like them. This bay is in thirty-five degrees and is a good port, and the country is good, with many valleys, plains, and groves.

On the following Monday, the 9th of the said month of October, they left the Bay of Los Fuegos (the Fires), and sailed this day some six leagues, anchoring in a large bay. From here they departed the next day, Tuesday, and sailed some eight leagues along a coast running from northwest to southeast. We saw on the land a pueblo of Indians close to the sea, the houses being large like those of New Spain. They anchored in front of a very large valley on the coast. Here there came to the ships many very good canoes, each of which held twelve or thirteen Indians; they told them of Christians who were going about in the interior. The coast runs from northwest to southeast. Here they gave them some presents, with which they were greatly pleased. They indicated by signs that in seven days they could go to where the Spaniards were, and Juan Rodriguez decided to send two Spaniards into the interior. They also indicated that there was a great river. With these Indians they sent a letter at a venture to the Christians. They named this town the Pueblo of Las Canoas [San Buena-Ventura]. The Indians dress in skins of animals; they are fishermen and eat raw fish; they were eating *maguey* also. This pueblo is in thirty-five and one-third degrees. The interior of the country is a very fine valley; and they made signs that in that valley there was much maize and abundant food. Behind the valley appear some very high mountains and very broken country. They call the Christians Taquimine. Here they took possession and here they remained until Friday, the 13th day of said month.

On Friday, the 13th of said month of October, they left the pueblo of Las Canoas to continue their voyage, and sailed this day six or seven leagues, passing along the shores of two large islands. Each of them must be four leagues long, and they must be about four leagues from the mainland. They are uninhabited, because they have no water, but they have good ports. The coast of the mainland trends to the west-northwest. It is a country of many savannahs and groves. On the following Saturday they continued on their course, but made no more than two leagues, anchoring in front of a magnificent valley densely populated, with level land, and many groves. Here came canoes with fish to barter; the Indians were very friendly.

On the following Sunday, the 15th day of the said month, they continued on their course along the coast for about ten leagues; all the way there were many canoes, for the whole coast is very densely populated; and many Indians kept boarding the ships. They pointed out the pueblos and told us their names. They are Xuco, Bis, Sopono, Alloc, Xabaagua, Xocotoc, Potoltuc, Nacbuc, Quelqueme, Misinagua, Misesopano, Elquis, Coloc, Mugu, Xagua, Anacbuc, Partocac, Susuquey, Quanmu, Gua, Asimu, Aguin, Casalic, Tucumu, and Incpupu.

All these pueblos are between the first pueblo of Las Canoas, which is called Xucu, and this point. They are in a very good country, with fine plains and many groves and savannahs. The Indians go dressed in skins. They said that in the interior there were many pueblos, and much maize three days' journey from there. They call maize Oep. They also said that there were many cows; these they call Cae. They also told us of people bearded and clothed.

This day they passed along the shore of a large island which must be fifteen leagues long. They said it was very densely populated and that there were the following pueblos: Niquipos, Maxul, Xugua, Nitel, Macamo, and Nimitapal. They called this island San Lucas. From here to the pueblo of Las Canoas it must be about eighteen leagues. The island must be about six leagues from the mainland.

On Monday, the 16th of the said month, sailing along the coast, they made about four leagues, and cast anchor in the afternoon in front of two pueblos. All this day, likewise, many canoes came with the ships and made signs that farther on there were canoes much larger.

On the following Tuesday, the 17th of the said month, they made three leagues, with favorable winds. Many canoes went with the ships from day-break, and the captain kept giving them many presents. All this coast which they have passed is very thickly settled. The Indians brought for them many sardines, fresh and very good. They say that in the interior there are many pueblos and abundant food. They ate no maize. They were dressed in skins, and wore their hair very long and tied up with long strings interwoven with the hair, there being attached to the strings many gewgaws of flint, bone, and wood. The country appears to be very fine.

Source: Moquin, Wayne, with Charles Van Doren, eds. *A Documentary History of the Mexican Americans.* New York: Praeger, 1971.

Thomas Gage, Description of His Travels in Central America (1648)

Central America is an isthmus located at the southernmost end of North America abutting South America. It is the shortest landmass between the Atlantic and Pacific oceans. Since the 18th century, the United States has seen Central America as strategically important to its political, military, and economic interests. During the Spanish colonial period, the early 1500s to 1821, Panama served as a center of commerce for Spain's colonies in America because Spain shipped trade items and slaves from Panama to Peru. On September 15, 1821, the colonies that made up the Captaincy General of Guatemala declared their independence from Spain. For two years, Central America was under the rule of Emperor Agustín de Iturbide, but on July 1, 1823, El Salvador, Guatemala, Honduras, Nicaragua, and Costa Rica formed the United Provinces of Central America. The following description was written by Thomas Gage, a British subject and a Spanish Dominican who spent two or three years in Guatemala City. Gage published a book in 1648 describing his travels in Latin America.

The isthmus of Panama, which runneth between the north and south seas, besides gold in it, is admirably stored with silver, spices, pearls, and medicinal herbs . . . Guatemala, seated in the midst of a Paradise on one side and a hell on the other [a volcano], yet never hath this hell broke so loose as to consume that flourishing city. True it is that many years ago it opened a wide mouth on the top, and breathed out such fiery ashes as filled the houses of Guatemala and the country about. . . . The trading of the city [Guatemala] is great, for by mules it partakes of the best commodities of Mexico, Oaxaca, and Chiapa, and, southward, of Nicaragua and Costa Rica. By sea, it hath commerce with Peru, by two sea ports and havens. . . . The Government of all the country about, and of all Honduras, Socomusco, Comayagua, Nicaragua, Costa Rica, Vera Paz, Suchitepéquez, and Chiapas is subordinate unto the Chancery [*Audencia*] of Guatemala; for although every governor over these several provinces is appointed by the King and Council of Spain, yet when they come to those parts to the enjoyment of their charge and execution office, their actions, if unjust, are weighed and judged, censured, and condemned by the Court residing in the city [of Panama]. . . . It is held to be one of the richest places in all America, having by land and, by the river Chagres, commerce with the North Sea, and by the south, trading with all Peru, East Indies, Mexico, and Honduras.

Source: Thompson, J. Eric S., ed. *Thomas Gage's Travels in the New World.* Norman: University of Oklahoma Press, 1958, 95, 183, 186, 187, 327.

Eusebio Kino, Explorations and Work in Pimería Alta (Modern-Day Arizona and Sonora)

(1687)

Jesuit Eusebio Kino was, by vocation, a missionary to the Indians and, by disposition, an explorer and cartographer. He lived among the Pima Indians from 1687 until his death in 1711 and explored the Southwest extensively during that time. He was the first to make an accurate geography of the region on the basis of actual travels. Perhaps most notable among his achievements was the conclusive demonstration that California was not an island. The area in which Kino worked was called the Pimería Alta, today southern Arizona and northern Sonora. He himself claimed to have made nearly 40 expeditions throughout the Southwest in all directions from his mission, and his many maps of the region were widely circulated in Europe, especially his famous 1705 map entitled "A Land Passage to California." Three chapters from Kino's memoirs are reprinted here. The first deals with his assertions about California and the second and third with his vocation—the conversion of the Indians.

CHAPTER VIII. COGENT REASONS AND CLEAR ARGUMENTS WHICH ESTABLISH THE CERTAINTY OF THE LAND PASSAGE TO CALIFORNIA

In case there should be some incredulous persons or someone ignorant of it, the continuity of these lands with California would be rendered certain and proved by the seven following convincing reasons or arguments:

1st. Because thus I saw it on October 9, 1698, from the neighboring high mountain of Santa Clara. And again in March of the past year, 1701, we saw this connection and passage by land to California, in the company of Father Rector Juan María de Salvatierra, for his Reverence came with ten soldiers and other persons to see this demonstrated, since some had contradicted us.

2d. Because in four other journeys inland which I have made, travelling fifty leagues to the northwest of the said hill of Santa Clara, which is near to and to the eastward of the arm and head of the Sea of California, and afterwards in going ten leagues more to the westward, along the Rio Grande, to where it unites with the Colorado River, and from this confluence forty leagues more to the southwest, along the same Colorado River to its mouth, no Sea of California has been found or seen, for it does not rise higher than barely to the latitude of thirty-two degrees. Hence it is plainly to be inferred that Drake, besides many other modern cosmographers, in their various printed maps, with notable discredit to cosmography, deceive themselves as well as others, by extending this sea, or arm, or strait of the Sea of California from thirty-two to forty-six degrees, making it thereby an island, and the largest in the world, whereas it is not an island but a peninsula.

3d. Because in this journey inland when I was saying mass on March 11 at the above-mentioned mouth of the Colorado River, in company with Father Rector Manuel Gonzales, the sun rose above more than thirty leagues of sea, at the head of this California arm or gulf. At the same time, from the same estuary we saw to the westward thirty leagues more of continuous land, as many more to the south and southwest, and many more to the north, northwest, and northeast. Therefore, this sea does not extend to the north.

4th. Because the natives nearest to that estuary, Quiquimas as well as Cutganes and Coanopas, both this time and on other occasions, gave us various blue shells which are found only on the opposite coast and on the other, or South Sea, where the ship from China comes. And they gave us this time some little pots which shortly before they had brought from that opposite coast, travelling ten leagues from the west by continuous land.

5th. Because these natives and others who came to see us from far to the southwest gave us various reports of the fathers of our Company, telling us that they wore our costumes and vestments, and that they lived down there to the southward with the other Spaniards at Loreto Concho, where the Guimies and Edues, or Laimones Indians obtained their food, and where Father Rector Juan Maria de Salvatierra and others were. And I having purposely asked them if those Guimies and Edues Indians down there planted maize, and what foods they lived on, they answered us that they did not plant maize nor beans, etc., but that their food was game, the deer, the hare, the mountain goat, the *pitajaya*, the *tuna*, the *mescal*, and other wild fruits, and that the Indians to the westward had blue shells, all being things and reports which it was plain to me were true, since I was there and lived with those Indians seventeen years ago.

6th. Because now in this journey inland and on other occasions I have found various things—little trees, fruit, incense, etc.—all species which are peculiar to California alone, and samples of which I bring, to celebrate with the incense, by the favor of heaven, this Easter and Holy Week, and to place five good grains of incense in the Paschal candle. Moreover, near this estuary we already have found some words of the Guimia language which I learned there, while missionary and rector of that mission of California, although unworthy, in the two trienniums of Fathers Provincial Bernardo Pardo and Luys del Canto, from the year 1681 to that of 1685.

7th. Because the ancient maps with good reason showed California as a peninsula and not as an island, as well as some modern ones, among them the universal map of my Father master of mathematics in the University of Ingolstadt, which is in my possession. He dedicated it to our Father San Ygnacio and to San Francisco Xavier, with this inscription: *de Universo Terrarum Orbe Opime Mentis* [To the well-deserving of the whole world].

And if some hostile and obstinate persons should maintain that some Quiquima Indians say that farther west the sea still extends to the northwest, these Quiquimas speak of the other sea, on the opposite coast, and not of this our Sea of California, of which, as some call it Red Sea, we may say, because we have found this passage, *Aparuit terra arida, et in Mari Rubro via sine inpedimento* [Dry land appeared and in the Red Sea a road without hindrance], as says the Church on August 8, on the day of the saints who have the Gospel: *Euntes in mundum universum. Predicate Evangelium omni creaturœe* [Go into all the world and preach the gospel to every creature]. . . .

CHAPTER X. TEMPORAL MEANS FOR THESE NEW CONVERSIONS AND FOR THE TOTAL REDUCTION OF THIS NORTH AMERICA, WHICH HITHERTO HAS BEEN UNKNOWN

I. First, there are already many cattle, sheep and goats, and horses; for, although in the past year I have given more than seven hundred cattle to the four fathers who entered this Pimería, I have for the other new conversions and missions which by the favor of heaven it may be desired to establish, more than three thousand five hundred more cattle; and some of them are already far inland, ninety leagues from here, and by the divine grace they can pass with ease to the Californias, Upper and Lower, as a certain important person is pleased to name them, the latter being in twenty-six and the former in thirty and more degrees of latitude.

II. There are in this very fertile and rich Pimería, which already has five missions with five fathers, many fields of wheat, maize, beans, etc; and produces all sorts of vegetables, garden products, and fruit trees, as in Europe. There are already vines for Castilian wine for the missions, a watermill, pack trains, fields, oxen, lands, level roads, beautiful rivers, abundant pasturage, good timbers for buildings, and mineral lands.

III. Of these new nations almost all are composed of industrious, docile, affable, and very friendly Indians; and only in some remote parts are there some Indians somewhat more barbarous and uncivilized, because of never having seen civilized people in all their lives.

IV. The temperature of these lands, which extend from thirty degrees of latitude to thirty-one, thirty-two, thirty-three, thirty-four, etc., is similar to that of Mexico and the better part of Europe, without excessive heat or excessive cold.

V. With these means and with these new conversions it will be possible to trade by sea and land with other near-by and remote provinces, nations, and kingdoms, with Sonora, Hyaqui, Cinaloa, Culiacan, with all New Galicia, with New Biscay, with Moqui, with New Mexico, which will be able to come to join hands with these provinces of Sonora, and even with New France.

CHAPTER XI. ADVANTAGES WHICH MAY RESULT FROM THESE NEW CONVERSIONS TO THE BENEFIT OF ALL THIS UNKNOWN NORTH AMERICA

I. First, with these new conversions the Catholic dominion of the royal crown of our very Catholic monarch Philip V, God preserve him, and our holy Roman Catholic Faith, will be extended.

II. Very extensive new lands, nations, rivers, seas, and people of this North America which hitherto have been unknown will be discovered and won; and, besides, thereby these Christian provinces will be more protected, safer, and more quiet.

III. Thereby will be removed the great errors and falsehoods imposed upon us by those who have delineated this North America with feigned things which do not exist, such as a crowned king whom they carried on a golden litter; a lake of quicksilver, and another of gold; a walled city with towers, etc.; the Kingdom of Axa; the pearls, amber, and corals of the Rio del Tizon, the Rio del Coral, and the Rio de Aganguchi, which they represent as emptying into this sea of California in thirty-five or thirty-six degrees, although this sea does not extend to that latitude; likewise the error of the Seven Cities, which some represent. Although at present they do not exist, ten years ago we saw some great houses at different places near the Rio Grande, whose structures, now fallen, indicate that they did exist a long time ago; and it is very possible that from them issued the people of Monte Suma, when they went to found the great City of Mexico.

IV. Since Father Mariano reprehends with reason those feigned grandeurs and riches, in particular when they wish to attribute them to the account of the Adelantado of New Mexico, Don Juan de Oñate, we shall be able to make drawings and true cosmographic maps of all these new lands and nations, of this passage by land to California, as well as of the very large volumed, fertile, and very populous rivers which empty into the head of this sea, and of the harbors and bays of the opposite coast and Sea of the South, of Gran Quivira, of Gran Teguayo, and of the neighboring Apachería, Moqui, etc. And as your Reverence, in the journey inland made two years ago with Señor Lieutenant Juan Mateo Manje, Father Francisco Gonzalvo, and me, which in going and returning was more than two hundred leagues, found these Pima nations, with some Opas and Cocomaricopas, already reduced to our friendship, so now the Yumas, Coanopas, Cutganes, Quiquimas, and many others to the north, northwest, and west are reduced, in this terra firma as well as in the neighboring California Alta; all of which lands combined are as large as all of Europe, and of the same climate and temperature.

Moreover, by the north, northeast, and east, can be found a road to Europe shorter by half than the one which we now use by way of Mexico and Vera Cruz; as also by the northwest and west one shall be able to go in time by land even very near to Japan, Great China, and Tartary; for the Strait of Anian, which authors place with such a variety of opinions, probably has no more foundation in fact than had this arm of the sea with which for us they incorrectly delineated California as an island. That route to Japan and Great China can be found by way of Cape Mendozino, and by the land of Yesso [Alaska, perhaps], and by the land which they call

Tierra de la Compañia, which by divine grace, with apostolic missionaries can become Land of the Company of Jesus.

V. The China ship can have a port call, as you have so much desired, on the opposite coast of California, where the many sick with scurvy which it is accustomed to bring will find relief. And it can have trade, very profitable for all, with the provinces of this Kingdom of New Biscay, for they told me seventeen years ago when I sailed in the Chinese ship from Matanchel to Acapulco that for a sheep they gladly gave an ivory tusk or a piece of China linen, which is usually forty *varas* [yards, approximately] long and which it is the custom to sell for a dollar a *vara*, because of the heavy freight charges entailed in carrying it by land from Mexico to these provinces of Sonora. And almost the same is true with respect to the other goods of this very rich Philippine galleon.

VI. We shall comply with what so Christianlike and so earnestly is charged upon us by the very Catholic *cédula* [certificate of instruction] of May [1]4, 1686, which the Royal Audiencia of Guadalajara gave me, inserted in a royal provision, when I was passing through that city on my return from California and coming to these new conversions. In that royal *cédula* his royal Majesty commands that with respect to the most essential point of the new conversions effort shall be made to make all haste possible as in a matter of chief concern to his royal Majesty, and a matter of conscience to him, just as to those of us who live nearest, and that the necessary expenses be not spared, because his royal Majesty recognizes that for all that is spent in those causes, so merciful, our Lord always returns to his royal crown very abundant and well known increase, which are the words of the royal *cédula.* And, indeed, we very plainly see that at the very same time that his royal Majesty, Don Carlos II, God preserve him, incurred the very great expense of the three ships for the conversion of California through Admiral Don Ysidro de Atondo y Antillon, there were discovered very near to and opposite said conquest and conversion the great riches and mines of the mining camps which are commonly called Los Frayles, Alamos, and Guadalupe; and the day of our Lady of Sorrows, day before yesterday, when I received the news of the six thousand *pesos* which his royal Majesty Philip V, God preserve him, gave to the new conversions of California, they gave me certain news of the treasure and rich mines which have just been discovered near here at Quisuani, Aygame, San Cosme, etc., and very near to the new conversion or mission of San Francisco Xavier of the Pimas Cocomacaques of Pimeria Baxa.

VII. In this way even with very great good fortune and profit to ourselves, by divine grace, we will bring it about that, so many souls being converted, *fiat unus pastor, et unum ovile*, and that all will help us to praise our most merciful God through all the blessed Eternity. All of which I commend very affectionately to the holy sacrifices and to the paternal, holy protection of your Reverence, whose life may our Lord preserve as I desire.

Source: Bolton, Herbert E. *Kino's Historical Memoir of Pimería Alta, 1683–1711.* vol. 1 Cleveland: Arthur H. Clark, 1919, 351–354, 357–362.

Louisiana Purchase
(April 30, 1803)

On April 30, 1803, Napoleon Bonaparte of France sold the Louisiana Territory, more than 800,000 square miles (2 million square kilometers) of land extending from the Mississippi River to the Rocky Mountains, to the United States for about $15 million. This acquisition put the United States at the Texas border, on the rim of New Spain (Mexico). European Americans viewed Texas as being controlled by a corrupt and intrusive European power. From the beginning, the United States was aggressive in its claims to Texas. U.S. president Thomas Jefferson insisted that the Rio Grande River was the western boundary of the Louisiana Territory. The United States claimed that it owned all the land to and including half of New Mexico. Jefferson instructed that the U.S. minister to Spain insist on the Rio Bravo (Rio Grande) but yield in case of the probability of armed conflict. With the Louisiana Purchase, the United States doubled its size and, more importantly, was free to navigate the Mississippi River. Although many considered the taking of more territory a violation of the U.S. Constitution, which did not specifically declare that the government had the power to purchase land, the Senate ratified the treaty on October 20, 1803. The following articles from the Louisiana Purchase treaty deal with the cession of the territory and accentuate the lack of clear boundaries. However, with regard to boundaries, the United States promised to honor the San Ildefonso Treaty.

ARTICLE I

Whereas by the Article the third of the Treaty concluded at St Ildefonso the 9th Vendémiaire on 1st October 1800 between the First Consul of the French Republic and his Catholic Majesty it was agreed as follows.

His Catholic Majesty promises and engages on his part to cede to the French Republic six months after the full and entire execution of the conditions and Stipulations herein relative to his Royal Highness the Duke of Parma, the Colony or Province of Louisiana with the Same extent that it now has in the hand of Spain, & that it had when France possessed it; and Such as it Should be after the Treaties subsequently entered into between Spain and other States.

And whereas in pursuance of the Treaty and particularly of the third article the French Republic has an incontestible [sic] title to the domain and to the possession of the said Territory—The First Consul of the French Republic desiring to give to the United States a strong proof of his friendship doth hereby cede to the United States in the name of the French Republic for ever and in full Sovereignty the said territory with all its rights and appurtenances as fully and in the Same manner as they have been acquired by the French Republic in virtue of the above mentioned Treaty concluded with his Catholic Majesty.

ARTICLE II

In the cession made by the preceeding [sic] article are included the adjacent Islands belonging to Louisiana, all public lots and Squares, vacant lands and all public buildings, fortifications, barracks and other edifices which are not private property. The Archives, papers & documents relative to the domain and Sovereignty of Louisiana and its dependances [sic] will be left in the possession of the Commissaries of the United States, and copies will be afterwards given in due form to the Magistrates and Municipal officers of such of the said papers and documents as may be necessary to them.

ARTICLE III

The inhabitants of the ceded territory shall be incorporated in the Union of the United States and admitted as soon as possible according to the principles of the federal Constitution to the enjoyment of all these rights, advantages and immunities of citizens of the United States, and in the mean time they shall be maintained and protected in the free enjoyment of their liberty, property and the Religion which they profess. . . .

ARTICLE VI

The United States promise to execute Such treaties and articles as may have been agreed between Spain and the tribes and nations of Indians until by mutual consent of the United States and the said tribes or nations other Suitable articles Shall have been agreed upon. . . .

ARTICLE X

The present treaty Shall be ratified in good and due form and the ratifications Shall be exchanged in the Space of Six months after the date of the Signature by the Ministers Plenipotentiary or Sooner if possible.

In faith whereof the respective Plenipotentiaries have Signed these articles in the French and English languages; declaring nevertheless that the present Treaty was originally agreed to in the French language; and have thereunto affixed their Seals.

Done at Paris the tenth day of Floreal in the eleventh year of the French Republic; and the 30th of April 1803.

Source: Louisiana Purchase Treaty, April 30, 1803; General Records of the U.S. Government; Record Group 11; National Archives.

El Grito de Dolores
(September 16, 1810)

At midnight on September 16, 1810, Father Miguel Hidalgo rang his parish bell in the city of Dolores, Guanajuato, and declared Mexico's independence. The declaration of independence was called El Grito de Dolores *(the Shout of Dolores). Hidalgo called for Mexican independence and the exile or arrest of all Spaniards in Mexico; he ended by calling out,*

"Mexicanos, ¡Viva México!" *(Mexicans, long live Mexico!). The exact words Father Hidalgo said have not been found, and the two quotations here are two renditions of what he might have said.*

El grito de Dolores, Fr. Miguel Hidalgo, September 15, 1810

"My children: a new dispensation comes to us today. Will you receive it? Will you free yourselves? Will you recover the lands stolen three hundred years ago from your forefathers by the hated Spaniards? We must act at once . . . Will you not defend your religion and your rights as true patriots? Long live our Lady of Guadalupe! Death to the gachupines!"

Source: Meyer, Michael C., and William L. Sherman, "Mexican Independence." In *The Course of Mexican History*. 2nd ed. New York: Oxford University Press, 1983, 287–288.

"My friends and countrymen: neither the king nor tributes exist for us any longer. We have borne this shameful tax, which only suits slaves, for three centuries as a sign of tyranny and servitude; [a] terrible stain which we shall know how to wash away with our efforts. The moment of our freedom has arrived, the hour of our liberty has struck; and if you recognized its great value, you will help me defend it from the ambitious grasp of the tyrants. Only a few hours remain before you see me at the head of the men who take pride in being free. I invite you to fulfill this obligation. And so without a patria nor liberty we shall always be at a great distance from true happiness. It has been imperative to take this step as now you know, and to begin this has been necessary. The cause is holy and God will protect it. The arrangements are hastily being made and for that reason I will not have the satisfaction of talking to you any longer. Long live, then, the Virgin of Guadalupe! Long live America for which we are going to fight!"

Source: "Father Hidalgo's *Grito de Dolores.*" Courtesy of Sons of DeWitt Colony Texas. http://www.tamu.edu/ccbn/dewitt/mexicanrev.htm.

Simón Bolívar, *Carta de Jamaica* (Letter from Jamaica), Kingston, Jamaica (September 6, 1815)

No Latin American hero is as revered as Simón Bolívar (1783–1830), the "Great Liberator" of Latin America. Bolívar believed a united hemisphere would strengthen it against foreign threats. On September 6, 1815, Bolivar wrote the Carta de Jamaica *in Kingston, supposedly as a response to a letter from an Englishman named Henry Cullen. In the letter, Bolívar reviews the historical successes in the struggle for Latin American independence and discusses the causes and justifications for independence. He also calls upon Europe to support the Latin American nations in their common struggle against Spain, and he reflects upon the future of Mexico, Central America, and South America. The following excerpt from the* Carta de Jamaica *discusses the centrality and importance of Central America to Latin American unity.*

It is a grandiose idea to think of consolidating the New World into a single nation, united by pacts into a single bond. It is reasoned that, as these parts have a common origin, language, customs, and religion, they ought to have a single government to permit the newly formed states to unite in a confederation. But this is not possible. Actually, America is separated by climatic differences, geographic diversity, conflicting interests, and dissimilar characteristics. How beautiful it would be if the Isthmus of Panamá could be for us what the Isthmus of Corinth was for the Greeks! Would to God that some day we may have the good fortune to convene there an august assembly of representatives of republics, kingdoms, and empires to deliberate upon the high interests of peace and war with the nations of the other three-quarters of the globe. . . . The states of the Isthmus of Panamá, as far as Guatemala, will perhaps form a confederation. Because of their magnificent position between two mighty oceans, they may in time become the emporium of the world. Their canals will shorten distances throughout the world, strengthen commercial ties between Europe, America, and Asia, and bring to that happy area tribute from the four quarters of the globe. There some day, perhaps, the capital of the world may be located—reminiscent of the Emperor Constantine's claim that Byzantium was the capital of the ancient world. . . . I am, Sir, etc. etc. Simón Bolívar

Source: Bolívar, Simón. "Reply of a South American to a Gentleman of this Island [Jamaica]." In *Selected Writings of Bolivar*, edited by Harold Bierck Jr., 118–119. vol. 1 New York: Colonial Press, 1951, 103–122.

Adams-Onís Treaty (1819)

The Adams-Onís Treaty is also known as the Transcontinental Treaty of 1819 or the Florida Purchase Treaty. Since before the United States achieved independence in 1783, Americans had designs on Spanish Florida, which they considered part of U.S. territory. Tension along the U.S.-Florida border was aggravated by frequent raids and the American belief that the Seminoles were a menace. These tensions increased in 1817, when President James Monroe ordered General Andrew Jackson to lead an expedition against Florida's Seminole Indians. Many scholars say the underlying reason for this expedition was to empower Monroe to put pressure on Spain—which was already having problems with independence movements throughout the Americas—to sell Florida. Another pretext was that Spain was harboring runaway African slaves in Florida. In 1818, Jackson invaded Florida, took control of Spanish forts, and executed British nationals. Jackson's raid led to an international incident with Britain and put pressure on Spain to enter into negotiations regarding Spanish Florida. The Adams-Onís Treaty of 1819, signed by Spanish foreign minister Luis de Onís and U.S. secretary of state John Quincy Adams, ceded Florida to the United States and settled a dispute regarding borders along the Sabine River in Texas. The following treaty articles specify the new borders.

ARTICLE 2. His Catholic Majesty cedes to the United States, in full property and sovereignty, all the territories which belong to him, situated to the Eastward of the Mississippi, known by the name of East and West Florida. The adjacent Islands dependent on said Provinces, all public lots and squares, vacant Lands, public Edifices, Fortifications, Barracks and other Buildings, which are not private property, Archives and Documents, which relate directly to the property and sovereignty of said Provinces, are included in this Article. The said Archives and Documents shall be left in possession of the Commissaries, or Officers of the United States, duly authorized to receive them.

ARTICLE 3. The Boundary Line between the two Countries, West of the Mississippi, shall begin on the Gulf of Mexico, at the mouth of the River

Sabine in the Sea, continuing North, along the Western Bank of that River, to the 32d degree of Latitude; thence by a Line due North to the degree of Latitude, where it strikes the Rio Roxo of Nachitoches, or Red-River, then following the course of the Rio-Roxo Westward to the degree of Longitude, 100 West from London and 23 from Washington, then crossing the said Red-River, and running thence by a Line due North to the River Arkansas, thence, following the Course of the Southern bank of the Arkansas to its source in Latitude, 42. North and thence by that parallel of Latitude to the South-Sea. The whole being as laid down in Melishe's Map of the United States, published at Philadelphia, improved to the first of January 1818. But if the Source of the Arkansas River shall be found to fall North or South of Latitude 42, then the Line shall run from the said Source due South or North, as the case may be, till it meets the said Parallel of Latitude 42, and thence along the said Parallel to the South Sea: all the Islands in the Sabine and the Said Red and Arkansas Rivers, throughout the Course thus described, to belong to the United States; but the use of the Waters and the navigation of the Sabine to the Sea, and of the said Rivers, Roxo and Arkansas, throughout the extent of the said Boundary, on their respective Banks, shall be common to the respective inhabitants of both Nations. The Two High Contracting Parties agree to cede and renounce all their rights, claims and pretensions to the Territories described by the said Line: that is to say—The United States hereby cede to His Catholic Majesty, and renounce forever, all their rights, claims, and pretensions to the Territories lying West and South of the above described Line; and, in like manner, His Catholic Majesty cedes to the said United States, all his rights, claims, and pretensions to any Territories, East and North of the said Line, and, for himself, his heirs and successors, renounces all claim to the said Territories forever.

ARTICLE 4. To fix this Line with more precision, and to place the Landmarks which shall designate exactly the limits of both Nations, each of the Contracting Parties shall appoint a Commissioner, and a Surveyor, who shall meet before the termination of one year from the date of the Ratification of this Treaty, at Nachitoches on the Red River, and proceed to run and mark the said Line from the mouth of the Sabine to the Red River, and from the Red River to the River Arkansas, and to ascertain the Latitude of the Source of the said River Arkansas, in conformity to what is above agreed upon and stipulated, and the Line of Latitude 42 to the South Sea: they shall make out plans and keep Journals of their proceedings, and the result agreed upon by them shall be considered as part of this Treaty, and shall have the same force as if it were inserted therein. The two Governments will amicably agree respecting the necessary Articles to be furnished to those persons, and also as to their respective escorts, should such be deemed necessary.

ARTICLE 5. The Inhabitants of the ceded Territories shall be secured in the free exercise of their Religion, without any restriction, and all those who may desire to remove to the Spanish Dominions shall be permitted to sell, or export their Effects at any time whatever, without being subject, in either case, to duties.

ARTICLE 6. The Inhabitants of the Territories which His Catholic Majesty cedes to the United States by this Treaty, shall be incorporated in the Union of the United States, as soon as may be consistent with the principle of the Federal Constitution, and admitted to the enjoyment of all the privileges, rights and immunities of the Citizens of the United States. . . .

ARTICLE 8. All the grants of land made before the 24th of January 1818 by His Catholic Majesty or by his lawful authorities in the said Territories ceded by His Majesty to the United States, shall be ratified and confirmed to the persons in possession of the lands, to the same extent that the same grants would be valid if the Territories had remained under the Dominion of His Catholic Majesty. But the owners in possession of such lands, who by reason of the recent circumstances of the Spanish Nation and the Revolutions in Europe, have been prevented from fulfilling all the conditions of their grants, shall complete them within the terms limited in the same respectively, from the date of this Treaty; in default of which the said grants shall be null and void—all grants made since the said 24th of January 1818 when the first proposal on the part of His Catholic Majesty, for the cession of the Floridas was made, are hereby declared and agreed to be null and void. . . .

Source: The Adams-Onís Treaty of 1819. *The Federal and State Constitutions Colonial Charters, and Other Organic Laws of the States, Territories, and Colonies Now or Heretofore Forming the United States of America.* Compiled and Edited Under the Act of Congress of June 30, 1906, by Francis Newton Thorpe. Washington, DC: Government Printing Office, 1909.

Plan of Iguala (February 24, 1821)

The Mexican war for independence lasted just over 10 years, from 1810 to 1821, and encouraged the rise of local caudillos (strongmen). It also created national heroes, such as Vicente Guerrero (1782–1831), a mule driver of African, Indian, and Spanish ancestry who became commander in chief of the Mexican Army. Eight years later, when Guerrero became president of Mexico, he abolished slavery.

The war also encouraged unity among many of the racial groups in Mexico. Along with Agustín de Iturbide (1783–1824), a former Spanish army officer, Guerrero agreed on the Plan de Iguala, known as the Plan of Three Guarantees, which called for independence, union with equality of races, and the Catholic religion. When Mexico was under Spain, it was called New Spain. The new nation of Mexico would be independent of Spain but ruled by a constitution. Guerrero joined with Iturbide to successfully overthrow Spain.

Plan or indications to the government that must be provisionally installed with the objective of ensuring our sacred religion and establishing the independence of the Mexican Empire: and it will have the title of the North American Government Junta [Assembly], proposed by Colonel D. Agustin de Iturbide to his Excellency The Viceroy of New Spain, Count del Venadito.

1st. The Religion of New Spain is and shall be catholic, apostolic and Roman, without toleration of any other.

2nd. New Spain is independent of the old and of any other power, even of our Continent.

3rd. Its Government shall be a Monarchy moderated with arrangement to the Constitution peculiar and adaptable to the kingdom.

4th. Its Emperor will be D. Fernando VII, and if he does not present himself personally for swearing in México within the term prescribed by the Courts, his Most Serene Highness the Infante [Crown Prince] Carlos, D. Francisco de Paulo, Archduke Carlos or other individual of the reining house that the Congress considers suitable will be called upon in his place.

5th. While the courts convene, there will be a Junta that will have that meeting and the assurance of compliance with the plan in all its extent as its objective.

6th. Said Junta, that will be denominated as Governing, must be composed of voters [speakers] of whom the official letter from his Excellency The Viceroy speaks.

7th. While D. Fernando VII presents himself in México to render a swearing, the Junta will govern in the name of His Majesty by virtue of the swearing of loyalty that it made to the nation; however the orders that he may have imparted will be suspended while he has not been sworn.

8th. If D. Fernando VII does not consider it worthwhile coming to México, while the Emperor to be crowned is resolved, the Junta or the Regency shall rule in the name of the nation.

9th. This government shall be supported by the army of the three warranties that will be discussed later.

10th. The courts shall resolve the continuation of the Junta, or of a Regency if one should substitute for it while a person arrives to be crowned.

11th. The courts shall immediately establish the Constitution of the Mexican Empire.

12th. All the inhabitants of New Spain, without any distinction among Europeans, Africans or Indians, are citizens of this Monarchy, with options to all employment according to their merits and virtues.

13th. The person of every citizen and his properties, shall be respected and protected by the government.

14th. The secular and regular cleric will be preserved in all its rights and pre-eminences.

15th. The Junta shall take care that all the branches of the state, and all the political, ecclesiastic, civil and military personnel remain without any alteration in the same state as they exist today. Only those that indicate to be in disagreement with the plan shall be removed, replaced by those more distinguished by virtue and merit.

16th. A protective army will be formed that shall be denominated of the three warranties, and under its protection it will take first the conservation of the Catholic, apostolic and Roman Religion cooperating by all means that are within its reach so that there will be no mixing of with any other sect and will attack opportunely the enemies that could damage it; second the independence under the manifested system; third the intimate union of American and Europeans therefore guaranteeing the bases so fundamental to the happiness of New Spain, sacrificing the life of the first to the last of its individuals before consenting to their infringement.

17th. The troops of the army will observe the most exacting discipline to the letter of the ordinances, and the chiefs and officers will continue afoot as they are today: that is in their respective classes with options to vacate employment and those to be vacated by those who would not wish to follow its flags or by any other cause, and with option to those that are considered of necessity or convenience.

18th. The troops of said army shall be considered of the line [regular army troops].

19th. The same will take place with those that follow this plan. Those that do not differ, those of the system prior to the independence that join said army immediately, and the countrymen who intend to enlist, shall be considered national militia troops, and the Courts shall dictate the form of all of them for the domestic and foreign security of the kingdom.

20th. Employment will be granted according to the true merit by virtue of reports from the respective chiefs and provisionally in the name of the Nation.

21st. While the Courts are established delinquencies will be processed in total arrangement with the Spanish Constitution.

22nd. Conspiring against independence shall be processed by imprisonment without progressing to any other action until the Courts decide the penalty for the gravest of the delinquencies after that of Divine Majesty.

23rd. Those who encourage disunion shall be watched and shall be considered conspirators against independence.

24th. Since the Courts to be installed shall be constituent, it will be necessary that the representatives [deputies] receive sufficient powers to that effect; and furthermore as it is of great importance that the voters know that their representatives will be to the Mexican Congress, and not to Madrid, the Junta shall prescribe the just rules for the elections and shall indicate the time necessary for those and for the opining of Congress. Since the elections may not be verified in March, its completion shall occur as soon as possible.

Source: Plan of Iguala, February 24, 1821. Courtesy of Sons of DeWitt Colony Texas. http://www.tamu.edu/ccbn/dewitt/iguala.htm.

Stephen Austin, Letter to Edward Lovelace or Josiah Bell (November 22, 1822)

The European American aggression into Texas in the 1820s was about slavery, not the desire for freedom or democracy. It was about more land and more slaves. In 1819, Moses Austin (1761–1821)—the father of Stephen Austin—received permission from the Spanish Crown to settle in Texas and bring other colonists. The settlers received vast land tracts that they did not, in most cases, have to pay for. In return for free and low-cost land, they promised to obey the laws, become Spanish subjects, and become Catholics. However, before Moses could comply with the terms of the contract, he died, and New Spain became Mexico. His son Stephen met with Mexican officials and made much the same agreement. From the beginning, the younger Austin considered slavery critical to the prosperity of the European American colonists. Texas after 1821 was part of the Mexican Republic that had won its freedom in that year. Although slavery had been legal under Spain, Mexican revolutionary leaders promised to abolish slavery. Thus, Austin went to Mexico City to protect the interests of the slaveholders who were part of his colony.

This letter, which discusses political affairs in Mexico City, may have been written to Edward Lovelace (d. ca. 1824), a planter from Louisiana who had accompanied Stephen Austin to Texas. However, the letter may also have been written to Josiah Bell (1791–1838) because it was found in the possession of Bell's wife. Bell was one of Austin's original 300 planters, so it is probable that the letter was to him. Regardless of the recipient, the letter makes clear that Austin was of the opinion that the only thing that could save Mexico was a monarchy.

Dear Sir:

When I arrived here Congress were sitting but progressing very slowly, the discord and jealousy manifested from the first day of the session of Congress against the Generalissimo Iturbide (now Emperor) was increasing daily and everything was at a stand[still]. There were three distinct parties in Congress, one for a Bourbon King, one for an Emperor from this country, and the other for a Republic, in this state of things the government was approximating towards Anarchy, when on the night of the 18 of May the army stationed in this city proclaimed Iturbide Emperor, the next day Congress elected him in due form and on the 21 he took the oath, these things put a stop to all business for some time—Agreeably to the Emperors Oath he could do nothing without the consent of Congress and this body moved most astonishingly slow and were more occupied in watching the Emperor than in attending to the interest of the country—On the 21 July the Emperor was crowned, and very soon after serious collisions began to arise between him and Congress, the latter wished to keep all power in their hands and things were getting worse every day all was at a dead stand, for Congress would do nothing for fear of granting a little power to the executive, and the Emperor could do nothing so long as Congress existed without its sanction—In this state of things it was in vain for an individual to urge his business. . . . Matters progressed in this manner from bad to worse and were again verging towards Anarchy; one dangerous conspiracy was discovered and quelled by the imprisonment of about 70, amongst whom were 20 members of Congress and at length finding that nothing but an extraordinary and desicive [sic] step could save the nation from the confusion and the established government from ruin, the Emperor desolved [sic] congress by a decree of his own on the 31 of October last and created a national Junta of his own choosing from amongst the members of Congress—since then things have gone on better and with more harmony. My business relative to the settlement is now, acting on and in less than 10 days I shall be dispatched with everything freely arranged. The principal difficulty is slavery, this they will not admit—as the law is all slaves are to be free in ten years, but I am trying to have it amended so as to make them slaves for life and their children free at 21 years—but do not think I shall succeed in this point, and that the law will pass as it now is, that is, that the slaves introduced by the settlers shall be free after 10 years—As regards all other matters there will be no difficulty, I will write you again from here after I get through and let you know the particulars. I am doubtful nothing can be done about getting land at or near Galveston, the government seems opposed to any settlement being formed so near the borders of the United States, when I return to Texas I will write you very fully—you must not be frightened at the name of an Imperial government, you like myself have lived under a Monarchy, when Louisiana belonged to Spain and I think we lived as happy then as under the government of the United States—The Emperor has his enemies and in the United States the Democrats will abuse him no doubt, but he is doing the best for his country. These people will not do for a Republic nothing but a Monarchy can save them from Anarchy.

Stephen F. Austin This is a true copy of the letter, recd from S. F. Austin. Received from Mrs. Bell and I presume was addressed to her husband Josiah H Bell.

Guy M. Bryan

Source: Stephen Austin. Letter to Edward Lovelace or Josiah Bell. November 22, 1822. Courtesy of Sons of DeWitt Colony Texas. http://www.tamu.edu/ccbn/dewitt/slaveryletters.htm.

Monroe Doctrine
(December 2, 1823)

President James Monroe (1758–1831) delivered this speech to a joint session of Congress on December 2, 1823. In it, Monroe outlines the foreign policy objectives of the United States and proclaims that European powers should no longer colonize or interfere with the affairs of the nations of the "Americas." The United States planned to stay neutral in wars between European powers and those between Spain and its colonies. But if the latter's wars spilled over to the Americas, the United States would not permit it. America was for Americans and no longer open to European colonization. Generally, Latin Americans have interpreted the Monroe Doctrine as an expression of the imperial designs of the United States toward Latin America. But, as explained by President Monroe in his speech, the United States saw the doctrine as a proclamation of anticolonialism.

Fellow-Citizens of the Senate and House of Representatives:

At the proposal of the Russian Imperial Government, made through the minister of the Emperor residing here, a full power and instructions have been transmitted to the Minister of the United States at St. Petersburgh [sic] to arrange, by amicable negotiation, the respective rights and interests of the two nations on the northwest coast of this continent. A similar proposal has been made by His Imperial Majesty to the Government of Great Britain, which has likewise been acceded to. The Government of the United States has been desirous, by this friendly proceeding, of manifesting the great value which they have invariably attached to the friendship of the Emperor, and their solicitude to cultivate the best understanding with his Government. In the discussions to which this interest has given rise, and in the arrangements by which they may terminate the occasion has been judged proper for asserting, as a principle in which the rights and interests of the United States are involved, that the American continents, by the free and independent condition which they have assumed and maintain, are henceforth not to be considered as subjects for future colonization by any European powers. . . .

It was stated at the commencement of the last session that a great effort was then making in Spain and Portugal, to improve the condition of the people of those countries, and that it appeared to be conducted with extraordinary moderation. It need scarcely be remarked, that the result has been, so far, very different from what was then anticipated. Of events in that quarter of the globe, with which we have so much intercourse, and from which we derive our origin, we have always been anxious and interested spectators. The citizens of the United States cherish sentiments the most friendly, in favor of the liberty and happiness of their fellow men on that side of the Atlantic. In the wars of the European powers, in matters relating to themselves, we have never taken any part, nor does it comport with our policy to do so. It is only when our rights are invaded, or seriously menaced, that we resent injuries, or make preparation for our defence.

With the movements in this hemisphere, we are, of necessity, more immediately connected, and by causes which must be obvious to all enlightened and impartial observers. The political system of the allied powers is essentially different, in this respect, from that of America. This difference proceeds from that which exists in their respective governments. And to the defence of our own, which has been achieved by the loss of so much blood and treasure, and matured by the wisdom of their most enlightened citizens, and under which we have enjoyed unexampled felicity, this whole nation is devoted. We owe it, therefore, to candor, and to the amicable relations existing between the United States and those powers, to declare, that we should consider any attempt on their part to extend their system to any portion of this hemisphere, as dangerous to our peace and safety. With the existing colonies or dependencies of any European power we have not interfered, and shall not interfere. But with the governments who have declared their independence, and maintained it, and whose independence we have, on great consideration, and on just principles, acknowledged, we could not view any interposition for the purpose of oppressing them, or controlling, in any other manner, their destiny, by any European power in any other light than as the manifestation of an unfriendly disposition towards the United States. In the war between those new governments and Spain we declared our neutrality at the time of their recognition, and to this we have adhered, and shall continue to adhere, provided no change shall occur, which, in the judgement [sic] of the competent authorities of this government, shall make a corresponding change, on the part of the United States, indispensable to their security.

The late events in Spain and Portugal, show that Europe is still unsettled. Of this important fact, no stronger proof can be adduced than that the allied powers should have thought it proper, on any principle satisfactory to themselves, to have interposed, by force, in the internal concerns of Spain. To what extent such interposition may be carried, on the same principle, is a question, to which all independent powers, whose governments differ from theirs, are interested; even those most remote, and surely none more so than the United States. Our policy, in regard to Europe, which was adopted at an early stage of the wars which have so long agitated that quarter of the globe, nevertheless remains the same, which is, not to interfere in the internal concerns of any of its powers; to consider the government de facto as the legitimate government for us; to cultivate friendly relations with it, and to preserve those relations by a frank, firm, and manly policy; meeting, in all instances, the just claims of every power; submitting to injuries from none. But, in regard to these continents, circumstances are eminently and conspicuously different. It is impossible that the allied powers should extend their political system to any portion of either continent, without endangering our peace and happiness: nor can any one believe that our Southern Brethren, if left to themselves, would adopt it of their own accord. It is equally impossible, therefore, that we should behold such interposition, in any form, with indifference. If we look to the comparative strength and resources of Spain and those new governments, and their distance from each other, it must be obvious that she can never subdue them. It is still the true policy of the United States to leave the parties to themselves, in the hope that other powers will pursue the same course.

Source: Message of President James Monroe at the commencement of the first session of the 18th Congress (The Monroe Doctrine). December 2, 1823. Presidential Messages of the 18th Congress, ca. 12/02/1823-ca. 03/03/1825; Record Group 46; Records of the United States Senate, 1789-1990; National Archives.

Decree No. 16: The Colonization of the State of Coahuila and Texas (1825)

In 1825, Texas was part of the Mexican state of Coahuila and, as such, was governed by the laws of Mexico and the state of Coahuila. The following are the laws of colonization for Coahuila and Texas, which European Americans and other colonists had agreed to uphold. However, almost immediately upon their arrival after 1822, European American colonists pressured the Mexican government to change these laws and grant them more autonomy. The Mexican state, on the other hand, sought to make the new settlers comply and obey the laws. This friction led eventually to conflict between the European American settlers in Texas and the Mexican government.

The Governor provisionally appointed by the Sovereign Congress of this State. To all who shall see these presents; Know that the said Congress have decreed as follows.

Decree No. 16. The Constituent Congress of the Free, Independent and Sovereign State of Coahuila and Texas, desiring by every possible means, to augment the population of its territory; promote the cultivation of its fertile lands; the raising and multiplication of stock; and the progress of the arts and commerce; and being governed by the Constitutional act, the Federal Constitution, and the basis established by the National Decree of the General Congress, No. 72, have thought proper to decree the following LAW OF COLONIZATION:

Art. 1. All Foreigners, who in virtue of the general law, of the 18th August, 1824, which guarantees the security of their persons and property, in the territory of the Mexican Nation, wish to remove to any of the settlements of the state of Coahuila and Texas, are at liberty to do so; and the said State invites and calls them.

Art. 2. Those who do so, instead of being incommoded, shall be admitted by the local authorities of said settlements, who shall freely permit them to pursue any branch, of industry that they may think proper, provided they respect the general laws of the nation, and those of the state.

Art. 3. Any foreigner, already in the limits of the state of Coahuila and Texas who wishes to settle himself in it, shall make a declaration to that effect, before the Ayuntamiento [town council] of the place, which he selects as his residence; the Ayuntamiento in such case, shall administer to him the oath which he must take to obey the federal and state constitutions, and to observe the religion which the former prescribes; the name of the person, and his family if he has any, shall then be registered in a book kept for that purpose, with a statement of where he was born, and whence from, his age, whether married, occupation, and that he has taken the oath prescribed, and considering him from that time and not before, as domiciled.

Art. 4. From the day in which any foreigner has been enrolled, as an inhabitant, in conformity with the foregoing article, he is at liberty to designate any vacant land, and the respective political authority will grant it to him in the same manner, as to a native of the country, in conformity with the existing laws of the nation, under the condition that the proceedings, shall be passed to the government for its approbation.

Art. 5. Foreigners of any nation, or a native of any of the Mexican states, can project the formation of any towns on any lands entirely vacant, or even on those of an individual, in the case mentioned in 35th article; but the now settlers who present themselves for admission, must prove their Christianity, morality and good habits, by a certificate from the authorities where they formerly resided.

Art. 6. Foreigners who emigrate at the time in which the general sovereign congress may have prohibited their entrance, for the purpose of colonizing, as they have the power to do, after the year 1840, or previous to that time, as respects those of any particular nation, shall not then be admitted; and those who apply in proper time, shall always subject themselves to such precautionary measures (if national security, which the supreme government, without prejudicing the object of this law, may think proper to adopt relative to them).

Art. 7. The government shall take care, that within the twenty leagues bordering on the limits of the United States of the North, and ten leagues in a straight line from the coast of the Gulf of Mexico, within the limits of this state, there shall be no other settlements, except such as merit the approbation of the supreme government of the Union, for which object, all petitions on the subject, whether made by Mexicans or foreigners, shall be passed to the superior government, accompanied by a corresponding responding report.

Art. 8. The projects for new settlements in which one or more persons offer to bring at their expertise, one hundred or more families, shall be presented to the government, and if found conformable with this law, they will be admitted; and the government will immediately designate to the contractors, the land where they are to establish themselves, and the term of six years, within which, they must present the number of families they contracted for, under the penalty of losing the rights and privileges offered in their favor, in proportion to the number of families which they fail to introduce, and the contract totally annulled if they do not bring at least one hundred families.

Art. 9. Contracts made by the contractors or undertakers, *Empresarios* [land contractors], with the families brought at their expense, are guaranteed by this law, so far as they are conformable with its provisions.

Art. 10. In the distribution of lands, a preference shall be given to the Military entitled to them, by the diplomas issued by the supreme executive power, and to Mexican citizens who are not Military, among whom there shall be no other distinction, than that founded on their individual merit, or services performed for the country, or in equal circumstances, a residence in the place where the land may be situated; the quantity of land which may be granted, is designated in the following articles.

Art. 11. A square of land, which on each side has one league or five thousand *varas*, or what is the same thing, a superficies of twenty-five million varas, shall be called a *sitio*, and this shall be the unity for counting one, two, or more sitios; and also the unity for counting one, two or more labors, shall be one million square varas, or one thousand varas on each side, which shall compose a labor. The vara for this measurement shall be three geometrical feet.

Art. 12. Taking the above unity as a basis, and observing the distinction which must be made, between grazing land, or that which is proper for raising of stock, and farming land, with or without the facility of irrigation, this law grants to the contractor or contractors, for the establishment or a new settlement, for each hundred families which they may introduce and establish in the state, five sitios of grazing land and five labors, at least the one half of which, shall be without the facility of irrigation; but they can only receive this premium for eight hundred families, although a greater number should be introduced, and no fraction whatever, less than one hundred shall entitle them to any premium, not even proportionally.

Art. 13. Should any contractor or contractors in virtue of the number of families which he may have introduced, acquire in conformity with the last article, more than eleven square leagues of land, it shall nevertheless be granted, but subject to the condition of alienating the excess, within twelve years, and if it is not done, the respective political authority shall do it by selling it at public sale, delivering the proceeds to the owners, after deducting the costs of sale.

Art. 14. To each family comprehended in a contract, whose sole occupation is cultivation of land, one labor shall be given; should he also be a stock raiser, grazing land shall be added to complete a sitio, and should his only occupation be raising of stock, he shall only receive a superficies of grazing land, equal to twenty-four million square bars.

Art. 15. Unmarried men shall receive the same quantity when they enter the matrimonial state, and for foreigners who marry native Mexicans, shall receive one fourth more; those that are entirely single, or who do not form a part of some family whether foreigners or natives, shall content themselves with the fourth part of the above mentioned quantity, which is all that can be given them until they marry.

Art. 16. Families or unmarried men who, entirely of their own accord, have emigrated and may wish to unite themselves to any new towns, can at all times do so, and the same quantity of land shall be assigned them, which is mentioned in the two last articles; but if they do so within the first six years from the establishment of the settlement, one labor more shall be given to families, and single men in place of the quarter designated in the 15th article shall have the third part.

Art. 17. It appertains to the government to augment the quantity indicated in the 14, 15, and 16th Articles, in proportion to the family industry, and activity of the colonists, agreeably to the information given on these subjects by the Ayuntamientos [town councils] and Commissioners; the said government always observing the provisions of the 12th article, of the decree of the general congress on the subject.

Art. 18. The families who emigrate in conformity with the 16th article shall immediately present themselves to the political authority of the place which they may have chosen for their residence, who, finding in them the requisites, prescribed by this law for new settlers, shall admit them, and put them in possession of the corresponding lands, and shall immediately give an account thereof to the government; who of themselves, or by means of a person commissioned to that effect, will issue them a title.

Art. 19. The Indians of all nations, bordering on the state, as well as wandering tribes that may be within its limits, shall be received in the markets, without paying any duties whatever for commerce, in the products of the country; and if attracted by the moderation and confidence, with which they shall be treated, any of them, after having first declared themselves in favor of our Religion and Institutions, wish to establish themselves in any settlements that are forming, they shall be admitted, and the same quantity of land given them, as to the settlers spoken of in the 14th and 15th articles, always preferring native Indians to strangers.

Art. 20. In order that there may be no vacancies between tracts, of which, great care shall be taken in the distribution of lands, it shall be laid off in squares, or other forms although irregular, if the local situation requires it; and in said distribution, as well as the assignation of lands for new towns, previous notice shall be given to the adjoining proprietors, if any, in order to prevent dissentions and law suits.

Art. 21. If by error in the concession, any land shall be granted, belonging to another, on proof being made of that fact, an equal quantity shall be granted elsewhere, to the person who may have thus obtained it through error, and he shall be indemnified by the owner of such land, for any improvements he may have made; the just value of which improvements, shall be ascertained by appraisers.

Art. 22. The new settlers as an acknowledgment, shall pay to the state, for each sitio of pasture land, thirty dollars; two dollars and a half for each labor without the facility of irrigation, and three dollars and a half, for each one that can be irrigated, and so on proportionally according to the quantity and quality of the land distributed; but the said payments need not be made, until six years after the settlement and by thirds; the first within four years, the second within five years, and the last within six years, under the penalty of losing the land for a failure, in any of said payments; there are excepted from this payment, the contractors, and Military, spoken of in the 10th article; the former with respect to lands given them, as a premium, and the latter, for those which they obtained, in conformity with their diplomas.

Art. 23. The Ayuntamiento of each municipality (*Comarca*) shall collect the above mentioned funds, gratis, by means of a committee appointed either within or without their body; and shall remit them as they are collected, to the treasurer of their Funds, who will give the corresponding receipt, and without any other compensation than two and a half per cent, all that shall be allowed him; he shall hold them at the disposition of the government, rendering an account every month of the ingress and egress, and of any remissness or fraud, which he may observe in their collection of all which, the person employed, and the committee, and the individuals of the Ayuntamientos who appoint them, shall be individually responsible and that this responsibility may be at all effectual, the said appointments shall be made viva voce, and information shall be given thereof immediately to the government.

Art. 24. The government shall sell to Mexicans and to them only, such lands as they may wish to purchase, taking care that there shall not be accumulated in the same hands, more than eleven sitios, and under the condition, that the purchaser must cultivate what he acquires by this title within six years, from its acquisition, under the penalty of losing them; the price of each sitio, subject to the foregoing condition, shall be one hundred dollars, if it be pasture land; one hundred and fifty dollars, if it be farming land without the facility of irrigation; and two hundred and fifty dollars if it can be irrigated.

Art. 25. Until six years after the publication of this law, the legislature of this state, cannot alter it as regards the acknowledgement, and price to be paid or land, or as regards the quantity and quality, to be distributed to the new settlers, or sold to Mexicans.

Art. 26. The new settlers, who within six years from the date of the possession, have not cultivated or occupied the lands granted them, according to its quality, shall be considered to have renounced them, and the respective political authority, shall immediately proceed to take possession of them, and recall the titles.

Art. 27. The contractors and Military, heretofore spoken of, and those who by purchase have acquired lands, can alienate them at any time, but the successor is obliged to cultivate them in the same time, that the original proprietor was bound to do; the other settlers can alienate theirs when they have totally cultivated them, and not before.

Art. 28. By testamentary will, made in conformity with the existing laws, or those which may govern in future, any new colonist, from the day of his settlement, may dispose of his land, although he may not have cultivated it, and if he dies intestate, his property shall be inherited by the person or persons entitled by the laws to it; the heirs being subject to the same obligation and condition imposed on the original grantee.

Art. 29. Lands acquired by virtue of this law, shall not by any title whatever, pass into mortmain.

Art. 30. The new settler, who wishing to establish himself in a foreign country, resolves to leave the territory of the state, can do so freely, with all his property; but after leaving the state, he shall not any longer hold his land, and if he had not previously sold it, or the sale should not be in conformity with the 27th article, it shall become entirely vacant.

Art. 31. Foreigners who in conformity with this law, have obtained lands, and established themselves in any new settlement, shall be considered from that moment, naturalized in the country; and by marrying a Mexican, they acquire a particular merit to obtain letters of citizenship of the state, subject however to the provisions which may be made relative to both particulars, in the constitution of the state.

Art. 32. During the first ten years, counting from the day on which the new settlements may have been established, they shall be free from all contributions, of whatever denomination, with the exception of those which, in case of invasion by an enemy, or to prevent it, are generally imposed, and the produce of agriculture or industry of the new settlers, shall be free from excise duty, Alcabala, or other duties, throughout every part of the state, with the exception of the duties referred to in the next article; after the termination of that time, the new settlements shall be on the same footing as to taxes with the old ones, and the colonists shall also in this particular, be on the same footing with the other inhabitants of the state.

Art. 33. From the day of their settlement, the new colonists shall be at liberty to follow any branch of industry, and can also work mines of every description, communicating with the supreme government of the confederation, relative to the general revenue appertaining to it, and subjecting themselves in all other particulars, to the ordinances or taxes, established or which may be established on this branch.

Art. 34. Towns shall be founded on the sites deemed most suitable by the government, or the person commissioned for this effect, and for each one, there shall be designated four square leagues, whose area may be in a regular or irregular form, agreeably to the situation.

Art. 35. If any of the said sites should be the property of an individual, and the establishment of new towns on them, should notoriously be of general utility, they can, notwithstanding, be appropriated to this object, previously indemnifying the owner for its just value, to be determined by appraisers.

Art. 36. Building lots in the new towns shall be given gratis, to the contractors of them and also to artists of every class, as many as are for the establishment of their trade; and to the other settlers they shall be sold at public auction, after having been previously valued, under the obligation to pay the purchase money by installments of one third each, the first in six months, the second in twelve months and the third in eighteen months; but all owners or lots, including contractors and artists, shall annually pay one dollar for each lot, which, together with the produce of the sales, shall be collected by the Ayuntamientos, and applied to the building of churches in said towns.

Art. 37. So far as is practicable, the towns shall be composed of natives and foreigners, and in their delineation, great care shall be taken to lay off the streets straight, giving them a direction from north to south, and from east to west, when the site will permit it.

Art. 38. For the better location of the said new town, their regular formation and exact partition of their land and lots, the government on account of having admitted any project, and agreed with the contractor or contractors, who may have presented it, shall commission a person of intelligence and confidence, giving him such particular instructions as may be deemed necessary and expedient and authorizing him under his own responsibility, to appoint one or more surveyors, to lay off the town scientifically, and do whatever else that be required.

Art. 39. The Governor in conformity with the last fee bill, *Arancel*, of notary public's of the ancient audience of Mexico, shall designate the fees of the commissioner, who in conjunction with the colonists shall fix the surveyor's fees; but both shall be paid by the colonists and in the manner which all parties among themselves may agree upon.

Art. 40. As soon as at least forty families are united in one place, they shall proceed to the formal establishment of the new towns, and all of them shall take an oath, to support the general and state constitutions; which oath will be administered by the commissioner; they shall then, in his presence, proceed for the first time, to the election of their municipal authority.

Art. 41. A new town, whose inhabitants shall not be less than two hundred, shall elect an Ayuntamiento, provided there is not another one established within eight leagues, in which case, it shall be added to it. The number of individuals which are to compose the Ayuntamiento, shall be regulated by the existing laws.

Art. 42. Foreigners are eligible, subject to the provisions which the constitution of the state may prescribe, to elect the members of their municipal authorities, and to be elected to the same.

Art. 43. The municipal expenses, and all others which may be considered necessary, or of common utility to the new towns, shall be proposed to the Governor, by the Ayuntamientos through the political chief, accompanied with a plan of the taxes, *arbitrios*, which in their opinion may be just and best calculated to raise them, and should the proposed plan, be approved of by the Governor, he shall order it to be executed, subject however to the resolutions of the legislature, to whom it shall be immediately passed with his report and that of the political chief, who will say whatever occurs to him on the subject.

Art. 44. For the opening and improving of roads, and other public works in Texas, the government will transmit to the chief of that department, the individuals, who in other parts of the state, may have been sentenced to public works as vagrants, or for other crimes; these same persons may be employed by individuals for competent wages, and as soon as the time of their condemnation is expired, they can unite themselves as colonists, to any new settlement, and obtain the corresponding lands, if their reformation shall have made them worthy of such favor in the opinion of the chief of the department, without whose certificate, they shall not be admitted.

Art. 45. The government in accord with the respective ordinary ecclesiastics, will take care to provide the new settlements with the competent number of pastors, and in accord with the same authority, shall propose to the legislature for its approbation, the salary which the said pastors are to receive, which shall be paid by the new settlers.

Art. 46. The new settlers as regards the introduction of slaves shall subject themselves to the existing laws, and those which may hereafter be established on the subject.

Art. 47. The petitions now pending relative to the subject of the law, shall be dispatched in conformity with it, and for this purpose they shall be passed to the Governor, and the families who may be established within the limits of the state, without having any land assigned them, shall submit themselves to this law, and to the orders of the supreme government of the Union, with respect to those who are within twenty leagues of the limits of the United States of America, and in a straight line of the coast of the Gulf of Mexico.

Art. 48. This law shall be published in all the villages of the state; and that it arrives at the notice of all others, throughout the Mexican confederation, it shall be communicated to their respective legislatures, by the secretary of this state; and the Governor will take particular care, to send a certified copy of it, in compliance with the 16th article of the federal constitution, to the two houses of Congress, and the supreme executive power of the nation, with a request to the latter, to give it general circulation through foreign states, by means of our ambassadors. The Governor pro tem of the state will cause it to be published and circulated.

Saltillo, 24 March, 1825

Signed, RAFAEL RAMOS Y VÁLDEZ, President

JUAN VICENTE CAMOS, Member & Secretary

JOSÉ JOAQUÍN ROSALES, Member & Secretary

Therefore I command all Authorities, as well Civil as Military and Ecclesiastical, to obey and cause to be obeyed, the present decree in all its parts.

Source: Decree No. 16: The Colonization of the State of Coahuila and Texas. 1825. Courtesy of Sons of DeWitt Colony Texas. http://www.tamu.edu/ccbn/dewitt/cololaws.htm.

Decree of Mexican President Vicente Guerrero Abolishing Slavery (September 15, 1829)

Between 1821 and 1829, the Mexican government attempted to regulate slave traffic in Texas and make European American colonists comply with Mexican laws. By 1829, Texas had a population of about 20,000, not counting slaves, who numbered just over a thousand. By this time, many Mexicans feared that the steady migration of European Americans into Texas was undermining its sovereignty, and Mexico moved to secure its borders. One of the ways suggested to stem American migration was to emancipate the slaves; the prosperity of the white colonists depended on slave labor. The abolitionists convinced Mexican president Vicente Guerrero, who was of Indian, African, and Spanish heritage, to sign the following decree abolishing slavery.

Abolition of Slavery. The President of the United Mexican States, to the inhabitants of the Republic. Be it known; That in the year 1829, being desirous of signalizing the anniversary of our Independence by an Act of national Justice and Beneficence, which may contribute to the strength and support of such inestimable welfare, as to secure more and more the public tranquility, and reinstate an unfortunate portion of our inhabitants in the sacred rights granted them by Nature, and may be protected by the Nation under wise and just Laws, according to the Provision in Article

30 of the Constitutive Act; availing myself of the extraordinary faculties granted me, I have thought proper to Decree:

1. That slavery be exterminated in the Republic.
2. Consequently those are free, who, up to this day, have been looked upon as slaves.
3. Whenever the circumstances of the Public Treasury will allow it, the owners of slaves shall be indemnified, in the manner which the Laws shall provide.

Mexico 15 Sept. 1829, A. D. JOSÉ MARÍA de BOCANEGRA.

Source: Decree of Mexican President Vicente Guerrero Abolishing Slavery. September 15, 1829. Courtesy of Sons of DeWitt Colony Texas. http://www.tamu.edu/ccbn/dewitt/chieftains.htm#guerroedict.

General Manuel de Mier y Terán, Letter to Lucás Alamán, *"¿En qué parará Texas? En lo que Dios quiera."* ("What is to become of Texas? Whatever God wills.")

(July 2, 1832)

Mexican general Manuel de Mier y Terán (1789–1832) led a boundary commission tour of Texas in 1828–1829. Mier y Terán was a seasoned and respected officer and after the tour was made commandant general of the Eastern Interior Provinces. In this capacity, he visited Galveston Bay in November 1831. His 1828 report had a sense of urgency, and he recommended strong measures to stop U.S. expansion into Texas. As a first step, he recommended placing more presidios or garrisons close to major settlements. Concerned with the growing trade with the United States, he urged closer trade ties between Mexico proper and Texas. Then he urged that more Mexican and European settlers be recruited to settle in Texas. These measures were not effectively implemented. In this letter to Lucás Alamán, the intellectual leader of the Mexican conservatives, Mier y Terán anticipated the Texas revolt of 1836 and the loss of Texas. This letter was the last Mier y Terán ever wrote, for he died the next day.

A great and respectable Mexican nation, a nation of which we have dreamed and for which we have labored so long, can never emerge from the many disasters which have overtaken it. We have allowed ourselves to be deceived by the ambitions of selfish groups; and now we are about to lose the northern provinces. How could we expect to hold Texas when we do not even agree among ourselves? It is a gloomy state of affairs. If we could work together, we would advance. As it is, we are lost. I believed, and with reason, that the withdrawal of the ministry would end the revolution. It only gave courage to those factions of discord who now hope to occupy all the country. There is commotion from Tampico to Mexico. The present state of affairs in Texas does not permit me to leave. The revolution absorbs the energies of men who should be working together.

From the twenty-fourth of last May I held a position in order to protect the states of San Luis and Tamaulipas from the military forces of the revolutionists, and to a certain extent overcome their influence in closing the principal means of communication; but it was impossible to stay their activities in Huasteca and other towns in Tamaulipas, from which places they were able completely to surround my camp. Particularly in Victoria did they make headway. The authorities and powers there were in a most critical position, since the legal existence of their government depended upon my success in this fracas. As individuals, they were about equally divided in their allegiance—some favored the government and some supported the revolution. Was ever a general faced with a more insuperable obstacle? I could expect no direct aid from the state government in pursuing a rigorous plan of war. Even when I received orders from Victoria, I realized under the circumstances that they were not constitutional. The effect has been to leave me isolated in Tamaulipas with my depleted forces. If I leave, the, state is lost. If I remain, all is lost. Martial law would be a precarious remedy, and one justified by the revolution; but our constitution makes no provision for such a law, and if it were changed so as to provide for such measures today, in Tamaulipas and everywhere in the federation it would produce such lamentable results, that it is best not to consider it. In the first place, it is an impossibility, and secondly, if it were not, I as commander would have to ask for my relief.

Moctezuma would not listen to reason. His forces now are larger than mine. His successes are due to numbers rather than to his generalship. . . . When I came through this country in 1829, on my way to Tampico, I noticed many places connected with the return of Iturbide to Mexico. I have seen the house where he spent his last night. The wall in front of which he was shot is still standing. This morning dawned diaphanous, radiant, beautiful. The sky was blue; the trees green, the birds were bursting with joy; the river crystalline, the flowers yellow, making drops of dew shine in their calyces. Everything pulsed with life, everything gave evident signs that the breath of God had reached nature. In contrast to these things the village of Padilla is alone and apathetic, with its houses in ruin and its thick ashen adobe walls; and my soul is burdened with weariness. I am an unhappy man, and unhappy people should not live on earth. I have studied this situation for five years and today, I know nothing, nothing, for man is very despicable and small; and—let us put an end to these reflections, for they almost drive me mad. The revolution is about to break forth and Texas is lost.

Immortality! God! The Soul! What does all this mean? Well, then, I believe in it all, but why does man not have the right to put aside his misery and his pains? Why should he be eternally chained to an existence which is unpleasant to him? And this spirit which inspires, which fills my mind with ideas—where will it go? Let us see, now; the spirit is uncomfortable, it commands me to set it free, and it is necessary to obey. Here is the end of human glory and the termination of ambition.

¿En qué parará Texas? En lo que Dios quiera. ["What is to become of Texas? Whatever God wills."]

Source: General Manuel de Mier y Terán. Letter to Lucás Alamán, "¿En qué parará Texas? En lo que Dios quiera." ("What is to become of Texas? Whatever God wills.") July 2, 1832. Courtesy of Sons of DeWitt Colony Texas. http://www.tamu.edu/ccbn/dewitt/teranmanuel.htm.

Diary Entry of José Enrique de la Peña (1836)

In this entry from his diary, Lieutenant Colonel José Enrique de la Peña (1807–1844), an officer on General Antonio López de Santa Anna's staff in 1836, gives an eyewitness account of the Battle of the Alamo. He reports the capture and execution of the legendary outdoorsman Davy Crockett. His account debunks the traditional story that Crockett, the former congressman from Tennessee, fought to the end, wielding his long rifle, "Betsy."

Shortly before Santa Anna's speech, an unpleasant episode had taken place, which, since it occurred after the end of the skirmish, was looked upon as base murder and which contributed greatly to the coolness that was noted. Some seven men had survived the general carnage and, under the protection of General Castrillón, they were brought before Santa Anna. Among them was one of great stature, well proportioned, with regular features, in whose face there was the imprint of adversity, but in whom one also noticed a degree of resignation and nobility that did him honor. He was the naturalist David Crockett, well known in North America for his unusual adventures, who had undertaken to explore the country and who, finding himself in Béxar at the very moment of surprise, had taken refuge in the Alamo, fearing that his status as a foreigner might not be respected. Santa Anna answered Castrillón's intervention on Crockett's behalf with a gesture of indignation and, addressing himself to the sappers, the troops closest to him, ordered his execution. The commanders and officers were outraged at this action and did not support the order, hoping that once the fury of the moment had blown over these men would be spared, but several officers who were around the president and who, perhaps, had not been present during the moment of danger, became noteworthy by an infamous deed, surpassing the soldiers in cruelty. They thrust themselves forward, in order to flatter the commander, and with swords in hand, fell upon these unfortunate, defenseless men just as a tiger leaps upon his prey. Though tortured before they were killed, these unfortunates died without complaining and without humiliating themselves before their torturers.

Source: de la Peña, José Enrique. *With Santa Anna in Texas: A Personal Narrative of the Revolution.* Carmen Perry, trans. College Station: Texas A & M University, 1997, 53.

Treaty of Velasco
(May 14, 1836)

The Treaty of Velasco was negotiated between officials of the interim government of the Republic of Texas and General Antonio López de Santa Anna (1794–1876) about three weeks after his capture by the Texans on April 22, 1836. Santa Anna did not have the authority to negotiate the treaty that gave Texas to the United States as all treaties had to be ratified by the Mexican Congress. Hence, the status of Texas was tenuous because it was legally still part of Mexico. Tensions between slave and free states in the United States stood in the way of U.S. annexation of Texas, although the United States kept troops poised at the border. This excerpt from the treaty includes a discussion of the prisoners of war taken during the Texas revolt (1836) and relations between the Mexican and Texas armies.

Articles of an agreement entered into, between His Excellency David G. Burnet, President of the Republic of Texas, of the one part, and His Excellency General Antonio Lopez de Santa Anna, President General in Chief of the Mexican Army, of the other part.

ARTICLE 1ST

General Antonio Lopez de Santa Anna agrees that he will not take up arms, nor will he exercise his influence to cause them to be taken up against the people of Texas, during the present War of Independence.

ARTICLE 2ND

All hostilities between the Mexican and Texian troops will cease immediately both on land and water.

ARTICLE 3RD

The Mexican troops will evacuate the Territory of Texas, passing to the other side of the Rio Grande del Norte.

ARTICLE 6TH

The troops of both armies will refrain from coming into contact with each other, and to this end the Commander of the Army of Texas will be careful not to approach within a shorter distance of the Mexican Army than five leagues.

ARTICLE 7TH

The Mexican Army shall not make any other delay on its march, than that which is necessary to take up their hospitals, baggage—and to cross the rivers—any delay not necessary to these purposes to be considered an infraction of this agreement.

ARTICLE 8TH

By express to be immediately dispatched, this agreement shall be sent to General Filisola and to General T. J. Rusk, commander of the Texian Army, in order that they may be apprised of its stipulations, and to this and they will exchange engagements to comply with the same.

ARTICLE 9TH

That all Texian prisoners now in possession of the Mexican Army or its authorities be forthwith released and furnished with free passports to return to their homes, in consideration of which a corresponding number of Mexican prisoners, rank and file, now in possession of the Government of Texas shall be immediately released. The remainder of the Mexican prisoners that continue in possession of the Government of Texas to be treated with due humanity—any extraordinary comforts that may be furnished them to be at the charge of the Government of Mexico.

ARTICLE 10TH

General Antonio Lopez de Santa Anna will be sent to Veracruz as soon as it shall be deemed proper.

The contracting parties sign this Instrument for the above mentioned purposes, by duplicate, at the Port of Velasco this fourteenth day of May 1836.

David G Burnet
Ant. Lopez de Santa Anna
Jas Collinsworth, Sec of State
Bailey Hardeman, Secy of Treasury
T W Grayson, Atty General

Ant. Lopez de Santa Anna
David G Burnet
Jas Collinsworth, Secretary of State
Bailey Hardeman, Secy of Treasury
T W Grayson, Atty General

Source: The Treaty of Velasco (Public). May 14, 1836. Archives and Information Services Division, Texas State Library and Archives Commission.

John L. O'Sullivan, Column on "Manifest Destiny," *United States Magazine and Democratic Review* (1839)

In 1846, the ideological rationale for the Mexican-American War was Manifest Destiny, a religious doctrine with roots in Calvinist and Puritan ideas. The concept is important because it influences U.S. foreign policy even today. According to the doctrine, God determines salvation, and he predestined the European race for salvation. The United States was the chosen land, and Americans were God's chosen people. Many European Americans believed God chose the United States to be the custodian of democracy, and hence, the nation had a mission—that is, God had predestined Western Europeans to spread his principles. Mexico, on the other hand, was a Catholic country. John L. O'Sullivan (1813–1895), a columnist and editor for the influential United States Magazine and Democratic Review, *coined the term "Manifest Destiny" in this 1839 column. O'Sullivan said it was the destiny of the United States to annex Texas and the Oregon Territory. This excerpt from the column lays out this ideology in passionate detail.*

The American people having derived their origin from many other nations, and the Declaration of National Independence being entirely based on the great principle of human equality, these facts demonstrate at once our disconnected position as regards any other nation; that we have, in reality, but little connection with the past history of any of them, and still less with all antiquity, its glories, or its crimes. On the contrary, our national birth was the beginning of a new history, the formation and progress of an untried political system, which separates us from the past and connects us with the future only; and so far as regards the entire development of the natural rights of man, in moral, political, and national life, we may confidently assume that our country is destined to be the great nation of futurity.

It is so destined, because the principle upon which a nation is organized fixes its destiny, and that of equality is perfect, is universal. It presides in all the operations of the physical world, and it is also the conscious law of the soul—the self-evident dictates of morality, which accurately defines the duty of man to man, and consequently man's rights as man. Besides, the truthful annals of any nation furnish abundant evidence, that its happiness, its greatness, its duration, were always proportionate to the democratic equality in its system of government. . . .

What friend of human liberty, civilization, and refinement, can cast his view over the past history of the monarchies and aristocracies of antiquity, and not deplore that they ever existed? What philanthropist can contemplate the oppressions, the cruelties, and injustice inflicted by them on the masses of mankind, and not turn with moral horror from the retrospect?

America is destined for better deeds. It is our unparalleled glory that we have no reminiscences of battlefields, but in defence of humanity, of the oppressed of all nations, of the rights of conscience, the rights of personal enfranchisement. Our annals describe no scenes of horrid carnage, where men were led on by hundreds of thousands to slay one another, dupes and victims to emperors, kings, nobles, demons in the human form called heroes. We have had patriots to defend our homes, our liberties, but no aspirants to crowns or thrones; nor have the American people ever suffered themselves to be led on by wicked ambition to depopulate the land, to spread desolation far and wide, that a human being might be placed on a seat of supremacy.

We have no interest in the scenes of antiquity, only as lessons of avoidance of nearly all their examples. The expansive future is our arena, and for our history. We are entering on its untrodden space, with the truths of God in our minds, beneficent objects in our hearts, and with a clear conscience unsullied by the past. We are the nation of human progress, and who will, what can, set limits to our onward march? Providence is with us, and no earthly power can. We point to the everlasting truth on the first page of our national declaration, and we proclaim to the millions of other lands that "the gates of hell"—the powers of aristocracy and monarchy—"shall not prevail against it."

The far-reaching, the boundless future will be the era of American greatness. In its magnificent domain of space and time, the nation of many nations is destined to manifest to mankind the excellence of divine principles; to establish on earth the noblest temple ever dedicated to the worship of the Most High—the Sacred and the True. Its floor shall be a hemisphere—its roof the firmament of the star-studded heavens, and its congregation [a] Union of many Republics, comprising hundreds of happy millions, calling, owning no man master, but governed by God's natural and moral law of equality, the law of brotherhood—of "peace and good will amongst men." . . .

Yes, we are the nation of progress, of individual freedom, of universal enfranchisement. Equality of rights is the cynosure of our union of States, the grand exemplar of the correlative equality of individuals; and while truth sheds its effulgence, we cannot retrograde, without dissolving the one and subverting the other. We must onward to the fulfilment of our mission—to the entire development of the principle of our organization—freedom of conscience, freedom of person, freedom of trade and business pursuits, universality of freedom and equality. This is our high destiny, and in nature's eternal, inevitable decree of cause and effect we must accomplish it. All this will be our future history, to establish on earth the moral dignity and salvation of man—the immutable truth and beneficence of God. For this blessed mission to the nations of the world, which are shut out from the life-giving light of truth, has America been chosen; and her high example shall smite unto death the tyranny of kings, hierarchs, and oligarchs, and carry the glad tidings of peace and good will where myriads now endure an existence scarcely more enviable than that of beasts of the field. Who, then, can doubt that our country is destined to be the great nation of futurity?

Source: "The Great Nation of Futurity." *The United States Democratic Review* 6, no. 23 (November 1839): 426–430. Courtesy of Cornell University Library, http://cdl.library.cornell.edu/cgi-bin/moa/sgml/moa-idx?notisid=AGD1642-0006-46.

The Treaty of Annexation—Texas: A Treaty of Annexation Concluded between the United States and the Republic of Texas

(April 12, 1844)

The Texas Annexation Treaty, negotiated in 1844, was not approved by the U.S. Congress until February 28, 1845. Most European Americans in Texas favored annexation to the United States, although a substantial number wanted to remain independent. Yet most Texans were southerners by birth, and they wanted unification with the United States. They also felt threatened by the British insistence that they emancipate their slaves. Reproduced here are excerpts from the Treaty of Annexation in which the United States recognized Mexican and Texan land grants and agreed to pay the debts of Texas.

ARTICLE II

The citizens of Texas shall be incorporated into the Union of the United States, maintained and protected in the free enjoyment of their liberty and property and admitted, as soon as may be consistent with the principles of the federal constitution, to the enjoyment of all the rights, privileges and immunities of citizens of the United States.

ARTICLE III

All titles and claims to real estate, which are valid under the laws of Texas, shall be held to be so by the United States; and measures shall be adopted for the speedy adjudication of all unsettled claims to land, and patents shall be granted to those found to be valid.

ARTICLE IV

The public lands hereby ceded shall be subject to the laws regulating the public lands in the other Territories of the United States, as far as they may be applicable; subject, however, to such alterations and changes as Congress may from time to time think proper to make. It is understood between the parties that if, in consequence of the mode in which lands have been surveyed in Texas, or from previous grants or locations, the sixteenth section cannot be applied to the purpose of education, Congress shall make equal provision by grant of land elsewhere. And it is also further understood, that, hereafter, the books, papers and documents of the General Land Office of Texas shall be deposited and kept at such place in Texas as the Congress of the United States shall direct.

ARTICLE V

The United States assume and agree to pay the public debts and liabilities of Texas, however created, for which the faith or credit of her government may be bound at the time of the exchange of the ratifications of this treaty; which debts and liabilities are estimated not to exceed, in the whole, ten millions of dollars, to be ascertained and paid in the manner hereinafter stated.

Done at Washington, the twelfth day of April, eighteen hundred and forty-four.

Source: The Treaty of Annexation—Texas. Treaties and Other International Acts of the United States of America. Edited by Hunter Miller. Vol. 4. Documents 80-121: 1836-1846. Washington, DC: Government Printing Office, 1934.

Ulysses S. Grant, Letter to His Fiancée, Julia Dent (July 25, 1846)

In the following letter to his fiancée, Julia Dent, Lieutenant Ulysses S. Grant (1822–1885) expresses horror over the Mexican-American War, saying that it was unjust. However, it was his duty to fight in the war against Mexico—the United States was his country, whether right or wrong. In this case, Grant considers the war unjust. Throughout his memoirs, Grant was critical of the war against Mexico because he considered it a U.S. war of aggression.

Since we have been in Matamoros, a great many murders have been committed, and what is strange there seems to be very week [weak] means made use of to prevent frequent repetitions. Some of the volunteers and about all the Texans seem to think it perfectly right to impose on the people of a conquered City to any extent, and even to murder them where the act can be covered by dark. And how much they seem to enjoy acts of violence too! I would not pretend to guess the number of murders that have been committed upon the persons of poor Mexicans and our soldiers, since we have been here, but the number would startle you.

Source: Simon, John Y. *The Papers of Ulysses S. Grant.* Vol. 1. London: Feffer & Simons, 1967, 102.

The Other Side: Or Notes for the History of the War between Mexico and the United States Written in Mexico (1846–1847)

The original articles excerpted here were written between September 1848 and May 1849, under the general title Apuntes para la Historia de la Guerra entre México y los Estados-Unidos. *The articles were attributed to 15 Mexican officers. One of the principal contributors was Ramón*

Alcaraz, an officer in the Mexican Army during the Mexican-American War (1846–1848), who wrote many books about the topic. Apuntes para la Historia *was translated into English in 1850 by Albert C. Ramsey and published as* The Other Side: Or Notes for the History of the War between Mexico and the United States. *The book was published in Mexico, Britain, and the United States. The book gave the Mexican side of the Mexican-American War. The following excerpts have been attributed to Alcaraz's eyewitness accounts from the various battles in which he participated.*

Matamoros is situated on the west bank of the Rio Bravo, in a vast plain, composed of wooden and brick houses, fourteen leagues distant from the coast. The proximity of the enemy indicated that they would little hesitate to attack a place presenting such important difficulties to its defenders. Open on all sides, except that where the river flowed, little resistance could be made towards the interior, and what increased the danger was that the fortifications which had existed were reduced now to a small redoubt. This had been constructed to the west of the city, and at some 600 yards distant from it, upon the bank of the river at the ford called the Anacuitas. . . .

To sustain the attack, they could not count on a sufficient force. The garrison was composed in the beginning of the battalion of Sappers, the 2d light, the 1st and 10th infantry regiments of the line, and the 7th of cavalry, the auxiliaries of the towns of the North, several companies of Presidiales, and a battalion of the National Guard of the city of Matamoros. The artillery consisted of 20 field pieces, served by one company. Two or three days after the coming of the Americans, the marines of Tampico arrived, the 6th infantry, and a battalion of the Guarda Costa of that place. These two sections being united, they formed a total of about 3,000 men.

The munitions were not scarce, if they were not abundant. But it was not so fortunate with provisions, because the necessary supply had not been obtained in time, and before the blockade of the port. From the interior of the country it was impossible to bring them, and much less now was there an opportunity.

On the 8th it was positively ascertained from the spies, that the enemy, in number about 3,000 men with an abundance of artillery and numerous wagons, were directing their march from the Fort of Isabel to the entrenched camp in front of Matamoros. The General-in-Chief at once determined to give battle; an opportunity which he had sought for so many days. At ten o'clock in the morning our cavalry went forth upon the spacious plain of Palo Alto: the infantry followed at two in the day, and there came in sight of the enemy.

The artillery of the Americans, much superior to ours, made horrid ravages in the ranks of the Mexican [A]rmy. The soldiers yielded, not overwhelmed in a combat in which they might deal out the death which they received—not in the midst of the excitement and gallantry which the ardor of a battle brings forth, but in a fatal situation in which they were killed with impunity, and decimated in cold blood. The action was prolonged for whole hours under such unfortunate auspices, and the slain increased every minute. The troops at last, tired of being slaughtered for no use, demanded with a shout to be led on to the enemy with the bayonet, for they wished to fight hand to hand, and to die like brave men.

The fire began to spread. Its sinister splendor illuminated the camp, in which a short time before resounded the roar of artillery, and in which now were heard heart-rending groans of our wounded. As most of these were from cannon-shot, they were horribly mutilated. The sight deeply saddened, and the misfortune was complete, when nothing could be done to alleviate their sufferings, for the surgeon who carried the medicine-chests had disappeared at the first fire, without breathing where he had deposited them. There was no other choice than to send some of them to Matamoros in the carts that had brought provisions. The rest were left abandoned on the 9th in the field.

—The Battles of Palo Alto and La Resaca,
Ramón Alcaraz (Mexican Army Officer), 1846

A little further on, they came up with the enemy on the field of battle known by the name of the Angostura. The ground which had to be passed over was formed of extensive and broad plains, in which it would not have been possible to resist the vigorous shock of our troops, especially of our beautiful cavalry. But where the enemy had halted to give battle, two successive series of hills and barrancas began, which formed a position truly formidable. Each hill was fortified with a battery and ready to deal its murderous fire upon any attempting to take it. The position presenting serious obstacles to an attack, manifested very plainly, that for the Mexicans to gain a victory they would have to sustain a heavy loss in men.

At the second charge of our troops, a lieutenant, D. José Maria Montoya, who was in the front rank, became mixed up with the Americans. Seeing himself alone, and not desiring to be killed nor taken prisoner, he availed himself of a stratagem to feign a parley, whereby he was carried into the presence of General Taylor. This was followed by his returning to our camp accompanied by two officers of their army, to have an interview with General Santa Anna. But Montoya, who had his reasons for not presenting himself, separated from the commissioners, who fulfilled their instructions.

General Santa Anna has not been embraced in this accusation. Friends and enemies have recognised [sic] the valor with which he constantly braved the fire. It is to be regretted his combinations did not correspond with his gallantry, that his errors dim the splendor of his merits, and that while it is painful to blame his conduct as a general, it is also pleasing to praise his courage as a soldier.

—The Battle of Buena Vista,
Ramón Alcaraz, February 1846

At dawn on the 18th, the roar of the enemy's artillery resounded through the camps, as a solemn announcement of a battle.

Some of our soldiers now began to leave their ranks, and to descend the opposite side, attempting to mingle with the wounded who were retiring, but General Santa Anna, observing it, ordered some of his adjutants to prevent this disorder and they, either on compulsion or by the stimulus of enthusiasm, succeeded in persuading the fugitives to return.

In the meantime, General Baneneli appealed to the last resource, and ordered his men to charge bayonets. They, eager to join in an action which they had only heard, immediately hastened this movement in full force to come up to where they were directed; but, surprised at finding themselves hand to hand with an enemy so superior in numbers and surrounded on all sides, were panic-struck in an instant, fell into disorder, and their commander in vain endeavored to keep them in their ranks. Being himself involved in the crowd with the chiefs of engineers and other officers who endeavored, sword in hand, to keep back the men, they were actually rolled together down the opposite declivity, borne along by the multitude, which poured onward like a torrent from the height.

Among the fire and smoke, and above the mass of blue formed by the Americans behind the summit of the Telégrafo, still floated our deserted flag. But the banner of the stars was soon raised by the enemy upon the same staff, and for an instant both became entangled and confounded together, our own at length falling to the ground, amidst the shouts and roar of the victors' guns, and the mournful cries and confused voices of the vanquished.

When the Telégrafo was lost, the 6th infantry had retreated to the positions on the right, where they capitulated with the other corps. The grenadier battalion, which had been drawn out from the battery of the centre to the foot of the hill, chiefly dispersed, in spite of the exertions made to collect it.

An enthusiastic officer harangued the troops at the pitch of his voice, assuring them that they had yet lost nothing, wishing to reanimate the spirit now dead in all that unfortunate crowd. General Baneneli, rushing in with his horse and full of wrath, poured forth a thousand horrible imprecations upon his soldiers, and with the butt of his pistol threatened particularly one of his captains. The General-in-Chief vented his rage upon the officers who had lost their positions; and the agitation of the multitude, and the difficulties of the ground, with the general dangers and desperation, rendered the scene indescribable.

Horrible, indeed, was the descent by that narrow and rocky path, where thousands rushed, disputing the passage with desperation, and leaving a track of blood upon the road. All classes being confounded, all military distinction and respect were lost, the badges of rank became marks for sarcasms, that were only meted out according to their grade and humiliation. The enemy, now masters of our camp, turned their guns upon the fugitives. This augmented more and more the terror of the multitude crowded through the defile, and pressed forward every instant by a new impulse, which increased the confusion and disgrace of the ill-fated day.

Cerro-Gordo was lost! Mexico was open to the iniquity of the invader.

—The Battle of Cerro Gordo,
Ramón Alcaraz, Mexican Army, April 1847

We will speak in the first place of Chapultepec, the key of Mexico, as then was commonly said, and whose reminiscences and traditions made it doubly important for the enemy, and moreover for the military projects they had conceived.

On the exterior it had the following fortifications. A horn-work in the road which leads to Tacubaya. A parapet in the gate at the entrance. Within the [e]nclosure which surrounds the woods to the south side, a breast-work was constructed, and a ditch eight yards wide and three in depth.

The artillery defending this fortification were 2 pieces of twenty-fours, 1 of eight, 3 field of fours, and 1 howitzer of 68, in all, 7 pieces.

The chief of the castle was General D. Nicolas Bravo and the second General, D. Mariano Monterde.

At dawn on the 12th, the enemy's battery, situated in the hermitage, opened its fire on the garita of the Niño Perdido, without any other object, as we can learn from the documents published by the American chiefs, than to call attention, and to properly be able to plant the ordnance which should batter Chapultepec in the places which we have mentioned.

In effect, in a few minutes, these batteries began to fire upon Chapultepec. At first, they caused no destruction. But rectifying their aim, the walls of the building commenced to be pierced by balls in all directions, experiencing great ravages also in the roofs, caused by the bombs which the mortar threw that, as we have said, was concealed in the court of the Molino. The artillery of Chapultepec answered with much precision and accuracy. The engineers worked incessantly to repair the damage done by the enemy's projectiles, and the troops quite behind the parapets suffered from this storm of balls. The most intelligent in the military art judge that the troops could have been placed at the foot of the hill to avoid the useless loss, leaving in the building only the artillerymen and the requisite engineers. This was not done, and the carcasses of the bombs and hollow balls killed and wounded many soldiers, who had not even the pleasure of discharging their muskets.

—The Battle of Chapultepec, Ramón Alcaraz

Source: Alcaraz, Ramón et al., eds. *The Other Side: Or Notes for the History of the War between Mexico and the United States Written in Mexico.* Translated by Albert C. Ramsey. New York: John Wiley, 1850, 33–38, 45–50, 122–129, 208–214, 353–365.

Abraham Lincoln, "Spot Resolutions" (December 22, 1847)

President James K. Polk (1795–1849) ordered General Zachary Taylor (1784–1850) into the disputed land between the Nueces and Rio Grande rivers to provoke the Mexican Army, which fired on Taylor's troops on April 24, 1846. Polk labeled this an act of war and called for hostilities with Mexico.

Abraham Lincoln (1809–1865), who was a freshman Whig congressman from Illinois at the time, questioned the "spot" where blood had first been shed in the Mexican-American War. Was it on U.S. soil? Was the president lying about the provocation? Lincoln was one of several congressmen opposing the war. On December 22, 1847, he introduced the "Spot Resolutions," in which he demanded to know the spot where American blood was spilled. This was important because Polk claimed that the Mexicans attacked U.S. troops on American soil. Lincoln's legislation was never acted upon by the full Congress. However, it earned him the nickname "Spotty Lincoln."

And whereas this House is desirous to obtain a full knowledge of all the facts which go to establish whether the particular spot on which the blood of our citizens was so shed was or was not at that time our own soil: Therefore, Resolved by the House of Representatives, That the President of the United States be respectfully requested to inform this House—

1st. Whether the spot on which the blood of our citizens was shed, as in his messages declared, was or was not within the territory of Spain, at least after the treaty of 1819 until the Mexican revolution.

2d. Whether that spot is or is not within the territory which was wrested from Spain by the revolutionary Government of Mexico.

3d. Whether that spot is or is not within a settlement of people, which settlement has existed ever since long before the Texas revolution, and until its inhabitants fled before the approach of the United States army.

4th. Whether that settlement is or is not isolated from any and all other settlements by the Gulf and the Rio Grande on the south and west, and by wide uninhabited regions on the north and east.

5th. Whether the people of that settlement, or a majority of them, or any of them, have ever submitted themselves to the government or laws of Texas or of the United States, by consent or by compulsion, either by accepting office, or voting at elections, or paying tax, or serving on juries, or having process served upon them, or in any other way.

6th. Whether the people of that settlement did or did not flee from the approach of the United States army, leaving unprotected their homes and their growing crops, before the blood was shed, as in the messages stated; and whether the first blood, so shed, was or was not shed within the enclosure of one of the people who had thus fled from it.

7th. Whether our citizens, whose blood was shed, as in his messages declared, were or were not, at that time, armed officers and soldiers, sent into that settlement by the military orders of the President, through the Secretary of War.

8th. Whether the military force of the United States was or was not so sent into that settlement after Gen. Taylor had more than once intimated to the War Department that, in his opinion, no such movement was necessary to the defence or protection of Texas.

Source: Printed Resolution and Preamble on Mexican War: "Spot Resolutions." The Abraham Lincoln Papers at the Library of Congress. http://memory.loc.gov/cgi-bin/query/r?ammem/mal:@field(DOCID+@lit(d0007000)).

Treaty of Guadalupe Hidalgo (1848)

With the Treaty of Guadalupe Hidalgo, Mexico ceded Arizona, New Mexico, California, and parts of Utah, Nevada, and Colorado to the United States. Mexico was forced to relinquish claims to Texas—recognizing the Rio Grande as the boundary (Article V) between the two *countries. The land cession amounted to about half of Mexico's territory. The United States paid Mexico $15 million in compensation for war-related damage to Mexican property and agreed to compensate American citizens for debts owed to them by the Mexican government. These debts were mostly related to the loss of runaway slaves who found refuge in Mexico. The treaty promised protection for the property and civil rights of Mexican nationals who resided on what was to become the U.S. side of the border. Finally, the United States promised to police its boundaries. The Senate ratified the treaty by a vote of 34–14 on March 10, 1848. It only passed by a one-vote margin because a two-thirds majority was required for passage. Article X, which guaranteed the protection of Mexican land grants, was deleted. The following are key articles of the treaty.*

ARTICLE V

The boundary line between the two Republics shall commence in the Gulf of Mexico, three leagues from land, opposite the mouth of the Rio Grande, otherwise called Rio Bravo del Norte, or opposite the mouth of its deepest branch, if it should have more than one branch emptying directly into the sea; from thence up the middle of that river, following the deepest channel, where it has more than one, to the point where it strikes the southern boundary of New Mexico; thence, westwardly, along the whole southern boundary of New Mexico (which runs north of the town called Paso) to its western termination; thence, northward, along the western line of New Mexico, until it intersects the first branch of the River Gila; (or if it should not intersect any branch of that river, then to the point on the said line nearest to such branch, and thence in a direct line to the same); thence down the middle of the said branch and of the said river, until it empties into the Rio Colorado; thence across the Rio Colorado, following the division line between Upper and Lower California, to the Pacific Ocean.

The southern and western limits of New Mexico, mentioned in the article, are those laid down in the map entitled "Map of the United Mexican States,["] as organized and defined by various acts of the Congress of said republic, and constructed according to the best authorities. Revised edition. Published at New York, in 1847, by J. Disturnell, of which map a copy is added to this treaty, bearing the signatures and seals of the undersigned Plenipotentiaries. And, in order to preclude all difficulty in tracing upon the ground the limit separating Upper from Lower California, it is agreed that the said limit shall consist of a straight line drawn from the middle of the Rio Gila, where it unites with the Colorado, to a point on the coast of the Pacific Ocean, distant one marine league due south of the southernmost point of the port of San Diego, according to the plan of said port made in the year 1782 by Don Juan Pantoja, second sailing-master of the Spanish fleet, and published at Madrid in the year 1802, in the atlas to the voyage of the schooners Sutil and Mexicana; of which plan a copy is hereunto added, signed and sealed by the respective Plenipotentiaries.

In order to designate the boundary line with due precision, upon authoritative maps, and to establish upon the ground land-marks which shall show the limits of both republics, as described in the present article, the two Governments shall each appoint a commissioner and a surveyor, who, before the expiration of one year from the date of the exchange of ratifications of this treaty, shall meet at the port of San Diego, and proceed to run and mark the said boundary in its whole course to the mouth of the Rio Bravo del Norte. They shall keep journals and make out plans of their operations; and the result agreed upon by them shall be deemed a part of this treaty, and shall have the same force as if it were inserted therein. The two Governments will amicably agree regarding what may be necessary to these persons, and also as to their respective escorts, should such be necessary.

The boundary line established by this article shall be religiously respected by each of the two republics, and no change shall ever be made therein, except by the express and free consent of both nations, lawfully given by the General Government of each, in conformity with its own constitution. . . .

ARTICLE VII

The River Gila, and the part of the Rio Bravo del Norte lying below the southern boundary of New Mexico, being, agreeably to the fifth article, divided in the middle between the two republics, the navigation of the Gila and of the Bravo below said boundary shall be free and common to the vessels and citizens of both countries; and neither shall, without the consent of the other, construct any work that may impede or interrupt, in whole or in part, the exercise of this right; not even for the purpose of favoring new methods of navigation. Nor shall any tax or contribution, under any denomination or title, be levied upon vessels or persons navigating the same or upon merchandise or effects transported thereon, except in the case of landing upon one of their shores. If, for the purpose of making the said rivers navigable, or for maintaining them in such state, it should be necessary or advantageous to establish any tax or contribution, this shall not be done without the consent of both Governments. The stipulations contained in the present article shall not impair the territorial rights of either republic within its established limits.

ARTICLE VIII

Mexicans now established in territories previously belonging to Mexico, and which remain for the future within the limits of the United States, as defined by the present treaty, shall be free to continue where they now reside, or to remove at any time to the Mexican Republic, retaining the property which they possess in the said territories, or disposing thereof, and removing the proceeds wherever they please, without their being subjected, on this account, to any contribution, tax, or charge whatever.

Those who shall prefer to remain in the said territories may either retain the title and rights of Mexican citizens, or acquire those of citizens of the United States. But they shall be under the obligation to make their election within one year from the date of the exchange of ratifications of this treaty; and those who shall remain in the said territories after the expiration of that year, without having declared their intention to retain the character of Mexicans, shall be considered to have elected to become citizens of the United States.

In the said territories, property of every kind, now belonging to Mexicans not established there, shall be inviolably respected. The present owners, the heirs of these, and all Mexicans who may hereafter acquire said property by contract, shall enjoy with respect to it guarantees equally ample as if the same belonged to citizens of the United States.

ARTICLE IX

The Mexicans who, in the territories aforesaid, shall not preserve the character of citizens of the Mexican Republic, conformably with what is stipulated in the preceding article, shall be incorporated into the Union of the United States and be admitted at the proper time (to be judged of by the Congress of the United States) to the enjoyment of all the rights of citizens of the United States, according to the principles of the Constitution; and in the mean time, shall be maintained and protected in the free enjoyment of their liberty and property, and secured in the free exercise of their religion without restriction.

ARTICLE X [STRICKEN BY U.S. AMENDMENTS]

ARTICLE XI

Considering that a great part of the territories, which, by the present treaty, are to be comprehended for the future within the limits of the United States, is now occupied by savage tribes, who will hereafter be under the exclusive control of the Government of the United States, and whose incursions within the territory of Mexico would be prejudicial in the extreme, it is solemnly agreed that all such incursions shall be forcibly restrained by the Government of the United States whensoever this may be necessary; and that when they cannot be prevented, they shall be punished by the said Government, and satisfaction for the same shall be exacted all in the same way, and with equal diligence and energy, as if the same incursions were meditated or committed within its own territory, against its own citizens.

It shall not be lawful, under any pretext whatever, for any inhabitant of the United States to purchase or acquire any Mexican, or any foreigner residing in Mexico, who may have been captured by Indians inhabiting the territory of either of the two republics; nor to purchase or acquire horses, mules, cattle, or property of any kind, stolen within Mexican territory by such Indians.

And in the event of any person or persons, captured within Mexican territory by Indians, being carried into the territory of the United States, the Government of the latter engages and binds itself, in the most solemn manner, so soon as it shall know of such captives being within its territory, and shall be able so to do, through the faithful exercise of its influence and power, to rescue them and return them to their country or deliver them to the agent or representative of the Mexican Government. The Mexican authorities will, as far as practicable, give to the Government of the United States notice of such captures; and its agents shall pay the expenses incurred in the maintenance and transmission of the rescued captives; who, in the mean time, shall be treated with the utmost hospitality by the American authorities at the place where they may be. But if the Government of the United States, before receiving such notice from Mexico, should obtain intelligence, through any other channel, of the existence of Mexican captives within its territory, it will proceed forthwith to effect their release and delivery to the Mexican agent, as above stipulated.

For the purpose of giving to these stipulations the fullest possible efficacy, thereby affording the security and redress demanded by their true spirit and intent, the Government of the United States will now and hereafter pass, without unnecessary delay, and always vigilantly enforce, such laws as the nature of the subject may require. And, finally, the sacredness of this obligation shall never be lost sight of by the said Government, when providing for the removal of the Indians from any portion of the said territories, or for its being settled by citizens of the United States; but, on the contrary, special care shall then be taken not to place its Indian occupants under the necessity of seeking new homes, by committing those invasions which the United States have solemnly obliged themselves to restrain. . . .

ARTICLE XV

The United States, exonerating Mexico from all demands on account of the claims of their citizens mentioned in the preceding article, and considering them entirely and forever canceled, whatever their amount may be, undertake to make satisfaction for the same, to an amount not exceeding three and one-quarter millions of dollars. To ascertain the validity and amount of those claims, a board of commissioners shall be established by the Government of the United States, whose awards shall be final and conclusive; provided that, in deciding upon the validity of each claim, the boa[rd] shall be guided and governed by the principles and rules of decision prescribed by the first and fifth articles of the unratified convention, concluded at the city of Mexico on the twentieth day of November, one thousand eight hundred and forty-three; and in no case shall an award be made in favour of any claim not embraced by these principles and rules.

If, in the opinion of the said board of commissioners or of the claimants, any books, records, or documents, in the possession or power of the Government of the Mexican Republic, shall be deemed necessary to the just decision of any claim, the commissioners, or the claimants through them, shall, within such period as Congress may designate, make an application in writing for the same, addressed to the Mexican Minister of Foreign Affairs, to be transmitted by the

Secretary of State of the United States; and the Mexican Government engages, at the earliest possible moment after the receipt of such demand, to cause any of the books, records, or documents so specified, which shall be in their possession or power (or authenticated copies or extracts of the same), to be transmitted to the said Secretary of State, who shall immediately deliver them over to the said board of commissioners; provided that no such application shall be made by or at the instance of any claimant, until the facts which it is expected to prove by such books, records, or documents, shall have been stated under oath or affirmation.

Source: Treaty of Guadalupe Hidalgo, February 2, 1848. Treaty of Guadalupe-Hidalgo [Exchange copy], February 2, 1848. Perfected Treaties, 1778–1945. Record Group 11. General Records of the United States Government, 1778–1992. National Archives.

President James K. Polk, Message to the Senate on Article X of the Treaty of Guadalupe Hidalgo

(February 22, 1848)

President James K. Polk (1795–1849) sent U.S. minister Nicholas Trist (1800–1874), a seasoned diplomat, to Mexico in the spring of 1847 to negotiate a treaty of peace ending the Mexican-American War. By August 1847, negotiations were well under way. However, President Polk was not pleased with the outcome of the negotiations and wanted more of Mexico's land. The Treaty of Guadalupe Hidalgo ceded 55 percent of Mexico's territory to the United States in exchange for $15 million in compensation for war-related damage to Mexican property. Polk actively campaigned against the inclusion of Article X of the treaty, which guaranteed the protection of Mexican land grants. He did not want strong guarantees to protect Mexican property—opining that the U.S. Constitution already protected Mexicans in the United States. Polk pressured senators to vote against the inclusion of Article X. The following presidential message to the Senate raises what Polk called serious flaws in Article X, saying there was no need for the article because U.S. law protected property rights.

IN EXECUTIVE SESSION, SENATE OF THE U. STATES.

WEDNESDAY, FEBRUARY 23, 1848.

The following message was received from the President of the United States, by Mr. Walker, his secretary:

To the Senate of the United States:

I lay before the Senate, for their consideration and advice as to its ratification, a treaty of peace, friendship, limits, and settlement, signed at the city of Guadalupe Hidalgo, on the second day of February 1848, by N. P. Trist on the part of the United States, and by plenipotentiaries appointed for that purpose on the part of the Mexican government.

I deem it to be my duty to state that the recall of Mr. Trist as commissioner of the United States, of which Congress was informed in my annual message, was dictated by a belief that his continued presence with the army could be productive of no good, but might do much harm by encouraging the delusive hopes and false impressions of the Mexicans; and that his recall would satisfy Mexico that the United States had no terms of peace more favorable to offer. Directions were given that any propositions for peace, which Mexico might make, should be received and transmitted by the commanding general of our forces, to the United States.

It was not expected that Mr. Trist would remain in Mexico, or continue in the exercise of the functions of the office of commissioner, after he received his letter of recall. He has, however, done so, and the plenipotentiaries of the government of Mexico, with a knowledge of the fact, have concluded with him this treaty. I have examined it with a full sense of the extraneous circumstances attending its conclusion and signature, which might be objected to; but, conforming, as it does substantially on the main questions of boundary and indemnity, to the terms which our commissioner, when he left the United States in April last, was authorized to offer, and animated, as I am, by the spirit which has governed all my official conduct towards Mexico, I have felt it to be my duty to submit it to the Senate for their consideration, with a view to its ratification.

To the tenth article of the treaty there are serious objections, and no instructions given to Mr. Trist contemplated or authorized its insertion. The public lands within the limits of Texas belong to that State, and this government has no power to dispose of them, or to change the conditions of grants already made. All valid titles to land within the other territories ceded to the United States will remain unaffected by the change of sovereignty; and I therefore submit that this article should not be ratified as a part of the treaty.

There may be reason to apprehend that the ratification of the "additional and secret article" might unreasonably delay and embarrass the final action on the treaty by Mexico. I therefore submit whether that article should not be rejected by the Senate.

If the treaty shall be ratified as proposed to be amended, the cessions of territory made by it to the United States, as indemnity, the provision for the satisfaction of the claims of our injured citizens, and the permanent establishment of the boundary of one of the States of the Union, are objects gained of great national importance; while the magnanimous forbearance exhibited towards Mexico, it is hoped may insure a lasting peace and good neighborhood between the two countries.

I communicate herewith a copy of the instructions given to Mr. Slidell in November 1845, as enjoy extraordinary and minister plenipotentiary to Mexico; a copy of the instructions given to Mr. Trist in April last, and such of the correspondence of the latter with the Department of State, not heretofore communicated to Congress, as will enable the Senate to understand the action which has been had with a view to the adjustment of our difficulties with Mexico.

Source: U.S. Senate, 30th Cong., 1st Sess., Executive Order 68. Congressional Record.

Deleted Article X from the Treaty of Guadalupe Hidalgo (1848)

Article X of the Treaty of Guadalupe Hidalgo used strong terms to guarantee the property rights of Mexicans and Indians who remained in the ceded territory. However, there was some question whether the article applied to Texas. There was also sentiment against leaving large amounts of land in Mexican hands. The debate was heated, and many U.S. senators did not want to make any concessions to the vanquished nation. On March 10, 1848, the Senate finally approved the Treaty of Guadalupe Hidalgo without Article X, which guaranteed the protection of Mexican land grants, and with changes made to Article IX that obligated the United States to police its boundaries. U.S. secretary of state James Buchanan (1791–1868) sent a letter to the Mexican Congress giving reasons for the elimination of Article X and the revision of Article

IX. He wrote that the U.S. Constitution already promised to protect private property. Article IX was changed because it violated precedents in treaties negotiated with France and Spain. The Querétaro Protocol was given to the Mexican Congress before the U.S. ratification of the treaty giving the reasons why the United States had changed the original. In short, it said "Trust us." The U.S. Constitution would protect Mexican Americans. The protocol's interpretation of the treaty, however, had no legal force.

ARTICLE X

All the land grants made by the Mexican government or by the competent authorities which pertained to Mexico in the past and which will remain in the future within the boundaries of the United States will be respected as valid, with the same force as if those territories still remained within the limits of Mexico. But the grantees of lands in Texas who had taken possession of them and who because of the conditions of the state since discord began between the Mexican Government and Texas, may have been impeded from complying with all the conditions of the grants, have the obligation of fulfilling the same conditions under the stated terms of the respective grants, but now counted from the date of the exchange of the ratifications of this Treaty; for failing to do this the same grants are not obligatory upon the State of Texas, in virtue of stipulations contained in this article.

Source: Article X, Treaty of Guadalupe Hidalgo, http://www.digitalhistory.uh.edu/mexican_voices/voices_display.cfm?id=62.

Querétaro Protocol
(May 26, 1848)

The Mexican Congress reluctantly ratified the Treaty of Guadalupe Hidalgo as amended by the U.S. Senate on March 10, 1848. One more vote against the treaty in the U.S. Senate would have meant the failure of the treaty because it would have lacked the required two-thirds majority. Article X was absent from the ratified version of the treaty, and changes to Article IX had lessened the obligation of the United States to protect Mexican property. The treaty passed the Mexican Congress by a one-vote margin and was ratified on May 19, 1848. Some Mexican legislators relied on a letter of protocol by American negotiators, known as the Querétaro Protocol, that assured Mexicans that their rights would be protected by the U.S. Constitution and that the deletion of Article X and parts of the other articles was in their interest. Many Mexican legislators did not trust the United States and wanted a guarantee of property rights as well as the inclusion of parts of Article IX that guaranteed Mexicans left behind in the ceded territories full citizenship, guaranteed immediate statehood to the Mexican Southwest, and obligated the United States to police its borders.

1st. The American Government by suppressing the IXth article of the Treaty of Guadalupe Hidalgo and substituting the IIId article of the Treaty of Louisiana, did not intend to diminish in any way what was agreed upon by the aforesaid article IXth in favor of the inhabitants of the territories ceded by Mexico. Its understanding is that all of the agreement is contained in the 3d article of the Treaty of Louisiana. Inconsequence of all the privileges and guarantees civil, political, and religious, which would have been possessed by the inhabitants of the ceded territories, if the IXth article of the treaty had been retained, will be enjoyed by them, without any difference, under the article which has been substituted.

2nd. The American Government by suppressing the Xth article of the Treaty of Guadalupe Hidalgo did not in any way intend to annul the grants of lands made by Mexico in the ceded territories. These grants notwithstanding the suppression of the article of the treaty, preserve the legal value which they may possess, and the grantees may cause their legitimate (titles) to be acknowledged before American tribunals. (Titles: those which were legitimate titles up to the 13th of May, 1846, and in Texas up to the 2nd March, 1836.)

Source: Protocol of Quéretaro. 106th Congress, 2d Session, S. 2022. http://www.digitalhistory.uh.edu/mexican_voices/voices_display.cfm?id=65.

Manuel Crescion Rejón, Commentary on the Treaty of Guadalupe Hidalgo (1848)

Many Mexican intellectuals expressed doubt as to the good faith of the United States in 1848. For them, the United States had unjustly invaded Mexico. In 1848, at the time the treaty was signed, Mexican diplomat Manuel Crescion Rejón (full name Manuel Crescencio García Rejón y Alcalá;1799–1849) predicted that Mexicans in the United States would be at the mercy of the European Americans and, because of their race, would be treated as second-class citizens in the United States.

Our race, our unfortunate people, will have to wander in search of hospitality in a strange land, only to be ejected later. Descendants of the Indians that we are, the North Americans hate us, their spokesmen depreciate us, even if they recognize the justice of our cause, and they consider us unworthy to form with them one nation and one society, they clearly manifest that their future expansion begins with the territory that they take from us, and pushing aside our citizens who inhabit the land.

Source: Reyes, Antonio de la Peña y Reyes. *Algunos Documentos Sobre el Tratado de Guadalupe-Hidalgo.* México, D.F.: Sec de Rel. Ext., 1930, 159. Quoted in Gonzales, Richard. "Commentary on the Treaty of Guadalupe Hidalgo." In *A Mexican American Source Book*, edited by Feliciano Rivera, 185. Menlo Park, CA: Educational Consulting Associates, 1970, 185.

Abiel Abbot Livermore, *The War with Mexico Reviewed* (1850)

Abiel Abbot Livermore (1811–1892), a minister of the Congregational Church in New England, opposed the Mexican-American War because he considered it unjust and a plot by slave states to secure more land. In 1850, he won the American Peace Prize for a graphic book, The War with Mexico Reviewed, *which extensively covered the atrocities of the war. Not much is known about Livermore, who continued to be involved in progressive causes, such as the abolitionist movement that sought to end slavery. In this excerpt from his book, Livermore quotes an eyewitness to the atrocities committed against Mexicans during the war. Livermore represents the progressive strain within American society that had worked for peace and questioned the motives for war.*

Again, the pride of race has swollen to still greater insolence the pride of country, always quite active enough for the due observance of the claims of universal brotherhood. The Anglo-Saxons have been apparently persuaded to think themselves the chosen people, anointed race of the Lord, commissioned to drive out the heathen, and plant their religion and institutions in every Canaan they could subjugate. . . . Our treatment both of the red man and the black man has habituated us to feel our power and forget right . . . The god Terminus is an unknown deity in America. Like the hunger of the pauper boy of fiction, the cry had been, "more, more, give us more." . . .

[He quotes one account:]

> Among the hundreds of the dead whom I saw there [at the Battle of Buena Vista], I was much touched by the appearance of the corpse of a Mexican boy, whose age, I should think, could not have exceeded fifteen years . . . [a bullet had struck him through the breast].

Source: Livermore, Abiel Abbot. *The War with Mexico Reviewed*. Boston: American Peace Society, 1850, 8, 11, 12, 139.

Samuel E. Chamberlain, *My Confession: The Recollections of a Rogue* (undated)

Samuel E. Chamberlain (1829–1908) was a soldier, artist, and author who traveled throughout the Southwest and Mexico. At the age of 15, he left home and joined the Second Illinois Volunteer Regiment that was headed for Texas. Once in Texas, he joined the regular army. He participated in border fights and rode with the Glanton gang, taking Mexican scalps. My Confession *documents European American racism and destruction during the Mexican-American War. The book was apparently based on Samuel Chamberlain's scrapbook, MC092, at the San Jacinto Museum of History in Houston, Texas. The book was published long after Chamberlain's death in 1908. The following excerpts are from a report from the Mexican city of Parras (Coahuila, Mexico).*

We found the patrol had been guilty of many outrages. . . . They had ridden into the church of San José during Mass, the place crowded with kneeling women and children, and with oaths and ribald jest had arrested soldiers who had permission to be present.

[He described a massacre by volunteers, mostly from Yell's Cavalry, at a cave:] On reaching the place we found a "greaser" shot and scalped, but still breathing; the poor fellow held in his hands a Rosary and a medal of the "Virgin of Guadalupe," only his feeble motions kept the fierce harpies from falling on him while yet alive. A Sabre thrust was given him in mercy, and on we went at a run. Soon shouts and curses, cries of women and children reached our ears, coming apparently from a cave at the end of the ravine. Climbing over the rocks we reached the entrance, and as soon as we could see in the comparative darkness, a horrid sight was before us. The cave was full of our volunteers yelling like fiends, while on the rocky floor lay over twenty Mexicans, dead and dying in pools of blood. Women and children were clinging to the knees of the murderers shrieking for mercy. . . . Most of the butchered Mexicans had been scalped; only three men were found unharmed. A rough crucifix was fastened to a rock, and some irreverent wretch had crowned the image with a bloody scalp. A sickening smell filled the place. The surviving women and children sent up loud screams on seeing us, thinking we had returned to finish the work! . . . No one was punished for this outrage.

Source: Chamberlain, Samuel E. *My Confessions*. New York: Harper & Row, 1956, 75, 87–88.

Defining the U.S.-Mexico Border

William D. Carrigan and Clive Webb, "The Lynching of Persons of Mexican Origin or Descent in the United States, 1848 to 1928"

European American people warred with Native Americans for two centuries. They also considered Mexicans to be Indians. Phrases such as "the only good Indian is a dead Indian" were part of their vernacular. European Americans transferred these racial and cultural attitudes to Mexicans upon moving into what was formerly Mexican land. This racism created barriers that reinforced inequality and led to a lack of protection under the law for Mexicans that is still present. The brutality was not confined to groups such as the Texas Rangers (formed in 1823), who were infamous for their brutal treatment of Mexicans, but also from ordinary people who saw Mexicans as intruders and a menace to the American way of life. Hence, in the name of justice, many white Americans executed hundreds of Mexican migrants and residents without any repercussions. This action gave rise to vigilante groups, often called Minute Men, who perpetuated atrocities. Lynchings were the worst of these atrocities. Studies, such as that from which the following excerpt is taken, suggest that 473 of every 100,000 Mexican migrant workers during this period died as lynching victims. The following excerpt describes the extent of the lynching of Mexicans in the Southwest in the 80 years after the end of the Mexican-American War.

Although no comprehensive work on the lynching of Mexicans was ever produced, several historians have addressed the subject of mob violence against Mexicans in more general terms. Despite the extensive documentation of anti-Mexican mob violence provided by these scholars, historians of lynching continue to ignore the brutal repression of Spanish-speakers in the United States. One reason is that no scholar has attempted to provide an actual count of Mexican lynching victims. Discussions of African American lynching victims in the South have rested upon an actual count of individual cases since the turn of the twentieth century. The treatment of Mexican lynching victims, by contrast, often rests upon impressionistic estimates. In 1949, Carey McWilliams wrote in North from Mexico that "vast research would be required to arrive at an estimate of the number of Mexican lynchings.". . .

Between 1848 and 1928, mobs lynched at least 597 Mexicans. Historian Christopher Waldrep has asserted that the definition of lynching has altered so much over the course of time as to render impossible the accurate collection of data on mob violence. It is therefore essential to familiarize the reader from the outset with the interpretation of lynching used to compile the statistics in this essay. The authors regard lynching as a retributive act of murder for which those responsible claim to be serving the interests of justice, tradition, or community good. Although our notion as to what constitutes a lynching is clear, it is still impossible to provide a precise count of the number of Mexican victims. We have excluded a significant number of reported lynchings when the sources do not allow for verification of specific data such as the date, location, or identity of the victim. The statistics included in this essay should therefore be considered a conservative estimate of the actual number of Mexicans lynched in the United States.

Frontier conditions undoubtedly fostered the growth of vigilantism in general. Nonetheless, the conventional interpretation of western violence cannot be applied to the lynching of Mexicans. The most serious criticism of the "socially constructive" model of vigilantism espoused by Richard Maxwell Brown is that it legitimates the actions of lawbreakers. There is an implicit presumption in the civic virtue of the vigilantes and the criminal guilt of their victims. In truth, the popular tribunals that put Mexicans to death can seldom be said to have acted in the spirit of the law. According to Joseph Caughey, vigilante committees persisted in their activities "long after the arrival" of the law courts. However, Anglos refused to recognize the legitimacy of these courts when they were controlled or influenced by Mexicans. Determined to redress the balance of racial and political power, they constructed their own parallel mechanisms of justice. This is precisely what occurred in Socorro, New Mexico, during the 1880s when an Anglo vigilance committee arose in opposition to the predominantly Mexican legal authorities. These committees showed little respect for the legal rights of Mexicans, executing them in disproportionately large numbers. Their actions therefore amounted to institutionalized discrimination. . . .

The lynching of Mexicans not only occurred in areas where there was a fully operating legal system but often involved the active collusion of law officers themselves. In February 1857, a Justice of the Peace assembled an unwilling audience of Mexicans outside the San Gabriel mission to watch as he decapitated Miguel Soto and then stabbed repeatedly at the corpse. The most systematic abuse of legal authority was by the Texas Rangers. Their brutal repression of the Mexican population was tantamount to state-sanctioned terrorism. Although the exact number of those murdered by the Rangers is unknown, historians estimate that it ran into the hundreds and even thousands. In March 1881, Rangers crossed the border into Mexico and illegally arrested Onofrio Baca on a charge of murder. Baca was returned without extradition orders to the United States where he was handed over to a mob "and strung up to the cross beams of the gate in the court house yard until he was dead." The terrorizing of Mexicans continued well into the twentieth century. On October 18, 1915, Mexican outlaws derailed a train traveling toward Brownsville, killing several passengers. Some who survived the crash were robbed and murdered by the bandits. The Rangers exacted brutal revenge. Two Mexican passengers aboard the train were shot for their supposed assistance of the raid. The Rangers then executed eight suspected Mexican criminals along the banks of the Rio Grande. . . .

Source: Carrigan, William D., and Clive Webb, "The Lynching of Persons of Mexican Origin or Descent in the United States, 1848 to 1928." *Journal of Social History* 37, no. 2 (2003): 412–417.

Unknown Author, "New Mexico—Its Social Condition" (1852)

Along with the European American merchants and U.S. soldiers who moved into the occupied territory along the Rio Grande, Protestant missionaries descended on the newly occupied territory that once belonged to Mexico. Much like the Spanish missionaries, they entered Mexico with their cultural and racial biases. They believed that the Mexicans were pagans and that through their conversion to Christianity, not only would their souls be saved but they would also become civilized. The following description by a Protestant minister comments on Mexicans in New Mexico and their "depraved" state.

He found there some 6,000 Mexicans who had never heard a gospel sermon. There were numbers of American traders there, and a host of gamblers. The state of society was most deplorable and alarming. It does not materially differ from the society of some of the other heathen territories. Ignorance, superstition and idolatry were prevalent in such a degree as I had never before heard of in any uncivilized country. There never had been a school-house or institution of learning of any kind for the instruction of the youth, neither were there any school books of any description.

The Mexicans are a depraved, lawless set of desperadoes. Gambling is a universal habit. I believe there is not a single Mexican, man or woman, boy or girl, of the age of eight years, but knows how to gamble. Mothers teach their children from infancy the art of gambling. They are trained up in the school of deception by their parents until able to deceive, cheat and gamble on their own hook. The most depraved and wicked are the greatest to be respected. Licentiousness in all its deplorable malignity—in the worst conceivable forms—stalks abroad at mid-day. Until this vice is checked, little can be done for the elevation of the people, and unless missionaries are sent there to teach them, their reformation is hopeless. It is a lamentable fact that since the conquest by the Americans, their vices have increased. The Americans have been instrumental in carrying among them.

Their christenings, their weddings, and their funerals are celebrated in the most debasing and humiliating debauchery.

Source: New York Daily Times, September 21, 1852, 6.

"Dame Shirley," Letter Concerning San Francisco Vigilante Committee Activities against Chileans (1852)

Mexicans were not the only victims of vigilantism after 1848. Chinese, blacks, and other Latinos were also targeted. Not all Latinos went to the mine fields, and a sizable colony grew in San Francisco, California. The following letter is from Louise Amelia Knapp Smith Clappe (1819–1906), who used the pseudonym "Dame Shirley," to her sister Molly in Massachusetts. In the letter, Dame Shirley views the activities of the San Francisco Vigilante Committee as an attempt to purge civic sins and as an improvement over more spontaneous lynchings.

This frightful accident recalled the people to their senses, and they began to act a little less like madmen, than they had previously done. They elected a vigilance committee, and authorized persons to go to The Junction and arrest the suspected Spaniards.

The first act of the Committee was to try a Mexicana, who had been foremost in the fray. She has always worn male attire, and on this occasion, armed with a pair of pistols, she fought like a very fury. Luckily, inexperienced in the use of fire-arms, she wounded no one. She was sentenced to leave the Bar by day-light, a perfectly just decision, for there is no doubt she is a regular little demon. Some went so far as to say she ought to be hanged, for she was the indirect cause of the fight. You see always, it is the old, cowardly excuse of Adam in Paradise—the woman tempted me, and I did eat—as if the poor frail head, once so pure and beautiful, had not sin enough of its own, dragging it forever downward, without being made to answer for the wrong-doing of a whole community of men.

The next day, the Committee tried five or six Spaniards, who were proven to have been the ringleaders in the sabbath-day riot. Two of them were sentenced to be whipped, the remainder to leave the Bar that evening, the property of all to be confiscated to the use of the wounded persons. Oh Mary! imagine my anguish when I heard the first blow fall upon those wretched men.

Source: Indian Bar, August 4, 1852. Louise Amelia Knapp Smith Clappe, The Shirley Letters from California Mines in 1851–1852: Being a Series of Twenty-Three Letters from Dame Shirley . . . to Her Sister in Massachusetts . . . Reprinted from the Pioneer Magazine of 1854–1855, Thomas C. Russell, ed. San Francisco: Thomas C. Russell, 1922, 263–264.

José María Loaiza, Claim for the Lynching of His Wife Josefa and His Banishment by a Mob in Downieville, California (July 4, 1852)

In 1851, a Downieville, California, kangaroo court sentenced a 26-year-old Mexican woman called Juanita (her real name was Josefa) to hanging. She was the first woman hanged in California. Early accounts minimized the gravity of the lynching, claiming that Juanita Loaiza was a prostitute who lived with a gambler, José María Loaiza. On July 4, 1851, during a drunken rage, Fred Cannon, a miner in Downieville, in Northern California, intentionally broke down Josefa's door and tried to force sexual favors from her. She ran him off. When Josefa and her husband approached Cannon the next day and asked him to pay for the door, he called her a whore. Josefa went to the door of her home and said, "This is no place to call me bad names; come into my house and call me that." Josefa stabbed Cannon with a knife. Although the miners wanted to lynch Josefa and José on the spot, they held a kangaroo trial. Cannon's body was displayed in a tent, dressed in a red flannel shirt, unbuttoned to show the wound. A pregnant Josefa was convicted. She was hanged from a bridge, while more than 2,000 men lined the river to watch. For years, the lynching of Josefa was excused because, according to the defenders of the vigilantes, she was a whore.

The following document from the Rodolfo F. Acuña Archives at California State University–Northridge presents an electronic mail message from Sacramento, California, historian Roberto

Carrillo Gantz in which he summarizes his research on the Josefa Loaiza lynching and exposes the lie that she was a prostitute. Gantz, who is a vocational instructor for Sacramento County, a historian, and a screenwriter, was moved by a Public Broadcasting television program about the California Gold Rush and the lynching of Josefa. He did quite a bit of research on the subject at the California State Library in Sacramento while researching the injustice for a screenplay. While browsing microfiche on the U.S. Mexican Claims Commission, he came across a claim made by Josefa's husband.

A claim made by José María Loaiza, filed against the U.S. government for "the lynching of his wife and the banishment of himself by a mob . . . July 4, 1852 . . . Downieville, California." The date was inaccurate but further research verified that it was Josefa's husband. Josefa and José María Loaiza were from Sonora. "Schedule of Mexican Claims against the United States," Senate Executive Document 31, 44th Congress 2nd Session. Docket Number 904. José María Loaiza made a claim for the lynching of his wife Josefa and his banishment by a mob on July 4, 1852 in Downieville, California. The claim was made on June 11, 1875. The claim was dismissed by the commissioner.

Source: Rodolfo F. Acuña Archives, Special Collections, California State University, Northridge.

Governor William Carr Lane, Manifesto Regarding the Drawing of the Boundary between Mexico and the United States (1853)

The Treaty of Guadalupe Hidalgo (1848) mandated a joint boundary commission to determine the boundary between the United States and Mexico. In December 1848, President James K. Polk (1795–1849) named Ambrose Sevier as U.S. commissioner, but Sevier (1801–1848) died before he could be confirmed to head the U.S. commission. John B. Weller (1812–1875), a former congressman from Ohio, replaced Sevier and on July 6, 1849, met with Mexican commissioner general Pedro García Conde (1806–1851). The joint commission ran a line from the Pacific Ocean to the Gila and Colorado rivers. They planned to meet in El Paso. Weller was forced to leave the commission because of political intrigue and infighting. He was replaced by John Russell Bartlett (1805–1886), and the commission resumed its work in the El Paso, Texas, area. Immediately, an impasse developed over the location of the southern boundary of New Mexico. Controversy developed when several serious discrepancies were found in the official Disturnell Treaty map used by the framers of the Treaty of Guadalupe Hidalgo (1848) to set the boundaries.

Bartlett and García Conde reached a compromise in the spring of 1851. This agreement resulted in a crisis that was not resolved until the Gadsden Purchase was negotiated in 1853. Federal, state, and local representatives from New Mexico and the rest of the country claimed that Bartlett had sold them out by giving "their" land to Mexico. The following document is an excerpt from a manifesto issued by New Mexico territorial governor William Carr Lane (1789–1863), a Whig who had served as mayor of St. Louis from 1837 to 1840. President Millard Fillmore

(1800–1874) appointed him to be the new governor of the New Mexico Territory in 1852. The statement inflamed Mexican authorities in neighboring Chihuahua who charged that the United States was attempting to goad Mexico into another war so they could seize more land.

The mere fact, without any other reason, that the President and Congress of the United States have disapproved and repudiated the provisional boundary line which has been run from the Rio Grande to the Gila, is of itself an ample justification of the act of the Government of New-Mexico in promulgating the proclamation of the 19th inst., and the want of special instructions from Mexico does not in the slightest degree invalidate this official act. Whatever your Excellencies may have heard to the contrary from persons as ignorant as presumptuous, it is none the less true that my authority is to be found in the laws and constitution of the United States, in the law of nations, in the treaty with Mexico, and in the duties of my office as Governor of this Territory.

Your Excellencies have affirmed that the southern boundary line of New-Mexico terminated at New-Mexico, twenty-two miles north of the provisional line of Mr. Bartlett, while a decree of the Mexican Congress fixes the line at El Paso; this decree has never, to my knowledge, been revoked.

In your communication your Excellencies frankly admit that Chihuahua never exercised its jurisdiction over the territory in dispute, before the running of Mr. Bartlett's line, notwithstanding it was entreated by the inhabitants so to do. And why did it not exercise its jurisdiction? I will answer for your Excellencies—it was because it was well known that the territory belonged to New-Mexico, and not to Chihuahua.

The error committed by Mr. Bartlett, when he determined the said line, induced Chihuahua into error, and it is now incumbent upon Chihuahua to correct it.

"If we should have to suspend for a time the work on one portion of the line, by reason of a difference of opinion, or any other cause, we may go on and determine some other part, so that, in case we should not agree as to the southern boundary line, and should therefore have to refer to our respective Governments, the work on the Gila may progress, should it be deemed expedient." To these reasonable propositions, Mr. Bartlett turned a deaf ear, and obstinately insisted upon his established line, without the concurrence of his colleagues, even though the latter had shown the said line to be wrong. . . .

Source: New York Daily Times, June 20, 1853, 3.

John Disturnell, Letter to the *New York Daily Times* on the Drawing of the New-Mexican Boundary

(May 6, 1853)

John Disturnell (1801–1877) was the most influential and well-known U.S. mapmaker of the 19th century. When the United States turned to an authority to establish the U.S.-Mexican border, they based their assumptions on Disturnell's map because it was the most authoritative. But his 1847 map was flawed and caused a dispute over the placement of the U.S.-Mexico boundary around the El Paso area. An error in the coordinates of the map raised the issue as to whether the lines in that area should be disputed. El Paso was incorrectly located on the official map 34 miles too far north and 100 miles too far east. The dispute was resolved by a compromise between U.S. boundary commissioner James Bartlett (1805–1886) and Mexican commissioner Pedro García Conde (1806–1851). This compromise caused an uproar, and U.S. politicos claimed that Bartlett had given away U.S. territory. In the following letter, Disturnell defended the Boundary Commission's compromise and called the Mesilla dispute of imaginary value and an attempt to take advantage of Mexico. The letter is fundamental to understanding the dispute and the European American maneuver of reannexation.

THE NEW-MEXICAN BOUNDARY

To the Editor of the New York Daily Times:

The article in your paper of the 5th inst., on the subject of "The Mexican Boundary," signed "W.H.S." is one-sided, and partly erroneous in regard to the matter in dispute. For a correct view of the subject, the public should read the article in the National Intelligencer of the 5th of April, signed "P.F.," which quotes from the instructions given to N.P. Trist, Esq., the Commissioner on the part of the United States, and who signed the Treaty of Peace and Limits, Feb. 2, 1848. Also refer to the Constitution of Chihuahua, as revised in 1847, which defines the northern boundary between New-Mexico, at 32° 57' 43" north latitude. Then examine a map of the Republic of Mexico, certified to by Don Garcio Conde in 1845, which valuable and authentic map is in the possession of the late Commissioner to settle the boundary between the two countries; and in conclusion, refer to the "Treaty Map," revised edition, 1847, which indicates, on careful examination, the line in dispute to run parallel to 32° 22' north latitude—being no doubt the fair and equitable boundary line, according to the letter of said Treaty.

As to the imaginary value of the Mesilla Valley, or tract in dispute, it has no force other than a greater inducement for a stronger party to despoil a weaker foe.

As regards the Treaty Map of the Republic of Mexico, which has of late so often been referred to, it was first published in the City of New-York, in 1828, being then considered the most correct map of Mexico, and certified to as such by competent authority. Since then, in many respects, the map has been improved and corrected from time to time, as new information has been received from the Departments at Washington and otherwise.

In December 1847, it was discovered that a geographical error existed in regard to the true position of El Paso, a frontier town of Chihuahua, which error was corrected from official documents, derived in Washington by the publisher of said map. In changing the boundary between New-Mexico and Chihuahua, the compiler was guided by new and supposed reliable American authority, which, however, seems to have been an error in regard to said boundary, according to the import of the able article in the National Intelligencer, and from an official map of Chihuahua, which has recently been shown to me by J. R. Bartlett, Esq., the late Commissioner on the part of the United States, to settle the boundary between the two countries, as called for by the Treaty of 1848.

Yours, &c.,

Source: New York Daily Times, May 7, 1853, 3.

Gadsden Purchase Treaty (December 30, 1853)

The U.S. minister to Mexico, James Gadsden (1788–1858), attempted to purchase Sonora and northern Mexico from Mexico. When Mexico was unwilling to sell this area, Gadsden used heavy-handed methods in the negotiations, threatening Mexican ministers that if they did not sell southern Arizona and parts of New Mexico, "we shall take it." Under pressure, Mexico ceded more than 45,000 square miles, of which some 35,000 were in southern Arizona, for $10 million. The Gadsden *(or Mesilla) Treaty settled the controversy surrounding where the boundary between the countries should be placed. The following excerpts from the treaty deal with the Mesilla Valley's transfer to the United States and the relief of the United States of responsibility for Indian raids emanating from U.S. territory.*

ARTICLE I

The Mexican Republic agrees to designate the following as her true limits with the United States for the future: retaining the same dividing line between the two Californias as already defined and established, according to the 5th article of the Treaty of Guadalupe Hidalgo limits between the two republics shall be as follows: Beginning in the Gulf of Mexico, three leagues from land, opposite the mouth of the Rio Grande, as provided in the 5th article of the Treaty of Guadalupe Hidalgo; thence, as defined in the said article, up the middle of that river to the point where the parallel of 31° 47' north latitude crosses the same; thence due west one hundred miles; thence south to the parallel of 31° 20' north latitude; thence along the said parallel of 31° 20' to the 111th meridian of longitude west of Greenwich; thence in a straight line to a point on the Colorado River twenty English miles below the junction of the Gila and Colorado Rivers; thence up the middle of the said River Colorado until it intersects the present line between the United States and Mexico.

For the performance of this portion of the treaty, each of the two governments shall nominate one commissioner, to the end that, by common consent the two thus nominated, having met in the city of Paso del Norte, three months after the exchange of the ratifications of this treaty, may proceed to survey and mark out upon the land the dividing line stipulated by this article, where it shall not have already been surveyed and established by the mixed commission, according to the treaty of Guadalupe Hidalgo, keeping a journal and making proper plans of their operations. For this purpose, if they should judge it necessary, the contracting parties shall be at liberty each to unite to its respective commissioner, scientific or other assistants, such as astronomers and surveyors, whose concurrence shall not be considered necessary for the settlement and of a true line of division between the two Republics; that line shall be alone established upon which the commissioners may fix, their consent in this particular being considered decisive and an integral part of this treaty, without necessity of ulterior ratification or approval, and without room for interpretation of any kind by either of the parties contracting.

The dividing line thus established shall, in all time, be faithfully respected by the two governments, without any variation therein, unless of the express and free consent of the two, given in conformity to the principles of the law of nations, and in accordance with the constitution of each country respectively.

In consequence, the stipulation in the 5th article of the treaty of Guadalupe Hidalgo upon the boundary line therein described is no longer of any force, wherein it may conflict with that here established, the said line being considered annulled and abolished wherever it may not coincide with the present, and in the same manner remaining in full force where in accordance with the same.

ARTICLE II

The government of Mexico hereby releases the United States from all liability on account of the obligations contained in the 11th article of the treaty of Guadalupe Hidalgo and the said article and the thirty-third article of the treaty of amity, commerce, and navigation between the United States of America and the United Mexican States concluded at Mexico, on the fifth day of April 1831, are hereby abrogated.

BY THE PRESIDENT: FRANKLIN PIERCE

Source: Gadsden Purchase Treaty (December 30, 1853). Statutes of the United States, Vol. 10. http://www.yale.edu/lawweb/avalon/diplomacy/mexico/mx1853.htm.

Special Correspondent, "A Tour in the Southwest" (1854)

Racial attitudes of European Americans toward Mexicans were formed by popular articles published by travelers along the almost 2,000-mile U.S.-Mexican border. The following excerpt is an account of a traveler along the Rio Grande that was printed in the New York Daily Times *in 1854. It speaks of Mexicans in racial terms and perpetuates stereotypes that were rampant at the time.*

It must be remembered that the Mexican population within the territory is large and increasing, and that it is a dark-colored, mixed race, including often no small proportion of African blood, so much so, that it requires the eye of an expert to distinguish many of those held as slaves, on account of their color, from others among the Mexicans who are constitutionally eligible to the highest offices. The Mexicans have no repugnance, but rather the contrary, to equality and the closest intimacy with negroes. But the intelligence, the enterprise, and the peculiar habits of mind which are the effects of early industrial training, that exist as most important elements in the Germans, as well as the rational regard for liberty, as a right of man, which they generally have, is wanting in the degraded Mexicans.

Source: New York Daily Times, June 3, 1854, 2.

Report of the Mexican Commission on the Northern Frontier Question (1875)

Juan Cortina (1824–1894) had become, according to European Americans, an outlaw for shooting a marshal who pistol-whipped an elderly servant of his mother and called Cortina a "greaser" when he intervened. The Texas press and many merchants demanded more troops and forts on the border. Many Mexicans charged that the hysteria was manufactured and that the threat was exaggerated. The motive, they believed, was to pressure the government to sustain military forts on the border so that the merchants could make fortunes through supply contracts necessary to maintain the forts and to ensure the flow of money spent by soldiers in the nearby towns. Considerable diplomatic pressure was put on the Mexican government to arrest Cortina, and many European Americans demanded that the United States invade Mexico. Tired of the accusations, the Mexican government conducted its own investigation. Some of the findings follow in a Mexican Commission Report that some historians consider one of the most important documents of its time.

Desirous of hearing the complaints of the sufferers of injuries received, the Commission issued copies of the regulations of the 21st November, and invited the citizens of Mexico and Texas to present their claims before them. They then set about to collect all the facts relative to cattle stealing on the United States frontier, whether favorable or adverse to the Mexican Republic. Besides this, and in compliance with the law of Congress, their duties extended to the hearing and investigation of the complaints of American citizens, and to this end the above-named regulations were issued, as follows:

Although testimonial evidence on all these points has been most useful and important, yet circumstantial proofs culled from the archives have in all cases been more conclusive. In those examined by the Commission are a series of regulations framed by the municipal and police authorities for the suppression of horse thieves in the towns lying on the bank of the river. Very few of these measures looked to the prevention of the traffic in stolen cattle from Texas, from which it would seem that this evil did not exist to the same extent; whilst on the contrary, the laws had in view the damages resulting from horse stealing in Mexico, and the transportation of the horses into Texas, proving that this was the greater traffic, and the one that needed greater legislation. Measures for the prevention of this crime have been issued in every town along the river, from which it may be deduced that like injuries were experienced in every village on the Mexican line; and as these preventive measures were constant and frequently repeated, it would seem that the injuries were constant and frequently recurring. . . .

The great weight of these proofs cannot be estimated from a few isolated measures of this kind, but must be judged as a whole; for whilst instituting a repressive system of horse stealing on the Mexican frontier for the Texan market, since 1848, they also indicate the robberies organized on the Texan shore of the Rio Bravo, in injury to Mexican proprietors.

They are contemporaries, at least, in the robberies committed in 1848, and which have since continued. Adolfo Glaevecke is one of those who have most actively engaged in horse stealing in Mexico, ever since the Rio Bravo has been the dividing line between the two nations.

Persons who have belonged to the police corps, accomplices of Glaevecke, and persons who have appeared in court at various times to reclaim stolen animals, have appeared before the Commission as witnesses against Glaevecke, so that with all the overwhelming testimony before them, the Commission feels confident to express an opinion as to his character. Glaevecke owns a horse pen on the Texas shore of the river, which used to bear the name of Santa Rita, but is now called Linero. On one side of this enclosure was the ford known as Tia Morales. Here the thieves in the employ of Glaevecke congregate, and to this pen, or enclosure, are the animals stolen in Mexico carried; driven for the most part across the ford Tia Morales. The evidence of title witnesses on this point is corroborated by documentary testimony. This ford was the object of the most active vigilance on the part of the authorities, and the extracts from the documents in Matamoros show that seizure was here often made of thieves and stolen animals, and that various enactments of law were made to guard the ford of Tia Morales.

Since 1848 to the present, for the space of twenty-five years, there has existed in Texas the trade in goods stolen in Mexico, without the attempt at interference on the part of the authorities to punish the offenders of law in this illicit traffic. During this same period the collection of droves of animals at certain periods of each year along the whole American line has been permitted, with the knowledge that these animals were stolen from Mexican territory. Finally, there had been tolerated the public organization of bands of robbers, who under the patronage of influential persons have gone to Mexico to steal for the benefit of their patrons.

We quote the following extracts from a correspondence dated at Rome, Star County, and published in a Texan newspaper:

> "In Guerrero, Mexico . . . I was informed by the city authorities that there was an organized band of robbers, whose constant occupation was to steal horses in Mexico and carry them to Texas, where they in return stole horses and cattle to bring back to Mexico. The three principal leaders are, Atilano Alvarado, Procopio Gutierrez, and Landin, the former being the foreman of Captain R. King, on whose rancho he has lived for a number of years, and is well known to the stock-raisers of that section of the country; our informer

says also, I am sure they have many accomplices and co-operators on the ranches of Texas on this side of the river and all along the coast. Procopio Gutierrez resides a part of the time in Texas, on San Bartolo rancho, Zapote county, with his adoptive father.

I crossed afterwards to the American side and investigated the matter in the most secret manner possible, and found all these things to be perfectly correct.

I asked several persons of the city whether they were doing anything to put a stop to the robbery. What can we do? they replied. Our sheriff lives on a ranch twenty-two miles from here: and has not come within the county.

For several months, and even he himself has aided in transporting the stolen animals through his rancho over into Mexico on the 10th or 12th of November. No one knows or can swear with any certainty that said cattle had been stolen, but it is presumed that the whole or a part of them were stolen, as the drivers kept away from the collector of customs and from the inspector of hides and cattle; and when an authority of the county connives in the robbery, instead of preventing it, there is nothing to be done against such powerful bands of robbers."—*Daily Ranchero*, Brownsville, January 12th, 1873, p. 84

The residents of Texas have complained constantly that the Mexican authorities have not taken all the necessary precautions to prevent the stealing of cattle on our borders; that the State of Texas has, to the contrary, done all in its power by way of keeping the laws. Now an investigation has become indispensable in order to ascertain what has occurred on both frontiers. . . .

The question relative to Texas presents four aspects—her legislation, her public administration, her police, and her administration of justice.

The Texas legislation is imperfect. It contains no efficacious, energetic means to prevent the robberies which take place in the branding pens, and which contribute to maintain a state of perfect disorder, in the prolongation of which the proprietors who give themselves up to these depredations are interested. To commit these depredations they require accomplices—men destitute of conscience, who rob for others without any other consideration than the pay which they receive; and it is certain that these men, accustomed not to respect property, rob on their own account whenever it is possible.

One of the proprietors who has distinguished himself most in these depredations is Ricardo King, owner of the estate Santa Gertrudis, county of Nueces. He has had as chief, Tomas Vasquez, accomplice in robberies of Mexican horses, and in the robberies of cattle committed in Texas, and Fernando Lopez, accomplice in the last. He has kept in his rancho this Atilano Alvarado, who is thought to be chief of a party of robbers stationed in Guerrero. They appear also in the dispatches drawn up before the Commission, the dates of which are not very accurate with regard to the robberies in which the individuals have participated who have been in his service. Ricardo King had a large band who ran constantly in all directions of the country marking calves, though they did not belong to him. It is impossible to admit that the people forming that party possessed any sentiments of morality. The laws of Texas offer no energetic remedies for this evil, and are insufficient.

His revolt was brought about by the following circumstances. He saw the sheriff at Brownsville dragging a Mexican along by the collar; [Juan] Cortina remonstrated with him; the sheriff made use of insulting language in his reply; Cortina then shot at and wounded him, and carried off the prisoner. This occurred on the 13th of July, 1859. On the 28th of September of the same year, he again appeared at Brownsville with some fifty men, and took possession of the town. Several of those who, it was alleged, had been guilty of outrage toward the "Texan Mexicans," were killed, and all the prisoners who joined him were released. At the request of various persons he left the city and retired to his ranch; he was disposed to lay down his arms and leave Texas; several parties saw him for this purpose, and he agreed to it, requiring only from four to six days to transfer to the Mexican side some cattle which some of his companions had, and divide his people into small parties of three or four each, to avoid their being pursued by the Mexican authorities at the time of their crossing the river. He did so, but shortly after he was told that one of his followers bad been hung at Brownsville, upon which he went into Texas and began gathering people together, giving his movement a more definite character.

It is worthy of notice that when the revolt assumed this aspect it was highly popular among the "Texan Mexicans," that is, among all the Mexican population which had settled in Texas before or after the Treaty of Guadaloupe [sic]. The fact that Cortina was joined by a large number of these, some of whom were land owners, can be attributed to no other reason. . . .

Richard King has in his service a large band; he makes use of it for depredating upon other people's cattle, by seizing all of the unbranded calves, which are then branded with King's brand, notwithstanding the ownership of the calves is shown by their following cows bearing other people's brands. These depredations are continuous, because King's band is almost always uninterruptedly in movement. He thus develops and maintains demoralization among a great number of people, because only men without principle could accept the position of instrument for the commission of such crimes. He has had among his herders the accomplices in robberies committed in Texas or Mexico, as, for example, Fernando Lopez and Tomas Vazquez: nevertheless, he states that his injuries amount to millions.

MONTEREY, May 15th, 1873

Source: Report of the Mexican Commission on the Northern Frontier Question: Investigating Commission of the Northern Frontier. New York, Baker & Goodwin Printer, 1875, 3, 13, 28, 39, 83–84, 105–106, 126–129, 176.

Horace Bell, *Reminiscences of a Ranger; or, Early Times in Southern California* (1881)

Horace Bell (1830–1918), an attorney, wrote his autobiography in a gossip-like fashion in which he described the lawless days of Los Angeles in the 1850s. Although he chased the "Mexican" bandit Joaquín Murrieta and contemporary gangs of Mexican bandits, he was, in the following excerpt, very critical of fellow European Americans in California, conceding that Murrieta and other Mexican rebels were justified in rebelling against white American racism and mistreatment.

On the morning following my arrival in the city of the Angels I walked around to take notes in my mind as to matters of general interest. First I went immediately across the street to a very small adobe house with two rooms, in which sat in solemn conclave, a sub-committee of the great constituted criminal court of the city. On inquiry I found that the said sub-committee had been in session for about a week, endeavoring to extract confessions from the miserable culprits by a very refined process of questioning and cross-questioning, first by one of the committee, then by another, until the whole committee would exhaust their ingenuity on the victim, when all of their separate results would be solemnly compared, and all of the discrepancies in the prisoner's statements would be brought back to him and he be required to explain and reconcile them to suit the examining committee; and the poor devil, who doubtless was frightened so badly that he would hardly know one moment what he had said the moment previous, was held strictly accountable for any and all contradictions, and if not satisfactorily explained, was invariably taken by the wise heads of the said committee to be conclusive evidence of guilt. Six men were being tried, all Sonoranians, except one, Felipe Read, a half-breed Indian, whose father was a Scotchman; all claimed, of course, to be innocent; finally one Reyes Feliz made a confession, probably under the hypothesis that hanging would be preferable to such inquisitorial torture as was being practiced on him by the seven wise men of the Angels. Reyes said in his confession that he and his brother-in-law, Joaquín Murietta, with a few followers, had, about a year previous, ran off the horses of Jim Thompson from the Brea ranch, and succeeded in getting them as far as the Tejon, then exclusively inhabited by Indians; that old Zapatero, the Tejon chief, on recognizing Jim Thompson's brand, arrested the whole party, some dozen in all, men and women, and stripped them all stark naked, tied them up, and had them whipped half to death, and turned loose to shift for themselves in the best way they could. Fortunately for the poor outcasts, they fell in with an American of kindred sympathies, who did what he could to relieve the distress of the forlorn thieves, who continued their way—as best they could toward the "Southern Mines" on the Stanislaus and Tuolumne, no mining being done south of those points at that time. In the meantime, brave old Zapatero, who was every inch a chief, sent Thompson's herd back to him—an act for which I hope Jim is to this day duly grateful.

At the time this confession was made, Joaquín was walking around, as unconcerned as any other gentleman; but when the minions of the mob went to lay heavy hand upon him he was gone, and from that day until the day of his death, Joaquín Murietta was an outlaw and the terror of the southern counties. Until that confession he stood in this community with as good a character as any other Mexican of his class.

Reyes Feliz denied all knowledge of the murder of General Bean. One of the prisoners, Cipriano Sandoval, the village cobbler of San Gabriel, also, after having for several days maintained his innocence, and denied any and all knowledge of the murder, came out and made a full confession. He said he was on his way home from the maromas (rope-dancers) at about 11 o'clock one night, it being quite dark. He heard a shot, and then the footsteps of a man running toward him; that a moment after he came in violent contact with a man whom he at once recognized as Felipe Read. They mutually recognized each other, when Felipe said: "Cipriano, I have just shot Bean. Here is five dollars; take it, say nothing about it, and when you want money come to me and get it." That was the sum total of his confession. All the others remained obdurate, and what I have related was the sum of the information elicited by the seven days [of] inquisition. The committee had certainly found the murderer of General Bean.

The fact was, I believe, that Bean, who kept a bar at the Mission, had seduced Felipe's mistress, an Indian woman, away from him, and hence the assassination. Three days after my arrival the "inquisitors" announced themselves as ready to report. In the meantime I went around taking notes in my mind. Los Angeles, at the time of my arrival, was certainly a nice looking place—the houses generally looked neat and clean, and were well whitewashed. There were three two-story adobe houses in the city, the most important of which is the present residence of Mrs. Bell, widow of the late Capt. Alex. Bell; then the Temple building, a substantial two-story, at the junction of Main and Spring Streets; and the old Casa Sanchez, on what is now Sanchez Street. The lower walls of the latter are still there, the house having been razed. The business of the place was very considerable; the most of the merchants were Jews, and all seemed to be doing a paying business. The fact was, they were all getting rich. The streets were thronged throughout the entire day with splendidly mounted and richly dressed caballeros, most of whom wore suits of clothes that cost all the way from $500 to $1,000, with saddle and horse trappings that cost even more than the above named sums. Of one of the Lugos, I remember, it was said his horse equipments cost over $2,000. Everybody in Los Angeles seemed rich, everybody was rich, and money was more plentiful, at that time, than in any other place of like size, I venture to say, in the world.

The question will at once suggest itself to the reader: Why was it that money was so plentiful in Los Angeles at the time referred to? I will inform him. The great rush to the gold mines had created a demand for beef cattle, and the years '48, '49, and '50 had exhausted the supply in the counties north of San Luis Obispo, and purchasers came to Los Angeles, then the greatest cow county of the State. The southern counties had enjoyed a succession of good seasons of rain and bountiful supply of grass. The cattle and horses had increased to an unprecedented number, and the prices ranged from $20 to $35 per head, and a man was poor indeed who could not sell at the time one or two hundred head of cattle, and many of our first class rancheros, for instance the Sepulvedas, Abilas, Lugos, Yorbas, Picos, Stearns, Rowlands, and Williams, could sell a thousand head of cattle at any time and put the money in their pockets as small change, and as such they spent it.

On the second evening after my arrival, in company with a gentleman, now of high standing in California, I went around to see the sights. We first went to the "El Dorado" and smiled at the bar. The "El Dorado" was a small frame building, a duplicate of the "Imprenta," wherein the *Star* was published; the room below being used as a bar and billiard room, while the upper room was used as a dormitory. The place was kept by an elegant Irishman, John H. Hughes, said to have been a near Kinsman of the late great church dignitary, Archbishop Hughes. John was a scholar, and without doubt, so far as manners and accomplishments went, was a splendid gentleman, and the whole community accorded to him the honor of being a good judge of whisky. The "El Dorado" was situated at about the southeast corner of the Merced theater.

Along toward the spring of 1853, the Rev. Adam Bland, without the fear of the virtuous community before his eyes, purchased the "El Dorado," pulled down its sacred sign, and profanely converted it into a Methodist church! Alas, poor Hughes! I believe it broke his heart. He never recovered from the blow. It broke his noble spirit, and a few years later, when a fair Señorita withheld her smiles from the brilliant Hughes, it was the feather that broke the camel's back, and the disconsolate Hughes joined the Crabbe filibustering expedition to Sonora and was killed.

From the "El Dorado" we betook ourselves to Aleck Gibson's gambling house on the plaza, where a well kept bar was in full blast, and some half dozen "monte banks" in successful operation, each table with its green baize cover, being literally heaped with piles of $50 ingots, commonly called "slugs." Betting was high. You would frequently see a ranchero with an immense pile of gold in front of him, quietly and unconcernedly smoking his cigarrito and betting twenty slugs on the turn, the losing of which produced no perceptible discomposure of his grave countenance. For grave self-possession under difficult and trying circumstances, the Spaniard is in advance of all nationalities that I know of.

From the great gambling house on the plaza we hied us to the classic precincts of the "Calle de los Negros," which was the most perfect and full grown pandemonium that this writer, who had seen the "elephant" before, and has been more than familiar with him under many phases since, has ever beheld. There were four or five gambling places, and the crowd from the old Coronel building on the Los Angeles street corner to the plaza was so dense that we could scarcely squeeze through. Americans, Spaniards, Indians, and foreigners, rushing and crowding along from one gambling house to another, from table to table, all chinking the everlasting eight square $50 pieces up and down in their palms. There were several bands of music of the primitive Mexican-Indian kind, that sent forth most discordant sound, by no means in harmony with the eternal jingle of gold—while at the upper end of the street, in the rear of one of the gambling houses was a Mexican "Maroma" in uproarious confusion. They positively made night hideous with their howlings.

Every few minutes a rush would be made, and may be a pistol shot would be heard, and when the confusion incident to the rush would have somewhat subsided, and inquiry made, you would learn that it was only a knife fight between two Mexicans, or a gambler had caught somebody cheating and had perforated him with a bullet. Such things were a matter of course, and no complaint or arrests were ever made. An officer would not have had the temerity to attempt an arrest in "Negro Alley," at that time.

I have no hesitation in saying that in the years of 1851, '52, and '53, there were more desperadoes in Los Angeles than in any place on the Pacific Coast, San Francisco with its great population not excepted. It was a fact, that all of the bad characters who had been driven from the mines had taken refuge in Los Angeles, for the reason that if forced to move further on, it was only a short ride to Mexican soil, while on the other hand all of the outlaws of the Mexican frontier made for the California gold mines, and the cut-throats of California and Mexico naturally met at Los Angeles, and at Los Angeles they fought. Knives and revolvers settled all differences, either real or imaginary. The slightest misunderstandings were settled on the spot with knife or bullet, the Mexican preferring the former at close quarters and the American the latter. . . .

As stated in the beginning of this history, on the arrest and confession of Reyes Feliz, Joaquín Murietta [another spelling], his brother-in-law, who had for one or two years been domiciled among the angels, decamped, and was not heard of until the spring of 1853, when he commenced a succession of bold and successful operations in the southern mines, beginning at San Andres, in Calaveras County. His acts were so bold and daring, and attended with such remarkable success, that he drew to him all the Mexican outlaws, cut-throats and thieves that infested the country extending from San Diego to Stockton. No one will deny the assertion that Joaquín in his organizations, and the successful ramifications of his various bands, his eluding capture, the secret intelligence conveyed from points remote from each other, manifested a degree of executive ability and genius that well fitted him for a more honorable position than that of chief of a band of robbers. In any country in America except the United States, the bold defiance of the power of the government, a half year's successful resistance, a continuous conflict with the military and civil authorities and the armed populace—the writer repeats that in any other country in America other than the United States—the operations of Joaquín Murietta would have been dignified by the title. . . .

There is little doubt in the writer's mind that Joaquin's aims were higher than that of mere revenge and pillage. Educated in the school of revolution in his own country, where the line of demarcation between rebel and robber, pillager and patriot, was dimly defined, it is easy to perceive that Joaquín felt himself to be more the champion of his countrymen than an outlaw and an enemy to the human race. . . .

Source: Bell, Major Horace. *Reminiscences of a Ranger; or, Early Times in Southern California.* Los Angeles: Yarnell, Caystile & Mathes, Printers, 1881, 23–29, 72, 108.

Manuel Retes, "Emigration to Sonora" (1858)

Francisco Ramírez, publisher of El Clamor Público, *at first advocated living under the American flag. He believed the U.S. Constitution would protect the rights of Mexicans in the United States. However, he was soon disillusioned by racism and the lynching of Mexicans, and he advocated the return to Mexico as the only means of achieving justice. Manuel Retes was an agent for the return-to-Mexico movement and regularly advertised in* El Clamor *with the support of Ramírez. This circular advertises a meeting at the home of the last Mexican governor, Pio Pico (1801–1894).*

EMIGRATION FOR SONORA

(Circular)

The Board responsible for promoting emigration to Sonora, informs its countrymen that registration in this county has started and so far has, amounts five hundred fifty to date. In view of the support for this movement . . . that has barely begun . . . the organizing board still has had no time to start in other counties; and considering that the number of those wishing to emigrate continue multiply, the Board Representative believes that it is now time this venture should be put under the protection and consideration of the Government of Sonora, and the Supreme Court of Mexico. . . . Accordingly, it is agreed as of 16 October a commissioner will be appointed on 1st of next January . . . all Hispanic American residents currently in this county are invited to a General Board meeting, with this end in mind, in this city, to be held at twelve noon, in the house of tiles of D. Pio Pico, located in the plaza. At this time, a discussion will be submitted to the General Board according to the terms proposed, the commissioner, to the [Sonoran] government, to be considered and discussed, and approved by all emigrants.

Chamber of Sessions, Los Angeles, December 16 of 1858.

Source: El Clamor Publico, Los Angeles, December 18, 1858; translated by Guadalupe Compean.

Miguel Antonio Otero II, *My Life on the Frontier* (1864–1882)

Miguel Antonio Otero II (1859–1944) was from a prominent New Mexico family. Like the elites of other territories and states taken from Mexico, he intermarried and had business dealings with prominent European Americans immigrating to the territory. Otero became governor of New Mexico Territory from 1897 to 1906. He was the son of Miguel Antonio Otero, a prominent businessman and New Mexico politician. The following passages are from his autobiography, a trilogy, which tells of life in New Mexico, largely from the viewpoint of an elite "New Mexican."

My father, Don Miguel Antonio Otero I, had declined a renomination as New Mexico delegate to the United States Congress because of a determination to retire from politics. He had also refused the appointment as Minister to Spain which President Lincoln . . .

It was my father's strong conviction that he devote his time and energies entirely to the business he had previously formed with David Whiting. Whiting & Otero was engaged in the multiform profitable activities of banking, outfitting, wholesaling. . . .

During our stay at Don Juan's home [upon returning to New Mexico,] we saw some of the lawlessness that prevailed in that part of the Territory. A band of Texa[n]s had debouched into northern New Mexico . . . and were rustling all the cattle and horses in the country. In their raids they had killed several herders who had opposed them. I saw the large herd of cattle these Texans had stolen near Las Vegas. The rustlers all wore chaps and were armed to the teeth with rifles and pistols.

The presence of this outfit was naturally a great source of excitement to Las Vegas people, and, as my father had arrived the day before, a delegation of the most prominent citizens of northern New Mexico appealed to him to do something to relieve the section from this scourge, their notion being that a man of my father's prominence might have some influence with the rustlers. My father undertook the mission, without much hope of success, and to our great delight he allowed my brother and me to accompany him.

We all rode out to their camp, located where East Las Vegas now stands. When my father asked for the leader of the band, a large, red-headed man with chin whiskers, weighing fully two hundred and twenty-five pounds, presented himself. My father urged him to have greater regard for the property of the citizens of New Mexico. When my father had finished, the leader of the Texans answered thus:

"These God damn greasers have been stealing our horses and cattle for the past fifty years, and we got together and thought we would come up this way and have a grand roundup, and that is why we are here. What is more, we intend to take all the horses and cattle we come across and drive them back to their old ranges in Texas, where they belong. My advice to you fellows is: Don't attempt to interfere with what we are doing unless you are looking for trouble."

My father did not attempt to argue the matter further, knowing that it was useless. I have never forgotten the episode, for it revealed that hostile and vengeful feeling displayed by the Texans which produced acts of lawlessness calculated to make the name "Tejano" a hated word among the New Mexicans. It is said that mothers were in the habit of censuring their children with the dire threat: "If you are not good, I'll give you to the Tejanos, who are coming back."

In this instance, as in many others, the New Mexicans were long suffering. The people of the northern part of the Territory had suffered heavily from these pillagers and reasoned that it would cost them their lives to interfere in any way with the northern ruffians. So they stood the losses and allowed the Texans to proceed on their way. Two days after my father made his plea, the whole herd and the Tejanos had disappeared in a southeasterly direction. It was afterwards learned that the leader of this band of marauders took the proceeds of the raid and invested it in Denver, erecting one of that city's largest office buildings.

After a pleasant renewal of friendship with their many acquaintances in Las Vegas, my parents started for Santa Fe on the Barlow & Sanderson Stage, taking all of us children with them. On our arrival, we took rooms in a building which stood just across the street from the old Exchange Hotel, called the "La Fonda," celebrated as being the end of the Santa Fe Trail (on the site where H. H. Dorman now has his real estate office), and here we remained until conveyances arrived to take us to my uncle's home at La Constancia.

My uncle's home was a typical hacienda, or country estate, located in the richest and most desirable part of the Territory—the valley of the Rio Grande, extending from Penña Blanca to El Paso, Texas. At such haciendas, the life was lavish and luxurious to a degree hard to imagine nowadays; in many respects it resembled the principality of some foreign prince. The owners of these haciendas were fittingly called "Don" and "Dona," titles of respect and honor.

Uncle Manuel and Aunt Doloritas were very fond of entertaining, and while we were there, they gave several dances. The dances usually lasted until sunrise, refreshments and wines being served from midnight on. A good hot breakfast was furnished [to] all the guests before they started for their homes.

Source: Otero, Miguel. *My Life on the Frontier 1864–1882.* New York: Arno Press, 1974, 1, 61–63.

María Amparo Ruiz de Burton, *Who Would Have Thought It?* (1872)

María Amparo Ruiz de Burton (ca. 1832–1895), one of California's first female novelists, wrote from the perspective of the Mexican elite of her time. Born in Baja, California, she moved to U.S. soil after marrying a European American captain. The following are excerpts from her first novel about a young Mexican girl as she is delivered from Indian captivity in the Southwest and comes to live in the household of a New England family. The author gives her insight into culture and perspectives on national history and identity clash. The passages criticize the dominant society's opportunism and hypocrisy and showcase northern racism. The novel is set in Massachusetts and New England. The main character is Dr. James Norval, a geologist, who returns home with dark-skinned María Dolores Medina, aka Lola. Norval had been captured by Indians along the Colorado River and encountered Lola and her mother, who were also captives. Lola's mother dies and Norval escapes with Lola, returning home. Lola's presence causes friction with Norval's racist wife, Jeminia. Through the tension, Ruiz de Burton critiques the hypocrisy of New England's Puritan society and northern righteousness. The first passage contrasts Norval's humanity with his wife's snobbery. The last passage discusses the French occupation of Mexico during this same period of the 1860s.

"What would the good and proper people of this world do if there were no rogues in it—no social delinquents? The good and proper, I fear, would perish of sheer inanity—of hypochondriac lassitude—or, to say the least, would grow very dull for want of convenient whetstones to sharpen their wits. Rogues are useful."

So saying, the Rev. Mr. [John] Hackwell scrambled up the steep side of a crazy buggy, which was tilting ominously under the pressure of the Rev. Mr. Hammerhard's weight, and sat by him. Then the Rev. Hackwell spread over the long legs of his friend Hammerhard a well-worn buffalo-robe, and tucked the other end carefully under his own graceful limbs, as if his wise aphorism upon rogues had suggested to him the great necessity of taking good care of himself and friend, all for the sake of the good and dull of this world. . . .

But Mrs. [Jeminia] Norval was so shocked at this that the doctor, tired as he was in body by his journey, and in mind by all the harassing little incidents and disputes which had occurred since his arrival, left the matter for that night to his wife's discretion. The child, then, was sent with Hannah to share her room for the night.

The doctor kissed Lola several times and embraced her to bid her good night, and she, sobbing as if her heart would break, and looking back several times as she left the room, went away to sleep the sleep of the orphan under that inhospitable roof. . . .

"Don't you know, doctor, that you kissed that Indian child more affectionately than you kissed your own daughters?" Mrs. Norval said fiercely to her husband when they had closed their bedroom door to the outer world.

"Maybe I did, for I pity the poor orphan. My daughters, thank God, have yet their parents to take care of them, but this poor little waif has no one in the world, perhaps, to protect her and care for her but myself."

"As for that, she'll get along well enough. She is not so timid as to need anybody's particular protection. Her eyes are bold enough. She will learn to work—I'll see to that—and a good worker is sure of a home in New England. Mrs. Hammerhard will want just such a girl as this, I hope, to mind the baby, and she will give her some of her castoff clothes and her victuals."

"Cast-off clothes and victuals!" the doctor repeated, as if he could not believe that his ears had heard rightly.

"Why, yes. We certainly couldn't expect Mrs. Hammerhard would give more to a girl ten years old to mind a little baby in the cradle."

"And how is she to go to school, if she is to mind Mrs. Hammerhard's baby for old clothes and cold victuals?" . . .

[Isaac in the land of the Aztecs] Don Felipe and Don Luis, therefore, had been among the firm and most prompt supporters of the republican government up to winter of 1863. In December of this year, however, and just about time of Isaac's arrival in Mexico, these letters which the two gentlemen perused so eagerly as Isaac was riding towards them had come. These letters said that there was a very strong probability—almost a certainty—that the Archduke Maximilian would accept the proposed throne of Mexico; that he still hesitated, but that, as a great field for a noble and lofty ambition was thus opened to him, and he was known to be of generous impulses, the friends of monarchism anticipated [he] would accept in the hope of effecting a great good by giving the Mexican people a stable government, which would bring to them peace and prosperity and raise them to a high rank among the civilized nations of the world.

Source: Ruiz de Burton, María Amparo. *Who Would Have Thought It?* Edited and introduced by Rosaura Sanchez and Beatrice Pita. Houston: Arte Publico Press, 9, 21–22, 196.

Statement by Tiburcio Vásquez (1874)

Tiburcio Vásquez (1835–1875), from the San Jose, California, area, was perhaps the best-known Mexican bandit of his time after Joaquín Murrieta (1829–ca. 1853), exemplifying what British historian E. J. Hobsbawm called a "primitive rebel" or "social bandit." He was not a revolutionary because his intent was not independence but instead a revolt against injustice. In his case, injustice was fueled by the racism of the times. His career spanned 15 years and, like Jesse James and even Bonnie and Clyde, he was supported by his people. In the following excerpt, he talks about his early life and why he became an outlaw.

I was born in Monterey County, California, at the town of Monterey, August 11, 1835. . . . I can read and write, having attended school in Monterey. My parents were people in ordinarily good circumstances; owned a small tract of land and always had enough for their wants.

My career grew out of the circumstances by which I was surrounded as I grew to manhood. I was in the habit of attending balls and parties given by the native Californians, into which the Americans, then beginning to become numerous, would force themselves and shove the native-born men aside, monopolizing the dances and the women. This was about 1852.

A spirit of hatred and revenge took possession of me. I had numerous fights in defense of what I believed to be my rights and those of my countrymen. The officers were continually in pursuit of me. I believed that we were unjustly and wrongfully deprived of the social rights which belonged to us. So perpetually was I involved in these difficulties that I at length determined to leave the thickly settled portion of the country, and did so.

I gathered together a small band of cattle and went into Mendocino County, back of Ukiah and beyond Fallis Valley. Even here I was not permitted to remain in peace. The officers of the law sought me out in that remote region, and strove to drag me before the courts. I always resisted arrest.

I went to my mother and told her I intended to commence a different life. I asked for and obtained her blessing, and at once commenced the career of a robber. My first exploit consisted in robbing some peddlers of money and clothes in Monterey County. My next was the capture and robbery of a stagecoach in the same county. I had confederates with me from the first, and was always recognized as leader. Robbery after robbery followed each other as rapidly as circumstances allowed, until in 1857 or '58 I was arrested in Los Angeles for horse-stealing, convicted of grand larceny, sent to the penitentiary and was taken to San Quentin and remained there until my term of imprisonment expired in 1863.

Up to the time of my conviction and imprisonment, I had robbed stagecoaches, houses, wagons, etc., indiscriminately, carrying on my operations for the most part in daylight, sometimes, however, visiting houses after dark.

After my discharge from San Quentin I returned to the house of my parents and endeavored to lead a peaceful and honest life. I was, however, soon accused of being a confederate of Procopio and one Sato, both noted bandits, the latter of whom was afterward killed by Sheriff Harry Morse of Alameda County. I was again forced to become a fugitive from the law-officers, and, driven to desperation, I left home and family and commenced robbing whenever opportunity offered. I made but little money by my exploits, I always managed to avoid arrest. I believe I owe my frequent escapes solely to my courage. I was always ready to fight whenever opportunity offered, but always tried to avoid bloodshed.

Source: Los Angeles Star, May 16, 1874.

Eulalia Pérez, Testimony Regarding Her Life in Mexican California (1877)

Eulalia Pérez (1766–1878) was the "keeper of the keys" at Mission San Gabriel Arcángel and the owner of Rancho del Rincón de San Pascual in Alta, California. She was born in Baja, California. Court records show that she lived to be 140, but her descendants agree that she was only 110 years old when she died. In the following passage, she described her duties as a housekeeper in a California mission in 1823. The testimony was taken by Hubert Howe Bancroft, who conducted some 100 interviews with descendants of the original Californios (Californians of Mexican extraction) to preserve the early history of the state. Of these 100 testimonies, 12 were from women.

I, Eulalia Pérez, was born in the Presidio of Loreto in Baja California.

My father's name was Diego Pérez, and he was employed in the Navy Department of said presidio; my mother's name was Antonia Rosalia Cota. Both were pure white.

I do not remember the date of my birth, but I do know that I was fifteen years old when I married Miguel Antonio Guillen, a soldier of the garrison at Loreto Presidio. During the time of my stay at Loreto I had three children—two boys, who died there in infancy, one girl, Petra, who was eleven years old when we moved to San Diego, and another boy, Isidoro, who came with us to this [Alta] California.

I lived eight years in San Diego with my husband, who continued his service in the garrison of the presidio, and I attended women in childbirth.

I had relatives in the vicinity of Los Angeles, and even farther north, and asked my husband repeatedly to take me to see them. My husband did not want to come along, and the commandant of the presidio did not allow me to go either, because there was no other woman who knew midwifery.

In San Diego everyone seemed to like me very much, and in the most important homes they treated me affectionately. Although I had my own house, they arranged for me to be with those families almost all the time, even including my children.

In 1812, I was in San Juan Capistrano attending Mass in church when a big earthquake occurred, and the tower fell down. I dashed through the sacristy, and in the doorway the people knocked me down and stepped over me. I was pregnant and could not move. Soon afterwards I returned to San Diego and almost immediately gave birth to my daughter Maria Antonia, who still lives here in San Gabriel.

After being in San Diego eight years, we came to the Mission of San Gabriel, where my husband had been serving in the guard. In 1814, on the first of October, my daughter Maria del Rosario was born, the one who is the wife of Michael White and in whose home I am now living. . . .

When I first came to San Diego the only house in the presidio was that of the commandant and the barracks where the soldiers lived.

There was no church, and Mass was said in a shelter made out of some old walls covered with branches, by the missionary who came from the Mission of San Diego.

The first sturdy house built in San Diego belonged to a certain Sanchez, the father of Don Vicente Sanchez, alcalde [administrator] of Los Angeles and deputy of the Territorial Council. The house was very small, and everyone went to look at it as though it were a palace. That house was built about a year after I arrived in San Diego.

My last trip to San Diego would have been in the year 1818, when my daughter Maria del Rosario was four years old. I seem to remember that I was there when the revolutionaries came to California. I recall that they put a stranger in irons and that afterwards they took them off.

Some three years later I came back to San Gabriel. The reason for my return was that the missionary at San Gabriel, Father Jose Sanchez, wrote to Father Fernando at San Diego—who was his cousin or uncle—asking him to speak to the commandant of the presidio at San Diego requesting him to give my son Isidoro Guillen a guard to escort me here with all my family. The commandant agreed.

When we arrived here, Father Jose Sanchez lodged me and my family temporarily in a small house until work could be found for me. There I was with my five daughters—my son Isidoro Guillen was taken into service as a soldier in the mission guard.

At that time, Father Sanchez was between sixty and seventy years of age—a white Spaniard, heavy set, of medium stature—a very good, kind, charitable man. He, as well as his companion Father Jose Maria Zalvidea, treated the Indians very well, and the two were much loved by the Spanish-speaking people and by the neophytes and other Indians.

Father Zalvidea was very tall, a little heavy, white; he was a man of advanced age. I heard it said that they summoned Zalvidea to San Juan Capistrano because there was no missionary priest there. Many years later, when Father Antonio Peyri fled from San Luis Obispo—it was rumored that they were going to kill the priests—I learned that Zalvidea was very sick, and that actually he had been out of his mind ever since they took him away from San Gabriel, for he did not want to abandon the mission. I repeat that the father was afraid, and two Indians came from San Luis Rey to San Juan Capistrano; in a rawhide cart, making him as comfortable as they could, they took him to San Luis, where he died soon after from the grueling hardships he had suffered on the way.

Father Zalvidea was very much attached to his children at the mission, as he called the Indians that he himself had converted to Christianity. He traveled personally, sometimes on horseback and at other times on foot, and crossed mountains until he came to remote Indian settlements, in order to bring them to our religion.

Father Zalvidea introduced many improvements in the Mission of San Gabriel and made it progress a very great deal in every way. Not content with providing abundantly for the neophytes, he planted [fruit] trees in the mountains, far away from the mission, in order that the untamed Indians might have food when they passed by those spots.

When I came to San Gabriel the last time, there were only two women in this part of California who knew how to cook [well]. One was Maria Luisa Cota, wife of Claudio Lopez, superintendent of the mission; the other was Maria Ignacia Amador, wife of Francisco Javier Alvarado. She knew how to cook, sew, read, and write and take care of the sick. She was a good healer. She did needlework and took care of the church vestments. She taught a few children to read and write in her home, but did not conduct a formal school.

On special holidays, such as the day of our patron saint, Easter, etc., the two women were called upon to prepare the feast and to make the meat dishes, sweets, etc.

The priests wanted to help me out because I was a widow burdened with a family. They looked for some way to give me work without offending the other women. Frs. Sanchez and Zalvidea conferred and decided that they would have first one woman, then the other and finally me, do the cooking, in order to determine who did it best, with the aim of putting the one who surpassed the others in charge of the Indian cooks so as to teach them how to cook. With that idea in mind, the gentlemen who were to decide on the merits of the three dinners were warned ahead of time.

One of these gentlemen was Don Ignacio Tenorio, whom they called the Royal Judge, and who came to live and die in the company of Father Sanchez. He was a very old man, and when he went out, wrapped up in a muffler, he walked very slowly with the aid of a cane. His walk consisted only of going from the missionary's house to the church.

The other judges who also were to give their opinions were Don Ignacio Mancisidor, merchant; Don Pedro Narvaez, naval official; Sgt. Jose

Antonio Pico—who later became lieutenant, brother of Gov. Pio Pico; Don Domingo Romero, who was my assistant when I was housekeeper at the mission; Claudio Lopez, superintendent at the mission; besides the missionaries. These gentlemen, whenever they were at the mission, were accustomed to eat with the missionaries.

On the days agreed upon for the three dinners, they attended. No one told me anything regarding what it was all about, until one day Father Sanchez called me and said, "Look, Eulalia, tomorrow it is your turn to prepare dinner—because Maria Ignacia and Luisa have already done so. We shall see what kind of a dinner you will give us tomorrow."

The next day I went to prepare the food. I made several kinds of soup, a variety of meat dishes and whatever else happened to pop into my head that I knew how to prepare: The Indian cook, named Tomas, watched me attentively, as the missionary had told him to do.

At dinner time those mentioned came. When the meal was concluded, Father Sanchez asked for their opinions about it, beginning with the eldest, Don Ignacio Tenorio. This gentleman pondered awhile, saying that for many years he had not eaten the way he had eaten that day—that he doubted that they ate any better at the King's table. The others also praised the dinner highly.

Then the missionary called Tomas and asked him which of the three women he liked best—which one of them knew the most about cooking. He answered that I did.

Because of all this, employment was provided for me at the mission. At first they assigned me two Indians so that I could show them how to cook, the one named Tomas and the other called "The Gentile." I taught them so well that I had the satisfaction of seeing them turn out to be very good cooks, perhaps the best in all this part of the country.

The missionaries were very satisfied; this made them think more highly of me. I spent about a year teaching those two Indians. I did not have to do the work, only direct them, because they already had learned a few of the fundamentals.

After this, the missionaries conferred among themselves and agreed to hand over the mission keys to me. This was in 1821, if I remember correctly. I recall that my daughter Maria del Rosario was seven years old when she became seriously ill and was attended by Father Jose Sanchez, who took such excellent care of her that finally we could rejoice at not having lost her. At that time I was already the housekeeper.

The duties of the housekeeper were many. In the first place, every day she handed out the rations for the mess hut. To do this, she had to count the unmarried women, bachelors, day-laborers, vaqueros—both those with saddles and those who rode bareback. Besides that, she had to hand out daily rations to the heads of households. In short, she was responsible for the distribution of supplies to the Indian population and to the missionaries' kitchen. She was in charge of the key to the clothing storehouse where materials were given out for dresses for the unmarried and married women and children. Then she also had to take care of cutting and making clothes for the men.

Furthermore, she was in charge of cutting and making the vaqueros' outfits, from head to foot—that is, for the vaqueros who rode in saddles. Those who rode bareback received nothing more than their cotton blanket and loin-cloth, while those who rode in saddles were dressed the same way as the Spanish-speaking inhabitants; that is, they were given shirt, vest, jacket, trousers, hat, cowboy boots, shoes, and spurs; and a saddle, bridle, and lariat for the horse. Besides, each vaquero was given a big silk or cotton handkerchief, and a sash of Chinese silk or Canton crepe, or whatever there happened to be in the storehouse.

They put under my charge everything having to do with clothing. I cut and fitted, and my five daughters sewed up the pieces. When they could not handle everything, the father was told, and then women from the town of Los Angeles were employed, and the father paid them.

Besides this, I had to attend to the soap-house, which was very large, to the wine-presses, and to the olive-crushers that produced oil, which I worked in myself. Under my direction and responsibility, Domingo Romero took care of changing the liquid.

Luis the soap-maker had charge of the soap-house, but I directed everything.

I handled the distribution of leather, calf-skin, chamois, sheepskin, Morocc[an] leather, fine scarlet cloth, nails, thread, silk, etc., everything having to do with the making of saddles, shoes, and what was needed for the belt- and shoe-making shops.

Every week I delivered supplies for the troops and Spanish-speaking servants. These consisted of beans, com, garbanzos, lentils, candles, soap, and lard. To carry out this distribution, they placed at my disposal an Indian servant named Lucio, who was trusted completely by the missionaries.

When it was necessary, some of my daughters did what I could not find the time to do. Generally, the one who was always at my side was my daughter Maria del Rosario.

After all my daughters were married—the last one was Rita, about 1832 or 1833—Father Sanchez undertook to persuade me to marry First Lt. Juan Marine, a Spaniard from Catalonia, a widower with family who had served in the artillery. I did not want to get married, but the father told me that Marine was a very good man—as, in fact, he turned out to be—besides, he had some money, although he never turned his cash-box over to me. I gave in to the father's wishes because I did not have the heart to deny him anything when he had been father and mother to me and to all my family.

I served as housekeeper of the mission for twelve or fourteen years, until about two years after the death of Father Jose Sanchez, which occurred in this same mission.

A short while before Father Sanchez died, he seemed robust and in good health, in spite of his advanced age. When Capt. Barroso came and excited the Indians in all the missions to rebel, telling them that they were no longer neophytes but free men, Indians arrived from San Luis, San Juan, and the rest of the missions. They pushed their way into the college, carrying their arms, because it was raining very hard. Outside the mission, guards and patrols made up of the Indians themselves were stationed. They had been taught to shout "Sentinel on guard!" and "On guard he is!" but they said "Sentinel open! Open he is!"

On seeing the Indians demoralized, Father Sanchez was very upset. He had to go to Los Angeles to say Mass, because he was accustomed to do so every week or fortnight, I do not remember which. He said to me, "Eulalia, I am going now. You know what the situation is; keep your eyes open and take care of what you can. Do not leave here, neither you nor your daughters." (My daughter Maria Antonia's husband, named Leonardo Higuera, was in charge of the Rancho de los Cerritos, which belonged to the mission, and Maria del Rosario's husband, Michael White, was in San Blas.)

The father left for the pueblo, and in front of the guard some Indians surged forward and cut the traces of his coach. He jumped out of the coach, and then the Indians, pushing him rudely, forced him toward his room. He was sad and filled with sorrow because of what the Indians had done and remained in his room for about a week without leaving it. He became ill and never again was his previous self. Blood flowed from his ears, and his head never stopped paining him until he died. He lived perhaps a little more than a month after the affair with the Indians, dying in the month of January, I think it was, of 1833. In that month, there was a great flood. The river rose very high and for more than two weeks no one could get from one side to the other. Among our grandchildren was one that they could not bring to the mission for burial for something like two weeks, because of the flood. The same month—a few days after the father's death—Claudio Lopez, who had been superintendent of the mission for something like thirty years, also died.

In the Mission of San Gabriel there was a large number of neophytes. The married ones lived on their rancherias with their small children. There were two divisions for the unmarried ones: one for the women, called the nunnery, and another for the men. They brought girls from the ages of seven, eight, or nine years to the nunnery, and they were brought up there. They left to get married. They were under the care of a mother in the nunnery, an Indian. During the time I was at the mission, this matron was named Polonia—they called her "Mother Superior." The alcalde was in charge of the unmarried men's division. Every night, both divisions were locked up, the keys were delivered to me, and I handed them over to the missionaries.

A blind Indian named Andresillo stood at the door of the nunnery and called out each girl's name, telling her to come in. If any girl was missing at admission time, they looked for her the following day and brought her to the nunnery. Her mother, if she had one, was brought in and punished for having detained her, and the girl was locked up for having been careless in not coming in punctually.

In the morning the girls were let out. First they went to Father Zalvidea's Mass, for he spoke the Indian language; afterwards they went to the mess hut to have breakfast, which sometimes consisted of corn gruel with chocolate, and on holidays with sweets—and bread. On other days, ordinarily they had boiled barley and beans and meat. After eating breakfast each girl began the task that had been assigned to her beforehand—sometimes it was at the looms, or unloading, or sewing, or whatever there was to be done.

When they worked at unloading, at eleven o'clock they had to come up to one or two of the carts that carried refreshments out to the Indians working in the fields. This refreshment was made of water with vinegar and sugar, or sometimes with lemon and sugar. I was the one who made up that refreshment and sent it out, so the Indians would not get sick. That is what the missionaries ordered.

All work stopped at eleven, and at twelve o'clock the Indians came to the mess hut to eat barley and beans with meat and vegetables. At one o'clock they returned to their work, which ended for the day at sunset. Then all came to the mess hut to eat supper, which consisted of gruel with meat, sometimes just pure gruel. Each Indian carried his own bowl, and the mess attendant filled it up with the allotted portion. . . .

The Indians were taught the various jobs for which they showed an aptitude. Others worked in the fields, or took care of the horses, cattle, etc. Still others were carters, oxherds, etc.

At the mission, coarse cloth, serapes, and blankets were woven, and saddles, bridles, boots, shoes, and similar things were made. There was a soap-house, and a big carpenter shop as well as a small one, where those who were just beginning to learn carpentry worked; when they had mastered enough they were transferred to the big shop.

Wine and oil, bricks, and adobe bricks were also made. Chocolate was manufactured from cocoa, brought in from the outside; and sweets were made. Many of these sweets, made by my own hands, were sent to Spain by Father Sanchez.

There was a teacher in every department, an instructed Indian.

Source: Hijar, Carlos N., Eulalia Pérez, and Agustín Escobar. *Three Memoirs of Mexican California, 1877.* Berkeley: University of California, Bancroft Library, 1988, 73–82.

Petition of Antonio María Pico et al. to the Senate and House of Representatives of the United States

(1859)

After California became part of the United States in 1848, land ownership became the major cause of hostility between the conquered and the conquerors. With the heavy immigration of European Americans, the question of the validity of Mexican land titles was raised. The discovery of gold brought hordes of new settlers who contested Mexican ownership of land. California had been an isolated Spanish colony and then a Mexican province. The governors had liberally handed out land. As in other former Mexican states and territories, the U.S. government, under the pretext of validating titles, encouraged squatters to compete for land titles distributed before 1848. Mexican law provided that any Californian wanting a land grant should apply to the governor. The applicant listed his or her name, age, country, and vocation as well as the quantity and description of the desired land. Surveying was very expensive, so the applicant typically made a hand-drawn map, or diseño, *laying out the boundaries of the grant. The U.S. system evolved at a different time in history and required a more involved process. The American process required that the land be surveyed and plotted on a grid system. In 1851, to clear up the confusion over land ownership in California, Congress established the California Land Commission, which placed the burden of proof of land ownership on the claimant. This was an expensive burden that included appeals of the commission's decisions to the federal courts. Land owners were required to hire attorneys, who often took their land as collateral. Litigation over land grants lasted years. The following is a petition by Antonio María Pico and other Californios to the U.S. Congress presenting their grievances.*

We, the undersigned, residents of the state of California, and some of us citizens of the United States, previously citizens of the Republic of Mexico, respectfully say:

That during the war between the United States and Mexico the officers of the United States, as commandants of the land and sea forces, on several occasions offered and promised in the most solemn manner to the inhabitants of California, protection and security of their persons and their property and the annexation of the said state of California to the American Union, impressing upon them the great advantages to be derived from their being citizens of the United States, as was promised them.

That, in consequence of such promises and representations, very few of the inhabitants of California opposed the invasion; some of them welcomed the invaders with open arms; a great number of them acclaimed the new order with joy, giving a warm reception to their guests, for those inhabitants had maintained very feeble relations with the government of Mexico and had looked with envy upon the development, greatness, prosperity, and glory of the great northern republic, to which they were bound for reasons of commercial and personal interests, and also because its principles of freedom had won their friendliness.

When peace was established between the two nations by the Treaty of Guadalupe Hidalgo, they joined in the general rejoicing with their new American fellow countrymen, even though some—a very few indeed—decided to remain in California as Mexican citizens, in conformity with the literal interpretation of that solemn instrument; they immediately assumed the position of American citizens that was offered them, and since then have conducted themselves with zeal and faithfulness and with no less loyalty than those whose great fortune it was to be born under the flag of the North American republic—believing, thus, that all their rights were insured in the treaty, which declares that their property shall be inviolably protected and insured; seeing the realization of the promises made to them by United States officials; trusting and hoping to participate in the prosperity and happiness of the great nation of which they now had come to be an integral part, and in which, if it was true that they now found the value of their possessions increased, that was also to be considered compensation for their sufferings and privations. . . .

They heard with dismay of the appointment, by Act of Congress, of a Commission with the right to examine all titles and confirm or disapprove them, as their judgment considered equitable. Though this honorable body has doubtless had the best interests of the state at heart, still it has brought about the most disastrous effects upon those who have the honor to subscribe their names to this petition, for, even though all landholders possessing titles under the Spanish or Mexican governments were not forced by the letter of the law to present them before the Commission for confirmation, nevertheless all those titles were at once considered doubtful, their origin questionable, and, as a result, worthless for confirmation by the Commission; all landholders were thus compelled de facto to submit their titles to the Commission for confirmation, under the alternative that, if they were not submitted, the lands would be considered public property.

The undersigned, ignorant then, of the forms and proceedings of an American court of justice, were obliged to engage the services of American lawyers to present their claims, paying them enormous fees. Not having other means with which to meet those expenses but their lands, they were compelled to give up part of their property, in many cases as much as a fourth of it, and in other cases even more.

The discovery of gold attracted an immense number of immigrants to this country, and, when they perceived that the titles of the old inhabitants were considered doubtful and their validity questionable, they spread themselves over the land as though it were public property, taking possession of the improvements made by the inhabitants, many times seizing even their houses (where they had lived for many years with their families), taking and killing the cattle and destroying their crops; so that those who before had owned great numbers of cattle that could have been counted by the thousands, now found themselves without any, and the men who were the owners of many leagues of land now were deprived of the peaceful possession of even one acre.

The expenses of the new state government were great, and the money to pay for these was only to be derived from the tax on property, and there was little property in this new state but the above-mentioned lands. Onerous taxes were levied by new laws, and if these were not paid, the property was put up for sale. Deprived as they were of the use of their lands, from which they had now no lucrative returns, the owners were compelled to mortgage them in order to assume the payment of taxes already due and constantly increasing. With such mortgages upon property greatly depreciated (because of its uncertain status), without crops or rents, the owners of those lands were not able to borrow money except at usurious rates of interest. The usual interest rate at that time was high, but with such securities it was exorbitant; and so they were forced either to sell or lose their lands; in fact, they were forced to borrow money even for the purchase of the bare necessities of life. Hoping that the Land Commission would take quick action in the revision of titles and thus relieve them from the state of penury in which they found themselves, they mortgaged their lands, paying compound interest at the rate of from three to ten percent a month. The long-awaited relief would not arrive; action from the Commission was greatly delayed; and, even after the Commission would pronounce judgment on the titles, it was still necessary to pass through a rigorous ordeal in the District Court; and some cases are, even now, pending before the Supreme Court of the nation. And in spite of the final confirmation, too long a delay was experienced (in many cases it is still being experienced), awaiting the surveys to be made by the United States Surveyor-General. . . . Congress overlooked making the necessary appropriations to that end, and the people were then obliged to face new taxes to pay for the surveys, or else wait even longer while undergoing the continued and exhausting demands of high and usurious taxes. Many persons assumed the payment of the surveyors and this act was cause for objection from Washington, the work of those surveyors rejected, and the patents refused, for the very reason that they themselves had paid for the surveys. More than 800 petitions were presented to the Land Commission, and already 10 years of delays have elapsed and only some 50 patents have been granted.

The petitioners, finding themselves unable to face such payments because of the rates of interest, taxes, and litigation expenses, as well as having to maintain their families, were compelled to sell, little by little, the greater part of their old possessions. Some, who at one time had been the richest landholders, today find themselves without a foot of ground, living as objects of charity—and even in sight of the many leagues of land which, with many a thousand head of cattle, they once had called their own; and those of us who, by means of strict economy and immense sacrifices, have been able to preserve a small portion of our property, have heard to our great dismay that new legal projects are being planned to keep us still longer in suspense, consuming, to the last iota, the property left us by our ancestors. Moreover, we see with deep pain that efforts are being made to induce those honorable bodies to pass laws authorizing bills of review, and other illegal proceedings, with a view to prolonging still further the litigation of our claims.

Source: Manuscript HM 514, Huntington Library, San Marino, California.

Las Gorras Blancas (The White Caps) Manifesto (1890)

Las Gorras Blancas (The White Caps) was a group of New Mexicans, mostly around the Las Vegas, New Mexico, area, who fought to retain community control of the common lands in the 1880s and 1890s. They conducted raids on white farmers who threatened native-owned land near Las Vegas, cut fences, and destroyed property. On August 12, 1890, LeBaron Bradford Prince (1840–1922), governor of the New Mexico territory, begged officials in Washington to send federal troops to patrol the area around Las Vegas. Many of the white ranchers had built fences to separate cattle from flocks of sheep belonging to the native inhabitants. The enclosure movement accelerated after 1870 with the introduction of cheap barbed-wire fencing. The following excerpt summarizes the grievances of the native farmers.

Not wishing to be misunderstood, we hereby make this our declaration.

Our purpose is to protect the rights and interests of the people in general; especially those of the helpless classes.

We want the Las Vegas Grant settled to the benefit of all concerned, and this we hold is the entire community within the grant.

We want no "land grabbers" or obstructionists of any sort to interfere. We will watch them.

We are not down on lawyers as a class, but the usual knavery and unfair treatment of the people must be stopped.

Our judiciary hereafter must understand that we will sustain it only when "Justice" is its watchword.

The practice of "double-dealing" must cease.

There is a wide difference between New Mexico's "law" and "justice." And justice is God's law, and that we must have at all hazards.

We are down on race issues, and will watch race agitators. We are all human brethren, under the same glorious flag.

We favor irrigation enterprises, but will fight any scheme that tends to monopolize the supply of water courses to the detriment of residents living on lands watered by the same streams.

We favor all enterprises, but object to corrupt methods to further the same.

We do not care how much you get so long as you do it fairly and honestly.

The People are suffering from the effects of partisan "bossism" and these bosses had better quietly hold their peace. The people have been persecuted and hacked about in every which way to satisfy their caprice. If they persist in their usual methods, retribution will be their reward.

We are watching "political informers."

We have no grudge against any person in particular, but we are the enemies of bulldozers and tyrants.

We must have a free ballot and a fair count, and the will of the majority shall be respected.

Intimidation and the "indictment" plan have no further fears for us. If the old system should continue, death would be a relief to our sufferings. And for our rights our lives are the least we can pledge.

If the fact that we are law-abiding citizens is questioned, come out to our homes and see the hunger and desolation we are suffering; and "this" is the result of the deceitful and corrupt methods of "bossism."

Be fair and just and we are with you, do otherwise and take the consequences.

The White Caps, 1,500 Strong and Growing Daily

Source: Las Vegas Daily Optic, March 12, 1890.

W. W. Robinson, *The Story of Mission Lands, Ranchos, Squatters, Mining Claims, Railroad Grants, Land Scrip, Homesteads*

(1948)

William Wilcox Robinson (1891–1972) was a prolific writer of pamphlets, articles, and books on the history of Southern California. In The Story of Mission Lands, Ranchos, Squatters, Mining Claims, Railroad Grants, Land Scrip, Homesteads, *Robinson described California's early Spanish land laws and institutions; he then selected San Pascual (Pasadena) as their archetype and narrated California's land history. He wrote about the changes in land institutions and laws that followed the Mexican-American War, profiling San Francisco and Los Angeles. The following passage describes the phenomenon of squatterism in California.*

Every American is a squatter at heart—or so it seems if we think of the tide of adventurous men that began moving west at the close of the Revolutionary War, men impatient of governmental authority and as contemptuous of the rights of Indians as of wild animals, men who believed land should be free as air. This tide finally reached the westernmost boundary of California.

Squatterism is as old as our country. George Washington, in 1784, was making entries in his diary about his experiences with squatters on lands he owned west of the Alleghenies. The squatter movement that began in the eastern states continued steadily west and farther west, greatly influencing the land policies of the government. It found its climax, but hardly its conclusion, when gold-hungry pioneers looked enviously and graspingly on the vast ranchos held by Californians under Mexican laws. Squatterism in California has never entirely died out, although shotguns gave way to lawyers. In recent years, with California rancho titles all settled, we still find mild flare-ups of the squatter spirit, for the desire to settle upon the good lands held by another person dies hard. Who does not want to get something for nothing!

Even before California became a part of the Union—September 9, 1850—the wagons of the immigrants were moving in and coming to a stop on the good valley lands of the rancheros. Squatters began early to organize into armed bands to get what they wanted. Some were interested in ranches. Some began staking out, or helping themselves to, lots on the outskirts of growing towns like San Francisco and Sacramento.

Many years were to elapse before a land commission, authorized under Act of Congress in 1851, and the courts to which its decisions could be appealed, could pass upon all of the 800 and more private land claims in California. Meanwhile, adventurous American immigrants, who believed—as in the popular song—that "Uncle Sam is rich enough to give us all a farm," found on their arrival that all the best land in California, or at least the most usable, was included in enormous grants made by the Mexican regime. To many of these "North American adventurers," as native Californians liked to refer to them, the great landowners were merely monopolists who, like the Indians, were obstructing the path or progress of civilization. After all, California had been captured, as well as bought, from Mexico.

No doubt some of these newcomers brought with them the honest notion that this territory obtained from Mexico was inevitably public land and that they, therefore, had the right to preempt and settle upon lands in California as freely as they had been doing upon any part of the public domain in other states. When they found the best areas under Mexican titles or held by speculators who had bought them up, clashes were inevitable. Hardly any part of California was free from violence. The story of squatterism in California is just one chapter in the story of mob law in America. . . .

In May 1853, Jack Powers, who was a squatter on land of Nicholas Den near Santa Barbara, barricaded himself with fifteen of his friends behind logs and wagons and defied the sheriff's attempt to oust him. They were armed with revolvers, rifles, and shotguns and were supplied with liquor and food. In the battle that developed there were killed and wounded on both sides.

Trespassers and squatters roamed and mined at will along the creek beds of John Charles Fremont's ore-rich Mariposas grant, and when the final survey showed valuable mines included within the rancho's boundaries, Fremont's settlement became an armed camp. Miners attempted to seize the mines they had worked. Bloodshed and riots followed.

Source: Robinson, W. W. *The Story of Mission Lands, Ranchos, Squatters, Mining Claims, Railroad Grants, Land Scrip, Homesteads*. Berkeley: University of California Press, 1979, 111–113, 126.

Herbert O. Brayer, *William Blackmore: The Spanish Mexican Land Grants of New Mexico and Colorado, 1863–1878*

(1949)

New Mexico was the most heavily populated Mexican province at the time of the signing of the Treaty of Guadalupe Hidalgo in 1848. Because so many people were dispossessed there as a result of land grabs, the Land Question—or the question of from whom the land was stolen—continues to be important to this day. Under Mexican law, two types of grants existed: private grants to individuals and communal grants, made to villages in frontier regions. Communal land grants were made to frontier settlers and to the pueblos for tribal use. The Mexican signers of the Treaty of Guadalupe Hidalgo wanted to protect property rights and believed the promises of U.S. negotiators that their property rights would be respected.

Further, Article VIII of the treaty provided that "property of every kind now belonging to Mexicans not established there shall be inviolably respected." However, in 1854, the Office of the Surveyor General of New Mexico was set up to review titles. It was supposed to respect Spanish and Mexican laws, usages, and customs in reviewing the claims. In all, this office reviewed approximately 180 claims (not including grants to pueblo villages) and confirmed 46 of these non-pueblo grants. In 1891, the Court of Private Land Claims was established to judge land-grant claims in New Mexico and the Southwest. In the next 13 years, the court reviewed 282 claims to land grants in New Mexico and confirmed 82. The following passages are by Herbert O'Brayer, the state archivist of Colorado, in his biography of William Blackmore (1827–1878), an infamous British entrepreneur and speculator in Spanish and Mexican land grants in Colorado and New Mexico who represented English mining interests in New Mexico after the Civil War. Here Brayer reviews Anglo-Saxon law and attitudes and their applicability to New Mexico and gives a brutal assessment.

Anglo-Saxon principles of law, taxation and land holding, as well as the new-found trade and commerce, also made definite, though for a time unnoticeable, inroads on the traditional economy of the territory. The terms of the [T]reaty of Guadalupe Hidalgo had pledged the United States to respect and protect the private property rights of the former Mexican citizens within the ceded territory. Unfortunately for the owners of New Mexico land grants, the methods devised by Congress for confirming their holdings became so involved, prolonged, and expensive, that many owners ultimately lost their lands instead of obtaining confirmation of them. The legal process established by the government was, in theory, relatively simple. A grant claimant was called upon to present his evidence of title to the newly created Surveyor General of New Mexico who examined the documents, held hearings, and, after determining the validity of the title to each grant, reported his findings to Congress with the recommendation that final confirmation be made by that body. In practice, however, the system failed to function so easily. Many of the grantees, unable to understand the English language, and naturally suspicious of the "gringo," flatly refused to submit their documents to the surveyor general, believing that they were well protected by the provisions of the treaty with Mexico.

To further complicate matters, a group of shrewd, and not too scrupulous Yankee lawyers, many of them ex-soldiers who had entered with the army of occupation or had settled in the territory after the Civil War, took advantage of the situation and within a few years had not only succeeded in obtaining control of many of the more important grants, but had actually obtained ownership of them. Since the native was dependent upon large tracts of land for the successful grazing of his flocks, this practice contributed largely to the breakup of the traditional economy by forcing the New Mexican to contract his operations or to seek other, less desirable lands. Impoverishment, dispossession, and the dislocation of population was the inevitable result. The method practiced by these representatives of "Yankee" law was to approach the native land grant residents and, after grossly exaggerating the intricacies of the confirmation process and their influence with officials both in Santa Fe and in Washington, to offer their services as attorneys for the claimants. The gullible land owners, desiring to avoid all personal contact with the new and frequently misunderstood government, readily consented. As only a few of the grantees could afford monetary remuneration, the astute lawyers generously agreed to accept payment in land. It took a good many acres at twenty-five to thirty-five cents an acre to pay the well-padded expense accounts and retainer fees charged by the counselors. Land became the usual media for payment of legal services by the natives. In one acknowledged instance, a noted Santa Fe attorney received title to more than 50,000 acres of one of the most valuable grants in the territory as payment for his efforts in defending a native charged with murder. The success of a small group of politically powerful attorneys in literally "cornering the land grant market," led to much controversy. This famous clique controlled territorial politics for more than half a century, exercising undue influence over the territorial courts, and obtaining powerful support both in Congress and in the executive branch of the federal government. . . .

Slowly, the process whereby over eighty percent of the grants were to be lost to their hispanic settlers and owners set in and destroyed the economic equilibrium of New Mexico. The changes wrought by the imposition of the Anglo-American culture were very real, but in 1870 were not readily discernible to the casual observer. The native New Mexican remained essentially a subsistence farmer, utilizing centuries' old agricultural methods and implements. . . .

Source: Brayer, Herbert O. *William Blackmore: The Spanish Mexican Land Grants of New Mexico and Colorado, 1863–1878.* Vol. 1. Denver: Bradford Robinson, 1949, 16–19.

U.S. Government Accountability Office, "The Concept of Common Lands Defines Community Land Grants"

(2007)

Land policy differs from country to country and is often based on the environment and tradition. For example, water laws in arid countries like Mexico and Spain differ from those in wet places like England. After the U.S. conquest of 1848, the United States was forced to follow Mexican water-use laws to avoid conflicts. In the Mexican tradition, water belonged to the public—or at least this was how it was supposed to work. The Spanish and Mexican governments followed a similar logic; to settle their northern frontier, the Spanish Crown, and later the Mexican government in the 18th and early 19th centuries, allowed the governors of California, New Mexico, and Coahuila y Tejas to grant or sell land to individuals and communities. The Spanish Crown distributed grants to groups of people to form towns or villages. The Treaty of

Guadalupe Hidalgo (1848) explicitly protected the rights of holders of private and communal lands. The original Article IX of the treaty also included language that required the immediate admission of former Mexican territories as states so the Mexican settlers would have a say in their governance. The U.S. government violated the treaty, and rather than simply accepting titles to Spanish or Mexican land grants, Congress required claimants to confirm the legality of their land grants through a lengthy and expensive legal process before courts or commissions. Meanwhile, the communal lands were privatized, and villagers lost their use of common lands and forests. Grantees had the burden of proof, which was often at an expense beyond their means. Judges and commissioners unfamiliar with Spanish and Mexican land law (let alone the Spanish language) weighed the evidence. Reproduced here are excerpts from a U.S. Government Accountability Office explanation of community land grants in the Southwest.

From the end of the seventeenth century to the middle of the nineteenth century, Spain and México issued grants of land to individuals, groups, towns, pueblos, and other settlements in order to populate present-day New Mexico. Academic treatises and popular literature typically divide these grants into two types: "individual grants" and "community land grants." Grants to towns and other settlements were modeled on similar communities created in Spain, where the king granted lands adjacent to small towns for common use by all town residents. Under Spanish and Mexican law in the territory of New Mexico, officials made grants to towns and other communities. Such grants were in keeping with Spanish laws, including the 1680 Recopilación de las Leyes de los Reynos de las Indias. However, local laws, practices, and customs often dictated how grants were made and confirmed.

After achieving independence from Spain in 1821, México continued to adhere to Spanish law by extending additional land grants to individuals to encourage settlements in unoccupied areas and to stave off U.S. encroachment on Mexican territory. The Mexican-American War began in 1846 and formally ended with the signing of the Treaty of Guadalupe Hidalgo in 1848. Under the treaty, México ceded most of what is presently the American Southwest, including the present day states of New Mexico and California, to the United States for $15 million. . . .

Land grant documents contain no direct reference to "community land grants" nor do Spanish and Mexican laws define or use this term. Scholars, land grant literature, and popular terminology use the phrase "community land grants" to denote land grants that set aside common lands for the use of the entire community. We adopted this broad definition for the purposes of this report.

To determine the meaning of the term "community land grants," we first reviewed land grant documents, and found that grant documents do not describe grants as community land grants. We also did not find applicable Spanish and Mexican laws that defined or used the term. However, as a result of our review of land grant literature, court decisions, and interviews with scholars, legal experts, and grantee heirs, we found that the term is frequently used to refer to grants that set aside some land for general communal use (ejidos) or for specific purposes, including hunting (caza), pasture (pastos), wood gathering (leña) or watering (abrevederos). Our definition coincides with the way in which scholars, the land-grant literature, and grant heirs use the term.

Under Spanish and Mexican law, common lands set aside as part of an original grant belonged to the entire community and could not be sold. Typically, in addition to use of common lands, settlers on a community land grant would receive individual parcels of land designated for dwelling (solar de casa) and growing food (suerte). Unlike the common lands, these individual parcels could be sold or otherwise disposed of by a settler who fulfilled the requirements of the grant, such as occupying the individual parcel for a continuous period. For example, the documentation for the Antón Chico grant, issued by México in 1822, contains evidence that common lands were part of the original grant. The granting document provided for individual private allotments and common lands. Congress confirmed the Antón Chico grant in 1860 and the grant was patented in 1883.

APPROXIMATELY FIFTY-TWO PERCENT OF ALL NEW MEXICO LAND GRANTS MAY BE CLASSIFIED AS COMMUNITY LAND GRANTS

[There were] three types of community land grants, totaling 152 grants, or approximately 52 percent of the 295 land grants in New Mexico. In 79 of the community land grants, the common lands formed part of the grant according to the grant documentation. Scholars, grant heirs, and others have found an additional 51 grants that they believe to contain communal lands; and we located 22 grants of communal lands to the indigenous pueblo cultures in New Mexico. . . .

The third type of community land grants . . . encompasses grants extended by Spain to the indigenous pueblo cultures in New Mexico to protect communal lands that had existed for centuries before the Spanish settlers arrived. For the most part, the pueblo settlements these colonists encountered in the sixteenth century were permanent, communally owned villages, where inhabitants engaged in agricultural pursuits. Spain declared itself guardian of these communities, respected their rights to land adjacent to the pueblos, and protected pueblo lands from encroachment by Spanish colonists. Spain made grants to these communities in recognition of their communal ownership of village lands. México continued to recognize pueblo ownership of land and considered pueblo residents to be Mexican citizens.

After the Treaty of Guadalupe Hidalgo, the Congress required the Surveyor General to investigate and report on pueblo claims. The Congress subsequently confirmed Spanish grants to 22 pueblos on the recommendation of the Surveyor General. . . .

Source: U.S. Government Accountability Office. http://www.gao.gov/guadalupe/commland.htm.

Latinos and Independence Movements South of the Border

(1848–1860)

Clayton-Bulwer Treaty
(1850)

The chief rival of the United States in the Caribbean and Central America was Great Britain, which had the mightiest navy in the world and maintained a global empire. Spain was on the decline. Most of its American colonies had won their independence; its last major colonies in the New World were Cuba and Puerto Rico. The United States and Great Britain competed over who would build and control an Atlantic-Pacific interocean canal throughout the 1850s. However, despite its bluster that the Americas were for Americans and its declaration of the Monroe Doctrine (1823), the United States could ill afford a war with Great Britain. In Central America, Great Britain claimed Belize, the Mosquito Coast, and the Bay Islands. The United States had treaties with Nicaragua and Honduras. To ease tensions, the United States and Great Britain signed the Clayton-Bulwer Treaty in 1850. The chief negotiators were U.S. secretary of state John M. Clayton and Great Britain's Sir Henry Lytton Bulwer. The treaty, which is excerpted here, stipulated that neither the United States nor Great Britain would ask for exclusive control of an interocean canal. The treaty said that neither the United States nor Great Britain would "occupy, or fortify, or colonize, or assume or exercise any dominion over Nicaragua, Costa Rica, the Mosquito Coast, or any part of Central America."

ARTICLE I

The governments of the United States and Great Britain hereby declare, that neither the one nor the other will ever obtain or maintain for itself any exclusive control over the said ship canal; agreeing that neither will ever erect or maintain any fortifications commanding the same or in the vicinity thereof, or occupy, or fortify, or colonize, or assume or exercise any dominion over Nicaragua, Costa Rica, the Mosquito coast, or any part of Central America; nor will either make use of any protection which either affords or may afford, or any alliance which either has or may have, to or with any State or people, for the purpose of erecting or maintaining any such fortifications, or of occupying, fortifying, or colonizing Nicaragua, Costa

Rica, the Mosquito coast, or any part of Central America, or of assuming or exercising dominion over the same; nor will the United States or Great Britain take advantage of any intimacy, or use any alliance, connection, or influence that either may possess, with any State or government through whose territory the said canal may pass, for the purpose of acquiring or holding, directly or indirectly, for the citizens or subjects of the one, any rights or advantages in regard to commerce or navigation through the said canal which shall not be offered on the same terms to the citizens or subjects of the other. . . .

ARTICLE VIII

The governments of the United States and Great Britain having not only desired, in entering into this convention, to accomplish a particular object, but also to establish a general principle, they hereby agree to extend their protection, by treaty stipulations, to any other practicable communications, whether by canal or railway, across the isthmus which connects North and South America, and especially to the interoceanic communications, should the same prove to be practicable, whether by canal or railway, which are now proposed to be established by the way of Tehuantepec or Panama. In granting, however, their joint protection to any such canals or railways as are by this article specified, it is always understood by the United States and Great Britain that the parties constructing or owning the same shall impose no other charges or conditions of traffic thereupon than the aforesaid govern[ments] shall approve of as just and equitable; and that the same canals or railways, being open to the citizens and subjects of the United States and Great Britain on equal terms, shall also be open on like terms to the citizens and subjects of every other State which is willing to grant thereto such protection as the United States and Great Britain engage to afford.

Source: Convention between the United States of America and Her Britannic Majesty; April 19, 1850.

The United States Democratic Review, "The Nicaraguan Question" (1858)

General William Walker (1824–1860), a 5-foot, 2-inch Tennessean, drifted into California in the 1850s and launched a series of filibustering expeditions against Mexico. He caught the imagination of European Americans in 1853, when he landed a party in Sonora, Mexico, and invaded Baja California. He was kicked out. But in 1855, he enlisted some 60 men and sailed for Nicaragua, where he led a successful coup. Walker was opposed by Commodore Cornelius Vanderbilt (1794 –1877), a wealthy banker who built a road through Nicaragua and then a railroad through Panama that joined the Atlantic and Pacific oceans. Costa Rica declared war on Walker and, in May 1857, forced him to surrender and leave Nicaragua. His departure did not end European American dreams of annexing Nicaragua. Walker led an invasion of Honduras, where he was captured and executed in 1860. His successes inspired debate on the "Nicaraguan Question," which concerned the status of Nicaragua within the U.S. sphere of influence. Although many Americans coveted its land, the thinking of most was influenced by racial doctrines that saw Nicaragua as a land of mongrels. The following excerpt from an article appearing in The United States Democratic Review *in 1858 deals with how Americans viewed*

Nicaraguans and the impediments to democracy there. The article argues that European Americans had good reason to disown the "abominable bastard democracies of Central and South America." This antipathy was overcome by the potential profits that would be derived from its rich lands.

The first objection to this method is that there are no democracies, in the American sense, nor can be, in the Spanish American republics. A collection of negroes, mestizoes, mulattoes, and renegades of all colors, without political ideas, a sense of right, or notions of common humanity, much less of progressive civilization, must not be dignified with the name of a Democracy. We resolutely protest against it, and the good sense of the nation will go with us. The same objections that apply to the sudden emancipation of Negro slave populations, apply to these misnamed democracies of Negroes and Indians. They are mere sluggish anarchies, liable at any moment to despotism, their natural end, or to barbarism, their natural and real condition. It is unbecoming the dignity of the Federal Government, or people of the United States, to lend themselves to such contemptible fallacies. If we disown Mormonism, as [many] good reasons can be found for disowning the abominable bastard democracies of Central and South America.

It has been proposed, in a spirit of opposition, and in order to turn the scale of immigration in favor of the North, to encourage northern laborers, artisans from Massachusetts, farmers with "subsoil ploughs," and McCormick's reapers, to immigrate in large bodies to Nicaragua. Those who propose an emigration of this character to Nicaragua are either very ignorant or very cruel. When we consider that the mortality of white men in Nicaragua is as great as at Cayenne or the mouths of the Niger, and that not one person in a hundred escapes the fever, the idea of sending shiploads of emigrants with "subsoil ploughs" will be abandoned. Subsoil ploughs will never be used in Nicaragua. Agricultural labor in that climate is simple: it consists only in "keeping down the weeds and killing vermin." The wealth of the soil is generally excessive and inexhaustible. One year of neglect turns a ploughed field into an impenetrable thicket of thorns and brambles.

It is hardly necessary to develop at large, or in many words, the commercial importance of the Nicaraguan Isthmus. It is in fact the key to the Pacific. During the last two years there has been a desperate struggle among the great steamship and transit owners of California and New York to gain exclusive possession of the Nicaraguan Isthmus. These steamship owners, independently of Southern sympathy, have been the real instigators and supporters of the private war waged by adventurers against the governments of Central America for the possession of the Isthmus. The ships of these ambitions speculators have transported armies with their provisions and munitions of war to obtain by force what they had failed to secure by negotiation. Not less than five thousand lives, in all, of white men, and some fifteen thousand of Central Americans have been destroyed by lead, steel, and fever, in this contest of transit monopolists. Another five or ten thousand are waiting to be shipped away and poured into the same deadly abyss.

If our intelligent but unprincipled speculators stand ready to throw entire armies into that Nicaraguan gulf which lies midway between New York and California, to fill it up even with human bones, over which to build a solid causeway for commerce, the Federal Government needs no other apology for laying its powerful hand upon the territory.

Without violating any individual or territorial right, without sacrificing the least interest of a political nature at home; without favoring the claims of South or North, or even so much as taking these into consideration, we may purchase the Nicaraguan right of way, and as much territory as may be necessary to open it for gradual and healthy colonization.

Source: The United States Democratic Review 41, no. 2 (February 1858): 115–123. New York: J & H.G. Langley, etc. Publishers.

New York Times, "The Cuban Scheme" (January 10, 1859)

The fervor to gain Cuba had not cooled by the end of the 1850s. The center of the southern lobby was the state of Louisiana, where U.S. senator John Slidell (1793–1871) proposed a bill in which the United States would set aside $30 million as an installment for the $100 million purchase of Cuba. Similar proposals had been made before 1859, but Slidell had a large following in the Senate. During the 1840s, he had served on a commission that attempted to purchase California and New Mexico from Mexico. The bill failed because, by this time, the die was cast in the struggle between the free and slave states, and the South did not have sufficient votes to pass the bill. The following New York Times *article calls for a more aggressive policy in acquiring Cuba and favored the Slidell bill.*

THE CUBAN SCHEME

Important Movement of Resistance among the Virginia Democracy.

From the *Richmond Enquirer,* Jan. 10

> The proposition of Sen. Slidell to place $30,000,000 "as an installment for the purchase of Cuba," in the hands of the President, is treated by the press with a superficial comment scarcely more satisfactory than the marked indifference to its passage or rejection, which seems to possess both Houses of Congress, with regard to most of the startling propositions, Executive or Legislative in their origin, which have distinguished the present session of Congress.
>
> Mr. Slidell's proposition will not, however, we sincerely trust, be allowed to pass through default of opposition, or by sufferance. The serious financial embarrassment in which it cannot fail to involve us, offers a very serious obstacle to a scheme which affords no perceptible promise of countervailing advantage.

When a proposition is made to raise the public debt (which, twelve months ago, stood at "0") by a single coup, to $100,000,000, we have the right to demand some substantial evidence of good to be accomplished, of benefit to be derived. What is the immediate object or necessity to be met by this appropriation of money to coax a purchase? The sum offered, however important at this time to our depleted treasury, is entirely too insignificant to tempt the cupidity of Spain. It is not even pretended that this $30,000,000 would be regarded as a sufficient equivalent for the purchase of Cuba. Indeed, it is regarded as a mere "installment" by the proposer himself.

In what manner, then, is this installment to be rendered an inducement to Spain for the sale of Cuba? In the earlier years of our Republic, when the galvanic wire of Alexander Hamilton had scarcely revived the pallid corpse of public credit, when our Government was as yet a mere experiment, when the permanency of the Union was as doubtful and more doubted than the solvency of the treasury, it was natural that foreign nations should demand some pledge in the way of prospective appropriation, before negotiating for the transfer of valuable territories. But now, will it be pretended that Spain doubts or can doubt the ability of the Federal Government, to raise and appropriate without delay or impediment the whole sum, however large, which may, and whenever it may be required for the purchase of Cuba? Equally flimsy would be the presence that this appropriation is necessary to convince Spain of the willingness of the Legislative Department of the Government, to cooperate with the Executive in the purchase of Cuba. Spain knows, England knows, France knows, everybody knows that both Legislature and Executive, as well as the people themselves, are only too desirous to secure this darling object.

Why, then, shall the appropriation be made? If it is intended as a link in the policy of practical argument by which it is attempted to force on us an increase of tariff duties—that line of vicious management which would increase expenditures, present and prospective, for the purpose of increasing the rates of taxation, only for the ultimate purpose of stimulating certain branches of industrial pursuit at the expense of all other pursuits and occupations—then we owe it to ourselves, and to the principles of the party to which we owe our honest loyalty, to crush this bantling as remorselessly as we would assail the protective system itself. Nay, the qualifying "if" is scarcely necessary, for whatever be the intent of Mr. Slidell's proposition, its tendency of domestic influence is obviously what we indicate.

But there is another supposition. The most probable of all, and one which will not fail to receive immediate credence in Europe, to be exclusion of all others; that this appropriation is intended, not as an installment of a round sum to be fixed by a future treaty as the amount of purchase money to be paid over to Spain, but a bonus to be employed in secret negotiation with Spanish officials, so as to induce the accomplishment of a treaty of purchase.

We will not pause to discuss the morality of such an arrangement, not the probability of such intent. Whether this be the intent or not, it will at once be recognized as such by European diplomatists, and this alone will be sufficient to delay the acquisition of Cuba. The ostentatious publicity which has unfortunately been given to diplomatic documents bearing on this question, and the loose, vague, devil-may-care tone of undetermined rashness and undefined purpose which has marked Congressional discussions on the same subject have already served to awaken and irritate the selfish apprehensions of England and France, to call into exercise all their resources of diplomatic management and powerful influence at the Court of Madrid to arouse in Spain, if not in Cuba, all the opposition of national jealousy. We have lost much ground, both as regards time and international confidence, by inopportune movements for the acquisition of Cuba.

At present, an abstinence from all public demonstration, if not an entire "masterly inactivity," is what is needed to ripen this fruit of territorial aggrandizement.

There are more reasons than one to justify such a conservative course, and to require its adoption. In order to succeed in any of the great objects of domestic or home policy, we must retrench not only the present rates of expenditure, but also the extravagant list of magnificent schemes which has received the sanction of the Executive. To accomplish anything at all we must refrain from attempting too much. The great Napoleon himself, with all the resources of an empire at his sole command, never ventured the simultaneous accomplishment of so many daring projects. The acquisition of Cuba, at a minimum expense of $100,000,000, the construction of a Pacific Railroad, at perhaps double the figure; a Mexican protectorate, international preponderance in Central America, in spite of all the powers of Europe; the submission of distant South American States; the repulse of unwarrantable demands, in which the selfish British policy of foreign encroachment is deeply interested; the enlargement of the navy; a largely increased standing army; a vital reactionary change in the mode of collecting revenue, directly opposed to the current of free-trade sentiment which is now drawing into its channel all the nations of the earth; a gigantic financial revolution, which contemplates a transfer of all the power over banking and industrial corporations from the hands of the States to those of the Federal Government. Involving a monopoly of monetary command at the centers of trade—what Government on earth could possibly meet all the exigencies of such a flood of innovations? What Treasury could afford the drain required to supply it?

No, this sort of thing is out of the question. This chasing after a multitude of objects will inevitably lose us everything of solid benefit, besides involving us in complicated embarrassments, which the wisdom of a subsequent century will hardly be sufficient to unravel. We want a Napoleon in the field. We want some man who can concentrate all the energies and resources, Governmental and national, on some one great point of reform or advancement. Abundant promises, magnificent and various, although mutually destructive, may indeed win for an Administration, an agglomeration of tolerance, not of support, from conflicting interests and interested contestants. But the Administration which aims to secure for itself, or for the party which it represents, the confidence and the earnest cooperation of popular support, or which aims still higher at the speedy accomplishment of great and beneficial public measures, such an Administration must be chary of promises, and must resort to a concentration of purpose, and a provident consolidation of public resources.

We must at once take hold on the first point of policy, the comparative importance and present urgency of which command the most immediate attention.

In the domain of foreign policy, a Virginia Representative, the Hon. A. G. Jenkins, seems to have recognized the clue to the disentanglement of our international complications. Before we can calculate the expediency of any other step, the abrogation of the Bulwer-Clayton Treaty must be effected.

Source: New York Times, January 21, 1859 (as obtained from the *Richmond Enquirer*, January 10, 1859), 2.

El Grito de Lares, Principles of Unity (1867)

The Puerto Rican independence movement gained ground in the 1860s. The leader was physician Ramón Betances (1827–1898), who had been exiled for sedition because he raised the issue of Puerto Rican independence. By the day's standards, Puerto Rico was heavily populated, with estimates of a million people. Although it was influenced by movements in Cuba, Puerto Rico was some 900 miles from Cuba and 1,000 miles from the United States. There was also a faction calling for greater Puerto Rican autonomy within the Spanish Empire. On September 23, 1868, rebels called for Puerto Rican independence from Spain. The movement was influenced by successful struggles throughout Latin America. However, the revolt was premature and failed. Only a year before, Betances and his fellow revolutionaries founded the Revolutionary Committee of Puerto Rico. They issued the following principles of unity, known today as El Grito de Lares *(the Cry of Lares), which formed the building blocks of the independence movement. After this point, Puerto Ricans formed a government in exile, operating from New York and Latin American capitals, where they solicited money for arms and supporters.*

THE TEN COMMANDMENTS OF FREE MEN

Abolition of slavery

The right to fix taxes

Freedom of worship

Free press

Free speech

Free trade

Freedom of assembly

Right to bear arms

Civil liberties of the citizens

Right to elect their own public officials

Source: World of Guazabara Federation. http://guazabara.com/GritodeLares.htm.

María Eugenia Echenique, "The Emancipation of Women" (1876)

In 1876, Argentine feminist María Eugenia Echenique (1851–1878) wrote the following critique on the role and rights of women. There was a budding feminist movement throughout Latin America at the time. Latinas were well acquainted with Harriet Beecher Stowe (1811–1896) and had read Uncle Tom's Cabin. *Stowe's views on emancipation were applied to the emancipation of women. In her journal, Stowe wrote, "I wrote what I did because as a woman, as a mother, I was oppressed and brokenhearted, with the sorrows and injustice I saw, because as a Christian I felt the dishonor to Christianity, because as a lover of my country I trembled at the coming day of wrath." While downplaying Stowe's views on race, many Latina feminist writers emphasized her views on gender inequality. The following excerpt is in the context of a six-month debate between María Eugenia Echenique and poet and novelist Josefina Pelliza de Sagasta (1848–1888) in the journal* La Ondina del Plata. *Echenique passionately advocates the emancipation of women.*

When emancipation was given to men, it was also given to women in recognition of the equality of rights, consistent with the principles of nature on which they are founded, that proclaim the identity of soul between men and women. Thus, Argentine women have been emancipated by law for a long time. The code of law that governs us authorizes a widow to defend her rights in court, just as an educated woman can in North America, and like her, we can manage the interests of our children, these rights being the basis for emancipation. What we lack is sufficient education and instruction to make use of them, instruction that North American women have; it is not just recently that we have proclaimed our freedom. To try to question or to oppose women's emancipation is to oppose something that is almost a fact, it is to attack our laws and destroy the Republic.

So let the debate be there, on the true point where it should be: whether or not it is proper for women to make use of those granted rights, asking as a consequence the authorization to go to the university so as to practice those rights or make them effective. And this constitutes another right and duty in woman: a duty to accept the role that our own laws bestow on her when extending the circle of her jurisdiction and which makes her responsible before the members of her family.

This, assuming that the woman is a mother. But, are all women going to marry? Are all going to be relegated to a life of inaction during their youth or while they remain single? Is it so easy for all women to look for a stranger to defend their offended dignity, their belittled honor, their stolen interests? Don't we see every day how the laws are trodden underfoot, and the victim, being a woman, is forced to bow her head because she does not know how to defend herself, exposed to lies and tricks because she does not know the way to clarify the truth?

Far from causing the breakdown of the social classes, the emancipation of women would establish morality and justice in them; men would have a brake that would halt the "imperious need" that they have made of the "lies and tricks" of litigations, and the science of jurisprudence, so sacred and magnificent in itself but degenerated today because of abuses, would return to its splendor and true objective once women take part in the forum. Generous and abnegated by nature, women would teach men humanitarian principles and would condemn the frenzy and insults that make a battlefield out of the courtroom.

"Women either resolve to drown the voice of their hearts, or they listen to that voice and renounce emancipation." If emancipation is opposed to the tender sentiments, to the voice of the heart, then men who are completely emancipated and study science are not capable of love. The beautiful and tender girl who gives her heart to a doctor or to a scientist, gives it then, to a stony man, incapable of appreciating it or responding to her; women could not love emancipated men, because where women find love, men find it too; in both burns the same heart's flame. I have seen that those who do not practice science, who do not know their duties or the rights of women, who are ignorant, are the ones who abandon their wives, not the ones who, concentrated on their studies and duties, barely have time to give them a caress.

Men as much as women are victims of the indifference that ignorance, not science, produces. Men are more slaves of women who abuse the prestige of their weakness and become tyrants in their home, than of the schooled and scientific women who understand their duties and are capable of something. With the former, the husband has to play the role of man and woman, because she ignores everything: she is not capable of consoling nor helping her husband, she is not capable of giving tenderness, because, preoccupied with herself, she becomes demanding, despotic, and vain, and she does not know how to make a happy home. For her, there are no responsibilities to carry out, only whims to satisfy. This is typical, we see it happening every day.

The ignorant woman, the one who voluntarily closes her heart to the sublime principles that provoke sweet emotions in it and elevate the mind, revealing to men the deep secrets of the All-Powerful; the woman incapable of helping her husband in great enterprises for fear of losing the prestige of her weakness and ignorance; the woman who only aspires to get married and reproduce, and understands maternity as the only mission of women on earth—she can be the wife of a savage, because in him she can satisfy all her aspirations and hopes, following that law of nature that operates even on beasts and inanimate beings.

I would renounce and disown my sex if the mission of women were reduced only to procreation, yes, I would renounce it; but the mission of women in the world is much more grandiose and sublime, it is more than the beasts', it is the one of teaching humankind, and in order to teach it is necessary to know. A mother should know science in order to inspire in her children great deeds and noble sentiments, making them feel superior to the other objects in the universe, teaching them from the cradle to become familiar with great scenes of nature where they should go to look for God and love Him. And nothing more sublime and ideal than the scientific mother who, while her husband goes to cafés or to the political club to talk about state interests, she goes to spend some of the evening at the astronomical observatory, with her children by the hand to show them Jupiter, Venus, preparing in that way their tender hearts for the most legitimate and sublime aspirations that could occupy men's minds. This sacred mission in the scientific mother who understands emancipation—the fulfillment of which, far from causing the abandonment of the home, causes it to unite more closely—instead of causing displeasure to her husband, she will cause his happiness.

The abilities of men are not so miserable that the carrying out of one responsibility would make it impossible to carry out others. There is enough time and competence for cooking and mending, and a great soul such as that of women, equal to that of their mates, born to embrace all the beauty that exists in Creation of divine origin and end, should not be wasted all on seeing if the plates are clean and rocking the cradle.

Source: Brians, Paul, Mary Gallwey, Douglas Hughes, Azfar Hussain, Richard Law, Michael Myers, Michael Neville, Roger Schlesinger, Alice Spitzer, and Susan Swan, eds. *Reading About the World*, translated by Francisco Manzo Robledo. Vol. 2. New York: Harcourt Brace Custom Books, 1999.

New York Times, "Cigarmakers Protesting" (1884)

Not every cigar maker in the United States in the late 19th century was Cuban, Puerto Rican, or Spanish, but they were among the best. At this point, not many Puerto Ricans had migrated to the United States. Puerto Rico was 1,000 miles away, and workers had to travel by water. Spaniards came by way of Cuba, which was only 90 miles away. There were also a large number of German cigar makers who had learned the craft in Europe. Samuel Gompers (1850–1924), a founder of the American Federation of Labor (AFL) in 1886, learned the craft from his father. His family came to New York, where a relatively few cigar sweatshops packed as many as 75 employees into a small space. Thousands of small children worked in these sweatshops and factories, helping their parents. Gompers worked his way up through the union and, in 1881, was sent as the delegate of the cigar makers to a conference that formed the Federation of Organized Trades and Labor Councils, which evolved into the AFL. Gompers was elected as this group's first president, and held the presidency for nearly 40 years. The following New York Times *article talks about a committee of workers from the AFL that was sent to Washington, DC, to lobby the Committee on Foreign Affairs not to sign a treaty with Spain that would lower the tariff on foreign-made cigars by 50 percent and allow the tobacco leaves to be imported to the United States duty free. Cuban American cigar makers played a role in union affairs. The stream of Cubans to the United States quickened after the 1868 Cuban war of independence broke out. There were more than 80 cigar factories by 1883. These factories employed almost 2,700 Cuban cigar workers. They founded the first trade unions in the U.S. South. The Cuban cigar makers were highly politicized. In 1864, cigar makers introduced* lectores *(readers), who workers paid to read them literary and political works as they rolled cigars. They were educated through these readings.*

CIGARMAKERS PROTESTING TO USE EVERY EFFORT TO HAVE THE TREATY REJECTED

The cigarmakers held a meeting yesterday afternoon at No. 189 Bowery to discuss the best means to prevent the ratification of the Spanish treaty, by which the import tax on cigars is to be reduced 50 per cent and the duty on tobacco leaf is to be abolished altogether. This was an adjourned meeting from a previous one, at which the cigarmakers expressed their unqualified opposition to the treaty as not only derogatory to the tobacco manufacturing interests of the country, but also as prejudicial to themselves as workingmen, as such a treaty would lower their wages to the level of those of European workmen, and cause them great sufferings, if it did not drive a great portion of that industry out of the country. All were agreed as to the necessity of opposing the ratification of the treaty, and the only question was what was the best method to do it.

For the first time in a long while, the manufacturers and workingmen were in unison, and behind the cigarmakers there stand many large cigar and tobacco manufacturing firms in the country. Among these are the firms of Lesano & Pendas, manufacturers of fine Havana tobacco cigars; Lichtenstein Brothers, Wengler & Co., Brown & Earle, McCoy, Sutro & Newmark, Sanchez, Hayga & Co., C. Upman, Kaufman Brothers, George P. Lies, Powell, Wenigman & Smith, A. A. Suma & Co., C. Bartolini, M. Stachelberg & Co., and M. Hutchinson & Co. Although none of these manufacturers have taken part in the meetings of the workmen or have been known to be present at any of them, they are not any the less interested in the agitation, and are working on their own account to obtain the same result—the rejection of the treaty by the Senate. A committee of 11 was appointed at the first meeting to go to Washington to appear against the treaty before the Senate Committee on Foreign Affairs or any other committee to whom it might be referred. There were a number of workmen, however, who wanted to call a mass meeting of cigarmakers to protest against the treaty, to pass resolutions demanding its rejection, and to discuss the subject more thoroughly, and another meeting was called for yesterday afternoon, at which Samuel Gompers presided.

A motion was made to hold a mass meeting, but that did not receive as much support as its friends expected. It was argued that while a great deal of indignation would undoubtedly be expressed, the reports of the arguments that would be made at the mass meeting would hardly be presented to the Senators, while the advocates of the treaty would be on the spot with all their arguments and persuasions. Nevertheless, some of the German cigarmakers insisted on a mass meeting being held, and Mr. Feltenberg, one of the Committee of Eleven, made an earnest appeal for one. The Senators, he declared, were the public servants of the workingmen, who had a right to demand the rejection of the treaty, and it was the duty of the Senators and of Congress to accede to the demands of the voters. All that the cigarmakers had to do would be to call a mass meeting and to make known their demands. Unless a mass meeting was called, Mr. Feltenberg threatened to resign from the committee, and, with his supporters, to withdraw from the agitation.

Another more philosophic delegate remarked that there might not be time enough to call and make preparations for a mass meeting upon a grand scale, and that meanwhile the enemy might steal a march upon them. Still another delegate who supported Feltenberg suggested that all cigarmakers and other trades unions throughout the country be requested to make demonstrations. Mr. Gompers, in reply to Mr. Feltenberg, remarked that it was true that workingmen had a right to make certain demands upon Senators and Congressmen, but when they did not have the power to enforce those demands it was unwise and a waste of time to make them. It was better to ask for what they wanted in a practical manner and to present their arguments in such a way as to obtain the desired result. The advocates of the treaty were on the spot, trying their utmost to make an impression upon the Senators and push the treaty through, while the workingmen were away in New York and other cities, far from the scene of action.

Mr. Gompers had acted as a committeeman to Washington upon a former occasion, and he knew that even if the Senators were honest in their intentions they were not posted on everything that came up before them. When he was last in Washington as a member of a committee they found that the Senators were to a great extent ignorant of the wants of the workingmen. Senator Allison requested Mr. Gompers to write out the workingmen's case just as he would write it for an entirely ignorant man, and the Senator would thus be enabled to use it in his argument on the floor of the Senate.

A black-eyed and black-haired woman came into the meeting room, and after giving her name to the Chairman, was introduced as Mrs. Velasquez, of Washington. She spoke English fluently and said that she was a Cuban and had come to help the cigarmakers. She was an old worker in Congress, although she wanted it to be understood that she was not a woman's rights agitator. She had been requested by several Senators to come on to New York and confer with the cigarmakers and sugar manufacturers. One hundred and forty members of Congress and 41 Senators were decidedly opposed to the treaty. The speaker said she was very well acquainted with Messrs. Edmunds, Blair, Sherman, Randall, and numerous other Senators and Congressmen. Mr. Foster's object in drafting the treaty was to further his own individual interests and the interests of his friends, and they would do all that lay in their power to push it through the Senate.

Mrs. Velasquez was not only opposed to the treaty, but she wanted to see Cuba annexed, and there were many in Washington who wanted that, too. Mr. Hill, of Ohio, was in her office on Saturday, and she had a letter from Senator Blair asking her to see the different societies in this city. She urged the cigarmakers to send representatives to Washington, where committees would arrive from New Orleans, California, and other places, and if the workingmen only showed sufficient interest in the matter the treaty would undoubtedly be rejected.

The motion to hold a mass meeting was finally tabled.

Source: "The Cigarmakers Protesting." *New York Times*, December 8, 1884, 1.

José Martí, "My Race" (April 16, 1893)

José Martí (1853–1895), referred to as the "Apostle of Cuban Independence," was born in La Habana (Havana), Cuba. He became politically active at a young age, helping to found an anticolonial newspaper, for which he was arrested and sentenced to six years of hard labor at age 15. In 1871, after serving three years, Martí moved to Spain, and, in 1878, he moved to Mexico City, where he joined other exiles from various Latin American countries. In 1881, Martí moved to New York, where he worked as a journalist and organized Cuban and Puerto Rican dissidents. In the following article, he reacts to the term "racist." Racism was fully developed within the Cuban community since colonial times—but in the United States it took on a new meaning.

"Racist" is becoming a confusing word, and it must be clarified. No man has any special rights because he belongs to one race or another: say "man" and all rights have been stated. The black man, as a black man, is not inferior or superior to any other man; the white man who says "my race" is being redundant, and the black man who says "my race" is also redundant. Anything that divides men from each other, that separates them, singles them out, or hems them in, is a sin against humanity. What sensible white man thinks he should be proud of being white, and what do blacks think of a white man who is proud of being white and believes he has special rights because he is? What must whites think of a black man who grows conceited about his color? To insist upon the racial divisions and racial differences of a people naturally divided is to obstruct both individual and public happiness, which lies in greater closeness among the elements that must live in common. It is true that in the black man there is no original sin or virus that makes him incapable of developing his whole soul as a man, and this truth must be spoken and demonstrated, because the injustice of this world is great, as is the ignorance that passes for wisdom, and there are still those who believe in good faith that the black man is incapable of the intelligence and feelings of the white man. And what does it matter if this truth, this defense of nature, is called racism, because it is no more than natural respect, the voice that clamors from man's bosom for the life and the peace of the nation. To state that the condition of slavery does not indicate any inferiority in the enslaved race—for white Gauls with blue eyes and golden hair were sold as slaves with fetters around their necks in the markets of Rome—is good racism, because it is pure justice and helps the ignorant white shed his prejudices. But that is the limit of just racism, which is the right of the black man to maintain and demonstrate that his color does not deprive him of any of the capacities and rights of the human race.

And what right does the white racist, who believes his race has superior rights, have to complain of the black racist, who also believes that his race has special traits? What right does the black racist who sees a special character in his race have to complain of the white racist? The white man who, by reason of his race, believes himself superior to the black man acknowledges the idea of race and thus authorizes and provokes the black racist. The black man who trumpets his race when what he is perhaps trumpeting instead is only the spiritual identity of all races—authorizes and provokes the white racist. Peace demands the shared rights of nature; differing rights go against nature and are the enemies of peace. The white who isolates himself isolates the Negro. The Negro who isolates himself drives the white to isolate himself.

In Cuba there is no fear whatsoever of a race war. "Man" means more than white, more than mulatto, more than Negro. "Cuban" means more than white, more than mulatto, more than Negro. On the battlefields, the souls of whites and blacks who died for Cuba have risen together through the air. In that daily life of defense, loyalty, brotherhood, and shrewdness, there was always a black man at the side of every white. Blacks, like whites, can be grouped according to their character—timid or brave, self-abnegating or egotistical—into the diverse parties of mankind. Political parties are aggregates of concerns, aspirations, interests, and characters. An essential likeness is sought and found beyond all differences of detail, and what is fundamental in analogous characters merges in parties, even if their incidental characteristics or motives differ. In short, it is the similarity of character—a source of unity far superior to the internal relations of the varying colors of men, whose different shades are sometimes in opposition to each other—that commands and prevails in the formation of parties. An affinity of character is more powerful than an affinity of color. Blacks, distributed among the diverse or hostile specialties of the human spirit, will never want or be able to band together against whites, who are distributed among the same specialties. Blacks are too tired of slavery to enter voluntarily into the slavery of color. Men of pomp and self-interest, black and white, will be on one side, and generous and impartial men will be on the other. True men, black or white, will treat each other with loyalty and tenderness, taking pleasure in merit and pride in anyone, black or white, who honors the land where we were born. The word "racist" will be gone from the lips of the blacks who use it today in good faith, once they understand that that word is the only apparently valid argument—valid among sincere, apprehensive men—for denying the Negro the fullness of his rights as a man. The white racist and the Negro racist will be equally guilty of being racists. Many whites have already forgotten their color, and many blacks have, too. Together they work, black and white, for the cultivation of the mind, the dissemination of virtue, and the triumph of creative work and sublime charity.

There will never be a race war in Cuba. The Republic cannot retreat and the Republic, from the extraordinary day of the emancipation of blacks in Cuba and from its first independent constitution of April 10, in Guaimaro, never spoke of whites or blacks. The rights already conceded out of pure cunning by the Spanish government, and which have become habitual even before the Island's independence, can no longer be denied now, either by the Spaniard, who will maintain them as long as he draws breath in Cuba—in order to continue dividing Cuban blacks from Cuban whites—or by the independent nation, which will not, in liberty, be able to deny the rights that the Spaniard recognized in servitude.

As for the rest, each individual will be free within the sacred confines of his home. Merit, the clear and continual manifestation of culture and inexorable trade will end by uniting all men. There is much greatness in Cuba, in blacks and in whites.

Source: From *José Martí: Selected Writings by José Martí*, introduction by Roberto Gonzalez Echevarria, edited by Esther Allen, translated by Esther Allen, 318–321.

José Martí, Letter to Manuel Mercado (May 18, 1895)

Cuban poet and journalist José Martí (1853–1895) lived in the United States for 15 years, where he grew increasingly disillusioned with white Americans. The Cuban war for independence from Spain had been going on for 30 years, and many Cuban rebels had hoped that the United States would help them. Martí had returned to his beloved island and in the heat of the battle warned his fellow revolutionaries to guard against possible U.S. intervention. The day before he was killed, Martí wrote an unfinished letter to Manuel Mercado (1838–1909) about his fear of U.S. imperialism in the region. Mercado was born in Michoacán, Mexico, where he met Martí. They formed a close friendship.

Dos Rios Camp, May 18, 1895

Mr. Manuel Mercado

My dearest brother: Now I can write, now I can tell you with what tenderness and gratitude and respect I love you, and your home that is my own—and with what pride and commitment. Every-day now I am in danger of giving my life for my country and duty—since I understand it and have the spirit to carry it out—in order to prevent, by the timely independence of Cuba, the United States from extending its hold across the Antilles and falling with all the greater force on the lands of our America. All I have done up to now and all I will do is for that. It has had to be concealed in order to be attained: proclaiming them for what they are would give rise to obstacles too formidable to be overcome. The nations such as your own and mine, which have the most vital interest in keeping Cuba from becoming, through an annexation accomplished by those imperialists and the Spaniards, the doorway—which must be blocked and which, with our blood, we are blocking—to the annexation of the peoples of our America by the turbulent and brutal North that holds them in contempt, are kept by secondary, public obligations from any open allegiance and manifest aid to the sacrifice being made for their immediate benefit. I lived in the monster, and I know its entrails—and my sling is the sling of David: Even now, a few days ago, in the wake of the triumph with which the Cuban people greeted our free descent from the mountains where six expenditionaries walked for fourteen days, a correspondent from the *New York Herald* took me from my hammock and hut and told me about the activities aimed at annexation—which is less fearsome because of the scant realism of those who aspire to it—by men of the legal ilk who, having no discipline or creative power of their own, and as a convenient disguise for their complacency and subjugation to Spain, request Cuba's autonomy without conviction, content that there be a master, Yankee or Spaniard, to maintain them and grant them, in reward for their services as intermediaries, positions as leaders, scornful of the vigorous masses, the skilled and inspiring mestizo mass of this country—the intelligent, creative masses of whites and blacks.

And did the *Herald* correspondent, Eugene Bryson, tell me about anything else? About a Yankee syndicate, backed by the Customs Office, in which rapacious white Spaniards have a deep hand, and that may become a toehold in Cuba for those from the North, whose complex and entrammeled political constitution fortunately leaves them unable to undertake or support this plan as the project of their government. And Bryson told me something else, though the truth of the conversation he reported to me can only be understood by one who has seen at close hand the vigor with which we have launched the revolution, and the disorder, reluctance, and poor pay of the raw Spanish army—and the inability of Spain to muster, either in or out of Cuba, the resources with which to fight this war, resources that, during the last war, it extracted from Cuba alone. Bryson told me about a conversation he had with Martinez Campos at the end of which he was given to understand that no doubt, when the time came, Spain would prefer to reach an agreement with the United States than to hand the Island over to the Cuban people. And Bryson told me still more: about an acquaintance of ours who is being groomed in the North as the United States' candidate for the presidency of Mexico, once the current President has disappeared. I am doing my duty here. The Cuban war—a reality that is superior to the vague and disparate desires of the annexationist Cubans and Spaniards whose alliance with the government of Spain would give them only relative power—has come at the right hour in America to prevent, even against the open deployment of all these forces, the annexation of Cuba to the Unites States, which would never accept the annexation of a country that is at war, and which, since the revolution will not accept annexation, cannot enter into a hateful and absurd commitment to crush, for its own benefit and with its own weapons, an American war of independence.

And Mexico? Will it not find a wise, effective, and immediate way of supplying aid, in time, to those who are defending it? Yes, it will, or I will find one on Mexico's behalf. This is life or death; there is no room for error. Discretion is the only option. I would have found and proposed a way already, but I must have more authority myself, or know who does have it, before acting or advising. I have just arrived. The constitution of a simple, practical government may take two more months, if it is to be real and stable. Our soul is one, I know that, and so is the connections', timeliness, and compromise. I represent a certain constituency, and I do not want to do anything that might appear to be a capricious expansion of it.

I arrived in a boat with General Maximo Gomez and four other men, taking the lead oar through a storm to land on an unknown, rocky stretch of one of our beaches. For fourteen days I carried my rucksack and rifle on foot across brambles and high places—rousing the people to take up arms as we passed through. I feel, in the benevolence of these souls, the root of my attachment to the pain of mankind and to the justice that will alleviate it. The countryside is undisputedly ours, to such a degree that in a month I've heard gunfire only once; at the gates of the cities we either win a victory or pass three thousand armed men in review, to an enthusiasm akin to religious fervor. We are going on now to the center of the Island where, in the presence of the revolution that has given rise to, I will lay aside the authority given me by the Cubans off the island, which has been respected on the island, and which an assembly of delegates of the visible Cuban people, the revolutionaries now in arms, must renew in accordance with their new state. The revolution desires full liberty for the army, without the nee imposed on it by a Chamber of Deputies with no real authorization, or by the suspicions of a younger generation that is its republicanism, or by jealousy and fear of the excessive future prominence of some painstaking and farsighted caudillo. However at the same time, the revolution wants concise and respectable republican representation—the same spirit of humanity and decency, full for individual dignity, in the republic's representatives as is revolutionaries on and keeping them at war. For myself, I understand that a nation cannot be made to go against the spirit that moves it, or to do without that spirit, and I know how to set hearts on fire and how to use the ardent and gratified state of those hearts for incessant agitation and attack. But where forms are concerned, there is room for many ideas, and the things of men are made by men. You own me. For myself, I will defend only that which I believe will or serve the revolution. I know how to disappear. But my ideas would not disappear, nor would my own obscurity embitter me. And as long as we have a form, we will work, whether the fulfillment of it falls to me or to others.

And now that matters of the public interest have gone first, I'll tell you about myself. Only the emotion of this duty was able to raise from coveted death the man who knows you best—now that

Najera no longer lives where he can be seen—and who cherishes the friendship which you distinguish him like a treasure in his heart. I know you have been scolding me, silently, since my journey began. We give him all our soul, and he is silent! What a disappointment! How callused his soul must be if the tribute and honor of our affection has not been enough to make him write one letter more, among all the pages of letters and newspaper articles he writes each day! There are affections of such delicate honesty.

Source: From *José Martí: Selected Writings by José Martí*, introduction by Roberto Gonzalez Echevarria, edited by Esther Allen, translated by Esther Allen, 346–349.

New York Times, "Interment of José Martí" (1895)

The following New York Times *article describes the burial of José Martí (1853–1895), the apostle for Cuban independence who died in military action. Martí was a poet, journalist, and* independista. *He is credited with creating sympathy for the Cuban Revolution in the United States, and in the mid-1890s took command of the armed struggle on the island. The following description of his burial ceremonies would be the equivalent for Americans of a description of George Washington's burial.*

INTERMENT OF JOSE MARTI

Official Documents Relative to the Death of the Insurgent

Correspondence of The United Press

HAVANA, June 1—The official documents relative to the burial of Marti have been published in full. An epitome of them is as follows:

"In the General Cemetery of Santiago de Cuba, at 8 a.m., May 27, there was a meeting of a military commission named by his Excellency the Military Governor of Santiago. Among the prominent men were Col. Sandoval, who commanded the troops at the engagement of Dos Rios, May 19; Gen. Garrich, Col. Caberro, and many others. The Governor's commission was read. It empowered them to proceed to the identification and burial of the body of the so-called chief of the rebels, one José Martí.

"Several of the senior officers knew Martí in his lifetime, having known him during the 1868 to 1878 rebellion, and several having seen him during recent engagements. After a close and careful scrutiny of the remains, they were unanimously of the opinion that the body before them was that of José Martí.

"Following the identification, Col. Sandoval, acting for the Spanish Government, authorized the sepulture of the body in Compartment No. 134 of the Bovedas.

"All the legal requirements having been complied with in every detail, the certificate of death and identification of the body of José Martí was signed by the following: Manuel Tejerizo, Enrique Ubieta Maurl, Enrique Yatue, Pablo A. de Valencia, José X. de Sandoval.

"At the conclusion of the official ceremonies, Col. Sandoval addressed the vast concourse, asking if any relative or friend of Martí was present. Such friend or relative was at liberty to step forward and take part in the last offices to the dead. No one offering to do so, Col. Sandoval addressed the people, saying that in the presence of death the past was forgotten. Martí had ceased to be an enemy of Spain, and the body before them was worthy of honorable and Christian burial.

"The coffin was then placed in its niche, and the opening was closed with the usual stone tablet. When this had been done, Gen. Salcedo, in an eloquent address, said that if Spanish soldiers knew how to overcome enemies, they knew also how to respect the vanquished and how to pay honors to the dead.

"This closes the Martí incident—the one and only Martí is literally and legally dead."

Source: "Interment of José Martí," *New York Times,* June 9, 1895, 5.

Los Angeles Times, "Porto Rico in Rebellion" (1895)

In 1850, Cuba had a population of 1.2 million—of whom 605,560 were white. That year 205,570 were free Africans, and the rest were slaves. According to a royal census in 1858, 300,430 Puerto Ricans were white, 341,015 were free Africans, and 41,736 were slaves. By 1894, the Cuban population had grown substantially—about 709,000 Spanish immigrants arrived between 1868 and 1894. Puerto Rico had a total population of about a million people. To the United States, the main difference between the two island nations was that Puerto Rico was 1,000 miles away whereas Cuba was only 90 miles away. And U.S. business interests had already invaded Cuba. Like in Cuba, Puerto Rico witnessed the growth of a pro-independence movement. Spain initially responded by conceding such colonial reforms as establishing the first national political parties, abolishing slavery, and briefly experimenting with a grant of autonomy under the Spanish Crown, which gave Puerto Rico representation in the Spanish parliament. Like other Latin American nations, Puerto Rico developed an identifiable culture. As with Cuba, Puerto Rico's struggle for independence came to a head in 1895. Puerto Rico had had a strong presence in the Cuban Revolutionary Party. The following Los Angeles Times *article predicts that Puerto Rico will soon declare its independence and describes the overall activities of the Puerto Rican Separatist Party as well as its independence activities in New York City,where it worked with the Cuban Revolutionary Party to raise, funds, seek volunteers, and win U.S. popular support.*

PORTO RICO IN REBELLION

NEW YORK, Dec. 11—A local paper says that in her struggle for independence Cuba has found a powerful ally in the Island of Porto Rico. According to the latest intelligence, Spain has now two insurrections on her hands, or will have if the plans maturing are carried into execution. Porto Rico has gone so far, it is said, as to issue a declaration of independence and will soon join her sister island in the active struggle for liberty. An army is being formed by the Separatist party of Porto Rico, and as soon as the leaders are ready the new campaign will open.

As in the Venezuelan affair, the revolutionists are Cuban patriots residing in this city, and the same secrecy attended their movements. At a meeting held at the home of Dr. Julio Hanna, business calculated to further harass the Spanish government was transacted. It was that the initial steps were taken in the country towards a revolution in Porto Rico. If these plans and those formulated by the leaders on the island are carried out the first blow against Spain will be struck in a very short time. It may be but a few days before the people of Porto Rico, the only Spanish province in the West Indies which is not revolting against the mother country, will be in arms against Spain.

The leaders here declare that a vigorous declaration of independence has been prepared by the leaders of the Porto Rican Separatist party and that it is their intention to issue this as soon as they feel sure that they can defend themselves against any action Spain may take. One of the most prominent Porto Ricans in New York declared that this may be in less than a week. The declaration of independence was prepared on the island and at least one copy of it was sent to this city for the leaders to pass upon. They have given it their approval and have so informed the Separatist party in Porto Rico.

In starting this new revolution in Porto Rico, the leaders are fully carrying out the original plans of Gen. José Martí, the late leader of the Cuban revolution, which were to first get the Cuban insurrection well under way and then to encourage, or rather create, a similar uprising in Porto Rico. There were to be two separate revolutions, the army of each of the two provinces acting independently as far as possible, but necessarily in conjunction when a crisis was reached, but each striving for the same object, the defeat of Spain. If a victory should be won, it was arranged that the sister island should form entirely separate governments, the republic of Cuba and the republic of Porto Rico.

In formulating this plan, Gen. Martí consulted prominent Porto Ricans who are now in this city, one of whom corroborated the above statement last night. These men are among those who are arranging the present proposed coup. Cuba's cause and Porto Rico's cause, they say, are identical.

Source: Los Angeles Times, December 12, 1895, 3.

U.S. Resolution on the "Recognition of the Independence of Cuba" and the Teller Amendment

(1898)

The following resolution was passed in response to a message sent to Congress by William McKinley, U.S. president from 1897 to 1901, asking for permission to intervene in Cuba and go to war with Spain. The support of the United States was important to the rebels because they did not have a navy and needed supplies and food. At this time, the United States considered Cuba and Puerto Rico vital to its interests in the Caribbean and Central America—both would become staging areas for future intervention and the building and protection of the Panama Canal.

The fourth and final resolution presented in the following document is known as The Teller Resolution, named for its author, U.S. senator Henry M. Teller (1830–1914), a Democrat from Colorado, who, like many Americans, feared that the United States had imperial designs on Cuba and that the war was a pretext for grabbing more territory. His resolution specified that the United States would not establish permanent control over Cuba and disclaimed any intention of annexing the island. It was passed without opposition in Congress. However, after Spanish troops left the island in 1898, the United States occupied Cuba until 1902, after which Cuba, for all intents and purposes, became a U.S. protectorate.

JOINT Resolution for the recognition of the independence of the people of Cuba, demanding that the Government of Spain relinquish its authority and government in the Island of Cuba, and to withdraw its land and naval forces from Cuba and Cuban waters, and directing the President of the United States to use the land and naval forces of the United States to carry these resolutions into effect.

Whereas, the abhorrent conditions which have existed for more than three years in the Island of Cuba, so near our own borders, have shocked the moral sense of the people of the United States, have been a disgrace to Christian civilization, culminating, as they have, in the destruction of a United States battle-ship, with two hundred and sixty-six of its officers and crew, while on a friendly visit in the harbor of Havana, and can not longer be endured, as has been set forth by the President of the United States in his message to Congress of April eleventh, eighteen hundred and ninety-eight, upon which the action of Congress was invited: Therefore,

Resolved, by the Senate and House of Representatives of the United States of America in Congress assembled, First. That the people of the Island of Cuba are, and of right ought to be, free and independent.

Second. That it is the duty of the United States to demand, and the Government of the United States does hereby demand, that the Government of Spain at once relinquish its authority and government in the Island of Cuba, and withdraw its land and naval forces from Cuba and Cuban waters.

Third. That the President of the United States be, and he hereby is, directed and empowered to use the entire land and naval forces of the United States, and to call into the actual service of the United States, the militia of the several States, to such extent as may be necessary to carry these resolutions into effect.

Fourth. That the United States hereby disclaims any disposition or intention to exercise sovereignty, jurisdiction, or control over said Islands except for the pacification thereof, and asserts its determination, when that is accomplished, to leave the government and control of the Island to its people.

Approved, April 20, 1898.

Source: "Recognition of the Independence of Cuba, 1898." *American Historical Documents, 1000–1904.* Vol. XLIII. The Harvard Classics. New York: P. F. Collier & Son, 1909–1914. Bartleby.com, 2001. www.bartleby.com/43/.

The Occupation: The United States in the Caribbean and Central America

(1898–Present)

Diary of General Máximo Gómez

(January 8, 1899)

Máximo Gómez Baez (1836–1905) was born in Santo Domingo. A member of the Spanish armed forces, he supported and fought in Cuba's Ten Years' War from 1868 to 1878, which was the first major insurgency and the beginning of the wars for independence. He traveled to the United States, where he met Cuban reolutionaries. Gómez bristled at the attitude of superiority European Americans displayed toward Cubans. In the following excerpt from his diary, he decries the American occupation of Cuba, saying that it was too high a price to pay for the military aid that Cubans received from the United States in the last year of the war. He concludes that the European Americans turned the Cuban victory from a joyous occasion to a bitter experience. Cuban nationalists from this time forward would accuse the United States of imperialism rather than solidarity with Cubans and other Latin American nations.

The Americans' military occupation of the country is too high a price to pay for their spontaneous intervention in the war we waged against Spain for freedom and independence. The American government's attitude toward the heroic Cuban people at this history-making time is, in my opinion, one of big business. This situation is dangerous for the country, mortifying the public spirit and hindering organization in all of the branches that, from the outset, should provide solid foundations for the future republic, when everything was entirely the work of all the inhabitants of the island, without distinction of nationality.

Nothing is more rational and fair than that the owner of the house should be the one to live in it with his family and be the one who furnishes and decorates it as he likes and that he not be forced against his will and inclination to follow norms imposed by his neighbor.

All these considerations lead me to think that Cuba cannot have true moral peace—which is what the people need for their happiness and good fortune—under the transitional government. This transitional government was imposed by force by a foreign power and, therefore, is illegitimate and incompatible with the principles that the entire country has been upholding for so long and in the defense of which half of its sons have given their lives and all of its wealth has been consumed.

There is so much natural anger and grief throughout the island that the people haven't really been able to celebrate the triumph of the end of their former rulers' power.

They have left in sadness, and in sadness we have remained, because a foreign power has replaced them. I dreamed of peace with Spain; I hoped to bid farewell with respect to the brave Spanish soldiers with whom we always met, face to face, on the field of battle. The words peace and freedom should inspire only love and fraternity on the morning of concord between those who were combatants the night before; but, with their guardianship imposed by force, the Americans have turned the Cubans' victorious joy to bitterness and haven't sweetened the grief of the vanquished.

The situation that has been created for this people—one of material poverty and of grief because their sovereignty has been curbed—is ever more distressing. It is possible that, by the time this strange situation finally ends, the Americans will have snuffed out even the last spark of goodwill.

Source: Sierra, J. A. and History of Cuba.com. http://www.historyofcuba.com/history/gomez.htm.

Rudyard Kipling, "The White Man's Burden" (1899)

In February 1899, British novelist and poet Rudyard Kipling (1865–1936) wrote the poem "The White Man's Burden: The United States and The Philippine Islands." Like American poet Walt Whitman (1819–1892), who supported the War against Mexico and the acquisition of half its nation in the 1840s, Kipling laid the justification for U.S. imperialism on racial and moral superiority. "The White Man's Burden" was published in McClure's Magazine *in February 1899, at a pivotal point in the U.S. debate over imperialism after the Treaty of Paris (1898) had given the United States control of Puerto Rico and the Philippines. Kipling's poem urged the United States to take up the burden of "civilizing" the former Spanish colonies—a thankless task but a noble undertaking. Beginning in 1899, native Filipinos revolted against U.S. dominance and began an insurgency lasting into 1902. Most Latin Americans resented the notion that they had to be civilized and Christianized, pointing to the fact that most were Catholics, hence they already were Christians.*

THE WHITE MAN'S BURDEN

Take up the White Man's burden—
Send forth the best ye breed—
Go send your sons to exile
To serve your captives' need
To wait in heavy harness
On fluttered folk and wild—
Your new-caught, sullen peoples,
Half devil and half child.

Take up the White Man's burden
In patience to abide
To veil the threat of terror
And check the show of pride;
By open speech and simple
An hundred times made plain
To seek another's profit
And work another's gain. . . .

Take up the White Man's burden—
And reap his old reward:
The blame of those ye better
The hate of those ye guard—
The cry of hosts ye humour

(Ah slowly) to the light:
"Why brought ye us from bondage,
"Our loved Egyptian night?"...

Take up the White Man's burden—
Have done with childish days—
The lightly proffered laurel,
The easy, ungrudged praise.
Comes now, to search your manhood
Through all the thankless years,
Cold-edged with dear-bought wisdom,
The judgment of your peers!

Source: Kipling, Rudyard. "The White Man's Burden." *McClure's Magazine* 12 (February 1899).

"La Miseria: A Los Negros Puertorriqueños," a Letter from Ramón Romero Rosa to Black Puerto Ricans (March 27, 1901)

Ramón Romero Rosa (1863–1907), a Puerto Rican anarchist, was dedicated to organizing the working class. He was a printer, playwright, and agitator. He used the theater to teach workers to defend themselves against the power of the ruling class. Romero Rosa opposed the ideology of individualism popular in the years after the Spanish-American War and expressed a strong racial consciousness. For Romero Rosa, the recognition of African culture was essential. European traditions had been superimposed on Puerto Ricans, hiding the African essence. "La Miseria: A Los Negros Puertorriqueños" *(Misery: To the Black Puerto Ricans) was a pamphlet circulated in 1899 and published in 1901. In it, Romero Rosa says that "the children of Africa brought over to settle this untamed region, constituted our first working people after the conquest." It was as if the African heritage had come out of the closet. The following excerpt is in response to a proposal from a member of the Puerto Rican elite that encouraged the exportation of black Puerto Ricans while promoting white immigration.*

TO BLACK PUERTO RICANS: MISERY

You unfortunate martyrs have doubly suffered unjust exploitation at the hands of the white slave trader of all times and of all ages. . . . listen to the horrible sentence just dictated against you by a miserable man, who if his skin is clear, it is because his entrails are dark. My pen refuses to write his name, because the ink, as black as ebony, is ashamed to trace it. However, it is important that you know who he is . . . so you can spit on his face. His name is Don Ramón de Castro Rivera.

This miserable creature, who if he is Puerto Rican dishonors his own origin, has written to the Civil Governor, cynically telling him the importance of keeping emigration at a ratio of two thirds Blacks and mulattos and one third white, and not to permit the immigration of Blacks onto the island; that as many whites as possible be brought to the island from the United States, but not a single Black, since there are already many on the island and there should be an effort to get rid of them, since there is absolutely no need for them. Also, he advocates the fomenting of the emigration of Blacks to Ecuador since there are few and there will be no complaints of this emigration. Oh, unspeakable the shame of this miserable creature! That means, that the country's Blacks, those unfortunate workers who created the wealth of Puerto Rico, today THERE IS NO NEED FOR THEM AT ALL and you must get rid of them: How is this unfortunate race repaid for their good service. In what miserable conditions they have placed this people of virtuous and honest men who have only worked and worked to produce the gold which has been wasted by the vagabonds of this earth; the white who only have known how to handle the shameful whip of slavery and prostitution. We are not to become unraveled with insults that is not or ever will be how we behave: our minds are fresh and our hearts are honest. But we shall take our notes to the neurotic brain of this miserable being and at least remind him certain points of the history of Blacks in Puerto Rico.

Listen, Ramón de Castro Rivera, and also listen, white exploiters of the Borinquen country, the wealth that today you hold hidden, has been extracted from the blood of Blacks. Listen to those features in the history of slavery in Puerto Rico. Four centuries and eight years have gone by since the first day, in the name of Christianity, the Spain of Catholic Kings robbed the natives of their land. Maybe the immortal Colón did not imagine that his discovery would be the major cause of slavery and infamous cruelty for the Black race.

However, what happened after the discovery was a crime against humanity: the Borinquen Indians, not only were pulled from their collective way of life, they were completely exterminated by the sharp arrows and sharp blades of the scribes of the Catholic Kingdom and bourgeois aristocracy of the middle ages. All perversity is disguised with a benevolent end; and to that we repeat, in name of Christianity and European civilization the natives were expropriated of their own land and massacred. In the name of Christianity, the conquest legalized the usurpation by the expropriators of the Borinquen, and with another horrific crime substituted the fully exterminated natives. And now we get into history. It was the commercial trade of this unfortunate race from Africa, this race that today you are asking for its annulment in Puerto Rico, the ones that populated this region and were once free in their country and owned their own piece of land and who were taken by force by the cursed slave-traders, with their white faces, and a heart of darkness. European aristocracy committed this horrendous crime. Understand correctly, it was the sons of Africa, the unfortunate beings who were brought to colonize this Indian land, the first working people after the conquest. And we would fail Reason and Justice, if the richness and wealth produced in this land is denied . . . to all unfortunate workers, twice slaves of the tyrannical patronage and of the state. Even today there is a scarcity of white workers arriving in Puerto Rico. The haciendas, the factories, the fields, the shops, and in all that is practical and useful the majority are black hands.

Ramón de Castro Rivera's white hands are only used to maneuver the shameful whip and to [hoard] the wealth which was produced and continues to be produced with the sweat and blood of Blacks.

Now Ramón de Castro Rivera can see, as well as all the white bourgeoisie criminals, that with the blood and sweat of Blacks who they no longer need, made and fomented the making of all the wealth of the bourgeoisie expropriators of yesterday and the [hoarding] bourgeoisie of today.

Miserable human being! You should kiss the Black hand that has been the source of inexhaustible richness, instead you lash out with those horrible words that so degrade us and enrage us.

Those of you who have a conscience and know civics, answer: what has been the rewards for blacks for their labor, either today or in the past?

Absolutely none! If we are to talk of those tragic and horrific times of marketing human flesh; if we are to speak of those inquisitional acts, in which the poor Black man, wearing nothing, but a pair of light shorts, with their ebony-color backs exposed to the elements of nature, having the hot sun rays reverberating of their backs, and subjugated by the infamous whip, was forced to perform in inhuman labor conditions; if we are to remember the crimes committed against Blacks who were not to lift their face to face the punisher, boss, manager, patron because it would make his blood boil and maybe even seek revenge.

Yesterday Anduza, another miserable creature like many other whites, requested the whip . . . for Puerto Rico, today Ramón de Castro Rivera requests the governor to get all Blacks out of the country, because they are no longer needed! What depravity have we reached! Maybe Anduza, as Castro Rivera, and all the white criminals, enslavers of Blacks, do not remember that their elders and maybe even themselves while taking all the wealth and delighting themselves in orgies, also prostituted black women, then sold their own children to the human trade. Blacks lived in dirty quarters and were forced to eat roots and fungi. To add to the vast inequity, basic education was denied to the Black people. And as a sublime rewarding law, a venerable black teacher, Rafael Cordero taught a group of white children who became luminaries in science and humanities.

Black Puerto Ricans know that yesterday Anduza requested the whip law and today Castro Rivera asserts that Black Puerto Ricans are no longer needed. Blacks must not emigrate: Puerto Rico belongs to them. Let the thieves emigrate. Comrades, defend yourselves!

Source: Sources for the Study of Puerto Rican Migration, 1879–1930. History Task Force/Centro de Estudios Puertorriqueños Research Foundation of the City University of New York, 1982, 30–33. Translated by Guadalupe Compeán.

Platt Amendment
(1903)

The Platt Amendment was a rider to the Army Appropriations Act, passed on March 2, 1901, that—for all intents and purposes—made Cuba a vassal of the United States. The United States would not evacuate its forces until Cuba stipulated that Cuba would not make a treaty or enter into debt with a foreign nation without the approval of the United States. Connecticut Republican senator Orville H. Platt (1827–1905) offered the amendment, which was similar to the Teller Amendment in the 1898 U.S. resolution on the Recognition of the Independence of Cuba, in which the United State resolved to go to war with Spain over Cuba. Like the Teller Amendment, the Platt Amendment said that the United States had no intention of annexing Cuba and would leave the country in the hands of the Cuban people. A critical difference between both amendments is that the Platt Amendment forced Cuba to lease Guantánamo Bay to the United States in perpetuity and gave the United States the right to intervene in Cuban affairs.

Article I. The Government of Cuba shall never enter into any treaty or other compact with any foreign power or powers which will impair or tend to impair the independence of Cuba, nor in any manner authorize or permit any foreign power or powers to obtain by colonization or for military or naval purposes, or otherwise, lodgment in or control over any portion of said island.

Article II. The Government of Cuba shall not assume or contract any public debt to pay the interest upon which, and to make reasonable sinking-fund provision for the ultimate discharge of which, the ordinary revenues of the Island of Cuba, after defraying the current expenses of the Government, shall be inadequate.

Article III. The Government of Cuba consents that the United States may exercise the right to intervene for the preservation of Cuban independence, the maintenance of a government adequate for the protection of life, property, and individual liberty, and for discharging the obligations with respect to Cuba imposed by the Treaty of Paris on the United States, now to be assumed and undertaken by the Government of Cuba. . . .

Article V. The Government of Cuba will execute, and, as far as necessary, extend the plans already devised, or other plans to be mutually agreed upon, for the sanitation of the cities of the island, to the end that a recurrence of epidemic and infectious diseases may be prevented, thereby assuring protection to the people and commerce of Cuba, as well as to the commerce of the Southern ports of the United States and the people residing therein. . . .

Article VII. To enable the United States to maintain the independence of Cuba, and to protect the people thereof, as well as for its own defense, the Government of Cuba will sell or lease to the United States lands necessary for coaling or naval stations, at certain specified points, to be agreed upon with the President of the United States.

Source: Treaty Between the United States and the Republic of Cuba Embodying the Provisions Defining Their Future Relations as Contained in the Act of Congress Approved March 2, 1901, signed 05/22/1903; General Records of the United States Government, 1778–2006, RG 11, National Archives.

"Porto Rican Labor for Panama Canal," Letter to the Editor of the *New York Times* (1904)

Puerto Ricans continued their diaspora after the U.S. occupation. Predictably, U.S. industry followed the flag, and the presence of U.S. corporations accelerated the commercialization of land and the uprooting of the small subsistence farmers. These displaced Puerto Ricans migrated to the cities, where there was limited work. At the same time, employment contractors heavily recruited Puerto Rican labor to work in Mexico, Hawaii, California, and Panama. The following letter to the editor of The New York Times *responds to the constant harping of American officials and citizens that Puerto Ricans should be grateful to the United States for liberating them and suggests that the people of Puerto Rico were in better financial condition under Spanish rule than U.S. occupation.*

PORTO RICAN LABOR FOR PANAMA CANAL

To the Editor of the New York Times:

The suggestion made to employ Porto Ricans for work on the Panama Canal has so much to recommend it that it is to be hoped that it will receive the consideration it merits.

Up to date the people of Porto Rico have little to be grateful for to the people of the United States. Having ceased to be Spaniards they expected to become Americans, yet this has not been granted to them.

The island appears to be less prosperous now than it was under the Spanish flag, and it would seem to be a duty to assist its people in every way possible. It is to our own interest to give employment to these people, as they will doubtless return with their earnings, in part at least, so that this money will serve to help develop our "Island Paradise." All things being equal, preference should be given to those under our own flag.

Source: New York Times, December 30, 1904, 8.

New York Times, "Taft to Porto Ricans" (1907)

In 1907, while visiting Puerto Rico, U.S. secretary of war William Howard Taft (1857–1830), who would later become president of the United States from 1909 to 1913, told the Puerto Rican people that they should be grateful to be a part of the United States. This remark was made in response to the chief justice of Puerto Rico's statement that it was his hope that Puerto Rican children would someday be American citizens—which at that time they were not. Taft replied that Puerto Ricans should be grateful that they had free trade with the United States but begged the question of citizenship, which he said should be left up to Congress. This was a thorny issue. The status of Puerto Ricans was left in the air. They were part of the United States but lacked the rights of American citizens. It was little consolation to have unlimited access to U.S. markets because those same markets were commercializing agriculture and driving Puerto Ricans from the island.

TAFT TO PORTO RICANS

Tells Them Difficulties Stand in Way of American Citizenship

SAN JUAN, Porto Rico, April 15—Secretary of War Taft, who arrived here yesterday on board the Government yacht Mayflower, spent the day in consultation with various heads of departments inquiring minutely as to details in an effort to ascertain the reasons for the grievances of the people. Among others, he conferred with Surgeon General Robert M. O'Reilly relative to the building now being used as a military hospital.

The Supreme Court and the Executive Council entertained the Secretary at luncheon. In a speech of welcome Chief Justice Quinones expressed the hope that the Porto Rican children now growing up would receive from the United States the great honor of American citizenship.

Secretary Taft made a brief reply, in which he said Porto Rico was free from many of the difficulties existing in the Philippines and Cuba, and he called attention to the fact that trade with the United States had brought prosperity and contentment to the island. Referring to citizenship, he said:

"I beg of you to think of those things which you do have; let me call your attention to them. You have what is desired by the Philippines and Cuba, namely, the unsurpassed markets of the United States. What I am saying is not intended to oppose citizenship, but there are difficulties in the way of securing the passage of such laws through Congress."

Source: New York Times, April 16, 1907, 5.

Luisa Capetillo, Letter on Women's Roles to Dr. Paul Vigne (1910)

Puerto Rican feminist Luisa Capetillo (1879–1922) was a committed anarchist and activist. Capetillo's book Mi opinión acerca de las libertades, derechos y deberes de la mujer *(My Opinion about the Liberties, Rights and Duties of Women) was published in 1911 and reprinted in 1913. Capetillo, born out of wedlock in the northern town of Arecibo, Puerto Rico, on October 28, 1879, to working-class parents, rebelled by wearing trousers. She was highly political and tied the misery of Puerto Ricans to low pay and poor working conditions. She championed workers' rights, especially the right to livable wages, and was an early advocate of gender rights. In the following letter, she discusses the role of women historically, particularly with regard to women entering the field of medicine as physicians.*

(From L'Avenir Médical of Paris)

The legislative elections, which have just been held, have not been favorable to feminism. One or another female candidate has run, but none has been able to sustain a true struggle until the end.

But this doesn't mean despair for those apostles of women's causes. All countries will continue to heed their aspirations, either under a timid veneer as in France, or in tumultuous abundance, as in England or in the Americas.

In fact, the feminist cause has had many important partisans among the strong sex. In 1877, Victor Hugo heatedly defended feminism in a letter to Leon Richer: "Women," wrote the poet, "are seen as lesser beings civically and as slaves, morally. Her [woman's] upbringing suffers from this double sense of inferiority; and from this all the suffering that man inflicts on her, which is unjust. Men have tipped the scales of the law, in whose equilibrium human consciousness is invested, putting all of the rights on their own little plates, and all the duties on the woman's. From this, the profound upheaval, from this, the slavery of woman. We need reform and this reform will be achieved for the benefit of civilization, of society, of light." The eminent philosopher, John Stuart Mill has written: "All of the egotistical inclinations, the cult of oneself, the injustice of self preference that dominates humanity, has its origin and roots in the way that current relations between men and women take place, and it is from these relations that such egotisms derive their principal force. Consider the vanity of the young man who when he becomes a man, is convinced that, without merit, without having done a thing on his own, and even if he is among the most frivolous and incapable of men, just by having been born a man, feels that he is superior to half of humanity without exception, when in that half one can find people whose superiority is capable of weighing over him every day and at every moment. By giving women the freedom to use their faculties, letting them freely choose the manner in which they want to exercise those faculties, by opening up the same work opportunities, and offering the same stimuli as those available to men, one of the principle benefits of such an endeavor would be to duplicate the total of intellectual faculties that humanity would have at its service."

But perhaps we should not follow these authors so far along this road, and instead, to return to what concerns our profession. We can agree that various women have undertaken this profession with great success.

Even in remote times, we have seen woman become interested in our art. In France, Diana of Poitiers and Marguerite of Valois are known for having practiced the art of medicine from antiquity.

Madame Necker, wife of the renowned minister of Louis XVI, was responsible for the reorganization of French hospitals.

In Germany, women doctors were numerous during the Middle [A]ges, and even more so in the fourteenth and fifteenth centuries.

And in our times there are many women who have devoted themselves to medicine. Miss Elisabeth Blackwell, who had been a primary school teacher, is the first in the United States to become a doctor, at Boston University in 1847, also having studied in Geneva and Paris. Only eight years after Boston, the University of Philadelphia began to admit women to medical school, and this example was quickly imitated by other universities. In 1874, for the first time, Madame Putnam-Jacobi became a professor at Mount Sinai's teaching hospital. Later, there have been women doctors in the Army and one could cite the example of Madame MacGee, who was appointed military surgeon in Puerto Rico, with the rank of lieutenant. Miss María Walcher had a similar position in the Union Army during the Civil War.

Without trying to make this brief analysis something more extensive, and even if we didn't recognize that women have the same aptitude as men to undertake study as arduous as that of medicine, we can safely conclude from the previously cited examples, that women, by force of will and energy, are quite capable of doing certain jobs that they previously had been denied. This theory is constantly disputed by those who claim women's inferiority due to sexual difference, which, it is said, seems to be an immutable law of nature. But there is nothing more false than to attempt in this way to uphold the permanent superiority of men. There are numerous animal species for whom this rule has been broken. Elephants, for example, when they migrate and are about to cross into rough terrain, send the females ahead, because they are considered more apt to find the safest road.

Among birds it is often the female that is dominant in the couple. The female sparrow is not bashful about harshly reprimanding the male; and the female tosses the male sparrow out of the nest when there isn't sufficient food for the both of them. The female pigeon makes the male sit on the eggs and guard the nest from ten to four every day, while she goes off and gets some fresh air.

Among birds of prey, the female is more ferocious than the male, a fact that is well known to falconers, who prefer the females. She is so unaffectionate that, when made prisoner, she will kill her male companion.

Even among insects, a husband's fate is frequently of a most humiliating nature. The queen bee has many suitors. Forced to dash after her, the most agile male catches up with her and is accepted; but the joy of this husband is ephemeral because of course he dies. The destiny of the rivals he overcame is more enticing. These well-fed and non-working bees take on the leisurely pace of a lord, but then one fine morning, the female worker bees realize that they are feeding lazy and useless beings, and massacre the males.

But the true epitome of female triumph in the animal realm is reached in the spider. In this species, the female is much heavier and much stronger than the male, which is why the male is reduced to slavery, immediately and until the moment of fertilization. Once mating is finished and there is no more need for his services, he is simply devoured.

An elegant solution to conjugal problems! But we trust that the amiable members of the female sex have yet tended toward such a solution, in spite of overwhelming us everywhere with their vindications, and in spite of the fact that they already greet in the figure of a liberated Eve—according to the phrase coined by Miss Odette Laguerre—the engenderer of a more worthy humanity.

Source: "Doctor Paul Vigne, Paris, 1910" is reprinted with permission of the publisher of Luisa Capetillo's *A Nation of Women: An Early Feminist Speaks Out*, edited by Felix V. Natos Rodriguez, translated by Alan West-Duran. Houston: Arte Público Press–University of Houston, 2005. 42–45.

Luisa Capetillo, Letter on Socialism to Manuel Ugarte (1911)

Puerto Rican feminist Luisa Capetillo (1879–1922) was a committed anarchist and activist. In addition to her focus on gender issues, she was involved in the political and labor struggles of the working class. She condemned the exploitation of workers by political parties, religious institutions, and capitalism. In this letter to Argentine writer Manual Ugarte (1878–1951), Capetillo defines the kind of socialist she was in the following letter.

I am a socialist because I want all the advances, discoveries, and inventions to belong to everyone, that their socialization be achieved without privilege. Some understand this to mean that the State regulate this socialization, I see it without government. That does not mean that I will oppose a government that regulates and controls wealth, as it needs to do, but I maintain my position in being decidedly against government per se: Socialist anarchism.

What I solemnly declare here is that to be a socialist it is necessary to have analyzed and understood psychology.

It is a mistake to think oneself as a socialist and accept the fanatical dogmas, rites, and practices of religion because Socialism is truth and imposed religions are erroneous.

Equally wrong is to think oneself a socialist and be an atheist, a skeptic, and a materialist. Socialism is not a negation, nor violence, nor a utopia. It is a real and tangible truth. Under socialism there isn't room for the cunning (no!) to live comfortably from the work of others. There is no deceit, nor the imposition or imperialism over the weak or ignorant. Socialism persuades with truth, it does not wound. In socialism we find pure reason, the harmony between all, sweetness of demeanor, equality in everything. It is truth not lies, sincerity not intrigue. Now I have said sweetness of demeanor, isn't that what religions preach? Let us analyze this further. Reason is a straight path, serene, peaceful, and impassive. Jesus was a rationalist. A person whose norms follow reason does not violate himself, does not run away, does not make fun of nor express joy at the evil of his enemy or adversary.

So a reasonable person does not have enemies, and should he have them he does not hate them. What are the results of this? If they are insulted or struck by a hand, or with hurtful remarks, and respond in kind, what do they get out of it? (I cannot accept that someone be struck or mistreated without motive). Well, you'll say, what about getting even, vengeance? But reason is serene, self-controlled, it is not vengeful or injurious, and a socialist, for the good and emancipation of humankind should be reasonable. Whoever has reason is in control of themselves, and is not the instrument of vengeance and its consequences: crime, violence, and all sorts of brutal passions.

Socialism is found within the luminous Christianity that shook the foundations of Roman power, because of its notion of fraternity. And universal brotherhood will be the implementation of socialism, which is selflessness, sweetness, modesty, temperance: "All for one and one for all." These are sure steps that lead us to human perfection, toward the freedom and the still undefined spiritual progress of a plurality of superior worlds.

Let us enlighten and purify ourselves, let us educate our wills to do good, and let us consume the fire of our passions under guiding reason, in an offering to human emancipation to achieve spiritual progress.

Source: "My Profession of Faith to Manuel Ugarte" is reprinted with permission of the publisher of Luisa Capetillo's *A Nation of Women: An Early Feminist Speaks Out*, edited by Felix V. Natos Rodriguez, translated by Alan West-Duran. Houston: Arte Público Press–University of Houston, 2005, 110–111.

# of Mexican Immigration to the United States

New York Times, "Opening Up Mexico" (1881)

In the early 1880s, the Mexican Central Railroad linked the center of Mexico to the United States, facilitating the U.S. exploitation of Mexico's natural resources and physically binding the two countries. The railroads paid peasants considerably more than they made on haciendas. Hence, the pull of the Mexican Central Railroad uprooted thousands, and eventually millions, of Mexican workers. The railroad also commercialized much of the nation's agriculture, encouraging the encroachment of large owners on peasant and communal farms. The railroads were crucial in forging the modern Mexican nation, setting the stage for the Mexican Revolution of 1910 and the development of the Southwest, which way built by Mexican labor. The following New York Times *article is on the building of the Mexican Central Railroad and its importance in economically exploiting Mexico.*

Luisa Capetillo It looks as though a new era was about to dawn for the Republic of Mexico. Until recent years it has been so disturbed by internal convulsions and external complications that it has failed to make the progress of which its situation and natural resources give promise. For a long time it had good reason for being distrustful of the United States; it could hope for no stimulus from its neighbors to the south, and European intrusion was justly regarded with suspicion and dread. Thus, isolated and impoverished by her struggles, Mexico has remained undeveloped and unprogressive, while the country to the north of her has been growing in wealth and prosperity. Latterly the barriers have been falling, especially those that prevented Mexico from sympathizing with and sharing in the advancement of her northern neighbor. The United States has no longer its old motive for encroachment, and Mexico has not its old reason for fearing the consequences of closer relations, and both are beginning to see that such relations might be made mutually profitable and helpful.

Mexico awakens to a desire for commercial and industrial activity and growth to find herself without lines of communication, without capital, and without any organization of her labor forces. The most that she can do to promote her own advancement is to open her doors to the enterprise of others, invite capital in to arouse her labor forces to activity, and give fair guarantees of profit to the undertakings which are to develop her industrial energies. The republic has no large navigable rivers which as natural highways do so much to promote the development of new countries. Its territory is compact, and rising from either coast to the plateaus of the Cordilleras, enjoys every variety of climate, soil, and production. Its harbor facilities are ample, but they are not connected with the regions of the interior in which there are so many elements of natural wealth. Railroads are the necessary instrumentality of her industrial and commercial growth. Without them she is nothing, and she has not the means of building them. She has shown evidence of appreciating her needs in the liberal charters which she has lately granted, especially to capitalists of this country. Since the reestablishment of the republic in 1867, one hundred and one acts have been passed by its Congress or initiated by the President under general legislative sanction for the encouragement of railroad construction. The various charters, agreements, and contracts represent 14,530 miles of road, for which subsidies amounting to over $171,000,000 were granted. Many of the contracts and concessions were made to the Governors of States for local lines of communication. Some charters have expired by limitation; some have been forfeited for one cause or another, and others will doubtless lapse, but there are several very substantial schemes on foot to which $69,000,000 in subsidies have been promised.

The most important of the Mexican railroad enterprises, and those of which most has been heard, are the Mexican Central, that of the Mexican Construction Company, the Sonora, the Mexican Southern, and the Tehuantepec Interocean Railroad. The first of these has recently been made familiar to our readers. It is in the hands of Boston capitalists concerned in the Atchison, Topeka, and Santa Fé system of communication, which will bring it into connection with the diverging lines eastward from Kansas City. The main line of the Mexican Central is more than a thousand miles in length, connecting the capital of Mexico with El Paso on the northern border. There it will not only have the eastern outlet already mentioned into our great railroad system, but will be brought into immediate connection with that of the Pacific coast. It has a large subsidy secured by a pledge of Customs revenue and liberal privileges, and work upon it is already going on with great energy. Its two branches diverging from the main stem near Leon will traverse the country north of the capital to either coast. The Sonora line is being constructed in the same interest, and will traverse a rich territory from the Gulf of California to Arizona. Both the Central and the Sonora are organized under Massachusetts law. The Mexican Construction Company is operating under the Sullivan and Palmer grant. It was a line from the City of Mexico to the Pacific at Manzanill[o], further to the south than that of the Central Company, and one from the same city to the Rio Grande at Laredo, where it will connect through Texas with our Southern system. The two lines include over 1,200 miles of length and are liberally subsidized. The Mexican Southern has been seeking a charter from this State. It is intended to cross the country from Anton Lizardo on the Gulf of Huatalco on the Pacific, with connections to Vera Cruz and Mexico on the one side and Tehuantepec on the other. Its line is over 500 miles, and it has a subsidy of $8,000 per kilometre. The Tehuantepec Interocean Railroad is under construction, and its main object is to form a connecting link for the commerce of the two oceans. These schemes are active and promising and will of themselves give Mexico a system of communication, which will stimulate development and set in motion the forces that are to regenerate that country. In a few years results may be looked for, and it will be surprising if Mexico does not enter upon a career of commercial and industrial growth in sharp contrast with her past lethargy.

Source: New York Times, March 8, 1881, 4.

Maud Mason Austin, "Teresa Urrea" (1896)

Teresa de Urrea (1873–1906) was known as la Niña de Cabora, Santa Teresa, Teresita, and La Santa. Her fame spread throughout northern Mexico and the southwestern United States. People would travel hundreds of miles to be healed by Teresa, who they believed performed miracles. For others, she held out hope that their redemption was near and that she would bring about a revolution. Born on October 15, 1873, in Sinaloa, Mexico, she was the natural child of Tomás Urrea and Cayetana Chávez. As a child, she moved to Cabora, Sonora, where she lived with her father on his hacienda. In her teens, Teresa had a seizure and fell into a coma for three months and 18 days. When she woke up, many considered it a sign that she was blessed. As word spread, thousands of pilgrims traveled to Cabora to visit La Santa. At the time, the end of the millennium was approaching, and many awaited the end of the world; this inspired millenarian movements that included Yaquis, Tarahumara, and villagers from as far away as Tomochic, Chihuahua. Because of her notoriety and the government's fear of her, Teresa and her father were forced to leave Sonora in 1892, taking refuge in the Nogales, Arizona, area. Within three years, they moved to Solomonville, Arizona, and then to El Paso, Texas. As revolutionists increased activity within Mexico and along the border, Mexican president Porfirio Díaz blamed Teresa. She moved away from the border to Clifton, Arizona, where rumors continued to circulate that she was going to head a revolution against Díaz. The president sent an agent to Clifton to spy on her. He wormed his way into her confidence and married her. Once they were married he tried to force her to return to Mexico where she would have been subject to Mexican authority. When she refused to return to Mexico, he shot her. This resulted in his arrest. Teresa continued to live in Clifton until she died in 1906. The following is an article describing her faith healings in the United States.

TERESA URREA

The Unlettered Mexican Girl who Claims to Heal the Sick.

(CONTRIBUTED TO THE *TIMES*.)

If, as Carlyle says, "matter exists only spiritually and to represent some idea, and body it forth," then Teresa Urrea the saint of Cabora, embodies charity, love, self-abnegation and all those cardinal virtues which pulpit orators bepraise. This picturesque "maravillosa sanadora," believing that all aspirations should be utilitarian in their scheme and show forth God's harmonies regardless of man's creeds, moves among her horde of afflicted devotees, giving with a touch and a smile great cheer to the sorrowing.

TERESA'S METHODS

She is an unlearned Mexican girl, born and bred in an isolated hacienda, in Sonora, where no hint of odylic force uses—which "from female finger-tips burnt blue"—could ever have reached her for imitation. She never could have heard of Gassner's strokes with the hand or of Franz Anton Mesmer, yet her method is theirs. She has had no education, so she cannot have read Deleuze, or Mayo, or Teste or Carpenter. Her chirography has been acquired, as she naively explains, with a piece of charcoal upon a board, yet she is associate editor of El Independiente a creditable weekly published in El Paso. . . . Tomochic are Mexicans, not Tarahumar[a]s—impelled by oppression and poverty, fanaticism and defiance, perhaps would have needed, even less than this girlish idol, to precipitate the horrors of Tomochic and San Tomas.

When 18 years of age, Teresita lay in a trance for three months. In this comatose state she began denouncing sectarianism and performing her wonderful curses—which her family, being, at that time, orthodox people, looked upon with small sympathy. It was in the succeeding year, when her fame was already abroad and the people coming to her from within 400 miles thereabouts by wagon, that Gov. Carrillo of Chihuahua, came to the little mountain pueblo of Tomochic to remove certain famous paintings from the church. These paintings were presumably by Murillo and very dear to the pride and hearts of the people. When the canvases were cut—the frames were imbedded in the walls—the people protested, defying the Governor and the jefe politico in defense of their altars. Carillo returned empty-handed and indignant, leaving some ill-will behind him.

This was in August 1891. The following December, Padre Manuel Gastelum came from Urnachic to preach to the Tomochitecos, and denounced Teresa from the pulpit as a heretic and evil-worker. But the people were sullen and only praised her good works. Much incensed, the good padre betook himself to Guerrero in high dudgeon and notified the authorities that the Tomochitecos were in revolt.

How meets Mexico any uprising or massing, political, ecclesiastical or incidental? Soldiers were sent at once from Guerrero. Thirty Tomochitecos, rudely armed, resisted them, but were routed and all prisoners shot. Having registered a vow that they would appeal to Teresa Urrea—now a sort of saint and prophetess by virtue of her fame and their superstitions—they repaired to Cabora, a pueblo on the Urrea estate. The girl's father, Tomas Urrea, an intelligent and comely Mexican, denies that the girl further inflamed them or led them. He characterizes the trouble as persecution and the government's well-known distrust of the populacho. But the troops fell upon all, and riot, incendiarism, and bloodshed followed. Women and children were shamelessly butchered and Tomochic burnt. Before this was accomplished, however, fifty-eight valiant rebels killed 580 pelon[e]s—soldiers—in one encounter, and it is not to be wondered at that Diaz laid his sword upon these poor creatures maddened by previous wrongs and oppressions. They fought not like men, but demons, shouting the names of Maria Santisima and Teresa until they were exterminated. 'Tis no wonder the soldiers dubbed them "tigres de la Sierra."

TERESA'S BANISHMENT

The Urrea family, abandoning large landed property, under pronounciamentos, escaped into Arizona; and Santa Teresa, her name still a talisman recklessly flaunted by the defiant Mexicans, innocently bore the responsibility of being a "leader of insurrections" in their campaigns.

This gentle girl could never have reveled in bloodshed. Expatriated, but undaunted, she finds on the American side of the Rio Grande at El Paso no armed opposition to her creed—which seems to be: Be good, and love. She leaves science to the wise, theories to investigators, pelf to the avaricious. Her surroundings are poor beyond compare. She sleeps upon a bed woven of raw-hide. When, if she chose, she could coin "pesos."

It may count for one's eternal salvation to wear one's skin away on bare boards like Wesley, but good workers seem to me more efficacious; and I see no difference between his self-torture and the crucifratres. He it was, too, who said: "A string of opinions is no more Christian faith than a string of beads is Christian holiness." Because Teresa Urrea is not orthodox—what freedom of thought was ever orthodox?—need we scoff at her honesty? And because she believes like Kardec—but in her own words that "God is a spirit and we a spark of Him, hence needing no mediations"—need we denounce her into a calabash, like the Kalmucks, and wait for the wind to turn them. Are texts to be used only as pretexts, constraining us to believe that "there is nothing true but doubt," and then to even doubt this? Such finished pyrrhonism in pulpit rationale threatens to have religion enveloped in hypotheses and God vanishing in mist; but the most callous is touched by the honest self-sacrifice which will thus serve the repulsively poor and afflicted.

Teresa Urrea does not profess to work miracles, neither is she attempting—as the malicious declare—to raise the dead and insurrections. But she nestles a suffering infant into her tender arms and hushes it; strokes the throbbing temples of the aged; feeds the hungry, and lays her pretty magnetic hands upon aching and distorted limbs, smiling into sad eyes in so truly saint-like a way as touches the unregenerate heart into respect and reverence such as must have brooded over the multitude about the shores of Galilee.

Somehow as I look at her wretched court the thought will come to me likening the poor hard herd about this earnest soul into animals gathering from the outskirts of civilization and returning home wearied but comforted to their several lairs.

It is only a little span here at best. Who dares to impugn or retard one infinitesimal movement toward.

O Heaven, whither? Sense knows not; Faith knows not; only that it is through Mystery to Mystery.

From God and to God

Source: Los Angeles Times, August 23, 1896, 18.

In re Ricardo Rodríguez
(1897)

From the beginning of the nation's existence, the question of race has been very important in the United States, setting the standard for who was considered an American. White Americans had similar racial attitudes toward Mexicans as they had toward Africans and Native Americans. They were looked upon as half-breeds— a mixture of races—as most Mexicans had Indian blood and some Spanish and African lineage. This became a problem when half of Mexico's territory was incorporated into the United States and Mexico insisted that its former citizens have the right of U.S. citizenship. By inference, the Treaty of Guadalupe Hidalgo (1848) made Mexicans white because without this status they could not be equal to U.S. citizens or immigrate to the United States. In 1897, Ricardo Rodríguez, who had been born in Mexico, applied for citizenship and was denied the right because immigration authorities said he was an Indian. Rodríguez had lived in Texas for 10 years. Federal attorneys argued against his eligibility on the grounds that Rodríguez was "not a white person, not an African, nor of African descent." U.S. district judge Thomas Maxey held that because Rodríguez knew "nothing of the Aztecs or Toltecs," he was not an Indian and thus had the right to become a naturalized citizen. The excerpt below is from Judge Maxey's convoluted ruling.

OPINION

. . . After a careful and patient investigation of the question discussed, the court is of opinion that, whatever may be the status of the applicant viewed solely from the standpoint of the ethnologist, he is embraced within the spirit and intent of our laws upon naturalization, and his application should be granted if he is shown by the testimony to be a man attached to the principles of the constitution, and well disposed to the good order and happiness of the same. It is suggested that the proof fails in this respect; and the objection appears to be based upon the ground, intimated in the briefs, of his inability to understand or explain those principles. That the applicant is lamentably ignorant is conceded, and that he is unable to read and write the testimony clearly discloses. Naturally enough, his untrained mind is found deficient in the power to elucidate or define the principles of the Constitution. But the testimony also discloses that he is a very good man, peaceable and industrious, of good moral character, and law abiding "to a remarkable degree." And hence it may be said of him, notwithstanding his inability to undergo an examination on questions of constitutional law, that by his daily walk, during a residence of 10 years in the city of San Antonio, he has practically illustrated and emphasized his attachment to the principles of the Constitution. Congress has not seen fit to require of applicants for naturalization an educational qualification, and courts should be careful to avoid judicial legislation. In the judgment of the court, the applicant possesses the requisite qualifications for citizenship, and his application will therefore be granted.

Source: District Court, W. D. Texas 81 F. 337; 1897 U.S. Dist. LEXIS 50, May 3, 1897.

Mariano Martínez, "Arizona Americans," Letter to the Editor of the *New York Times* (1904)

This is an eloquent letter to The New York Times *from Mariano Martínez, a Mexican American in Arizona, in response to editorials written by the paper essentially condoning the vigilantism of a mob that had taken the law into its own hands and broke into Mexican homes abducting the lawfully adopted white babies. This unlawful act was then given de facto approval by authorities in Clifton-Morenci, Arizona. Martínez defended the Mexican race, asking who was an American? He questioned the* Times's *definition of what an American was; many Mexicans in Arizona had been born there and voted. Was being an American based on color? Martínez was tired of the superior attitude of recent white immigrants whose time in the United States could not match that of many Mexicans who had been in Arizona for generations.*

To the Editor of *The New York Times*:

I have read carefully your editorial about the experience of the Sisters of the New York Foundling Asylum who endeavored to place their charges in Mexican families in Arizona.

I believe that you, being a true American, love truth and justice above everything, and therefore I desire to inform you that the Mexican families to whom these children were to be given were carefully selected before the American children arrived, both from a moral and from a financial point of view. The priest did his duty without race prejudice. He read the circular about the distribution and conditions of those orphans, both in English and Spanish. The Mexicans applied and complied with the requirements for the adoption of the American children. The English-speaking population was indifferent. Nearly all of the Mexican families referred to own their own farms, ranches, cattle, &c. and are better able financially to take care of themselves than the "Americans of Arizona." The heads of these Mexican families and their children were born and raised in Arizona under the American flag. They are able to write and speak both the Spanish and English languages, and they do not butcher it as do your so-called "Arizona Americans," who are composed of Swedes, Norwegians, Serbians, Canadians, and Dutch, who have been shipped from the old country to work our mines and make out of this portion of the United States a dumping ground. The majority of the "Arizona Americans" are not even entitled to cast a vote because they have not been in this country long enough. Probably the only claim you have to call them "Americans" is that they have blue eyes, red hair, a face full of freckles, and long feet. The "low-down" Mexicans whom you refer to [we didn't by the way] are nearly all native-born American citizens and voters, as the great register of Graham County will prove. They have absolute respect for law and order. They know that the United States has laws which must be respected, and that it is strong and able to enforce them, without having to resort to mob violence, like your so-called "Arizona Americans."

My parents were born in this Territory. I was born and raised in Tucson, Arizona. I was educated in the public schools, and I always considered myself an American, though of Mexican parents. Since I have read your editorial about the assault on the Sisters by the mobs of Clifton and Morenci, I have been wondering whether I have a right to call myself an American citizen and to vote the Democratic ticket next November or not. The heads of the Mexican families you refer to are in the same position as myself.

Source: New York Times, October 31, 1904, 8.

New York Times, "Big Man Hunt in Texas" (1901)

The Texas Rangers continued to unjustly persecute the Mexican population of South Texas into the 20th century. At the turn of the century, the hunt for an alleged horse rustler, Gregorio Cortez (1875–1916), polarized Mexicans and white Americans. In 1901, a sheriff mistakenly accused Cortez and his brother of stealing a horse. When the sheriff shot Cortez's brother, Gregorio shot the sheriff, and a huge manhunt followed. It seemed as if the whole state of Texas was chasing Cortez. During this period, Cortez's wife and children were incarcerated and his friends were harassed. He was finally caught and convicted after several trials. Cortez was lionized by Mexican balladeers. The following article reports on the hunt for Gregorio Cortez.

AUSTIN, June 17—The killing of Sheriff Robert M. Glover of Gonzales County, Sheriff W. T. Morris of Karnes County, and "Tony" Schnabel, a well-known ranchman, by Mexicans, during the last few days, has aroused the authorities of every county in Southwest Texas, and large posses of determined men, headed by the Sheriffs of Travis, Hays, Bee, Bexar, Falls, Bastrop, Kerr, Kendall, Star, Atascosa, Webb, and several other counties are hunting for the guilty men. Mayor Emmett White of Austin is in the field with a large body of men. Gov. Sayers to-day directed a detachment of the State Rangers to join in the pursuit, and altogether there are probably 500 men searching for the Mexican fugitives.

This big man hunt has excited the Mexican population of Southwest Texas, and hundreds are leaving their homes on the farms and ranches and flocking into the towns for protection. As fast as they arrive, they are disarmed by the police and placed under guard. Every Mexican home in town and country is being searched for some clue that will lead to the capture of the men who committed the recent murders. The leaders of this band is known to be Gregorio Cortez, and it is said that he has with him a dozen or more Mexicans who will fight to the last should there be an effort made to capture them.

Cortez's home is a short distance south of Austin, and that locality is being watched by Mayor White and his posse. They believe that Cortez will make his way to his home, and his presence there is expected any time. Gov. Sayers has taken every precaution to protect the Mexicans from mob violence when they are captured.

Source: New York Times, June 18, 1901, 1.

Anonymous, *"El Corrido de Gregorio Cortez"* (ca. 1901)

Gregorio Cortez (1875–1916) became a folk hero among Mexican Americans in the early 1900s after shooting a sheriff and being chased by the Texas Rangers. On June 12, 1901, Cortea was approached by Karnes County sheriff W. T. "Brack" Morris. After a misunderstanding in which Morris shot Cortez's brother, lawmen, including the Texas Rangers, chased him for nearly two weeks. During this period, he was immortalized and portrayed as a Mexican who stood up to the gringos. The following is a corrido, *a folk song used to tell a story.* Corridos *are very common among northern Mexicans. The earliest border* corrido *can be traced to Juan Cortina (1824–1894), who shot a white marshal in 1859 for mistreating one of his mother's young servants. Today* corridos *frequently protest injustice and racism in the United States. The following* corrido *tells of a Mexican, outnumbered—as is usually the case in a* corrido*—and defending his rights with a pistol in hand against the Texas Rangers who were unjustly chasing him.*

In the county of El Carmen
A great misfortune befell;
The major sheriff is dead;
Who killed him no one can tell.
At two in the afternoon,
In half an hour or less,
They knew that the man who killed him
Had been Gregorio Cortez.
They let loose the bloodhound dogs;
They followed him from afar.
But trying to catch Cortez
Was like following a star.
All the rangers of the county
Were flying, they rode so hard;
What they wanted was to get
The thousand-dollar reward.
And in the county of Kiansis
They cornered him after all;
Though they were more than three hundred
He leaped out of their corral.
Then the Major Sheriff said,
As if he was going to cry,
"Cortez, hand over your weapons;
We want to take you alive."
Then said Gregorio Cortez,
And his voice was like a bell,
"You will never get my weapons
Till you put me in a cell."
Then said Gregorio Cortez
With his pistol in his hand,
"Ah, so many mounted Rangers
Just to take one Mexican!"

Source: From *With His Pistol in His Hand: A Border Ballad and Its Hero* by Américo Paredes, 3. Copyright 1958, renewed 1986. By permission of the University of Texas Press.

New York Times, "Mexicans Burn American Flag" (1910)

The lynching of Antonio Rodríguez, a Mexican youth in Rock Springs, Texas, who was accused of murdering a white woman in early November 1910, unleashed anti-American demonstrations and riots throughout Mexico. By this time, there was considerable resentment toward European

Americans because of the racism and unequal treatment suffered by Mexican workers in the United States. The protests created tensions not only between Mexicans and Americans but also between the government of Mexican president Porfirio Díaz who ruled Mexxico between 1877 and 1911 and the United States. Díaz supported European American official protests and apologized for the riots and destruction of "American property."

MEXICANS BURN AMERICAN FLAG

Rioters in Guadalajara Wreck Americans' Houses—Police Save Consulate.

ANOTHER RIOT AT DIAZ

MEXICANS BURN AMERICAN FLAG Sunday Bullfights Banned in Mexico City for Fear of More Trouble, and 51 Arrests Made.

GUADALAJARA, Mexico, Nov. 11—An American flag was burned amid cries of "Death to the Gringos" last night during riotous demonstrations against Americans because of the lynching of the Mexican Rodriguez in Texas. Depredations committed by the rioters were not made known until late to-day, when the danger of a further outbreak seemed unlikely.

Conservative estimates to-day place the damage to property of Americans at from $5,000 to $10,000. The rioters wore themselves out about midnight. The efforts of Government officers to preserve order prevented further rioting to-day, but a spirit of unrest prevailed and renewed violence was feared.

Manuel Cuestra Gallarde, candidate for Governor, is doing everything possible in conjunction with the commander of the Federal troops to maintain peace. American Consul Samuel Magill has been assured by Mexican officers that there will be no further trouble.

[Later last] night a high iron fence surrounding the Methodist Missionary Institute was torn down by the mob and the windows in the building were smashed.

Glass doors and windows in the houses of C. N. Strotz, W. L. Kline, the Rev. R. C. Eilot, C.E. Coruthers, and Dr. W. H. Swayze in the American colony were demolished. Plate-glass fronts in the American Banking Company Building, the German Drug Store, the Commercial Banking Company offices, the National Candy Company, the West End Realty Company, the hardware store of Carlos Hering, and the American Drug Company's store were broken. Windows were also demolished in the Cosmopolitan Hotel and an American restaurant.

C.E. Myers of Joplin, Mo., and Cliff Munger of York, Penn., railroad employees, were beaten and kicked by rioters, but they were not seriously injured.

Source: New York Times, November 12, 1910, 5.

Plan of San Luis Potosi (November 20, 1910)

By 1910, Mexicans wanted a change; Porfirio Díaz (1830–1915) had ruled Mexico for three decades. Much of the popular support coalesced around Francisco Madero (1873–1913), a wealthy hacienda owner from Coahuila who campaigned against Díaz in Mexico's 1910 presidential elections. When Madero lost, his followers claimed that the election was stolen by Díaz, who ordered Madero arrested and imprisoned on charges of treason. Madero fled to San Antonio and issued the Plan of San Luis Potosi, calling for the nullification of the elections. In the following excerpts, Madero called upon Mexicans to take up arms against the government. Not all revolutionists accepted the leadership of Madero, however. The Magonistas, the followers of Ricardo Flores Magón (1874–1922), fought under their own banner, as did the followers of Emiliano Zapata (1879–1919), the agrarian leader from the state of Morelos in southern Mexico.

People, in their constant efforts for the triumph of the ideal of liberty and justice, are forced, at precise historical moments, to make their greatest sacrifices.

Our beloved country has reached one of those moments. A force of tyranny, which we Mexicans were not accustomed to suffer after we won our independence, oppresses us in such a manner that it has become intolerable. In exchange for that tyranny, we are offered peace, but peace full of shame for the Mexican nation, because its basis is not law, but force; because its object is not the aggrandizement and prosperity of the country, but to enrich a small group who, abusing their influence, have converted the public charges into fountains of exclusively personal benefit, unscrupulously exploiting the manner of lucrative concessions and contracts.

The legislative and judicial powers are completely subordinated to the executive; the division of powers, the sovereignty of the States, the liberty of the common councils, and the rights of the citizens exist only in writing in our great charter; but, as a fact, it may almost be said that martial law constantly exists in Mexico; the administration of justice, instead of imparting protection to the weak, merely serves to legalize the plundering committed by the strong; the judges instead of being the representatives of justice, are the agents of the executive, whose interests they faithfully serve; the chambers of the union have no other will than that of the dictator; the governors of the States are designated by him and they in their turn designate and impose in like manner the municipal authorities.

From this it results that the whole administrative, judicial, and legislative machinery obeys a single will, the caprice of Gen. Porfirio Diaz, who during his long administration has shown that the principal motive that guides him is to maintain himself in power and at any cost.

For many years, profound discontent has been felt throughout the Republic, due to such a system of government, but Gen. Diaz with great cunning and perseverance, has succeeded in annihilating all independent elements, so that it was not possible to organize any sort of movement to take from him the power of which he made such bad use. The evil constantly became worse, and the decided eagerness of Gen. Diaz to impose a successor upon the nations in the person of Mr. Ramon Corral carried that evil to its limit and caused many of us Mexicans, although lacking recognized political standing, since it had been impossible to acquire it during the 36 years of dictatorship, to throw ourselves into the struggle to recover the sovereignty of the people and their rights on purely democratic grounds. . . .

In Mexico, as a democratic Republic, the public power can have no other origin nor other basis than the will of the people, and the latter can not be subordinated to formulas to be executed in a fraudulent manner. . . .

For this reason, the Mexican people have protested against the illegality of the last election and, desiring to use successively all the recourses offered by the laws of the Republic, in due form asked for the nullification of the election by the Chamber of Deputies, notwithstanding they recognized no legal origin in said body and knew beforehand that, as its members were not the representatives of the people, they would carry out the will of Gen. Diaz, to whom exclusively they owe their investiture.

In such a state of affairs, the people, who are the only sovereign, also protested energetically against the election in imposing manifestations in different parts of the Republic; and if the latter were not general throughout the national territory, it was due to the terrible pressure exercised by the

Government, which always quenches in blood any democratic manifestation, as happened in Puebla, Vera Cruz, Tlaxcala, and in other places.

But this violent and illegal system can no longer subsist.

I have very well realized that if the people have designated me as their candidate for the Presidency it is not because they have had an opportunity to discover in me the qualities of a statesman or of a ruler, but the virility of the patriot determined to sacrifice himself, if need be, to obtain liberty and to help the people free themselves from the odious tyranny that oppresses them.

From the moment I threw myself into the democratic struggle, I very well knew that Gen. Diaz would not bow to the will of the nation, and the noble Mexican people, in following me to the polls, also knew perfectly the outrage that awaited them; but in spite of it, the people gave the cause of liberty a numerous contingent of martyrs when they were necessary and, with wonderful stoicism, went to the polls and received every sort of molestation.

But such conduct was indispensable to show to the whole world that the Mexican people are fit for democracy, that they are thirsty for liberty, and that their present rulers do not measure up to their aspirations.

Besides, the attitude of the people before and during the election, as well as afterwards, shows clearly that they reject with energy the Government of Gen. Diaz and that, if those electoral rights had been respected, I would have been elected President of the Republic.

Therefore, and in echo of the national will, I declare the late election illegal and, the Republic being accordingly without rulers, provisionally assume the Presidency of the Republic until the people designate their rulers pursuant to the law. In order to attain this end, it is necessary to eject from power the audacious usurpers whose only title of legality involves a scandalous and immoral fraud.

With all honesty, I declare that it would be a weakness on my part, and treason to the people who have placed their confidence in me, not to put myself at the front of my fellow citizens, who anxiously call me from all parts of the country, to compel Gen. Diaz by force of arms, to respect the national will.

Source: United States Congress, Senate Subcommittee on Foreign Relations, Revolutions in Mexico, 62nd Congress, 2nd Session. Washington, DC: Government Printing Office, 1913, 730–736.

New Mexico Constitution (1912)

There was considerable controversy over the admission of New Mexico and Arizona as states. New Mexico had had a sufficient number of inhabitants to qualify since 1848. Indeed, the Treaty of Guadalupe Hidalgo (1848) between Mexico and the United States called for rapid admission of territories within the Mexican cession as states. But the feeling in Congress was that the territory had too many nonwhites—too many Indians and Mexicans. Deals were cut, and even the Catholic Church opposed statehood for New Mexico in return for control of education in the territory. New Mexico and Arizona were split in 1863. The same objections were made to Arizona's admission. Finally, when New Mexico was granted statehood in 1912, its constitution explicitly affirmed the protections provided by the Treaty of Guadalupe Hidalgo that ended the war between the United States and Mexico. It also guaranteed the rights of those left behind in the conquered territory. The following excerpts from the Constitution of New Mexico refer to those articles that protected the rights of those of Mexican extraction.

ARTICLE II

Sec. 5. Rights under Treaty of Guadalupe Hidalgo preserved. The rights, privileges, and immunities, civil, political, and religious, guaranteed to the people of New Mexico by the Treaty of Guadalupe Hidalgo shall be preserved inviolate. . . .

ARTICLE VII

Sec. 3. Religious and racial equality protected; restrictions on amendments. The right of any citizen of the state to vote, hold office, or sit upon juries, shall never be restricted, abridged, or impaired on account of religion, race, language, or color, or inability to speak, read, or write the English or Spanish languages except as may be otherwise provided in this Constitution; and the provisions of this section and of section one of this article shall never be amended except upon a vote of the people of this state in an election at which at least three-fourths of the electors voting in the whole state, and at least two-thirds of those voting in each county of the state, shall vote for such amendment. . . .

ARTICLE XII

Sec. 5. Teachers to learn English and Spanish. The legislature shall provide for the training of teachers in the normal schools or otherwise so that they may become proficient in both the English and Spanish languages, to qualify them to teach Spanish-speaking pupils and students in the public schools and educational institutions of the State, and shall provide proper means and methods to facilitate the teaching of the English language and other branches of learning to such pupils and students. . . .

Sec. 10. Educational rights of children of Spanish descent. Children of Spanish descent in the State of New Mexico shall never be denied the right and privilege of admission and attendance in the public schools or other public educational institutions of the State, and they shall never be classed in separate schools, but shall forever enjoy perfect equality with other children in all public schools and educational institutions of the State, and the legislature shall provide penalties for the violation of this section. This section shall never be amended except upon a vote of the people of this State, in an election at which at least three-fourths of the electors voting in the whole State and at least two-thirds of those voting in each county in the State shall vote for such amendment.

Source: Excerpt of New Mexico Constitution, 1912. Zia Net. Entire Constitution found at http://www.zianet.com/drbill/govnmt/nmconst.htm.

Los Angeles Times, "Race War in Arizona; Death List Is Sixteen" (1914)

Mostly unrecorded in history books are the race riots in Arizona mining camps during the 1910s when white miners tried to drive Mexican miners and their families from the copper camps. In places like Ray, Arizona, gun battles broke out, and dozens of Mexicans were killed. These racial encounters were encouraged by copper and mining barons throughout the Southwest. Most notable were the Ludlow Massacres of 1914 in Colorado, where the National Guard shot down miners in cold blood, and the Bisbee Deportation of 1917, where nearly 1,200 strikers were rounded up, put on trains, and dumped in the middle of the desert. The violence described in this Los Angeles

Times article took place around the segregated mining camps of Ray, Arizona, in 1914–1915, when white miners attacked Mexicans, killing at least a dozen.

GLOBE (Ariz.) Aug. 19—Four Americans and twelve Mexicans were reported killed in a series of clashes in and near Ray today and tonight, according to information received here late tonight.

Deputy Sheriff Finn Brown and two Mexican horse thieves were killed today when officers and a band of Mexican outlaws first clashed. This fight occurred in Devil's Canyon near Ray.

Early tonight the third Mexican was killed by Deputy Sheriff Henderson, when that officer and Deputy O'Neil were ambushed by the thieves. The horse of O'Neil was shot from beneath him.

Two more Americans and two Mexicans were killed when a posse late tonight came upon the outlaws. The Americans killed in this clash were Earl and Frank Miller, brothers.

Infuriated at the news of the death of members of the posse, American residents of Ray tonight invaded the Mexican section of town, driving the terror-stricken men, women and children of the section from their homes.

One American and seven Mexicans were killed when a number of the Mexican residents resisted the attack upon their homes. The others fled to the hills.

Reports said that many Americans were searching the hills near Ray tonight, bent upon killing every Mexican they meet.

Officers and citizens who have been sworn in as deputies, were sent to patrol the entire section to prevent a spread of the race rioting, if possible.

Source: Los Angeles Times, August 20, 1914, I3.

Plan de San Diego (1915)

The Plan de San Diego (1915) is still very controversial. Mexican revolutionist Ricardo Flores Magón (1874–1922) criticized the plan, while others have justified it or even denounced it as a terrorist document. The most popular view is that it was proclaimed during a period of intense oppression of Mexicans from 1915 to 1920, when the Texas Rangers and other authorities lynched and hounded Mexicans. They used the Mexican Revolution and the hysteria surrounding the supposed presence of German spies in Mexico as a pretext to harass Mexicans. In response to the violence, a small group of Mexican Americans proclaimed the "Plan of San Diego," a revolution, on January 6, 1915, in the Texas town of San Diego. The manifesto called for the raising of a liberating army made up of Mexican Americans, African Americans, and Japanese, to "free" the states of Texas, New Mexico, Arizona, California, and Colorado and form an independent republic. It called for the death of white males. The manifesto fanned nativist brutality, and federal reports indicated that more than 300 Mexicans or Mexican Americans were summarily executed in the South. What is amazing is that a couple dozen Mexicans could create so much fear. The following excerpt is from a book by Charles H. Harris III and Louis R. Sadler on atrocities committed against Mexicans.

On February 20, 1915, at 2:00 there would occur an uprising against the United States government to proclaim the liberty of blacks from the "Yankee tyranny" that had held them in "iniquitous slavery since remote times" and to proclaim the independence of Texas, New Mexico, Arizona, Colorado, and California, "of which States the Republic of Mexico was robbed in a most perfidious manner by North American imperialism."

To achieve these objectives, an army would be formed under the leadership of commanders named by the Supreme Revolutionary Congress of San Diego, Texas. This army, known as the "Liberating Army for Races & Peoples," would fight under a red and white banner bearing the inscription "Equality & Independence."

Each commander was assigned certain cities to capture; once he had done so, he would amass their weaponry and funds in order to provide the necessary resources to continue the struggle. Commanders would account for everything to their superiors.

Upon capturing a city, especially a state capital, commanders must immediately appoint municipal authorities to preserve order and assist the revolutionary cause.

"It is strictly forbidden to hold prisoners, either special prisoners (civilians) or soldiers; and the only time that should be spent in dealing with them is that which is absolutely necessary to demand funds (loans) of them; and whether these demands be successful or not, they shall be shot immediately without any pretext."

"Every foreigner who shall be found armed and cannot prove his right to carry arms, shall be summarily executed, regardless of his race or nationality."

"Every North American over sixteen years of age shall be put to death; and only the aged men, the women, and the children shall be respected; and on no account shall the traitors to our race be spared or respected."

"The Apaches of Arizona, as well as the Indians (Redskins) of the territory" would have their lands returned, so that they would assist the revolutionary cause.

All appointments and ranks of subordinate officers in the revolutionary army, as well as those of other conspirators who might wish to cooperate with the cause, would be reviewed by their superiors.

"The movement having gathered force, and once having possessed ourselves of the States alluded to, we shall proclaim them as an Independent Republic, later requesting (if it be through expedient annexation to Mexico, without concerning ourselves at that time about the form of government which may control the destinies of the common mother country."

When the revolutionary movement had obtained independence for the blacks, the revolutionaries would grant them a banner, "which they themselves shall be permitted to select," and the revolutionists would aid them in obtaining "six States of the American Union, which states border on those already mentioned," so the blacks could form an independent republic of their own.

"None of the leaders shall have the power to make terms with the enemy, without first communicating with their superior officers of the army, bearing in mind that this is a war without quarter; nor shall any leader enroll in his ranks any foreigners unless said foreigner belong to the Latin, the Negro, or the Japanese race."

It is understood that upon the triumph of the cause, no member of this conspiracy would fail to recognize his superior, nor to aid others seeking to destroy "what has been accomplished by such great work."

As soon as possible, each local junta would select delegates who would elect a Permanent Directorate of the Revolutionary Congress. At this meeting the powers and duties of the Permanent Directorate would be determined, and the revolutionary plan could be amended or revised.

It was understood that the revolutionists would achieve the independence of the blacks, and that "on no account will we accept aid, either moral or pecuniary, from the Government of Mexico; and it need not consider itself under any obligations in this, our movement."

Source: Harris, Charles H. III, and Louis R. Sadler. *The Texas Rangers and the Mexican Revolution: The Bloodiest Decade, 1910–1920*. Albuquerque: University of New Mexico Press, 2004, 210–212.

New York Times, "Immigration Bill Enacted over Veto" (1917)

Called the Literacy Act, this 1917 legislation barred all illiterate immigrants over the age of 16 from coming to the United States; it reduced European immigration to the United States to a trickle because most immigrants were not literate. It excluded most Asians but the bill exempted Mexicans because they were vital to agriculture and the railroads, and the bill's sponsors could not have gotten the support of western growers without the exemption. The following excerpts from a New York Times *article give the background of the act, which was passed over the veto of President Woodrow Wilson (1856–1924), who did not believe the literacy provision was warranted.*

WASHINGTON, Feb. 5.—By a vote of 62 to 19 the Senate today repassed the Immigration bill, containing the literacy test, thus enacting it into law despite the President's veto. The House repassed the bill over the veto last week by a vote of 287 to 106. By this action, the first time a veto by President Wilson has been overridden, Congress has at last ended a fight for the restriction of immigration by the literacy test which began in 1897, when President Cleveland vetoed the measure. President Taft also vetoed the provision, and President Wilson has done so twice. The first time Mr. Wilson refused his signature, the bill was repassed by the Senate with a sufficient majority to override the veto, but failed of the necessary two-thirds vote in the House. The law goes into effect May 1.

The literacy test, President Wilson declared in his recent veto message, is unjust in principle, constituting a test, not of character but of opportunity. He also objected that the provision of the bill which permits immigration officials to exempt from the operation of the test foreigners who, in their judgment, are fleeing from religious persecution would raise delicate questions which might involve this nation in international difficulties. . . .

VOTE ON REPASSAGE OF THE BILL

The vote today was non-partisan, 34 Democrats and 28 Republicans voting for the bill and 11 Democrats and 8 Republicans voting to sustain the veto. . . .

SAYS JAPAN HAS OBJECTED

"I am authorized to say to the Senate," he went on, "that the Japanese Embassy has called attention to this language. The State Department feels that the clause may be the occasion of some misunderstanding, and is exceedingly desirous that nothing shall be done which will cause the Japanese Government to feel that we have in any way impinged upon the understanding that now exists."

Under the present wording, the bill excludes by geographical limitation Asiatics coming from certain countries. Japan was expressly omitted from this restriction at the request of the State Department because the immigration of Japanese labor is now forbidden by a "gentlemen's agreement" between the two nations, and the Japanese Embassy objected to having Japan discriminated against specifically while the Japanese Government was carrying out this agreement faithfully.

"Senators from the Pacific Coast attempted to secure definite restriction of the Japanese in spite of this, but the Senate refused to permit it. The conference committee which framed the final draft of the bill finally agreed on a clause, to follow the geographical restriction paragraph, reading, "And no alien now in any way excluded from or prevented from entering the United States shall be admitted to the United States." This, Sen. Reed asserted, was objectionable to the Japanese as referring to the existence of the agreement.

It was said by an official at the State Department today, however, that some misunderstanding must have occurred, as, so far as he knew, the Japanese Embassy had made no objection to the bill in its present form. The final draft of the bill was decided upon after Secretary Lansing had conferred with the committee on this particular point.

Sen. Smith of South Carolina, Chairman of the Immigration Committee, answered Sen. Reed with the declaration that the present state of international affairs emphasized the necessity for a pure, homogeneous American people, such as the bill was intended to protect.

Source: New York Times, February 6, 1917, 12.

Amendment to the Espionage Act of 1917 (1918)

The Espionage Act, which was passed on June 15, 1917, made it a crime for a person to convey information with the intent to interfere with the operation or success of the armed forces of the United States. The offense was punishable by a maximum fine of $10,000 and 20 years in prison. The act was passed to suppress all dissent and was used against progressives. Many of those deported were Latinos who belonged to labor unions. The law intimidated activists. It was important because it was in large part directed against the foreign-born and was thus within an antiforeign tradition in this country that dated from the Alien and Sedition Acts of 1798. The following are excerpts from a 1918 amendment to the Espionage Act.

Be it enacted by the Senate and House of Representatives of the United States of America in Congress assembled, That section three of title one of the Act entitled "An Act to Punish Acts of Interference with the Foreign Relations, the Neutrality, and the Foreign Commerce of the United States, to Punish Espionage, and Better to Enforce the Criminal Laws of the United States, and for Other Purposes," approved June fifteenth, nineteen hundred and seventeen, be, and the same is hereby, amended so as to read as follows:

Section 3. Whoever, when the United States is at war, shall willfully make or convey false reports or false statements with intent to interfere with the operation or success of the military or naval forces of the United States, or to promote the success of its enemies, or shall willfully make or convey false reports or false statements, or say or do anything except by way of bona fide and not disloyal advice to an investor or investors, with intent to obstruct the sale by the United States of bonds or other securities of the United States or the making of loans by or to the United States, and whoever, when the United States is at war, shall willfully cause or attempt to cause, or incite, or attempt to incite, insubordination, disloyalty, mutiny, or refusal of duty in the military or naval forces of the United States, or shall willfully obstruct or attempt to obstruct the recruiting or enlistment services of the United States, and whoever, when the United States is at war, shall willfully utter, print, write, or publish any disloyal, profane, scurrilous, or abusive language about the form of government of the United States or the Constitution of the United States, or the military or naval forces of the United States, or the flag of the United States, or the uniform of the Army or Navy of the United States into contempt, scorn, contumely, or disrepute, or shall willfully utter, print, write, or publish any language intended to incite, provoke, or encourage resistance to the United States, or to promote the cause of its enemies, or shall willfully display the flag of any foreign enemy, or shall willfully by utterance, writing, printing, publication, or language spoken, urge, incite, or advocate any curtailment of production in this country of any thing or things, product or products, necessary or essential to the prosecution of the war in which the United States may be engaged, with intent by such curtailment to cripple or hinder the United States in the prosecution of war, and whoever shall willfully advocate, teach, defend, or suggest the doing of any of the acts or things in this section enumerated, and whoever shall by word or act support or favor the cause of any country with which the United States is at war or by word or act oppose the cause of the United States therein, shall be punished by a fine of not more than $10,000 or the imprisonment for not more than twenty years, or both: Provided, That any employee or official of the United States Government who commits any disloyal act or utters any unpatriotic or disloyal language, or who, in an abusive and violent manner criticizes the Army or Navy or the flag of the United States shall be at once dismissed from the service. Any such employee shall be dismissed by the head of the department in which the employee may be engaged, and any such official shall be dismissed by the authority having power to appoint a successor to the dismissed official.

Section 4. When the United States is at war, the Postmaster General may, upon evidence satisfactory to him that any person or concern is using the mails in violation of any of the provisions of this Act, instruct the postmaster at any post office at which mail is received addressed to such person or concern, to return to the postmaster at the office at which they were originally mailed, all letters or other matter so addressed, with the words "Mail to this address undeliverable under Espionage Act" plainly written or stamped upon the outside thereof, and all such letters or other matter so returned to such postmasters shall be by them returned to the senders thereof under such regulations as the Postmaster General may prescribe.

Source: Amendment to the Espionage Act of 1917. 40 U.S. Statutes at Large 553–554 (1918).

Lon C. Hill, Testimony before Albert B. Fall Committee (1920)

In 1919–1920, Congress investigated claims of brutality toward Mexicans. In Texas, there were calls for the abolition of the Texas Rangers, who many claimed wantonly lynched Mexicans. University of Texas historian Walter Prescott Webb (1888–1963), who wrote The Texas Rangers *in 1935, later excused the Rangers, blaming Mexicans for the violence on the border. He supported the testimony of Lon C. Hill (1862–1935), a Texas businessman who testified at the Senate hearings. Hill blamed Ricardo Flores Magón for the violence and Mexicans for creating the overreaction. It was, according to Hill, a matter of preemptive strikes against terrorists.*

Q. Now, what was the general condition about that time among the citizens on the border down there—did they feel safe under the protection of their flag?

A. No, sir; no. They were just in this fix, gentlemen: All the Americans . . . the biggest part of them, were going this way [indicating].

Q. Which way?

A. Up north, up the railroad, getting out of that country. And all the Mexicans were going that way [indicating towards Mexico], and the people, they came into town and lived—the people that lived out in the country. . . . They brought their women and children into town, and a great many just got on the train, left their chickens and hogs and cows, and everything else, and just went to Corpus and San Antonio, and went from there to Canada—just scattered all over the country. . . .

Q. What were the objects of those raids?

A. Well, Senator, . . . that is a question that bothered us down there for a good little while. What were they up to? Now, when the thing first started we couldn't understand . . . why those fellows there would want to come over there and steal a few cows . . . and run across the river. . . . We got to investigating . . . and we found out that they had been sending off a lot of money through the post office . . . and they sent a world of money to Los Angeles, California . . . to a firm known as the Magnon Bros.

Q. Ricardo Magnon? [sic]

A. I think he is the fellow. Well, they sent worlds of money over there, and they had all kinds of literature from California on this I.W.W. stuff. . . . Well, now, they would send this money off, and then they would order guns and ammunition . . . lots of it . . . and it . . . got noised around . . . that they were trying to take that country and they said they were going to run all of the Gringos out of there. Well, to my mind and to the other fellows', that was absolutely inconceivable . . . how a bunch of Mexicans would take a fool idea in their heads that they were going to kill all those Americans and take all that country; it was just laughable to us that they really meant it. But they were coming . . . they would tell us coming . . . in bunches and take your horses and burn up your houses and kill you and then, after a while, they were just going to come over in a great big army and take the whole country. . . . Well . . . the inside dope . . . we could never get it from the leaders . . . but we would get hold of some fellow, and they would tell us . . . and ask them what in the name of goodness is the matter with you Mexicans; are you all going crazy here? Well, what are you up to; what are you going to do?

"Well," they said, "we have organized, and we have got some foreigners going to help us, and we are going to take all the land back that you Gringos stole from us before the constitution of 1857."

Q. What term did they use to describe these foreigners?

A. Well, "enrejados" [sic] something like that.

Q. Extranjeros?

A. That is it; that is the name.

Q. Do the Mexicans . . . by the term "extranjeros" . . . mean Mexican citizens?

A. No; they don't.

Q. Do they mean Americans?

A. No; they don't; them fellows didn't; they meant Alemans, to come out and tell you the right of it.

Q. Aleman means a German?

A. Aleman means a German. They would tell you they had instruction not to kill any Germans and not to molest any Germans and . . . there was a whole raft of Germans came down there and lived down there, and on both sides of that river, too. They . . . would say that they were going to take the country between the Rio Grande and the Nueces. . . .

Q. And they were going to take it back?

A. Yes, sir; and the Aleman was going to help them, furnish them ammunition, money, and everything.

Source: Fall, Albert B. United States Congress. Senate Committee on Foreign Relations. Investigation of Mexican affairs preliminary report and hearings of the Committee on Foreign Relations, United States Senate, pursuant to S. res. 106, directing the Committee on Foreign Relations to investigate the matter of outrages on citizens of the United States in Mexico. Washington DC: Government Printing Office, 1920, 1253.

Ricardo Flores Magón, Letter to Harry Weinberger (May 9, 1921)

Ricardo Flores Magón (1874–1922) was an anarcho-syndicalist thinker from Oaxaca, Mexico. He was thrown into prison for writing and publishing articles critical of Mexican dictator Porfirio Díaz (1830–1915), who ruled Mexico from 1876 to 1911. When Magón was threatened with prison, he fled to Texas and established the Partido Liberal Mexicano *(PLM) in 1905. In the United States, he rallied other dissidents around the banner of the PLM and published the newspaper* Regeneración (Regeneration). *The PLM published denunciations of Díaz, smuggled arms into Mexico, and conducted border raids. Magón was charged with violating U.S. neutrality laws. He refused to support Francisco Madero (1873–1913) and his followers, who overthrew Díaz in 1910. Magón led a separate anarchist revolt in Baja California, resulting in more prison time in the United States. The following is a letter Magón sent from Leavenworth Prison to his attorney, Harry Weinberger. The letter conveys the essence of Magón, who was offered freedom in return for renouncing his principles—something he refused to do.*

Post Office Box 7

Leavenworth, Kansas

May 9, 1921

Mr. Harry Weinberger

Counselor at Law

New York City

My Dear Mr. Weinberger:

Your letter of the 25th of last April and a copy of Mr. Daugherty's letter to you received. You want me to furnish you with data regarding the sentence which ended on January 19, 1914; but in order for you to judge whether I have been the victim of a conspiracy bent on keeping in bondage the Mexican peon, or not, I am going to furnish you with an abstract of the persecution I have suffered ever since I took refuge in this country. I must, before going any further, beg your pardon for my keeping your attention from other business undoubtedly more important than mine.

After years, many years, of an unequal struggle in the press and the political clubs of the City of Mexico against the cruel despotism of Porfirio Diaz; after having suffered repeated incarcerations for my political beliefs ever since I was 17 years old, and having almost miraculously escaped death at the hands of hired assassins on several occasions in that dark period of the Mexican history when the practice of the government was to silence truth's voice with the firing squad, or the dagger, or the poison; after the judiciary, by judicial decree of June 30, 1903, forbade me not only to write for my own journals but to contribute for theirs as well, having my printing plants successively sequestrated by the government and my life being in peril, I decided to come to this country, which I knew to be the land of the free and the home of the brave, to resume my work of enlightenment of the Mexican masses.

The 11th day of January, 1904, saw me set my foot on this land, almost penniless, for all that I had possessed had been sequestrated by the Mexican Government, but rich in illusion and hopes of social and political justice. *Regeneración* made its reappearance on American soil in November 1904. On the following December, a ruffian sent by Diaz entered my domicile, and would have stabbed me in the back had it not been for the quick intervention of my brother, Enrique, who happened to be near by. Enrique threw the ruffian out of the house, and showing that this brutal assault on my person had been prepared by certain authorities, and the possible failure of the ruffian's attempt foreseen, at the falling of the latter on the sidewalk, a swarm of agents of the public peace invaded the premises. Enrique was made a prisoner and jailed, and finally condemned to pay a fine for disturbing the peace. Embolded by the protection he enjoyed, the ruffian again forced his entrance into my house. This time I telephoned the police; the man was arrested, and I was summoned to appear in court the following day early in the morning. When I arrived at the police court the man had already been released. . . . Being my life was so lightly regarded by those who claim to have been empowered with authority to safeguard human interests and life, I decided to move southward, and in February 1905, *Regeneración* resumed publication at St. Louis, Mo. In October, same year, trouble broke loose against me. A Mexican Government official, by the name of Manuel Esperon y de la Flor, who maintained the worst type of slavery in the district under his command, for he used to kill men, women, and children as feudal lords used to do, was chosen by Diaz to come and file against me a complaint for what he deems to be a slanderous article which had been printed in *Regeneración*, and dealing with the despotism he displayed on the unfortunate inhabitants of the district under his control. A charge of criminal libel was preferred and I was thrown into jail with my brother, Enrique, and Juan Sarabia. Everything in the newspaper office was sequestrated—printing plant, typewriter machines, books, furniture, and so on—and sold before a trial had taken place. A detail that illustrates the connivance between the Mexican and American authorities to persecute one, may be seen in the fact that the postmaster at St. Louis called me to his office with the apparent purpose of getting from me some information as to the financial status of the newspaper, but in reality to let a Pinkerton detective see me, that he might identify me later. The detective was already in the postmaster's office when I arrived there in compliance to his summons. This same detective led the officers who arrested me. After months of languishing in a cell, I got released on bail, to find that the second-class privilege of *Regeneración* had been canceled by the Postmaster General on the flimsy pretext that more than half of the regular issues of the newspaper circulated in Mexico, and that extradition papers were being prepared in Mexico to ask my delivery to the Mexican authorities. I paid my bondsman the amount of my bail, and on March 1905, I took refuge in Canada, for I was certain that death awaited me in Mexico. At that time, the mere asking by Diaz for a man he wanted was enough to spirit a man across the line to be shot. While in Toronto, Ontario, *Regeneración* was being published in St. Louis. The Diaz agents found at last my whereabouts. I was informed of their intentions and evaded arrest by moving to Montreal, Quebec. Few hours after my having left Toronto, the police called at my abandoned domicile. I ignore until today how could Diaz throw the Canadian authorities against me.

While in Montreal, my Mexican comrades in Mexico were planning an uprising to overthrow the savage despotism of Porfirio Diaz. I secretly moved to the Mexican frontier on September 1906, to participate in the generous movement. My presence in El Paso, Texas, though kept strictly unknown, was discovered by American and Mexican sleuths, who on the 20th of October, same year, assaulted the room where I had to confer with some of my comrades. Antonio I. Villarreal, now Minister of Agriculture in Obregon's cabinet, and Juan Sarabia, were arrested. I escaped. A price was put on my head. A $25,000 reward was offered for my capture, and hundreds of thousands of leaflets bearing my picture and a description of my personal features were circulated throughout the Southwest, and fixed in post offices and conspicuous places with the tempting reward. I succeeded, however, in evading arrest until August 23, 1907, when, with Librado Rivera and Antonio I. Villarreal, I was made prisoner in Los Angeles, Cal., without the formality of a warrant.

The intention of the persecutors was to send us across the border, this being the reason of their actions without a warrant, as they had done to Manuel Sarabia on June of the same year. Sarabia was one of my associates. Without a warrant, he was arrested at Douglas, Ariz., by American authorities, and in the dead of night delivered to Mexican rurales, who took him to the Mexican side. The whole Douglas population arose against such a crime, and the unrest which it produced was so intense that Sarabia was sent back to the United States three or four days later, where he was immediately released. We avoided being kidnapped into Mexico by voicing in the street the intentions of our captors. A big crowd gathered, and it was necessary for our abductors to take us to the police station, and to rapidly manufacture a charge against us. Our lawyer, Job Harriman, got an affidavit, which I think was sent to the Department of Justice, wherein it is alleged that one Furlong, head of a St. Louis detective's agency, confessed that he was in the employment of the Mexican Government and paid by it, and that it was his purpose to kidnap us across the Mexican border.

Charge after charge was proffered against us, ranging in importance from resisting an officer to robbery and murder. All these charges were successfully fought by Harriman, but in the meantime our persecutors were forging documents, training witnesses, and so forth, until at length they finally charged us with having broken the neutrality laws by giving material assistance to patriots to rise in arms against Porfirio Diaz. The forged documents and trained witnesses were examined by the United States Commissioner at Los Angeles, and as a result we were, after more than 20 months' incarceration in the county jail, sent to Tombstone, Ariz., to be tried. The mere reading of the depositions made by the government witnesses before the United States Commissioner at Los Angeles, and then before the judge of our trial at Tombstone, shows that they committed perjury in either place, or in both. Experts for the defense proved that the exhibited documents were gross forgeries. We were, however, sentenced to 18 months' imprisonment, which we served in Yuma and Florence, Ariz., being released on August 1, 1910, after three years spent behind prison bars.

Regeneración appeared again in September of the same year, this time in Los Angeles. Cal. On June, 1911, I was arrested with my brother, Enrique, Librado Rivera, and Anselmo L. Figueroa, charged with having violated the neutrality laws by sending men, arms, and ammunition to those fighting in Mexico against that form of chattel slavery known as peonage, which has been the curse of four-fifths of the Mexican population, as everybody knows. Jack Mosby, one of the prospected witnesses for the prosecution, said on the stand that the United States District Attorney had promised him all kinds of benefits if he perjured against us. Fake testimony was introduced by the prosecution, as proven by affidavits sworn by its witnesses after the trial was over, affidavits which must be on file in the Department of Justice, as they were sent there in 1912. In June 1912, after a year of fighting the case, we were sent to McNeil Island to serve the 23 months' imprisonment to which we were condemned, having been released on January 19, 1914. Figueroa died shortly afterward as a result of his imprisonment.

On February 18, 1917, I was arrested with my brother Enrique, for having published in *Regeneración* articles against the treachery committed by Carranza, then President of Mexico, against the workers, and for having written that the Mexicans who at the time were being assassinated by Texas Rangers deserved justice rather than bullets. I got a sentence of one year and one day, for I was expected to live only a few more months, having been taken from a hospital bed to be tried. Enrique got three years. We appealed and finally succeeded in getting bond, under which we were released pending the appeal.

On the 21st of March 1918, I was arrested with Rivera for having published in *Regeneración* the "Manifesto" for which I was given 20 years' imprisonment and Rivera 15. The wording and meaning of the "Manifesto" were construed as seditious by the prosecution, that is, as aiming at the insubordination and revolt of the military and naval forces of the United States. Any sensible person who happened to read the "Manifesto" would not draw such a conclusion, for in reality the "Manifesto" is only an exposition of facts and a fair warning to all mankind of the evils those facts might produce. In one of its paragraphs it is clearly stated that no one can make a revolution on account of it being a social phenomenon. The "Manifesto" was aimed at the prevention of the evils a revolution carries, itself the revolution being regarded from a scientific standpoint as a world-wide inevitable result of the unsettled conditions of the world. The "Manifesto" does not refer in the least to the policies of the American Government in the last war, nor gives aid and comfort to its enemies. It is neither pro-German nor pro-Ally, and does not single out the United States in its brief review of the world conditions. It was enough, however, to secure for me a life term behind prison bars. The persecution, this time, was exceedingly severe. My poor wife, Maria, was incarcerated during five months, and is now free on bond awaiting trial for having notified my friends of my arrest, that they should assist me in my legal defense.

After reading this extremely long and dreadfully tedious statement of facts, how could any person believe that I have rightfully been prosecuted and in no way persecuted? In each case, and in defiance of the law, bail has been fixed at enormous rates so as to prevent me making use of the privilege. As to the veracity of my assertions, my honor as a life-long fighter for justice is hereby solemnly pledged.

Mr. Daugherty says I am a dangerous man because of the doctrines I assert and practice. Now, then, the doctrines I assert and practice are the anarchist doctrines, and I challenge all fair-minded men and women the world over to prove to me that the anarchist doctrines are detrimental to the human race. Anarchism strives for the establishment of a social order based on brotherhood and love, as against the actual form of society, founded on violence, hatred, and rivalry of one class against the other, and of members of one class among themselves. Anarchism aims at establishing peace forever among all the races of the earth by the suppression of this fountain of all evils—the right of private property. If this is not a beautiful ideal, what is it? No one thinks that the peoples of the civilized world are living under ideal conditions. Every conscientious person feels himself shocked at the sight of this continual strife of man against man, of this unending deceiving of one another. Material success is the goal that lures men and women the world over, and to achieve it no vileness is too vile, no baseness is too base, to deter its worshippers from coveting it. The results of this universal madness are appalling; virtue is trampled upon by crime, and artfulness takes the place of honesty. Sincerity is only a word, or at the most, a mask under which fraud grins. There is no courage to uphold the convictions. Frankness has disappeared and deceit forms the slippery plan on which man meets man in his social and political intercourse. "Everything for success" is the motto, and the noble face of the earth is desecrated with the blood of the contending beasts. . . . Such are the conditions under which we civilized men live, conditions which breed all sorts of moral and material torture, alas! And all sorts of moral and material degradation. At the correction of all these unwholesome influences [is] the anarchist doctrines' aim, and a man who sustains these doctrines of brotherhood and love can never be called dangerous by any sensible, decent person.

Mr. Daugherty agrees on my being sick, but he thinks that I can be taken care of in my sickness in prison as well as it could be done on the outside. Environment is all-important in the treatment of diseases, and no one would ever imagine that a prison cell is the ideal environment for a sick man, and much less when the presence in prison of such a man is owing to his having been faithful to truth and justice. The government officials have always said that there are not in the United States, persons kept in captivity on account of their beliefs, but Mr. Daugherty says in his letter to you: "He, in no manner, evinces any evidence of repentance, but on the contrary, rather prides himself upon his defiance of the law. . . . I am of the opinion, therefore, that until he indicates a different spirit than that expressed in his letter to Mrs. Branstetter, he should at least serve until August 15, 1925." The quoted paragraphs, and the part of Mr. Daugherty's letter in which he says I am regarded dangerous on account of my doctrines, are the best evidence that there are persons kept in prison owing to their social and political beliefs. If I believed that it is not persecution, but prosecution, that has been exerted against me; if I believed that the law under which I was given a life term in prison was a good law, I would be set free, according to Mr. Daugherty. That law was undoubtedly a good law but to a few persons, those who had something to gain with its enactment. As for the masses, the law was a bad one, for thanks to it thousands of young American men lost their lives in Europe, many thousands more were maimed or otherwise incapacitated to earn a livelihood, and thanks to it the colossal European carnage, where scores of millions of men were either slain or maimed for life, received momentous impulse and bred the tremendous financial crisis which is threatening to plunge the world into chaos. However, as I have stated before, I did not violate this law with the issuance of the "Manifesto" of March 16, 1918.

As for the matter of repentance to which Mr. Daugherty gives so much importance, I sincerely state that my conscience does not reproach me with having done wrong, and therefore, to repent of what I am convinced is right would be a crime on my part, a crime that my conscience would never pardon me. He who commits an anti-social act may repent, and it is desired that he repents, but it is not fair to exact a vow of repentance from him who all he wishes is to secure freedom, justice and well-being for all his fellow men regardless of race and creed. If someone ever convinces me that it is just that children starve, and that young women have to choose of two infernos one, prostitution, or starvation; if there is a person who could drive out of my brain the idea of not being honorable to kill within oneself that elementary instinct of sympathy which prompts every sociable animal to stand by the members of its species, and that it is monstrous that man, the most intelligent of beasts, has to wield the weapons of fraud and deceit if he wants to achieve success; if the idea that man must be the wolf of man enters my brain, then I shall repent. But as this will never be, my fate is sealed. I have to die in prison, branded as a felon. Darkness is already enshrouding me as though anxious of anticipating for me the eternal shadows into which the dead sink. I accept my fate with manly resignation, convinced that some day, long perhaps after Mr. Daugherty and myself have breathed our last, and of what we have been there only remained his name exquisitely carved in a marble flag upon his grave in a fashionable cemetery, and mine, only a number, 14596, roughly scraped in some plebeian stone in the prison graveyard, justice shall be done me.

With many thanks for the activity you have shown on my behalf, I remain, sincerely yours,

Source: Magón, Ricardo Flores. Collected Works http://dwardmac.pitzer.edu/Anarchist_archives/bright/magon/works/letters/harry050921.html.

Walter Prescott Webb, *The Texas Rangers: A Century of Frontier Defense* (1935)

Walter Prescott Webb (1888–1963) was a giant among Texas historians. He was president of the American Historical Association and a professor of history at the University of Texas at Austin. Throughout his writing career, he was an apologist for the Texas Rangers, a special police force first organized in the 1820s to deal with Indians. Webb described the Rangers as the protectors of civilization. They had to be ruthless to deal with Mexicans and Indians who were treacherous, according to Webb. In excusing the Rangers in the following excerpt from his book, he does not use facts but the testimony of a wealthy rancher who was notoriously anti-Mexican. Webb wrote or edited more than 20 books. The Texas Rangers: A Century of Frontier Defense *(1935) is still considered by some to be the definitive study of this frontier law enforcement agency and is often quoted by Texas historians. The problem is that he excludes the Mexican side of the controversies and, in the following excerpt from his book, twists the congressional testimony of wealthy real estate devoper Lon C. Hill.*

The testimony of Lon Hill indicates the confusion that existed in the minds of the Americans when the Mexicans began their inexplicable raids. There were strange rumors of great plans that were [afoot] to take Texas, but as Hill said, it was inconceivable "how a bunch of Mexicans would take a fool idea in their heads that they were going to kill all those Americans and take all that country." The mystery was deepened when the Americans learned that some of their own Mexicans, people who had lived in close harmony with them for years, were joining the raiders.

Source: Webb, Walter Prescott. *The Texas Rangers: A Century of Frontier Defense*. Austin: University of Texas Press, 1935 and 1965, 482. Copyright renewed 1993.

Geographical Review, "Overcrowded Porto Rico" (1916)

Before the European American occupation began in 1898, Puerto Rico was a nation of subsistence farmers called jibaros. *The U.S. occupation introduced laws that favored the expansion of plantations and corporate interests that were attracted to the island because of low production costs. The further commercialization of agriculture led to a drastic decline in the number of small farmers, many of whom were uprooted and forced to seek employment in factories in the cities of the island and on the U.S. mainland. Many ended up on plantations in Hawaii and Arizona, where workers were in great demand. Problems for small farmers increased when Puerto Rican islands like Vieques came under the control of the U.S. Navy. The lack of land caused poverty and hunger. U.S. policy makers attempted to explain this poverty, and the diaspora of Puerto Ricans, by raising the pretext of overpopulation. The following excerpt is from a* Geographical Review *article that illustrates the American sentiment at the time that the island of Puerto Rico was overcrowded compared with other nations. This mind-set would influence future U.S. policy in Puerto Rico.*

The gross area of the island, land, and water, including the small adjacent and dependent islands, is 3,435 square miles, and the present population therefore is nearly 350 to the square mile. This is a greater density than that of China proper (200 to the square mile in 1910) or of India (175) or of Japan (362). It is more than ten times greater than that of the United States proper (30.9) and over three times as great as that of New England (105.7). In fact, there are only two states in the American Union that have more people per square mile, viz., Massachusetts (419) and Rhode Island (509), and in these states about three-fourths of the people live in cities and depend upon manufactures, while in Porto Rico only about 10 per cent of the people live in cities of more than 10,000 population and there are almost no manufactures. In short, if we consider both the area and the industrial development of this little island there is perhaps no region in the world, save Java, more densely populated.

The island is about four-fifths mountainous, much of it so steep that it can hardly be cultivated, and yet this great population is so evenly distributed over its whole surface that the center of population is only about 5 miles in a straight line from the geographical center of Porto Rico. Moreover, the population has been produced by the natural increase of the people of the island. There is practically no immigration and, according to the census of 1910, only about one percent of the people are of foreign birth.

Furthermore, the population is still steadily increasing. The first census, taken by the Americans in 1899, enumerated in round numbers 953,000 persons in Porto Rico. At the present time they exceed that number by 250,000. By comparison with the census taken by the Spanish government in 1887, which enumerated 732,000, we find that in the twenty-two years immediately preceding the coming of the Americans there was an increase of 221,000 people, or about 30 percent, while in the sixteen years since the American annexation there has been an increase of 250,000, or about 27 percent. To put it another way, during the latter part of the Spanish period, the average annual increase was about 1.3 percent, while during the whole of the American period, it has been 1.6 percent. The increase last year, according to the official reports of births and deaths, was 24,000, or 2 percent, of the whole population. This rapid increase in population has been made possible by the commercial expansion and industrial development that has followed the American occupation. . . .

Source: Geographical Review, 1, no. 3 (March 1916): 211–212

Rafael George Gatell, "Porto Ricans and America," Letter to the Editor of the *New York Times* (1921)

The issue of race irritated better-off Puerto Ricans, who disagreed with the characterization of Puerto Ricans as a hybrid people. In the following letter to the editor, New York Times *reader Rafael George Gatell took issue with this characterization, claiming that Puerto Rico was 100 percent white, populated by descendants of the Spanish or French. He said that there were three purely white social clubs and denied the recent claims of former Consular Agent L. S. Delaplaine that the American flag had recently been disrespected by Puerto Ricans. Gatell insisted that Puerto Ricans were grateful to the United States for all it had done for them and happy that the Americans were in Puerto Rico.*

To the Editor of *The New York Times*:

I have read in today's edition of your paper various statements made by L. S. Delaplaine Jr., formerly in the Consular Service of the United States in South America, regarding conditions prevailing in the island of Porto Rico. Fortunately, many sensible and friendly Americans have visited the island in the last years and do not share in the least this gentleman's opinions.

In the first place, Mr. Delaplaine states that "the native Porto Rican is the greatest hybrid on earth." This is not so. The native Porto Rican is 100 percent white and is a descendant either from Spanish or French people. Naturally, there are colored Porto Ricans as well as there are colored Americans. In San Juan, which is the capital of the island, there are three social organizations, as follows: The Union Club (American), Spanish Casino, and

Porto Rican Casino. They are all composed of the most refined and well educated Americans, Spaniards, and Porto Ricans, and are the places by which our race should be judged and not by visiting the colored section of the city.

The Porto Ricans are grateful for what the United States had done for them, and that has been proved by facts in the recent World War. The quotas assigned to the island for Liberty Bond and Red Cross subscriptions were always oversubscribed and our loyalty to the flag demonstrated by the spirit of patriotism with which we accepted the Compulsory Military Service law. But that was not all. Hundreds of Porto Ricans enlisted voluntarily in the United States Army, and I have the honor to be one of them.

While I must admit that we have now better roads and schools than previous to the American domination beginning in 1898, it should not be forgotten that these roads and schools were built with money from the Porto Rican Treasury and not from the Federal Treasury, as Mr. Delaplaine states. Therefore, the native Porto Ricans, through taxes, paid for their roads and schools. As a matter of justice I should say that the Military Road from San Juan to Ponce, considered one of the best roads in the whole world, was built during the Spanish domination and is a masterpiece of the Spanish civil engineers.

It is the first time that I have heard that the American flag has been hissed by my countrymen and I doubt it, as I know them too well. To show how the present generation is Americanized it would be sufficient to ask a schoolboy who was Washington or Lincoln? On the other hand, if one inquired about prominent Porto Ricans, he probably might not know who they were.

Mr. Delaplaine says that the Porto Ricans have no desire to be civilized, but he certainly did not see negroes being lynched and burned alive.

His last compliment is calling us dirty. He saw the poorer suburbs of the cities. I wish that Mr. Delaplaine would visit certain sections of the east side of New York City. He will be certainly shocked. But it would not be fair for a Porto Rican tourist to call New York unclean, as the east side is only a part of the city.

The American colony at San Juan will undoubtedly disapprove the action of this gentleman, aimed to destroy the brotherhood between Americans and Porto Ricans.

Source: New York Times, February 27, 1921, XX3.

Luis Muñoz Marín, "The Sad Case of Porto Rico" (February 1929)

Luis Muñoz Marín (1898–1980) was one of Puerto Rico's most prominent politicos. After the U.S. takeover of the island, there were three political parties in Puerto Rico—the Alliance Party, the largest; the Unionist Party under Antonio R. Barceló (1868–1938); and the Socialist Party under Santiago Iglesias (1872–1939) and Rafael Martínez Nadal (1877–1941). These parties represented the divergent political tendencies on the island. Muñoz Marín at first joined the Socialists but later became a liberal. Puerto Ricans were faced with dire problems in the 1920s. Thirty percent of the farms had been wiped out between 1910 and 1920, and 50 percent of Puerto Rican farmers worked on small farms of 1–10 acres. Absentee ownership was a major problem, and fewer than 500 people owned one-third of the land. Added to this was the insult over the question of statehood. Puerto Ricans grew painfully aware that most Americans harbored racist views toward them. The following excerpts are from an article in which Luis Muñoz Marín describes conditions on the island and reacts to the consequences of American investment and cultural Americanization. The article is important for understanding the man who would become the first democratically elected governor of Puerto Rico in 1949.

Two major problems perplex the old Spanish province of Porto Rico, arising out of its enforced relationship to the United States. One deals with the consequences of American economic development, the other with cultural Americanization. Both go to the root of the drama now being acted on that gorgeous stage; both are portentous in their potentialities.

The American flag found Porto Rico penniless and content. It now flies over a prosperous factory worked by slaves who have lost their land and may soon lose their guitars and their songs. In the old days, most Porto Rican peasants owned a few pigs and chickens, maybe a horse or a cow, some goats, and in some way had the use of a patch of soil. Today, this modest security has been replaced by a vision of opulence. There are more things that they can't have and what they can imagine has widened monstrously. While there are many more schools for their hungry children and many more roads for their bare feet, their destiny is decidedly narrower now than it was when they were part and parcel of one of the most interesting and incompetent nationalities in the world.

In 1898, Porto Rico was a semi-feudal country, typical of the old Spanish provinces in America, willing and capable of assuming with a natural grace and a natural awkwardness its position in the Spanish commonwealth of provinces, or to venture into a simple, old-fashioned Latin-American national form. Its economics were those developed by Spain in the tropical New World: fiscally rotten, socially humble, and sound. Culturally, it was a slow, calm place. Racially, it shared with Costa Rica one peculiarity: a predominantly unmixed European peasantry—if Spain be Europe.

Schools were few, roads were fewer; chickens laid eggs under thatched cottages, goats cavorted outside and were corralled for a milking and sometimes killed for a stuffing, the squeal of pigs and not of factory whistles woke up the countryside. Pale, wiry, mustached, sleepy-eyed men tumbled out of hammocks pulling up their trousers for the day, and barefooted women in terribly starched dresses of many colors began preparing strong coffee in iron kettles and serving it steaming in polished cocoanut shells. Although Porto Rico was not then one of the great sugar producing centers of the world, there was usually sugar at the bottom of the cocoanut and the sleepy-eyed man stirred it lazily with a wooden spoon, tasting it with his eyes and his nose. Inside the hut, the brats wailed; one of them soothed itself by finding five eggs, certified by cackles, under the floor, another by plucking from the wall the image of the Virgin, printed in screaming blue and red. The men left for the field to cut cane, to lead the oxen on their sugar grinding merry-go-round, to prune or pick the coffee bushes in the sloping shade of the tall guavas, to pick and seed the cotton, or sift the tobacco leaves, or spade in their masters' truck field. As they wound their way along the coastal plain or twisted along the precipitous mountain paths, a very few pennies jingled in their pockets.

At noon the jíbaro comforted himself, for two cents, with a tumbler of rum bought at the store under the Ceiba tree, and went home to a meal of codfish with sweet potatoes and rice mixed with beans. The rice and beans were plentiful; he ate of them until he had enough, and then he slept. After the day's work, he loafed in the starlight, sang fantastic songs, usually depicting a topsy-turvy grandeur of some sort, made love to one or two girls, and then went home and made love to his wife.

On a Sunday, he might, with a number of his friends, carve a barbecued pig, get drunk in the shade, and go to a cockfight. If there was sickness in the family, the master of the plantation would send his doctor, and the master's wife might send some quinine or rhubarb or cadillo leaves. I don't believe he ever went to bed hungry or muddled through a spell of sickness without attention.

As he could not read, it was unlikely that he would discover that Porto Rico's total production for the year came to something less than $9,000,000 and that 950,000 human beings were living, sleeping, eating, drinking, feasting, gambling, singing, and loving on that money.

His master, the feudal lord, rose out of an enormous mahogany bed, washed his hands and face in cold water out of an enameled bowl with a design of roses, and breakfasted on a cup of coffee, rolls, butter, and cheese. Then he shouted for his horse and rode over his land, seeing that everyone was at work, inquiring after those who were sick or lazy, listening to gossip, giving advice on marriages. It was not until later in the morning that, coming upon a secluded bend of the stream where the Pomarrosas bent over the water, he took off his clothes and bathed. . . .

It is close contact with the United States rather than the influence of the small group of resident Americans that has given a decided, if superficial, direction to the institutional life of the island. The Y.M.C.A. has its swimming pool, its basketball court, its inspirational talks, but I doubt that such implied notions as Christ's disapproval of cigarettes get much serious attention from the local young men. Rotary slaps backs, sings, and hears speeches in a bored and genial way, but when I gave it a somewhat fantastic talk on the culture of light-skinned ladies as an index of civilization, the members really had a good time. The Elks and Odd Fellows play with their rituals, charity becomes slightly organized, evangelical preachers thunder in the villages, Holy Rollers roll in the back alleys, three or four prominent citizens become Protestants and are considered funny, women are beginning to be feared as the rolling-pin follows the flag, virginity still abounds and often attains to old age, but is perceptibly on the wane.

It is probably through the women that the largest doses of Americanism are being administered. The Latin-American attitude in this respect is confusing to a narrowly egalitarian world. Certainly we are wont to make a sharp nonsensical distinction between good and bad women—there is hardly any middle ground between chastity and prostitution. But this has not heretofore meant that the mere goodness of good women gave them any appreciable influence on the social point of view. Good women have been powerless and tame among us, and have grown smug in the consciousness of their hard luck. Generally speaking, there were only four things Latin women could be: old maids, wives, mistresses, or prostitutes. Now, they can be girls. They can be girls for a long time.

They can also be stenographers, bookkeepers, telephone operators, shop assistants, and feminists. They may speak in public and harass legislators.

Porto Rican politicians may now be publicly accused of keeping mistresses. The charge doesn't come near defeating them, but evidently there is some suggestion in the atmosphere that makes it seem relevant. Twenty years ago, it would have seemed preposterous to advance such an argument as in any way affecting a man's fitness for office. . . .

Will this [Americanization] ever come about? Will the island retain its historical personality? An unqualified answer to either of these questions would necessarily fall short of the possibilities. Perhaps a more absurd fate is in store for us. Perhaps we are destined to be neither Porto Ricans nor Americans, but merely puppets of a mongrel state of mind, susceptible to American thinking and proud of Latin thought, subservient to American living and worshipful of the ancestral way of life. Perhaps we are to discuss Cervantes and eat pork and beans in the Child's restaurant that must be opened sooner or later. Perhaps we will try not to let mother catch us reading the picaresque verses of Quevedo. Perhaps we are going to a singularly fantastic and painless hell in our own sweet way. Perhaps all this is nothing but a foretaste of Pan-Americanism.

Source: Marín, Luis Muñoz. "The Sad Case of Porto Rico." *The American Mercury* (February 1929).

"Cubans vs. Porto Ricans," Letter to the Editor of the *New Republic* Responding to "Porto Rico: A Colonial Responsibility"

(1929)

The following letter responds to "Porto Rico: A Colonial Responsibility," a February 6, 1929, article in the New Republic *regarding President Calvin Coolidge's (1872–1933) controversial speech that Puerto Ricans should be grateful to be part of the United States. The author called the article silly and goes beyond the Coolidge statement advising Puerto Rican gratitude. The letter is an expression of the racism of the times.*

SIR:

The editorial, "Porto Rico: A Colonial Responsibility" in the New Republic of February 6 is—how shall I term it without hurting feelings?—well, silly. I am disappointed with you for publishing it. On what grounds does the writer of that editorial base the statement: "Cuba and Santo Domingo and (in theory) Haiti are inhabited by peoples intellectually more backward than the Porto Ricans?" I know nothing about the Haitians and little about the Dominicans (though I am one of a large number who believe the Dominican, Máximo Gómez, was the greatest military intelligence in the history of the Americas). But I do know the other races sufficiently well to challenge the assertion that Cubans are intellectually inferior to Porto Ricans.

The fact is, the Porto Ricans are living in the best of all possible worlds for them. They are a supine, stodgy, spiritless race. They have not even as yet developed a spirit of nationalism at a time in the world's history when among cultured peoples nationalism has started on the way to join the family, the clan, and the city fetishes in the realm of the dodo. Had the Porto Ricans existed two thousand years ago they would inevitably have been the slaves of whatever virile people wanted them, if any. . . .

W. Z. W.

Washington, D.C.

Source: "Cubans vs. Porto Ricans." *The New Republic.* April 10, 1929, 230.

Memoirs of Bernardo Vega

(1977)

Bernardo Vega (1885–1965) arrived in New York from Puerto Rico in 1916, just before the U.S. involvement in World War I. Originally a cigar maker in Puerto Rico, Vega, like so many Puerto Rican immigrants, found employment in munitions factories. As a reader for cigar makers, he achieved an extraordinary education with a highly developed class consciousness. The Memoirs of Bernardo Vega *tell of the Puerto Rican struggle for justice from a socialist perspective during the early development of the Puerto Rican community in New York. They also describe life in the city, how Puerto Ricans adjusted to this new environment, their past times, and their organization.*

The Battery, which as I found out later is what they call the tip of lower Manhattan where our ferry from Staten Island docked, was also a port of call for all the elevated trains. The Second, Third, Sixth, and Ninth Avenue lines all met there. . . . The train snaked along at breakneck speed. I pretended to take note of everything, my eyes like the golden deuce in a deck of Spanish cards. The further along we moved, and as the dingy buildings filed past my view, all the visions I had of the gorgeous splendor of New York vanished. The skyscrapers seemed like tall gravestones, I wondered why, if the United States was so rich, as surely it was, did its biggest city look so grotesque? . . .

We returned by the same route, but got off the bus at 110th Street. We walked up Manhattan Avenue to 116th, which is where the Leon brothers—Antonio, Pepín, and Abelardo—were living. They owned a small cigar factory. They were part of a family from Cayey that had emigrated to New York back in 1904. The members of that family were some of the first Puerto Ricans to settle in the Latin barrio of Harlem. In those days the Nadals, Matienzos, Pietris, Escalonas, and Umpierres lived there too; I also knew of a certain Julio Ortiz. In all, I'd say there were some one hundred and fifty Puerto Ricans living in that part of the city around the turn of the century.

Before our countrymen, there were other Hispanics here. There was a sizable Cuban colony in the last quarter of the nineteenth century, members of the Quesada, Arango, and Mantilla families, as well as Emilia Casanova de Villaverde. They must have been people of some means, since they lived in apartments belonging to Sephardic Jews on 110th Street facing Central Park.

As I was saying, when I took up residence in New York in 1916, the apartment buildings and stores in what came to be known as El Barrio, "our" barrio, or the Barrio Latino, all belonged to Jews. Seventh, St. Nicholas, and Manhattan Avenues, and the streets in between, were all inhabited by Jewish people of means, if not great wealth. [Then] 110th Street was the professional center of the district. The classy, expensive stores were on Lenox Avenue, while the more modest ones were located east of Fifth Avenue. The ghetto of poor Jews extended along Park Avenue between 110th and 117th and on the streets east of Madison. It was in this lower-class Jewish neighborhood that some Puerto Rican and Cuban families, up to about fifty of them, were living at that time. . . .

In those years, and for a long time to come, the Socialist Party, the Cigarmakers' Union, and the Seamen's Union were the only groups that were concerned about defending foreign workers. The other labor unions either showed no interest, or were too weak to do anything, as in the case of the Dressmakers' Union, which later became the powerful International Ladies' Garment Workers' Union. . . .

As soon as I had assured myself of a job at the cigar factory, I enrolled in a public school on 86th Street off First Avenue. The other students were mostly Hungarians and Germans. The class was taught by a little teacher of Irish descent. One night she talked of the advantages of being a United States citizen and how to go about becoming one. "How can I become an American citizen?" I asked. She replied that you just have to follow the steps she had outlined. I responded by pointing out that, unlike our Hungarian and German classmates, Puerto Ricans do not really have any citizenship. Outside of Puerto Rico our natural citizenship is not recognized. Without any citizenship to give up, it would seem pretty hard for us to become Americans.

A bit flustered, the teacher could only restate what she had said before: that you just have to give up your own citizenship, follow the steps, and there you have it. And it was the same for everyone who was a resident of the United States!

"Yes, for everyone," I said, "except Puerto Ricans."

The teacher did not like my attitude. She must have thought that I was trying to make her look stupid in front of the whole class. She called the principal who, informed of the situation, felt it his duty to save the teacher from ridicule. After hemming and hawing, he concluded by saying that the problem was that so little is known about Puerto Rico here in the United States.

This incident wouldn't be worth mentioning if it weren't for what happened as a result: they transferred me to a school so far from where I was living that I had to give up my studies. I would have been better off if I hadn't said anything. Which is how I learned that keeping your mouth shut is the key to "success" in the United States. . . .

Cigar workers bought and circulated a wide assortment of books, especially works expressing the most advanced ideas published in America and Europe. There were also many newspapers and magazines advocating all kinds of social and political doctrines. In New York City there were several newspapers published in Spanish: the anarchist Cultura Proletaria; the more general-interest El Heraldo; Las Novedades, an old-time Spanish paper founded in 1887; and La Prensa, a daily that began publishing in 1913. There were a few monthly magazines, too, such as El Comercio.

This variety reflected the cultural, political, and civic environment of the Hispanic community in New York in 1917. Cigar makers and their families made up more than 60 percent of the Puerto Rican population. . . .

In about 1918, entertainment for Puerto Ricans in New York was confined to the apartments they lived in. They celebrated birthdays and weddings and, of course, Christmas Eve, New Year's Day, and the Feast of the Epiphany. But always at home, with friends and neighbors.

There would be dancing, and between numbers somebody would recite poetry or hold forth about our distant homeland. At some of the parties there were charangas, lively groups of Puerto Rican musicians. But most of the time we played records. By that time, Columbia Records was recording danzas, aguinaldos, and other kinds of music from back home.

Almost every family owned a Victrola, and many even had a Pianola. The fact is that once this music gained in popularity, Puerto Ricans were exploited mercilessly. Pianolas cost about $500.00, on credit. Many was the worker who wound up losing what little he earned by falling behind on his payments. Not to mention the times a family would move and have to leave their Pianola behind . . . just getting it from one place to another cost more than moving the rest of their belongings!

Those boisterous Puerto Rican parties would often disturb neighbors of other nationalities, which led to some serious conflicts and unpleasant quarrels.

And there were some less innocent events as well. In the more spacious apartments in Harlem, some people threw parties on Saturdays and Sundays that weren't just family parties, but full-scale dances with a cover charge and all. And once you were in they'd take you for whatever else you had, for drinks and tidbits. Which is not the least of the shameful things that went on.

There was none of that in the homes of the tabaqueros. . . .

Source: Iglesias, Cesar Andreu, ed. *Memoirs of Bernardo Vega: A Contribution to the History of the Puerto Rican Community in New York.* Translated by Juan Flores.

# of Latino Immigrants in the Early 20th Century

Bylaws of *La Liga Protectora Latina* (1920)

La Liga Protectora Latina *(the Latin Protective League) was organized in Phoenix, Arizona, in 1915 by Mexican American leaders to ensure that members had health, accident, and death benefits. It shared members with other mutual aid societies, such as* La Alianza Hispano Americana *(the Spanish American Alliance) (1894), but it was much more involved in political struggles, including campaigning against the 80 percent law, which excluded noncitizens from the workplace (80 percent of the workforce had to be native-born Americans).* La Liga *also sponsored adult and other educational programs. The following is a copy of the society's by-laws showing the sophistication of early Mexican American organizations, which have been dismissed by some historians.*

First chapter. Denomination, address, objective, and principles.

Art. 1. This Society was called "Liga Protectora Latina" (Latin Protective League) when it was created and will continue to bear the same name.

Art. 2. This Society was organized in Phoenix, Arizona, on February 10, 1915, where it was incorporated and legally authorized to exercise its duties according to the laws of that state on August 30, 1915.

Art. 3. Its legal address and primary branch of business will be Phoenix, Arizona, under the government of the Supreme Board of Directors, which will execute its authority over the Branches established or those that will be set up in the State of Arizona, in other states of the American Union, and Latin-American countries where its extension and development will be pursued.

Art. 4. The Latin Protective League is a POLITICAL, FRATERNAL, AND EDUCATIONAL Corporation whose objective is to:

I. Pursue unity and development of brotherhood between Latinos regardless of nationality.
II. Aid members in need in case of illness and if they should die, attend their funerals, and offer a pecuniary death benefit to the

member so that it is received according to the ordinances.

III. Pay attention to the Legislatures and other departments within the State of Arizona and everywhere else so that laws or dispositions are not issued whose objectives might deprive Latinos of their privileges and rights as citizens or of their individual guarantees sanctioned by the Constitution of the United States and present treaties.

IV. Try to defend members of the Institution and people of Latin descent before all officials or courts so that they receive the same treatment and law enforcement as individuals of other races.

V. Encourage Latino voters to exercise their political rights by guiding and unifying their vote toward the interests of our race during general elections in order to help citizens of Latin descent or those who are not hostile toward our race obtain positions in the Executive, Legislative, and Judicial Branches.

VI. Promote intellectual, moral, and economic improvement of Latinos through proper educational systems, English and Spanish classes, by establishing Cooperatives, Savings Banks, and other similar methods.

VII. Harmonize the interests of the diverse economic elements by establishing mutual agreement and respect for individual rights, by abstaining from the use of violence and class struggle, and by trying to solve conflicts that may appear with the set of the principles of conciliation and arbitrage.

Art. 5. PROTECTION, EQUALITY, AND JUSTICE are the principles that the Latin Protective League adopts, and condensed in them you will find the objectives that they pursue as they are listed in the previous article.

Art. 6. The "Protection" principle forces all League members to wait and help all individuals of the race, especially their comrades in all situations in which that protection is necessary. The manner and cases in which it is necessary to provide protection for the Society will be arranged by the ordinances and regulations.

Art. 7. The "Equality" principle indicates that the Latin Protective League advocates the exercise of political rights, including carrying out public tasks of popular election and jury duty by Latinos, as well as the identical treatment in labor fields, political and private fields, and the abolition of laws and practices that try to establish race distinctions which prejudice Latinos or residents of the same origin in the United States.

Art. 8. When the Latin Protective League proclaims the "Justice" principle, it intends to obtain for its members, and Latinos in general, unbiased and just decisions in civil trials and the granting of all guarantees that the laws concede a defendant in criminal liability cases.

Art.9.Allbanners,emblems,badges,correspondence, stamps, and other objects of the Supreme Court and its Branches will have the name of the Corporation inscribed and next to it the following words, "PROTECTION, EQUALITY, JUSTICE" or its initials "P.E.J." which will be used as the formal closing on the Society's official and private correspondence as well as between its members.

Second chapter. Motto, coat of arms, and the use of social badges.

Art. 10. The motto of the Latin Protective League is "One for all. All for one." It represents the mutual aid and brotherly love as the basis of our Institution. They should also be inscribed in the objectives addressed in the previous article.

Art. 11. The Society's coat of arms will have the shape, allegory, and emblem that are drawn here:

All for one. One for all.

Source: Rosales, F. Arturo, ed., *Testimonio: A Documentary History of the Mexican American Struggle for Civil Rights*. Houston: Arte Publico Press–University of Houston © 2000, 114–115. Reprinted with permission of the publisher.

R. N. McLean and Charles A. Thompson, "Spanish and Mexican in Colorado" (1924)

The Rev. Robert N. McLean (1882–1964) was the associate director of the Presbyterian Board of Missions in the United States. The U.S. Presbyterian Church was heavily involved worldwide in missionary work in such countries as China, Ireland, Puerto Rico, and Mexico. Mexicans in the United States were seen as an extension of those in Mexico, where many native ministers were trained and schools established. McLean belonged to the more progressive arm of the Presbyterian Church, often advocating for the material well-being of Mexicans. In the following article, McLean says the condition of the Spanish-speaking in Colorado was deteriorating. The excerpt describes the work of contract laborers and the importance of sugar beets in attracting Mexicans to the United States. The Immigration Acts of 1917, 1921, and 1924 had severely restricted the labor supply of central and southern Europeans. In 1924, the Great Western Sugar Company in Colorado hired thousands of Mexicans from New Mexico and sent enganchadores *(labor contractors) into Mexico to contract with more than 10,000 Mexicans to fill the void. These workers were brought into Colorado at a time when sugar production was expanding and there was a lack of housing and other facilities. Church people like McLean were the few voices raised that were pro-immigrant.*

Traveling through the beet fields of Colorado, or across the broad grazing lands, one thinks of the state as comparatively level. But if one attempts to cross from one tableland to tableland—"parks" they call them—one is convinced of the fact that one is indeed upon the backbone of America.

Colorado is high—so high in fact that only one fourth of the area lies below 5,000 feet, while about two thirds of its surface ranges between 6,000 and 14,000 feet. Lots of potatoes are raised in Colorado, but boiled with difficulty in almost every corner of the state.

And Colorado is large. Within its borders the Plymouth fathers could have found land to make twelve states the size of Massachusetts. Although it is seventh in size among the states of the Union, its total population in 1920 was only 939,629; this means a little more than nine persons to the square mile. Still it must be remembered that some of the square miles of Colorado are too vertical for anyone even to try to stand upon them.

Colorado also is diverse in its topography, as well as in its crops. There are no less than nine clearly defined districts. Beginning with the non-irrigated prairie section in the eastern part of the state, one passes to the broad valley watered by the Arkansas in the southeastern part. Across the La Veta pass, where the road crosses the divide at an elevation of ten thousand feet, one comes to the San Luis valley, where since the early days of the Spanish adventurers, millions of sheep have grazed. Another . . . over the mountains to the west, and we are in the great San Juan basin, fertile in resources, and needing only adequate transportation facilities to awaken it from slumber. Then there is the valley of the South Platte, the valleys of the Colorado and tributary streams in the central western part, the mountainous mineral districts, and the broad upland grazing lands known as north central and south parks. But whether it be plain, or valley it is always Colorado—Colorado with her face set toward the days which are to be.

Colorado is diverse also in her population groups; and it is a diversity which is exemplified even among the Spanish people which this survey studies. The earliest Americans of European blood were the Spanish Americans living principally . . . bordering upon New Mexico. These people have lived in Colorado for fifty or sixty years; in fact they were there when the Anglo-American appeared, and so were really the first settlers. They are descended from immigrants from New Mexico, who though they passed through old Mexico on their way from Spain, did not dwell there for any considerable length of time, and so supposedly kept their blood free from any Indian tinge. Having been born on American soil, these Spanish Americans are citizens. Because they are native to the United States are sometimes referred to by Anglo-Americans as "native Mexicans," in distinction to the Mexicans born south of the border who are "old Mexico Mexicans." The Spanish used by these people is in many instances extremely archaic. The expressions upon the lips of the Spanish Americans can be found outside the pages of the writers of Spain's golden age. The isolation which distances furnished for so many years has been replaced by an isolation of language and blood; and the people have therefore perpetuated many of the [errors] . . . of Spain during her age of gold.

The Mexicans are those who were born south of the Rio Grande in the Republic of Mexico, and who have emigrated to the United States, usually within the last five or ten years. They are not American citizens, and usually do not wish to become so.

In many cases their skin is slightly darker than that of the Spanish Americans. The Spanish Americans are more phlegmatic, more taciturn than are the old Mexico Mexicans. It is harder to move . . . them; but they "stay put" better than their neighbors from the south. Also they are very much more "Catholic" in the narrow sense of the word than are the Mexicans. The immigrant Mexicans have seen the effects of unchecked Romanism in governmental affairs. They have learned to identify church and state, and there has resulted a decided reaction against both. Hence, while Protestantism makes less apparent headway among the Spanish Americans, the results gained are more permanent.

In addition to the descendents of the early settlers there are people of Spanish blood in southern Colorado, Las Animas and Huerfano counties, in the southeastern part of the state, and also lie southeastern end of the mountainous belt. In all, these districts contain about 25,000 persons. The San Luis valley has approximately 5,000 and the San Juan valley to the west between 2,000 and 3,000. For the state, a total of 35,000 is probably a fair estimate.

According to the census of 1920, Mexicans were found in fifty-two of the sixty-three counties of Colorado. In eighteen of these counties there was a population of 100 or more Mexicans. Their work as section hands on the railroads probably does more to give them this wide distribution, than any other cause. Their work in the coal mines attracts them in considerable numbers to the eastern edge of the mineral belt, in Weld, Boulder, Fremont, Huerfano, and Las animas counties. But they are found in greatest numbers in the South Platte and Arkansas valleys drawn by the demand for labor for the beet fields. The two industrial centers of Pueblo and Denver also possess a considerable colony of Mexicans. Pueblo has 5,000; Denver a steady population of about 2,000, which is augmented to two or three times that number during the winter, by beet workers who come there after the close of the beet season and remain until the spring work begins. In 1920 the census showed that in the whole state there were 10,894 Mexicans. With regard to the situation at present, it is impossible to give anything more than an estimate. But considering all the industrial and agricultural fields in which the Mexican is now found, the figure suggested by Mr. José Esparza, the Mexican consul of Denver, of 22,000–25,000, does not appear improbable, if we understand it to include the migratory beet workers. Thus, with 25,000 Mexicans, and 35,000 Spanish Americans, we have 60,000 people of Spanish speech in the state.

And there are more to follow. Experimentation as to the adaptability of the soil of the San Luis valley for beet culture is being made. Colorado, the diverse, the gigantic Rocky Mountain state is just coming into her kingdom.

Source: New York, Board of National Missions, Presbyterian Church in the U.S.A., 1924, vii–x.

Adolfo Romo v. Tempe School District (1925)

According to Arizona State University historian Arturo Rosales, the "first successful desegregation court case of Mexicans took place in Tempe, Arizona, in 1925. Mexican families, whose ancestors helped found the city in the 1870s, succeeded in overturning a segregation policy in effect since 1915. However, segregation continued for children of the recently arrived or from poorer families until the 1940s." The following are excerpts of the Superior Court's ruling in favor of Adolfo "Babe" Romo and other parents who sued the district to admit Mexicans to the 10th Street School in Tempe, Arizona. The parents were supported by local mutualistas *(mutual aid societies) such as La Alianza Hispano Americana (the Spanish American Alliance) and* La Liga Protectora Latina *(the Latin Protective League). In Tempe, not only the schools were segregated but also the swimming pools.*

THE COURT: This is an action brought by the plaintiff Adolfo Romo against the Board of Trustees and Superintendent of School District No. 3 of Maricopa County, comprising the town of Tempe wherein he prays for a writ of mandamus requiring the defendants to admit his four children to the public schools of said district upon equal terms with all other children of school age residing within said school district. The plaintiff in his complaint says that he and his children are of "Spanish-Mexican" descent; that the defendants Trustees of School District No. 3 have entered into an agreement with the Board of Education of the Tempe Normal School of the State of Arizona, whereby one of the two school buildings of School District No. 3, known as the "Eighth Street School" has been set apart, designated and declared to be a "Normal Training School" and its use, insofar as it relates to "primary or elemental education," shall be restricted to "Spanish-American" or "Mexican-American" children; that the children required to attend said Eighth Street School pursuant to said agreement are taught exclusively by "student teachers"; that the plaintiff presented his four children to the defendant, Superintendent of School District No. 3 on September 14th, 1925, and requested their admission to the public schools of School District No. 3, but that said defendant, acting under the orders and directions of defendants Board of Trustees of School District No. 3, refused and still refuses to admit said children to the public schools of said School District No. 3 but required and directed them to report to the authorities of the said Normal Training School pursuant to said agreement; that by reason of the said acts of defendants, the children of plaintiff, as well as all other Spanish-American and Mexican-American children entitled to be admitted to the public schools of School District No. 3, are, on account of their race or descent, and without regard to their age, advancement, or convenience, segregated, excluded, and compelled to attend the Eighth Street School taught exclusively by student teachers of the Normal Training School of the Tempe State Teacher's College.

An alternative writ was issued and the defendants filed their return to the writ and answer to plaintiff's complaint, admitting that plaintiff's children are entitled to admission to the public schools of School District No. 3, if they reside with him in said district, but deny that said children have been refused admission to said schools; alleging that for purposes of convenience and advantage to the children of Spanish-American and Mexican-American extraction and descent, all such children, including the children of [the] plaintiff, admitted to the first six grades of elemental education were located in what is commonly called the Eighth Street School and taught by teachers able to speak and understand the Spanish language; that the course of education in said Eight Street School is the same in every respect and the same character of, surroundings, advantages, and equipment prevail therein, as is maintained by the defendants in any other school in said district, and that teachers of the same grade in ability are employed in said Eighth Street School as are employed in said Tenth Street School. . . .

This action, having come on for trial upon the complaint of the plaintiff herein, the return and answer of the defendant thereto, and having been tried by the court sitting without a jury, and the court having filed its findings of fact herein, and the court having determined as conclusions of law, that the relator is entitled to a permanent peremptory writ of mandamus, as prayed for in the complaint.

NOW, upon motion of Edward B. Goodwin and Harold I. Janson, attorneys for said plaintiff:

IT IS ORDERED, ADJUDGED, AND DECREED, that the said Adolfo Romo, plaintiff herein, have a permanent peremptory writ of mandamus, and that the same do issue forthwith directed to and commanding the said defendants, William E. Laird, I. H. Daniel and I. F. Waterhouse, as members of, and constituting the Board of Trustees of Tempe School District No. 3, and G. W. Persons, Superintendent of Tempe School District No. 3, Maricopa County, Arizona, upon the pain and peril that shall fall thereon for refusal, that they and each one of them, shall admit the children of Adolpho Romo, namely, Antonio Romo, age fifteen; Henry Romo, age fourteen; Alice Romo, age eleven; and Charles Romo, age seven, on the same terms and conditions to the public schools of said Tempe School District No. 3, Maricopa County, Arizona, as children of other nationalities are now admitted.

Done in open court this 5th day of October, a.d. 1925.

Source: Excerpt is reprinted with permission of the publisher of *Testimonio: A Documentary History of the Mexican American Struggle for Civil Rights,* F. Arturo Rosales, ed. Houston: Arte Publico Press–University of Houston, 126–127. © 2000.

Anonymous, "Life, Trial, and Death of Aurelio Pompa" (1928)

A corrido *is a folk ballad popular among Mexicans who, to this day, record popular events, tragedies, and injustices in verse form. This* corrido *was transcribed by the great Mexican anthropologist Manuel Gamio (1883–1960), who did groundbreaking work on the Mexicans in the United States. This ballad was sung in the United States by Mexicans who protested the execution of Aurelio Pompa for the shooting and death of a white foreman who had verbally and physically abused him. Pompa was from Sonora, Mexico. After he was mistreated and beaten by a white foreman, he went home, got a gun, and shot the foreman to death. After mistrials, Pompa was convicted and sentenced to death in 1924. The Mexican community unsuccessfully sought a reprieve.*

I am going to tell you the sad story
Of a Mexican who emigrated out here—
Aurelio Pompa, so he was called.
Our compatriot who died there,
Out there in Caborca, which is in Sonora,
The humble village where he was born,
"Come on, mother," he said one day,
"Over there, there are no revolutions.

Goodbye, friends; goodbye, Maria,"
He said to his betrothed very sadly.
"I promise you that I will return soon,
So we can get married, God willing."
"Goodbye, Aurelio," said the girl,
And she went sobbing to pray.
"Look after him, Virgin Mary,
I have a foreboding he will not come back."
The priest and his friends
Along with his sweetheart went to talk
And to beg poor Aurelio
Not to leave his native village. Such advice was useless
And so were the entreaties of his mother.
"Let's go, mother, over there is the dollar,
And I swear I am going to earn a lot of them."
Four years ago in the month of May
The two of them went to California
And through misfortune on the very same date
Died there in prison.
A carpenter who was very strong
Struck the poor young fellow cruelly,
And Aurelio Pompa swore to be revenged
For those blows he had received.
Filled with rage he told his mother about it
And the poor old woman advised him,
"Por Dios, forget it, dear son."
And good Aurelio forgave him;
But one afternoon, when he was working
With three friends at the railroad station
The carpenter came by mocking at him
And aroused poor Pompa.
The three friends advised him
To leave him alone and go his way,
And then the carpenter, with a hammer,
Very offensively threatened him.
Then Pompa, seeing the danger,
Fired in self-defense
With a revolver and face to face
As a man he killed him.
The case came to court, the jury arrived,
And the Yankee people sentenced him.
"The death penalty," they all demanded,
And the lawyer did not object.
Twenty thousand signatures of compatriots
Asked for his pardon from the Governor.
All the newspapers asked for it too,
And even Obregon sent a message.
All was useless; the societies,
All united, asked his pardon.
His poor mother, half-dead already,
Also went to see the Governor. . . .
"Farewell, my friends, farewell, my village;
Dear mother, cry no more.
Tell my race not to come here,
For here they will suffer; there is no pity here.
The jailor asked him:
"Were you Spanish?" and he answered,
"I am a Mexican and proud of being so
Although they deny me a pardon."
This is the story of a compatriot
Who four years ago came there
And through misfortune on the same date
Died in a dreadful way in a prison.
Los Angeles, Calif.

Source: Gamio, Manuel. *Mexican Immigration to the United States: A Study of Human Migration And Adjustment*. New York: Dover Publications, Inc., 1971, 104–105.

Lina E. Bresette, "Mexicans in the United States: A Report of a Brief Survey" (1929)

The National Catholic Welfare Council (NCWC) of the American Catholic bishops, which met annually from 1919 to 1966, was established largely in response to Protestant efforts to convert Mexicans. Reproduced here are excerpts from a report by sociologist Lina E. Bressette on the status of Mexicans in the United States. The report is important because, although the overwhelming majority of Mexicans were Catholics, little was known about them. The following brief survey indicates who they were and where they worked. It draws attention to the reaction of nativist groups, such as the Ku Klux Klan, to their presence.

Mexican labor is becoming an increasingly basic factor in certain lines of industry. Most of the Mexicans who come to the United States work at unskilled labor. They are much in demand for the reason, expressed by many employers, that they are "not radical," "easily controlled by those in authority," and "willing to take orders." In the North, East, South and West, the Mexican is being used. Lumbering, agriculture, mining, grazing, railroad construction, all demand his labor. They furnish the great supply of transient labor for the perishable crops of the Southwest. Much of their work is seasonal and they drift from one occupation to another, from state to state, and between seasons are often idle and unemployed. It is reported that in the Imperial Valley in California each year, Mexican labor picks "25 tons of raisins, 25 tons of walnuts, 5 million boxes of lemons, and 25 million boxes of oranges." In Texas thousands of acres of Bermuda onions are cared for by the Mexicans. Families are to be found in large numbers in the beet areas of California, Utah, Colorado, Montana, Wyoming, North Dakota, Michigan, and Ohio. In three counties of Colorado, 18,000 cared for 110,000 acres of beets, more than two thirds of its entire beet acreage.

They travel with the crops and the jobs. Whole families of them may be seen loaded in old and half broken-down Fords going from the oranges to the cantaloupes, then to the grape picking, and then, to the walnuts. From the beet fields they go to whatever work is offered them. In the Southwest they are the principal highway builders and almost exclusively the railroad section hands. They pick much of the cotton in Texas and Arizona, they tend vineyards, citrus orchards, walnut groves and melon fields in California, they care for the sugar beets in Colorado, Wyoming, Montana, and California, they are in the copper mines of Arizona. . . .

The General Secretary of the I.W.W. [Industrial Workers of the World] claims that "a large number of Mexican workers have joined and are joining the I.W.W., mainly Colorado miners and beet workers of Colorado and other Western states." The Knights of Columbus Welfare Committee of one state denies that the I.W.W. has made much progress, but adds, that "when representatives of the I.W.W. and other radical groups go into the fields and talk with the Mexicans, who are already conscious of the discrimination against them, about labor unionism, exploitation, inequality, and injustice, they have used the existing bad conditions effectively to attract and secure followers." The chairman of this Committee says a deplorable economic exploitation of the Mexicans and Spanish-speaking people is taking place under the very noses of the Catholics; who ought to be the first to raise their voices in protest and to help introduce reforms for better working conditions. The Knights of Columbus Welfare Committee in Colorado and representatives of the Knights of Columbus, particularly in New Mexico and Texas, and a number of the Bishops have on many occasions spoken against their bad working conditions. . . .

Of course, the walls of prejudice and mistrust are breaking down gradually, and as the two groups come to know each other, there is more mutual esteem. So far, there has been very little intermarriage.

In Walsenburg, the Ku Klux Klan has been active, and has done much to drive the two groups apart. Last January, the sheriff and the chief prohibition officer were shot, and shortly after that the Klan held a parade. As a result, feeling has been very bitter. Said a leading Spanish American, "The Klan has made the Spanish Americans a solid group again. We were drifting apart, away from the church, away from our old friends. But this has brought us all together again. But you know this bitter feeling . . . there's a fellow in town whom I chummed with at school since we were kids. We sat in the same double desk, went to picnics and parties together. I was at home at his house, and he at mine. When mother made some Spanish dish that he especially liked, we had him over . . . our wives were friends in the same way. And now he's leader of the Klan, and ready to knife me in the back at any time. Gosh darn it, it hurts to believe it. . . ."

The Spanish population of this section is maintained principally by agricultural activities. In Alamosa, there are railroad shops and a newly established lumber mill, but otherwise the occupation of the people is dominantly agricultural. Many of the Spanish Americans own their farms, small holdings running 80 to 160 acres. They raise grains, potatoes, and peas, and some stock though less sheep than formerly. Many others are agricultural laborers. Housing, educational, and health conditions are largely similar to those among the rural population of Las Animas and Huerfano counties. . . .

Source: Social Action Department, National Catholic Welfare Conference, Washington, DC, 1929, iii, 16, 17, 19.

Constitution of the League of United Latin American Citizens (1929)

By the 1920s, a sizable middle-class Mexican American community had emerged in the United States. These middle-class Mexican Americans challenged the political and social hegemony of the Mexican elites who had dominated business and even Spanish-language newspapers. Mutualistas *(mutual aid societies) were the most popular form of organization. With veterans from World War I returning, second-generation Mexican Americans began forming their own issues that were focused on conditions in the United States rather than in Mexico. The League of United Latin American Citizens (LULAC) was formed in 1929; it was a middle-class Mexican American group that demanded equal participation in American life. It was in favor of better education, the end of segregation in schools and public facilities, and the abolition of other forms of racism. It limited its membership to U.S. citizens and fought vigorously for civil rights. LULAC paid for attorneys who brought lawsuits against school districts and established precedents for abolishing school segregation. LULAC also secured the right of Mexican Americans to serve on juries. The organization was important because it focused on second-generation Mexican Americans instead of serving the needs of the immigrant community.*

To develop within the members of our race the best, purest, and most perfect type of a true and loyal citizen of the United States of America.

To eradicate from our body politic all intents and tendencies to establish discriminations among our fellow citizens on account of race, religion, or social position as being contrary to the true spirit of Democracy, our Constitution, and Laws.

To use all the legal means at our command to the end that all citizens in our country may enjoy equal rights, the equal protection of the laws of the land and equal opportunities and privileges.

The acquisition of the English language, which is the official language of our country, being necessary for the enjoyment of our rights and privileges, we declare it to be the official language of this organization, and we pledge ourselves to learn and speak and teach same to our children.

To define with absolute and unmistakable clearness our unquestionable loyalty to the ideals, principles, and citizenship of the United States of America.

To assume complete responsibility for the education of our children as to their rights and duties and the language and customs of this country; the latter, in so far as they may be good customs.

We solemnly declare once [and] for all to maintain a sincere and respectful reverence for our racial origin of which we are proud.

Secretly and openly, by all lawful means at our command, we shall assist in the education and guidance of Latin Americans and we shall protect and defend their lives and interest whenever necessary.

We shall destroy any attempt to create racial prejudices against our people, and any infamous stigma which may be cast upon them, and we shall demand for them the respect and prerogatives which the Constitution grants to us all.

Each of us considers himself with equal responsibilities in our organization, to which we voluntarily swear subordination and obedience.

We shall create a fund for our mutual protection, for the defense of those of us who may be unjustly persecuted and for the education and culture of our people.

This organization is not a political club, but as citizens we shall participate in all local, state, and national political contests. However, in doing so we shall ever bear in mind the general welfare of our people, and we disregard and abjure once and for all any personal obligation which is not in harmony with these principles.

With our vote and influence we shall endeavor to place in public office men who show by their deeds, respect and consideration for our people.

We shall select as our leaders those among us who demonstrate, by their integrity and culture, that they are capable of guiding and directing us properly.

We shall maintain publicity means for the diffusion of these principles and for the expansion and consolidation of this organization.

We shall pay our poll tax as well as that of members of our families in order that we may enjoy our rights fully.

We shall diffuse our ideals by means of the press, lectures, and pamphlets.

We shall oppose any radical and violent demonstration which may tend to create conflicts and disturb the peace and tranquility of our country.

We shall have mutual respect for our religious views and we shall never refer to them in our institutions.

We shall encourage the creation of educational institutions for Latin Americans and we shall lend our support to those already in existence.

We shall endeavor to secure equal representation for our people on juries and in the administration of governmental affairs.

We shall denounce every act of peonage and mistreatment as well as the employment of our minor children of scholastic age.

We shall resist and attack energetically all machinations tending to prevent our social and political unification.

We shall oppose any tendency to separate our children in the schools of this country.

We shall maintain statistics which will guide our people with respect to working and living conditions and agricultural and commercial activities in the various parts of our country.

Source: Weeks, O. Douglas. "The League of United Latin-American Citizens: A Texas-Mexican Civic Organization." *Southwestern Political and Social Science Quarterly*, December 1929, 257–278.

Emory S. Bogardus, "The Mexican Immigrant and Segregation" (1930)

The following article is by University of Southern California sociologist Emory S. Bogardus (1882–1973). In 1915, Bogardus founded one of the first sociology departments in the United States at the University of Southern California. He served as president of the American Sociological Society in

1931. From the Chicago School, he encouraged a host of students to conduct community studies of Mexican communities. This treasure trove of theses and dissertations is now in the University of Southern California library. The following excerpts are about living conditions for Mexicans in Los Angeles in the 1920s. Here, Bogardus profiles the town of Santa Ana, which is east of Los Angeles in Orange County.

1. THE MEXICAN COMMUNITY

Nearly every city in the southwestern part of the United States has its Mexican community. The native-born portions may range from descendants of families who lived in the area when the given region was a part of Mexico to the young children who are known as second-generation Mexicans. Irrespective of these diversities, a significant observation is the relative uniformity with which a Mexican community may be found as an integral or adjacent part, not only of every American city or town in the Southwest, but of the rural districts as well.

Often the Mexican community is the original part of the American city. It may have a history extending back a century or more; it may have stood still as a small Mexican village for decades; and then in the latter part of the nineteenth century, or more recently, have become a center of settlement by American immigrants from the Middle West [Midwest] or from the eastern sections of the United States. Differences in the history of the settlement of the two groups and in culture traits are pronounced and significant; they account for many of the current conflict problems.

In S. A., a city of 25,000 [assumed to be Santa Ana], there is first of all the typical Mexican community located "beyond the railroad tracks." This is relatively large, static, unsanitary. "Beyond the railroad tracks" means a part of town where living conditions are naturally the least desirable and the poorest. The lowest levels of Mexican immigrant culture are found here. An important sidelight is thrown upon this situation by the following observation of a Mexican who feels somewhat deeply on the matter. "Why did the Mexicans come to this part of town? Because it was low and swampy, and not good, and that is where the Americans want the Mexicans to go—to the places where the Americans will not go themselves. The rents also have something to do with the situation." Nearly every city of size in the Southwest has an area such as the one referred to here. It is an area of first settlement, which sooner or later becomes the parent of areas of second, and even third, settlements.

In S. A. there is an area of second and one of second and third settlement combined. The process of moving out from the area of first settlement is most interesting. The area of second settlement in S. A. was established in part by members of the younger generation residing in the first-settlement region. They grew dissatisfied with the environment and sought a better district in the opposite side of town. Newly married Mexican couples were not content to live "beyond the tracks." They have settled in a much better part of town and have become so well established there that Mexicans from this district together with Mexicans from the first are starting a third Mexican district. But who are the Mexicans that leave the old district? In the main, they represent families who can afford to live in better houses and pay higher rents. These invade the American community, where they can get larger yards, gas, electric lights, and inside plumbing, and where the streets are paved. They are persons who have developed the desire to live in the type of houses that Americans live in, and in American neighborhoods, if possible. Some of these young married couples want to buy a home like Americans have, preferably a stucco one, for are not "all Americans moving into stucco houses?"

As rents become cheaper in some American quarters, there is a tendency for the more wide-awake Mexicans to break into an American community. "Lower rents in American sections and the desire to put the children into schools with American children have been responsible for much of the shifting in population." Sometimes there is a wholesale migration, due to the activities of subdividers. American real estate men have been active in promoting such plans.

2. SEGREGATION

Both the urban and rural Mexican immigrant communities are segregated from American communities. This segregation is partly spatial and partly psycho-social. One of the self-evident results of segregation is the failure of the Mexican immigrant to become an American citizen. It is in this connection that illustrative materials may be presented for the study of the segregation problem. Although there are two million or more Mexicans in the United States, and although many have been in the country many years, the number who have taken out citizenship papers is almost negligible. After those who were born in this country are eliminated, the percentage is still very low. In 1927, only 112 Mexicans became citizens, while in 1926 the number was but 78. In the Belvedere Gardens Mexican community in Southern California, where there are 40,000 or more Mexicans, the total number of registered voters in 1928 was about 250. Many of these belonged to other races.

Hence the general impression is supported by the facts—the Mexican immigrant is not becoming naturalized. When this situation is charged against the Mexican and to his lack of appreciation of American opportunities, he is likely to refer to the situation in Mexico, where there are many Americans who have lived in that country for many years and who show no higher rate of becoming citizens in Mexico than Mexicans do here. It is claimed that the American in Mexico is profiting by oil and other resources of Mexico but refuses to become a Mexican citizen, and that therefore the Mexicans in our country are simply following the example of Americans in Mexico. It is also pointed out that Mexicans feel that Mexico is in some ways superior to the United States and that the culture of our people is not wholly superior to that of Mexico.

An important attitude is expressed by those Americans who claim that since the Mexican immigrants are enjoying the advantages of living in the United States they should become citizens and assume their full responsibility for the problems of the country. Since large sums of money are spent that their children may have an education in this land, since public health aid is theirs, and since many of them are the recipients of assistance, it is asserted that they should put their shoulder to the wheel of American life. It is also claimed that the Americans in Mexico who live there many years and who profit greatly should become citizens in their adopted country.

Mexicans sometimes state that they are expecting to return to Mexico, and hence cannot be asked to become citizens here. While it is true that large numbers of those who come are definitely expecting to return, and while many who are here have at least the vague hope of returning to their native land some day, it nevertheless is a fact that large numbers do not return and are actually making no effort toward that end. It is also true that some who go back to Mexico are dissatisfied with the home country after having lived for a time in the United States, and come again to this country, but even then they do not seek citizenship here. . . .

Source: Bogardus, Emory S. "The Mexican Immigrant and Segregation," *The American Journal of Sociology* 36, no. 1 (July 1930),: 74–76.

Robert C. Jones and Louis R. Wilson, "The Mexican in Chicago" (1931)

Not all white Americans were anti-Mexican, and many pro-immigrant groups started settlement houses that had roots in the abolitionist movement against slavery. This tradition was strongest on the East Coast and in the Midwest, where historical memories of abolition were most vivid.

These areas also saw the greatest immigration to their urban cities. The Southwest had no such tradition, and a lot of the Mexican migration was initially to rural areas. Chicago was important to the history of Mexicans because, by the 1920s, a significant number of Mexicans had migrated there. Chicago was an ethnic city with a steady migration of European immigrants who fed the city's growth by building the railroad network, the stockyards, factories, and skyscrapers. In 1889, to ameliorate the exploitative conditions under which these immigrants lived, Jane Addams (1860–1935) and Ellen Gates Starr (1859–1940) cofounded Hull House, one of the first settlement houses in Chicago. At first, its main mission was to give social and educational opportunities to working-class people, many of whom were recent immigrants. Social workers and scholars associated with Hull House did studies of the surrounding neighborhood, which, by the late 1930s, had a substantial number of Mexican residents. The following excerpts are from an article describing Mexicans at Hull House.

Through the open windows of a second-story room opposite Hull House on a midsummer Saturday evening come the jazz strains of a gospel hymn being lustily sung in Spanish. If we were to trace this music to its source it would lead us into the midst of a revival meeting of the Pentecostals. There in a crowded room we would find a Mexican evangelist, eyes shining and face flushed by his enthusiasm, leading the singing, while an orchestra made up of a cornet, two drums, three triangles, and a piano beats out the rhythm with a will. But we do not wish to loiter long within doors. There are other interesting things to be seen along South Halsted during this twilight hour. The strange Spanish signs upon the shop windows put us in the mood for exploration, and we turn our steps southward along the Mexican Boulevard.

First we pass a restaurant whose brilliantly painted walls are covered by designs reminiscent of that Indian . . . Cortez and his followers so ruthlessly destroyed in their conquest of Mexico.

In the next block we pause before the window of a music store and glance at the display of ukuleles, guitars, violins, and wind instruments. This little shop makes phonographic records of music as played and as sung by Chicago's finest Spanish-speaking artists. And from here the records may find their way to the portable phonographs in the box-car homes of Mexican railroad workers all over the United States, or even in the little far-away shacks which house the migratory laborers in the sugar-beet fields.

Across the street a Mexican woman of middle age, straight black hair caught up in a knot at the back of her head, modestly garbed in a long brown skirt and green silk waist, stands beside her husband. They are looking at the primitive metates in the window of a grocery store—those crude, stone ironing boards with their stone rollers for crushing the water soaked kernels of corn into the paste from which the Mexican bakes his thin cakes of unleavened bread, his tortillas. The woman is evidently considering a purchase. A well dressed young Mexican man set him off as a person to be sneered at and hated. . . .

The crowded conditions of housing in smoke-filled neighborhoods together with the low economic level result in ill health among many, especially among the babies.

But there is a strain upon the moral health also. This is due to the great proportion of single men and the small number of women in the colonies. The thwarted sex life of the men is all too apt to break across the normal social restraints, and these dangers are aggravated by the fact that many married couples, struggling to make a living, fill their houses with roomers and boarders. There is another phase of this same peril. The Mexican girl finds an entirely different standard of women's dress prevailing in this country. There is a freedom which in Mexico would have constituted an open invitation to male advances. Often enough, economic necessity itself demands of the girl that she dress in modern fashion if she would win a job. Once persuaded of this, she is apt to go to extremes in her modernity. The men do not understand.

THE MEXICAN IMMIGRANT'S REACTION TO THE PROTESTANT MESSAGE

Although accurate statistics as to the number of Protestants in Mexico are not available, a good estimate would be that not more than one out of every two hundred of the entire population claimed that faith. In Chicago, however, one Mexican out of about every thirty is a member of a Protestant denomination or sect. What accounts for this difference? First of all, a much larger number of Protestant Mexicans have migrated from Mexico than their percentage of the total population there would indicate. Then, from the time they leave Mexico, the Mexicans are constantly being ministered to both materially and spiritually by the Protestant missionaries—in the cotton and beet fields, on the railroads and in the larger industrial centers. Many are won to the new faith.

A great protest has risen on the part of the Roman [Catholic] Church against what they call a proselytizing movement. It has been said that the Protestants have disorganized the religious life of the Mexicans by showing them supposed weaknesses in the Catholic Church and have offered them nothing in return; that they have "bought" members through their social service and relief work and that since "the Mexicans are one hundred percent Catholic they are not subjects of missionary endeavor. . . . "

It should be remembered, however, that there are very few Catholics in Mexico whose faith has been developed and shaped by systematic instruction and enlightened teaching. The Catholicism of the Mexican is principally a folk Catholicism developed through tradition and which has incorporated within itself a great deal of Indian and Spanish superstition. However beautiful it may be, however blind the devotion, such a faith is inadequate when the individual moves to a new and more complex environment where a multitude of new problems must be met. In Chicago, at least, in spite of occasional prejudice, some blindness, and ignorance, and at times overzealousness, the service of the Protestant Mexican missions has been to gather up the bewildered, those who are lost and those who are actively striving to find a better way of living. Very few persons whose lives were strongly organized about the Catholic Church have been taken from that church although many have been given a broader view of their faith and a new appreciation of others.

The Protestant Mexican Churches in Chicago have made four outstanding contributions to the religious life of the people they are striving to serve: (1) They have furnished a church home for those Mexicans who claim the Protestant faith; (2) They have provided groups where individuals who are seeking a "better life" mutually stimulate each other; (3) They have furnished an organization and standards about which many disorganized individuals have been able to orient their lives; [and] (4) Through competition they have stimulated the Roman [Catholic] Church to action in serving its people, moving it to give greater attention than formerly to the intellectual development of its members and to furnish them with more adequate social life through the Catholic Societies.

But let us see what the Mexican himself thinks of the churches and missions with which he comes in contact. Of course, the variety of reactions is as great as the variety of individuals. Many are indifferent. . . .

Epitenio Gonzales is an artist whose life is largely centered around his art and the social settlement in which he has his studio. He is quite indifferent to all forms of organized religion, although he still says that he is a Catholic. He says: "My impression is that a comparatively small number of Mexicans go to church. That is probably due to a number of reasons. I don't go because I don't care much about it, and I work so that I stay in bed Sunday morning. I also go to parties and dances Saturday night and stay up late. I think a lot of Mexicans see that the Americans do not go to church so they follow their example. There are a lot more things to do here than in Mexico. . . . "

Most of the members of the Mexican Protestant Churches in Chicago belong to the lower middle class. It is difficult for a person of different standards and ideas to find a place in them.

Darío Orozco is a student who has had educational opportunities which place him on an intellectual level superior to that of most of his fellows. He was born and raised a Protestant. On being asked why he was one of the few educated Mexicans who regularly attended a Mexican Mission Church, he answered: "The reason why I go to the Mexican Church instead of to an American is because I was brought up to believe that I had an obligation to help my countrymen, especially those who have not had as much opportunity as I have had. I know a number of young Mexicans here who are Protestants but who either go to American churches or don't go to any church. They all have had a better education than the average and some of them are students here. The real reason they don't come is because they don't fit in with the other members of the church."

Darío has learned the often difficult way of getting along with his less privileged countrymen on a basis of equality and without condescension. There are no widely differing Mexican Protestant churches in Chicago, so that those belonging to different social classes must work together in close communion with one another or not at all. . . .

José Mendoza is a quiet, sensitive, mystical man who likes to dream. Although he has been attending the Protestant Church for two years, the beautiful ritual of the Roman Church still has a strong appeal and he sends his children to a Parochial School.

"When I came to Chicago five years ago I don't know what went wrong with me. At times, I thought that I must be crazy. I was very unhappy and at times I even wanted to take my life. My wife knew that I wasn't happy and told me to go to the Catholic Church and confess myself. I would go but I wasn't satisfied. When I heard the church bells ringing, I felt glad but after I had gone to Mass I felt sad again. No one seemed to care about me. Everything was strange and there didn't seem to be anything which would satisfy me. Finally, one day when I was crossing the street, one of my little boys ran ahead of me. As he was crossing, a taxicab rounded the corner at full speed. It swept my boy off the curb and killed him. It was a terrible blow. . . . It was at the time of the loss of this child that I found the Protestant Church. It was just about then that I heard it rumored where I could find a Protestant Church. I knew that they had the Bible there; and that was what I wanted. I felt that if I could find that Book I could find some satisfaction for my disturbed mind."

Source: Comity Commission of the Chicago Church Federation, Chicago, Illinois, 1931, 7, 19–21.

Devra Anne Weber, "The Organizing of Mexicano Agricultural Workers: Imperial Valley and Los Angeles 1928–34, an Oral History Approach" (1973)

In 1927, the Confederación de Uniones Obreras Mexicanas *(Federation of Mexican Workers Union) (CUOM) was founded in Los Angeles to organize and consolidate Mexican workers. CUOM organized to protect rural and urban Mexican American workers against unfair deportation and labor practices. It asked the federal government to further restrict immigration from Mexico. Hence, CUOM adopted the policy of the American Federation of Labor that advocated restricting immigration from Mexico. CUOM held that as long as corporate growers had an unlimited pool of cheap labor from Mexico, there would be no success in organizing Mexicans into unions. The only weapon that unions had was the strike, which could not succeed if employers had large numbers of workers who would cross the picket line. In the following excerpts, University of California–Riverside historian Devra Weber reproduces CUOM's constitution.*

A confederation of Mexican unions, Confederatión de Uniones Obreros Mexicanos (CUOM), was the forerunner of the Mexican Union involved in the El Monte berry strike of 1933. CUOM was organized in 1927 following a meeting of the Federation of Mexican Societies at which a resolution was passed calling upon affiliated mutual aid societies to lend moral and financial support to organizing trade unions of Mexican workers. This confederation of Mexican labor unions was modeled after the Mexican union the Confederación Regional Obrera Mexicana (CROM) and exhibited a similar philosophy, a mixture of radical rhetoric combined with adherence to legal and nonviolent tactics. The declaration of principles and the constitution capture the mixture of rhetoric and tactics. They also give the reader an indication of the tone of the union.

That the exploited class, the greater part of which is made up by manual labor, is right in establishing a class struggle in order to effect an economic and moral betterment of its conditions, and at last its complete freedom from capitalist tyranny. . . .

That in order to be able to oppose the organization, each day more complete and intelligent, the exploited class must organize as such, the base of its organization being the union of resistance, in accord with the rights which the laws of this country concede to native and foreign workers.

That the corporations, possessors of the national and social wealth, being integral parts of the associates of industry, commerce, and banking, the disinherited class must also integrate by means of its federation and confederation into a single union of all labor of the world.

The 1929 constitution added that—

[Since] the results in the industry are obtained through the efforts of man, the Confederación de Uniones Obreros Mexicanos does acknowledge that the industries must be in the hands of those who are capable of maintaining said industries of production.

The militant tone of the union, reminiscent in part of Magonista ideology, is modified by some of its specific principles.

To organize all Mexican workers in the United States in unions according to Sindical principles.

To establish a solid pact with the American and the Mexican working men that any difficulty in the future may be solved mutually.

To establish likewise solid relations with the organized labor of Mexico (Confederación Regional Obrero Mexicana) and to try to stop the immigration of unorganized labor into the United States which is harmful to the working men in both countries.

To do away with the exploitation of Mexican victims in the so-called employment agencies, and to get the unions to constitute their own employment department in which supply and demand can be carried on without a fee so that the workingman's economical interests may not suffer.

To constitute prevision offices with the exclusive object of illustrating to Mexican laborers who for the first time come to the United States as well as those who already reside here, all that is referent to working systems, job revenues, contract forms, interpretations, translations from English to Spanish or vice versa, working men's insurance indemnization [indemnification], etc., etc.

To keep Mexican laborers from being exploited in the so-called commissary stores that still exist in some regions of the United States by submitting in their place cooperative stores in which the working man can get all his needs at just prices.

To study and resolve in accord with the Mexican government the best systems of repatriation so that those wishing to go back will form agricultural cooperatives and receive the best guarantees.

To negotiate with the Mexican government so that the immigration of Mexican labor into the United States may be regulated.

The new union also proposed to:

Animate by all possible ways the conservation of our racial and patriotic principles.

To promote a strong cultural campaign giving preference to the education of our children, for which we shall build school and libraries as is possible. . . .

To raise a beneficence fund towards helping our indigent countrymen and to build up or help other Mexican societies for the establishment of exclusive Mexican hospitals, orphan asylums, alm houses, etc.

Constitute committees of defense which will have competent lawyers, paid by the Mexican colonies themselves so that those with the help of the consulate can effectively defend Mexicans who are put in jails, in many cases by mere ignorance of the law.

Although the union pledges to uphold syndicalist principles, "a revolutionary doctrine by which workers seize control of the economy and the government by the general strike and other direct means," they emphasized they would adhere to the existent legal system which had been devised and operated under a society in which the worker's inferior role was maintained. It appears that international class solidarity is subjugated to nationalist interests and economic security.

By March, 1928, CUOM claimed 2,000 to 3,000 members even though only 200 paid dues. . . .

Source: Weber, Devra Anne. "The Organizing of Mexicano Agricultural Workers: Imperial Valley and Los Angeles 1928–34, An Oral History Approach." *Aztlan Journal* (University of California Los Angeles) 3, no. 2 (1973), 326–328.

Steve Zuckerman, "Didn't Think I Was Great, Fighter Said" (1979)

Mexican boxer Bert Colima (1902–1979) was the idol of the Los Angeles Mexican community. In the 1920s, the Los Angeles Times *printed almost 1,000 articles featuring him. Many of his most exciting matches were fought in the Grand Olympic Auditorium, which opened in 1925 and was used for boxing matches during the 1932 Olympics. Thanks to Colima, the Grand Olympic Auditorium became a landmark boxing venue and drew multitudes of Mexicans, whose attendance made the Olympic profitable. The following article, written at the time of Colima's death in 1979, is among the most memorable, capturing the essence of Colima and his importance to the Mexican community.*

"I wasn't a great fighter," Bert Colima once said. "But I made a lot of friends—Mexicans, Americans, everybody. . . . So I figure I came out ahead of the game." . . .

"He was the greatest Mexican-American boxer ever to appear in California," said Everett Sanders, former state athletic commission member. "He was the biggest attraction Jack Doyle's Vernon arena ever had." . . .

It always was a sellout when Colima fought. His fans urged him on, shouting, "Geeve eet to heem Co-lee-mah." Or they would cry "Andale, Co-lee-mah, Andale!" ("Hurry up, go after him Colima"). . . .

Colima was born in 1902 in Los Nietos, near Whittier. His real name was Ephraim E. Romero, but he seldom used it and in 1947 he had his name legally changed to that of his mother's home town, Colima, Mexico.

Colima fought 65 times from 1921–1929. He won 56, lost 9, and scored 20 knockouts.

Source: Zuckerman, Steve. "Didn't Think I Was Great, Fighter Said." *Los Angeles Times*, November 5, 1979, 20.

Paul J. Dosal, "The Building of El Círculo Cubano" (1902–1918)

By 1930, the Puerto Rican and Mexican communities had substantial barrios (neighborhoods). The largest Puerto Rican mainland community was in New York City in neighborhoods such as Spanish Harlem. The third-largest Latino group was the Cubans, who, in some cases, had been in the United States throughout the last quarter of the 19th century. They formed established communities with a bevy of social and self-help organizations that helped them survive economic and personal disasters. The social club El Círculo Cubano (the Cuban National Club) was formed in 1899 by Cuban Spanish War veterans in Ybor City, which was named after cigar manufacturer Vicente Martínez Ybor (1818–1896) in the 1870s. Along with various mutualistas *(mutual aid societies),* El Círculo *has had a continual presence in south Florida. In the early 1900s, Afro-Cuban war veterans also founded the* Sociedad la Union Martí-Maceo, *a mutual aid society in Tampa. It coexisted with El Círculo, which, at first, welcomed white and Afro-Cubans but soon afterward divided along racial lines. Some Cubans maintain that this segregation was a response to the South's Jim Crow laws, which mandated the separation of the races. The members of both of these organizations worked in Tampa's cigar factories. These two organizations have survived to this day, but when the Great Depression of the 1930s decimated the cigar industry, members were hard put to keep these groups alive. It was a time when the cigar factory owners threw the lectors who read to the workers out of the factories, and the community fell on bad times. Even so, President Franklin D. Roosevelt's (1882–1945) Works Progress Administration used* El Círculo *during the Depression to record Cuban American performers. The significance of* El Círculo *and* La Unión *was that they survived disasters like the Great Depression, kept together by a small group who wanted to preserve their presence as a people. Survival often meant receiving donations from Cuba and meant the sacrifices of many Cubans.*

When the Cuban National Club changed its name to El Círculo Cubano in 1902, the club had less than two hundred members and it operated out of the old offices of the Cuban National Club at the corner of 14th Street and 9th Avenue. In 1905, under President Eladio Paula, the Cuban Club began construction of a new and larger clubhouse at the corner of 14th Street and 10th Avenue.

The cornerstone of the new building was dedicated in an impressive ceremony on October 31, 1905. Nearly 2,000 people showed up to witness an event of great symbolic importance, as evident by the presence of the consuls of Cuba, Spain, and Italy. However, construction of the club did not actually begin until the summer of 1907, financed by a loan of $14,500. On November 14, 1907, the new building at the corner of 14th Street and 10th Avenue (where the club is currently located) was formally inaugurated in another ceremony with the Mayor, city council, and three foreign consuls in attendance. The red-brick building consisted of two stories facing 10th Avenue with a 1,500-seat theater that was "comfortable and modern in every detail." The clubhouse also boasted a boardroom, a small library, classrooms, a billiard room, and a cantina, where members came to relax after work.

In 1914, the club allowed the wives and children of members to join the club and membership increased from 1,120 in 1914 to 2,625 in 1916. Then, the club's progress was interrupted. After a theatrical performance on the night of April 30, 1916, a fire started on the stage and nearly consumed the entire building before it was put out. The fire was a great setback to the Cuban Club. Insurance covered only a portion of the losses, which meant that the club had to raise more money to rebuild their institution. Under the leadership of Dr. Alfredo Kohly, the club moved quickly to raise $70,000 to build an even grander clubhouse on the same spot. The club borrowed $35,000 from the Pacific Mutual Life Insurance Company and raised another $10,000 by selling $20 and $5 bonds to its members. In addition, members approved a 10-cent increase in their weekly fees and organized a series of fundraising events to raise the necessary money. At the suggestion of Rafael Martínez Ybor, the Cuban Consul, the club also appointed a committee in Cuba to solicit donations on the island. Thanks to this committee, which included heroes of Cuba's independence movement like Gen. Emilio Nuñez and Fernando Figueredo, the club obtained donations from a number of prominent Cubans, including President Mario G. Menocal, who contributed $1,000.

The club contracted with the firm of Bonfoey & Elliott to design a concrete, fire-proof building with three stories and a basement. Actual construction was placed with the firm of McCracken and Hyer in Nov. 1916. At 9:30 a.m. on February 25, 1917, the club dedicated the cornerstone at the corner of 10th Avenue (now Palm Avenue) and 14th Street. With Mayor McKay in attendance, Dr. Kohly dedicated a cornerstone in which were placed local newspapers and valuable documents relating to the history of the club.

When completed in 1918, the neoclassical structure was the most beautiful building in Ybor City, featuring a spacious theater and a magnificent grand ballroom on the top floor. In the basement, members could enjoy a gymnasium, complete with two bowling lanes, a wading pool, lockers, and a shower. On the third floor, there was a small library, classroom, ladies room, and the boardroom. But the crown jewel of the entire building was the stained glass window bearing the Cuban coat of arms, which induced some to call the Cuban Club a "cathedral for workers." Soon after the building opened, two new crises—a flu epidemic and a prolonged labor strike—threatened the financial condition of the club, forcing the members to work hard to pay off their debts for another decade.

Source: El Círculo Cubano de Tampa (Tampa Cuban Club). http://en.wikipedia.org/wiki/Circulo_Cubano_de_Tampa.

Victor S. Clark, *Porto Rico and Its Problems* (1930)

Economist Victor S. Clark's (1868–1946) study of Puerto Rico and its problems in the 1930s was conducted under the auspices of the Brookings Institute. It was one of the most comprehensive studies of Puerto Ricans to date and was laden with racial biases. Nevertheless, it gives insight into Puerto Rico, Puerto Ricans, and why Puerto Ricans were migrating to the mainland. In 1899, General John Eaton (1829–1906), U.S. commissioner of education to Puerto Rico, led a campaign to Americanize Puerto Ricans through an English-only policy in public schools in Puerto Rico. Eaton proposed the teaching of English only by all teachers, the preferential hiring of English-speaking teachers, and the examination of high school and normal school candidates in English. Clark approved of this policy and called Puerto Rican Spanish a "patois," implying that it was a dialect of the uneducated. Previously, in 1908, Clark had produced highly biased and negative studies of Mexicans in the United States.

Nearly one and one-half million people live in Porto Rico, of whom all but a minute minority were born in the Island and are descended from ancestors who have lived there for centuries. The only numerically important additions to this stock since the early Spanish migrations of the sixteenth and seventeenth centuries were African slaves. These and an indeterminate Indian element, which was absorbed during the first years of settlement, but has probably contributed a trace of blood to a constantly widening circle of descendants, have blended with the original Iberian colonists until it is impossible to draw an exact line between white and colored. A pure negro type is encountered in the port towns and the former slave plantation districts on the coast, while peasants as fair as north Europeans are not infrequently met upon the mountain trails of the interior. As a rule, the propertied and professional classes are white, while the laboring classes, exclusive of the peasant mountaineers, are in varying degrees colored. Soldiers and other temporary sojourners have constantly diluted the African blood of the coast towns since the cessation of the slave trade, and merchants, planters, and civil servants from Spain, and occasionally political refugees from Latin America, have recruited the commercial and official classes. According to the census, in 1920 approximately 73 percent of the population was white and 27 percent colored, but this is hardly more than a statistical guess.

Race lines are not as strictly drawn in Porto Rico as on the mainland. Intelligent, educated, and forceful colored men and women are found in all walks of life, where they associate without apparent discrimination with whites. Negroes are numerous in the teaching profession, and colored pupils attend, on terms of equality, public schools and higher educational institutions. An advertisement inserted in an Island paper by a Porto Rican automobile mechanic, residing in an upstate city in New York, for a wife who among other qualifications must be either white or mulatto, illustrates a race attitude of the common people.

Nevertheless, race is a potent sociological force in Porto Rico. African slavery drove the poor whites into the mountains, as it did in our Southern States, where isolation and absence of cultural and economic opportunities perpetuated or created a special type, the mountain peasant or "jibaro," of whom we shall hear abundantly in the following pages. He presents some parallels with the cabin dwellers of the southern Appalachians, but today is succumbing to the influence of good roads, public schools, and commercial agriculture. As yet, however, his economic status is depressed below a normal subsistence level. Generations of civic and spiritual neglect have given him some of the primitive mores of the indigenees [indigenes]. His family ties are often merely consensual, and his children therefore technically illegitimate; but he is not immoral in an anti-social sense.

Among the floating laborers of the coast towns and low-land plantations, survivals of slave mores still persist. Family ties, even when normally more formal than in the mountains, are apparently less binding, and result in the type of illegitimacy that is accompanied by a high infant mortality. Both the birth rate and the death rate of the colored Porto Ricans, who are relatively more numerous on the coast than elsewhere in the Island, exceed those of the whites. The causes for the high mortality appear to be social and economic rather than physiological. In fact, it is hard to escape the inference, unverifiable though it may be, until more research than hitherto has been devoted to the subject, that whites suffer a climatic handicap, at least as compared with full-blooded blacks, throughout the West Indies.

The common people in the country look to the United States for help and guidance with a degree of faith and hope that is naïvely childlike. The promise of aid from the United States, their newly gained political democracy, which they are slowly learning how to manipulate, and their increasing acquisition of knowledge through a still inadequate but improving school system, offer their only prospect of escape—and that at best seems a long way off.

In 1914 and 1926, strikes in the principal cigar factories of the Island failed to win their objective, and are said partly to account for the action of the largest of the tobacco corporations in transferring most of its manufacturing from the Island to the mainland. Waves of labor agitation, marked by strikes, rise and subside as if they were the result of a psychic contagion. In most cases, however, they represent impulsive resistance to some worsening of the condition of the workers and not infrequently accompany one of those general depressions that are liable to affect, from time to time, a relatively small and isolated community whose prosperity is largely dependent upon one or two staple crops. It is not strange, therefore, that they have had little observable effect upon the material condition of the working people. The main accomplishments of the labor movement have been achieved through political action.

Moreover, English is the chief source, practically the only source, of democratic ideas in Porto Rico. There may be little that they learn to remember, but the English school reader itself provides a body of ideas and concepts which are not to be had in any other way. It is also the only means which these people have of communication with and understanding of the country which they are now a part. The utility of instruction in English and indeed of education generally has been severely limited by the almost complete lack of books and periodicals among the common people of the Island. The seeds sown by an elementary education, such as that now offered in Porto Rico, can hardly be expected to germinate and fructify into an improving citizenship in a soil devoid of reading matter.

Yet so long as private enterprise must be depended upon, publications wait on general literacy. To break through this difficulty, we recommend that the Insular Department of Education undertake the publication and free distribution of a periodical dealing with current events and important practical matters related to health, diet, homemaking, and community life. It should be a first principle in the Department's management of this periodical that it should be completely exempt from political influence and free from bias. It should be printed in both Spanish and English.

The Commission wishes to warn against the assumption that large expenditures for building and equipment are necessary before this work can begin. For automobile repair work a shed, a discarded car which the Government Bureau of Transportation or a garage might furnish from its junk heap, the simplest tools, and a mechanic-teacher would form an adequate starting equipment. The most outstanding objection to be urged against the present work in manual training is the unduly expensive equipment which is provided for work which at best is inadequate. The criticism of unduly expensive equipment is valid in the case of home economics equipment in some high schools. School equipment should include but little more than the kind of tools with which the students will be obliged to work when they practice their skill in home or shop. In order to acquaint them with better equipment of a sort which they might conceivably acquire, a small margin beyond this might be provided. The length of courses offered in such industrial schools or courses should be governed not by any preconceptions about courses of fixed period of length but by the time necessary for a student to acquire the skill concerned.

Source: Clark, Victor S. (Victor Selden). *Porto Rico and Its Problems*. Clark, Victor S. (Victor Selden), 1868–1946, Washington, DC: The Brookings Institution, 1930, 8, 9, 39, 52, 81, 82, 88.

Acción Feminista Dominicana's Statement of Principles (ca. 1931)

Acción Feminista Dominicana *(Dominican Feminists for Action) was founded in the Dominican Republic on May 14, 1931. Although many groups were labeled feminist, they were established to promote family values and were limited to "good women." This nascent women's organization had the blessing of Dominican dictator Rafael Trujillo (1891–1961). The organization was limited to literate women at a time when 70 percent of Dominicans were illiterate. Hence, the masses were denied participation. In the Caribbean, as in most places, the status of women was critiqued as paternalistic societies came under fire. Once they gained access to better education, many women became teachers, writers, union leaders, and intellectuals—and coalesced to form feminist leagues. The ability for women to meet opened many to more radical forms of action as many were influenced by communist and socialist literature and other political movements.*

This group will be made up of women of good conduct, who have reached their eighteenth birthday and who know how to read and write. Its main goal is to tend to the betterment of the intellectual, social, moral, and legal condition of women, as well as to campaign for social defense against alcoholism, prostitution, and narcotic drugs, and the like, to fight for the passage of laws for the protection of mothers, children, adolescents, the aged, and the blue-collar workers. To advocate for the establishment of tribunals for children, to work to instill in women the understanding of the necessity to be frugal and to dissuade them from spending on unnecessary luxuries; to persuade Dominicans not to sell their land to foreigners; to fight so that our traditions are preserved and to sponsor every idea that would mean the advancement and welfare of the Republic.

The Acción Feminista aspires to enroll in its rank all their compatriots, so that a true feminist union will result, formed by ladies and young ladies who live, some by their rents and incomes, others by teaching, by industry, blue-collar work, students, and so on. One of its principal goals will be to accustom Dominican women to the agreement of thought and of mutual tolerance and protection, at work. The Acción Feminista wishes to make mothers truly conscious of their mission; it wishes to prepare mothers to earn a livelihood in a dignified manner for themselves and their families, should the need arise; it wishes [for] even women with means to receive such training so they are prepared to administer their fortune and make them fit to sustain the moral and material equilibrium of the home, because lest we forget, whosoever says balance at home, says balance in the fatherland.

Feminism will tend to bring about the happiness of women by preparing them so that they always marry for love, and not of necessity and in a hurry with the first to come for fear of facing the demands of life; it will work so that laws are passed that would support marriage and the stability of the family.

Source: De Filippis, Daisy Cocco, ed. *Documents of Dissidence: Selected Writings by Dominican Women.* New York: CUNY Dominican Studies Institute, 2000, 61–62.

Eleanor Roosevelt, "Our Island Possessions" (1934)

The Great Depression devastated the Puerto Rican economy. To improve relations, First Lady Eleanor Roosevelt (1884–1962) made a trip to the Caribbean in the summer of 1934. Roosevelt, an involved first lady, wrote a regular column in the magazine Woman's Home Companion, *in which she shared the following impressions of Puerto Rico. She describes the poverty, the impact of the Great Depression, the needlework cottage industry, and her opinion that the women received fair wages in the garment factories. But regardless of the first lady's impressions, needleworkers were far from happy, and labor unrest persisted.*

Many times I wonder whether the people of the United States have any real interest in our insular possessions. I doubt if many of us even know that we own the Virgin Islands or Puerto Rico or Hawaii. We do realize the Philippines are in our possession chiefly, I think, because we have disagreed so much as to whether they ought to be given their freedom or not; and I think it is generally realized that we control the Canal Zone, particularly since the fleet came through!

Occasionally when our navy planes make a flight to Hawaii someone says, "I suppose we do have some interest in that island in the Pacific." A few people every winter take a trip to Puerto Rico or the Virgin Islands and discover that they do not have to have passports, but even so, few of us fully take in the fact that these islands are a part of the United States of America and that what befalls them and their people is of great interest to us as American citizens.

Last winter I took a trip by air, leaving Miami early in the morning, spending a night in Haiti and arriving at three o'clock the next afternoon in the Virgin Islands after stopping only for a few minutes in Puerto Rico. I had been told that the Virgin Islands had been costing our government each year a little more until finally Congress had become convinced that it would be more economical to spend enough to rehabilitate the people and try to make them self-supporting. They have, therefore, begun to work out a real plan.

The population of these islands is partly white and partly colored. The last owners were Danish and many of the customs and habits are those inherited from Danish rule and many, many of the people have been accustomed to turning to the government or to the heads of big plantations for complete guidance and care. So the first thing that needs to be done is to build up a sense of self-reliance and initiative.

On landing at St. Thomas, which is on the whole the loveliest of these islands, we drove over a road made by C.W.A. [Civil Works Administration] labor to the top of a mountain where we could look down on the sparkling green water of the bay beyond. There are beautiful beaches for bathing on

St. Thomas and apparently sharks do not frequent the waters, at least near the shore, for I bathed there the following morning without receiving any warning as to these dread animals.

We visited the hospital for children, held a meeting of the women in the school, went to the operative stores which will, I think, be more successful as the workers get better teaching, then drove off to what will shortly be a new hotel. It is being erected in a most charming spot, on top of a steep hill where the old tower known as Bluebeard's Tower looks across at another hill where Blackbeard's Tower stands. . . . Bluebeard's Tower is being preserved so visitors may walk to the top and get a view of the harbor. The hotel is being built around three sides of a square. The dining room is to have a porch for dining al fresco. I can hardly wait to go down and stay in this hotel and I hope that the methods of travel both by air and by water will shortly be improved so that a trip to St. Thomas will be a pleasant winter holiday, financially within the reach of anyone of moderate means.

There are two other islands within easy reach of St. Thomas: St. John where the bay trees grow which once produced the bay rum our fathers used, and St. Croix. We visited St. Croix which has two small towns and some agricultural land, flat and not as interesting, but more productive. Here agricultural and housing experiments are being tried.

On the third day of the trip I visited Puerto Rico. If you want to know anything of this island and its people you must spend several days there, and you will enjoy all these days and wish you could stay longer for its scenery is beautiful and varied. Mountains, rich valleys, seashore, and plains are all combined in an island one hundred miles long and thirty miles wide. Puerto Rico has a better rainfall than the Virgin Islands and we hope that the frequent hurricanes of the past three years are not going to continue for hitherto she has only suffered occasionally from these. They have done a great deal of harm, practically ruining the coffee plantations and citrus and coconut groves.

On this account, many Puerto Ricans have gone from the rural districts into the outskirts of the cities where dangerous slums have been formed. The population of about 1,600,000 people cannot be fed by what is produced on the land no matter what improved methods of agriculture are instituted. We are at last waking up to the fact that a long-term plan must be made for this island and it is at present being worked out, including all the government departments concerned and a committee of Puerto Ricans themselves.

There are questions of education and questions of health and economic questions that we could discuss at length, but the industry which largely employs women will probably be of primary interest to the women of our country. This is the needlework industry. In some districts even little girls in the school are never without their needlework. When the women are not doing housework and as soon as a little girl has eaten her lunch between school sessions, this handwork is taken up. To make it more profitable, the women should be taught to work with more exactness and perhaps with greater perfection and detail, although many of them do very beautiful work now. A few of them who work in the factories earn fair wages, but for sewing done in the home they are paid absurdly low wages. For drawing threads and cutting a dozen handkerchiefs out of a piece of cloth, a woman receives one and one-half cents a dozen; for whipping the edges and doing a small embroidered design in each corner, a woman receives three cents per dozen.

The finished handkerchief is sold for seven cents a dozen in a retail shop in the United States. The material used is so poor that it will certainly not last as long as would a machine-made handkerchief of slightly better material. Another example is the nightgowns scalloped on neck and sleeves with a hand-embroidered design and hand-sewn seams.

A woman receives two dollars a dozen for these and spends two weeks making them. The manufacturer sells them to a distributing agent in United States for somewhere around eight dollars a dozen and you buy them from a department store for one dollar and ninety-five cents each, twenty-three dollars and forty cents a dozen.

The standards of living in Puerto Rico are low. The population is increasing rapidly. This island is closely tied to our country the people are constantly coming here to establish themselves and we are sending some of our own people to Puerto Rico to work and live on the island. Therefore, let us take a more intelligent interest in our beautiful possession with its possibilities for a happy people who unfortunately have been buffeted by nature and exploited by man. So women, let us think a little about our future citizens in all these islands and try to bring about, wherever our flag lies, conditions of which we can be proud.

Source: Roosevelt, Eleanor. "Our Island Possessions." In *Woman's Home Companion*, October 1934. Women in World History, a project of the Center for History and New Media, George Mason University. http://chnm.gmu.edu/wwh/modules/lesson16/lesson16.php?s=5.

Chicago Defender, "Harlem Relief Is Poor; Misery Caused Race War" (1935)

The Chicago Defender *reported on an incident in Harlem that broke out after an alleged false report over the shooting of a 16-year-old Puerto Rican.* The Defender, *a newspaper that was black owned and militant in its defense of black Americans and other minorities, describes the unrest and attributes the causes of confrontations in Harlem to a 55–65 percent unemployment rate and the uneven appropriation of government relief; Harlem received only about one-third of the relief provided to other parts of New York. The mainstream press blamed the discontent on communists but, according to* The Defender, *the real culprit was poverty.*

REDS NOT TO BLAME

The Harlem disturbance can be laid to economic causes and poor housing conditions, one leader said. The false report that 16-year-old Lino Rivers, a Porto Rican youth, had been killed in S. K. Kress' 5 and 10 cent store was sufficient to start the fireworks.

That the unemployment situation may have had something to do with the outbreak is evidenced by the fact that between 55 and 65 percent of the people of Harlem are jobless and that the relief given Colored people is about one-third of that given in other sections of the city, and as a consequence they live in misery and poverty.

The committee was further told that the relief for a family in Harlem is $31 per month lower than for families in other sections of the city.

Unless Mayor LaGuardia takes steps to have this situation remedied, it is likely that there will be more riots and perhaps the 650 police on duty this time won't be sufficient to handle the trouble the next time.

Source: Chicago Defender, March 30, 1935, 1.

Arthur Garfield Hays, "Defending Justice in Puerto Rico" (1937)

One of the most infamous days in Puerto Rican history was the Ponce Massacre of March 21, 1937. This event occurred during the administration of U.S.-appointed governor Blanton Winship (1869–1947), who was the military governor of Puerto Rico from 1934 to

*1938. Winship governed the island in alliance with the sugar barons and elite Puerto Ricans. He is generally blamed for the massacre in which the police shot and wounded 100 demonstrators, killing 20—including one woman and a seven-year-old girl. The Puerto Rican Nationalist Party had organized a march in the southern city of Ponce to protest the prolonged incarceration of Nationalist Party leader Pedro Albizu Campos (1891–1965). They also demanded Puerto Rico's independence from the United States. Winship threw fuel on the fire by revoking the permits for the protest a short time before it was scheduled to begin. As "*La Borinqueña*" (the national anthem of Puerto Rico) was played, the demonstrators began to march. The militia ordered a halt and then began to shoot. Police shot and clubbed the horrified marchers, following them to the entrance of their houses as they tried to get away. About 150 demonstrators were arrested in what was one of the bloodiest episodes in Puerto Rican history. This account was written by an attorney for the American Civil Liberties Union and appeared in the* Nation, *a progressive weekly magazine.*

In the fall of 1935, five members of the Nationalist Party of Puerto Rico sought to make their way to a meeting which students at the Puerto Rico University were to hold to protest against certain remarks made by Pedro Albizu Campos, the Nationalist leader. The story is that the Nationalists were stopped by the police, that they shot at the police, and that, as a result of the fracas, four of the five Nationalists in the automobile were killed. It was said that they carried bombs and guns.

In February, 1936, Col. Riggs, head of the insular police, was assassinated by two Nationalists. The assassins were seized and, while in the hands of the police, were shot. Although Col. Riggs was popular with the Puerto Ricans and was himself a believer in independence, the cold-blooded murder of the two Puerto Rican "martyrs" aroused not only the Nationalists but great numbers of Puerto Ricans who opposed Nationalist methods. Americans thought of the murder of Col. Riggs; Puerto Ricans thought of the murder of the two assassins.

Albizu Campos and other Nationalist leaders were charged with conspiracy to overthrow the government of the United States and later, in July 1936, were convicted and sentenced to six years in jail. Gov. Blanton Winship apparently felt it was necessary to deal with the Nationalists with a heavy hand and acted to suppress not only those who were militantly demanding Puerto Rican freedom but also a united front of groups opposed to the conviction of Albizu Campos. Parades and meetings of Nationalists and other protesting groups were prohibited. The Puerto Ricans take seriously their Organic Act guaranteeing the rights of free speech and assemblage, and resentment grew apace.

On March 21, 1937, the Nationalists announced that they would hold a parade and meeting in the town of Ponce. A permit was first given by the mayor of the town. At the last moment it was canceled. The insular police commanded by Col. Orbeta, who was acting under orders of the Governor, prohibited the parade as it was about to start. The national hymn of Puerto Rico was played, the crowd cheered, the parade advanced. Suddenly there was shooting, and when it was all over, it appeared that the casualties were 20 killed—including those who died later, among whom were two police officers—and from 150 to 200 wounded, among whom were 6 police officers.

Gov. Winship reported to Washington that several "divisions" of the so-called" Army of Liberation" had arranged a concentration in the town of Ponce, that a parade was forbidden; that nevertheless the Nationalists insisted upon proceeding; that when the command "Forward march!" was given, a Nationalist fired a shot killing a policeman on the left of the chief of police and another Nationalist fired a shot killing a policeman on the right of the chief of police; that fighting then broke out from all sides as well as from roofs and balconies where Nationalists were stationed, and that casualties resulted. He ended his report by commending the patience and consideration of the police.

The leading citizens of Ponce formed a committee of prominent citizens of San Juan and asked that they make an investigation. The proposed commission consisted of Emilio Belaval, president of the Athenaeum, who acted as secretary; Mariano Acosta Velarde, president of the Puerto Rican Bar Association; Lorenzo Pineiro, president of the Teachers' Association; Dr. Manuel Diaz Garcia, president of the Puerto Rican Medical Association; Antonio Avuso, editor of the Imparciale [sic]; Francisco M. Zeno, editor of the *Correspondencia*; and Davilla Ricci, assistant editor of the *Mondo*. None of the commission were Nationalists. Request was made to the American Civil Liberties Union to appoint the chairman of the commission, and the writer was so appointed. The commission undertook to investigate not only the events of Ponce on March 21 but the general subject of civil rights and liberties in Puerto Rico.

Hearings were held at Ponce beginning Friday, May 14, and were thereafter adjourned to San Juan. Evidence as to what happened on March 21 was adduced not only from disinterested eyewitnesses but from a series of photographs which tell the story in incontestable fashion. Photographs show that the "divisions" of the "Army, of Liberation" consisted of about eighty young men wearing black blouses and white trousers, about twelve girls dressed in white as nurses, and a brass band of about six pieces. The Nationalists, known as "cadets," carried no arms; the girls did not even have Red Cross kits.

A photograph shows the scene just before the shooting. About eighteen policemen, armed with revolvers, shotguns, and tear-gas bombs, stood in front of the line of these eighty boys and twelve girls; about twenty policemen armed with Thompson submachine-guns were in the rear; a number of armed police were on the street along the side; a crowd of men, women, and children stood across the way watching the parade. The Nationalists had brought their wives, mothers, and children along to see the parade. The evidence showed that there was no shooting whatever from any roofs or balconies, and this was confirmed by the district attorney of police, Perez Marchand, who made the first investigation and who later retired as district attorney because, according to him, he was not given a free hand in his inquiries. One of the photographs shows a policeman actually firing at the crowd and other policemen drawing their guns, all in menacing posture. The police who were wounded or killed seem to have been caught in a cross fire.

The commission unanimously reported that the people of Puerto Rico have properly described the occurrence as the "massacre of Ponce."

I shall never forget the photograph of those cadets whom newspapers have described as "ruffians" and "gangsters," standing quietly with their hands at their sides waiting to be shot—defenseless but not one of them running away.

Source: Hays, Arthur Garfield. "Social Worker Visits Spanish Loyalist Men." Reprinted with permission from the July 3, 1937, issue of *The Nation*.

Thyra Edwards, "Social Worker Visits Spanish Loyalist Men" (1938)

In the period from 1936 to 1939, the Spanish Civil War against fascism consumed progressives. In 1936, the military, led by General Francisco Franco (1892–1975), overthrew the Spanish republican government. Franco's forces were supported by Nazi Germany and fascist Italy. About 2,800 Americans volunteered to defend the Republic of Spain. They formed a little known, but well-respected, legion called the Abraham Lincoln Brigade. The conflict was an ill-fated war that ushered in a brutal dictatorship. The Abraham Lincoln Brigade fought alongside 35,000 other volunteers from other countries, large numbers of which came from Latin America. Together with the Spaniards, they fought to protect democracy. Labor activist Basil Cueria was one of many Cubans in the United States who volunteered to fight in the Abraham Lincoln Brigade during the Spanish Civil War. This article appeared in the Chicago Defender, *one of the few U.S. newspapers to report objectively on this conflict that set the stage for World War II.*

MADRID, Spain, Feb. 11—Captain Basil Ceuria [Cueria], tall, broad, muscular, dark brown, nearly swung Joaquin Ordoci off his feet in the warmth of his rugged embrace. Ordoci, vice president of the Cuban Federation of Labor, was visiting Cubans in the Spanish trenches. Many of them, as he, exiled from Cuba under the terror of the fascist, Machado. Singly and in groups these Cubans gathered around him, embracing him, clapping him heavily on the back eager and hearty in their greeting.

ANXIOUS TO HEAR STORY

None was warmer than Basil Cueria. Race man. Captain of the machine gun company of the 46th division, whose headquarters we were then visiting. And none was more heartily responded to. I, of course was restless for the greetings to end so that I might have an opportunity talk to Cueria and get his story—why he came to Spain and how and what he thought of it all, now that he is here.

He came in January, he said, and by way of the U.S.A. He is one of hundreds of Cuban trade unionists and liberals whom the Fascist Machado persecuted until they had to flee the country at the risk of their lives. He came to New York in 1933 and began earning his living as a professional baseball player with the Cuban Stars and subsequently with the Havana Red Stars.

When Italy invaded Ethiopia he found himself again involved in the struggle against oppression—the thing that had forced him to leave Cuba. He became active in the various groups and communities aiding Ethiopia and in these groups found many of his exiled Cuban compatriots—including Ordoci.

JOINS INTERNATIONAL BRIGADE

From Ethiopia, Mussolini advanced into Spain. And Cueria with other Cuban compatriots (there are 200 of them in El Campeseno's division) made the difficult and devious journey to Spain joining the International Brigade, aiding the Spaniards, despoiled of their regular army, in successfully holding back Mussolini's advance.

Cueria arrived in Spain the 6th of January. By February 11th, after a hurried month of intensive training, he entered the fight on the Jarama front. By the 17th he had advanced to the front line trenches and "started battering the fascists." Shortly he became a machine gunner in the Lincoln battalion of the International brigade.

There on the Jarama front, he says, fighting was at high speed and in a continuous cold rain. "But I was very enthusiastic," he adds.

"In our trenches we fight fascism. If we're defeated, the working class of the world is defeated."

Source: Chicago Defender, February 12, 1938, 12.

Congressman Vito Marcantonio, "Five Years of Tyranny" (1939)

New York congressman Vito Marcantonio (1902–1954) represented East Harlem from 1935 to 1950. His constituents included Italians, Puerto Ricans, and African Americans who supported his controversial politics. He pushed for civil rights legislation before it was popular. Marcantonio gave this speech before Congress on August 14, 1939, in which he outlined the grievances against the administration of the military governor of Puerto Rico, Blanton Winship (1869–1947). The congressman blamed Winship for the Ponce Massacre of 1937, when police shot down 20 peaceful demonstrators. Marcantonio presented these charges to Secretary of the Interior Harold L. Ickes (1874–1952) several months before he gave this speech, which has become one of the most important in Puerto Rican history.

Ex-Governor Blanton Winship, of Puerto Rico, was summarily removed by the President of the United States on May 12, 1939. I had filed charges against Mr. Winship with the President during two visits that I had with him, and subsequently, on April 27, 1939, I wrote a letter to the President filing additional charges in support of my request for the removal of Mr. Winship. During my visits at the Executive Office of the President of the United States, I informed him of many acts of misfeasance as well as nonfeasance, among which were the tyrannical acts of the Governor, in depriving the people of Puerto Rico of their civil rights, the corruption and rackets that existed, and were made possible only by the indulgence of the governor, and the extraordinary waste of the people's money. . . . My written, as well as oral, charges were transmitted by the President to Secretary Ickes, of the Department of the Interior.

The Secretary of the Interior, by code, wired Mr. Blanton Winship to return to the United States. In response to this wire, Mr. Winship came here and visited the Secretary of the Interior. The Secretary of the Interior demanded that Mr. Winship resign. Mr. Winship flatly refused to resign, and stated that inasmuch as he was a Presidential appointee, he would not resign until he had had an opportunity to appeal to the President. After various unsuccessful efforts, Mr. Winship finally saw the President, and pleaded that he be permitted to remain Governor of Puerto Rico on the ground that his resigning while he was under fire might be misinterpreted. What the President told Mr. Winship I do not know. I do know, however, that he made a very unfavorable impression on the President. When Mr. Winship left the White House with the bravado which is characteristic of a swivel chair general, he invited friends of his and newspapermen to visit him in Puerto Rico in September of 1939, thereby giving the impression that he would remain as Governor.

On May 11, 1939, I took the floor in the House of Representatives, objecting to exempting Puerto Rico from the provisions of the wage-and-hour amendment, and in that speech I made an attack on Mr. Winship, and revealed that I had made charges against him, and stated specifically that the charges were being investigated by the Department of the Interior at the request of the President of the United States. The following day, the President made the announcement that Admiral William D. Leahy would succeed Mr. Winship as Governor of Puerto Rico. Up to and including the time that this terse announcement was made, Mr. Winship had not resigned. Even a school child knows that the announcement of one's successor before one has resigned is tantamount to dismissal. Blanton Winship was dismissed by the President of the United States.

He devoted all of his time since he was kicked out as Governor to two tasks: first, to that of self-glorification; and second, to further damage the best interests of the people of Puerto Rico.

In the second category, his activities were in keeping with his 5 years of terror in Puerto Rico. He acted the part of a slimy lobbyist, and fought by means fair and foul to have the wage-and-hour law amended so that the sugar companies could continue to pay 12 1/2 cents an hour instead of 25 cents an hour, and thereby gain $5,000,000 a year; so that the exploiters of labor in Puerto Rico could continue to pay the intolerable wages they have been paying, a wage system which was made possible under his regime, so that the system of abysmal wage slavery could be perpetuated in Puerto Rico. Up to the very closing days of Congress, this kicked-out governor fought to have Puerto Rican workers removed from the protection of the wage-and-hour law. He made a frantic appeal to the

Speaker, Hon. William Bankhead, to suspend the rules and recognize someone who would offer the amendment which would have removed Puerto Rico from the provisions of the wage-and-hour law. This was done after he, together with his stooge and personal lobbyist, James J. Lanzetta, had made all efforts and failed to have the Barden and other amendments considered by the House, which not only would have affected the workers of Puerto Rico but would have also exempted 2,000,000 workers in the United States from the protection of the Fair Labor Standards Act. The welfare of 2,000,000 workers in the United States meant nothing to Blanton Winship or his appointee.

The sacrificing of 2,000,000 workers in the States and the sacrificing of labor's welfare in the States, as well as in Puerto Rico, meant nothing to these gentlemen who were hell-bent on doing the bidding of the financial and industrial corporations of Wall Street that have kept the workers of Puerto Rico in the tentacles of imperialism and wage peonage. I take this occasion to praise the patriotism and statesmanship of our Speaker, Hon. William Bankhead, who treated the dismissed and disgraced ex-Governor of Puerto Rico with a flat and patriotic "no." This "no" was given after I had spoken to the Speaker, who had promised me that there would be no suspension of the rules, or the considering of any legislation that would exempt Puerto Rico from the provisions of the Fair Labor Standards Act, at this session of Congress.

In the face of these activities, treacherous and detrimental to the people of Puerto Rico, I felt that I should no longer remain silent. I felt that I should not permit this ex-Governor or his stooges to any longer use the prestige of his office which he so disgraced, to the benefit of the exploiters of the Puerto Rican people. I would be derelict if I did not tear off the cloak of virtue in which this destroyer of liberty, protector of grafters, and exploiter of the people of Puerto Rico had enshrouded himself. Therefore, Mr. Speaker, here is his record:

In his 5 years as Governor of Puerto Rico, Mr. Blanton Winship destroyed the last vestige of civil rights in Puerto Rico. Patriots were framed in the very executive mansion and railroaded to prison. Men, women, and children were massacred in the streets of the island simply because they dared to express their opinion or attempted to meet in free assemblage.

Citizens were terrorized. The courts became devoid of any prestige because of the evil influence exerted upon them by politicians who acted with the connivance and consent of Mr. Winship. American workers were persecuted and shot down whenever they sought to exercise their right to strike, or to organize and protest against the abominable wages that were paid to them by Mr. Winship's pals. The insular police were militarized and transformed from an honest police organization to an organization of provocateurs and murderers, such as existed in the darkest days of czarist Russia. Nero played the fiddle while Christians were massacred in the days of ancient Rome. Winship drank cocktails and danced in the Governor's palace while the police ruthlessly killed and persecuted Puerto Rican citizens. The following are just a few cases illustrative of Winship's Neroism. Neither time nor space permits me to give a full history, or the list of victims, of which the American people know very little or nothing at all.

On Palm Sunday, March 21, 1937, in Ponce, the second largest city in Puerto Rico, the police forces fired with machine guns, rifles, and pistols into a crowd of marching Nationalists. Seventeen were killed, more than 200 wounded. The Nationalists were going to hold a meeting and a parade in Ponce on March 21. The mayor, Tormes, issued a permit. One hour before the time set for the parade, and when the demonstrators were ready to march, the mayor canceled the permit on frivolous grounds. As Winship pointed out in a statement issued after the massacre, the parade was called off by the mayor at the request of Gov. Blanton Winship and Police Chief Col. Orbeta.

Gov. Winship went out of San Juan. Col. Orbeta went to Ponce and concentrated there a heavy police force, among which he included all the machine gunners. For many days, the government had been planning action in Ponce.

Chief of Police Guillermo Soldevilla, with 14 policemen, placed himself in front of the paraders; Chief Perez Segarra and Sgt. Rafael Molina, commanding 9 men, armed with Thompson machine guns and tear-gas bombs, stood in the back; Chief of Police Antonio Bernardi, heading 11 policemen, armed with machine guns, stood in the east; and another police group of 12 men, armed with rifles, placed itself in the west.

The demonstrators, at the order of their leader, and while "La Borinqueña," the national song, was being played, began to march. Immediately, they were fired upon for 15 minutes by the police from the four flanks. The victims fell down without an opportunity to defend themselves. Even after the street was covered with dead bodies, policemen continued firing. More than 200 were wounded; several were killed. Men, women, and children, Nationalists and non-Nationalists, demonstrators, and people passing by, as well as the people who ran away, were shot. They were chased by the police and shot or clubbed at the entrance of their houses. Others were taken from their hiding places and killed. Leopold Tormes, a member of the legislature, told the reporters how a Nationalist was murdered in cold blood by a policeman, after the shooting, in his own arms.

A 7-year-old girl, Georgina Maldonado, while running to a nearby church, was shot through the back. A woman, Maria Hernandez, was also killed. Carmen Fernandez, aged 33, was severely wounded. After she fell down, a policeman struck her with his rifle, saying, "Take this; be a Nationalist." Maria Hernandez was a member of the Republican Party, and while running away, was clubbed twice on her head by a policeman. Dr. Jose N. Gandara, one of the physicians who assisted the wounded, testified that wounded people running away were shot, and that many were again wounded through the back. Don Luis Sanchez Frasquieri, former president of the Rotary Club in Ponce, said that he had witnessed the most horrible slaughter made by police on defenseless youth. No arms were found in the hands of the civilians wounded, nor on the dead ones. About 150 of the demonstrators were arrested immediately afterward, several of them being women. All the Nationalist leaders were also arrested. They were a released on bail. More than 15,000, as was reported by El Mundo, a Puerto Rican newspaper, attended the funerals at Ponce, and more than 5,000 at Mayagüez.

The above is not a description of the Ponce events by a Puerto Rican Nationalist. It is from a speech of Rep. John T. Bernard, of Minnesota, in Congress and appeared in the Congressional Record of April 14, 1937: "Does not this bring to mind the Boston Massacre in 1770 and the shooting of Russian peasants by the czar in 1905? Remembering the events of Easter Week in Dublin, 1916, do not you agree with Jay Franklin, Washington commentator for the Stern papers, that Puerto Rico is the Ireland of the Caribbean?"

April 16 is a legal holiday in Puerto Rico. It is the anniversary of the birthday of Jose de Diego, former speaker of the House of Delegates, noted orator, poet, jurist, and outstanding advocate of independence. Every year, the Nationalist Party celebrates a mass, a demonstration, and a meeting in his honor. Wreaths of flowers are deposited on his tomb. Another demonstration and a meeting are held to honor Manuel Rafael Suarez Diaz, a martyr to the cause of independence. Flowers are deposited on his tomb also.

In 1937, a few weeks after the Palm Sunday massacre, the city manager of San Juan, under Winship's pressure, denied permits for these meetings and demonstrations. As was even reported in the New York newspapers, although the ecclesiastical authorities gave authorization to hold the Mass on the 16th, the Cathedral was closed, and policemen posted at its doors. The cemeteries were closed and the Puerto Rican people forbidden to go in groups larger than two to deposit flowers on the graves of the patriots. Gen. Winship again mobilized the Regular Army and National Guard, subject to call.

Arthur Garfield Hays, attorney for the American Civil Liberties Union, went to Puerto Rico and investigated the Palm Sunday massacre, and his conclusion as reported in the report of the American

Civil Liberties Union was as follows: "The facts show that the affair of March 21 in Ponce was a massacre."

Governor Winship tried to cover up this massacre by filing a mendacious report. . . . However, the photographs that were brought to Secretary Ickes by a committee consisting, among others, of former Congressman Bernard of Minnesota, and myself, photographs of children shot in the back and of police wantonly firing on unarmed people from four sides, could not be ignored. What did the tyrant do? Instead of ceasing the terror, he continued it; and immediately had arrested the friends of people who had been killed, on charges of conspiracy to commit murder. Two trials were held. The first trial resulted in a mistrial, and in the second trial the defendants were acquitted.

In the meantime, the reign of terror continued. While the victims of the Ponce massacre were being tried for murder, the police forces were given a free hand to continue the orgy of murder.

(Here, as well as in the next omission indicated below, Congressman Marcantonio described in detail a number of killings by the police.)

An indignant public opinion forced the Government to convene the grand jury, which . . . bitterly assailed the practices of the police and tried to determine the responsibility, if any, of the Governor. . . . They left the door open for further inquiries. Gov. Winship got the law (providing for investigation and indictment of public officers, including the Governor, by a grand jury) repealed soon afterward. So that at the time of the Ponce massacre, denounced in this House by Congressman John T. Bernard on April 14, 1937, in the brilliant and moving speech which appears in the Congressional Record of that date, page 4,499, and to which I referred above, the district judges of Ponce denied a petition made by prominent citizens of that community, who represented every sector of public life, when they asked for the convening of a grand jury to investigate the case. As the law now stands, the citizens are helpless when the aggression originates with the top public officials, because the prosecutors are appointed by and are to a great extent responsible to the Governor.

A frame-up "a la Medici" was something at which Mr. Winship would not stop. Dr. Pedro Albizu Campos, a Harvard graduate and leader of the Nationalists, together with several of his followers, were indicted under a post-Civil War statute of a conspiracy to insurrect against the Government of the United States. They were framed at the Governor's palace. Mr. Rockwell Kent, famous American artist, describes what took place at a cocktail party in the Governor's palace immediately after the first trial, and I quote from his letter to Sen. Henry F. Ashurst, chairman of the Senate Judiciary Committee, dated May 21, 1939:

I was present in San Juan during the progress of the first trial of Albizu Campos for treason, and I was a guest of Gov. Winship's at a cocktail party on the terrace of his residence a few hours after the conclusion of that first trial through a disagreement of the jury. The party was a large one and the guests were mainly Americans, tourists and residents of San Juan, and upper-class Puerto Ricans. There was naturally a great deal of talk about the trial, and much of this talk centered about Judge Cooper, who had presided. The comments were heatedly pro-government; and in my hearing condolences upon the miscarriage of justice were repeatedly voiced to the judge. These were received without rebuke. At that party, a Puerto Rican friend of mine introduced me to a Mr. Cecil Snyder as the prosecuting attorney in the Campos case. We three withdrew for conversation to a corner of the terrace. My friend complimented Mr. Snyder upon his brilliant summing up and deplored the judge's failure to bring in a conviction. Mr. Snyder assured him that he had already received a dispatch from Washington telling him to go ahead with a new trial and that the Department of Justice would back him until he did get a conviction.

Mr. Snyder drew a paper from his pocket and handed it to my friend, saying, "This is to be my next jury. What do you think of them?" I recall that my friend was familiar with the name and position of all but one of those listed, and that he assured Mr. Snyder that they could be counted upon for a conviction. This appeared to agree with Mr. Snyder's own knowledge. The jury of the second trial of Albizu Campos contained several men whose connections were identical with those in the list submitted to my friend by Mr. Snyder. How the prosecuting attorney could determine in advance who would compose his next jury, I don't know. I do state as a fact that Mr. Snyder said, "This is to be my next jury." I have subsequently given this information all possible publicity. The defense counsel at the Ponce trials asked me to come to Ponce to testify to what I knew about Federal prejudice. I was accompanied on the plane by the Federal marshal of San Juan. He spent literally hours of the trip attempting to persuade me not to go to Ponce, not even to leave San Juan. He urged me to put myself under his protection, to stay with him at the Condado Hotel, to meet his friends, who, he said, were the people I ought to know in Puerto Rico, and to avoid association with friends of the defendants. He warned me that my life would be in danger from the moment I set foot in Puerto Rico. From the moment of my arrival in Puerto Rico I was viciously attacked in the government-controlled evening paper. Before my appearance on the witness stand, it was published that Cecil Snyder and the prosecuting attorney of Ponce, after a session together of some hours the night before, had agreed that I should not be permitted to testify. It was rumored in Puerto Rico that if I did testify, I would be immediately arrested.

A suggestion as to the origin of these rumors is contained in a statement attributed to Cecil Snyder and published in a recent issue of Ken. I was not permitted to testify, although the entire matter of my testimony was put into the record by the defense counsel. You will recall that the Ponce trials resulted in the acquittal of all the defendants. As a result of these experiences my own feeling is, naturally enough, one of serious distrust of Federal Law enforcement in Puerto Rico.

Sincerely yours,

Rockwell Kent

The trial took place, and by a prejudiced jury, by jurors who had expressed publicly, bias and hatred for the defendants, Campos and his colleagues were railroaded to jail. Mr. Speaker, these innocent men languish in Atlanta Penitentiary today because they were convicted by a fixed jury, a jury representing the economic interests of Wall Street in Puerto Rico. They did the bidding of Blanton Winship. An idea of what took place in the jury room is contained in the following letter to President Franklin Delano Roosevelt by Elmer Ellsworth, one of the jurors who convicted Campos:

(The letter, written in support of a petition for clemency, concludes …)

I cannot refrain from saying that my associates on the jury seemed to be motivated by strong, if not violent, prejudice against the Nationalists and were prepared to convict them, regardless of the evidence. Ten of the jurors were American residents in Puerto Rico and the two Puerto Ricans were closely associated with American business interests. It was evident from the composition of the jury that the Nationalists did not and could not get a fair trial.

Very sincerely yours,

Elmer Ellsworth

This frame-up is one of the blackest pages in the history of American jurisprudence. The continuance of this incarceration is repugnant to our democratic form of government; it is repugnant to our Bill of Rights and out of harmony with our good-neighbor policy. There is no place in America for political prisoners. As long as Puerto Rico remains part of the United States, Puerto Rico must have the same freedom, the same civil liberties, and the same justice which our forefathers laid down for us. Only a complete and immediate unconditional pardon will, in a very small measure, right this historical wrong.

When we ask ourselves, "Can it happen here?" the Puerto Rican people can answer, "It has happened in Puerto Rico."

Source: Congressional Record of August 14, 1939. http://www.cheverote.com/reviews/marcantonio.html.

Herschel T. Manuel, "Results of a Half-Century Experiment in Teaching a Second Language"

(1952)

The battleground between U.S. government administrators who demanded the Americanization of Puerto Rico through English-only programs and Puerto Rican educators who advocated bilingual programs that included instruction in Spanish was set during the 1920s and 1930s. Caught in the crossfire were the children of Puerto Rican parents. The failure to include Spanish contributed to a high dropout rate among Puerto Rican children. Sociologist Herschel T. Manuel (1887–1976) was an education professor at the University of Texas from the 1920s through the 1960s. He conducted important studies on Mexican children and was a strong advocate of bilingual education. Manuel began his study of Mexicans in 1929. He was outraged by the lengths to which many Euro-Texans went to deny these children education. He converted from objectivism to a purposivism, which meant moving from describing what was to reaching for what should, and could, be. The following excerpts show the devastating effects of English-only education on Puerto Rican children.

Table 1 Median Scores (Spanish) of Puerto Rican Pupils in Comparison with Median Scores (English) of Continental Pupils

Continental U.S. Grade Level	General Reading	Natural Sciences	Social Studies	Language Usage
1.8	2.2			
2.8	2.8			
3.8	3.6			
4.8	4.2			
5.8	5.1			
6.8	5.7	7.0		
7.8	6.6	7.8	6.6	6.1
8.8	7.8	8.8	8.0	6.8
9.8	9.1	9.9	8.5	7.8
10.8	10.6	11.1	8.9	8.3
11.8	12.0	11.7	10.0	8.8
12.8	12.3	12.3	10.8	8.8
13.8	13.8	13.8	11.7	11.3

Note: The table shows, for example, that at the close of the eighth month of the first grade the Puerto Rican pupils achieved a score (in Spanish) equal to the average score achieved (in English) by Continental pupils at the end of the second month of the second grade.

Administration of the English edition of the tests in the Continental United States makes possible a comparison of achievement in Puerto Rico with achievement in corresponding grades in the States. Table 1 compares the scores of urban Puerto Rican pupils on the Spanish edition with the scores of urban Continental pupils on the English edition. Point scores have been translated into grade scores on the basis of Continental norms.

In non-specialized reading the Puerto Rican pupils have at the end of the first grade a somewhat higher score than the Continental pupils.

This advantage changes to a deficit in the middle grades, but in the senior high school and first year of college, the pupils in Puerto Rico read about as well as pupils in the States. The scores of Puerto Rican pupils in the specialized reading materials of the natural sciences follow closely Continental norms but are lower in the social studies and in Language Usage.

With reference to English it may be said that in the high school the average Puerto Rican pupil reads English at the level of efficiency of a Continental English-speaking pupil two and one-half or three grades below the level at which the Puerto Rican pupil is enrolled and that from fifteen to twenty percent of the high school pupils read English as well as or better than the average Continental pupil of the same grade. In Language Usage, on the other hand, fewer than one percent of the high school pupils have scores reaching the medians of Continental pupils. Since the language of every-day life is predominantly Spanish, one can understand that there is much less opportunity for expression in English than there is for reading.

These, then, are the measured results of a half-century of effort to teach English to Spanish-speaking pupils. This paper must come to an end with little effort to interpret the results either in terms of the Puerto Rican situation or in relation to the broader problems of language teaching. To a linguist, the results must be evidence of remarkable progress in a job that is inherently difficult—the teaching of a language which is little used out of school by most of those who are trying to learn it. The Puerto Rican people themselves may well be proud of their accomplishments. On the other hand, the results lend a note of realism to education in the Island. It will be a long time before the desires of the people for English can be completely satisfied. The results bring home to all of us the difficulties of teaching a second language to an entire population.

Source: Manuel, Hershel T. "Results of a Half-Century Experiment in Teaching a Second Language." *The Modern Language Journal* 36, no. 2 (February 1952): 76–77.

Memoirs of Bernardo Vega, the Great Depression Years, 1929–1939 (1977)

Bernardo Vega (1885–1965) came to the United States in 1916. The Memoirs of Bernardo Vega *tell of his journey, Puerto Rico, and his struggles. In these excerpts, Vega discusses the Great Depression years and their impact on the Puerto Rican community in New York. Vega also describes the radical community's relationship to Cuban exiles and the Spanish Civil War (1936–1939) and the war against fascism. Vega's focus was on the survival of the working class.*

In the spring of 1931 we concentrated on an effort that was being made to send an armed expedition to Cuba. A ship and ample military supplies had been purchased, and over 150 volunteers awaited orders to set sail from New York. Our group was defeated, though, when it came time to select the commander of the expedition. I was anything but pleased when Gen. Menocal was named to head the revolt against Machado. It seemed to me that [was] nothing more than replacing one bigwig with another, and I resigned. But even then I continued to help organize the arm[ed] expedition.

The plans were upset by Machado's spies, who revealed our preparations to the American authorities. Some of the volunteers, including most of the leaders, were arrested. Only thirty-three men made it to the ship, which was anchored outside of United States. The rest never made it.

Nevertheless, despite all the problems, the expedition managed to land in Cuba. Machado met it with a sizable army. The revolutionaries fought bravely but were defeated. Three of those who came out alive were members of Flor Roja: Montiel, Alvaro Moreno, and Sabis Vega.

On February 3, 1932, the Democratic Party presidential candidate addressed the nation in the first of what were to be well-known fireside chats. The working class, and the American people in general, listening on their radios, were impressed by Franklin Delano Roosevelt's reassuring words. In simple terms he described what he proposed to do, if elected, to return the country to prosperity. He would launch large-scale public-works projects giving jobs to millions of unemployed people; he would have the government take the initiative in exploiting the vast sources of hydroelectric power; he would bring together the best brains the country had to offer. . . . That speech, and the many that followed, spread a spirit of optimism across the United States.

By that time, 15 million workers were unemployed. New York was one of the cities most seriously affected. The winter of 1932 was particularly harsh, and in the middle of February the whole city was blanketed in snow. Around twelve thousand men were hired by City Hall to clean up the streets. Many Puerto Ricans jumped at the opportunity to make some money, and what a sight it was to see them wrapped up in rags, their necks covered with old newspapers, swinging their shovels and shivering to the bone.

On September 29, 1933, the Fusionists nominated a Puerto Rican, M. Vivaldi, to run for the state assembly from the 17th district. The Fusion Party established an Hispanic division based in Harlem. The leadership included Vivaldi, Enrique Torregrosa, Victor Fiol, Salguero Font, Florencio Ruiz, Antonio Gonzalez, Felix Caro, J. D. Lopez, Miguel Collazo, and Luis Caballero.

Meanwhile the trade union struggle of Puerto Rican workers continued to grow, especially among hotel and restaurant workers and in the needle trades. Many of our countrymen were employed in those lines of work, and during the year they held several work stoppages and mass pickets.

The Harlem section of the Communist Party put up candidates for the state assembly and city council. These candidates won the support of the Liga Antiimperialista Puertoriqueña, the Centro Obrero Español, and several labor unions.

Heading up the Fusionist forces, La Guardia carried out an extremely effective electoral campaign. He kept his rivals in the traditional parties constantly on the defensive. He campaigned in the poor neighborhoods and explained what measures he would take if elected mayor. To the surprise of all the local newspapers and to the shame of Tammany Hall, the Fusionists swept the election by a margin of over 200,000 votes. And thus began Fiorello La Guardia's reign in City Hall.

The newly founded Club Hostos quickly became the center of many activities, including classes in Spanish and in Hispanic culture for children and young people, and a vast number of lectures and meetings. Filiberto Vazquez, for example, gave a talk on the "Foundations of the Nationalist Struggle in Puerto Rico," and Max Vazquez gave one on "Russian Literature Before the Revolution of 1917," which gives an idea of the kinds of topics that were discussed at the club.

The Junta Nacionalista also sponsored a number of public events, one of which concerned the Congreso Estudiantil Inter-Americano being held in Costa Rica. The event centered around a report delivered by the delegate of the students from Puerto Rico, Francisco Pagán Rodríguez.

An equally active group was the Liga Antiimperialista Puertoriqueña. The Cuban intellectual, Leonardo Fernández Sánchez, one of the most admired orators of the time, came to speak in its hall. The theme of his speech was Puerto Rico, and particularly the relationship between the agrarian problem and sugar production.

In May 1933 a famous incident occurred between the [multi]millionaire John D. Rockefeller and Diego Rivera, the Mexican painter. Diego Rivera had contracted to paint a series of murals in Rockefeller Center, for which he was to be paid a small fortune. The artist presented an elaborate plan of the project, which was accepted. But after he had finished his first mural, Rockefeller hit the ceiling when he recognized a picture of Lenin stretching out his arms to clasp hands with a Negro and a soldier. The leading representative of U.S. finance capital demanded that Diego Rivera paint something else; this, in his opinion "was not a work of art."

Diego refused of course. The whole city was talking about the controversy. A huge picketline was organized in front of Rockefeller Center. But the millionaire would not give in. The mural ended up being destroyed by that "great patron of the arts." Diego Rivera's principled stand won admiration throughout the world.

Meanwhile, the Roosevelt years did not seem to bring many changes in our Island's fortunes. Our hope that, with the New Deal, governors with somewhat greater intellectual and administrative competence would be appointed were destroyed by bitter reality. The first to receive the appointment, strictly for the support he mustered in Florida during the election campaign, was a certain Gore. No sooner had he taken office than, on a visit to his home state, he declared that "independence would bring ruin" to Puerto Rico. If Puerto Rico were independent, he went on, it would lose free entry of its sugar into the United States. Florida would be the beneficiary, since it would be able to take the Island's share of the sugar market. For that reason, he extended an invitation to the large landowners in Puerto Rico to move their sugar plantations and mills to Florida. He not only ranted and raved along these lines, but he even went so far as to suggest the massive emigration of Puerto Rican workers to Florida. We protested against that idea in New York, and even got a campaign going in Puerto Rico. Our position caught on, and the hair-brained scheme never got off the ground.

Another public act that was to prove damaging to Puerto Ricans was committed by the First Lady, Mrs. Eleanor Roosevelt. On her return from a well-publicized trip to Puerto Rico in April 1934, she spoke at a benefit held in her honor by the Women's Trade Union League in New York. She told of the deep impression the dire poverty she found on the Island had made on her, and went on to say: "Tuberculosis is widespread everywhere, just as it is in the Puerto Rican community here in New York . . . I assume that none of you will be hiring any of them in your homes, but however careful we may be in rearing our children, they can still come into contact with one of those sick people in the streets or in the schools. And tuberculosis is an extremely contagious disease. . . ." Those were her words, spoken without malice and with the best of intentions. But the consequences, at least in the short run, could only hurt Puerto Ricans, especially those living in New York. Thousands of us were working in restaurants and cafeterias, and came into contact with food that was served to the public. The chances of finding, and of holding onto, jobs in that kind of work became dimmer than ever. It was even harder on all the Puerto Rican women working as domestics and nursemaids. And so, to add to the usual discrimination, the population was led to fear that our countrymen would infect them with tuberculosis!

"Isn't that something. Even when they try to do us a favor, they only bring more harm to Puerto Ricans. . . . " That's what I said to myself, and I decided that we had to do something about it.

In January 1938, Puerto Rican dockworkers—first in San Juan, and soon in every port on the Island—went out on strike. This strike action was of particular historical importance for two reasons: first of all, because the seamen working the ships, organized by the National Maritime Union of the CIO, totally supported the strike; and secondly because new elements, clearly identified with the Partido Comunista Puertoriqueño, played a leading role in the labor movement for the first time. In New York, a strike solidarity committee was formed, made up of Manuel Ortega, Harry de la Cruz, Joaquín Rosado, Aracelio Pagón, Juan N. Maissonet, Consuelo Marcial, Jose Martinez, Homero Rosado, Juan Emmanuelli, J. Enamorado Cuesta, A. Pacheco Padro, and G. Concepción de Gracía.

On the initiative of José Camprubi, the editor of the Spanish daily *La Prensa*, another effort was made to bring the Puerto Rican organizations together in an alliance that would represent the entire community. Some of those who carried through on the idea were the legislator Oscar García Rivera, J. M. Vivaldi, Caban Soler, Cesar G. Torres, and Laura Santiago. After a series of meetings the Confederación de Sociedades Puertoriqueñas was founded with J. M. Vivaldi as president and Tomás Gares, José Santiago, García Angulo, Laura Santiago, and Angel Vidal as vice-presidents. Named to the board of directors were Isabel O'Neill, Vicente Medina, and Gregorio Domenech, among others.

The campaign in support of the Spanish Republic and against the arms embargo culminated in a huge rally at Madison Square Garden. The featured speakers were the Spanish leaders Juan Negrin, José Bergamin, and Carmén Meana. The gathering approved messages to the President and the Congress of the United States demanding that the embargo be lifted. Aside from what it paid at the door, the audience wound up contributing over $20,000 to the cause. And it is worth pointing out that the Puerto Rican workers did not scrimp in their economic support for the heroic struggle of the Spanish people.

Source: Iglesias, Cesar Andreu, ed. *Memoirs of Bernardo Vega: A Contribution to the History of the Puerto Rican Community in New York*. Translated by Juan Flores.

the Great Depression of the 1930s

"What Was the Lemon Grove School Desegregation Case All About?" (1931)

In the early 1900s, Lemon Grove, California, acquired its name when large citrus groves were planted and citrus became the area's major industry. The area attracted large numbers of Mexican workers who formed a colonia *(colony or enclave). In January 1931, Lemon Grove Grammar School principal Jerome Green, acting under instructions from school trustees, turned away Mexican children at the schoolhouse door. The Mexican parents refused to accept inferior schools, and the "Lemon Grove Incident" resulted in one of the first successful school desegregation court decisions in the history of the United States. The following document provides an analysis based on the transcripts of the Superior Court case and* The Lemon Grove Incident, *a 1985 documentary produced by KPBS Television in San Diego, California.*

During the labor struggles in the Imperial Valley, the children of Mexican immigrants throughout Southern California were increasingly segregated into separate classrooms called Americanization schools. It is not known how widespread segregated schools were in metropolitan San Diego. In semirural regions of San Diego it is probable that segregation prevailed.

One notable challenge to the Americanization school came from the Mexican immigrant parents living in Lemon Grove, a rural hamlet near San Diego where the main employers were citrus growers. This has come to be known as the Lemon Grove Incident, thanks to the research of Robert Alvarez, Jr. and the documentary film [*The Lemon Grove Incident*] produced by Paul Espinosa. This was the first successful legal challenge to the segregation of Mexicanos in the public schools in the United States.

On July 23, 1930, the Lemon Grove school board began to discuss what to do with the more than 75 Mexican students who were attending the local grammar school. It was decided to build a separate school for them but no notice was given to the parents of the Mexicano students.

On January 5, 1931, the principal of the Lemon Grove Grammar School, Jerome T. Greene stood at the door of the school and directed the incoming Mexican students to go to the new school building, a wooden structure that came to be called "La Caballeriza" (the barn). Instead, the students returned home and thereafter their parents refused to send their children to the separate school. This became known in the press as the "Mexican student strike," but in reality it was their parents who, with the support of the Mexican consul in San Diego, decided to oppose segregation of their children. They formed a group called El Comité de Vecinos de Lemon Grove and asked the Mexican consul, Enrique Ferreira, for advice. Ferreira put the parents in touch with Fred C. Noon and A. C. Brinkely, two lawyers who had worked for the consul in the past and from there they filed a writ of mandate to prevent the school board from forcing their children to attend the segregated school. They chose a student, Roberto Alvarez, to be the plaintiff in the class action suit.

The San Diego district attorney argued that the new school was appropriate because it was in the Mexican neighborhood and large enough for all the students; that most of the students were below grade level in their knowledge of English; and that they would receive better instruction in this Americanization school. Incidentally, they suggested that American students would benefit by not having contact with Mexican students.

On February 24, 1931, Judge Claude Chambers began hearing the case. Fred Noon, the Mexican parents' lawyer called ten witnesses to the stand to challenge the school board's contention that the Mexican children were educationally backward. Most of the students had been born in the United States and spoke English. At least one student spoke no Spanish at all. In the interrogatory, Judge Chambers dramatically revealed the injustice of the differential treatment of Mexican students:

Judge Chambers:	When there are American children who are behind, what do you do with them?
Answer:	They are kept in a lower grade.
Judge Chambers:	You don't segregate them? Why not do the same with the other children? Wouldn't the association of American and Mexican children be favorable to the learning of English for these children?
Answer:	(silence)

In the final arguments, the judge was convinced that there was no reason to segregate the Mexican children and that the separation would probably hurt them academically in terms of learning the English language and customs. He ruled against the Lemon Grove school district and ordered them to reinstate the children in the regular school. While it was a victory for Mexicano students, the judge had held that their segregation violated state law which allowed for the segregation of African and Indian children. Thus the logic underlying the verdict did not challenge racial segregation, and it would remain for later court cases to outlaw that kind of injustice.

The Lemon Grove case was the first legal victory of Mexicanos to challenge their separation in the school system. Unfortunately the case did not set a precedent in other districts and segregation continued outside of Lemon Grove. Nevertheless, the dramatization of the incident in the documentary film *The Lemon Grove Incident* served to educate new generations about the struggles of their ancestors to achieve justice.

Source: San Diego Mexican & Chicano History, R. Griswold, 1998. http://www-rohan.sdsu.edu/dept/mas/chicanohistory/chapter07/c07s02.html.

Robert N. McLean, "The Mexican Return" (1932)

The Presbyterian Church and the United Presbyterian Church were very active among Mexican Americans and Spanish-speaking peoples in the southwestern United States. Evangelization efforts began in the 1800s. Presbyterian mission work among Mexican Americans was described as difficult because it was among "poor and illiterate people." The missionaries were often confronted with an ecclesiastical bureaucracy and limited funds. Like Catholic missionaries, they were paternalistic. Robert N. McLean (1918–1932) was a superintendent of the missions, taking over from his father, Robert McLean, also the head of the missions and a renowned missionary. The Presbyterians began missions in Mexico around 1872. The Presbyterian Church USA (Northern Presbyterian Church), the Presbyterian Church US (Southern Presbyterian Church), the Associate Presbyterian Church, and the Congregationalist Church in the United States built on the work of previous missionaries, many of whom were recruited from the ranks of the missions in Mexico. The Mexican Revolution (1910–1920) hastened the Mexicanization of the church, which expanded its work in the 1920s on both sides of the border. In the following article, which appeared in The Nation, *a progressive weekly magazine, McLean advocates for the interests of the Mexican population and criticizes the massive repatriation of Mexicans and the passage of laws to exclude Mexicans from employment on public works projects. He reminds the reader why Mexicans came here in the first place.*

The train was ready to go. Hand upon throttle, the engineer leaned from his cab. Behind him were ten plush-upholstered day coaches, loaded with six hundred Mexicans who were "going home." The windows were filled with brown faces, some sad, some eager; along the sides of the cars were little groups of country relief agents and workers from various churches and community houses, who under one pretext or another had succeeded in crashing the gates. Outside, a massed wall of humanity pressed against the iron fence. For one who was going, ten had come to say goodbye. It was just like the other trains which had been leaving Los Angeles on Thursday mornings—like the others but different, because inside the red-plush coaches were different people with different stories of suffering, hunger, and heartache. "All aboard!" sang the conductor, and the train began to move out of the station. As one car rolled by, a mother was seen comforting a little girl of about ten. And then these words, spoken in perfect English, floated through the window: "I don't want to go to Mexico! All my friends are in Brooklyn Avenue school, and I want to stay here!" But the train gathered momentum and swept out of the yards.

The press has had much to say during the past few months about the Mexicans who have gone home, but little has been said about the thousands of United States citizens who have been carried away by their parents to a land which they have never seen. Nor have we faced the fact that many of the parents who are taking these United States–born children out of the country, have been here so long that in their habits and ways of living they are far more "American" than Mexican.

The Mexican labor invasion of the United States—and the subsequent return—is one of the largest, most interesting racial movements in all history. In a time of economic stress such as the present we lose all sense of perspective. We forget why the Mexican came and why he has tarried so long, and we are blind to the injustices which are forcibly uprooting him from communities where he has cast his lot, built his home, and begotten his children. All we can see at such a moment as this is bread lines. And men of dark complexion are holding jobs which "white" men ought to have.

In August of 1931, a new law went into effect in California which makes it practically impossible for a contractor to employ Mexicans upon a public job. That, of course, means the bulk of the cement work and the work with pick and shovel—jobs which have been the recognized portion of the Mexicans for a dozen years. Even if the law permitted the employment of the "bronze" laborer, so strong is the social pressure now being exerted that few employers would care to defy it. At least one paving concern has temporarily gone out of business because it cannot carry on without Mexicans and the law will not permit them to be used. In one California community a contractor took refuge in the town hall in order to escape from a mob infuriated because he was using Mexican labor.

Even in times of economic strain and stress the foreign laborer is entitled to a square deal. Back of the lines of race and blood there are certain facts which merit consideration. The Mexican laborer came to this country to render a particular contribution at a time of particular need. The war depleted for a time our labor supply, while speeding up our industries. We had less labor and we needed more. Bursting shells on the fields of France proclaimed copper king. The large companies operating in southeastern Arizona, the greatest copper-producing district of the world, worked their mines to the utmost, leasing mineral land they could not work to other operators. Mexicans poured into Bisbee, Douglas, Miami, Globe, Ray, Jerome, and Morceni [Morenci], and have been there ever since. At about the same time, large areas of new citrus plantings began to come into bearing, and Mexicans by the thousand came to California to pick oranges. It was of prime importance during the war that transportation should not be interrupted, and Mexicans came over to man the section gangs and tamp the ties. Mexicans have been tamping ties on the railroads of the Southwest ever since, and have spread out along other lines into the North and East. The Mexican laborer came because we invited him and because we could not get along without him.

But it might be thought that after the national emergency was passed and our soldiers had returned from France, the Mexicans could have gone home. Not so. A number of new factors conspired not only to hold here the Mexicans already arrived, but to draw hundreds of thousands of their friends and relatives. First must be mentioned the new irrigation projects. The Roosevelt Dam, the Elephant Butte, the Yuma project, the extension of the ditches in the Imperial Valley—all brought vast new acreages under cultivation. The lower Rio Grande valley almost overnight changed from a desert into a garden, and hands beckoned across the river for help to work the crops. The Salt River valley of Arizona, feeling the miraculous touch of water, grew long staple cotton and called for Mexicans to pick it. When the bottom fell out of the cotton market, the growers quickly switched to lettuce and kept their Mexicans to "chop" it. In the Imperial Valley of California the lettuce acreage grew, until last season a total of eleven thousand cars rolled out of the valley to Eastern markets. Vying with lettuce, cantaloupes demanded Mexican labor, and during last May and June it took 21,400 cars to haul the melons to our breakfast tables. There is a common impression abroad that one American can do the work of three Mexicans. But no race can compete with the Mexicans in picking cantaloupes. Even the Japanese employ them, and the growers say that only a Mexican seems to have that sixth sense which tells when a cantaloupe is ready for the crate.

During the time of our agricultural expansion, the growers of oranges, grapes, cotton, melons, and winter vegetables not only invited the Mexicans, but even bid actively and acrimoniously among themselves for the amount of Mexican labor which was available. And whenever anyone suggested that the supply was beginning to exceed the demand and that perhaps society was paying a stiff price for its Mexican labor in the social costs involved, the growers sped their representatives to Washington to lobby against the various bills which were successively introduced to put Mexico upon a quota basis.

One cannot say or write anything about the Southwest without eventually bumping up against the fact that Los Angeles has grown. But while it grew from a city of less than half a million at the close of the war to over a million in 1930, it was compelled to build new houses and school buildings, lay new sewers and water mains, and pave hundreds of miles of new streets. Often it was in such a hurry about it that the streets were paved before the sewers were laid, but the work had to be done in a hurry and Mexicans did it. While the Mexican laborer was needed in both agriculture and industry, we were glad to have him hold the job in which he was employed.

We were perfectly willing that he should do our dirty work for us. We became "labor conscious." We developed the phrase "the work no white man will do"! Americans could not stand the heat of the desert, and so Mexicans tamped the ties and built the bridges.

Americans would not pick cotton—unless they were "cheap white trash"—and so the Mexicans did it. Americans would not labor in the heat with pick and shovel, and so Mexicans speedily filled the ranks of all the labor gangs. Americans would not "chop" lettuce all morning and then spend all afternoon trying to find out whether it was the grower or the contractor who was supposed to pay them. And so it was the Mexican laborers who jumped on the trucks at dawn and drove out to the lettuce fields to chop until noon. We developed a racial superiority toward certain types of labor, which came to be thought of as Mexican jobs. Thus the "bronze" man became the hewer of wood and the drawer of water in the Southwest. Simultaneously the large employers contrived to maintain the labor reservoir at a high level. It paid to keep the Mexicans both numerous and hungry.

Some day, perhaps, somebody with a flair for statistics will try to evaluate the contribution which the Mexican laborer has rendered in the building of an empire in the Southwest. He has done all the common work on practically every one of California's two hundred crops. He has maintained the lines of transportation. Every industry has been dependent upon him. And as is always the case with the common laborer, he has put much in and taken little out. Today, under the strain of economic adversity, we forget that during these years the Mexican has become part of our community life. We forget that his children have been born here and educated in our schools. We forget that by the sweat of his brow he has earned a place in our economic life. We are sending him home. There is little gratitude in our hearts.

But the most amusing thing about it all—amusing were it not so tragic—is the attitude taken by our own border immigration service toward this army of Mexican laborers. When we needed them we forgot our own laws, closing our eyes while Mexicans crossed the line. There were not enough men to patrol the border, there were no funds for deportation, and anyway the crops were perishing for want of pickers. As one official said, "I just have to shut my eyes to keep from crowding them off the sidewalk when I come down to work in the morning." It has been estimated that seven out of ten who came over between 1919 and 1929 came illegally; and most of them found it so easy to come that they are unconscious of any wrongdoing. Hundreds say naively: "I just crossed the bridge and nobody asked me any questions." Now the line is practically closed to the common laborer, and our reinforced border patrol, with plenty of money for deportations, is running up and down roads stopping Mexicans and asking dramatically: "How in the world did you get across the line?" And unless they can prove a legal domicile they are deported or told that they will be deported if they do not go of their own accord. In all this we have done little law-making. We have, indeed, armed our border service with a new law which makes it a felony for a foreigner to enter illegally. Otherwise our laws are as they were. They have been changed only by interpretation. But always more laws have been made by interpretation than by legislation.

Briefly, then, the Mexicans who are going home may be divided into five classes. First, there are those who are being deported—and Mexican deportations have reached as high as half of all those in the country. Second, there are those who are going because they have been told they will be deported unless they go voluntarily.

Third, there is the great class made up of those who know they are here illegally, and who tremble every time there is a knock at the door or an American speaks to them upon the street. Composing the fourth class are those whose way is being paid to the border by county relief agencies, which often make their grants of relief dependent upon the promise to return to Mexico at some later date. And the fifth class is made up of those who have long been out of work, and having sacrificed their homes for a fraction of what they are worth, are using the proceeds to go back to Mexico in the hope that things may be a little better and in the conviction that they cannot be any worse. During the first ten months of 1931, the number returning to Mexico outnumbered those entering the United States by 75,337.

Just what effect will this mass movement have upon the Southwest? And what will be its effect upon Mexico? Nobody expects the present depression to last forever. And when it is over the "white" man who has wrenched the pick and the shovel from the hands of the Mexican laborer, in order to drive the wolf from the door, will drop them and turn to other pursuits. Again there will be "work no white man will do." And when that time comes, unless we are willing to let our crops rot in the fields, we shall either beg the Mexicans to come back or import Negroes, Filipinos, and Porto [Puerto] Ricans. We shall find then that we have exiled both producers and consumers. And what about Mexico? Is anyone so simple as to believe in this period of world depression that Mexico is able to absorb an army of new laborers every month? What are they doing? What of the man who barefoot and with his belongings done up in a blanket left his ancestral village ten years ago—a village where life moves placidly along as it did in the seventeenth century? When he returns driving a secondhand car, will he drop back quietly into the niche from which he came? And if not, into what niche will he fit? What will the Americanized Mexican do to Mexico?

Source: McLean, Robert N. "The Mexican Return," 165–166. Reprinted with permission from the August 24, 1932, issue of *The Nation*. http://www.thenation.com.

Miriam Allen Deford, "Blood-Stained Cotton in California" (1933)

In October 1933, the largest agriculture strike in California history until that time occurred when 18,000 cotton pickers and their families, led by the Cannery and Agricultural Workers Industrial Union, called a strike after planters offered them 60 cents per hundred weight of cotton picked. Eighty percent of the strikers were Mexicans. The growers, assisted by police, formed armed vigilante squads and shot down 11 strikers, killing 3. They intentionally starved at least 9 children to death. The strike was broken by government intervention, which resulted in the growers agreeing to pay 75 cents per hundred weight. The Nation, *a progressive weekly magazine, was one of the few publications to give fair coverage to the strike; mainstream newspapers labeled it a communist revolt, which it was not. The following article from* The Nation *describes the strike.*

Three Mexicans murdered in cold blood; nine helpless children starved to death; 113 men and women under arrest on charges ranging from rioting to criminal syndicalism, not counting eight ranchers indicted for murder—that is the record of California's cotton pickers' strike, which was officially settled after it had raged through six counties of the lower San Joaquin Valley for more than three weeks.

Somewhat similar is the record of many strikes in many places, but there are ramifications of the cotton pickers' strike that are decidedly unusual. This is probably the first strike on record in which one of the demands of the strikers was higher pay for the bosses. The reason for this is that everyone, including the strikers, grants that the growers cannot at present afford to pay more than the sixty cents per hundred pounds which was offered. The pickers went on strike for a dollar a hundred; the compromise on which settlement was made was seventy-five cents. The differences, the growers were given to understand, would be made up by a grant of a million dollars from the Federal Land Bank at Berkeley; but when the growers had grudgingly accepted the higher rate, they were calmly informed by George Creel, the NRA [National Recovery Administration] regional director, who, with Timothy Reardon of the State Industrial Board, had been chiefly instrumental in bringing about the compromise, that he did not mean they would get any more money—he meant that they had already received a federal loan of a million dollars in the past!

This is sad news for the growers, who are just about on their last legs now after years of depression. Most of them are in pawn to the gin operators and the finance companies, the real villains in the piece, who financed the picking in advance on the basis of a sixty-cent rate. Three-quarters of the $9,000,000 crop was contracted for before it was ripe, at seven to eight cents a pound—most of it, it is said, on orders from Japan, in itself a significant statement. The few independent growers who held out because they were economically better fixed are now getting from ten to twelve cents a pound. The new textile code allows fifteen cents a pound for raw cotton. It is easy to see that the California cotton growers are not going to buy any Rolls Royces this season.

However, no sympathy need be wasted on them. Their treatment of the strikers and of the strike organizers has been execrable. It is easy, of course, to understand their psychology—that of the economically depressed poor white who lynches a Negro because he dare not attack the owner of his miserable farm. The cotton growers, faced with their first chance in years to make even a bare living, desperate and unnerved and just beginning to hope again, suddenly found themselves confronted with stubborn resistance from the submissive Mexican peons they had imported to do the grinding work of picking, which relatively few white workers will attempt. They could do nothing but grumble at the gin operators and the finance companies, but here was a chance for a real catharsis. The striker was the scapegoat. The growers and their law-enforcement officials fell upon him viciously. When they had turned the beautiful southern San Joaquin into a shambles, they blandly blamed the Communists—that is, the Cannery and Agricultural Workers [Industrial] Union. The pickers, they said, really wanted to work and were delighted to receive sixty cents a hundred pounds—a wage at which at the best a full-grown man can earn about $1.20 a day, out of which he must take the cost of his picking sacks; an entire family of husband, wife, and small children (all of whom usually work) can earn no more than $2. (The average family wage under the sixty-cent scale was $7.20 a week!) The only reason they walked out and stayed out, said the growers, was that they were afraid of the organizers.

Long before there was any actual bloodshed, it was being deliberately planned at growers' meetings in Kings and Tulare counties. There and in Kern County deputies so called—practically all of them ranchers or members of ranchers' families were being sworn in by the hundred, and all were heavily armed. An independent grower accused a prominent member of the "Protective Association" hastily formed by the ranchers of having urged that the members arm themselves and end the strike by violence.

And then, on the same day, Pedro Subia was shot to death at a struggle on a ranch near Arvin, Kern County, and Dolores Hernandez and Delfino Davila were murdered at Pixley, Visalia County. The only unusual feature of the shooting of Subia was that nine of his fellow strikers, including one woman, were arrested for his murder, the charge being that one of the strikers, Alonzo Andrews (all those arrested were Americans in this case), had killed him while attempting to attack a deputy sheriff who was endeavoring to disperse the crowd. There was plenty of testimony that the strikers were unarmed, and Andrews was not even present at the affray. On investigation, the Kern County grand jury refused to return murder indictments, and the nine are now held on charges of rioting.

In the Pixley killings, there could be no question of who did the shooting. Both the strikers and the growers had been holding all-night meetings, in separate places. At dawn, the meetings broke up and the two factions met face to face. The strikers were returning to their camp; they were entirely unarmed, even as to pick-handles or stones. There was some altercation, and then a young rancher yelled, "Let them have it, boys!" A volley of shots followed, and Hernandez fell dead. The killing of Davila was even more atrocious. He approached with his hands up, was shot, and fell, wounded, on his face. As he lay there helpless, growers pumped lead into his back. Davila was the Mexican consular representative at Visalia.

Then the armed ranchers they themselves behind their cars ambushed the strikers but there was no retaliation. The pickers had nothing to retaliate with. Eleven growers were indicted for murder by a very apologetic, reluctant, and slow-moving grand jury made up of their fellow ranchers. Eight are now held without bail, three having provided an alibi.

The heart and soul of the cotton pickers' strike was Pat Chambers, Communist organizer, who had been active in the earlier strikes of peach and grape pickers. Under the name of John Williams he is now in jail in Visalia on two criminal-syndicalism charges, bail having been fixed at $10,000. There have been rumors of attempts to lynch him. When Creel and the State's fact-finding committee—Archbishop Hanna of San Francisco, Professor Ira B. Cross of the University of California, and President Tully C. Knoles of the College of The Pacific—endeavored to negotiate with the strikers and asked for spokesmen, the strikers insisted unanimously that they had no spokesmen—that nobody could speak for them but Pat Chambers. Nothing could induce them to change their minds. It was a deliberate piece of tactics to keep official attention focused on Chambers and thus save his life.

The strikers' largest tent colony, after they were evicted from their cabins on such ranches as had any, was at Corcoran, where nearly 4,000 persons—twice the population of the town itself—were huddled in the space of two city blocks, without water or sanitation. Typhoid, dysentery, pink-eye, and diphtheria broke out. Children died from lack of food. Just before the settlement, federal relief was secured; after the compromise it was withdrawn, and no credit will be extended for food until after the picking of one bag of cotton. Gov. Rolph refused repeated appeals for the State militia, saying county officials should be able to handle the situation—officials notoriously in sympathy with the growers, using tear-gas on strikers, and looking the other way up to the point of actual murder. Now the State Highway Patrol is in charge and martial law practically exists.

The growers are sore because they feel they were fooled about that million-dollar subsidy. The rains have started and the cotton will brown. Some pickers, mostly Negroes, have been imported from Texas and more are on the way. The strikers say they will not return unless the union is recognized, their comrades are released from prison, and all armed forces are withdrawn from the area. The growers will not dream of granting any one of these demands. As Sheriff Buckner of Kings County puts it, "The situation is still full of dynamite."

Source: Deford, Miriam Allen. "Blood-Stained Cotton in California," 705. Reprinted with permission from the December 20, 1933, issue of *The Nation*. http://www.thenation.com.

Chicago Defender, "Another Case of Racial Prejudice" (1936)

Before the Depression, Chicago was the capital of the Mexican community in the Midwest; more than 25,000 Mexicans and Mexican Americans lived in the city. This group included families but there were also large numbers of single men who worked on railroads, in meatpacking plants, and at steel mills. The community was made up not only of workers but also of a growing middle class. The Depression hit this community hard, and by the end of the 1930s, about 16,000 Mexicans remained; thousands had been repatriated or deported to Mexico. In Chicago, traditionally an ethnically divided city, the divisions were worsened by the Depression, and this led to racially motivated incidents. The following article, which appeared in the Chicago Defender*, describes an incident that occurred when police reacted to a 26-year-old Mexican man and a 21-year-old white woman talking to each other. The* Chicago Defender *was unique in protecting the interests of minorities. An African American newspaper founded in 1905 by Robert Sengstacke Abbott (1870–1940) the* Defender *used bold headlines and red ink and spoke out against lynching, racism, and segregation. It published articles on injustices to groups other than black Americans. In the following article, the* Defender *chastised the bigotry and injustice of the arrest and trial of two young people of different races who were just talking to each other.*

Eleanor Swimmer, 21, white, a student of respectable attainment and supposed to have been born free, and George Rojas, 26, Mexican, also presumably free-born, were sitting on top of the retaining wall along the Illinois Central railroad embankment eating peaches. As we understand the law, it is no crime to eat peaches—but, with a widely divergent opinion, along comes Policeman Daniel Lahey. Whose ancestors, judging by his surname, did not come over in the Mayflower.

Now here is the story: The policeman immediately began to see red. It was a white woman in company with a Mexican. He arrested them and took them into the Municipal Court on a charge of disorderly conduct: viz, eating peaches in public. The case was called before his Hon. Judge Harold P. O'Connell. Attorneys for the white woman and the Mexican, for some reason or other, and probably well founded, asked for a jury trial. Twelve American citizens, not quite so deep-seated in racial hatred could find no crime committed by an intelligent white woman and an intelligent Mexican eating peaches together. As a result they were discharged.

Intelligent and civilized people must view with alarm some of the decadent ideals of America's system both in its everyday life and its judicial procedure. The whole scheme smacks of hypocrisy, chicanery, and littleness. It made our whole set-up look like a debauchery of civilization. It is all pretense, hate, prejudice, and bigotry built upon political and social idiosyncrasies which are not conducive to the perpetuation of real American ideals.

Could a Communistic government be any worse than our pretended democracy?

Source: Chicago Defender, October 17, 1936, 16.

Philip Stevenson, "Deporting Jesús" (1936)

In 1936, Jesús Pallares, founder of the 8,000-member coal miners' union Liga Obrera de Habla Española *(The League of Spanish-Speaking Workers), was deported back to Mexico as an "undesirable alien." Pallares, who was from Chihuahua, had migrated to the United States to work as a miner. In 1923, he participated in the Dawson, New Mexico, strike. The following article from* The Nation *describes Pallares's deportation, a favorite device of management to break unions.*

On June 29, Jesús was deported as an undesirable alien. Jesús Pallares is a skilled miner and an accomplished musician. He has spent twenty-three of his thirty-nine years in the United States. For nineteen years he worked here, supporting his family—of the remaining four years, two in childhood were spent in school, the last two on relief. Born in the state of Chihuahua, Mexico, Jesús joined the Madero revolution at the age of fifteen, fought four years, and mustered out in 1945 with part of his lower jaw missing. He entered the United States legally and obtained work as a miner. As miners' standards went, Jesús did well. He was an exceptional worker. There never was a time when he could not get a job. On the whole, he got along with his bosses. In 1923, during an unorganized strike at Dawson, New Mexico, when anarchists among the men wanted to blow up the tipple in answer to company violence, Jesús convinced them of the anti-labor effect of such tactics, and prevented catastrophe. Labor's best weapon, he contended, lay in solidarity of organization.

The onset of the Depression, 1930, found him working for the Gallup-American Coal Company, a subsidiary of the Guggenheim giant, Kennecott Copper. In 1930, Gallup was unorganized. So when Jesús found himself being paid but irregularly for his prospecting work on a new entry, he kicked—as an individual—and like individual protestors in all depressed coal fields, was promptly fired.

Jobs were scarce now. For the first time Jesús was up against it to support his wife and four children. But after several months of unemployment he obtained work at Madrid, New Mexico. Madrid is typical of thousands of marginal and submarginal coal camps. The town is company owned. The miners' homes are sagging, rotting shacks. Floors slant, roofs leak, plaster has fallen, doors lack panels, paint, and kalsomine have peeled away. The shacks can hardly have cost $100 per room to build fifty years ago. Yet today they rent for about $60 per room per year. Miners live in company houses—"or else." Payment is chiefly in scrip, good only at the company store, and there is a company coal racket whereby miners who get about eighty cents a ton for loading coal are charged $3 a month for fuel winter and summer. The prices for powder and caps are exorbitant, and the miners are docked every month for an Employees Fund of which the company steadfastly refuses to give any accounting.

At first Jesús got by in Madrid. But as bad times got worse, his earnings shrank. The summer of 1933 brought wholesale layoffs and misery. The company, in order to nullify Section 7-a of the NIRA, established a company union. Jesús joined, only to discover that the union concerned itself with the boss's problems rather than the miners'. In Gallup the miners had defeated the company union, organized independently, gone on strike, and won substantial gains. So Madrid, too, sent for organizers.

But Madrid was tougher to organize than Gallup. The company was forewarned by the Gallup struggle. And the entire town, including the streets, was company property. Union organizers ran great risks in entering Madrid at all. Yet enter they did, thanks to Jesús and others who smuggled them in on the floors of cars, covered with blankets and bags of groceries. To this, the company replied by spying on the union through its "lapdogs" (anti-unionists).

Jesús was elected local union organizer. But the union's demands remained a dead letter. Jesús and his aides decided to ask the aid of the federal government in enforcing Section 7-a. When the company prohibited all union meetings in Madrid, the unionists walked four miles to Cerrillos for meetings, passed resolutions, drew up petitions, framed protests, and sent them to the coal board, to Gen. Johnson, to Sen. Cutting, to the state Labor Commissioner. From the coal board came a promise of a hearing—if the miners would withhold their strike and wait. And wait they did—weeks—and sent more telegrams—and waited more weeks. Not until the tail-end of the busy season—February, 1934—did T. S. Hogan, chairman of the Denver District Coal Board, arrive in Madrid for an "impartial" hearing.

The affair was a farce. Jesús, attempting to present the case of his fellow union members, was repeatedly interrupted, not only by Superintendent Oscar Huber and his faithful lapdogs, but also by government representative Hogan, who refused to recognize Jesús as the leader and spokesman of the majority. By patience and persistence, in spite of organized heckling, Jesús did manage to cover the question of the coal-code wage-scale, even forcing an admission from Huber that code rates were being violated. "Now about the house-rents," Jesús continued. But he got no further. At that point, Huber asked for the floor, adroitly changed the subject, and that sorest of all points with the Madrid miners—house-rents—was never mentioned again!

Results of the Hogan hearing were zero. Grievances went unredressed. Union meetings continued to be prohibited. A new coal code went into effect, only to be violated even more flagrantly by the company. Plainly, the men must either strike or lie down. They struck—in the slack season. The strike failed. Jesús was marked for riddance.

Under the NRA he could not be fired for union activity. He finished work in his "room" in the mine and was assigned a new location. His eighteen years' experience told him that he could make at best sixty-seven cents a day here—and the mine was then working only one day a week—while his rent alone amounted to $3 per week. Yet the boss refused him any better location. Then a fellow worker offered to share his place with Jesús. It showed a good seam of coal, and both could make a living there. Jesús asked the superintendent's permission to accept this offer.

"No. Take the place assigned you, or none," Huber said.

The alternative was peonage—progressive indebtedness to the company. Jesús refused. His fifth child was expected shortly. His savings went for food. Arrears on his rent to the company piled up. He was told to vacate his house or be evicted. He stayed put; the child arrived. Asked by a fellow miner, "What is it, boy or girl?" Jesús replied:

"I think it's Bolshevik!"

Soon after the birth, Jesús was charged with "forcible entry" of his house. The "court" was the company office, the justice of the peace a company employee. Superintendent Huber, furious that Jesús had made a public hearing necessary, clung like Shylock to his pound of flesh. Evicted, blacklisted as a miner, Jesús moved to Santa Fe and for the first time in his life went on relief. The family of seven lived in one room, on two cents per meal per person—the starvation standard still current in New Mexico's relief.

Jesús protested his eviction to NRA Compliance Director J. J. Dempsey—today a New Deal Congressman. Dempsey refused to act and passed the buck to Hogan of the coal board. Hogan did not even bother to reply. Jesús then appealed to the National Labor Board. Chairman Garrison wrote to Hogan urging him to act. Hogan disregarded even this. He never acknowledged Jesús's letters.

The native New Mexicans, a Spanish-speaking peasant people, had never been successfully organized. Yet they were half the population of the state.

If organized in their own interest, instead of the interest of the railroads and mines, they could be a force to help themselves out of their 300-year-old bondage. At least they could end racial discrimination in relief. So in the fall of 1934, Jesús began organizing for the Liga Obrera de Habla Espanola (Spanish-Speaking Workers League), which concerned itself specifically with the problems of the Spanish-American rank and file. In November, there had been a few hundred members. By February, 1935, the Liga had grown to some 8,000. The politicos were frightened out of their wits. Jesús was elected organizer for the whole district, serving without pay and hitch-hiking to organize the most remote hamlets on his days off from FERA [Federal Emergency Relief Fund] work.

In January, the Democratic state legislature had hatched a criminal-syndicalism bill which would have made it a felony punished by fourteen years' imprisonment to be seen in public with a copy of *The Nation* or any printed matter advocating "any change in industrial ownership." The bill passed the House with only two dissenting votes. Sen. Juan Sedillo, opposition leader, had given up all hope of defeating it. The steering committee, itself a majority of the Senate, had unanimously recommended its passage. On the morning that it was to be passed, 700 members of the Liga Obrera, carrying placards of denunciation in two languages, swept past astonished police at the Capitol, filled the Senate galleries, and demanded the defeat of this fascist gag legislation. Senators took one look—and changed their votes. To the acute chagrin of its big-business sponsors, the bill was beaten.

This time Jesús had won the enmity not merely of one coal company but of the organized rulers of New Mexico. On April 23, 1935, he was arrested while at work on his FERA job and jailed on deportation charges. After three weeks' confinement, a secret hearing was held in an attempt to prove Jesús active in "communistic" organizations. N. D. Collear, federal immigration inspector, acted not only as an initiator, investigator, and prosecutor, but also as judge and jury, and even as court interpreter!

To the amazement of Jesús, he found his opening remarks at the Hogan hearing of the year before cited as "evidence" against him. Jesús had said: "We have been most patient. . . . Mr. Hogan, I hope you come here to bring us full justice, if justice exists for the working man. If you cannot see that we get it, we shall find other ways of getting it for ourselves."

Obviously Jesús referred to the strike which had been postponed at Hogan's request. At the deportation hearing it was offered as evidence of "communistic" activity!

Here is an item from the testimony of a Madrid lapdog:

Q. Have you ever heard him make inflammatory speeches about the government?

A. No, not exactly—he urges the Mexicans to fight for their rights.

On such trumpery charges, Jesús was held for deportation under $1,000 bond pending a review of the case. The bond was promptly furnished, and Jesús was a "free" man—as free as a labor organizer can be in a vigilante-ridden state—as free as an alien can be who faces deportation and separation from his American-born children.

He continued his task of organizing the Liga Obrera so successfully that the rulers of New Mexico redoubled their efforts to be rid of him. After all, the government's case against Jesús was weak, involving only trade-union activity—a constitutionally guaranteed right. Could he not be provoked into open violence?

As a leader in the Liga Obrera, Jesús often accompanied delegations to the local relief office presenting cases of discrimination or deprivation. Recently, a worker in that office has disclosed in a sworn affidavit the methods employed against Jesús "in an effort to create reasons for his deportation." Says Esther Cohen, formerly of the New Mexico ERA [Emergency Relief Administration]:

Attempts were made by my office to intimidate Pallares by withholding relief and by inventing reasons by which he could be removed from relief jobs which were the only types of employment open to him. He was repeatedly called into my office where threats were made to starve his family in order to involve him in an argument which the relief agency hoped would give rise to violence on his part, which in turn would give sufficient reason for a complaint to the Labor Department. Such violence never took place, even though situations were carefully prepared in advance such as the placing of a hammer on the supervisor's desk within his easy reach. Nevertheless a complaint was made to Washington on the vague and flimsy basis that Pallares was a "troublemaker."

I gave Pallares's case history to Mr. Colyear [N. D. Collear], the immigration officer from Washington, who stated that he found no data therein which would incriminate Pallares to the extent of seriously considering deportation. He wondered if it would be possible to extract some information from Pallares himself by any means available which would further the plan to get him out of the way.

Towards this end Pallares was once again called into the office and this time a stenographer was placed where he could not see her and Colyear was also listening behind the closed door where Pallares could not see him. Again threats were made to "starve out" his ailing pregnant wife and six American-born children to whom he was passionately devoted, if he did not admit that he was interested in organizing his friends into an unemployed council.

At the hearing on his case before the Labor Department's Board of Review last spring, Jesús was represented by an attorney for the American Committee for the Protection of Foreign Born. Among the papers on file in the case, two remarkable documents came to light, the existence of which had hitherto been kept secret.

The first was a letter to Secretary of Labor Perkins from Gov. Clyde Tingley of New Mexico, urging that Jesús's deportation be "expedited" on the extraordinary grounds that the Liga Obrera was "the New Mexico branch of the Communist organization." But the Governor, fully aware of how preposterous this charge was, and how unethical his interference in a federal judicial question, had been cautious enough to mark his letter "Personal and Confidential."

The second document was a telegram to the Immigration Bureau in Washington, so incautious as to be worth quoting in full:

Having trouble with Jesús Pallares on strike in this county. I understand he is under bond on account of the strike at Gallup, New Mexico, where the sheriff of that county was killed last spring. He is an alien from Old Mexico. We must act at once to save trouble and maybe lives in this county.

Francisco P. Delgado, Sheriff [of San Miguel County]

In four sentences, the telegram managed to utter five deliberate falsehoods or innuendoes: 1. The sheriff's trouble was not with Jesús but with the strikers at the American Metals Company's mine at Terrero, New Mexico, who embarrassed him by their accurate shouts of "Scab!" 2. Jesús was not on strike—did not even live in the sheriff's county. 3. Jesús was under bond for deportation, not for strike activity in Gallup or elsewhere. 4. At the time of the death of Gallup's sheriff, Jesús was living 230 miles away in Santa Fe—was totally unconnected with the event. 5. The deportation of Jesús could not possibly save "trouble and maybe lives" so long as the sheriff insisted on breaking the strike by armed force and violence.

Curiously enough, two truths did creep into the sheriff's wire: first, that Jesús was indubitably "an alien from Old Mexico"; second that "we"—that is, New Mexico officials and the Bureau of Immigration—were acting in concert to railroad Jesús out of the country. And they have had their way. Jesús is deported.

Source: Stevenson, Philip. "Deporting Jesús." Reprinted with permission from the July 18, 1936, issue of *The Nation*. http://www.thenation.com.

William S. Taylor, "Some Observations of Marginal Man in the United States" (1940)

William S. Taylor was an African American educator. Early on, African American educators became interested in what was happening with Latinos and Mexicans. The following article from the Journal of Negro Education *describes the problem of assimilation of the "marginal man" in American society. The excerpts describe the Mexican community in Texas in 1940 and how Mexicans fit into this marginalization. Taylor also dissects the different classes of Mexicans in Texas and Chicago.*

CLASSES OF MEXICANS

In Mexico one finds that the important racial element is the European Spaniard. It is interesting to note that there are three important classes of Mexicans: (1) Whites of Spanish descent; (2) mestizo, the middle class; and (3) Indians, the lowest class. Attempts at assimilation by Mexican social leaders have caused a change from caste to class. There are many classes of mixed blood, e.g., the Indian and European, the Negro and Indian, and the Negro and white (mulatto).

The writer has attempted to present a historical background of the various culture strains so that a sympathetic understanding might be had by the reader for what is to follow.

MEXICANS IN AUSTIN AND SAN ANTONIO, TEXAS

The Mexicans in and about Austin, and San Antonio, more or less follow the same culture patterns as do their native fellows that live about urban centers in Mexico. A stranger visiting either Austin, or San Antonio for the first time will be peculiarly interested in the dress, language, and general characteristics of the Mexicans met upon the streets.

The writer has lived in Austin, Texas, i.e., in 1926 through 1938, when he was employed at Samuel Huston College as director of physical education. Here, he has had many opportunities to drive over to San Antonio, a distance of eighty-one miles. The native Mexican life is more picturesque around San Antonio due to its proximity to the Mexican border.

Without a doubt, the most important fact in the life of the Mexican, is racial isolation. The long preponderance of Spanish culture can be attributed to this fact. The birth and death rate of the Mexican indicate a primitive community, having very low vitality. Some of the factors affecting the Mexicans are: (1) undernourishment and indifference; (2) racial tendencies; and (3) a prevalence of vices by the Indian.

Attempts at assimilation as has been heretofore stated, has caused a change from caste to class. The highest class is called white, the middle class is called mestizo, and the lowest class is called Indian. The dominant religion among those who are not pagans is the Catholic religion. The Mexican families are patriarchal. This fatherly worship as it were, seems more or less intuitive. True clans still persist as safe foundation stones. The father is respected and obeyed implicitly by the members of the household.

Delicious Mexican foods like enchiladas, hot tamales, tortillas, chile con carne, and frijoles, make up the better portion of the national diet.

The typical Mexican dress has disappeared from the sidewalks of Austin. This is true of the higher classes even in San Antonio, but not so with the peon and the Indian. A hat of plaited straw, with the big brim curving, and mounting to a high-peak is called a sombrero. The Mexican's hat is his pride and joy, so to speak. His hat carries his money, his lunch, and his cigarettes. His costume is similar to that of a cowboy, which is found all over Mexico, especially among the ranchero. The women of the upper classes wear dresses designed in France for the most part. Many women of the middle class can be seen wearing the mantilla up and down Red River Street in Austin, and on Commerce Street in San Antonio. The mantilla is a beautiful silk scarf, three to four yards in length, and about a yard wide. The peon women wear anything from calico to just plain rags.

Labor is more or less upon the guild plan, i.e., basically patriarchal. The industrial and agricultural workers are for the better part Indians and half breeds. The Mexican workers on the cotton farms and in the mills are poorly paid.

The writer has seen the greasy, peon type of Mexican walk right into a drug store, sit down at the soda fountain with his dirty overalls, and wait his turn to be served. The attendant shows by his facial expression that he despises serving him, yet he knows that he must not discriminate against this man of dark color because he is a Mexican. A Negro in a white man's drug store in Texas would not dare to sit down, and he had better not ask for a soda.

The dominant white class of Mexicans are readily taken into the white man's culture. The middle class, or mestizo, more or less herd together like the Indian. Color of the skin is an important factor as to their choice of assimilation. If the skin is white, or nearly white, the Mexican will partake of the white man's culture. If the skin is brown, yellow, or dark brown, he may elect to stay among his own group as the case is most of the time. On the other hand he may mingle with the Negro, especially if the Negro involved is a pretty girl.

MEXICANS IN THE MAXWELL STREET DISTRICT, CHICAGO

Unlike their fellows who live close to native soil, the Mexicans living on the west side of Chicago have adapted themselves to their man-made environment. The writer spent several hours on Easter Monday, 1937, in observing this district. Quite a number of the Mexicans and Negroes have intermarried. The type of family life is that of the emancipated family. In this area one sees the typical "touch-an-go" sort; living in cramped quarters, a kitchenette- apartment affair; the interest of both the wife and husband outside of the home; home meaning a place to rest one's weary bones at night; in most cases the type of family that feels itself free from all neighborhood and community ties. This type of family more or less leads a "hand to mouth" existence. There are hardly any children if any. The husband if he will work, finds employment as a day laborer, stockyard hand, shoe shiner, stevedore, presser, and as a waiter. Usually it is the wife who is the bread winner. In many instances she is employed as a domestic, i.e., cooking, washing, ironing, and housekeeping, all for one salary if she works in a private family. Of course there are those that are exceptions to this rule. The writer has noticed a goodly number of the Mexican women working as waitresses in public restaurants, and as store keepers in small retail stores.

What do these observations show? They clearly manifest that the Maxwell district is a poorly organized community. The life currents are all dammed up which makes for stagnant institutions. These poor people have not a chance at assimilation, for the poorer they are, the weaker is community cohesion. Along this line Bogardus states: "Whatever increases distance between groups weakens assimilation and lessens unity."

It is in the finely organized community where is found abundant and joyous life. Here is where one gives and shares.

Source: Taylor, William S. "Some Observations of Marginal Man in the United States." *Journal of Negro Education* 9, no. 4 (October 1940): 606–608.

Luisa Moreno, "Non-Citizen Americans of the Southwest: Caravan of Sorrow"

(March 3, 1940)

Luisa Moreno (1907–1992), the first Latina to serve on the executive committee of the United Cannery, Agricultural, Packing and Allied Workers of America (UCAPAWA), was born into a wealthy Guatemalan family. Moreno crossed group lines and worked largely among Mexican workers. At first she worked in New York's garment industry before joining UCAPAWA. In 1938, El Congreso de los Pueblos de Habla Español *(the Congress of Spanish-Speaking Peoples) held its first national conference in Los Angeles. The principal organizer was Luisa Moreno, who traveled throughout the United States and generated considerable interest in the conference. Representatives came from all over the United States: Spanish and Cuban cigar makers from Tampa, Florida; Puerto Ricans from Harlem; steelworkers from Pennsylvania, Illinois, and Indiana; meat packers, miners, and farm workers from many localities; and elected officials from New Mexico. The congress was broadly based—representatives included workers, politicians, youth, and educators. The* congreso *claimed more than 6,000 members from 1938 to 1940. On March 3, 1940, Moreno addressed the Panel on Deportation and Right of Asylum of the Fourth Annual Conference of the American Committee for the Protection of the Foreign Born in Washington, DC. She titled her speech, parts of which follow, "Caravan of Sorrow."*

Long before the "Grapes of Wrath" had ripened in California's vineyards a people lived on highways, under trees or tents, in shacks or railroad sections, picking crops—cotton, fruits, vegetables, cultivating sugar beets, building railroads and dams, making barren land fertile for new crops and greater riches . . . [they had been brought] by the fruit exchanges, railroad companies, and cotton interests in great need of underpaid labor during the early post-war period . . . [she condemned] today the Latin Americans of the United States are alarmed by an 'anti-alien' drive. . . . These people are not aliens. They have contributed their endurance, sacrifices, youth, and labor to the Southwest. Indirectly, they have paid more taxes than all the stockholders of California's industrialized agriculture, the sugar companies, and the large cotton interests, that operate or have operated with the labor of Mexican workers.

Source: Supreme Council of the Mexican American Movement Papers, Urban Archives, California State University Northridge.

Norman Humphrey, "The Migration and Settlement of Detroit Mexicans"

(1943)

Mexicans had been recruited to work in Michigan since at least the 1880s, mainly as seasonal labor in the sugar beet fields. The Michigan Sugar Company, which had plantations and processing plants in Clinton, Gratiot, Lapeer, Saginaw, and Tuscola counties, recruited them. Many Mexican workers had been born in Texas. In the 1920s, the auto and steel companies also recruited large numbers of Mexican workers, and the number of Mexicans in the Midwest increased as immigration restrictions stemmed the flow of European ethnics. The Great Depression hit this community hard, and many Americans partially blamed Mexicans for the hard times. Americans wanted to save money on public services (such as public school education for immigrant children) that were provided to Mexicans by sending them back to Mexico, even though many of those "repatriated" to Mexico had been born in Texas. The following article from Economic Geography *by Wayne State University professor Norman Daymond Humphrey (1911–1955) focuses on Mexicans in Detroit in the 1930s.*

With the onset of the depression of the '30s, the number [of Mexicans in Detroit] declined. At first the Mexican consul, Ignacio Batiza, attempted to institute a relief program in Detroit for his charges; but eventually a repatriation program began to take form. On October 10, 1931, sixty-nine Mexicans left Detroit, and it was significantly the Detroit Department of Public Welfare in cooperation with the Mexican government that made their return possible.

Regarding the group which left, Batiza said: "The Mexican colony of Detroit is young. The majority of the 15,000 Mexicans have not been in the United States more than five years. They have not yet adapted themselves to the American ways and have been hit hard by the current depression." He estimated that five-sixths of the 50,000 Mexicans had gone from the area by the end of 1932, "more than half of whom returned to Mexico." Actually, by the end of 1932, 1,500 Mexicans had been sent from Michigan, and lesser numbers went back from other nearby states. Most of these removals were made as voluntary repatriations.

The motives for returning to Mexico were primarily economic. Unable to find employment in Detroit, the breadwinner who was willing to return felt certain that he would obtain agricultural work in Mexico. The Mexican government offered to supply repatriates with land and with the tools to work it. Such were the main incentives operating on the Mexican to return to the homeland. In addition to this force pulling the immigrant, there was a strong force pushing him out which took one form in hostility manifested toward him by relief workers.

The exact Mexican population of Detroit at any one time is difficult to ascertain. The most accurate figure is that of the Federal Census which in 1930 enumerated 6,515 Mexicans in Detroit. The official estimate of the Detroit Board of Education Statistical Bureau for 1934 (the estimate including all Mexican children whether born in the United States or in Mexico) stated that 278 families were enumerated and that the total population was 1,946 persons. In the same year Consul Batiza placed their number at 4,000.

Source: Humphrey, N. D. "The Migration and Settlement of Detroit Mexicans." *Economic Geography* 19, no. 4 (1943): 360–361.

Ella Winter, *And Not to Yield: An Autobiography* (1963)

The 1933 San Joaquin cotton strike that involved 18,000 cotton pickers in the San Joaquin Valley of California attracted intellectuals such as journalist Ella Winter (1898–1980) and African American poet and author Langston Hughes (1902–1967), who were horrified by the violence and gross constitutional violations that took place during the strike. Winter was married to muckraking reporter Lincoln Steffens (1866–1936), and the couple formed a circle of activists who supported human rights causes. The following excerpt from Winter's autobiography describes the Corcoran Camp during the October 1933 cotton strike. Corcoran was one of five makeshift camps populated by strikers after they were evicted from cabins the growers provided for the workers and their families. A grower tactic was to starve out the strikers, and at least nine children starved to death during this strike. The growers also shot and killed three strikers.

It was dark when the car showed up at Camp Corcoran—the tent city the size of a block which those thousands of cotton pickers squatted to sit out their strike. A few people stood about a make-shift gate. Was this the entrance? Someone came to our car. . . .

We stumbled along in almost pitched darkness among tents, people, burning oil stoves, refuse, wretched and smell[s] as in the shack towns, smells of greasy cooking, stale fish, damp clothes, and sewerage. An occasional dim lantern lit up the mud we struggled through; there were small muffled sounds that gave the feeling of a crowded city, though we could not see the crowds. A sick baby wailed—and I had a sense, in the darkness, of people waiting, waiting. . . .

"Viva la Huelga!" (Long live the strike!) Came a cry out of the blackness. We stopped outside the dirty evil-smelling tent . . . a figure brought a swaying lantern, by whose murky yellow beam we could just make out a bunch of bedding, a broken chair, some gaping children. A frowsy woman came out with a bundle, a tiny wizened baby whose face was almost black—black as I had seen them in Vienna; his tiny eyes gazed unseeing. . . .

"The baby's dead!" Mexicans stood around unmoving, wondering, I supposed, who these strange people were, commiserating all of a sudden with a wretchedness they had always lived in.

Source: Winter, Ella. *And Not to Yield: An Autobiography*. New York: Harcourt, Brace & World, 1963, 196–197.

Allan Turner, "A Night That Changed San Antonio: Woman Recalls Leading Labor Riot in 1939" (1986)

The Great Depression took many Mexican women out of the household. Many joined unions, as Chicana or Mexican American women organizers across the country revolted against oppressive conditions. One of the best known was Emma Tenayuca (1916–1999), a native-born San Antonian who was one of few Mexican Americans to graduate from high school. By the mid-1930s, she was involved in organizing striking Mexican workers of both genders. Although she was abruptly replaced by professional union organizers, she was an early leader in the pecan shellers' strikes of San Antonio, which involved 12,000 pecan shellers. Right-wing forces in the city saw her as a Soviet agent, and indeed she was a member of the Communist Party. A devout Catholic, she joined the Communist Party because of the racism and inequality in Texas. There were threats on her life but she was beloved by the workers. The following article from the Houston Chronicle*, based on a 1986 interview with Tenayuca, recalls the 1939 riot in San Antonio that broke out while Tenayuca was speaking to labor activists inside the Municipal Auditorium. After this event, Tenayuca was blacklisted and driven from the city. She has since become an icon in Mexican American history.*

SAN ANTONIO—Night fell, and the depression-era patriots, armed with a truckload of bricks, came to save America from Red agitator Emma Tenayuca.

Five thousand strong, they boiled up Martin Street toward Municipal Auditorium, where several dozen communists vainly struggled to rationalize the latest dictum from Josef Stalin: the Soviet-German Non-Aggression Pact of 1939.

Bricks flew like curses as the leaders of the mob—a Catholic priest, a Jew, and a Lebanese immigrant—whipped the throng to a frenzy.

Tenayuca, though only 22 [years old] that sweltering August night, had already earned the hatred of a sizable portion of the community.

For years she had been involved in labor activities on the city's desperately poor Hispanic West Side. She had led strikes, been jailed, shepherded delegations of the unemployed to City Hall and—most annoyingly—proudly proclaimed her allegiance to the Communist Party.

Although communist activities stirred bitter controversy, they never spawned violence until party members received permission from liberal Mayor Maury Maverick, Sr., to use a small meeting room in Municipal Auditorium.

"It was crazy," recalled George Bartholomew, former *Chronicle* photo editor who was then working as a San Antonio newspaper photographer. Bartholomew was knocked unconscious in the melee.

"They had brought up a flatbed truck loaded with bricks," he said. "I was running up to it to get a photograph of it, thinking a photo with the license plate would help investigators. That's the last thing I remember.

"I was a lot in sympathy with Emma. Hell's bells, she was a frail little girl fighting for the poor Mexicans. I was trying to protect her. I don't think the community as a whole gave a damn—she was just a little pebble in a great big ocean. But those leading this mob kept waving the hammer and sickle and the red flag. They yelled communist long enough to start a fire, and, by God, they did."

More than 20 people were injured, at least 14 of them policemen. After breaking windows, the mob stormed the building to slash auditorium seats.

Fire hoses ended the riot. But the riot shattered illusions, ended hopes, and crippled political careers. Almost 50 years have elapsed since that night—a night in which, some thought, San Antonio was plucked from the grip of revolution.

It was a night that changed the city. Today, the San Antonio communist menace lives only in the troubled dreams of retired generals. Cheap labor reigns. And last week, Henry B. Gonzalez, the city's septuagenarian congressman, punched out a detractor who dared call him a communist.

It was a night that changed lives.

Tenayuca grew disenchanted with communism, enrolled in college and became a teacher. Though well informed and opinionated, she has lived in relative obscurity since her return to the city in the early 1960s.

Her husband, Homer Brooks, a sometimes communist [and] gubernatorial candidate, went to sea.

Maverick, a New Deal Democrat who had become mayor in 1939 after a term in Congress, never again held elective office.

"The First Amendment—that's why my father authorized use of the auditorium," said Maverick's son, attorney Maury Maverick, Jr. "The constitution doesn't exclude communists from the right of free speech. My father spent his life fighting for the Bill of Rights."

But Maverick, Jr.—who later was among four state legislators voting against a bill to outlaw the Communist Party in Texas—added: "I've got no rosy-hued glasses on about this thing. I've got a cocklebur under my saddle for the Communist Party. My father sent word to the party leaders that if they used the auditorium, it would ruin him. They met there anyway."

For days, strange autos circled ominously around the Maverick home. Tenayuca and her husband received death threats.

The senior Maverick, an astute political veteran, often expressed dismay that the riot had been led by ethnic and religious minorities. "He was seriously depressed and he was not a bitter or remorseful kind of guy. He always warned me that the destruction of freedom of speech could come from any direction—from the majority or from the minority."

Maverick, Sr., described the outburst as the worst display of Nazism in the nation. Weeks later, in routinely declaring "dog week," Maverick—still troubled by the riot—observed even dogs let other dogs bark.

Tenayuca said: "It was just a very bad time to organize a communist meeting. Coming right on the heels of the non-aggression pact, there was a lot of anger in this country. You could almost expect this type of reaction."

Almost half a century has elapsed since that night—a night that has taken its place in San Antonio folklore. Most of the principals—Maverick, Sr., the priest, the police chief—are dead. But Emma Tenayuca remembers.

Tenayuca, who now lives in a tidy bungalow a short distance from Mission San Jose on the city's South Side, was only a child when her father took her to the Hay Plaza—a social and political gathering spot on the western edge of downtown.

"There was always someone at the plaza making a speech or talking or discussing or reading the latest papers," Tenayuca said. "I was aware of a large number of people who came there and were contracted to work in the fields. I became aware that this was where they brought their problems to. There were cases where they weren't being paid, of incidents of beatings.

"I remember this—and it's still quite vivid—that once I was there with my grandfather and a man from some place in the Valley was there with his family. He told the story of having worked at this particular farm, and, after the crop was harvested, he and his family had been awakened about 2 o'clock in the morning and the farmer and his sons were armed with shotguns. Yes, they put them off the land without paying them. I was very disturbed about this. There was a little collection taken up for the family."

In 1920, San Antonio's population stood at 202,000—up from 119,000 a decade earlier. Slightly more than 40 percent were Hispanic. Among those recent arrivals were thousands of Mexicans who had fled the Mexican Revolution.

Tenayuca's family, however, had been in the country much longer. Her mother's family—the Zepedas—arrived with the first wave of Spanish settlers at the end of the seventeenth century. Her father's family was Indian.

"My father was interested in one method of livelihood, and that was farming, being independent. Before he met my mother, he had already struggled along and bought that place. Mother was the first one to move into that place. It was not the happiest marriage. There was quite a bit of difference between my mother's background and my father's background, and my father was always regarded as Indian—not quite acceptable to Mother's family," Tenayuca said.

Tenayuca was one of 11 children, the second-oldest girl.

She and her sister were reared by her maternal grandparents in the strictest of Catholic homes.

"I had a lot of catechism before I went to school. I learned my prayers in English and Spanish. Certain customs were followed in the house. There was grace observed. It was not just a question of prayers; it was a question of sitting down and really thanking God and being grateful that we had something to eat and that we weren't sick and were able to eat."

In keeping with her devout Catholic upbringing, Tenayuca at age 12 sought admission to a convent. "They told me to come back when I was 14, and by then I was no longer interested. But, for a time, the life of a nun appealed to me."

Although exposed to politics, Tenayuca said the awareness of poverty was kept at bay.

"I knew some youngsters were not dressed as well as I was and possibly did not eat as well," she said. "I knew that they traveled in trucks. But I was aware of injustices. There always was some politicking here. I remember going to the West Side on this occasion with my father. There was a park, a big gathering place for political campaigns. The speakers afterward handed out sandwiches—but they didn't contain meat. Each had a $5 bill inside.

"There was a certain section of Anglo-Americans who maintained power, handing out a certain number of jobs. I don't think I remember a Mexican-American mayor, but there always was a Mexican deputy sheriff, policeman, fireman. These were political jobs. My father had nothing but disdain for them and I shared his disdain."

Citing wages as low as $2 a week, excessive penalties for defective work, and inadequate sanitary facilities, between 300 and 400 female workers walked off the job at the Finck Cigar Co. in early August 1933. The strike lasted about four weeks, with dozens of young women, wearing pink ribbons bearing the words "Starvation Bound," picketing the company's West Side factory.

The strike was brought to a close when company president Ed Finck agreed to comply with National Recovery Administration wage standards of $9 a week for rollers and bunch makers and $7.50 a week for strippers.

The strike made front-page headlines daily as rumors of violence grew. The news stories spoke of the strikers "laying siege" to the plant, and stories were told of the throwing of animal feces on women who attempted to cross the picket lines. Auto windows were smashed and police—under the direction of Police Chief Owen Kilday—stationed as many as 15 officers at the plant.

The strike proved a training ground for Tenayuca.

"The workers just got tired," Tenayuca said. "They were angry. There was a system in which they rolled the cigars by hand at that time and the foreman would come say these are rollovers, rolled improperly, put them over by the side and the workers wouldn't be paid for them. So, this was a spontaneous strike, mostly women.

"We had at the time a sheriff, Albert West, and he had his picture taken with a brand new pair of shiny boots and made the statement that he was going out on the picket line and kick those women. Yes, definitely, I saw that picture myself. So I went out on the picket line. There were some other kids in high school who went, but I was the only one who went a second or third time."

Today, the cigar factory remains in operation under the direction of Bill Finck, a man Tenayuca describes as "a devout Catholic—a member of my tribe."

Finck, a former state legislator and county treasurer, recalled his father "wasn't too enthusiastic about her (Tenayuca)."

Contrary to the assertions of the strikers, Finck said, his father was "a very intelligent man. Everyone liked him. He loved the cigar business. He was a helluva good tobacco man—not a fat, old greedy businessman by any means. He would have been better off shutting this plant down. He didn't make that much money. Liberata Fernandez—born in 1916, as was Tenayuca—was among cigar workers who declined to join the strike. "I just thought it was better to work," she said. "We just didn't want to be in any trouble.

Fernandez, one of several current employees who had opposed the strike, has worked at the company continuously since age 13.

As the depression deepened, Tenayuca became increasingly involved in radical activities, drifting into a leadership role in the Workers Alliance, a communist-dominated organization for the unemployed. Through the mid-1930s, she organized workers around such issues as the use of immigration authorities to intimidate disgruntled Hispanic workers. At its height, the Workers Alliance claimed approximately 10,000 members in San Antonio. In July 1937, Tenayuca was among five Workers Alliance members arrested for disorderly conduct when police dispersed hundreds who had gone to the Works Progress Administration headquarters in the Gunter Hotel building to protest the layoff of 30 workers.

Tenayuca was acquitted. But days later, police raided the Alliance's Travis Street office, wrecking furniture, ransacking files, and beating up a couple of hapless party workers.

"You and your men should be granted a pay increase due to your attitude toward the Workers Alliance difficulty," Justice of the Peace Bat Corrigan telegraphed Police Chief Kilday.

"I suggest that we do our best to eliminate these foreign agitators and give the Americanized radicals all the works possible."

Gov. James V. Allred, though, warned that the Texas Rangers would be sent to San Antonio if such incidents continued. And the American Civil Liberties Union [ACLU] called for the impeachment of Kilday, Police Commissioner Paul Wright, and Mayor C.K. Quinn for the raid.

"San Antonio has established a new low in lawlessness," ACLU Chairman Harry Ward wrote Allred.

The stage was set for the fury that was to come.

By the mid-1930s, San Antonio had become one of the nation's pecan shelling capitals, with as many as 20,000 men, women, and children—most of them Hispanic—working in dimly lit, ill-heated, unsanitary processing plants throughout the West Side.

In St. Louis and other major nut processing centers, much of the tedious work had been mechanized. But, in San Antonio, where thousands of workers flooded the job market, cracking, picking, and cleaning were performed by hand. That arrangement was far cheaper than installing machinery. In December 1934, a National Recovery Administration investigator found workers in 14 shelling plants averaging $1.29 for a 34.8-hour week.

The work was seasonal—fall to spring—and informal. Laborers disgruntled by working conditions, or by the smallness or toughness of the nuts, would frequently move to other sheds.

"They were sweatshop conditions," recalled Ruben Munguia, Sr., who worked as a sheller in the winter of 1934–35. "Guys worked long hours, from 6 a.m. to 8 or 9 p.m. for pennies."

Munguia, 67, owner of a San Antonio print shop and uncle of San Antonio Mayor Henry Cisneros, typified the sheds as being 20 feet wide and 40 to 60 feet long. "There would be benches running the full lengths of the walls and tables like picnic tables, benches with no backs."

Each shop housed 100 or more workers, and, until 1936 when a city ordinance required running water in such facilities, sanitation in them was minimal.

"Workers could talk," Munguia said, "but they had to keep working diligently. You had to to make any money at all. Try it yourself. Go home and see how many pecans you can shell in an hour. See how little it is."

A WPA study of the period found hunger and sickness rampant on the West Side.

In 1938, more than 72 percent of the tuberculosis deaths in the city were among Mexican Americans, even though the group accounted for only about 40 percent of the population. Infant mortality during the first year for Mexican Americans stood at 120 per 1,000 live births; the rate for blacks, 68 per 1,000 live births; for non-Hispanic whites, 36.

One-sixth of children aged 8 to 9 in pecan shelling families had never completed the first grade.

On Jan. 31, 1938, agents for the monolithic Southern Pecan Shelling Co. announced that shellers' wages would be cut to 5 cents a pound for pecan pieces and 6 cents a pound for halves—down one cent from the previous rate.

On Feb. 1, 6,000 pecan workers—many of them members of the Workers Alliance—hit the bricks, electing Tenayuca honorary strike chairman. On the second day, the number of strikers had increased to 10,000.

Days after the strike began, Tenayuca and two other strikers were in jail. Six hundred indignant strikers appeared at the jail to call for her release. Three hundred strikers were arrested on Feb. 7; by the time the strike ended a month later, 1,000 workers had been arrested on such charges as obstructing the sidewalk, disturbing the peace and unlawfully assembling.

Tear gas was used to rout strikers six or seven times during the strike's first two weeks. "I did not interfere with a strike," Police Chief Kilday later told a commission investigating the strike. "I interfered with a revolution."

"There was very little support from Mexican organizations here, though, because I was a communist," Tenayuca recalled. "You read where Chief Kilday said he was stopping a revolution. There was no revolution. People were hungry and he didn't know. He had never been hungry himself. He was a devout Catholic—but there have been many changes in the church since then."

Munguia remembered: "The Catholic Church was the only group fighting communism back then per se. Hundreds of people followed her (Tenayuca) and even more would have followed her like Joan of Arc except that she was tainted by Communism. Myself, I never really believed she was a communist."

There was no question of Tenayuca's allegiances in the minds of others, however. And the CIO, under whose United Cannery and Agricultural Processors and Agricultural Workers of America the San Antonio Pecan Shellers Union was chartered, received intense pressure to relieve Tenayuca of her leadership role.

At first, Tenayuca said, she resisted. Then, convinced that stepping aside would aid the strike, she acquiesced. "I knew we had not developed the leadership to take care of the negotiating. I knew that I was a good organizer, but when it came to negotiating, that was something else," she explained in a 1983 article in the *Texas Observer*.

"She was a little girl with no financial backing," Munguia said. "She had no clout and the biggies did. It was almost natural that she would be shoved aside."

Tenayuca continued working with strikers in secondary roles until a settlement—splitting the difference in wages—was reached in March 1938. The contract was supplanted the following year, though, when the National Fair Labor Standards Act mandated a 25-cent-an-hour minimum wage in the pecan shelling industry. Thousands of shellers were left jobless when shop owners suddenly found installation of automated equipment economical.

"After the Municipal Auditorium riot, she just dropped out of sight," Munguia recalled. "You'd still see her name on the list of labor organizations—but she hadn't done very much."

Tenayuca recalled her confusion and dismay over the Stalin-Hitler non-aggression pact marked the beginning of her disenchantment with the Communist Party. "That was one of the weaknesses of the party—following a line," she said. "I don't think there was a communist in the country who wasn't puzzled . . . I decided I would never join a political party again."

The riot left her stunned.

Initially, she found employment as an office worker.

"I maintained good relations with a number of people in the labor movement, but, eventually, I felt—what the mischief! I went to California."

Enrolled in San Francisco State University, Tenayuca obtained degrees in English and education. In 1968, she returned to San Antonio, teaching in a succession of Catholic schools before joining the Harlandale Independent School District.

She retired in 1981, but has continued to work as a substitute teacher. She has also worked with a variety of labor and Hispanic-advocacy programs.

She remains a socialist.

"I did not consider all my work here in vain. I was quite young—I hadn't started formulating theories or developing any ideas or doing any amount of writing that could be influential.

"If there should be any criticism against any of these people, let me say this: We were fighting against poverty, starvation; fighting against the high infant death rate, disease, and misery. Believe me, I think I'm very sure I'd do the same thing again."

Source: Turner, Allan. "A Night That Changed San Antonio/Woman Recalls Leading Labor Riot in 1939." *Houston Chronicle* (2 Star Edition), December 14, 1986, 1.

Oral History Interview with Valentín S. Herrera about Mexican American Life in Morenci, Arizona

(ca. 1996)

Valentín S. Herrera (1920–?) was a longtime resident of the mining camps of Clifton-Morenci-Metcalf, Arizona, which have been among the world's top producers of copper from 1880 to the present. The Morenci camp was isolated, which contributed to a strong feeling of place among the residents. It was a Mexican camp that had been built by the labor of Mexicans from Chihuahua in the early 1870s. During the Great Depression, the mining industry came to a standstill and many miners and their families were forced to move out—either they were repatriated or sought work elsewhere. Those who stayed behind scraped together an existence. Some 50 years later, Herrera tells of his resourcefulness and his family's experiences during the Great Depression.

THE DEPRESSION

In [the Depression] I lived there in Duncan. My father did not work. We worked on the ranches, picking cotton, potatoes. They used to plant a lot of potatoes in those years. I worked little jobs here and there where I found them. My mother died, I think in 1928. They gave relief and my father went to get relief but he had four horses and because he had four horses he was not entitled. (laughs)

There were jobs, WPA. I worked in the WPA. Quico Alvidrez was in charge and I would go and go but he would never give me a job. I guess I was not old enough yet. He went on vacation and they put an Americano from Morenci in charge. I applied and he hired me. I think I worked two or three pay periods and Quico Alvidrez returned and as soon as he got back, threw me out [of the program]. You worked 11 days per month and they paid you $44. I think I worked three weeks. I think he got angry because the gabacho [pejorative term for a White male, non-Hispanic] put me in. I do not know. I did not go to the CC camp. In the WPA I worked on that road there by the Apache Grove. They made the highway, there on the cut just before you go up the hill. I helped make that cut using just a pick and shovel. You worked only 11 days and got $44. That way everybody could work. Everybody got a chance.

I never saw much difference. I ate. (laughs) I helped a lot of people that is why they help me. Manuel [my brother] and I were alone in the house. We both worked in Carlyle, where I told you we worked in the mine. We rented a house there in the town. It had three bedrooms, the house. It was a green house. We would come from Carlyle and stay here [Duncan] on the weekend. Five days we stayed in Carlyle. We had a house there. We camped there.

That night we came home; I took a bath, got cleaned up and went to the movies. I got out about ten o'clock at night. It was in the winter and it was so cold, even the ice shimmered! There was a fence by the house and there were some trees. They were big mulberry trees. I walked along the path in the dark without a light. A little kid cried. It was a woman and a man. They were young; they were not old. I asked them what they were doing. They were hobos. That is how people traveled during the Depression. I said, "It's too cold. There's going to be a bad freeze and that child is gonna be cold. I'll tell you what. You guys go with me. I live just a little piece from here. I got an extra room where you can get out of the cold." I did not know if it was her husband. I still think to this day that he was a tramp that tagged along with the lady. (laughs) Her name was Mary, I think.

I showed them the room. I always had a sack of potatoes and flour, hundred pounds. Lard, everything. We had food. I asked them, "Have you eaten?" The little boy was crying from hunger.

(laughs) I said to them, "If you want, there is potatoes, food. There is lard. There is flour. If you want to and you're hungry, if you guys haven't eat, you go ahead and make something to eat." She got the frying pan, the big cast iron frying pan I used to use, and flour and she made biscuits.

I was seventeen or so, it had not been long since I got out of school. There was a bed there and they slept there. The next morning, we got up. Manuel and I did not have to go to work. He [the man] left. He told us he was going to the mine to look for work. He never returned. She stayed there [with us] broke. She did not have a penny. There she stayed with her child. We left her there [in our house] alone and went to work at Carlyle. She stayed with us for months. She did not have anything, poor lady except what we gave her. She was from Oklahoma. When the work in Carlyle ended, they cut us back and that is when we decided to go to Phoenix. We had already sent her [to Oklahoma]. She had already left.

We went to Phoenix and we were there when she returned to Duncan. She went straight to the house and knocked on the door. By then Quica [my sister] lived there. She was married to Lencho. She told them, "They don't live in Duncan. They live in Phoenix or someplace." The little boy was not even a year old. I had lots of cans of milk. I bought cases of it. We drank milk in our coffee. We would leave her there in the house and we would stay over there the whole week in Carlyle. She already knew [our schedule]. She earned her money because she knew we would come on Friday and dinner would be ready.

All the others in my family had gone to California. They lived in El Centro. Manuel and I did not go because we worked in Carlyle. I do not know if that woman is still alive. The little boy would be about sixty years old or more. It was about 1938. We respected her. We would go to the movies often. We paid a dime for the movies. A nickel for the popcorn, I think. We used to go every day when we were off. She would stay there alone. She was not old. She seemed old to us but she probably was about 25 years old.

This is how I bought food during the Depression. I would buy a sack of potatoes. They planted a lot of potatoes there in Duncan. I would go to pick them and they would give you half a sack of the second pick. I would choose them at midday when we stopped to eat and got half a sack of only good potatoes. It would be ready. When I took my sack home, I took only number one potatoes. The next day, another one. Sometimes we had two or three sacks of potatoes. Paulo used to hang out with us and his father had a pickup, an old one, Model A. We used to go pick potatoes and I got half a sack of good potatoes. Then Manuel and I put it together and it was a full sack. Paulo Magallanes. On Saturday, we would load up the little truck and go to Lordsburg and sell it. Number one potatoes! Two dollars a sack! They bought it from us.

There in Duncan, everybody burned wood. Many were lazy. They did not have firewood. When I lived there, I had the horses there to one side of the house in a corral a little further than from here to the highway [about eighty feet]. I had the horses, the wagon, everything. When I did not have anything else to do. When I did not have to go to work, I would get up at six in the morning if I felt like it. I would eat breakfast and I would put together two sandwiches in bread. I used to make biscuits. I would put them in my pocket and a container of water. I would put the harnesses on the horses and I would hitch them to the wagon.

You know where the cemetery is in Duncan? By that cemetery, I would go up to the countryside. There were a lot of little mesquite trees, dried up. I would hit them with a hatchet and they would come out by the roots. I went alone and cut wood. I would come back to the house about three in the afternoon. If I got hungry while I was there, I ate the sandwiches I took. I would come back with the wagon full of firewood. I would get home and those that did not have firewood would buy it from me for two quarters the bucket. I have always looked for ways to make it. I had to eat!

In Glendale when I got to Phoenix, there was a street there and there was a big grocery store belonging to Jews. On this side of the store was a pool hall. In front of the pool hall was a big tree. That mulberry (points to a large tree in the yard) is small. It was thick like this (demonstrates with his arms not meeting). Huge! It was dry. It had been [that way] for a long time. When I got there, the guy from the pool hall wanted to cut it down. I told him I would do it. I asked for two hatchets and a saw, a big one to cut trees. I told the guy, "The tree is mine. All the firewood is mine. Get me the hatchets and the saw and a lot of long rope." The people saw me as very young and they said to me, "It's going to fall on top of the pool hall." (laughs) I said, "It will fall where I want it to fall. You do not know me. I am used to do work. I will cut down that tree and it will fall where I want it to."

I got the rope and I climbed up like a monkey to the top and tied the rope. I crossed the street where there was another big tree and I tied the other end to it. On this side, I cut with the saw to about the middle and then I cut with the hatchet. Afterwards I changed to the saw, Manuel and I. It had to fall to the other side. The rope was pulling it. When it was almost ready to fall, I gave notice to the cops to block the street. There were not many cars, but so no one would come along and get hurt. There it went! (laughs) It fell where I wanted it on top of the street. It was so dry that it splintered. Right away the people gathered. There was no firewood. A dollar a bucket! We sold all of it! We worked until it got dark. (laughs)

All of the branches that broke off, I cut small with the hatchet. Only the trunk was left. We cut it in big pieces. No one could steal it in the night, it was too heavy. The next day we came and cut it into pieces and we sold all of it.

I taught Richard [my son], he has learned a lot from me. "When you want to cut a tree. You make it fall where you want it to fall, not where it wants to fall. Look, this way I have cut many trees. I taught him how. When his father-in-law died, there was a tree that was next to the house and was hitting it. It was a big tree. She [his mother-in-law] wanted it cut but her sons did not know how. Richard was there. They laughed at him, even Evelyn [his wife]. They said, "It will fall on top of the house." Richard said, "No, my father showed me how to work. My father knows the works and he knows what he taught me." He did it like I showed him. I learned everything working on the ranches, watching.

Source: In the Shadow of the Smokestack, an Oral History of Mexican Americans in Morenci, Arizona. http://www.elenadiazbjorkquist.net/interviewees.html.

Latinos, World War II, and the Aftermath

J. Brooks Deton Jr., "Negro Fate in U.S. Tied to Puerto Rico Freedom" (1943)

A large part of the Puerto Rican population was of dark complexion and, correspondingly, they suffered the same discrimination as African Americans. The Chicago Defender, *a leading African American newspaper published in the United States since 1905 to advocate for the interests of black people, drew the correlation between white supremacy in the United States and the occupation of Puerto Rico. The following article from the* Defender *criticizes the U.S. military presence on the island and the obsession with communism. The article draws a parallel between southern politicos on the mainland and American attitudes and policies toward Puerto Rico.*

"The fate of the Negro, the Jew, the laboring classes, in fact most of America's minorities will be decided by what happens to Puerto Rico."

How could occurrences in a little sub-tropical island outpost 1,150 miles from Florida affect the condition of minorities here at home? Absurd! No, not quite! The link between freedom for Puerto Rico and freedom for the Negro is understandable.

I didn't realize Puerto Rico's significance either some seven weeks ago when a silver-winged Pan American clipper finally rested its big, sleek, bird-like frame on the military airport of Puerto Rico's capital, San Juan.

LEARNS TRUTH

There amidst the island's squalor, poverty, and disease where month-old babies die when half-grown because emaciated mothers cannot nourish them properly; where greedy, powerful sugar corporations have gobbled up the richest, most fertile land, leaving 85 percent of the masses landless and destitute; where disease-ravaged cripples plaintively beg to eke out an existence, I learned this truth.

There I saw a struggle in progress. Not just between Puerto Ricans—those like Munoz Marin and members of the Popular Party who have tried to change these conditions, and representatives of the sugar interests who have fought to keep them like they are—but a struggle in which reactionary Americans have entered and in which they are fighting bitterly, relentlessly.

I found that Puerto Rico is merely another battleground of the continuing struggle for reactionaries in resisting every social and economic advance the masses make. I found that the same Americans who rant and rave against the Negro, the Jew, and labor here at home are the ones who are determined to choke off any improvement in Puerto Rican conditions.

AFRAID OF INFILTRATION

Why should American interests be so intent in strangling reforms within the island? Because they are afraid that some of them might eventually infiltrate into the United States jeopardizing their vested interests.

That's the reason Congressman Doummengeaux (Dem. La.), a member of the Bell investigating group, gave a Puerto Rican leader for his vicious attack on the reform program. It's the reason Representative Crawford (Rep. Mich.) gave when a resolution into Congress to repeal the reform laws passed by the insular legislatures.

At no time did they argue as to the need of these laws in Puerto Rico. They were merely concerned with their probable effect on American economy. It must be remembered that Rep. Doummengeaux is from Louisiana and another member of the committee, Rep. McGhee, is from Mississippi. Crawford is a vest pocket edition of another Michigan reactionary, Clare Hoffman.

Why are Doummengeaux and McGhee so concerned? They come from the south. And Puerto Rico's economy resembles that of the south: both are agricultural areas; both have one-crop economies, the south cotton, Puerto Rico, sugar; and both viciously exploit their landless workers. We call them tenant farmers and sharecroppers in the south. In Puerto Rico they're aggregados.

GOOD FOR DIXIE

If Puerto Rico's law providing for land redistribution were allowed to be successful, wouldn't some bright young economists get an idea that it should be tried in Dixie? And what would happen to Reps. McGhee and Doummengeaux if Negroes and poor whites became respectable landowners? They'd vote! And these cohorts of infamy would lose their power and their jobs as congressmen.

No wonder McGhee is reported to have said during a recess between hearings of the Bell committee, "I hate the New Deal and all it stands for." Don't that sound just like Rankin or Tabor or Bilbo. You can count their votes in advance on any bill like anti-poll tax, anti-lynch, or anti-strike legislation.

Crawford's pet peeve was the insular law which provided for the establishment of a Development Authority. It's the organization the Puerto Rican legislature created to provide a banking institution to develop new industries in the island. Crawford wanted to kill it because it meant government in industry and no reactionary wants that to happen, even when private funds are not available.

For over a year and a half stories supposedly emanating from the island have viciously attacked Gov. Rexford Guy Tugwell, who has been made to appear as a tyrant ruling without the consent of the people; as the most hated man in the island.

REPORTS NOT TRUE

I traveled the length and breadth of Puerto Rico, up in the verdant peaked mountains by horseback along trails which no auto could travel, down in sugar cane-covered valleys and in quaint, picturesque Spanish-type cities. Everywhere I went I talked to the workers. I found that relatively few of them knew Tugwell, but they all knew President Roosevelt and Munoz Marin, their own local leader, both of whom enjoy a popularity unrivaled by anyone else on the island.

And Gov. Tugwell is the President's appointee. It's Marin's program he's helped to execute. In fact, Tugwell was appointed as governor after the controversial reform laws were passed. Gov. T. Swope of Pennsylvania was governor at that time, and it was he who signed these bills, making them law after the insular legislature passed them.

My own impression is that Tugwell has sought no personal glory himself. That he's been loyal to his chief—to the ideals that were originally incorporated in the New Deal program. That he's been self-effacing and he's tried to carry out the program agreed to by a majority of the insular legislators.

He is hated, however, by one group of islanders and continental Americans alike. In the island, the sugar interests talk as if he's something akin to the black plague. At a party one of their representatives refused to even stay in the same room with him.

Here at home, anyone who hates the New Deal philosophy hates Tugwell. He's been too close to it. To destroy him is a step in killing social legislation. This is the reason then for stories grossly misrepresenting his position in the island.

Remember, Puerto Rico is a battlefront. It's just another area in which the big American fight—the underdog vs. entrenched power—continues. We can't afford to lose there anymore than we can on the home front.

Source: Chicago Defender (National Edition), July 31, 1943, 7.

Lucius C. Harper, "The Puerto Rican in Our Midst" (1951)

Although New York was the principal port of entry for Puerto Ricans, small numbers of immigrants moved to Chicago from New York in the 1930s. By the late 1940s, they moved into Milwaukee, Wisconsin, after being recruited to work in the tanneries. The movement into Chicago was predictable; the city had many factories, office buildings, and homes, and private employment companies heavily recruited Puerto Ricans to work in these sectors. In Chicago, Castle, Barton, and Associates recruited Puerto Rican men to work as laborers in the foundries and placed Puerto Rican women in households. Most single men and women soon sent for family members once they established stable jobs and residences. The Chicago Defender, *a leading African American newspaper published in the United States since 1905 to advocate for the interests of black people, noted the growing presence of Puerto Ricans and introduced them to their readers. The following* Defender *article reaches out to the newcomers.*

The next time you meet a Puerto Rican—and you will be meeting more of them right along—there are a few things you might remember about him. First of all, he is a United States citizen by virtue of an Act of Congress passed some thirty odd years ago, and he has all the rights and privileges of any other citizen.

Secondly, the beautiful island he comes from is as much a melting pot as the United States itself. Native Indians, Spaniards, Negroes, French, Dutch, and other Europeans, all have made their contribution to the island character. The Puerto Rican is a well-stirred mixture; and whether his skin is white or dark brown or one of the many in-betweens he considers himself an equal part of the whole.

Puerto Rico is a small but modern land, where the roads and schools and stores and factories are proportionately fewer than here, but they are not unlike our own.

Since World War II, many new industries have been started in Puerto Rico and thousands of people have learned new industrial skills. Many thousands more have been and are being trained in vocational and technical schools. But the mainstay of Puerto Rico is agriculture. And there's the rub.

In this little area 100 miles long and 35 miles wide live more than 2,000,000 people. Yet despite their dependence on agriculture, only about half the land is arable. This is the reason 350,000 Puerto Ricans have entered the States in the past six years. It's the reason many more of them will probably come in the next six years.

Make no mistake about it. The pleasant young man with the wide and friendly smile didn't bring his pretty wife and his three lively children to the mainland because he wants to see baseball games and hear snappy music. He has plenty of that at home and much more besides. He has a warm, vacation climate that has never brought him snow. He doesn't know what winter clothes are. He feels the softness of the trade winds and watches the breezes stir the palm trees—he listens to the kind of music he loves, and he's a happy man. Happy that is, except for one all-important thing. He can't make a decent living in his island paradise.

So he comes to the States and he brings with him a lot of energy and ambition, a lot of ability to learn, and determination. And he brings a happy, generous spirit. We have everything to gain from his coming here and a lot to learn from him, just as he has a lot to learn from us.

The thousands of Puerto Ricans who have come to New York, Chicago, and other cities in the past three years will likely be followed by many more. It will be happier for all of us if we accept each individual for what he himself is and for what he can do, rather than try to label him "black" or "white" or "rural and dumb" or "city and slick." Because we'll be meeting Puerto Ricans of every degree of skill from the common laborer to the doctor and the engineer. Some of them will be "country boys." Others will be city people with a different set of manners and customs. We'll get the most from them if we give them our friendship and understanding.

Source: Chicago Defender, December 8, 1951, 11.

Citations for Valor: Fernando Luis García, Pablo Ramírez, and Pedro Rodríguez

(ca. 1951–1952)

In July 1950, some 20,000 Latinos were serving in the armed forces. During the three years of the Korean War, 148,000 Latinos volunteered or were drafted. Approximately 60,000 Puerto Ricans served in Korea. The number of Puerto Ricans might have been higher because mainland statistics were often not counted. Many of them fought in the historic all-Latino 65th Infantry Regiment. Members of 65th Infantry fought in temperatures 35 or 40 degrees below zero, and the casualties were heavy. The unit was unique because it had been organized soon after the United States took control of Puerto Rico in 1899. The 65th Infantry unit participated in nine major battles in Korea. In December 1950, Chinese troops caught the United Nations forces off-guard as thousands of Chinese soldiers crossed the 38th Parallel into South Korea. The 65th helped prevent a disaster by staying behind and preventing the Chinese from annihilating U.S. Marines as they retreated. Throughout the conflict, numerous Puerto Rican soldiers were cited for bravery. Among them were Private Fernando Luis García, Lieutenant Pablo Ramírez, and Sergeant Pedro Rodríguez. The following are copies of their citations and proof that they won the Borinquens' rights with their blood.

MARINE PFC FERNANDO LUIS GARCÍA (1929–1952) BORN IN PUERTO RICO

MEDAL OF HONOR CITATION:

Private First Class Fernando L. Garcia

Rank and organization: Private First Class, U.S. Marine Corps, Company I, 3d Battalion, 5th Marines, 1st Marine Division (Rein.).

Place and date: Korea, September 5, 1952.

Entered service at: San Juan, P.R.

Born: October 14, 1929 Utuado, Puerto Rico

Citation:

For conspicuous gallantry and intrepidity at the risk of his life above and beyond the call of duty while serving as a member of Company I, Third Battalion, Fifth Marines, First Marine Division (Reinforced), in action against enemy aggressor forces in Korea on September 5, 1952. While participating in the defense of a combat outpost located more than one mile forward of the main line of resistance during a savage night attack by a fanatical enemy force employing grenades, mortars, and artillery, Private First Class Garcia, although suffering painful wounds, moved through the intense hail of hostile fire to a supply point to secure more hand grenades. Quick to act when a hostile grenade landed nearby endangering the life of another Marine, as well as his own, he unhesitatingly chose to sacrifice himself and immediately threw his body upon the deadly missile, receiving the full impact of the explosion. His great personal valor and cool decision in the face of almost certain death sustain and enhance the finest traditions of the United States Naval Service. He gallantly gave his life for his country.

PABLO RAMIREZ

SILVER STAR

General Orders # 92 - 11 APRIL 1951

Second Lieutenant Pablo Ramirez, 0954382, Infantry, Company "A," 65th Infantry, 3d Infantry Division, United States Army. On 1 February 1951, Lieutenant Ramirez led his platoon in an assault on Hill 449 in the vicinity of Kalgok, Korea. In the initial phase of the assault, an enemy mortar barrage killed one of the men of the platoon and wounded two others. The platoon was disorganized by the terrific barrage, but Lt. Ramirez immediately reorganized his men and continued the attack on the hill in spite of the mortar and small arms fire. He discovered two wounded men and evacuated them. Upon reaching a third man, he was killed by a second mortar barrage. The bravery and gallantry displayed by Lt. Ramirez was an inspiration to his men and exemplifies the highest traditions of the military service. Entered the military service from Puerto Rico.

PEDRO RODRIGUEZ

Organization: Headquarters 3d Infantry Division

G.O. # 196 - 17 June 1951

1st Citation:

Master Sergeant Pedro Rodriguez, RA6674697, Infantry, Company "F," 65th Infantry, 3d Infantry Division, United States Army. On 24 March 1951, near Kopi-Dong, Korea, Sgt. Rodriguez, acting as platoon leader in the absence of a commissioned officer, was leading his unit to secure Hill 476, when the enemy opened fire from a well-camouflaged machine gun nest. Although he did not know the exact location of the gun, Sgt. Rodriguez ordered one squad to fix bayonets and assault the general area from which the fire was coming. After the enemy weapon fired again, Sgt. Rodriguez charged the position, yelling and shooting his rifle demoralizing the enemy and causing him to flee in haste, taking his gun with him, but leaving ammunition and rations behind. The gallantry and extreme devotion to duty displayed by Sgt. Rodriguez reflect great credit upon himself and the military service. Entered the military service from Puerto Rico.

PEDRO RODRIGUEZ

Organization: Headquarters 3d Infantry Division

G.O. # 261 - 8 July 1951

2nd Citation:

Master Sgt. Pedro Rodriguez, RA6674697, Infantry, Company "F," 65th Infantry, 3d Infantry Division, United States Army. On 31 March 1951, near Choksong-Myon, Korea, Company "F" was attacking Hill 398, defended by a firmly entrenched enemy supported by mortars. At some distance from the top of the hill, the lead platoon was halted by intense machine gun fire and fragmentation grenades, suffering several casualties. When Sgt. Rodriguez received the order to move his platoon to assist the stalled unit, he ran forward and led his troops in a furious assault, causing the enemy to retreat hastily, thereby relieving the besieged lead platoon. Continuing his charge, Sgt. Rodriguez pursued the fleeing enemy and covered by friendly machine gun fire, he personally searched the area to rout any enemy troops which might have been left behind. The aggressive leadership and personal gallantry exhibited by Sgt. Rodriguez reflect the highest credit upon himself and the military service. Entered the military service from Puerto Rico.

Source: Courtesy of Medal of Honor Recipients, Hispanics in America's Defense. http://www.neta.com/1stbooks/medal2.htm. GetNet, Korean War Educator. http://www.koreanwar-educator.org/topics/silver_star/p_silver_star_citations_r.htm.

Langston Hughes, "Simple Says Puerto Ricans Must Have Poro in Their Blood" (1953)

African American writer and poet Langston Hughes (1902–1967) was not only a leader in the black community but also in the human rights movement in the United States. In the mid-1940s, he became a regular columnist for The Chicago Defender, *an African American newspaper. Previously, Hughes had defended the cause of Mexican farm workers and had written scathing indictments against gross violations of the civil rights of African Americans. The following* Defender *article is an example of his witty observations on the changing complexion of Chicago when Puerto Ricans were becoming more numerous—it builds bridges between the black and Puerto Rican communities.*

"How come some of these colored Puerto Ricans have got such good hair?" asked Simple, as a couple of brownskin Puerto Ricans passed.

"It must be their Spanish blood," I said.

"Then why don't my Indian blood work the same way, daddy-o?"

"Maybe you haven't got enough Indian blood." I said.

"You mean to offset my colored blood—which is really powerful? But them Puerto Ricans have got colored blood too, and it is not powerful enough to curl their hair up like mine."

"Did you say, curl?"

"I said, curl," said Simple. "Straight as them Puerto Ricans' hair is, they must be related to Madam Walker or Rose Meta on their grandma's side, else they are born with Poro in their blood. Where do Puerto Ricans come from, anyhow, speaking all Spanishified and everything—which if Puerto Rico belongs to the United States, they ought to speak English."

"Puerto Rico used to belong to Spain," I said, "and we won it from the Spaniards in the Spanish-American War."

"Which I know our white folks regret," said Simple, "because when they won they lost."

"Why do you say that?"

"Because all them colored Puerto Ricans is coming up here flooding the USA with colored blood and they got enough Negroes in the USA already—with us—so I known they do not want any more."

"Puerto Ricans are not classed as Negroes," I said.

"The only reason they is not is because they speak some other lingo. Some of them is dark as me."

"But you've already remarked on the difference in their hair."

"White folks pays no attention to hair. Look at some of our New Orleans Creoles, handsome mens and goodlooking womens, pretty as a picture with hair like Moses, yet Jim Crowed right on. But Americans do not Jim Crow Puerto Ricans."

"I expect they do down South," I said.

"They don't up North," contended Simple. "Them Puerto Ricans go anywhere they want to in New York. But just let me, born here, try—and the man at the door says 'Whoa! No go! No-ooo-ooo!' And I am stymied—just because I do not speak Spanish. I think I am going to night school and learn me one term of it—you know five or six lessons. Then I am going to walk right up to the Stork Club and say, "Speegingee spagody aw dee ouse.' And they will let me right in, though I be the color of Josephine Baker."

"My dear fellow," I said, "you are not quite the color of Josephine Baker."

"She's pushing me," said Simple. "But with my new language, that will make no difference. I will jump on a train and run down to Baltimore or Washington and register at the biggest hotels there by just saying, 'Bendos Kneeous, s'il vous play!'"

"I fear you are mixing up both French and Spanish."

"Them white folks would not know the difference," said Simple. "They would not be cultured like me. Besides I would walk in with so much dignity, acting so much like a gentleman that they would not know who I were. And I would sail up to the desk like royalties with out crowns in our suitcase."

"You would be sailing under false pretenses," I said. "Instead of trying to pass for something you are not, you would do better to demand your rights for what you are, a pure American Negro."

"I been demanding my rights all these years as a pure American Negro and ain't got them yet," said Simple. "So what's wrong with demanding them now in Spanish?"

"You can answer that question yourself," I said.

"The answer is, I don't speak Spanish," said Simple.

Source: *Chicago Defender* (National Edition), November 21, 1953, 11.

New York Times, "Woman Terrorist Freed of 'Intent'" (1954)

Puerto Rican Nationalists had attempted to force a plebiscite on Puerto Rican independence from the beginning of the U.S. occupation. Repression of the Puerto Rican desire to end U.S. occupation led to police brutality toward the Nationalists, the imprisonment of Pedro Albizu Campos (1891–1965) and others, and the Ponce Massacre of 1937, during which police shot down 19 people and wounded more than 100. In 1950, two Nationalists, Oscar Collazo (1914–1994) and Griselio Torresola (1925–1950), attacked Blair House, where President Harry Truman

(1884–1972) was temporarily staying while repairs were made to the White House, failing in an attempt to assassinate him. Three secret service men were wounded, Torresola was killed, and Collazo was captured. Two years later, in 1954, Puerto Rican Nationalists Lolita Lebrón, age 34 (1919–2010); Rafael C. Miranda, age 25; Andrés Figueroa Cordero, age 29; and Irving Flores Rodríguez, age 29, led a failed attack on Congress. They fired 29 shots in the House of Representatives chamber, wounding five congressmen. A note was found on Lebrón saying: "Before God and the world my blood claims for the independence of Puerto Rico. My life I give for the freedom of my country."

The group also protested the imprisonment and torture of Dr. Albizu Campos (1893–1965), head of the Nationalist Movement and the father of the Puerto Rican Independence Movement. Lebrón received a sentence of 50 years and eight months in prison. The rebels were charged with assault with intent to kill. The following excerpt from a New York Times article describes the attack.

Mrs. Lebrón was one of four Puerto Rican nationalists who fired a volley of shots in the House chamber. Five members of Congress were wounded.

Her companions, Rafael Cancel Miranda, Andres Figueroa Cordero, and Irving Flores Rodriguez, were found guilty yesterday of assault with intent to kill and assault with a dangerous weapon.

They face a possible prison sentence of 125 years. Attorneys for the defendants said tonight they would file a motion for a new trial for the men on the ground they could not be convicted on both counts.

Source: "Woman Terrorist Freed of 'Intent.'" *New York Times*, June 18, 1954, 15.

Dan Wakefield, "Puerto Rico: Rebels Find a Welcome" (1957)

In the 1950s, in the midst of the Cold War with the Soviet Union, the United States considered Cuba and Puerto Rico essential to its defense of the Caribbean and Central America. Part of the U.S. policy was to maintain control by supporting dictators. However, in the aftermath of World War II, populist movements in Latin America demanded democracy and an end to dependence on the United States. Puerto Rico stood at the crossroads of these political upheavals during the 1950s. Political exiles held court in San Juan, Puerto Rico, planning their revolutions. The two most notable revolutionary hot spots were Cuba and Santo Domingo. Cuban dictator Ruben Fulgencio Batista Zaldívar (1901–1973) was a friend of the United States. He joined the Cuban Army and rose to the rank of sergeant, emerging as a strongman. Batista was in and out of the presidency. By the 1950s, the Cuban people had tired of his corruption and promotion of Havana as the sin capital of the hemisphere. During the decade, Fidel Castro (ca. 1926–) led a revolt against Batista that lasted a half dozen years, successfully ending in 1959. Castro was favored by many Puerto Ricans. Another U.S. favorite was Dominican dictator Rafael Trujillo, who ruled the Dominican Republic for 31 years. With the support of the United States, Trujillo ruled until his assassination in 1961. Before and after the revolts, political and economic refugees fled to the United States and Puerto Rico. The following article from The Nation *talks about revolutionary movements overthrowing these dictatorships.*

San Juan, Puerto Rico

In a makeshift meeting hall above a café in San Juan's suburbs, a small, enthusiastic audience sat before the flag-draped pictures of José Martí and Fidel Castro—dead and living symbols of Cuban freedom—and cheered a series of speakers who denounced the dictatorial regimes of Batista and Trujillo. The audience, generously sprinkled with the special apparel of political exiles, dark glasses, was made up of men and women from three different Caribbean countries who are joined in a fraternal, informal community of opposition to the current neighboring dictators.

The Cubans and Dominicans are exiles from their native countries, and the Puerto Ricans are their sympathetic hosts.

The Puerto Ricans, proud of their own democracy, are pleased to have their island serve as a port in the extended dictatorial storms, and the exiles find much popular support here, as well as official protection. There is also mutual support and camaraderie between the exile groups, of different countries. The meeting above the café was staged to raise funds for Cuba's 26th of July Movement, which organizes outside support for Castro; it was attended not only by Cubans and Puerto Ricans, but also by the leaders of the main Dominican party in exile. This mutual sympathy is part of a long tradition in the Caribbean—in fact, it is one of the few existing inter-island traditions. For, despite their geographic proximity, the countries of this area have had surprisingly little contact, political or social. One of the few has been that between the exiles and their temporary hosts. Since all the countries in the region have experienced the problems of either colonial rule or home-grown dictatorship or both, the people are immediately sympathetic to neighbors fighting the same sort of battle. Before the rise of Batista, the Cubans used to turn out to cheer the Dominican exiles leaving or returning from Havana on their perennially abortive attempts to overthrow Trujillo. Now the Cubans have a dictator of their own, and the Dominicans sit in San Juan and cheer the representatives of Fidel Castro, who stop through to raise funds to fight Batista.

The Puerto Ricans have had a happier recent history, but they don't have to go too far back to find reasons for sympathizing with neighbors fighting dictatorship. When the Spanish took over the island on the second voyage of Columbus, Ponce de Leon and his merry men nearly managed to exterminate the entire native Indian population of the island in two generations, brought Negro slaves from Africa, and went on to rule for four centuries. It was not until 1897 that Puerto Rico managed to gain a home-rule government from Spain; and it was one year after that hard-earned triumph that America captured the island from the Spaniards and Puerto Rico was right back where it started from as a colony. The country has made another, shorter rise now to self-rule, working it out of the Americans in little more than half a century (1898–1952).

Democracy is popular today in Puerto Rico in both idea and practice. The Castro men who came here to organize the 26th of July Movement said they had received more wide-spread support in Puerto Rico than anywhere else they had been. Their meeting in San Juan was attended by some of the outstanding leaders of the Puerto Rican Government and trade-union movement.

More important, it was also attended by a man from the Puerto Rican security police who took names of people not known to him and who asked questions of Francisco Javier Guilliani, leader of the Dominican Populist Party, the largest political group in exile from Trujillo. The interest of the island security police in these affairs is not prompted by government disapproval, but rather by the fact that the exiles and their friends are in constant danger from agents of the dictators. Trujillo has a large delegation of agents in San Juan, centered in the Casa Dominicana—billed as a "cultural center" for Dominicans away from home—and not only the exile leaders, but their Puerto Rican sympathizers, are often threatened and sometimes attacked by Trujillo's men.

That the threats are not to be taken lightly is proved by the long history of "extra-territorial" assassinations of Dominicans who oppose Trujillo.

The recent, highly publicized disappearance of Dr. Jesus de Galindez from New York City is only one in a series of deaths and kidnappings of men who spoke or worked against the Dominican dictator. Sergio Bencosme, one of the first outstanding Trujillo opponents, was murdered in New York; Mauricio Baez, a trade-union leader who spoke against Trujillo at an inter-American labor conference, was murdered in Havana; Andres Requena, a newspaperman who wrote a book attacking the Trujillo regime, was shot and killed in New York; Manuel José Hernández, leader of another anti-Trujillo movement, was stabbed and killed in Havana. Dr. Jesús de Galindez is one of a long line of assassins' victims.

It is one of the continual sources of suspicion and distrust of the U.S. Government among the people of the Caribbean that it proclaims democracy and gives diplomatic and financial support ($250,000 a year in Point Four funds, plus military aid) to a dictatorial regime with this record of slaughter—a record which does not even touch on the massacres and individual killings on Trujillo's own island.

No Dominican exile has yet been killed in Puerto Rico, but that can be credited more to the work of the island security police than to any lack of enterprise on the party of Trujillo's agents. This June, a Dominican-born man named Rafael Rivera Rosas went one night to the office of Dominican exile leader Francisco Guilliani and was beaten up and knifed by four attackers. The next day a note was delivered to Guilliani that read: "If this was not death for him, it will be death for you, Mr. Guilliani." Hector Landrón, a Puerto Rican radio news broadcaster, interviewed some Dominican exiles on his program and spoke in sympathy with their cause, and the next day received a phone call threatening his life if he continued such broadcasts.

The Rosas attack, which capped growing reports of threats and attacks by Trujillo agents, prompted a statement from Puerto Rico's Governor Munos [sic] Marín:

The alleged activities and attacks, carried out by persons said to represent a foreign government, against residents of our country should deeply concern everyone in Puerto Rico. Commonwealth police have strict orders to investigate those acts with the utmost energy. We cannot tolerate the extension to the peaceful and democratic life of Puerto Rico of dictatorial power from other countries.

There has been no public reaction to all these incidents from the U.S. Government. According to recent news dispatches, a U.S. Congressional committee is coming here to investigate communism, which is about as lively a movement in the Commonwealth as existentialism is in Dubuque, Iowa. But the committee will no doubt diligently search for Communist threats to Puerto Rican security, while Trujillo's men move unnoticed all around them, threatening life and limb of those who oppose the dictator.

Francisco Guilliani has been to Washington to ask for Congressional opposition to the current Dominican tyranny, but his only real support has come from Rep. Charles Porter of Oregon, who has asked the United States to cut its aid Trujillo. The other officials Guilliani saw—including such noted liberal Senators as Jacob Javits—were "privately sympathetic" but would go no further, Guilliani said.

In the meantime, Guilliani attends to the exiles. As head of the Dominican Populist Party, he is the leader of some 3,000 Dominican exiles now living in Puerto Rico. He is the man most often contacted by Dominicans who come to San Juan in escape from Trujillo, and he helps them find apartments and jobs and get established here.

But Guilliani is concerned with political as well as "domestic" action. He leads a weekly picket line outside the Dominican Embassy here on Saturdays, makes broadcasts to the Dominican Republic and sends in news and literature of his own party's promises and activities. His aim is not so much to draw people out of the Dominican Republic, but to establish a sympathetic following within it for his party and its stated principles of democratic politics. The Populist Party has never attempted any military attack on Trujillo's regime, and they say that they are planning none. Guilliani has little hope of an uprising within the tight military control that Trujillo has imposed upon his country with the help of U.S. arms aid and a national budget that devotes 55 percent of its total to the military. "We will just have to wait till Trujillo dies," Gilliiani says. "Then we will return, and with the help of our followers inside the country, set up a democratic government and democratic elections before another dictatorship starts."

But the waiting strategy is not shared by all the exiled Dominicans. The smaller, elite Dominican Revolutionary Vanguard Party, which also has headquarters in San Juan, is led by Horacio Ornes, who has already made one assault on Trujillo's regime with a revolutionary invasion force. When asked if he intends to lead another, Sr. Ornes—a tall, handsome, mustached man who could easily play the movie role of a Latin revolutionist—smiles broadly and says "Who knows?"

The Ornes party is composed mainly of professional men and intellectuals—doctors, lawyers, writers, professors, and former Trujillo diplomats. "One of the best ways of getting out of the country," Ornes explains, "is to join the diplomatic corps." Trujillo's state department has a long list of diplomats—including Ornes—who defected after being assigned to posts outside the country. But defection is always dangerous, whether it be from the diplomatic corps or merely from Dominican civilian life to civilian life in another country with affiliation to an exile party. Dr. Tancredo Martínez, one of the top officers of the Ornes party, became the most recent in the list of Dominican exiles assassinated abroad when he was shot down this September in Mexico City.

The Cuban exiles have had much less trouble from their home dictator's agents abroad than the Dominicans have had from theirs. One of the representatives of Fidel Castro who had come to Puerto Rico to help organize the 26th of July Movement said that Batista's agents, once outside the country, are just as afraid as the exiles they spy on. "Batista's spies know that our friends and brothers are with Castro in the Sierra Maestra, and that some of us have been there too. Bastista's men know how we feel, and when they get outside the country and meet us on equal terms—they know they are in just as much danger from us as we are from them."

Compared to Trujillo, Batista is still a novice at the dictator business, and his agents are no doubt suffering a cultural lag in the conduct of extraterritorial intrigue.

But the greatest threat that hangs over all the exiles, whether or not they are ever approached by a dictator's agent, is one that is seldom articulated. This is the possibility that when the great day finally comes and the dictator is overthrown, the man or party the exiles have lived and worked for may turn out to be just another dictator. It has happened often enough in the past, and the two Dominican exile parties both suspect that, if the other came to power, the result would be the establishment of another dictatorship. The leaders do not come right out and say so, for they all are bound for the moment by the common cause against Trujillo. But Ornes and Guilliani claim that the other's party would be "less democratic" than his own if it were ever returned to power.

In the case of the Cubans, all hope and faith rest with the young man leading the revolutionary forces from the ranges of the Sierra Maestra—Fidel Castro. His followers are confident of his good intentions, although he has no program except the immediate one of getting rid of Batista. The Cubans working for Castro at home and in exile seem to have the kind of faith in his "democratic ideals" that is held by Hacinto Vázquez, a young man who represents the 26th of July Movement in Puerto Rico. When asked of some proof of Castro's democratic ideals, Vázquez cited the fact that the revolutionary leader was always referred to and has asked to be referred to, as "Dr. Castro," when he might well have assumed the title of "General" or "Commander" of the revolutionary forces.

On such thin threads hangs the hope of the exiles, and that of the mass of their countrymen still at home in our neighboring island dictatorships.

Source: Wakefield, Dan. "Puerto Rico: Rebels Find a Welcome," 384–386. Reprinted with permission from the November 23, 1957, issue of *The Nation*. http://www.thenation.com.

Elena Padilla, *Up from Puerto Rico* (1958)

The following excerpts from the book Up from Puerto Rico *give an ethnographic view of Puerto Ricans living in an East Harlem slum during the post–World War II years. The book depicts the subculture and the stratification of the community as based on time of arrival, use of Spanish or English, skin color, hair texture, age, sex, education, and rural or urban origin. The book is a classic, showing the cultural and racial conflict Puerto Rican youth encountered in the period.*

Among Puerto Ricans . . . the terms "Hispano" and "Latino" are used and preferred to "Puerto Rican" for self-identification. . . .

In the past, Hispanos or Latinos were a small minority of intellectuals and middle-class professionals from Puerto Rico, Spain, and Latin America who lived in New York. By 1950, the Spanish-speaking socially mobile persons of lower-class origins, who now considered themselves in a higher social position than the recent lower-class migrants from Puerto Rico, were calling themselves Hispanos. More recently, the term has been extended to include all Spanish-speaking persons who reside in New York, regardless of their social and economic class.

In Puerto Rico, a Puerto Rican is someone born on the island, which is his country. He may be a member of the upper, the middle, or the lower class; he may come from either country or city; he may be a farmhand, a farmer, or a banker; he may be a millionaire, a salaried employee, or a wage earner. But whatever else he is, he is Puerto Rican and is not regarded as a member of an ethnic or minority group.

In New York, the terms "Hispano" and "Latino" have been substituted for that of "Puerto Rican," because the latter, in more ways than one, has become a "bad public relations" identification for New York Puerto Ricans. It is associated with unfavorable pictures of the behavior and respectability of Puerto Ricans, which are not necessarily true or real. Even when used in Spanish and by Puerto Ricans themselves, it may convey an assumption of undesirable characteristics of the persons referred to. . . .

When referring to friends, or to persons considered "decent and respectable," the term "Hispano" is preferred by Eastville Puerto Ricans. Recently arrived migrants soon learn that they are to call themselves Hispanos and drop their identification as Puerto Rican. They will probably not deny their country, but will resort to the linguistic subterfuge of Hispano to protect themselves from being characterized in a derogatory manner. They will tend to emphasize their particular home towns and municipalities in Puerto Rico, for to be accepted among Hispanos, it is important to know something specific about one's past and where one came from. . . .

One of the common forms of relating personally . . . is by initiating a conversation in which one identifies oneself as Hispano, in the sense of Puerto Rican, and by establishing this clearly. This particular approach to personal relations suggests three major social features of the Puerto Rican group. First, that being Puerto Rican and referring to oneself as Hispano is an entree for social relationships, and second, that the participants in the relationship have to establish the authenticity of their being Puerto Rican by showing some particular knowledge of the island, such as being conversant with a specific municipio, town, or city, and then a particular street there. Thus the identification is narrowed down to a level that no foreigner can reach. . . . Third, the identification also calls for establishing that one belongs to a particular family. One's status must be defined and acceptable if a personal relationship of any continuity is to be formed.

Hispanos classify themselves into three major groups with reference to life-experience and time spent in New York City. Those who have lived here for many years (los que llevan muchos años aquí) are the first. Those who grew up in this country, including the second generation, nacidos y criados (born and brought up), and those born in Puerto Rico who come to New York in early childhood comprise the second. Recent migrants, those who have come in the last several years from Puerto Rico, and who are referred to in derogatory terms . . . as "Marine Tigers" are the third. (Marine Tiger was the name of one of the Liberty ships, which made a number of trips between San Juan and New York after the war, bringing many thousands of Puerto Ricans to the States. It lent its name to the new "greenhorns," and the name has continued to stick.)

Source: From *Up from Puerto Rico*, by Elena Padilla, 32–35.

Edwin Maldonado, "Contract Labor and the Origins of Puerto Rican Communities in the United States" (1979)

The increase of Puerto Ricans leaving the island was dramatic during and after World War II. In 1941, about 1,000 left Puerto Rico, a number that thereafter doubled annually. By 1945, 14,800 had left the island, and from 1946 to mid-1947, another 25,000 left. The stimulus was widespread unemployment; 80,000 people were jobless in Puerto Rico. On June 1, 1947, The New York *Times reported that 75 percent of Puerto Rican immigrants on the U.S. mainland did not find the Promised Land and were unable to adjust. In February of that year,* The New York Times *reported that Puerto Rican families were breaking up because of a lack of housing. Homeless youths, age 16 to 20, were reported to be on the increase. It was not uncommon for 12 to 15 Puerto Ricans to be living in a single room in East Harlem. New Yorkers blamed the low price of airfare for bringing Puerto Ricans to the Big Apple. White nativists called for stemming Puerto Rican immigration, which after the war was flowing at the rate of 2,000 to 3,000 immigrants a month. In the context of this influx, racism increased, especially in New York, the destination for 90 percent of the islanders. Nativists claimed that Puerto Ricans were putting a strain on the schools and social services. They blamed parents for undoing the work of the schools by speaking Spanish to their children. In this post–World War II era, 160,000–600,000 Puerto Ricans lived in New York City. The following excerpt from the* International Migration Review *reports on a survey performed by Columbia University on Puerto Ricans in New York City and the recruitment of contract workers.*

In the autumn of 1947, the New York daily press started a campaign against the continuing influx of Puerto Ricans into that city. The government of Puerto Rico commissioned a survey by Columbia University and an investigation by the Department of Labor from which was framed a Statement of Motives on December 5, 1947 with respect to emigration. This statement, among other things, said that the Puerto Rican government "neither encourages nor discourages" migration to the United States or any foreign country. The government did, however, state its obligation to cooperate with municipal agencies in the United States to ease the adjustment of Puerto Ricans who, as American citizens, had every right to migrate to the states. Also, Puerto Ricans who wished to migrate would be guided to those areas where their labor was needed so as not to depress wages.

While the Puerto Rican government enunciated a policy neither encouraging nor discouraging migration, it still considered migration an effective way of relieving unemployment and overpopulation. Although Puerto Ricans as a group chose the United States as the primary area of resettlement, the government of Puerto Rico, over a period of years, discussed with officials in Washington and among themselves the feasibility of colonizing Puerto Ricans in Latin America. This interest waned in the post–World War II period as agricultural and industrial employment opened up in the United States. Not only would the Puerto Rican government turn its attention to working with mainland employers, but as colonies began to expand in the cities, other Puerto Ricans would make the decision to come to the mainland.

These workers were often the advance guardsmen who settled in urban communities on the mainland and made it possible for other Puerto Ricans to learn of these cities and leave the Island for the states. Whether it was industrial workers contracted to work in such places as Lorain, Ohio in 1947 and in Gary, Indiana in 1948, or agricultural contract laborers who drifted into cities such as Milwaukee, Wisconsin or Buffalo, New York looking for higher wages, these workers provided the nucleus from which ethnic communities arose on the mainland. . . .

Contract labor and the creation of communities in the United States was not a phenomenon peculiar to Puerto Ricans. The ethnic composition of the South Chicago, Illinois community is a product of labor recruitment by the nationally based steel corporations in that area. The first rolling mills along the Calumet River were constructed and manned by Native Americans, Scandinavians, and German immigrants. By the end of the nineteenth century, the steel mills began to recruit Poles, and Slovenes were brought in during the first decade of the twentieth century. During World War I, another ethnic group was added to the South Chicago community when the steel mills found it necessary to recruit Mexicans to fill the heavy demand for wartime labor.

The recruiting of labor in Puerto Rico began as early as the United States occupation of the Island after the Spanish-American War. At that time, agents from Hawaii came to Puerto Rico to recruit cane field labor. The plantation system introduced into Hawaii in the nineteenth century demanded a dependable labor supply and part of native resistance to conquest was a refusal to work under harsh conditions. As an alternative, foreign workers were recruited. The first big wave consisted of Chinese; the second of Japanese; the third of Filipinos and smaller groups of Portuguese, and later Puerto Ricans, Koreans, Spaniards, and Russians followed. For this trip, over a thousand Puerto Ricans were recruited. . . .

The recruitment of several hundred Puerto Rican men and women for domestic and foundry work in Chicago created a storm of controversy. By the middle of 1946, a private Chicago Employment Agency, Castle, Barton, and Associates, in agreement with the Insular Department of Labor, established an office on the Island for the purpose of recruiting migrant workers for the Chicago area. Two types of work were offered: general household service and unskilled foundry work. The employment agency offered contracts which guaranteed a full year of work.

In a report issued in November of 1946, the problems of the workers contracted for work in Chicago were brought out. The Department of Labor did not require proof of age and several of the girls were under sixteen. Many of the workers were allowed to leave without health certificates and some were later returned after failing to pass health examinations given by the Chicago Hardware Foundry Company. The report noted that the Department of Labor undertook no responsibility for supervising conditions under the contracts. The Commissioner of Labor visited the men at the Chicago Hardware Foundry Company and was aware of the conditions there. When forty-six of the men wrote to him complaining of the conditions, he replied that they had entered into the contracts voluntarily and that the Department of Labor would take action only in case of explicit violation of the contracts.

The workers were transported to Chicago in cargo planes. They were charged $150 for the trip and $60 for agency fees. The girls were charged half this amount, with the remainder being paid by the employer. The regular passage rate from San Juan to Chicago at that time was $131.80 and no tax was paid if the tickets were purchased in Puerto Rico. The workers were allowed only twenty pounds of luggage while on regular passenger flights fifty-five pounds were allowed. . . .

The contract provided that the girls received $60 per month as well as room and board. From this was deducted $10 per month to pay for the girl's share of the trip from Puerto Rico and $8.33 toward the return trip. The wages paid the girls was substantially below the prevailing wage for similar work in Chicago. No limitations were set in the contract for hours to be worked and some girls complained of working at least fifteen hours per day. The agency would transfer girls from one employer to another without explanation and sometimes with less than a day's notice. At least eighteen girls at the time of the report were unable to continue under these conditions and had broken their contracts and left their employer.

The foundry workers received $.88 per ½ hour with time and a half for overtime over forty hours a week. This was the rate established for common labor by the contract between the Chicago Hardware Foundry Company and the United Steelworkers of America. After the many deductions, though, a standard paycheck of $35.40 would shrink for some of the workers down to one dollar for a week's work.

The men were housed in four old passenger coaches on company property. Three of the coaches were wooden and were heated by coal stoves placed six inches from uninsulated walls. Two lightweight blankets were provided for each man and most of the men lacked warm clothing. When the men first arrived, their food consisted of cornflakes and milk for breakfast, soup and three slices of bread for lunch and three slices of bread for dinner. A one-day strike protesting the food resulted in some improvements. Men who were injured or ill were charged for their full living expenses and one man who injured his back was hospitalized for seven days and informed later that his hospital bills amounted to one hundred dollars and would be deducted from his wages. The case was investigated by the United Steel Workers of America to determine whether the Illinois Workmen's Compensation Act had been violated.

The condition of the Chicago workers was carried in the Puerto Rican newspapers. There were charges of mistreatment from some quarters and justification from the recruiting agency. Sen. Vicente Géigal Polanco went to Chicago at the behest of Múñoz Marín, then President of the Puerto Rican Senate, to get a first-hand account of this episode. As a result, legislation was drafted which tried to curb the worst abuses of the contract labor system.

Source: Excerpts from Maldonado, Edwin. "Contract Labor and the Origins of Puerto Rican Communities in the United States." *International Migration Review* XIII (1979): 103–114.

Jesús Colón, *How to Know the Puerto Ricans* (1982)

Puerto Ricans produced an incredible number of intellectuals during the postwar period. Jesús Colón (1901–1974), born in Cayey, Puerto Rico, is known as the Father of the Nuyorican Movement, a group of Puerto Rican poets, musicians, and artists who lived in New York

City. Like so many early intellectuals, he had links to the cigar industry. On the island of Puerto Rico, he was hired as a lector to read stories and articles about current events to the workers. This occupation educated and politicized Colón, who became a socialist. Migrating to New York, he got involved with left-wing politics and wrote a column for The Daily Worker. *His best-known work is* A Puerto Rican in New York, *which describes New York and the Puerto Rican community during the post–World War II years. The following excerpt from How to Know the Puerto Ricans is a humorous account of how to recognize a Puerto Rican in New York.*

One of the questions that we are most frequently asked is: "How can I get to the Puerto Ricans?" This is not a strange question to ask in a city like greater New York with more than 600,000 Puerto Ricans living, working, and struggling along with the rest of our city's inhabitants. This is a question that is crying for a correct answer, not only in our city, but in many other great cities throughout the nation where the Puerto Ricans have gone to live.

We have to admit from the start that we have no complete answer to open the door to the Puerto Ricans' houses, minds, and hearts. We have to confess that every day we are adding to that answer by our personal experience, by our going around with our American friends or by listening to what others have done—or have failed to do—in winning entrance to a Puerto Rican home and from there, to their confidence, friendship, and love. This, of course, is something that cannot be gotten in one day or in a number of weeks. Sometimes it takes months. Sometimes it takes years.

So, please excuse us if, in presenting what we have learned ourselves or added to our knowledge from the experience of others, we might sound at times a little critical, preachy, or even sermonizing. The theme lends itself to committing such errors.

The first thing we must realize is that the Puerto Ricans have been exploited for hundreds of years. That strangers have been knocking at the door of the Puerto Rican nation for centuries, always in search of something, to get something, or to take away something from Puerto Ricans. This has been done many times with the forceful and openly criminal way of the pirate.

Pirates with such tragically "illustrious" names as Cumberland and Drake. In one of those pirates' assaults around the middle of the seventeenth century, the bells of the cathedral in San Juan, Puerto Rico, were stolen and sold by one of their buccaneer ships in a little town known as New Amsterdam, just being built along the shores of the Hudson River.

So, in the words of one of my Puerto Rican friends, when one of those 200 percent Americans asks us why do Puerto Ricans have to come to New York? We can answer: "We come to take back our bells."

After the Spanish grandees, the French and English pirates and many others came to deprive us of whatever of value we have in our Puerto Rican land. Many came with the iron fist often hidden in the velvet glove. Many with the unctuous "love" and missionary ways of the do-gooders who come to "help" us. And we always had to listen to the chant that what was being done was "for our own good." Then came the imperialists: the pirates of the "American Century."

So when you come to knock at the door of a Puerto Rican home you will be encountered by this feeling in the Puerto Rican sometimes unconscious in himself—of having been taken for a ride for centuries. He senses that 99 persons out of 100 knock at his door because they want something from him and not because they desire to be his friend—a friend solving mutual problems that affect them both.

That is why you must come many times to that door. You must prove yourself a friend, a worker who is also being oppressed by the same forces that keep the Puerto Rican down. Only then will the Puerto Rican open his heart to you. Only then will he ask you to have a cup of black coffee with him in his own kitchen.

Before you come to understand a person, to deserve a people's love, you must know them. You must learn to appreciate their history, their culture, their values, their aspirations for human advancement and freedom.

There is much you can learn by speaking to the Puerto Ricans every time you get a chance at work or in the casual contact of everyday life.

We must always be ready to learn from the colonial people. They have much to teach. We do not have to elaborate the point to readers of this column. Their grueling struggle against economic, political, and social oppression has steeled the colonial world and taught its people many a way to combat imperialism and war. We colonial people have also much to learn from the working class of the imperialist countries. But if you want to open that door, don't assume a know-it-all attitude and superior airs just because you were born in the United States. This "superiority" attitude of the imperialist exploiters is unfortunately reflected sometimes in the less developed members of our own working class.

You can acquire much information by reading what is published about the Puerto Ricans in our papers and in the progressive weekly and monthly publications. There are some books with much valuable factual information and many incorrect conclusions. We have to be careful about such books.

Source: How to Know the Puerto Ricans by Jesús Colón. International Publishers, 2nd ed. (June 1982).

Mexican Americans, World War II, and the Aftermath

Felipe Valdés Leál, "El Soldado Raso" (1943)

"El Soldado Raso" ("The Buck Private"), *a popular song during World War II, was often sung nostalgically by young Mexican American soldiers as they went into battle. It was recorded by popular Mexican singer Pedro Infante (1917–1957) in 1943. The song asks the* Virgén Morena *(the brown Virgin Mary), to take care of the soldiers' mothers while they are at war. If they die, it should be remembered that Mexicans are brave and are not afraid to die. The song is ironic because while the soldiers were risking their lives fighting for democracy in Europe and the Pacific, many Mexicans in the United States went to segregated schools, could not eat at certain white-only diners, and could only swim in pools on days that were not reserved for white people.*

BUCK PRIVATE (EL SOLDADO RASO)

I am going as a buck private,
I am going to the front lines
with brave boys
who leave beloved mothers,
who leave sweethearts crying.
Crying on their farewell.
I am leaving for the war content,
I got my rifle and pistol,
I'll return as a sergeant
when this combat is over;
The only thing I regret:
leaving my mother alone.
Brown Virgin,
send me your blessing,
never allow
heaven to steal her from me
My lovely Guadalupe
will protect my flag
and when I find myself in combat,
far away from my land,
I will prove that my race
knows how to die anywhere.
I leave early tomorrow
as the light of day shines
here goes another Mexican
who knows how to gamble his life,
that gives his farewell singing:
singing to his motherland.
Brown Virgin,
I entrust my mother;
take care of her she is so good,
take care of her while I'm away.

Source: Acuña, Rodolfo F. *Occupied America: A History of Chicanos*. Translated by Guadalupe Compeán. New York: Longman, 2000, 265.

Isabel González, "Step-Children of a Nation: The Status of Mexican-Americans" (1947)

Although historically there have been virulent anti-immigrant groups in the United States, there have also been organizations that have sought to protect immigrants. For instance, settlement houses were set up in northern cities to help African American immigrants adjust to cities. In 1889, Hull House in Chicago was the first settlement house for immigrants. The Quakers founded the American Friends Service Committee in 1917, and to this day the organization is involved with protecting immigrants. After World War I, antiforeign sentiments grew to hysterical proportions as the Russian Revolution transformed Russia into a communist state. The Great Depression fanned nativism, and many activists in the United States were threatened with deportation. Roger Baldwin (1884–1981), of the American Civil Liberties Union initiated the American Committee for Protection of Foreign Born (ACPFB) (1933–1982) to defend the rights of immigrants. Some members of the committee were communists, others were not. Central to these groups was the protection of constitutional rights regardless of race, color, nationality, and creed.

The end of World War II saw a resurgence of anti-immigrant hysteria. Many labor union leaders were threatened with deportation, among them Mexican American and Latino organizers. Much of the hysteria was fueled by the Cold War. The enormity of the Mexican repatriations of the 1930s weighed on the minds of many pro-immigrant groups that established chapters in such places as Los Angeles, where there was a huge Mexican population. At the federal level, antiunion and anti-immigrant laws were passed, such as the McCarran Internal Security Act (1950) and the McCarran-Walter Immigration Act (1952), which the ACPFB fought. Because of this, the committee was placed on the U.S. attorney general's subversive list, and its tax-exempt status was revoked. In the 1950s, much of its work revolved around the protection of Mexican immigrants. The following excerpt is from an ACPFB pamphlet authored by Isabel González of Colorado; the pamphlet talks about deportations brought against Mexican American union leaders for union activities.

There are approximately five million people of Mexican origin in the United States. Of these, some three and one half million are American citizens who live principally in the West and Southwest. The other million and a half are non-citizens, and constitute the largest group of non-citizens in the country.

Why is it that so many Mexicans in the United States have failed to become citizens? Is it because they do not wish to enjoy the privileges of citizenship; or is it because they do not feel a loyalty to the United States; or is it because, as some say, the Mexican people are too ignorant to meet the qualifications for citizenship?

Could it be, however, that obstacles are placed in the way of Mexicans who seek citizenship; or could it be because their depressed status of the Mexican people as non-citizens bears profits for certain economic interests? Could it be also that the U.S. Government has helped some economic interests in their search for cheap labor to lure Mexicans into this country only to suppress and terrorize them once they are here?

Anyone who has tried to assist a Mexican immigrant in the preliminaries to citizenship is well aware of the difficulties involved. It is no accident that the bulk of naturalized citizens in the U.S. are those who entered after 1924, when regulations for entry were enforced and some sort of orderly accounting maintained. A large number of quasi-immigrants who remain unnaturalized, even though they have spent their lives in the U.S. and speak perfect English, quite frankly admit that they remain alien because they have neither the finances nor the courage to tackle the job of proving that they entered legally. Even the older immigrant, after he has given you all the customary reasons about having a "hard head" for the learning of English and history, is likely to settle on the difficulty of proving entry as the main deterrent. They often remember some "paisano" who tried to become a citizen and will tell you: "Look at Juan Martínez. He was going to be a citizen. And where is he now? Back in Juarez and his wife and children starving here."

Humberto Silex, of El Paso, Texas, former regional director of the International Union of Mine, Mill and Smelter Workers of America, CIO, is a leader of the Mexican American people of the Southwest. He has devoted his life to advancing the economic status of Mexican Americans, seeking to eliminate discrimination and defending their democratic rights as residents and citizens of the United States. Born in Nicaragua in 1902, Humberto Silex entered the United States legally in 1920. He is married to a legally resident alien of Mexican birth and is the father of seven American-born children. In 1946, the Department of Justice attempted to deport Mr. Silex on the basis of a 30-minute visit he made to Mexico for lunch one day in 1945. The attempt to deport Humberto Silex was defeated. Now the Justice Department is trying to prevent Mr. Silex's naturalization, for which he filed in 1942. Hearings on Mr. Silex's petition for citizenship were held in the Federal District Court in El Paso, Texas, on October 9, 1947, and a decision is expected shortly.

Refugio Ramón Martínez, of Chicago is a member of the staff of the United Packinghouse Workers of America, CIO. Born in Mexico in 1903, Mr. Martínez entered the United States legally in 1924. He is married to an American citizen and is the father of two American-born children. In 1947, the Justice Department started deportation proceedings against Mr. Martínez on the ground that, from 1932 to 1934, he was a member of the Communist Party of the United States. (More than 100 other legally resident non-citizens face deportation on this same charge.) A test case will be taken to the United States Supreme Court, which has never ruled on this question. We maintain that non-citizens are entitled to the protection of the Bill of Rights, to freedom of speech and belief, and cannot be deported because of their political opinions. After he was ordered deported, Mr. Martínez requested that the hearings in his case be reopened since he was not represented by counsel at his original hearings. No date has as yet been set for the new hearings. The 1947 National Convention of the United Packinghouse Workers of America pledged full support to Mr. Martínez in his fight against deportation. Jack Freeman, Chicago attorney, is representing Mr. Martínez in his deportation case. (Humberto Silex and Refugio Ramón Martínez are two of the more than 100 foreign-born Americans who are being defended by the American Committee for Protection of Foreign Born). Additional information concerning these cases—as well as ways in which you can help fight the attempt to deprive the foreign born of their constitutional and democratic rights—can be obtained by writing to the American Committee for Protection of Foreign Born, 23 West 26th Street, New York 10, N.Y.

Source: Gonzalez, Isabel. *Step-Children of a Nation: The Status of Mexican-Americans.* New York: American Committee for the Protection of Foreign Born, 1947, 3, 12–14.

"Election of Roybal—Democracy at Work," from Remarks of Representative Chet Holifield in the House of Representatives

(1949)

The Community Service Organization (CSO) began organizing in Boyle Heights, California, in 1947. the group worked for immigrants' rights and against police brutality, conducted leadership training, and encouraged voter participation. The CSO spearheaded voter registration drives that led to the 1949 election of Edward Roybal (1916–2005) to the Los Angeles City Council. Roybal initially ran for this position in 1947, but he came in third. In 1949, Roybal ran again, becoming the first Mexican American since 1887 to win a seat on the Los Angeles City Council. The CSO had chapters throughout California and trained such organizers as Dolores Huerta (1930–), César Chávez (1927–1993), and Tony Rios (1925–1999). Roybal became a legendary figure in Mexican American politics. The following excerpt is from comments made before the House of Representatives by California Democratic party representative Chet Holifield (1903–1995), in whose congressional district the grassroots election of Roybal to the Los Angeles City Council took place. Roybal's election gave hope to the Mexican American World War II GI generation that they would see an end to racial injustices.

Congressional Record

Proceedings and Debates of the 81st Congress, First Session

Extension of Remarks of Hon. Chet Holifield of California in the House of Representatives

Tuesday, August 9, 1949

Mr. Holifield: Mr. Speaker, it is not commonly known, but within the city of Los Angeles and its immediate environs is located the second greatest Mexican American population center in the world. Mexico City, Mexico, is the No. 1 population area in this respect.

We are proud of the contribution which American citizens of Spanish and Mexican descent have made to the cultural, social, educational, and political life of our community. Within my congressional district many thousands of these good citizens reside. One group in my district which has organized and achieved a highly respected position among my constituents is the Community Service Organization. I want to compliment them on the active leadership they are taking in assisting their fellow citizens integrate themselves into every phase of our community.

In the recent Los Angeles City councilmanic elections, one of our highly respected American citizens of Mexican ancestry, Edward R. Roybal, was elected to the important position of city councilman of the Ninth District, which is located in my congressional district.

Mr. Roybal was supported not only by Spanish-speaking citizens but by other good American citizens of Jewish, Negro, Japanese, Italian, and Philippine descent. In fact, people of all races and religions joined together to elect this fine young man to one of our most respected civic positions.

The election of Edward R. Roybal proves that the people of my district respect the intrinsic worth of the individual; it also proves that the majority of the people of my district are willing to rise above the prejudice, intolerance, and bigotry which precludes an individual from leadership because of his racial origin or his religious affiliation.

I am proud that the people of my district really believe in democracy. I am proud that they have demonstrated their belief by joining together and electing this worthy young man to public office. I am confident that Edward R. Roybal will acquit himself with great honor to the citizens of all races and religions, who have shown their trust and confidence in him by electing him to this position of leadership in our community.

Mr. Speaker, under leave to extend my remarks, I include in the Record, an editorial which appeared in the *Los Angeles Daily News* of July 1, 1949, on the subject matter of my remarks:

THE LATIN ONE-EIGHTH

Today something new is being added to Los Angeles' city government.

When Edward R. Roybal takes office today as Ninth District city councilman, he becomes the first local citizen of Mexican-American ancestry to win councilmanic stature in more than 70 years.

Roybal's election also says that after nearly a century of civic silence, Los Angeles' Spanish-speaking citizens—who constitute the city's numerically biggest minority—have raised their voices clearly and unmistakably. The estimated 250,000 residents of Mexican American descent—those who comprise the Latin one-eighth of metropolitan Los Angeles and make it the largest Spanish-speaking city outside of Mexico—are learning to make use of the most effective channel open to democracy's cultural minorities—the ballot. Through this channel they may succeed in drawing the attention of the rest of the community to the needs of their neglected neighborhoods.

More importantly, the rising political consciousness of this Latin one-eighth promises the beginnings of a valuable bridge-building job.

During the modern years of Los Angeles' emergence as the third city of the Nation, a gulf has separated most Mexican American citizens from the rest of the community. This gulf has been caused by many things: by language, by custom, by educational and economic factors. It's a gulf that isn't going to be bridged overnight. But a start toward bridging it at its most strategic point can be made and is being made at the precinct polling place. For it is here citizens begin to achieve social recognition and municipal attention on a par with that accorded other segments of the population. It is here citizens start to become responsible coparticipators in the life stream of the community and Nation.

What happened May 31 in Los Angeles' populous East Side ninth councilmanic district was no accident. Councilman Roybal received more than 20,000 out of a total of approximately 35,000 votes cast because 2 years ago a civic-minded group known as the Community Service Organization set about to accomplish a task of social engineering among residents of the East Side. In 6 months' time prior to the 1948 elections, the community service group registered 15,000 Spanish-speaking residents and many other thousands from the Jewish, Negro, Japanese American, Italian, Filipino, and Anglo neighborhoods of Los Angeles' most cosmopolitan area. What followed was a great upsurge of intergroup cooperation which rolled up a total of 138,132 votes for Richard Ibañez as candidate for judge of Superior Court Office No. 2 and gave to José Chávez nearly quadruple the 1946 votes cast for him in the fifty-first assembly district contest. Neither candidate was elected; but the way was paved, nevertheless, for strengthened future effort, as the Roybal election testifies. On May 31, 1949, the Ninth District registered 7 percent more votes than any other district in the city.

The Community Service Organization is the local project of the Chicago-founded Industrial Areas Foundation [IAF]. Established 10 years ago in the stockyards neighborhood by Bishop Shiel, head of Chicago's Catholic Charities, and G. Howland Shaw, former Assistant Secretary of State, the foundation went to work with adults in slum communities to solve the problems of juvenile delinquency. Most notable IAF innovation was the Back-of-the-Yards Neighborhood Council, a small, tightly knit citizens' group dedicated to neighborhood improvement.

In East Side Los Angeles, the community service people are furthering the Back-of-the-Yards objectives. And they seem to be proving, by orderly, democratic methods, that it's possible for any people, regardless of race, religion, or national origin to tear down the ripped and twisted remnants of the old barbed barriers of hostility and prejudice, walling off citizens of various religious and ethnic backgrounds—proving it's possible for people to go forth arm in arm and become sharing partners in all the manifold, rich experiences that make up the thing we call the democratic process.

Yes, something new has been added to Los Angeles' civic life. The municipal household has a brighter, more up-to-date look. And the local precedents shattered by Roybal's election indicate democracy is stepping steadily forward on the home front—that the distance of caste and culture is shrinking to fit the shrunken world.

Source: Congressional Record, Proceedings and Debates of the 81st Cong., 1st Sess.

Los Angeles Times, "Texans Combat Red Propaganda" (1950)

Half of the 2,000-mile border with Mexico was along Texas. Discrimination was so bad there that in 1943 Texas governor Coke R. Stevenson (1888–1975) established a Good Neighbor Commission to monitor and ameliorate the abuses. The reason for the commission was Mexico's refusal to send braceros *(guest workers) to Texas and the damage that refusal was doing to the image of U.S. democracy. Mexico lifted the ban in 1945 but abuses continued and the commission continued to try to ameliorate conditions. Some Texans blamed communists for stirring up trouble. This article from the* Los Angeles Times *talks about the continuing racism toward Mexicans in Texas and indicates the growing militancy of the Mexican American community in fighting for their rights.*

AUSTIN, Tex., Sept. 30 (AP)—Joe Márquez and Roberto Robles had had a long trip from Chihuahua City, Mex., to the cotton farm in Central Texas.

At 4 o'clock they wanted to quit and cook supper. The farmer wanted them to stay and pick a few more pounds to make full bale of cotton. They could not make themselves understood nor could they understand the farmer.

Roberto got excited and got close to the farmer's face. The farmer got excited, too, and grabbed hold of Roberto's shirt.

The story came out in a Mexican paper under the headline "Mexicans Are Treated Like Animals in Texas."

The Texas Good Neighbor Commission saw the story. They asked a man in the community who spoke Spanish fluently to see what it was all about. . . .

They were just tired after their trip from Chihuahua and could not make themselves understood. They are making about $10 a day picking cotton and are sorry about the whole misunderstanding. . . .

"We have no way of proving such stories are Communist inspired," said Neville Penrose, Ft. Worth oilman who is chairman of the Texas Good Neighbor Commission.

"We do know that Communist elements in the Mexican press play up cases of discrimination out of all proportion to the original incident." . . .

Source: "Texans Combat Red Propaganda." *Los Angeles Times*, October 1, 1950, A26.

Carey McWilliams, "Nervous Los Angeles" (1950)

Carey McWilliams (1905–1980) was best known for his strong commitment to progressive causes. He wrote the first history on Mexicans in the United States, titled North from Mexico *(1949), and wrote extensively about social issues in California. McWilliams headed the Sleepy Lagoon Committee, which protected 22 Mexican American youths who were unjustly indicted for murder. He also wrote about the condition of migrant farm workers and the internment of Japanese Americans. McWilliams edited* The Nation *magazine from 1951 to 1975 and wrote numerous muckraking books on agriculture. In the 1950s, McWilliams grew concerned when anti-Mexican hysteria was renewed in Los Angeles, where newspapers whipped up their readers with stories about Mexican American hoodlums and stereotyped Mexican youths as gang members who traveled in "wolf packs." Reproduced here are excerpts from an article that appeared in* The Nation.

I. THE "WOLF-PACK" CRUSADE

Los Angeles, May 24

The Los Angeles press has launched another of its lurid campaigns against juvenile "hoodlums," with special emphasis on Mexican American delinquents. These "crusades" are always started when there is a dearth of sensational local news and when racial tensions have predisposed people to hunt for scapegoats. The agitation whipped up in 1942 reached such a pitch of intensity that the Coordinator of Inter-American Affairs sent emissaries to plead with the press to stop featuring Mexican names in "crime" news. The press was most accommodating: thereafter Mexican Americans were simply identified as "pachucos" and "Zoot Suiters," and a year later Los Angeles was disgraced by the ugly Zoot Suit riots.

In any given period, a certain number of acts of juvenile hoodlumism will be committed in a city the size of Los Angeles. It is always possible, therefore, to make it appear that juvenile crime has shown a spectacular increase simply by beginning to feature reports of it. In the middle of April, the local press began to carry stories of gang assaults. But "gangs" are a rather thread-bare phenomenon. And so they soon became predatory "packs" striking down their victims in dark alleyways and unlighted parking lots. Each newspaper used its own special formula. One showed savage cartoons of "wolf packs," with the foam of madness dripping from their fangs; another invented the term "rat packs," and described bedraggled boys who fought like "rats" and possessed other "rat-like" characteristics: You would have imagined that a hundred or more juvenile rowdies had organized an attack on the community. In point of fact, the community had organized an attack on the youthful gangs by means of slanted news stories, "let's-not-be-soft" editorials, and news photographs which showed all too clearly excellent police cooperation in obtaining shots calculated to arouse public feeling.

Of course the names of the youngsters arrested, and certainly of those whose pictures were displayed, just happened to suggest that juvenile delinquency is a Mexican American cultural trait. The press of Los Angeles, mindful of the unfortunate role that it played in the Zoot Suit riots of 1943, has not been guilty of designating the participants as Mexican Americans. But it has not hesitated to mention their Spanish names or to publish editorials headed "Hoodlumism Is Not a Racial Problem." By elaborately disclaiming any bias, these editorials have clearly implied that hoodlumism was identical with Mexican American status.

Particular arrests and incidents have been handled in an interesting fashion. For example, the *Los Angeles Daily News* of May 6 featured a story under the headline "12 Jailed in New Attacks of L.A. Rat Pack." The names of those arrested in the first incident described were all of Spanish origin. There is nothing improper about giving the names of individuals arrested by the police, but the same edition of the same paper carried another story, not quite so prominently featured, with the mild head: "Beverly Hills Boys Held in Vandalism." These little darlings had merely driven through the streets of Beverly Hills in a station wagon, shooting out the windows of sixteen store buildings with an air gun. When Beverly Hills boys indulge their destructive impulses, they are presented as "vandals"; when Mexican American boys commit similar acts they are "wolves" and "mad dogs" and "rats." Moreover, the Beverly Hills vandals were not identified by name but merely described as "over-privileged youths," and "sons of prominent families." By contrast the other boys were named and were indiscriminately labeled "warped-minded little weaklings," "rats who in typical fashion swarm out of hiding," and so on.

The cause of the current acts of juvenile delinquency is not mysterious. The youngsters of many underprivileged groups, always first to be hit by hard times, are beginning to feel the economic squeeze which has thrown 180,000 people out of work in Los Angeles. With their parents unemployed, they are painfully poor, and since they in turn find it increasingly difficult to get part-time jobs they swarm about the city streets with nothing to do, frustrated in all their desires. The epithets applied to them convey to these youngsters a perfectly clear suggestion of the way they are regarded by the dominant groups.

Like a person suffering from acute paranoid delusions, the community has picked up a club and knocked down a handy victim, and now complains bitterly that it has been attacked. The present outburst, however, is unique in a number of respects: the Mexican American community through the Community Service Organization has promptly and intelligently protested; at [least] one newspaper, the *Los Angeles Mirror*, has declined to join wolf pack; and Chet Huntley, KNX's influential and enlightened news commentator, has been doing a fine job in undercutting the press campaign.

Source: McWilliams, Carey. "Nervous Los Angeles," 570–571. Reprinted with permission from the June 10, 1950, issue of *The Nation*. http://www.thenation.com.

Lyle Saunders and Olen E. Leonard, *The Wetback in the Lower Rio Grande Valley of Texas* (1951)

By the 1950s, Americans had whipped themselves into a frenzy, crying that they had lost control of their borders and calling for massive deportation of Mexicans. Operation Wetback (1953–1955) began in California and Arizona and coordinated 1,075 Border Patrol agents along with state and local police agencies. The operation was headed by the commissioner of the Immigration and Naturalization Service, General Joseph May Swing (1894–1984), an appointee of President Dwight Eisenhower (1890–1969) and a crony of Ike's from his army days. Swing promised to get tough on the "wetbacks." In 1953, Attorney General Herbert Brownell Jr. (1904–1996),who was charged with protecting civil rights, suggested that shooting a couple of "wetbacks" would dissuade them from coming across the U.S. border. Between 1953 and 1955, more than 1 million Mexican Americans a year were deported, and many more were frightened into leaving. Mexican Americans denounced this as a reign of terror. The following excerpt from Lyle Saunders and Olen E. Leonard's study of undocumented workers in the Rio Grande River appeared a couple of years before the operation, and documents the building hysteria and varying points of view of the undocumented.

Once he has crossed the river, the wetback faces an uncertain future. What will happen to him is largely dependent on the kind of people he comes in contact with and what their attitudes toward him are. If he is very lucky, he will meet an employer who will hire him at wages much higher than he could earn in Mexico. He will work for a few months, regularly sending a share of his earnings to relatives or friends on the other side. And, in time, he will return to his own country, where he may live for six or eight months on his accumulated savings. If he is very unlucky, he will be apprehended almost immediately by U.S. Border Patrol Inspectors and taken to one of their detention stations in the Valley. There, he will be detained for a day, questioned, written up on official forms, and finally sent to Edinburg, where he will remain in the county jail until the next session of the District Court in Brownsville. There, if his bad luck holds, he may be sentenced to from sixty days to a year in a federal prison. If, on the other hand, his luck is average, he will work a little while, earn a little money, enter into limited relationships with local citizens, and ultimately be permitted to return voluntarily to Mexico, neither much better nor much worse off for his experiences.

There are, in broad terms, four categories of people with whom the wetback is likely to come in contact. They are: employers, native Spanish-speaking people, Anglos in general, and public officials. That is to say that the kind of relationships established with anyone on this side of the river and the kind of treatment received by the wetback from any individual or group on this side will be determined largely by two sets of factors; the ethnic affiliation of the person or group with whom he interacts (i.e., whether they are "white" or "Mexican") and the nature of the relationships entered into (e.g., employer–employee, immigration official–alien; landlord–renter; storekeeper–customer, etc.). These four broad categories are not mutually exclusive, nor are they the only possible ones which might be used in describing the roles and attitudes and practices affecting the Spanish-speaking population of the Valley, both wetback and citizen. It enables the rationalization of the raw, sometimes vicious, sometimes paternal exploitation of wetback labor with the statement that "they never had it so good in Mexico"; it justifies the hiring of aliens in preference to citizens with the explanation that local citizens won't do agricultural work. It minimizes the often difficult position of the wetback by calling attention to great opportunities he enjoys there that presumably are not available to him in Mexico. It justifies the $2.00 and $2.50 a day wetbacks are paid in the Valley by comparing them to the five or ten pesos they might earn daily at home. It lends credence to the feeling that "A Mexican who has become Americanized is ruined" meaning that he then wants adequate wages, decent working conditions, and other privileges enjoyed by American citizens. It provides a reason for residential, recreational, and other types of segregation, and at the same time allows the admission to the select society of the "whites" of a few Spanish-speaking citizens whose membership in old families, business skills, economic standing, or ability to compete successfully are such as to make it difficult to group them with the wetback or "the lower class Meskins [pejorative distortion]."

The complete story of the development of Valley attitudes toward the wetback and the association of those attitudes with the native Spanish-speaking population would be long and difficult. Something of their general nature, however, can be depicted in an account of three fairly typical interviews on the matter in the Valley.

The first was with a Valley politician, a current member of the Texas legislature. His statement was as follows:

The local situation is not so bad. It works out to just about the best advantage of everyone. The farmers need labor; the wetbacks need work; and the local Spanish-speaking people have a gypsy spirit which makes them want to travel. They just can't resist going north each year, and it is fortunate that there are wetbacks around to take their place. Then, too, the local Spanish-speaking people are tending to leave agriculture. They don't like the hard work. They are beginning to want to get white-collar jobs. A few of them are going to school where they are being trained for non-agricultural work. So again, it is a good thing there are wetbacks around.

Relations in the Valley between English-speaking and Spanish-speaking people are good. The people eat together and visit together. They don't intermarry much. Although there is no discrimination in the Valley, of course there is segregation in a few things, but that is for hygienic, not racial reasons. Spanish-speaking people live in their own part of town and have their own businesses. They prefer it that way. They are excluded from swimming pools and barber shops. The exclusion from pools is because it is not possible to tell the clean ones from the dirty, so we just keep them all out. We just can't have all those dirty, possibly diseased people swimming with our wives and children. Recently a group of Mexicans here working on food-handling jobs were found to be suffering from syphilis. One had a leg that was just a mass of sores. Mexicans are excluded from barber shops because of the fact that some of them have lice in their hair or scalp diseases. Another resident whose attitudes reveal other aspects of the local stereotype of the Spanish-speaking group is quoted at length below. He is an employee of the Texas Employment Commission and has a Master's degree awarded on the basis of a thesis written on education in Mexico. This academic work and the fact that he had lived for 35 years in the Valley gave him, he thought, deep insight into the "nature" of the local people.

The Mexicans are creatures of impulse. They don't think with the cold, hard-headed logic of Anglos, but always act hastily in accordance with emotions and without considering consequences. Mentally they are all children. Oh, there are a few exceptions, of course, but I am talking about the lower class Mexicans. They have behind them five hundred years of burden bearing and animal-like living and just can't adjust to civilization in the way a white man does. They are extremely lazy and won't work, even for 50 or 60 cents an hour. The City of Edinburg has to hire wetbacks because it can't get citizens who will work steadily on the job. All the governmental agencies have to hire them (wetbacks) if they want to get any work done. Good Mexicans, however, are the best people in the world. They are hard working, docile, and very loyal. One of them will do anything for you. But the majority aren't worth much.

Mexican children don't get any training and they are allowed to do just about what they please. I've seen them in public places, doctors' offices, bus stations, and the like, where I wanted to get up and smack them one—kicking their parents, yelling, tearing things up, and the parents sitting calmly letting them do it. By the time they are twelve they all carry knives. They'll cut up anybody. They're just creatures of impulse. Human life doesn't mean a thing to them. Of course they're all cowards. Even a Mexican's dog won't attack a white man. By the time they're grown up something happens to them. They develop a strong loyalty to their family. If a man has six or seven kids working, he takes their pay and sits in the shade all day claiming he is "seek." That's what a Mexican lives for—to get a bunch of kids that he can put to work so that when they are ten or twelve he can retire. A grown man, even if he's married, has to ask his father's permission to do anything. And anyone of them is likely to quit a good job at any time just to come back and be with his family. They have no sense of responsibility. I (Texas Employment Commission) got twelve Edinburg boys jobs in a Boeing plant in California during the war. None of them had ever made $10 a week in his life before, and at Boeing they were paid $300 a month. But in a couple of months they were all back. Just because their mother got a cold or somebody in the family died they quit a good job and came running home.

The working class of Mexicans are all dirty. And they have a smell, a peculiar Mexican smell. Sometimes I have to back away from this counter they smell so bad. It hurts my nose if I stay close. It is a different smell from that of dirty Anglos or Negroes. It's a sort of sour, acid smell. A Negro, now, smells like a goat, but the Mexicans smell even worse. About 80% of them have lice in their hair, the women especially. They believe that lice help them have babies, and the one thing a Mexican woman lives for is to please her husband by presenting him with a baby every ten or eleven months. One of the main forms of recreation of Mexican women, especially those who live on farms or in small towns where there isn't much to do, is to sit around picking lice out of each other's hair. Sometimes when a Mexican woman is brought into the hospital at Edinburg, her friends or relatives smuggle in some lice to replace those the nurses take out of her hair when they clean her up.

Mexicans don't want to learn English and don't want their kids to know it. They keep the kids in school until they reach the third grade and then yank them out and put them to work. If a family has enough of them working, the father can retire and take things easy. They ought to be forced to learn English. We ought to have a law saying no one could work unless he learned English. Of course, those that do know English aren't much better off. They don't get any better jobs than the others.

Around here Mexicans get paid about 20% lower than whites for the same kind of work. They just have no sense of responsibility and can't do good work. They have to be supervised all the time. Housemaids get $10–$12 a week for about 48 hours. Some women pay less. And they have to watch the Mexicans all the time to see that the work is done right. Good Anglo secretaries get about $150–$250 a month; the average is around $167. Good Mexican secretaries, even those who have the advantage of being bilingual, get $100–$150. The difference lies in the fact that the Mexican girls just aren't capable of holding the better jobs.

A third illustration of the attitude of Valley Anglos toward "Mexicans" (whether alien or citizen) is a report of a conversation with a Valley farmer, a man who has owned a large acreage located west of Mission. Our research group had been his guests at dinner and afterwards we were discussing the perennial topic of conversation in the Valley—the wetbacks. Our host began:

The wetback comes into the Valley because the local people won't work. They're all inherently lazy and they just can't be persuaded to work, especially in agriculture. They lack initiative and ambition; they are content to go north and earn some money during the summer and then return here and live on it the rest of the year. They've been spoiled by too many advantages; too many welfare, educational, and other services. If you give a man something for nothing, you ruin him. And the local Mexicans know they can get services whether they work or not. As soon as you begin to Americanize a Mexican he's no longer any good. He just won't work any more.

Why is it, we asked, that all the people we see doing hard work in the Valley are Mexicans?

That's town work, he said, yard work, filling station work, construction work, and stuff like that.

But hard work, we asked, it is hard work, isn't it? Yes, but for that they get six or eight dollars a day.

Would they work in agriculture for six or eight dollars a day? They might.

What would they work for in agriculture? I don't think they'd work at any wage. Would they work for, say, $15 a day?

Yes.

Ten dollars a day? Yes. Eight dollars a day? Yes, they would. Five dollars a day? No.

Then they would work if the wages were from five to eight dollars a day?

No, they won't work in agriculture. We had a few working on our farm. They wouldn't do an honest day's work. When we leased the farm, the man we leased to had to let them go and get wetbacks. Wetbacks are good workers. We get a lot of them. Some of them have been with us for years. There are a couple of places on our farm where they cross over. They come by the hundreds. They've worn a sort of road up from the river. They come in a pitiful condition, with nothing, and we give them work at good wages, much better than they'd get in Mexico. I've got four boys working on my farm who have been with me for five years. Their home is about forty miles across the border and they go back every once in a while. But they always return. They're clearing a bit of land for themselves there. They're hard-working boys. And very dependable. One time their father came over. He told me that if his boys didn't do what they were told, just to let him know. We've got some other families on the farm that have been there a long time.

Source: Saunders, Lyle, and Olen E. Leonard. *The Wetback in the Lower Rio Grande Valley of Texas.* Austin: University of Texas, 1951, 65–69.

Patricio Morgan, *Shame of a Nation: A Documented Story of Police-State Terror against Mexican-Americans in the U.S.A.* (1954)

Passed in the McCarthy era of Cold War hysteria, the McCarran-Walter Act (1952) required all members of the American Communist Party, among other groups, to register with the attorney general. In 1950, Democratic senator Pat McCarran (1876–1954) of Nevada, who led the Senate Internal Security Subcommittee, sponsored the McCarran Internal Security Act. Association with groups that had been placed on a list of subversive organizations by the U.S. attorney general warranted placing the foreign-born under suspicion and surveillance. In 1952, McCarran joined Democratic congressman Francis Walter (1894–1963) from Pennsylvania to offer amendments to immigration laws. Although the bill ended blanket exclusion of immigrants based on race, it was insidious in other respects. Strict quotas were placed on immigrants from what were termed "undesirable" regions, such as Asia. Leftists were made special targets, and anyone with progressive ideas could be denied entry to the United States. Those already here were subject to summary deportation. Leftists, or those determined to have radical ideas, even if they were naturalized citizens, could be denaturalized and deported. President Harry S. Truman (1884–1972) vetoed the McCarran-Walter Act but it was passed over his veto. This excerpt from Patricio Morgan's A Documented Story of Police-State Terror Against Mexican-Americans in the U.S.A. *documents the campaign against Mexican Americans. Deportation proceedings were brought against labor activists, many of whom were Mexican Americans. They were pressured to inform on friends who were suspected of being leftist; even widows were pressured to inform the Federal Bureau of Investigation of their dead husbands' associates. The following excerpts provide narratives of a sampling of cases.*

These are the men, and women, the children who are exploited and mistreated by profit-greedy employers, who are haunted and hunted by U.S. authorities armed with the club of deportation, now reinforced by the onerous McCarran and Walter-McCarran Laws.

These laws have abolished the statute of limitations and create retroactive grounds for deportation, though the U.S. Constitution prohibits the making of such ex-post-facto laws.

These laws themselves legalize many of the practices used illegally for many years past against Mexican Americans by the Justice Department and its Immigration and Naturalization Service.

U.S. immigration officials, however, continue to disregard the few protections still maintained under the present laws, in their deportation moves against people of Mexican citizenship.

The Los Angeles Committee for Protection of Foreign Born, drafting a bill to remove these inequities, points out the special legislation is necessary to prohibit the lawless behavior, the terror, the police-state raids of U.S. immigration authorities against Mexican workers and their families.

Mrs. Josefina Yanez, executive secretary of the Committee's Eastside Branch, declared recently: "The role of the immigration authorities—their dragnet operations wherein they swoop down upon fields, factories and entire communities—is so well-known and feared in any Mexican community that the word[s] 'Los Federales' (the Federals) strikes terror not alone to the noncitizen but to Mexican American citizens of the first, second, and third generations."

Among the Mexican-born Americans now being defended against the McCarran Act deportation by the Los Angeles Committee [for Protection of Foreign Born], seven have been in this country for well over 40 years; three have lived in the United States for more than 30 years; three others have lived here over 20 years.

Seventeen have U.S.-born families, including sons, daughters, and grandchildren in every branch of the U.S. Armed Forces.

Twenty-two of them are trade unionists, members of the CIO Steelworkers Union, the AFL Laborers Union, CIO Packinghouse Workers Union, Independent International Longshoremen's and Warehousemen's Union, CIO Steelworkers Union, Railroad Brotherhood Unions, and others.

Steelworker, machine operator, packinghouse worker, tool grinder, railroad worker, furniture worker, sheet metal worker, moulder, shoe worker, laborer, fruit picker, fruit packer, agricultural worker: the roster of Los Angeles' Mexican-born deportees is adequate proof that the Walter-McCarran Law is aimed straight at the heart of American labor.

With this law, under pretext of hunting "illegals" and "subversives," immigration service officers serve as a terroristic police force in Mexican communities, as a strike-breaking, union-busting force in the fields, shops, and factories.

It is not easy, under the ever-changing U.S. immigration laws, to prove U.S. citizenship or legal permanent residence status. Not everyone has proof at hand, of his place of birth, or evidence of legal entry.

Furthermore, against those who have such evidence there still remains the charge, under the McCarran and Walter-McCarran Laws, of former membership in the Communist Party, the Workers Alliance and its Unemployed Councils of the early Depression '30s.

Proof of these ugly facts is shown in four typical case histories of Los Angeles' Mexican-born deportees:

Justo Cruz, 66, is a skilled machine operator in a Santa Ana County woolen mill. He came to the United States with his family as a young man of 19 years. His father and mother died here. His two children were born here. Justo Cruz helped build the railroads of this country; he worked in the fields and orchards, tilling and harvesting the million-dollar crops of the big U.S. growers.

In the 1933 Depression, when agricultural workers—if they found work at all—were paid as low as eight cents an hour, 75 cents for a sunrise to sundown day, Justo Cruz, with thousands of other impoverished workers, joined the Workers' Alliance.

Together with members of the Alliance's Unemployed Councils, Justo Cruz fought for relief for the jobless, against arrests and evictions, for the social security and unemployment insurance that is taken for granted by every U.S. worker today.

The Workers' Alliance (a product of the Depression '30s, no longer existent today) and other organizations which fought for jobs and to get living wages and working conditions; to end discrimination against minorities, including Mexican citizens and noncitizens, now have been declared "subversive" by the U.S. Attorney General. Membership, when Cruz and other workers joined the Alliance in the early '30s, was perfectly legal. Today, retroactively under the Walter-McCarran Law, it is a "crime," punishable by deportation if a noncitizen or a naturalized citizen; by fine and prison sentences if a U.S.-born citizen.

Acting under the Walter-McCarran Law and its predecessor, the McCarran Act, U.S. immigration officers first went to Cruz' employer and tried to get him fired from his job. His employer replied: "If business gets so bad that I have only two men working in the mill, one of them will be me. The other will be Justo Cruz."

Failing in this, the immigration department authorities arrested Cruz. He was taken to Terminal Island, the immigration department's Los Angeles detention center. There he was kept on $5,000 bail.

But Justo Cruz, and three others from Orange County arrested at the same time, had learned how to fight in those Depression years. As a member of the Orange County Community Chest in Santa Ana, as a member of the Mexican Festival Association and the Funeral Benefit Society in the Santa Ana Mexican community, Cruz had become known throughout California as a leader. He fought against segregation of Mexican children in the Orange County schools.

When his townsmen learned of his arrest, they rallied to free him. Together with the Los Angeles Committee for Protection of Foreign Born they managed to raise the staggering sum of $16,000 bail for Cruz and the other three victims.

The Committee's panel of lawyers fought through the hearings wherein the same U.S. Immigration Service whose officers had harassed, arrested, and imprisoned him now served as prosecutor, judge, and jury.

These officials scorned the facts of Cruz' long and honorable residence (45 years) in this country; his contributions to the U.S. as a hard working laborer and skilled workman. They ignored the hardship which Cruz' deportation would cause his two motherless U.S.-born children, both tubercular and depending for their very lives on their father's earnings and care.

Justo Cruz, on December 18, 1952, was ordered deported to Mexico. Delegations of trade unionists, nationality groups, and community leaders voiced protests and attorneys went to the U.S. Bureau of Immigration Appeals, fighting to win a stay of deportation.

Though again ordered to surrender for deportation on January 28, 1953, Justo Cruz is still here. Application for suspension of the deportation order now rests with Attorney General Herbert Brownell who has authority under the hardship clause of the Walter-McCarran Law to grant Cruz a permanent stay.

Hear now the story of Maria Cruz, widow of Jesus Cruz who was deported last year only to die in Mexico.

Mrs. Cruz, now 51, was brought with her mother and older sister to the U.S. by her father at the age of five and has lived here continuously. She is the mother of two children already made fatherless through deportation and death.

A son, Joseph, is one of our nation's heroes, who won the much-prized Oak Leaf Cluster as a U.S. Air Force gunner who distinguished himself in many hazardous missions over Germany in the thick of the fighting of World War II. Her second son, Carlos, 14, is in junior high school. Both are U.S.-born citizens.

Maria Cruz has broken no laws. She entered this country legally, paid the small crossing fee, and was registered with her mother and sister as required.

When the Walter-McCarran Act became law, she registered as demanded and, again meticulously obeying U.S. law, always carried her registration card with her.

When her registration card was stolen by a purse snatcher, as a law-abiding, legal resident, she reported it to the police and to immigration authorities.

When she asked for a substitute card, she was seized by the U.S. immigration authorities.

"Just a couple of questions, so that you can get your registration card back," they falsely told her.

Instead they questioned her, harassing her for three solid hours while exhibiting her dead husband's picture.

The questioning summed up to demands that she act as a stool pigeon against her own husband and against his friends and associates.

Four months later, Federal agents came to her home and arrested her. Only her well-decorated son's angry protests stopped a matron from the immigration office from inflicting further insults by searching her for "weapons and narcotics."

Maria Cruz, honorable, respected, legal and law abiding resident of the United States for the past 46 years, was held in Terminal Island on trumped up charges, including "illegal entry" and—a newly thought-up charge since her original questioning—"membership in the Communist Party."

This latter charge, it appeared from the questioning, was based on the fact that she had once belonged to the CIO Cannery Workers Union and had been active in that union in the early days of CIO organization in California.

While at Terminal Island, Mrs. Cruz—whose soft, dark eyes spark with anger at indignities against others, talked with penniless young Mexican women, who had come to seek jobs in this country and were being held for $500 bail by immigration authorities.

They told her of the rude, pawing hands of immigration officers in the corral at San Ysidro, hands which had insultingly "covered our whole bodies while the officers called us ugly, dirty names." No matron was on duty, they declared, at the border detention center.

She also talked to a Canadian woman, married to a U.S. citizen and who had lived here for 26 years. Her son is now serving in the U.S. Navy. Yet this woman, too, was held for deportation under terms of the Walter-McCarran Law.

Should Maria Cruz be deported, her U.S.-born sons would be orphaned, with the same alternative—exile from their land, the United States, the country that one brave son has heroically fought for.

Agapito Gomez, now 46, has lived in this country since he was 21. He worked for the Santa Fe and Southern Pacific Railroads as a section hand for the sum of 3½ cents per day, living in the miserable boxcar quarters that the multi-million dollar companies think good enough for thousands of Mexican workers that labor on their right-of-ways.

Later, he worked at grueling, back-breaking labor, picking celery, cabbage, and cauliflower on the fertile truck farms around Downey, Norwalk, Montebello, and Gardena. His pay was 10 cents an hour, $7.50 weekly.

Agapito Gomez believed he belonged here. He had a permit card showing permanent residence and the right to stay. His wife, Sophia, is U.S.-born, his two children, Georgia and Albert, were born here.

It was not easy to save on the $35 per week he made as a farm laborer in the costly war years of the early '40s. But Sophia and Agapito saved and stinted [zapping the stinted] and finally bought a little house. Later, by dint of more hard pinching, they bought another with a big yard for the children.

When, during World War II, the United States needed manpower and industry opened its doors to minority labor, Gomez went into a steel foundry. He became a crane helper and joined the union, the United Steelworkers of America, CIO.

Then came the McCarran Act. The witch hunt began. Honored families of the Southwest; permanent, legal residents; parents of U.S. native-born children were pilloried because they had once belonged to a relief organization or had joined in early efforts of the CIO to organize workers in field and factory.

Gomez was one of these. On December 17, 1951, two immigration service agents came to Agapito Gomez' Norwalk home. They wanted names: names of his fellow-unionists, names of organizations, and accounts of his past activities.

When Agapito Gomez refused to become an informer, they took away his prized permit card.

These men, sworn to uphold the Constitution and the country's laws, did not tell Gomez his rights, including the right against illegal search and seizure of property, and the basic right of counsel.

Nine months later, they returned. This time they arrested Gomez, took him to Terminal Island, held him on $500 bail. His wife appealed to the Los Angeles Committee for Protection of Foreign Born, which services deportees. Two days later, bail was obtained for his release.

The panel of attorneys which works with the Committee filed motions with the Bureau of Immigration Appeals and in the Federal Courts for a stay of the deportation order, pending court review.

On November 29, 1958, Gomez was again arrested and ordered to surrender for immediate deportation. Again, attorneys obtained a restraining order, this time in the Federal District Court in Washington, D.C. Agapito Gomez is now temporarily free on $1,000 bail, pending judicial review. Also living under threat of deportation and separation from his wife, his friends, and the land which he has called his own for over 40 years, is another Mexican trade unionist, José Noreiga.

Noreiga, now 57 years old, came to this country when he was 25.

As a construction worker in Texas and California and, later, as a longshoreman at the Los Angeles harbor, he learned the importance of unions to the worker. In 1928, Noreiga joined the longshore union, then the International Longshoremen's Association (ILA).

Arrested, with hundreds of other strikers in the maritime strike of 1923, Noreiga served a short jail sentence and, returning to the docks, found himself blacklisted.

He went to San Bernardino, worked in a packing shed and during the depths of the Depression was responsible for raising thousands of dollars in food contributions for needy workers and their families.

Noreiga returned to the docks in 1937, and again went on strike in the maritime struggle along the Pacific Coast which culminated in the formation of the International Longshoremen's and Warehousemen's Union (ILWU). During the war years, he continued maritime work as an active member of the Wilmington unit of Warehousemen's Local 26.

His harassment by immigration officers started in 1952, with interrogations at his home. A year later, his Coast Guard Port Security Pass was taken away, which meant that areas in which he could work were limited. In February of this year, he was arrested and held at Terminal Island detention center on $2,000 bail.

As with Justo Cruz, Mrs. Maria Cruz, Agapito Gomez, and many others, objectives of the immigration officers were made plain in the questioning of Noreiga.

His union activities; his work in the San Bernardino community among "Hooverville" dwellers, impoverished victims of the great Depression; the books he read, made him suspect with U.S. immigration officers. They even questioned the presence on his wall of a picture of the great Mexican liberator, Benito Juarez, who can be compared to Washington in our country.

Fellow-members of the Longshoremen's and Warehousemen's Union rallied to Noreiga's defense. A Jose Noreiga Defense Committee was formed in Local 26. Aim of this Committee was not alone to stop the deportation of fellow trade unionists, but to fight for total repeal of the Walter-McCarran Law.

Letters, speakers, appeals for funds for legal aid; delegations, petitions, and wired protests to the U.S. Immigration Service and to California congressmen, showed efforts of organized and continuing determination to stop deportations and to win for Noreiga and others the right to stay here.

The Los Angeles Committee for Protection of the Foreign Born, through its panel of attorneys, is also carrying the Noreiga case to the highest courts to prove that participation in union organization, in the Workers Alliance and political organizations of their choice which helped men fight for an extra pound of beans for their hungry children during the Depression is not a crime as Walter, McCarran, McCarthy and other police-state advocates profess.

On the contrary, such action is a privilege guaranteed by the United States Constitution to every resident of the U.S.

The terroristic raids, the wholesale arrests, the mass deportations of Mexican workers and their families in the United States today can be compared with only two other periods in U.S. history.

Source: Morgan, Patricio. *Shame of a Nation: A Documented Story of Police-State Terror against Mexican-Americans in the U.S.A.* Los Angeles: Los Angeles Committee for Protection of Foreign Born, 1954, 37–47.

Beatrice Griffith, *American Me* (1954)

American Me *describes the social life of Mexican Americans in the post–World War II era, particularly in Southern California. Beatrice Griffith was a social worker in the Mexican American community. In her book,* American Me, *she interweaves personal stories showing the shameful and ruthless exploitation of Mexican labor and the flagrant injustice, and discrimination Mexicans faced. The following is one of the stories from the book, which has long been out of print. The title,* American Me, *was also used by Mexican American actor and director Edward James Olmos in a 1992 film,* American Me, *about prison life. The significance of* American Me *is to remind people that Mexican Americans have been raised in the United States.*

We go every July from Los Angeles to pick the fruits in the summer hills of Hanford. We lived in tents and would get up early in the grey morning when it was cold. Then we all ate outdoors over a little fire. Everybody getting up from their tents and talking and calling to each other and cooking the beans. Then we go to work and stand on our feet from seven in the morning until six at night. Gee, man, I would get so tired. You know, in the fruits you dream, sleep, walk, breathe, and talk apricots yellow and big and soft all around you. You pick 'em, you dump 'em, you squash 'em, you peel 'em, you cut 'em, you count 'em. Everything is apricots. How many you pick? How many you peel? How much buckets or trays? Always it is to eat and smell apricots. 'Cause apricots is pennies and sometimes they are silver dollars after you pick them a long time. Now we get lots more money in the fruits 'cause there is a war, and now can go to the carnival with rich money like the boss of the ranch.

This day I tell you the boss came and paid the checks. Man, it was great. To all the working people and kids he paid them. My father and mother and me and my brother gots a hundred dollars for working three weeks, would you believe it? When I saw that check I told my mother she was fooling. The boss was just playing a game. But she said it was real money, and when I heard that I jumped up crazy I guess. I told her that check was a lot of school dresses. She said that in that check was a couch that made a bed at night for my father and brother who are tired to sleep on the little iron bed by the washing machine. And it was clothes for my brother and my father, and in it was a car. Would you believe it? A little broken car was in that check? And sure it was. Oh, I tell you, all was happy that night for getting money and lots clothes and food and stuff in that check.

At this camp was my new boy friend, Mokey. He was clean and handsome, not too tall—just right for me with a big smile and a handsome nose. He always looks like a movie actor in his Levis. And he walks with a swing real sure, like the Negro baseball player at school—who never hurries, just reaches out and grabs the ball so slow he count the stitches on them. It was Mokey who helped Freddie and my cousin Ramon fix a good shower for us when we got to camp. They took some rubber hose and put it up high, then spread branches to spray from the water. Then they made it private with boards, and we had a shower. Sure, there was a little hole down by our legs and the boys used to look in and sing and yell.

This night of getting paid was excitement, Jijola! All the kids call from the tents about going to the carnival near Fresno. My old aunt who remembers the little Jamaicas in Mexico, and who is with a young heart still, comes to our fire to talk over the war, and her boy who is a prisoner in Bataan, and the long fights and revolutions of the Mexicans, with my father. My aunt is a very beautiful woman with smooth brown skin and a proud face. She knows everything, all things in the heart of a girl. She had eight with five in the grave behind the adobe house on the hill. It is like all those dead girls were making her heart sweet with their wants of living in their dark graves. She brought my father a little bottle of her old, old wine this night, and he goes with her and my mother to sit by the fire, where others from the fields are sitting and eating under the trees in the night.

My cousin Ramon from Hanford has a little truck that's green and cute named Benito, that will take us to town. To get to this truck and Ramon, Mokey and me walk through the fields to the long dusty road. In the fields was sometimes little rabbits and birds, and there was always haystacks all bunched to jump on real quick and run. With Mokey, he loved those rabbits and sometimes would catch one and rub it soft on his face. Always it was like that. Sometimes he look at a little black fly, so careful how his wings is made, and his head put on by God. And he looks so long at the plants to see their little veins and how is a leaf put on that his sister tell him, "What you see in that plant, a picture of a pretty girl, a blondie maybe?" Then Mokey tell her to go lay an egg—and a big one.

Walking across the fields into the dark hills far away with Mokey was keen. He took my hand and said, "I wish Felix and Frankie could see this sky. Man, they knew this country, they worked this country."

"Mokey, you know lots, what makes wars anyway? All my brothers too are gone to war and they weren't mad at anybody—except the cops." I looked at him but he only shake his head.

"Lucy, I don't know. Sister at church says wars is from all the people's sins. But my mother says it's the big heads make 'em, and the little people slave 'em. I tell her, wars just don't happen. It's from the people bumping and pushing and getting mad at each other, I guess. Maybe they're afraid." He stopped and cut two sunflowers, then he stuck each one in my braids. "Now let's run, I'll race you to the truck," and so we did.

Inside the truck without much paint was lots [of] kids already. Everybody was happy and singing and calling to everybody, pushing and laughing. All the kids sit tight in the truck cause it goes to pieces lots of times and the sides all fall down. You always hit hard when you drive cause the tires go flat sometimes. Then Ramon and the boys stuff rags into the tires when they go flat so we ride lots of hitting together. Manuel, he's my cousin they call Jitterbug Sánchez, 'cause he's a good dancer, his picture is in the paper for the prize fight, well Manuel brings his good guitar to sing some ranchero songs and some songs for love. All sing "Soldados Rasos," and are happy for smiling and yelling, 'cause all are happy for living, I guess.

When we come onto the long highway that goes to Hanford this night I tell you about, two policemen in their white car stopped the truck because they see us Mexicans inside. But my cousin Ramon, who's been to high school and who is smart knowing all about maps and what means a filibuster and the United States Congress, says to that cop, "This is a free country ain't it? We can sing in this little truck if we want can't we? The man who says Mexicans can't sing for breaking the law in this truck doesn't know his country."

So the cops, seeing my cousin was smart said, "Oh, wise guy, huh?

"Okay, let's see your draft cards. All of you."

But only my cousin had a card from the draft, only he was eighteen.

The cops look hard at his draft card and then tell us, "Okay, cholos, go on,"

And so we go down the long bright highway into the streets of the town. Lots of people and kids were holding hands and walking down the streets. Little cars from the ranches and fruit camps passed us, some fast with only one light, some honking horns, but everybody was laughing and calling. Mokey waves his arms and says some dirty words to the car in back of us that gives us a big bump. The boys all pile out to look, then pile in again when they see it was nothing.

Pretty soon we come to the carnival. You know it's the place before you get there 'cause the music comes right through the trees and houses and into our truck. And you can see high up in the pink sky the Ferris wheel going swing around the stars. And the voice of the ticket man you can hear a little, just like the radio from the boss's house in the night on the ranch. Only sometimes you cannot hear it with the crickets, like it went around the posts and cars and barns to get to us who were listening.

At the carnival everything was excitement, and all the kids pile out. First thing I see is my cousin Danny. My cousin Danny, I tell you, was fun like Cantinflas in the Mexican movies.

The flying baskets with skirts and legs swinging in the sky stopped, and Mokey and me got in a gold basket. Adelita and Manuel sit in a red one, and soon the music begin and we are whizzing in the sky with all the stars falling around and down down to the ground. Then we jerked up high almost to a pink cloud, and Mokey held me tight, with the air whirring around us like a dive bomber. There was little screams coming from around like they was whistles that got stuck, but it was only the girls liking the hugging I think.

When we got out from the gold basket Mokey and me was still hugging like in the movies. All the peoples and tents and music and little screams was going around dancing in my head like a jitterbug. Up the streets some kids was riding on the merry-go-round and yelling and laughing to catch the gold ring from the horses and lions. Mokey and me watched Felix showing how strong he was from working and getting hard muscles in the hay fields that summer. He hit the wood block bang with the big hammer, and hit it so hard the little bell at the top in the dark would ring. The other guys was laughing and making fun of him showing off big for Theresa, him that didn't know she was going steady with two marines.

The tin woman in the next show was laughing too, but always she is laughing. Whenever you walk or ride in that carnival, or down the near streets, you hear her big laugh, in the night or day, you always hear it.

Across the carnival street, behind the wire fence, was the place where the little green and yellow and red automobiles go bump and crash around the big floor with music and fun. In one of the automobiles was an old man with red hair waving his arms and bumping the other autos like a borrachito. He had a white duck he won in the carnival and waved that duck over his head like a flag I think.

Pretty soon down the carnival street come all the kids singing and laughing and shouting. All their arms was around each other like a chain. In the middle was Danny with his arms full of Kewpie dolls.

Danny was always like the miracle man in the circus. Always he could go to a carnival with nothing but poor money, some pennies and nickels, and come home with hams and ducks and alarm clocks and Kewpies. Only never before tonight was there so many Kewpies.

He gave a Kewpie to Mokey for some tickets to ride the little automobiles. Then he yelled us, "Come on, let's have a race!"

We all piled in the cars, red, green, yellow—all the cars that was empty gets full. Danny put all his Kewpie dolls around him and piled some more in the other cars. Then the race began. Que suave! Man it was swell. My heart was pumping up and down like some jumping beans. I got scared bumping so many cars and my heart went black and my ears go clank . . . clank, but it was fun.

Danny banged my car, Mokey hit him, then Manuel and Adelita and Ramon and Rosie all was banging cars and yelling. Everybody got bumped, nobody got hurt and the music was loud like in the circus. The American kid bumped Mokey and laughed, and Mokey bumped him back. Then they was bumping, laughing and pushing, each car a little faster and a little harder. Pretty soon then the American guy looked away, and Mokey gave him a hard bump. Then they was getting mad for reals. The American kid called him, "Dirty Mexican, I'll fix you!"

Mokey tell him, "Who do you think you are, calling me dirty Mexican?"

The guy banged him hard and say, "Well, I'm me, American me. That's who I am!"

So Mokey banged him hard on the head with a pink Kewpie and yell him, "Yeah? Well I'm American me too. American inside, but Mexican on top!"

Danny throws a Kewpie to Mokey who jumps high in his car to catch it. Then all the kids begin to make trouble for purpose, all bunching and popping out of the cars to fight and hit. Danny throws us all his Kewpies, and the fight was on hard. The Kewpies was going over the cars hitting kids, busting on the floor with broken pieces getting smashed and run over. Everybody was mad with anger falling down and busting like a bomb in that place. The Kewpies was going zoom like big bullets. The cars was driving hard and spinning and bumping. Adelita's car she whirled in a circle, round and round. The air was thick and hot with kids. Some stand up in their cars the better to hit. The cars all jammed up in bunches. Everybody was all mixed up and tangled, hitting hard, zam the next one to him.

The manager or somebody cut off the electricity. Ramon yells, "Cops coming!"

Then it was a fight to get out that door with everybody running and tripping and getting socked. The American kids beat it out first, running through all the carnival people to where their cars was parked. We got in our truck, but before Ramon got the engine started everything was all mixed up again, with the American kids and us all yelling and hitting and pulling hair and getting socked. But we finally got going and drove bumping down the street by the popcorn man and the carnival people. Some of those kids was hanging on the truck but we banged their hands and they let go.

Ramon drove fast going down that big road in our truck. Danny turned off the lights so the cops wouldn't see our truck and we rode into the very night across the fields to the highway. Like Danny, Mokey's hands was bloody and his clothes was torn, and his breath was breathing hard—but he put his arms tight around me in that little ride.

It was quiet in the dark with the trees and fields and hills. Only could we hear the kids whispering and the car going fast like the wind, and the loud crazy laughing of the tin woman at the carnival following us down the road into the mist to our tents across the black fields.

Soon we would be in bed in our tents by the camp in the fruits, and I would put my head from under the tent and Mokey put his from his tent in the dark and stars, and we would talk and talk so long, our heads by the dark ground. All swell, until our mothers say, "Quit your talking and long gossip." And then we would go to sleep in the warm tent for morning to wake us to move on to pick the prunes.

But now, this little minute, I was sitting tight close to Mokey. I ask him, "Mokey, knowing about pushing and bumping and hating and all that, doesn't keep people from getting mad, huh?"

Mokey hugs me tighter. Then he kissed me soft soft, the first kiss.

For Mokey knows that to be a gentleman means always please the lady for what she wants.

Source: Griffith, Beatrice. *American Me*. New York: Pennant Books, 1954; Castaneda Shular, Antonia, Tomas Ybarra-Frausto, and Joseph Sommers, eds. *Literatura Chicana*. Englewood Cliffs, NJ: Prentice Hall, 1972, 250–255.

Octavio Paz, *The Labyrinth of Solitude: Life and Thought in Mexico* (1961)

Not everyone had a flattering opinion of Mexican American youth during the 1950s. At the extreme, European Americans saw the pachuco, *the Zoot Suiter, as a mongrel who was neither Mexican nor American. The* pachuco *was a grotesque image of Mexicans. The Nobel Prize laureate poet Octavio Paz (1914–1998) shows that white Americans were not the only people dealing in stereotypes. The following is an excerpt from Paz's* The Labyrinth of Solitude.

When I arrived in the United States I lived for a while in Los Angeles, a city inhabited by over a million persons of Mexican origin. At first sight, the visitor is surprised not only by the purity of the sky and the ugliness of the dispersed and ostentatious buildings, but also by the city's vaguely Mexican atmosphere, which cannot be captured in words or concepts. This Mexicanism—delight in decorations, carelessness and pomp, negligence, passion and reserve—floats in the air. I say "floats" because it never mixes or unites with the other world, the North American world based on precision and efficiency. It floats, without offering any opposition; it hovers, blown here and there by the wind, sometimes breaking up like a cloud, sometimes standing erect like a rising skyrocket. It creeps, it wrinkles, it expands and contracts; it sleeps or dreams; it is ragged but beautiful. It floats, never quite existing, never quite vanishing.

Something of the same sort characterizes the Mexicans you see in the streets. They have lived in the city for many years, wearing the same clothes and speaking the same language as the other inhabitants, and they feel ashamed of their origin; yet no one would mistake them for authentic North Americans. I refuse to believe that physical features are as important as is commonly thought. What distinguishes them, I think, is their furtive, restless air: they act like persons who are wearing disguises, who are afraid of a stranger's look because it could strip them and leave them stark naked. When you talk with them, you observe that their sensibilities are like a pendulum, but a pendulum that has lost its reason and swings violently and erratically back and forth. This spiritual condition, or lack of a spirit, has given birth to a type known as the pachuco. The pachucos are youths, for the most part of Mexican origin, who form gangs in Southern cities; they can be identified by their language and behavior as well as by the clothing they affect.

They are instinctive rebels, and North American racism has vented its wrath on them more than once. But the pachucos do not attempt to vindicate their race or the nationality of their forebears. Their attitude reveals an obstinate, almost fanatical will-to-be, but this will affirms nothing specific except their determination—it is an ambiguous one, as we will see—not to be like those around them. The pachuco does not want to become a Mexican again; at the same time he does not want to blend into the life of North America. His whole being is sheer negative impulse, a tangle of contradictions, an enigma. Even his very name is enigmatic: pachuco, a word of uncertain derivation, saying nothing and saying everything. It is a strange word with no definite meaning; or, to be more exact, it is charged like all popular creations with a diversity of meanings. Whether we like it or not, these persons are Mexicans, are one of the extremes at which the Mexican can arrive.

Since the pachuco cannot adapt himself to a civilization which, for its part, rejects him, he finds no answer to the hostility surrounding him except this angry affirmation of his personality. Other groups react differently. The Negroes, for example, oppressed by racial intolerance, try to "pass" as whites and thus enter society. They want to be like other people. The Mexicans have suffered a less violent rejection, but instead of attempting a problematical adjustment to society, the pachuco actually flaunts his differences. The purpose of his grotesque dandyism and anarchic behavior is not so much to point out the injustice and incapacity of a society that has failed to assimilate him as it is to demonstrate his personal will to remain different.

It is not important to examine the causes of this conflict, and even less so to ask whether or not it has a solution. There are minorities in many parts of the world who do not enjoy the same opportunities as the rest of the population. The important thing is this stubborn desire to be different, this anguished tension with which the lone Mexican—an orphan lacking both protectors and positive values—displays his differences. The pachuco has lost his whole inheritance: language, religion, customs, beliefs. He is left with only a body and a soul with which to confront the elements, defenseless against the stares of everyone. His disguise is a protection, but it also differentiates and isolates him: it both hides him and points him out.

His deliberately aesthetic clothing, whose significance is too obvious to require discussion, should not be mistaken for the outfit of a special group or sect. Pachuquismo is an open society, and this in a country full of cults and tribal costumes, all intended to satisfy the middle-class North American's desire to share in something more vital and solid than the abstract morality of the "American Way of Life." The clothing of the pachuco is not a uniform or a ritual attire. It is simply a fashion, and like all fashions it is based on novelty—the mother of death, as Leopardi said—and imitation.

Its novelty consists in its exaggeration. The pachuco carries fashion to its ultimate consequences and turns it into something aesthetic. One of the principles that rules in North American fashions is that clothing must be comfortable, and the pachuco, by changing ordinary apparel into art, makes it "impractical." Hence it negates the very principles of the model that inspired it. Hence: its aggressiveness.

This rebelliousness is only an empty gesture, because it is an exaggeration of the models against which he is trying to rebel, rather than a return to the dress of his forebears or the creation of a new style of his own. Eccentrics usually emphasize their decision to break away from society—either to form new and more tightly closed groups or to assert their individuality through their way of dressing. In the case of the pachuco there is an obvious ambiguity: his clothing spotlights and isolates him, but at the same time it pays homage to the society he is attempting to deny.

This duality is also expressed in another, perhaps profounder way: the pachuco is an impassive and sinister clown whose purpose is to cause terror instead of laughter. His sadistic attitude is allied with a desire for self-abasement which in my opinion constitutes the very foundation of his character: he knows that it is dangerous to stand out and that his behavior irritates society, but nevertheless he seeks and attracts persecution and scandal. It is the only way he can establish a more vital relationship with the society he is antagonizing. As a victim, he can occupy a place in the world that previously had ignored him; as a delinquent, he can become one of its wicked heroes.

I believe that the North American's irritation results from his seeing the pachuco as a mythological figure and therefore, in effect, a danger. His dangerousness lies in his singularity. Everyone agrees in finding something hybrid about him, something disturbing and fascinating. He is surrounded by an aura of ambivalent notions: his singularity seems to be nourished by powers that are alternately evil and beneficent. Some people credit him with unusual erotic prowess; others consider him perverted but still aggressive. He is a symbol of love and joy or horror and loathing, an embodiment of liberty, of disorder, of the forbidden. He is someone who ought to be destroyed; [he] is also someone with whom any contact must be made in secret, in the darkness.

The pachuco is impassive and contemptuous, allowing all eight contradictory impressions to accumulate around him until finally, with a certain painful satisfaction, he sees them explode a tavern fight or a raid by the police or a riot. And then, in suffering persecution, he becomes his true self, his supremely naked self, as a pariah, a man who belongs nowhere. The circle began with provocation has completed itself and he is [ready] now for redemption, for his entrance into the society that rejected him. He has been its sin and its scandal, but now that he is a victim it recognizes him at last for what he really is: its product, its son. At last he has found new parents.

The pachuco tries to enter North American society in secret daring ways, but he impedes his own efforts. Having been off from his traditional culture, he asserts himself for a [moment] as a solitary and challenging figure. He denies both society from which he originated and that of North America. When he thrusts himself outward, it is not to unite with what binds him but rather to defy it. This is a suicidal gesture because the pachuco does not affirm or defend anything except his exasperated will-not-to-be. He is not divulging his most intimate feelings: he is revealing an ulcer, exhibiting a wound. And that is also a grotesque, capricious, barbaric adornment. A wound that laughs at itself and decks itself out for the hunt. The pachuco is the prey of society, but instead of hiding he adorns himself to attract the hunter's attention. Persecution redeems him and breaks his solitude: his salvation depends on his becoming part of the very society he appears to deny. Solitude and sin, communion and health, become synonymous terms.

If this is what happens to persons who have long since left their homeland, who can hardly speak the language of their forebearers, and whose secret roots, those that connect a man with his culture, have almost withered away, what is there to say about the rest of us when we visit the United States? Our reaction is not so unhealthy, but after our first dazzled impressions of that country's grandeur, we all instinctively assume a critical attitude. I remember that when I commented to a Mexican friend on the loveliness of Berkeley, she said: "Yes, it's very lovely, but I don't belong here. Even the birds speak English. How can I enjoy a flower if I don't know its right name, its English name, the name that has fused with its colors and petals, the name that's the same thing as the flower? If I say bugambilia to you, you think of the bougainvillea vines you've seen in your own village, with their purple, liturgical flowers, climbing around an ash tree or hanging from a wall in the afternoon sunlight. They're a part of your being, your culture. They're what you remember long after you've seemed to forget them. It's very lovely here, but it isn't mine." . . .

Yes, we withdraw into ourselves, we deepen and aggravate our awareness of everything that separates or isolates or differentiates us. And we increase our solitude by refusing to seek out our compatriots, perhaps because we fear we will see ourselves in them, perhaps because of a painful, defensive unwillingness to share our intimate feelings. The Mexican succumbs very easily to sentimental effusions, and therefore he shuns them. We live closed up within ourselves, like those taciturn adolescents—I will add in passing that I hardly met any of the sort among North American youths—who are custodians of a secret that they guard behind scowling expressions, but that only waits for the opportune moment in which to reveal itself.

I am not going to expand my description of these feelings or discuss the states of depression or frenzy (or often both) that accompany them. They are all apt to lead to unexpected explosions, which destroy a precarious equilibrium based on the imposition of forms that oppress or mutilate us. Our sense of inferiority—real or imagined—might be explained at least partly by the reserve with which the Mexican faces other people and the unpredictable violence with which his repressed emotions break through his mask of impassivity. But his solitude is vaster and profounder than his sense of inferiority. It is impossible to equate these two attitudes: when you sense that you are alone, it does not mean that you feel inferior, but rather that you feel you are different. Also, a sense of inferiority may sometimes be an illusion, but solitude is a hard fact. We are truly different. And we are truly alone.

This is not the moment to analyze our profound sense of solitude, which alternately affirms and denies itself in melancholy and rejoicing, silence and sheer noise, gratuitous crimes and religious fervor. Man is alone everywhere. But the solitude of the Mexican, under the great stone night of the high plateau that is still inhabited by insatiable gods, is very different from that of the North American, who wanders in an abstract world of machines, fellow citizens, and moral precepts. In the Valley of Mexico man feels himself suspended between heaven and earth, and he oscillates between contrary powers and forces, and petrified eyes, and devouring mouths. Reality—that is, the world that surrounds us—exists by itself here, has a life of its own, and was not invented by man as it was in the United States. The Mexican feels himself to have been torn from the womb of this reality, which is both creative and destructive, both Mother and Tomb. He has forgotten the word that ties him to all those forces through which life manifests itself. Therefore he shouts or keeps silent, stabs or prays, or falls asleep for a hundred years.

The history of Mexico is the history of a man seeking his parentage, his origins. He has been influenced at one time or another by France, Spain, the United States and the militant indigenists of his own country, and he crosses history like a jade comet, now and then giving off flashes of lightning. What is he pursuing in his eccentric course? He wants to go back beyond the catastrophe he suffered: he wants to be a sun again, to return to the center of that life from which he was separated one day. (Was that day the Conquest? Independence?) Our solitude has the same roots as religious feelings. It is a form of orphanhood, an obscure awareness that we have been torn from the All, and an ardent search: a flight and a return, an effort to re-establish the bonds that unite us with the universe.

Nothing could be further from this feeling than the solitude of the North American. In the United States man does not feel that he has been torn from the center of creation and suspended between hostile forces.

Source: Paz, Octavio. *Labyrinth of Solitude and Other Writings,* 12–20.

Anthony Quinn, *The Original Sin: A Self-Portrait* (1972)

Anthony Quinn (1915–2001), undoubtedly the greatest actor of Mexican ancestry in the United States, was born in Chihuahua. He was a two-time Academy Award winner, earning Oscars for his roles in Zorba the Greek *and* Viva Zapata. *His grandfather was an Irish immigrant to Mexico and his mother was Mexican. He put his career in jeopardy by supporting the Sleepy Lagoon defendants—22 Mexican American youths who were indicted for the alleged murder of José Díaz (17 stood trial). The leader of the Sleepy Lagoon defendants was Henry Leyvas, whose mother was Quinn's mother's godchild. These excerpts from Quinn's autobiography give the reader a window into the lives of Mexican Americans during the war years. These excerpts also express the culture conflict that Quinn experienced, as told to his therapist.*

"Here it is. It tells about your being born in Mexico during the revolution." [The psychiatrist says.]

"Yes. April twenty-first, 1915."

"It goes on to say that your mother and father both fought on the side of Pancho Villa. Correct?"

"Yes, I suppose so."

"Why do you say it like that?"

"I mean the period is all mixed up. I'm sorry. Yes, they did fight with Pancho Villa."

The doctor nodded. "I'm afraid all I know about the Mexican Revolution is what I saw in the picture *Viva Villa* with Wallace Beery. Was Villa like that?"

"I thought Beery was great in the part, but I don't think he caught the burning intensity of Villa."

"What do you mean?"

Then I told him an anecdote related to me by my father, about when Villa rode to the top of the hill and saw the Pacific Ocean for the first time. He had stared at the ocean's immensity for many minutes without saying a word. Then he'd reined his horse and started back down the hill.

His lieutenant, riding behind him, said, "Quite a sight, eh, jefe?"

"It's too small to quench my thirst," Pancho had said over his shoulder.

"That's quite a remark," said the doctor. "When did your father tell it to you?"

"When I was a kid."

"And it stayed with you all these years?"

"Yes."

"Do you feel the ocean is too small to quench your thirst, Mr. Quinn?"

"Yes."

If there had been any doubt in the doctor's mind about my being sick, I felt it had been dispelled by my answer. To hell with him. Let him earn his money, I thought. The man had a good poker face, however, and went on examining the clippings.

"It goes on to say here that your father was an Irish adventurer and your mother an Aztec princess."

I had to laugh out loud.

He looked up. "Why do you laugh? Isn't it true?"

"My father was part Irish, that part is true. But I was laughing at the Indian princess crap."

"My wife and I thought it was very romantic when we read it."

"I guess that's what Paramount Pictures publicity wanted you to feel. They didn't think it was romantic enough for my mother to be plain Mexican."

"Why was that?"

"What the hell, Doc, you live in Los Angeles. You know what most people here feel about Mexicans."

"I don't. I've only been here a couple of years, Tony. May I call you Tony?"

The question about Mexicans irritated me. He had begun to look like a red-necked Texan already.

"Sure, if I can call you by your first name."

He roared with laughter. "You can call me anything you want—and that isn't all you're going to call me before you're through."

"Well, being a Mexican in Southern California is not exactly an open sesame. For years they used to have signs at dance halls and restaurants: 'No Mexicans allowed.' Mexicans were lazy, thieves, greasy; they were either Zoot Suiters or pachucos, marijuana smokers. . . . "

"He started coming around when I began acquiring things I thought would please him. [His other self or alter ego] The first time I saw him was when I bought the jazzy house on Sunset Boulevard. He was standing on the lawn one day wondering what the hell I was doing with such a mansion. It was during the war and big houses were going a begging so I thought what the hell, I'll buy it. The boy began to make me feel guilty about it so I used to let people use it to raise money for good causes. The only time I ever saw the son of a bitch smile approvingly was the night I gave a party to raise funds for the 'Sleepy Lagoon' case. That night the kid and I walked around the garden like real pals."

"What was the 'Sleepy Lagoon' case?"

"Around 1944 or 1945, twenty-two Mexican boys were being tried for murder. It seems there had been a party in East L.A. and it had ended in a rumble, which wasn't unusual at those parties. Some kids from another gang had tried to crash, there had been this fight, and one boy had been killed. Twenty-two Mexican boys were rounded up and now they were being tried for murder. Certain groups in Los Angeles were up in arms; they felt the kids' were being railroaded. They called it another Scottsboro case, where a group of Negroes had been found guilty of rape in the South. The case was becoming a political football. Some Los Angeles papers were saying that Mexicans had bad Indian blood in them which made them violent. They were fermenting a great deal of anti-Mexican feeling.

"I was making a war picture at Camp Pendleton at the time and one Saturday, after I'd finished work, some marines who were working with us came and asked if I wanted to join them. They were going up to Los Angeles to 'beat up some Mexicans.' Those poor misguided bastards. They were trying to tell me they considered me one of them. I guess my name being Quinn, they never thought I was Mexican. I got into a fight with the asshole who had invited me. He was a big bruiser. I guess luckily someone pulled us apart.

"One day I got a call at the studio from my mother. She asked if I had read about the 'Sleepy Lagoon' case. Christ! Even my mother was caught up in it. I said of course, the papers talked of nothing else.

"'One of the boys' names is Leyvas.' "'So?'

"'You wouldn't remember her but when we first arrived in Juarez from Chihuahua she was the first person to help us. We were starving and she made us some scrambled eggs.'

"I had to laugh thinking how Mother remembered the menu. She went on. 'Anyway, she called this morning and was crying. It seems that everything points to the fact that her son will go to the electric chair.'

"'Yes, I know,' I said. 'It looks like he was the ringleader.'

"'I promised her that you would get him off,' my mother announced.

"'You what?'

"'They have no money, Tony. They can't afford a good lawyer.'

'All she wants is for her son to get a fair trial. All these years she's never asked for a favor in return.'

"'Mama, I can't become involved in a murder case. Jeez, you've read the papers. Everybody who has come to the defense of the kids is being called a Communist. That's all I would need. Mama, we could be run out of the country!'

"'Maybe we wouldn't be in the country if it wasn't for Trini Levas.'

"'Why, because she fed us some scrambled eggs?' 'Perhaps she saved our lives.'

"'Christ, Mama, how much do we have to pay for those goddamned scrambled eggs? All right, I'll give you a thousand dollars. You can give it to her. That should be more than enough payment for those eggs.'

"'No, Tony. She doesn't want the money. She wants her son.'" I argued. I pleaded for her to let me off the hook. She wouldn't.

"That night I called a friend of mine. He and his wife, Goldie, were good people. They were always fighting for causes. Whether it was the lettuce strikers, the dock workers, or the 'Sleepy Lagoon' case.

"I told them I would like to help the boys. What could I do?

"He said there was a committee being formed for their defense. I could help them raise money.

"I had had no experience with such things so I took the direct approach. I went to actors and directors that I knew and asked for cash. Most of them responded generously. Some were afraid they would be implicated politically. One famous star who had made his reputation playing gangster parts turned me down flat. He said the whole movement for the defense of the kids was being run by 'Reds.'

"I began making speeches at ladies' club luncheons. The papers picked up the news and one day I was called in by Darryl Zanuck, at whose studio I was then under contract. He told me that my involvement was endangering the investment they had in my pictures.

"'Darryl, you have been one of the most courageous men I've ever seen in this business,' I told him. 'You've made pictures like *The Ox-Bow Incident*, *Grapes of Wrath*, *Gentleman's Agreement*.

You've never been afraid. Why do you want me to run scared now?'

"I explained the circumstances that had caused me to become involved. Now that I was in it, I said, I had begun to realize there were some ugly forces working against the boys.

"He nodded and said, 'A hell of an expensive plate of scrambled eggs!'

"When I walked away, I didn't know whether I would be dropped by the studio. I wasn't. I have always been proud to know that some people in my business stand for more than mere self-interest. Darryl Zanuck certainly proved it that day.

"Soon after, there was a big benefit party at my house in Beverly Hills. We charged a huge entrance fee and some of the most famous people in Hollywood came to entertain, all for the cause.

"That night as I went about the garden welcoming the guests, 'the boy' walked beside me. I had never seen him so happy. It was the first time in years he seemed to approve of me. I thought he'd leave me alone after that. He didn't."

The doctor had listened patiently. Once or twice I'd seen him scribble on the papers he kept on me.

"Tony, would you mind discussing your political views with me someday?"

I must have given him a strange look because he threw back his head and laughed.

"I am not a representative of the Un-American Activities Committee." The pains they had caused friends of mine kept me from joining in his laughter.

"No, Doc, I have nothing to hide. Let me say at the outset that I wouldn't give a damn if you were from the Un-American outfit. Sometimes I almost wished they had called me. To tell you the truth, I think 'the boy' hoped they would. He always prods me to stand up and be counted. I have never been a Communist. I have never attended a cell meeting and, believe it or not, I was never proselytized or asked to join any so-called subversive movement. I was pro-labor for humanitarian reasons. I was anti-Fascist and anti-Nazi because they preached racial and nationalistic superiority, which was diametrically opposed to my philosophy. . . .

"My wife and I are looking for a farm to buy, and when we saw your charming house my wife let out a scream, 'There it is, exactly the house we are looking for.'

"The woman looked agape, first at me and then over toward my wife, sitting in the car. Then she turned and saw the tire tracks that had destroyed her beautiful, neat field.

"'Tomorrow,' I jumped in, 'I will send some workmen to hoe and replant the field.'

"'What's your name?' she asked, beginning to soften. "'Anthony Quinn,' I smiled.

"'Could it be that you're Irish?' she asked, with a faint brogue." I nodded. 'My grandfather was from Cork.'

"'Was he now?' she smiled. 'Me and my husband come from Killarney.'

"'Is that a fact?'

"'Well,' she said finally, 'won't you and you dear wife come to the house and join us for a spot of tea?'

"During tea, the lady scoffed at my offer to have her field fixed.

"She assured us that she had three very able-bodied Mexicans working for her who would fix it in no time. Katie shot me a warning glance and I made no comment. She promised us that if she ever thought of selling we would be the first to hear about it. As we left her house, she said that she was sure that I could charm a snake, like all good Irishmen.

The doctor enjoyed the story. "Is it true, Tony? I mean, are there moments when you can tell that you're being Mexican or Irish?"

"Yes."

"Which is easier to live with?'"

"The Irish, but then nobody ever called me a dirty mick. I never had to take a beating because I was Irish. I only had the shit kicked out of me because I was Mexican. So I decided to be it most of the time."

"What do you suppose your life would have been like if you'd spent more time charming your way through life, rather than fighting it the way you do?"

"Christ only knows. Anyway, it had all been decided back there when I was a kid and fought against the Irish kids on the banks of the Los Angeles River, on the side of the Mexican boys."

"Do you ever wonder about your Irish parentage?"

"Yes, often. I have a picture of my grandfather. He's a blond version of my father. When I was a kid I would stare at him for hours. I wanted to love him so much. I made up all sorts of stories about him, then I'd stop myself because I wondered if he could love his dark grandson."

"And now?"

"I love him very much, but I'm still afraid. I wonder if he approves of me."

"Don't you think he would be proud of all you've done?"

I laughed. "Doctor, the kid doesn't think I've done a damn thing. I don't know if Father and my grandfather would agree with him."

"What about your mother's father? How do you feel about him?"

"Fuck him. He's one ghost I've killed and buried. He didn't have the balls to acknowledge his responsibility."

The doctor made an imaginary cross in the air. "One down, and how many ghosts to go?"

"An army."

"Don't you feel we're getting rid of some of them?"

"Yes, some of them have lost by default. They've died on me." The doctor started to tidy up his desk. I got up to put my jacket on. "When are you supposed to leave for Europe to start your new picture?"

"In a week or ten days."

"Well, we have to win the war soon, don't we? Where the hell do we find the bomb to blow up all the ghosts?"

As we headed down the hall, the doctor repeated that we'd have to work hard. He felt it would be dangerous for me to go to Europe in the middle of therapy. He explained that there were postoperative complications that could develop from mental therapy, just like those from any major operation. He walked me to my car. "The man you're going to play, Paul Gauguin, was a driven man himself, wasn't he?"

"Yes, poor bastard; but at least he made it."

"Did he think he'd made it?"

Source: Quinn, Anthony. *The Original Sin: A Self-Portrait.* Boston: Little, Brown and Company, 1972, 10–11, 81–84, 293–294.

Beverly Beyette, "Ralph Lazo Remembers Manzanar" (1981)

The following Los Angeles Times *article tells the story of 16-year-old Ralph Lazo (1924–1992), who did not think it was right that his Japanese American friends were taken to concentration camps, so he elected to go with them. He lived at Manzanar, which is in the Owen's Valley of California. Manzanar was in a desolate portion of the state where water had been diverted to Los Angeles. During World War II, Manzanar was a concentration camp for Japanese and Japanese American residents. Lazo was horrified at this injustice and registered as an American-born Japanese and voluntarily went to Manzanar for two years. The Japanese American community produced a docudrama,* Stand Up for Justice, *based on this profile of courage.*

If there was a moment of truth, an instant in which Ralph Lazo had determined that he would go with his Japanese-American friends to internment camp, perhaps it was during a wartime winter day in 1942 when he was helping a neighbor at an "evacuation sale." . . .

Lazo, a Mexican-American, was stunned. The Temple Street neighborhood in which he'd grown up was a multi-ethnic mix of Basques, Jews, Japanese-Americans. He'd played basketball on a Filipino Community Church team. . . .

Now, by government order, his friends were to be taken away from their homes, forced to sell or abandon their property. "It was immoral," says Lazo, "it was wrong, and I couldn't accept it."

[Lazo elected to go to the camp with his Japanese friends . . .]

He did not have to lie, to tell officials that he was of Japanese ancestry. "They didn't ask," he says. He grins. "Being brown has its advantages." . . .

For the next two years, Lazo would live at Manzanar, the relocation camp behind barbed wire fences in the dusty, desolate Owens Valley. There he would graduate from high school (Manzanar class of '44), play football, emcee Saturday night dances in the rec hall, learn to speak a little Japanese. . . .

[Lazo remembered . . .]

It was a good day—"There was this great feeling of having shared a common experience . . . ," says Lazo. "I had to be careful, not for me—I can take care of myself—but for my children." . . .

The heros [sic], he'll tell you, are the men, women and children who were imprisoned behind that barbed wire, who lived there with dignity. . . .

No Germans or Italians were ever evacuated. But on the premise that there was a real threat of a Japanese invasion of the West Coast, the mass evacuation of persons of Japanese ancestry was begun that March.

Source: Beyette, Beverly. "Ralph Lazo Remembers Manzanar." *Los Angeles Times*, April 2, 1981, H1.

Interview with Hector P. García, Founder of the American G.I. Forum (1992)

Hector P. García (1914–1996) was a physician from Corpus Christi, Texas. He spent his life working to better conditions for Mexican Americans. He witnessed segregated schooling, limited professional opportunities, and poverty for Mexican Americans living in the United States. As a child, he picked cotton and other crops. García was also the founder of the American G.I. Forum. In this interview, he talks about his childhood and the founding of the forum.

Q: Why did your father feel it necessary to emigrate from Mexico?

A: We were born in Mexico during the time of the Mexican Revolution. So by this time, one of his brothers had emigrated to Mercedes, Texas, and started his business. The situation in Mexico was not only very unstable, but dangerous. Especially, in northern Mexico where we came from—things were pretty bad and pretty wild. We didn't emigrate to come and work over here, we emigrated on a business venture with my brothers and sisters and father and mother.

Q: You say that you didn't know what discrimination was until you got to the University of Texas. What was it about your growing up before you went to the University of Texas that you didn't know what discrimination was? Was it an all-Mexican town?

A: We lived across the tracks in Mercedes. See, it was an accepted fact [at] that time that all the Mexican students would go to the segregated schools. And nobody knew the difference, that it was unconstitutional. We went along and at school our main job was to get a good education. In other words, we were not fighting discrimination and segregation because we did not know that it really existed. It was an accepted fact that in South Texas we were divided by the railroad tracks. Mercedes was no different. We accepted the fact that we went to the segregated schools. But at the University in Austin we found out also that there was discrimination against the Jewish people and also there were very few blacks. In fact, the blacks hardly attended the University of Texas schools 'til much later.

Q: How did you know that there was only one Mexicano admitted to the University of Texas Medical School every year? Was that official policy?

A: One Mexicano out of one hundred applicants, and out of one hundred people who went to school there was only one Mexicano. I was the one for that year. My brother, Dr. José Antonio García was the one in his year. Dr. Clotilde García, my sister, was one in [her] year. So it's an accepted fact that I know a lot of our own men that wanted to apply to medical school. They did apply but they didn't get in.

Q: When the Three Rivers incident thing happened with Pvt. Longoria, you already had a sense of what that injustice was before that event happened?

A: Oh, yes. We learned when we went to World War II. We went to fight a Nazi System—[in] which they thought the German was superior to anybody else. And of course we knew about some of the Jewish people being put to death. And the Germans were not accepting anybody except Aryan Germans as first-class citizens. We come back here and get involved in the Longoria case out of Three Rivers in 1948. We had segregated schools, segregated campuses, segregated hospitals. The hospital had segregated wards for Mexican American patients. As a doctor, I could not put a patient in the hospital because the so-called Mexican American wards were filled up, and although the Anglo ward would have one patient, they would not allow me to put a Mexican patient with the Anglo.

Q: Do you have a sense that [the] episode of Three Rivers set the stage for the political awakening of Mexican Americans in the state? Do you think it was that important?

A: I think that was a catalyst for our people—and not only Mexican American people, but also Anglo people—to realize the fact of the extent and seriousness of the injustices. Of a man who died for his country in World War II in the Philippines, being refused the use of the chapel. So he brought us up to the knowledge that we were denied the rights and the Anglo people began to see also the fact that it was an injustice. So I think it was a catalyst to start moving Mexican American people and to try to achieve first-class citizenship. And then try to erase all of those things—both in discrimination and segregation and violation of our rights—to eliminate them, to achieve what we wanted to achieve which was first-class citizenship.

Q: When all that was happening, were you aware that you were part of a historic event?

A: Oh no, I was merely trying to do my duty. I was still working in medicine. And I decided, like the rest of the people, that it was a great injustice. I didn't consider it an organized plan and I didn't consider it a historical event. It was a single event at that time of trying to bury Felix Longoria with full military honors: first, if possible, in Three Rivers, Texas; if not, in Arlington National Cemetery in Washington, D.C.

Q: But is it a fair statement to say that your previous military experience and your training as a doctor to be compassionate toward people, did all those things come together to create a very unique opportunity for you as an individual?

A: I certainly think the fact that I had been involved as an officer of the United States Army, the fact that I was a doctor, which showed me compassion for my people. All of those things gave me the ability to organize the American G.I. Forum. Not only locally, but citywide, nationwide. Which is an organization made up of American veterans of Mexican origin. We're now fighting for their civil rights after we have fought for our military rights in World War II. I felt capable of handling the situation. Now the fact also that our people had received military training made it very easy for me to organize them into a national organization because sure, we didn't have the education, we only had the military experience.

Q: When you were involved in all these things—the gaining of medical care for Mexican American veterans, and the educational lawsuits and the poll tax—did you get a sense that you were involved in a moment to uplift a whole community, a whole population? Did you think in those terms?

A: Once I got started, involved in matters concerning education, civil rights, hospitalization, the real estate restrictions—I got a feeling we were moving our Mexican American people way ahead of their time—faster than I ever thought. I thought unless we move this way, it will take us 50 years to achieve what we achieved within the American G.I. Forum in less than 10 years. I knew we were pushing a people ahead of time.

Q: And was that a feeling that you and people like Gus García and James Deanda and the others—was that something you all talked about? Or was it each person acting individually?

A: We called people like Gus García and Dr. George I. Sánchez and Jimmie Deanda and Cris Aldrete . . . we would talk about these things. And we realized what we were doing. Within the structure of this group of people who were knowledgeable. Our mentor, our director really was George I. Sánchez from the University of Texas. Our legal brain as far as arguing was Gus García. Our legal brain as far researching was Carlos Cadena from San Antonio. I was more or less the catalyst in all those movements. The American G.I. Forum was the "roots" group of people trying to work together to get this thing moving. So all of us together, we knew what we were doing. We worked together, although we didn't have a master plan or an idea. We only moved in the direction where things were happening that demanded our action.

Q: Did you ever consider political life?

A: People got the impression or idea that I would eventually seek a political office, and I felt that if I ever sought a political office, that would prove to them that I was only doing this for political satisfaction or getting some money for politics, which I never intended. I made up my mind I would not run for any political position, either for pay or no pay, because then you get involved in stopping the movement which I was trying to do on a voluntary basis. A movement of love and faith and respect, a movement that would convince me to work with the Constitution of the United States and state of Texas.

Q: When did you first begin to have such a love for those two Constitutions? How did that happen?

A: Well, I studied history at the university level. Consequently, because I certainly did not know about being a natural-born citizen here, I had to learn the Constitution to become a citizen. When I became a citizen, that's when I learned about the Constitution. I knew all the rights, all the things that it gave us. And then, of course, I also served on the United States Commission on Civil Rights. I did a lot of studying then, and my belief in the Constitution became stronger.

Q: What about when you started winning some of those legal cases? Did that reinforce your understanding and belief in the Constitution?

A: When we started winning a lot of the legal cases, my belief in the Constitution got stronger. In fact, for instance, the Minerva Delgado case in 1948 . . . the Constitution says that you could not segregate us . . . the courts decided you could not segregate us because of our origins because the Constitution always said in Texas that you could not have separate schools for the Mexican Americans. It was there all the time. Even today, I still have an abiding [faith in] the Constitution of Texas and the United States. It's important that you have the voting rights act, the civil rights act, which enforces very, very much all our efforts.

Source: García, Hector P. Founder, American G.I. Forum. Interview conducted in 1992. Courtesy of KERA-TV, Dallas, Texas. http://www.justiceformypeople.org/interview_hgarcia.html.

Leigh E. Smith Jr., "Company E Survivor Recalls Days as Prisoner of War" (1995)

During World War II, Company E of the 141st Regiment of the 36th Texas Infantry Division was called the Mexican Americans' company. It was made up almost entirely of Mexican Americans from the El Paso, Texas, area. Only the officers were white. In nearly a year of combat in Italy and France, the 141st Infantry Regiment sustained heavy casualties—1,126 killed, 5,000 wounded, and more than 500 missing in action. The all-Mexican company earned 31 Distinguished Service Crosses, 12 Legion of Merits, 492 Silver Stars, 11 Soldier's Medals, 1,685 Bronze Stars, and numerous other commendations and decorations. The following article is based on an interview with Ricardo Palacios Jr., who survived the Rapido River crossing below Monte Cassino in Italy. Palacios was later taken prisoner. In the interview, Palacios addresses the bravery of Mexican Americans in World War II, which is often left out of contemporary histories and documentaries of the war.

On the night of January 21, 1944, Ricardo Palacios, Jr., prepared to cross central Italy's Rapido River in assault boats with his platoon, members of Company E, 141st Infantry Regiment, and 36th Infantry Division. The boat crossing failed, so the company pulled back and waited for the engineers to build a pontoon bridge.

The bridge consisted of small rubber pontoon boats tied together with wooden planks over the tops and rope rails for the men to use as they walked across. The bridge was about 36 inches wide.

The Germans were waiting for them, however, and casualties were heavy. "I remember getting up early the next morning to see what was going on. All I could see was a lot of pieces of bodies scattered all over from both sides," Palacios said.

The survivors were now on the enemy side of the river and were rounded up by German soldiers. Palacios remembers: "The first time I heard a German officer say 'Auf Stehen,' I thought I better get up. I had a bar of chocolate in my back pocket. That was the first thing he went for—the chocolate bar. I knew he was an officer because you can distinguish them, very sharply dressed, even in combat.

"He looked at me and said, 'Amerikaner Hund.' I didn't know what he was saying. He had fire in his eyes. You knew he was mad. Later on, I asked him at the POW camp what 'Amerikaner Hund' meant. He said, 'American Dog. You're a dog.'"

January 21 will always remind Palacios of the day he became a prisoner of war. That day he also turned twenty-one years old.

Palacios continues, "Right after they took the chocolate bar, two other sergeants from the unit and I were brought over to a wall near the white house. A couple of German soldiers were pointing machine pistols at us and a German sergeant gave them an order. I said to myself, 'This is it. They're going to shoot us.'

"I closed my eyes as they brought the machine guns up to aim, and I heard a loud noise. One German had slapped his leg so it would sound like a gun shot. I opened my eyes and they were laughing. They were young soldiers like us, nineteen or twenty years old. They thought it would be funny. It's a helluva feeling," he says.

When Palacios was captured, he was moved from place to place and put with other Americans who were captured at the river. He recalls encountering three friends from the unit. "I met up with Edwardo Lalo Romo, Raul Caracena, and Eduardo Carreón, all from El Paso. We saw each other at the first camp. We were really happy to see each other." Palacios was interned in several POW camps including Stalag II B and a sub-camp of Dachau. "I remember having nothing to eat until we reached Dachau POW camp near Munich," he said. His final destination was Stalag III B prison camp near Buchenwald, where he arrived in March 1945. Palacios recalls the processing and interrogation vividly:

"You come from Mexico?" a German soldier asked.

"No sir."

"You don't understand English? I can get somebody in Spanish."

"I understand English, I understand Spanish."

"Your parents come from Mexico?"

"Yes sir. But I was born in the United States."

The Germans who interrogated Palacios and his fellow Hispanic prisoners could not believe these men were in the American army. They assumed that since El Paso is so close to the Mexican border, the Mexican Army had joined the American Army in the fighting.

The Germans were always very efficient when keeping records of prisoners. They wrote everything down, took fingerprints and photographs and kept all the information on a prisoner card [issued] to each prisoner. Palacios was able to obtain his card when fellow prisoners ransacked the administration building of the camp after the Germans deserted it to escape the Russian advance. He keeps it in a plastic folder along with postcards he wrote to his mother while he was imprisoned.

Palacios weighed 130 pounds when captured. When he was freed, he weighed only 98 pounds. On April 22, 1945, Palacios and the other prisoners of Stalag III B were liberated by Russian soldiers. Shortly after, he was returned to American troops in Hidelshiem, Germany.

"After Hidelshiem, we were taken to Camp Lucky Strike near Le Havre, France. We stayed there for about two weeks where we were examined, debriefed, and nutritionally rehabilitated. I was given a seven-day leave to London where I really enjoyed myself. Later I was sent back to the United States to a POW rehabilitation center in Santa Barbara, California, where I adjusted to civilian life and was discharged from the Army."

Source: Smith, Leigh E. "From the Editors." *Borderlands* 13, no. 2 (Spring 1995). El Paso Community College Local History Project. http://www.epcc.edu/ftp/homes/monicaw/borderlands/13_el_paso_company_e.htm.

Catherine Lavender, "On *Salt of the Earth* (1953)" (1998)

Salt of the Earth *(1953) was a movie made at the height of the McCarthy witch-hunt era; it was the only U.S.-made film to be blacklisted in the United States. Made by blacklisted filmmakers Herbert J. Biberman (director) and Michael Wilson (writer), it is based on a 1950 strike by zinc miners in Silver City, New Mexico. In this film about social injustice, characters such as Ramón and Esperanza Quintero, a Mexican American miner and his wife, grow as a consequence of struggle. When an injunction against the male strikers comes down and prevents them from picketing, the women take over the picket line, leaving the men to housekeeping duties. It has a strong treatment of the gender question. The following 1998 article places the strike in a historical context.*

THIS IS THE REAL LIFE STORY OF NEW MEXICAN MINERS

Films entertain but they also contain a message for viewers. Sometimes that message is explicitly stated, and at other times it is given through metaphor and allegory. These messages are a product of the time in which the film is made and are central to the meaning of the film. Films, then, can be read on the level of the story being told (the narrative of events) or on the level of the message being conveyed. The filmmaker hopes that the audience will react to the film and will leave with something to think about.

In order to examine the narrative and the internal message of *Salt of the Earth*, it is necessary to understand the Cold War context in which the film was made and seen by its original audience. One of the greatest changes facing Americans after the end of World War II was the nation's unprecedented position as a leader in world affairs. Many hoped that America's new industrial and military might would be used to build a better, more secure postwar world. The Soviet Union also emerged from the war as a world leader, and one which, although it had been allied with the United States during the war, many U.S. leaders viewed with suspicion.

Many Americans believed that Russian Communists were dedicated to the overthrow of capitalism and democracy and were intent on world domination. The Soviet Union, a nation twice invaded by the West in the twentieth century, also viewed the United States with suspicion, believing that it posed an ongoing threat to its security. To counter further invasion, it sought to dominate bordering nations in Eastern Europe and to build its military might. Both nations engaged in acts that collectively raised tensions, generating a "cold war" between them.

Americans responded with rising concern to each Communist "victory"—the extension of Soviet governance over Eastern Europe, captured spies, the development of a Soviet atomic bomb, the successful 1949 Chinese Communist revolution. The House Committee on Un-American Activities (HUAC) charged that Communist agents and spies were actively subverting American life, the American economy, and government. Most states, and many public and private institutions such as colleges and universities, joined the federal government in requiring loyalty oaths and establishing loyalty review boards. Many of these abrogated the constitutional rights of those under suspicion.

Among the industries most affected by the hysteria was the film industry. By 1947, HUAC had charged ten screenwriters—Communists, former Communists, and liberals—who came to be known as the "Hollywood Ten," with contempt of Congress for the refusal to name prominent Communists in Hollywood. Hollywood moved to remove the "blemish" of communism from its reputation; in late 1947, fifty motion picture executives devised a "black list" of suspicious people who would be prevented from taking jobs in the industry. No studio would hire a blacklisted writer, actor or actress, director, or producer. Unable to find jobs, a number of blacklisted film artists formed their own production company in 1951. They were looking for good stories when told about a strike by Local 890 of the Mine, Mill and Smelter Workers Union against the New Jersey Zinc Company in Bayard, New Mexico. The local was composed largely of Spanish and Mexican Americans. The Mine, Mill and Smelter Workers Union had been expelled from the CIO in 1950 for alleged Communist influence.

The movie was to be the story of the miners fighting against a giant company, of Chicanos and Anglos, and of miners and their families. The miners were to play themselves, and it was to be filmed on site. The crew was made up of blacklisted technicians, and only two professional actors would appear in the film: blacklisted Will Geer (the Sheriff, and who later went on to play the Grandpa on *The Waltons* on television), and Mexican actress Rosuara Revueltas (Esperanza). The final result, *The Salt of the Earth*, was a controversial film. Not only was the film about striking miners, whom the general public viewed to be either Communists or communist influenced, but the story focused on a Chicano community at a time when attitudes about Chicanos were changing. Throughout the Great Depression, official attitudes toward Mexican immigration and transborder migration had grown increasingly hostile, as Anglos clamored in the depressed economy to take jobs that had traditionally belonged to Mexican immigrants. Throughout the 1940s and 1950s, the movement towards closing the porous border at the Rio Grande had culminated in "Operation Wetback" in 1953, a government program designed to find and deport illegal Mexican aliens. These tensions were made more complex by the fact that many "Mexican American immigrants" had, in fact, been on their lands longer than those lands had been a part of the United States, becoming U.S. citizens by virtue of the Treaty of Guadalupe Hidalgo that ended the Mexican American War in 1848.

Source: Lavender, Catherine J. On "Salt of the Earth." 1953. The College of Staten Island of the City University of New York. http://www.library.csi.cuny.edu/dept/history/lavender/salt.html.

"Confidential Cabinet Meeting Decisions" (October 6, 1960)

Plans to sterilize Puerto Rican women took shape as early as 1900 as European American nativists grew concerned about the growth of what they considered less desirable races. Sterilization was a program pushed by powerful financiers and industrialists who were influenced by social Darwinism. They believed heredity, among other factors, determined intelligence. In the United States, they pushed for antimiscegenation laws and the sterilization of the "feeble minded." American social scientists and politicos were concerned with the growth of the island population, even though it was substantially below that of other Caribbean nations. William Moran, director of the U.S.-Puerto Rican Reconstruction Administration, testified before a 1965 U.S. Senate Population Crisis Hearing that the driving force behind the introduction of massive birth control programs in the colonial government's maternal child health services during the 1930s was unemployment and the Great Depression. During this time, 160 private hospitals were opened to exclusively or primarily deal with sterilizations. As a consequence, it was reported that by the mid-1960s just over a third of the Puerto Rican women of child-bearing age had been sterilized—two-thirds were in their early 20s, and most of them were poor. Sterilization programs were condoned by President John F. Kennedy's (1917–1963) program for Latin America known as the Alliance for Progress.

The following document is puzzling because these programs were well known and had occurred since at least the 1930s. However, they were not common or public knowledge. According to the document, on October 6, 1960, in a meeting between Puerto Rico's governor Luis Muñoz Marín (1898–1980) and his cabinet, the governor was informed that some companies favored by the government would hire women only if they agreed to undergo surgical sterilization. The governor acted surprised and ordered a complete investigation. One does not get a sense of moral outrage but the document does tie sterilization to the economic policies of colonial government.

1. Prepare statistics on the government revenue collected by taxes with revenue from the decade of 1930–40, and also the savings resulting from when the Republicans lowered the salaries of teachers and other public functionaries.
2. Compare the 1940 budget made by the PER with the 1941 budget made under the PPD.
3. Sierra will write an explanation on the diverse methods of collecting statistics about unemployment and how the system used in Puerto Rico differs from that used in the United States.
4. Sierra will send facts about unemployment among 4th year graduates.
5. Cancio will report on the laws that cover sterilization.
6. [Department of] Health will report on what has been the practice and regulation of this issue [sterilization] and the ways to provide information on contraceptives, specifically on who to give it to.
7. The Department of Justice should prepare legislation prohibiting job discrimination against un-sterilized women.
8. [Department of] Justice will prepare an amendment to the Law about electoral funds so that rich candidates cannot spend their own funds in excess of $300.
9. Agriculture will send many facts to refute the allegation that the PPD has abandoned and persecuted agriculture.
10. Moscoso [José Teodoro Moscoso Mora (1910–1992)] will send statements of experts to the sugar industry claiming negligence on the part of Puerto Rican sugar producers in not dedicating more funds to investigation efforts.

Following are some of the issues that arose or were mentioned in debate:

1. The argument of the PER that they did not have sufficient funds in their 8 years of governing.

The Governor indicated that the PER has been using this argument as an excuse for what happened during their time in government. The counterarguments are they had more money in special funds than they claim, and furthermore, they didn't collect what they could have from personal income taxes. He asked for statistics on the government revenue collected through said taxes and also about the savings resulting from when they lowered the salaries of teachers and other public functionaries.

As a demonstration of the way in which one could govern favoring economic development and protecting the poor, he mentioned that it would be interesting to compare the revenue made in 1940 by the PER and the 1941 revenue under the PPD.

2. Unemployment

Ferré alleges that there are currently 90,000 unemployed, and the Governor asked about the certainty of that number. Sierra said that allegation was false, and explained the many ways of collection statistics on unemployment and how the system used in Puerto Rico differs from the system used in the United States. The Governor asked him to write an explanation on this topic.

He also asked Sierra for facts about unemployment among 4th year graduates, because he had the impression that these young people had the least opportunities for work, and for that reason, they emigrate.

3. Sterilization

The Governor asked Moscoso about the allegation of Ferré that some of the industries of Cayey refused to employ women that were not sterilized. Moscoso informed him that the Industrial Association has proposed to respond to Ferré in the newspapers.

Independently of what the Industrial Association does, the Governor asked Cancio for a report on sterilization laws, and Salud for a report on the practice and regulation on this issue. Salud should also report on ways to gain information on.

Source: "Cabinet Meeting Decisions" (Puerto Rico). October 6, 1960. Women in World History. http://chnm.gmu.edu/wwh/modules/lesson16/lesson16.php?menu=1&s=12.

José Yglesias, "Right On with the Young Lords" (1970)

The Young Lords emerged as the leading Puerto Rican youth organization of the late 1960s. Its direct action and defense of the barrio attracted idealistic Puerto Rican youth. The following excerpt from a New York Times *article describes a Young Lords uprising against New York officials over the lack of sanitation services in East Harlem.*

Suddenly in East Harlem last summer people began throwing garbage and wrecked furniture into the middle of the streets. Traffic was stopped frequently, mid-town businessmen avoiding the clog of the East River Drive found themselves inside stifling cars in an area whose residents looked upon their discomfiture with little sympathy. . . . The Mayor's office got the message and a 24-hour pickup of garbage was begun. For a while, El Barrio, that part of Harlem where the first Puerto Rican migrants settled, was cleaner than anyone remembered. With this "garbage riot," the Young Lords first made their presence felt in New York. . . .

The rush thereafter by young Puerto Ricans to join the Lords . . . was so great that the organization had to close its rolls temporarily and take steps . . . to prevent police and F.B.I. agents from infiltrating. . . . "We believe armed self-defense and armed struggle are the only ways to liberation. . . . We want a socialist society."

Source: "Right On with the Young Lords." *New York Times*, June 7, 1970, 215.

Al Burt, "Miami: The Cuban Flavor" (1971)

In the case of most revolutions, the elites leave the country. It happened to the Mexicans in 1913, when massive numbers left Mexico after the overthrow of Mexican dictator Porfirio Díaz (1830–1915). After Fidel Castro took over Cuba in 1959, many wealthy Cubans, many of whom were supporters of Cuban dictator Fulgencio Batista (1901–1973), sent thousands of Cuban children to the United States in the early 1960s in a U.S.-sponsored operation known as Operación Pedro Pan *(Operation Peter Pan). The operation was initiated by the U.S. government, the Roman Catholic Church, and anti-Castro Cuban dissidents, and ran from December 26, 1960, to October 23, 1962. The mass exodus of 14,000 unaccompanied children from the Caribbean island nation was touted as a save-the-children operation that would take youngsters away from communists. These children were followed by thousands of political refugees.*

Although Cubans migrated to New York and elsewhere, their capital became Miami, which was about 90 miles from Cuba and shared the same climate. The first wave of immigrants were professionals, the better educated, and mostly white people. They received government support and were soon able to dominate the city's life. Miami became the exiles' center of anti-Castro activity. The following article from The Nation discusses Cuban Americans in the 1960s and the formation of a Cuban American community.

Miami, more renowned in the past for a brassy exterior than a loving heart, is undergoing a Cuban transplant that may change that image. The city has been Latinized, and there is, loose on the streets and in the bistros, the famous quality that prompted tourists visiting pre-Castro Cuba to marvel at what "good" people Cubans were.

Last spring, a Cuban exile robbed a secondhand clothing store, beat up a woman clerk (also Cuban), took $20, and fled into a Cuban neighborhood. He did not find the cover he expected. In minutes, the word spread and 300 angry Cubans gathered to help the pursuing police. When the man was dragged out of a vacant rooming house, the Cubans cheered and applauded. Then, emotionally carried away, they charged upon the robber. Police hustled him into their car, but some of the crowd beat on the roof and windows until it pulled away.

That incident tells much about the Spanish-language community (some 90 percent Cuban) in the Miami area. It numbers an estimated 318,000 in a city population of 1.3 million and is expected to reach 428,000 within five years. The instincts of this group are winningly human, but its brakes could be improved. In the case of the clothing-store robber, he offended the Cuban sense of honor, not for stealing but by beating a woman. He had to be caught and punished and the Cubans were eager to help with both jobs. In all human affairs, the Cubans' multifaceted impact on Miami has ranged from the beautiful to something less.

They have given Miami a flavor it lacked. Their gift for living whether they are rich or poor, seems both more festive and more real than the native style. Theirs is a mixture of pleasure seeking, understanding for human frailty, pride, devotion to church and family that are being lost in the computer age. Practice may fall short of the ideals, but human weaknesses are shrugged off, when not enjoyed.

To the motorist on the street with a flat tire or with a stalled car, or in any number of other fixes that focus notice on the individual in distress, the Cuban can be a cheering sight. The chances are that he will be more sympathetic than the native, more willing to inconvenience himself for the sake of a stranger.

The Cubans have done well in most areas—business, education, politics—with the major exception of their efforts against Fidel Castro, the man who sent them into exile. While most everything else they have touched has prospered (their annual earning power is estimated at nearly $600 million), the anti-Castro movements have foundered.

In the peak days of 1964, there were more than 300 active and militant anti-Castro exile groups in Miami, but they have dwindled to a handful. Those that are left still picket, demonstrate, and protest, but they also tend to bicker among themselves. With a few heroic exceptions, their efforts have sputtered out on the shores of Florida rather than in Cuba.

The Cubans cluster, perhaps because their orientation toward tradition is not understood in the larger community. They stress inherited custom and law and order. Police say that, except in traffic offenses, they are more law-abiding than the average Miamian. The exile community has been embarrassed, though, by increasing involvement of a few Cubans in narcotics traffic, particularly cocaine. After some forty Cubans had been arrested in Miami as part of a nationwide attack on drug smuggling, one federal narcotics officer announced that there was a Cuban Mafia. He described it as exceptionally violent.

Most Cubans will tell you that the one great political lesson of their lives was taught them by Castro. To them, it was a lesson of betrayal and it has left them highly suspicious of liberal thought and devoted to a kind of evangelical anticommunism. In a local election, some Cubans grumbled because one candidate had a travel agency that did business with Aeroflot, the Russian airline, and that another was unsuitable because a peace symbol hung on his office wall. The John Birch Society and similar conservative groups have recruited among Cubans with some success, limited, however, because most Cubans believe in a cradle-to-grave government care that enrages conservatives.

During the early days of the Cuban influx, when droves of uprooted professionals and technicians were trying to find outlets for their skills, a "clandestine" system of service developed. A wide variety of unlicensed or nonunion Cubans, from barbers to carpenters to doctors, quietly peddled their trades at bargain prices to fellow Cubans in need. Today, the signs of Cuban success are numerous. Rather than Miami's downtown core degenerating into a shell of empty stores and "for rent" signs, as has happened in other cities, Cubans have moved in. There and in nearby neighborhoods they have created Little Havana, not as boisterous and attractively sinful as pre-Castro Havana but with a touch of the same style.

A walk down the Tamiami Trail, or through parts of the southwest section of the city, has the smell and flavor of Cuba. Street conversations are in Spanish; the signs are in Spanish; the food, coffee, and businesses are Cuban; the people read Spanish-language newspapers and listen to Spanish-language radio stations or watch Spanish-language television.

An estimated 6,000 Cuban businesses now operate in the area (current hard times may eliminate some), producing everything from hand-rolled cigars to shoes to boats and furniture. The Cuban labor force numbers more than 65,000 and is expected to reach 100,000 in less than five years. Some 35,000 Cuban children go to public schools. Cuban doctors (nearly 600 are now licensed in Florida) abound in the hospitals.

This vast bilingual pool has helped attract thirty regional Latin American offices to serve international corporations. Even so, some Cubans still complain that they have difficulty making the telephone operator at the fire station or police station understand them when they speak Spanish. The situation is being corrected.

One exception to the general rule of successful relocation, an exception to be found, perhaps, in any American community today, is the behavior of Cuban youth. To the despair of their parents and grandparents, many are adopting North American ways. It becomes a generation gap of extraordinary width, for as older Cubans try to maintain traditions at home, many of the young spend their time outside the home trying to acquire new customs.

An outstanding example has been a young Cuban football player at the University of Florida, Carlos Álvarez (refugee vintage: 1960). A sophomore pass receiver, Álvarez was chosen on most of the all-American teams. He was an instant hero. But when he became a U.S. citizen, let his hair grow stylishly long, and criticized the war in Vietnam, some Cubans felt that Álvarez was abandoning his heritage.

It is odd that, though the United States is conducting one of the most unusual refugee operations in history—an airlift which has brought 230,000 Cubans to this country—many Americans are not even aware of it. Until 1962, regular commercial flights were available from Cuba. After they were curtailed, some refugees arrived by small boat and via legal transit through Spain and Mexico. But most of those now in Miami have come since 1965, when President Johnson inaugurated the airlift as a humanitarian gesture to unite families separated by the revolution. These have received U.S.-paid transportation, federally supervised food and health care, plus their own welfare system, and job settlement.

It works as follows. Twice each day, a U.S. plane takes off from Miami International Airport, flies to Cuba, and returns home with a load of refugees. In Miami, this is called the Freedom Airlift. The arrivals, as might be expected, are both tearful and joyous, and moving even to a non-Cuban spectator. The planes bring in some 800 new Cubans each week, or between 3,000 and 4,000 a month. Some 230,000 have been flown from Cuba since the flights began in December 1965.

The United States charters the planes for $800,000 a year, and welcomes the refugees to these shores with a welfare program that will cost U.S. taxpayers $112 million in 1971. It is a program unique in this era, when more than 20 million refugees are shuffling across various borders, searching for a place to survive. But, of course, what the Cubans have done with this U.S.-subsidized new start may also be unique.

Castro has challenged the propaganda aspect of the airlift by declaring that if the United States made a like offer to people in northeast Brazil, as one example, the same outpouring would result. Others have suggested that the offer might also empty Harlem. Nor does there seem much doubt that the Haitian refugees who try to flee to the Bahama Islands, and are refused permission by U.S. authorities there to continue on to the United States, would welcome such an opportunity. Jamaican migrant workers who cut sugar cane in Florida and must return home at the end of the season (some try to "escape" and stay) would be receptive. The examples could go on and on, for the immigration quota of 120,000 for the Western Hemisphere has a long waiting list.

In local politics, Cubans have yet to realize their potential, partially because many have not yet become citizens but also because exile politics and the yearning for home have diverted their attention. So far, their influence has been mostly vocal, but that is sometimes considerable, because Cubans are skilled, through their anti-Castro experiences, in the arts of propaganda. However, politicians already are looking ahead to the day when the exiles may be 20 percent or more of the registered voters in the Miami area. That would give them a political edge over the black community, which is already 50,000 smaller.

Cuban views seldom mesh with those of the blacks, who have the same ambitions and feel much more frustrated. To Cubans, the blacks often seem suspiciously liberal. Rivalry between the two minorities is spurred by feelings among the blacks that the Cuban is a Johnny-come-lately who walked in (with white complexion, for the most part, and with better education) and skimmed the cream off whatever opportunity there was in Miami. Blacks have grumbled that Cubans were better received and that the federal umbrella of assistance extended to Cubans has been broader than that extended to them.

In some cases, this argument is more emotional than factual, but certainly the Cubans did benefit from a crash program of help and did find open arms in the community. For example, blacks do not have a job resettlement program enabling them to move to other parts of the country, as do the Cubans. The program was designed to spread the Cuban influx to the rest of the country. Federal officials cite a 70 percent resettlement figure. Nevertheless, the Cuban population in the Miami area has increased 100,000 in the last three years as the airlift has brought in from 105,000 to 120,000. These figures indicate that many resettled Cubans become dissatisfied in colder climates and return to Miami.

An unemployed but employable Cuban male head of family can still get $100 a month welfare, but the U.S. citizen in similar circumstances gets nothing. A riot in the Miami black community during the 1968 Republican National Convention brought on a presidentially appointed commission to study the causes. It found that black resentment toward Cuban welfare was one factor. Studies are now under way to determine exactly what welfare differences exist so that they may be corrected.

A recent county survey disclosed that the 1969 median income for blacks was $5,350; for Cubans, $6,550. By 1985, the Cuban income was projected to rise to $9,400; the blacks, $7,800. Other complicating factors are a housing shortage, questions about the security screening given arriving Cubans, and crowding in the schools.

Apparent inequities in welfare caught the eye last summer of William Clay, a young black Congressman from East St. Louis, and so angered him that, as a member of a House Subcommittee on Labor, he began a movement that almost ended not only the airlift but the Cuban Refugee Program as well. Rep. Clay contended there should be one welfare system for all. In a letter dated May 20, he asked President Nixon "to take immediate action to terminate the Cuban airlift operation and make a public announcement of our future posture toward Cuba and its citizens."

This did not go over well at the White House, where the prevailing attitude has been a desire to ignore Cuba (Vice President Agnew has called U.S. policy one of "benign neglect"). Exiles, once enthusiastic about candidate Nixon, have been openly disappointed about his failure as President to move against Cuba. Not wishing to estrange them still further, Nixon preserved the airlift.

But though Clay made no headway with the Administration, he continued the argument. "No longer can this policy be couched or obscured in 'refugee' terminology," he said. "The real refugees of Cuba left in the early 1960s when they had to flee for sanctuary. They were the ones who opposed Castro politically and who faced oppression and mistreatment at the hands of the Castro regime. . . . Though the United States does not recognize Castro, our government volunteers to handle his social and economic problems. Our policy to solve these problems is at the expense of and detriment to American citizens. . . . "

Clay's attempt to stop the airlift came to a vote in the House and failed by 45 to 40 (attendance was not at its best that day). He vowed to continue the fight. One of his opponents, Rep. Otto Passman of Louisiana, made his feelings clear with this comment: "There is a lot of jealousy growing up because these Cubans are willing to work and it embarrasses some of those people who would rather live on a handout."

The common complaint about the airlift, as publicized by Clay, was gently and humorously explored in the 1969 movie, *Popi*. In it, a Puerto Rican slum dweller in New York City, working at three jobs, decided that the only way he could give his two sons a better life was to pass them off as Cuban refugees arriving in Miami. Then, the United States would be moved to help.

In any case, the airlift will eventually wind down because Cuba stopped accepting names for the waiting list in May 1966. A State Department official has estimated that the present list will require another four or five years of the airlift.

Also waiting in Cuba is an impatient group of 800 Americans and their families. When arrangements were made in 1965 to take care of Cubans who wished to leave, these Americans were forgotten. Cuba does not permit them to be part of the airlift, and only a few have been allowed to leave on special flights to Mexico. The United States sends some $15,000 a month in interest-free subsistence loans to those still in Cuba who need help.

Meanwhile Miami, already brimming with Cubans, gets a fresh batch every day on the airlift. They arrive to find a page out of their past coming alive again.

Source: Burt, Al. "Miami: The Cuban Flavor," 299–301. Reprinted with permission from the March 8, 1971, issue of *The Nation*. http://www.thenation.com.

Nicholas M. Horrock, "F.B.I. Releases Most Files on Its Programs to Disrupt Dissident Groups" (1977)

COINTELPRO, an acronym for Counterintelligence Program, encompassed a number of initiatives the Federal Bureau of Investigation (FBI) conducted between 1956 and 1971. Its purpose was to neutralize political dissidents, and it came about in response to the reversal of a law that outlawed the Communist Party in the heat of the Cold War. When Congress reversed the policies developed in large part by the House Committee on Un-American Activities and Senator Joseph McCarthy (1908–1957), the FBI responded by organizing COINTELPRO, a program designed to neutralize those who could no longer be prosecuted but were persons FBI director J. Edgar Hoover (1895–1972) considered dangerous subversives. A "communist front organization" was defined as anyone Hoover called a communist or a fellow traveler, that is, a person who may not be a communist but is sympathetic to its goals. The FBI used these programs to conduct surveillance on individuals and organizations, often disrupting the organizations by infiltrating them. Nationalists were discredited. The following excerpt from a New York Times *article memorializes the release and declassification of COINTELPRO documents—many of which are available on the Internet today.*

The bureau [FBI] had Cointelpros against Yugoslavian groups, Cuban groups, and the Socialist Workers Party, as well as the Puerto Rican nationalists, left-leaning antiwar radicals, black extremist groups, and white militants. There was no clear formula that caused a particular group to become a target, though only one traditional criminal organization was ever involved.

Source: Horrock, Nicholas M. "F.B.I. Releases Most Files on Its Programs to Disrupt Dissident Groups." *New York Times*, November 22, 1977, 26.

"Socialism" from "Pastoral Letter of the Nicaraguan Episcopate" (November 17, 1979)

Liberation theology, a movement within the Catholic Church to give a political voice to the poor, was popular in Latin America from the 1960s through the 1990s. It came about during a time of church reform and was a reaction to developmentalism, which led to a greater dependence of Latin American countries on U.S. markets. The marketplace, rather than ameliorating the plight of the poor, had worsened it, hastening a decline of small farms. Popular sentiment turned to a nationalism that encouraged populist leaders. Progressive priests and ministers encouraged lay participation in the church, setting the stage for a movement for basic education.

The Second Vatican Council was convened by Pope John XXIII in 1962 and brought about sweeping reforms. By the time Pope Paul VI closed the Second Vatican Council in 1965, these changes gave a theoretical justification for activities developed under the auspices of a theology of progress, authentic secularization, and human advancement. Christian groups were reformed to bring about social and political liberation (freedom). In the definition of liberation theology, religious salvation was not defined by prayer, the next world, or even faith but in the faithful's relationship to the material world. In Central America, religious orders such as the Jesuits, Maryknolls, and Franciscans actively formed comunidades de base (base communities) and organized study groups to raise the consciousness of believers. Jesus Christ was a liberator, and according to the theology of liberation, the mission of Christianity is to bring justice to the poor and oppressed. Rather than discouraging political activism, liberation theology encouraged it. Liberation theology also acknowledged that the church had been an ally of the ruling elite. Immediately, the new consciousness was at odds with the rich, who blamed the priests for the discontent and protests that led to the fall of Nicaraguan dictator Anastasio Somoza (1925–1980). The following article from The Nation includes a pastoral letter from the Nicaraguan bishop that gives the Church's stance on socialism. It takes a sharp turn from previous Church policy.

It [is] expressed, at times even with anguish, the fear that the present Nicaraguan process is headed toward socialism. People have asked us, the bishops, what we think about that. If, as some think, socialism debilitates people by usurping their character of being free protagonists of history, if it aims to submit people blindly to the manipulations and dictates of people who arbitrarily exercise power, such a spurious or false socialism we could not accept. Neither could we accept a socialism which takes from man the right to have a religious motivation to his life or to express publicly those motivations and convictions, whatever be his religious faith.

Equally unacceptable would be to deny to parents the right to educate their children according to their convictions [and] other rights of the human person. If, on the other hand, socialism signifies, as it ought to signify, pre-eminence of the interests of the majority of Nicaraguans and a model of a nationally planned economy that is progressively participatory, then we have nothing to object to. A social plan that guarantees the common destiny of the wealth and resources of the country and permits the satisfaction of the fundamental necessities of everyone and an improvement of the human quality of life seems to us just. Socialism implies a growing diminution of injustices and the traditional inequalities between city and country, between the remuneration for intellectual and manual work; if it signifies participation of the worker in the control of the process, thereby overcoming economic alienation, there is nothing in Christianity which would contradict this process. Rather, Pope John Paul II just recalled to mind in the United Nations the problems caused by the radical separation between work and property.

If socialism supposes power [is] exercised from the perspective of the great majority and increasingly shared by the organized people in a manner which leads toward a true transferal of power to the popular classes. Again one will find in the faith only motivation and support. If socialism produces cultural processes that awaken the dignity of our masses and encourages them to assume responsibilities and to demand their rights, then we are dealing with a humanization which converges with the human dignity that our faith proclaims. With respect to the class struggle, we think that one [of the] things [is] the dynamic fact of the class struggle which ought to produce just transformation of societal structures, and another thing is class hatred which is directed against persons and contradicts radically the Christian obligation to conduct oneself by love.

Our faith assures us that it is a fundamental Christian obligation to master the world, transforming the land and the rest of the resources for production. In order to permit people to live and to make of this Nicaraguan land a land of justice, solidarity, peace, and liberty, in which everyone will acquire a sense of the Christian announcement of the reign of God.

What is more, we have confidence that the revolutionary process will be something original, creative, profoundly national, and in no manner a simple imitation of other processes. With the majority of Nicaraguans, what we aim for is a process that will lead finally toward a fully and authentically non-capitalist Nicaragua, neither dependent nor totalitarian.

Translated by James Russell

Source: Lernoux, Penny. "The Church Revolutionary in Latin America," 623–624. Reprinted with permission from the May 24, 1980, issue of *The Nation*. http://www.thenation.com.

Linda Ocasio, "Portrait of an Organizer: Edgar deJesus" (1996)

In the 1960s, in Chicago, the Young Lords transformed from a street gang into a political organization. In prison, José "Cha Cha" Jiménez (1948–), one of the seven founders of the Young Lords street gang, met Fred Hampton and other Black Panther Party members. The Black Panthers were organized to promote civil rights and to defend the African American community. They were militant, dressed in uniforms, and wore black berets. Jiménez found common ground with the Panthers. Upon his release from prison, Jiménez transformed the Young Lords into a politically conscious organization committed to the liberation of the Puerto Rican people. The group believed in political control of the community and the responsiveness of its institutions to the community. Chapters spread to New York and elsewhere. The following is an excerpt from a portrait of Edgar deJesus, a Young Lords organizer.

When Edgar deJesus was growing up in East Harlem in the late 1960s, he was surrounded by the sights and sounds of a generation awakening to its own power. The Young Lords, a group of young Puerto Ricans committed to seizing the day on behalf of a community, commandeered a local church as the site for a children's breakfast program. It was the beginning of a community offensive that demanded respect and better services for the residents of the neighborhood known as El Barrio. "The offensive was happening in front of our faces," deJesus recalls. "It focused everyone on poverty."

Seared into his memory are the discussions that erupted over the dinner table or on the street about the causes of poverty. "It's illogical to have poverty in the richest country in the world," he remembers thinking. "It was the simple concept of why is there a division of rich and poor." DeJesus also recalls his father, a hotel waiter and shop steward, arguing vigorously in defense of the trade union movement as crucial to the economic stability of Latino families like his own.

DeJesus, now 40, is the assistant manager and director of organizing for the NY/NJ Regional Joint Board of the Union of Needle-trades, Industrial and Textile Employees (UNITE). The 350,000-member union was formed in July 1995 by a merger of the International Ladies' Garment Workers' Union (ILGWU) and the Amalgamated Clothing and Textile Workers Union (ACTWU). It is not only in his official UNITE capacity that deJesus is influencing the labor movement; he is also a member of the New York City Hispanic Labor Committee in East Harlem and the AFL-CIO Labor Council on Latin American Advancement.

Through his participation in these advisory bodies, deJesus has helped articulate a northeast Latino perspective on NAFTA and issues of trade that provided an important counterpoint to the pro-NAFTA drumbeat of the Clinton Administration and Latino business leaders. "Eddie managed to build a very solid roundtable of Latino unionism, including Puerto Ricans, Cubans, and Dominicans," says Hector Figueroa, an analyst with Service Employees International Union (SEIU). "He has made unions more sensitive to the needs of Latinos, especially in the Northeast, which tend to be overlooked."

Figueroa also credits deJesus with helping to reconnect the labor and civil rights movement, an alliance that has unraveled in the 33 years since Martin Luther King Jr. marched on Washington, D.C., with black and white union leaders at his side. "Eddie makes a contribution on a national agenda. He moves the labor movement, not just the Latino issues within the labor movement," says Figueroa. DeJesus also has ties with the Puerto Rican movement: he is a board member of the

Institute for Puerto Rican Policy and a former vice president of the National Congress of Puerto Rican Rights.

For deJesus, his stint as a teenage Puerto Rican activist lit the fire for a lifelong commitment to social justice. "I wouldn't be here if it weren't for that experience," he says. His experience is significant for the U.S. labor movement, as it seeks to re-energize itself, in part by addressing the issues of minority communities that it had ignored in the past.

By the time Eddie joined with the Young Lords in 1973–1974, the group had splintered and evolved into the Puerto Rican Revolutionary Workers Organization, a Marxist-Leninist group. That group eventually crumbled, fueled by paranoia and mistrust, which deJesus and others now attribute to deliberate government subversion—a fate common to radical left political groups in the 1970s. "From 1975 to 1976 was the most demoralized period in my life," deJesus says. After dropping out of Brooklyn College, he took refuge in family, marrying his high school sweetheart, Yolanda. Together they went to work in a bookbinding factory on 10th Avenue in Manhattan.

In addition to what he observed on the streets of East Harlem, deJesus had another influence shaping his political and organizing principles: his father. "My father was my first teacher of trade unionism," deJesus says. "My father made it clear, that if it weren't for the union, we wouldn't have anything." The evidence was all around him: Puerto Rican families who had a least one parent in a union stayed together and were financially stable, whether they lived in East Harlem, the Bronx, or the Lower East Side.

However, deJesus' first experience with a union was not what he expected at all. At the bookbinding factory he joined with coworkers to decertify a Teamsters local that was not representing the Latino workers. "They were disgruntled with the union and the union reps," he recalls. The experience gave him a chance to put into practice his beliefs about what a union should do for its members. "I was seeing in reality what I had theorized about," he says. Later, he and his wife moved on to a metal factory; she did clerical work for a jewelry workers union and he became a metal spinner.

By 1980, much of the fury that had splintered the Puerto Rican movement began to fade for deJesus, and he started contacting activists that he had lost touch with in Chicago and Canada. He reconnected to the Puerto Rican movement through the National Congress of Puerto Rican Rights, where he established a labor task force. Through the task force, he published for two years a newspaper called *El Obrero Boricua* (*The Puerto Rican Worker*). "We became the more activist Latino voice of the labor movement," he says. At that time he was also working with the Workers Education Center in Manhattan, which melded radical politics with labor-rights awareness. In 1985, he completed a study of Puerto Rican workers in New York City.

DeJesus began to draw the attention of older Latino labor leaders, including Edward Gonzalez, a onetime organizer for the ILGWU who taught at Cornell University's School of Industrial and Labor Relations. "He looked at my work with the task force and put me into labor law courses at Cornell," deJesus recalls. Gonzalez also did something more. He introduced deJesus to trade union veterans. "They were not radicals, just basic trade unionists who spent all their lives building unions," deJesus recalls. "That was probably the beginning of my left politics merging with my trade unionism in practice." After two years at Cornell, deJesus headed the school's Puerto Rican Latino Studies program for trade unionists.

From there, he worked as an organizer, business agent, and eventually administrator for the Capmakers Union Local 2 of ACTWU. Today he oversees organizing for the New York/New Jersey region of UNITE from his office in Union City, NJ. And the Latino communities he works with are not just Puerto Ricans, Cubans, and Dominicans. In the textile mills of Passaic and Paterson, Colombian and Peruvian workers predominate, and with them comes a more militant legacy of activism, deJesus observes: "They're used to the state negotiating with unions and general strikes. There, negotiations are done region or statewide. Here, it's done factory by factory."

In addition to reaching out to the Latino community in all of its diversity, DeJesus says strengthening the link between labor and the civil rights movement is a continuing effort. Recalling the 1963 March on Washington, he has a tone of wistfulness as he lists some of the unions that linked arms with Rev. King: the UAW, AFSCME, and the Steelworkers. "I'm waiting for that to happen with the Latino labor movement," he says.

Source: Ocasio, Linda. "Portrait of an Organizer: Edgar deJesus." *NACLA Report on the Americas* 30, no. 3 (November/December 1996): 27.

Frances Negrón-Muntaner, "Feeling Pretty: West Side Story and Puerto Rican Identity Discourses" (2000)

As with most people living in the United States, the question of identity has been important to Latinos and Puerto Ricans in particular. Although Puerto Ricans use the term "Latino" in the cultural sense, they generally identify themselves as Puerto Rican, Boricua, Borinquen, or borincano, which comes from the Taíno name for the island. The Taíno Indians were the first inhabitants of Puerto Rico. In the 1960 census, more than 95 percent of the inhabitants of Puerto Rico identified as Puerto Rican. Immigration to the U.S. mainland slowed down—whereas during the decade from 1950 to 1960, there were 470,000 Boricua who left the island, in the 1960s only 214,000 would leave. There were other patterns affecting identity: in 1940, 88 percent of mainland Puerto Ricans lived in New York City; by 1970, only 59 percent lived there. In the 1960s, Puerto Ricans were the second-largest Spanish-speaking group in the United States, second only to Mexican Americans. Nearly 2.3 million Puerto Ricans lived on the island and 892,513 on the mainland. In the 1960s, the second generation of immigrants to the mainland was now larger. More youth were influenced by black Americans, and they attempted to construct an identity for the U.S. boricua community. Other Spanish-speaking people lived among them but had not reached a critical mass; they remained "more immigrant" and looked to their home country for identity. Although Puerto Ricans continued to look to the island, they were building a unique group identity. Over time many had become "Nuyoricans" (Puerto Ricans raised in New York).

Puerto Rico itself was at the meeting point of the English-speaking and Spanish-speaking Americas and was greatly affected by the anticolonial rhetoric of the day. Part of this identity discourse was portrayed in movies and through expressions of racism in the greater society. This discourse would influence other Spanish-speaking groups who shared physical and, finally, cultural space and would result in the fusion of Puerto Rican music with that of other Caribbean peoples, especially with Cubans and Dominicans. Many Latinos credit music with helping maintain the identity and unity of the disparate groups. New York was the center of much of this fusion, although in the 1960s Chicago had begun to rival it. The following excerpts are from a critical review of West Side Story, *a Broadway musical that was also a 1961 film criticized by Puerto Ricans and other Latinos because it used a white actress in the main role and stereotyped Puerto Ricans.* West Side Story *was billed as a Puerto Rican Romeo and Juliet in which the white guy gets the girl.*

There is no single American cultural product that haunts Puerto Rican identity discourses in the United States more intensely than the 1961 film *West Side Story*, directed by Robert Wise and Jerome Robbins. Although neither the first nor last American movie to portray Puerto Ricans as gang members (men) or as sassy and virginal (women), hardly any Puerto Rican cultural critic or screen actor can refrain from stating their very special relationship to *West Side Story*. Jennifer López, the highest paid Latina actress in Hollywood today, recalls that her favorite movie was *West Side Story*. "I saw it over and over. I never noticed that Natalie Wood wasn't really a Puerto Rican girl. I grew up always wanting to play Anita [Rita Moreno's Oscar-winning role], but as I got older, I wanted to be María. I went to dance classes every week." Journalist Blanca Vázquez, whose editorial work in the publication Centro was crucial in creating a space for critical discourse on Latinos in media, comments: "And what did the 'real' Puerto Rican, Anita, do in the film? She not only was another Latina 'spitfire,' she also sang a song denigrating Puerto Rico and by implication, being Puerto Rican. . . . I remember seeing it and being ashamed." For Island-born cultural critic Alberto Sandoval, the film became pivotal in his own identity formation: "'Alberto, I've just met a guy named Alberto.' And how can I forget those who upon my arrival would start tapping flamenco steps and squealing: 'I like to be in America?' As the years passed by I grew accustomed to their actions and reactions to my presence. I would smile and ignore the stereotype of Puerto Ricans that Hollywood promotes."

Without a touch of irony, Leonard Bernstein has written about the extent to which he researched Puerto Rican culture in New York before writing the score: "We went to a gym in Brooklyn where there were different gangs that a social organization was trying to bring together. I don't know if too much eventually got into *West Side Story*, but everything does help." The "superficiality" of the way that Puerto Ricans were represented in the book made one of the original *West Side Story* producers, Cheryl Crawford, insist that "the show explains why the poor in New York, who had once been Jewish, were now Puerto Rican and black. . . . " When someone said the piece was a poetic fantasy, not a sociological document, she replied, "You have to rewrite the whole thing or I won't do it." Hence, if *West Side Story* was never intended to be "real" and doesn't feel real to Puerto Rican spectators, what accounts for its reality effects?

For many Puerto Rican spectators who identify with the narrative, *West Side Story* is a morality play about "our" everyday problems: racism, poverty, and the destructiveness of violence. An example of this pedagogical reading is exemplified by Actor's Playhouse, a Miami-based theater group that recently staged the musical to a group of "at risk" young adults who were mostly Latinos. The purpose was "to show them the devastating consequences of associating with gang members who use violence as their primary way of solving differences. This benign view of the film, however, was not shared by the government officials who pulled *West Side Story* out of the Brussels World's Fair "on the grounds that it was bad publicity for America." Hence, far from the homogeneous reading some critics have given the film as a piece of racist propaganda against Puerto Ricans, *West Side Story* endures in part due to the many discursive uses and "real" identifications it allows.

Several key discourses and histories of Puerto Rican–American representation coalesce in this text. First, the film—although not an entirely predictable Hollywood musical . . . perseveres in a long tradition of representing Latinos as inherently musical and performative subjects, ready to wear their sexualized identity for a white audience at the drop of a hat. Consistent with this history, the "Puerto Rican music" found in *West Side Story* is an American-made fusion of a wide range of rhythms with no discernible or specific national origin. In this sense, despite *West Side Story*'s dramatic elements, Latinos are doing exactly what they are expected to do, particularly at a time of significant racial and social unrest in the United States: singing and dancing the night away.

Source: Negrón-Muntaner, Frances. "Feeling Pretty: West Side Story and Puerto Rican Identity Discourses." *Social Text 63* 18, no. 2 (Summer 2000): 84–85. Reprinted with permission of Duke University Press.

Antonia Pantoja, *Memoir of a Visionary: Antonia Pantoja* (2002)

Because of such factors as the brutal suppression of Puerto Rican nationalists during the 1930s and 1950s and the growth of the middle class, the number of Puerto Ricans demanding independence from the United States declined. Many seemed resigned to remaining a colony within the United States. However, encouraged by the anticolonial rhetoric of the time, many Puerto Rican youth took up the cause of independence and considered Nationalists such as Pedro Albizu Campos (1891–1965) and Lolita Lebrón (1919–2010) role models and martyrs to the cause of freedom. Both had been imprisoned for their political beliefs and actions. Because they did not compromise their ideals, young Puerto Ricans identified more with the Nationalists than with Puerto Rico's accommodationist former governor, Luis Muñoz Marín (1898–1980). Within this context, the status of Puerto Rico was debated. Moreover, the 1960s saw a surge in second-generation Puerto Ricans in the United States, and although inspired by Campos, Lebrón, and love for the island, their issues focused on the mainland. The following excerpts are from the memoirs of Antonia Pantoja (1922–2002). Pantoja was the founder of one of the premier organizations in the 1906s for the empowerment, education, and leadership development of Puerto Rican youth, ASPIRA, a nonprofit agency with offices in six states. The organization took its name from the Spanish word "aspira," *which means aspire. Pantoja was a Puerto Rican activist in the 1960s, and she is still remembered today. These excerpts from her memoirs show the link between the younger generation of Puerto Ricans in the 1960s and their beloved island.*

Our family was one of the many families that grew up poor in Puerto Rico, surrounded by a society where privilege, abundance, and opportunities existed for others. The families of Barrio Obrero, a workers' community, survived and enjoyed the benefits of a strong internal social structure of belonging and respecting one another. The struggles of living in this community, under these circumstances, affected me in both positive and negative ways. I was born in Puerta de Tierra, a slum of the Old San Juan city. San Juan is a walled city, and the wall had two doors: Puerta del Mar, which still exists, and the door to the land, Puerta de Tierra. These doors in the wall were made for people to escape in case an invader would win a battle and the inhabitants had to escape either by sea or by land. The land door does not exist anymore because the wall was demolished on that side as the city grew. Today, there is only a small piece of the wall where the door used to be. The people left behind as San Juan grew were poor families that rented railroad-type apartments in houses made of wood.

I must have been two or three years old when we left Puerta de Tierra and moved to Barrio Obrero. We were a poor family in a poor neighborhood. In Barrio Obrero, the streets were numbered from 1 to 17. Avenida Borinquen, the main avenue, had a plaza from streets 12 to 15. As you traveled away from Avenida Borinquen toward the water, called El Cafio, the land became muddy, and when it rained, the waters flooded over the banks. The people who lived between Avenida Borinquen and Avenida A had sturdy houses. The first four houses were made of cement and the rest were made of wood. Houses below Avenida A did not have inside toilets or showers. They had outhouses. Barrio Obrero was built as a housing project for workers and their families who had lived in overcrowded areas. Other homes were built in the muddy areas by homeless, poorer people who had moved from rural areas.

Families living in Barrio Obrero did not pay rent. They paid taxes at the end of the year. This left us with the basic expenses of food, clothing, transportation, and medical care. In our family, we had a generous contributor to the food supply. We had a prolific breadfruit tree that fed us for years. You could add oil, vinegar, and codfish flakes to the breadfruit when there was money to buy luxuries. This tree was particularly important to us when Grandfather lost his job and after he died.

Barrio Obrero was a good neighborhood to grow up in. We all knew each other. There was a spirit of belonging, and we identified with one another. We knew of other neighborhoods, like Sunoco, but we always felt more united and proud of our own community. For other people, we were just a poor neighborhood, but we knew that we were more. Famous people were our neighbors. The Cortijos, a well-known family of musicians, lived in Barrio Obrero. Our neighbors were carpenters and cement workers who worked in the local factory.

Racial identity was not a major issue among the members of my neighborhood. We were a people of many colors and many shades. Some had straight hair; some had kinky hair, like mine; others had red or blond hair. This mixture was typical of the poor Puerto Rican neighborhoods. Although I would be considered a grifra (the name given to a person who has kinky hair, but has features associated with a Caucasian background), my mother was a black person with Negroid features, as were my grandmother and grandfather.

In the new home in Barrio Obrero, we had a place where we could have meetings. On some evenings, many men friends and coworkers of my grandfather would come to the house. They spoke loud, banged on the table, and used vulgar and dirty words and phrases. They were all workers who lived in the neighborhood. I would be put to bed and prohibited from coming to the parlor. However, I would get up and sit by the entrance of the living room to watch and listen. I was not allowed to participate or be seen. These men were angry at the tobacco factory owners. They wanted to get paid more money for their work. They wanted to form what was called a sindicato, a workers' union. My grandmother would bring coffee and large serving dishes full of serenta, slices of potatoes, tomatoes, yautfa, yuca, avocado, rings of white onions, red sweet peppers, and sliced codfish.

I did not realize that my work would be of such future historical importance to my community and to the city. It was only when I became the executive director of ASPIRA that I began to realize that our work would change the lives of many Puerto Rican youths and their families. As I write this book today, I continue to learn about the full impact of the work that we have had.

With the experience that the Forum gained in creating its first institution, the board began an examination of new problems that it could address. At the same time, a new public policy was announced by the federal government to designate funds for assisting the poor in establishing instruments for their own empowerment. Our board felt that we had the experience, knowledge, and philosophical understanding to work on a project that could address the community's poverty. We were an institution that had worked before anyone ever mentioned the War on Poverty. We had worked, placing our time, intelligence, energy, and personal funds together, to develop the organization. We had tested experience. We felt called upon to establish a citywide effort to assist all the existing Puerto Rican organizations in our community to develop the best War on Poverty effort in the city of New York. This commitment led the Forum to embark on its second project, the Puerto Rican Community Development Project in 1964.

ASPIRA, THE MOST IMPORTANT WORK OF MY LIFE

If you asked me, "What was the most important and impacting work that you have ever done?" I would reply, "The founding of ASPIRA." ASPIRA occupies a very special place in my heart. Trying to tell the story will be very difficult. Don Miguel de Unamuno, the Spanish philosopher and novelist, once said that a sheet of paper is dead and incapable of transmitting the emotions one wishes to convey. My words are clumsy in English and may be unable to capture the feelings that I wish to transmit. I will try, however.

The idea for a youth project began out of the early work of PRACA [Puerto Rican Association for Community Affairs] and its youth conferences. The conceptualizing of the idea continued throughout my education as a social worker and during [my] association with Puerto Rican youths while working at the Union Settlement House. The ideas lived in my mind and on pieces of paper, the full implementation did not come about until Dr. Horne supported the effort through the Commission on Intergroup Relations. This . . . period actually spans over seven years, ending in 1961. As I reflect on it now, I had begun to consider many theories of group work and development when I was a student at the New York School of Social Work, but I had not begun to think of program ideas. When I graduated from the School of Social Work, I went out of my way to find a job in the Puerto Rican community commonly called "El Barrio" in East Harlem. I could not be employed in a Puerto Rican agency, since they were nonexistent. I opted for the best substitute in selecting the Settlement House on 104th Street between Third and Second Avenues. I was employed as the director of the adult program. There were only two Puerto Ricans on the staff. Although situated in the heart of El Barrio, the Settlement House did not attract many Puerto Ricans because they did not speak English.

While working at the Settlement, I continued to share an apartment with Helen, but we had moved to a small unit in a renovated apartment building on 97th Street, between Lexington and Third Avenues. While we lived there, I found myself relating more and more to the Puerto Rican community. Helen would accompany me to some of the activities, but most of the time I would attend alone. Our lives began to go in separate directions. After a big disagreement, we separated our lives, and I continued to live in the apartment until I applied to buy a cooperative apartment at La Salle and 125th Street. The meetings of PRACA could now be held comfortably in my new apartment, since it was big and beautiful. My house became the center of activity for the younger professionals in the Puerto Rican community. I began to be considered the center of the group.

The original idea that I presented to Dr. Horne was called "New Leaders in New York." It was to organize youths into clubs that would become the vehicles to encourage them to find their identity, learn leadership skills by working on problems that their communities suffered, complete high school, and enter college to pursue a career that would allow them to give back to their community. The idea had germinated in my mind as a result of various experiences that I had when I arrived in New York. The idea began to haunt my thoughts after having heard discussions from Puerto Rican high school students who attended the youth conferences that PRACA was holding. These conferences were organized and held by the youths themselves, who were the leaders and speakers telling us how powerless and insignificant they were made to feel by their classmates and teachers. The students discussed their fear of speaking in their classes, their shame because of their native language, their fear of the gangs from other ethnic groups, and their fear of the police. I was deeply concerned about what I was hearing.

The implementation of my ideas would not come easily. I had to pursue many different persons and approaches before I could succeed. At the Settlement House and through the activities of PRACA, I had become more deeply committed to a program of action that would change the lives of these young people. As I would walk to my job in El Barrio, I would see a group of Puerto Rican teenagers standing in front of the Settlement, engaging in what seemed to me a strange ritual: taking turns spitting. I would say, "Good afternoon." There would be no answer. One early evening as I prepared to visit the adult club meeting, I noticed a young man leaning against the wall in front of the door to my office. He seemed to be a member of the group that I had seen spitting in front of the building. I said hello and he responded.

I seized the opportunity to ask if he was a member of the youth program on the fourth floor. He replied no, but said that he had come to speak with me if I had the time. When I said that I had the time, he sat down and opened with a barrage of questions, one right after the other.

What was my position in the Settlement House? Since I had an accent, was I a Puerto Rican? Did I go to school in New York?

I answered the questions as he asked them. Then I asked one question, "What is the game that I see you and your friends playing outside? The spitting?"

"It's a contest. Whoever spits the farthest, wins."
"Wins what?" I asked.

"Wins nothing."

We continued to talk about the fact that he lived in the Bronx, but came to East Harlem to visit his friends. He worked in a shoe factory downtown. His name was Eddie Gonzalez, and he was seventeen years old. He was one of fourteen children. He had dropped out of school to help support his family. The Gonzalez family was on welfare, but he had to supplement their income, since sixteen members needed his help. Eddie confessed that he was sorry that he had dropped out of school, but he considered it too late to return. I shared my experiences of going to night school and using vocational services to plan to complete college. I encouraged him to consider that he was young enough to return to school to complete his high school education at night and still continue to help his family. He argued that he was too old to return to school. I shared my experiences of attending night school with many adults who were his age or older.

I invited Eddie to join the group called HYAA. Later on, Eddie did complete his education and left his own impact on the city of New York by helping a whole generation of Puerto Ricans to obtain leadership positions in the labor unions. He developed a union leadership institute at Cornell University.

The experience with Eddie propelled me into writing the project for leaders of the new immigrants in the city. My idea was to pick up youth and provide a way for their "hanging out together" (the clubs), following a behavior that was natural to their age group. In the clubs, they would learn about their culture and the country of their parents, and also learn how to survive in the school and the neighborhood. The club would provide opportunities to develop feelings of self-worth and appreciation for their culture as they learned leadership skills to work in their communities. The clubs would substitute for the gangs that were already becoming popular protective groups for Italian, Polish, and black youths.

I worked on my idea of developing youth clubs by researching how the Jewish community had developed its youth programs. I also studied the literature on youth gangs and their origins. This information was becoming available through the city's newly organized agency, the Youth Board, an agency that had been formed to work mission, objectives, and a work plan. Everyone agreed that this new leadership program should not become a service agency; instead, in form and methods, it should be a movement. However, we all were wise enough to understand that it had to render some service if it was to be successful in raising funds.

The very important act of naming the project engaged the group in discussions that clearly indicated a philosophical position and a profound understanding that to work with youth we had to impart values, optimism, and the decision to succeed. We wanted an upbeat name, one word to express belief in one's self. The word aspira was finally selected. It was chosen because to aspire is upbeat. We all wished the meaning would be "I will aspire and I will attain." The Spanish command form ASPIRA, of the verb aspirar, was perfect.

We made fast progress in organizing ASPIRA. Dr. Horne's introduction to Mr. Sol Markoff, executive director of the New York Foundation, went a long way toward making our proposal more fundable. Horne introduced me to four other foundations. A couple of board members and I met with representatives of these foundations to present and defend the proposal. We were all novices in such matters, but we were able to obtain interviews with five funding sources: the New York, the Field, the Hofueimer, the Rockefeller Brothers, and the Taconic Foundations. Sol Markoff became our mentor and our facilitator during these interviews. All five foundations approved requests for funding. In fact, after a few months of functioning, we approached the Taconic Foundation. They suggested that I increase the amount requested, and funded us for three consecutive years, pending the positive evaluation of each year's work.

In the autumn of 1961, we received letters from the five foundations accepting our proposals and assigning funds. The Forum board called a meeting to discuss what to do, since we now had funds to start the project, but no one had ever had the experience of administering an institution. At the meeting, they all concluded that I should resign my position with the city of New York to come and direct ASPIRA. I postponed an answer until I had spoken with Dr. Horne. He agreed with the board: I should leave the Commission and become the first executive director of ASPIRA. He acknowledged that it was risky to leave the security of city employment, but he said that I was the only person who could get ASPIRA going. It must be understood that I had never directed an institution, but with the help of all my friends, I took the job. And I learned on the job as problems emerged and needed to be resolved.

The physical work and good social times were accompanied by long and arduous hours of discussion and decisions. We wanted to develop a program that would work with youths in groups because we believed that that way, it would be economically feasible to reach large numbers of young people. I had been a group worker, and I also knew that the adolescents would be most influential on each other. We planned for the groups or clubs to be organized in schools, in churches, on street corners, in billiard parlors, or wherever young people congregated. The youths would be asked to organize their own ASPIRA clubs, and by following a list of eight required steps, they would be accepted into a federation of clubs. Once the groups completed the eighth step, they would be initiated through a ceremony called areyto. The idea of the areyto had been borrowed from a ceremony of the native Taínos (the original inhabitants of the island of Puerto Rico who used the ceremony to celebrate their leaders).

From the beginning, ASPIRA adopted three major objectives in working with youth:

To organize a youth movement in the Puerto Rican community that would learn leadership skills, problem identification, and problem-solving skills, and to work through the clubs and the club federation in resolving the problems of the Puerto Rican community of New York.

To help club members study the history and the culture of Puerto Rico, as well as the history of their parents' immigration to New York, and to use this knowledge to develop a commitment to and positive identification with their community, in order to strengthen their participation in the life of their community.

To stay in high school, to graduate, and to identify a field, profession, or area of work in which the youths could earn a livelihood and acquire the skills to work as a leader in the community. The federation bylaws spelled out the number of youths allowed in each club, the naming of the club, the community projects to be selected for the club's work, the selection of career study areas, the assignment of a staff person, and the training and responsibilities of personnel to work with youth.

Our planning went very well. However, immediately upon opening our doors for service, a series of internal problems with the board and members of the community emerged. The members of our board had never served before on the board of directors of an institution. The Puerto Rican community of New York had never had an institution that offered services with a staff and formal offices. So, neither the board nor the community knew how to relate to their new institution.

An example of the kind of problem that I had to resolve with my own board came very early in the life of ASPIRA. At one of the early board meetings, the chairperson requested monies to establish a bar for the meetings. I would not approve the expenditures of grant funds for purchasing rum, beer, gin, ice, cheese, crackers, lemons, or mixers. I added that the idea was a good one, however, and I placed $20 as my donation to support the idea of the bar. I requested that board members do the same. I further requested that a proposition be introduced for a vote that would establish the policy that funds donated to ASPIRA could not be spent on activities or items for the benefit of the board, because it violated our tax-exempt status. A long and heated discussion followed with the board finally approving a policy that established the board's respect for donated funds and our responsibility to use funds only for the objectives of the specific donation. Even though I felt good about the end result of this first struggle, I was upset because it resulted in a tense relationship between the chair of the board and myself.

Problems that we encountered as we began to be known in the community were created by our community's lack of knowledge and experience in relating to an institution and in the feelings of some community members that felt they had a privileged status because they knew members of the board. For example, members of the community who considered themselves "important" would bring or send their children to request scholarships without belonging to or working in the clubs. In other instances, board members would send relatives or friends to obtain jobs for which they had no skills or for jobs that did not exist. The examples were numerous, but they always reflected a desire to obtain special privileges or resources. These problems and complaints were discussed at our board meetings, and were at times used by others to say that ASPIRA was not serving the community. I held firm in refusing to compromise our funding obligations and our mission and philosophy. As ASPIRA became better known, these problems diminished.

The most serious and destructive problems came from other youth and educational agencies and from non-Puerto Ricans. Very serious examples of these were hate letters, tapes, and recordings sent to me personally and to ASPIRA. Threats of violence were received whenever there was a news article announcing our receipt of a grant. I opened a file on these letters, following the advice of the police. Other less violent attacks came from people in the audiences at conferences where I was invited to speak. Members of the audience would angrily ask why we were segregating our youths into separate clubs and why we Puerto Ricans needed help in adjusting to the city when other newcomers had to make it on their own. Other youth-serving agencies attacked the idea of our setting up a separate new agency instead of bringing the funds and our youths into already existing programs. Fortunately, no physical attacks were ever made, only threats. From these experiences, I learned how to handle myself and to deflect the attacks. Sometimes I would respond directly and harshly. Other times, I thought it best to throw the questions back to those who challenged our work.

By far, the most difficult opposition came from the Board of Education, which wrote to ASPIRA saying our counselors would not be allowed to counsel the students because they were not licensed. I wrote back stating that we did not want the licensed counselors of the Board of Education to counsel our children because their advice was destructive to our youths' future. In the end, this was a function of ASPIRA that the board could not control, since our educational planning and counseling was conducted in the clubs at ASPIRA's offices. Later on when we had many clubs, they met at schools, but by then ASPIRA had enough strength to overcome the Board of Education's protests.

One of the really destructive acts of the Board of Education was not to allow the organizing of ASPIRA clubs in schools with high enrollments of Puerto Rican students unless a teacher was present at all times. This was fought vehemently by ASPIRA at the Board of Education level because it involved the attendance of teachers in meetings after school hours, for which they were not compensated. ASPIRA collected information on other student organizations, such as Hillel, NAACP

[National Association for the Advancement of Colored People], Catholic and Protestant clubs, and other ethnic youth clubs, such as the Irish, Spanish, and Italian clubs. ASPIRA was able to win recognition for its clubs, but the issue of the presence of a teacher advisor to be present at all meetings remained. The youths were able to convince some teachers to fulfill this requirement.

The club programs grew to be very impressive in membership size, number, and impact. The ASPIRA Club Federation became a very powerful organization with very successful programs. The most notable ones were the summer leadership study trips to Puerto Rico, the annual conference to evaluate and plan the federation program, the Areyto Leadership Initiation Ceremony, the Annual Graduation Dance, and the Annual Colleges and Universities Fair. The important fact about the model of the work in clubs was that it was invented by the youth.

About two weeks after we opened the offices on West 72nd Street in Manhattan, a young woman came in and asked if she could meet with the director. I received her and she proceeded to tell me, "I am a high school student in Brooklyn. I read in the newspaper that ASPIRA is organizing Puerto Rican youths in high schools. I came to inform you that I already have organized my own club in our high school. We met and decided that I should come to find out how you will work with us. We are ready."

"We think that in order to make a reality of the idea that Aspirantes have the strength to be a force in the fight for the rights of Puerto Rican students and adults, the clubs should be organized into a federation of clubs called the ASPIRA Club Federation (ACF)." On the blackboard, they drew a scheme showing the relationship of each club to the federation and the relationship of the ACF to the ASPIRA board of directors. It was a delight to see the youths already becoming a force for change, seeing themselves as joining the strength of loose clubs to a body that could influence the board of ASPIRA. I presented their scheme to the board of directors, since it included the proposal that the ACF elect three members to the board of directors of ASPIRA! The proposal was accepted, and today in New York and in the ASPIRAs in other states, the ACF elects five members to the board of directors of the agency. The ACF in New York also proposed to the staff of ASPIRA that an association of parents of club members be organized.

The expectation was that the ASPIRA Club Federation could be an instrument of power for the Aspirantes, to be exercised against the power of the overall society when it used its strength to oppress the youth. This principle was tested in a demonstration staged in front of Gov. Nelson Rockefeller's house. The ACF was protesting the City University of New York [CUNY] raising its admission requirements. The governor had approved these "higher" standards. The CUNY tuition-free colleges were the institutions that most of the college-bound Puerto Rican high school graduates attended. Most Aspirantes planning to attend CUNY held jobs after school while in high school in order to contribute to their families' income and in order to buy clothing and books for themselves. The announcement of the higher required grade point so late in the school year gave them no opportunity to raise borderline averages. The ACF and the parents' association mounted a picket of a three-ring line consisting of a man, a woman, and a student, symbolizing a mother, a father, and their child. The picket was led by parents holding a casket they borrowed from one of the Puerto Rican funeral parlors. On the casket, they placed a very large sign that said, "Rockefeller, you killed the future of high school Puerto Rican youth who worked all year to attend CUNY and now cannot make it." The picket line circled the block where Gov. Rockefeller had his New York City home. The press and television covered the orderly picketing, chanting, and marching. The mounted police were there the whole time to keep order. We, the ASPIRA staff, were deployed at key spots across the street from the picketing to prevent provocateurs from causing trouble. A student and a parent were spokespersons to the press and television. Leaflets explaining the situation were distributed. It was a successful demonstration. The governor's office asked ASPIRA, the ACF, and the parents' association to meet and give them a list of the affected students. All students affected entered college the next autumn.

The reader will understand why ASPIRA became the most important work of my life. In terms of numbers, ASPIRA of New York alone, from 1963 to 1999, can easily be shown to have touched the lives of approximately 36,000 young people from Puerto Rican and other Latino groups. This is a conservative estimate, using the number of thirty clubs a year with twenty members each—and we know some years we had many more clubs, and some were larger. But numbers do not tell the complete story. So I must tell you about the principles, the values, the philosophy upon which we, the founders, built the model of service. The most important of these has been the grounding of ASPIRA in the knowledge and value that people are born, grow up, and develop fully and best in a community. We believe that the uprooting of our children from their community has been deadly to their ability to learn and to their sense of worth. The immigrant family did not have the supportive environment of an extended family, neighborhood, and friends. Human beings live in families and in communities because they need these for their survival and development of their full potential. I challenge this society to test these statements and to find out if these are the reasons why our youths have so many problems in the United States.

A second principle upon which ASPIRA was founded is that there is a continuous developmental chain that prompts the emergence and maintains the growth of leadership from one generation to another. In order to provide a community with those leaders, it needs to identify and solve its problems and to guide the group through good and difficult times. That leadership emerges in a continuum through the contact and education of potential leaders from one generation to another. The potential leaders must have the opportunity to challenge and take over the mantle of leadership from older, established leaders.

Potential leaders must engage in the educational process that affords them the opportunity to learn history, new technology, and skills that will help them to identify problems and learn how to solve them. Leaders, new and old, must engage in the development, nurturing, and demonstration of ethical commitment to their communities.

Another important pillar in the founding of ASPIRA was the need to establish an institution that would insure that the youth of our community would be educated to acquire the knowledge and skills available to grow fully to their maximum potential. We also hoped to insure that they could occupy positions at all levels of the institutions of the society and earn a living, but also contribute to the needs of their family, their community, and the total society.

The challenge we imposed on ourselves was to invent a model that would operate on those principles, values, and philosophical commitments. We succeeded in doing so. Today, there are Aspirantes who went through the process and are in leadership and professional positions throughout the city of New York and in many other cities across the country. They work in corporations; in city, state, and federal agencies as top leaders; in universities; in social and educational agencies at top-level positions as scientists, entrepreneurs, and artists. Some have returned to serve as staff or board members of ASPIRA in various states. They make real the commitment that they pledged while they were members of a club. Many of the Aspirantes are engaging in organizing new agencies to deal with community problems. Others have played central roles in organizing ASPIRAs in other states. Today, there are seven ASPIRAs: in Connecticut, New York, Pennsylvania, Illinois, Florida, and Puerto Rico. They are served by a national office in Washington, D.C.

I left ASPIRA of New York in 1966. For several weeks, I drove across the United States to see the rest of the country. The real and most important reason for my trip was to disconnect myself from the organization. I wanted very much for the board to select a new director without any input from me.

I had been in the position since 1961, and I felt that it was time to leave. I was the only director that the board and staff had ever known. We had learned together and grown together as a family. I was leaving the agency to take a teaching position at the Columbia School of Social Work, my alma mater. I was leaving the agency in the hands of Yolanda Sánchez, the program director who had been my student, while a new director was being selected. Louis Nuñez was the assistant director of the institution. In these two persons, I believed that there was significant experience and sense of continuity to move forward. I also had decided to leave because my philosophy of leadership has always been that the top person must step down to open up opportunities for new people. In spite of my convictions that I was making the right decision for myself and the agency, I felt sad because I was leaving friends and an organization that had become a big part of my life, and its people had become family to me.

Since leaving ASPIRA, I have been fortunate to have visited all of the affiliates and to attend conferences, participate in the inauguration of new centers, and in graduations at their schools. I am most satisfied and feel a great sense of pride to know that the work that we began in 1961 continues and has made an impact on the lives of thousands of young people.

Whenever I travel to give speeches, receive awards, or attend conferences, I always meet Aspirantes who share their accomplishments with me and thank me for having made the resources of the institution available. I have heard their wonderful stories as I travel from one end of the country to the other. I hear these stories from faculty, elected officials, businessmen, artists, scientists, writers. Without a doubt, I feel enormously proud as I refer to all these people as "the children that I had."

When I hear of the problems of any affiliate, it pains me in a very personal way. Over the years, I have heard negative comments and criticism of ASPIRA. From time to time, I am told that individuals have used an affiliation with ASPIRA to advance their own careers. With regard to those who have claimed a relationship to the founding of the institution, I can only say that many persons supported our efforts, including Puerto Rican teachers, community leaders, and aspiring political figures. I wish to acknowledge the support of the community in our work. For those who have used positions on the board or staff for personal advancement, I have nothing to say.

Criticism is difficult to accept. ASPIRA has been accused of "creaming," by serving students who are already bound for college while not maintaining sufficient activities to reach and motivate the truly needy. I know that, over time, the ASPIRAs may have yielded to the obligations of funding sources and reshaped their original objectives. I have always directly criticized the pattern of fundraising that obligates an institution to one major source of funding or to a governmental funding base that too frequently controls and alters the original mission of an institution. Also, I have always been clear that it is vital to maintain the base of ASPIRA as a Puerto Rican entity, although other populations are served.

Over the years, I have been asked to meet with ASPIRA students.

While I lived in Puerto Rico, they would visit me yearly as part of their annual trips. I have always been asked questions regarding the origins, mission, and objectives of the institution and the relevance of maintaining an institution that is Puerto Rican. I have not always felt that my insistence on maintaining certain founding principles has been well received by new boards, but I have been consistent in my position that ASPIRA is not simply a service entity. It is supposed to be a movement with a national network that acts as an advocate for youths and their community. The ASPIRA bilingual education consent decree, won at court, was one of the major efforts that grew out of this tradition. Many Young Lords Party members and leaders in "the student revolts" developed or reinforced their sense of cultural identity and affiliation as members of ASPIRA clubs. Members of the first graduating clubs of ASPIRA entered college and formed the pivotal base of movements for Puerto Rican Studies programs at universities.

The charge that ASPIRA was founded as a conservative social service entity is simply not true. I challenge any critic to review the original documents to determine the true nature of our intent and our commitment to social change.

Source: Excerpt is reprinted with permission of the publisher of *Memoir of a Visionary: Antonia Pantoja* by Antonia Pantoja. Houston: Arte Público Press–University of Houston, 24–25, 93–109. © 2002.

Time Magazine, "Revolt of the Mexicans" (April 12, 1963)

In the 1960s, Crystal City, Texas, a small town of 10,000 in the Winter Garden region of southwest Texas, had a majority Mexican population. The Political Association of Spanish-Speaking Organizations (PASO) chose the city for a get-out-the-Mexican-vote drive and ran a slate of candidates for the city council. PASO had been born out of the Viva Kennedy Clubs of 1960, which helped elect John F. Kennedy to the U.S. presidency. PASO's slate of candidates for the city council was successful, Juan Cornejo, a local Teamsters Union business agent, was elected along with four other Mexican Americans. The electoral coup only lasted two years, but it lit a spark for later successes. In 1963, it spawned such leaders as José Angel Gutiérrez (1944–), who founded the Mexican American Youth Organization in 1967 and La Raza Unida Party in 1969. In 1969, La Raza Unida Party began its takeover of the city. When this Time *article was published, it caused a stir among Mexican Americans nationally. The feeling was that the group had finally made it on the national scene. The sleeping giant had awakened, and it was going to become a national power group. For them,* Time *magazine was the big time.*

[In] Crystal City stands a statue of Popeye, a symbol of the town's claim that it is "the spinach capital of the world." Otherwise, Crystal City (pop. 10,000) is like a lot of other farm towns in South Texas. Mexican Americans outnumber Anglo Americans four to one, but the Anglos run the place. . . .

The revolt in Crystal City was managed by a three-year-old Texas organization called Viva Kennedy during the presidential campaign, now named PASO (short for Political Association of Spanish-Speaking Organizations) dedicated to the advancement of Mexican Americans. PASO chose Crystal City as a test site for a get-out-the-Mexican-vote drive. . . . Says Albert Fuentes, the PASO official who led the campaign: "We have done the impossible. If we can do it in Crystal City, we can do it all over Texas. We can awake the sleeping giant." On Election Day, the Mexicans have learned, all South Texans are equal.

Source: Excerpt from *Time* magazine, April 12, 1963. http://www.time.com/time/magazine/article/0,9171,828075,00.html.

Marcos de León, "Statements of Philosophy and Policy as They Pertain to the Acculturation and Education of the Mexican-American" (1964)

By the end of the 1950s, considerable political activity developed among the Mexican American GI generation—veterans of World War II and the Korean War. Angry because the Democratic Party had failed to support Mexican Americans for statewide office in 1958, Mexican American Democrats met in Fresno, California, in 1959 and founded the Mexican American Political Association (MAPA). In 1960, when John F. Kennedy ran for president, many MAPA chapters were incorporated into the Viva Kennedy Clubs. After the 1960 presidential campaign, there was an effort to form a nationwide Mexican American political group. However, Texans were not able to agree on joining MAPA because of the word "Mexican," which they believed would offend European American Democrats. Instead, they formed the Political Association of Spanish-Speaking Organizations (PASO).

However, the biggest issue for Mexican American activists during the 1960s was the failure of the education system, which many believed could be improved through the political process. According to the 1960 census, the median grade completed in the Southwest was 7.1 years for Latinos and 12.1 years for whites; in California it was 8.6 and 12.2 years for Latinos and whites, respectively; and in Texas it was 4.8 and 11.5 years, respectively. Mexican Americans underscored how whites had benefited from post–World War II programs whereas Mexican Americans were falling further behind. Much of the gap was caused by the stubborn and nativist insistence on teaching only in English. The League of United Latin American Citizens, which had been formed in 1929, proposed a preschool program that would teach students 400 words in English. These 400 words would help the transition of Spanish-speaking students and give them a head start. One of the innovators of the time was Los Angeles schoolteacher Marcos de León, who said that the Mexican was a marginal person who had a hamburger in one hand and a taco in the other. The following piece was not published but de León handed out thousands of copies to educators in the 1960s as he appeared on countless panels. It was one of the few works of the period on Mexican American children and one of the first to address the differences between assimilation and acculturation.

I. PRINCIPLES

1. The purposes of education in American Democracy, as defined by the Educational Policies Commission specifying the function of the school are to be implemented as basic principles.

II. CONCEPTS

To strengthen the underpinnings of these principles and make the acculturative process a smoother and more stable process, the following concepts are offered as imperatives.

(a)

Accept the reality of the Anglo Saxon and Hispanic ethic as they exist in the Western Hemisphere, meeting and throwing circles of influence over one another in the Southwest, creating a permanent and perpetual historical cultural continuum through the movement of peoples.

(a)

This cultural buffer area forms the framework for the process of acculturation affecting both groups, from which emanates two subconcepts; the culture within a culture concept and the function of the school having to become twofold, i.e., perpetuating the core of values of the cultures of which the school is a functional part.

(a)

Within this framework any "long- or short-term goal" educational program to be effected has to be based on the values, cultural potential, and educational needs of both communities, together with the needs of all individuals, including ages, abilities, interests, cultural differences, and socioeconomic status. This is the motivation, the "glue" that will hold it together.

(a)

Embrace a functional theory of culture and its relation to the growth of human personality and how such a person adjusts to a maximum [of] the demands of the two cultures: bilingual in the true sense, and the proud inheritor of both the Anglo Saxon and Hispanic traditions, thus permitting greater social mobility, participation, and acceptance as a useful citizen to his community and the nation. This entails a broader acceptance of the acculturation process as an educational precept.

III. RECOMMENDATIONS

The school-community idea be given greater depth in meaning, better purpose in implementation. These two entities have long been geometrical parallel lines: Never meeting to explore and exploit their potential.

(a)

The creation of a core of counselors to serve as liaison workers between school and community, establish and supervise programs in which the leadership of both school personnel and community are to be utilized to a maximum. Wherever possible, these counselors should be bilingual, especially, where the demand for Spanish exists as the spoken vernacular.

To Strengthen Cultural Awareness and Self-Image:

(a)

Spanish should be taught as early as possible on the Elementary level and coordinated with the English Program and made a "must" or a strong elective for non-academic students in the Junior and Senior High Schools;

(a)

Units on History, Literature, Art, Music, regional dress, and foods concerning Spain, Mexico, and other Latin American Countries be developed in the present courses in Social Studies, Home Economics, and Art, not only for the purpose expressed above, but also to create a more informed general citizenry.

Establish a definite and specific program for compensatory education with the objective of supplementing the normal education effort and preparing the Mexican American child to compete and achieve within the existing education program:

(a)

Such programs whether in the Elementary, Junior High, or Senior High School should have continuity as determined by (1) "e" under Concepts; (2) stipulations made by Federal and State Authorities.

(a)

These programs can be extensive and costly as the "Higher Horizon Program" in New York City, or smaller target areas can be selected involving the community, curriculum, guidance, counseling, attendance, and tutorial areas as specific projects.

(a)

While it is recommendable that such programs be made available for the Elementary, Junior High, and Senior High Schools, it is strongly recommended that a great deal of concentrated effort be placed within pre-school, the Elementary, and Junior High Schools.

The total concept of education as to philosophy and program can certainly be extended and implemented in the area of Adult Education.

It is strongly recommended that the potential leadership in the various schools as well as the community be utilized to affect any program within the District.

(a)
In-service training for teachers and community leaders is recommended, preferably in small groups with the technique of the workshop at its best.

(a)
Utilize panels, speakers, and seminars for this purpose, correlating any effort with compiled materials in a kit containing historical, sociological, and statistical materials, and recommendations as to philosophy and programs.

Develop continuing flexible programs of testing, guidance, and counseling which will permit the discovery as early as possible of the potential and creativeness of each child, the identification and development of the academically able student, the so-called "slow gifted" and the culturally different child, motivating him toward definite educational goals, thus preventing him from becoming misplaced within the school as to ability and interest and thus becoming a drop-out.

Expanding and modernizing the vocational program of the comprehensive high school so as to give adequate adaptability to a technological[ly] changing community.

In reference to community relations and communications it is urged that bulletins be developed which are more meaningful to the general public and more interesting in format especially when they are intended to be sent home, and that Spanish be used in the appropriate areas.

Recruit, hire, and place bilingual teachers, counselors, and administrators who have understanding of the Mexican American child and his community.

Consultants should be utilized to the fullest extent to (1) aid school personnel set-up projects; (2) act as consultant for such, for teachers' in-service training, and in-service training for community leaders.

Source: de León, Marcos. Unpublished manuscript. 1964.

Voting Rights Act (1965)

Blacks and Mexicans had been systematically disenfranchised by poll taxes in Texas, which charged people a fee to vote. Moreover, the state administered literacy tests, which purposely excluded Mexicans and African Americans. Further, it was impossible to get minorities elected because of gerrymandering that mapped secure white majority districts. Mexican American organizations, such as the League of United Latin American Citizens and the American G.I. Forum, had sued to no avail. The civil rights movement led by Martin Luther King Jr. brought new urgency to the issue, pressuring Congress to pass the Voting Rights Act, which President Lyndon B. Johnson (1908–1973), signed on August 6, 1965. The act, excerpts of which are reproduced here, abolished poll taxes and established the legal mechanism for voting rights.

An Act to enforce the Fifteenth Amendment to the Constitution of the United States, and for other purposes.

Be it enacted by the Senate and House of Representatives of the United States of America in Congress assembled, That this Act shall be known as the "Voting Rights Act of 1965." . . .

SEC. 2

No voting qualification or prerequisite to voting, or standard, practice, or procedure shall be imposed or applied by any State or political subdivision to deny or abridge the right of any citizen of the United States to vote on account of race or color.

SEC. 3

(a) Whenever the Attorney General institutes a proceeding under any statute to enforce the guarantees of the Fifteenth Amendment in any State or political subdivision, the court shall authorize the appointment of Federal examiners by the United States Civil Service Commission in accordance with Section 6 to serve for such period of time and for such political subdivisions as the court shall determine is appropriate to enforce the guarantees of the Fifteenth Amendment

(1) as part of any interlocutory order if the court determines that the appointment of such examiners is necessary to enforce such guarantees or (2) as part of any final judgment if the court finds that violations of the Fifteenth Amendment justifying equitable relief have occurred in such State or subdivision: Provided, That the court need not authorize the appointment of examiners if any incidents of denial or abridgement of the right to vote on account of race or color (1) have been few in number and have been promptly and effectively corrected by State or local action, (2) the continuing effect of such incidents has been eliminated, and (3) there is no reasonable probability of their recurrence in the future.

(b) If in a proceeding instituted by the Attorney General under any statute to enforce the guarantees of the Fifteenth Amendment in any State or political subdivision the court finds that a test or device has been used for the purpose or with the effect of denying or abridging the right of any citizen of the United States to vote on account of race or color, it shall suspend the use of tests and devices in such State or political subdivisions as the court shall determine is appropriate and for such period as it deems necessary.

(c) If in any proceeding instituted by the Attorney General under any statute to enforce the guarantees of the Fifteenth Amendment in any State or political subdivision the court finds that violations of the Fifteenth Amendment justifying equitable relief have occurred within the territory of such State or political subdivision, the court, in addition to such relief as it may grant, shall retain jurisdiction for such period as it may deem appropriate and during such period no voting qualification or prerequisite to voting, or standard, practice, or procedure with respect to voting different from that in force or effect at the time the proceeding was commenced shall be enforced unless and until the court finds that such qualification, prerequisite, standard, practice, or procedure does not have the purpose and will not have the effect of denying or abridging the right to vote on account of race or color: Provided, That such qualification, prerequisite, standard, practice, or procedure may be enforced if the qualification, prerequisite, standard, practice, or procedure has been submitted by the chief legal officer or other appropriate official of such State or subdivision to the Attorney General and the Attorney General has not interposed an objection within sixty days after such submission, except that neither the court's finding nor the Attorney General's failure to object shall bar a subsequent action to enjoin enforcement of such qualification, prerequisite, standard, practice, or procedure.

SEC. 4

(a) To assure that the right of citizens of the United States to vote is not denied or abridged on account of race or color, no citizen shall be denied the right to vote in any Federal, State, or local election because of his failure to comply with any test or device in any State with respect to which the determinations have been made under Subsection (b) or in any political subdivision with respect to which such determinations have been made as a separate unit, unless the United States District Court for the District of Columbia in an action for a declaratory judgment brought by such State or subdivision against the United States has determined that no such test or device has been used during the five years preceding the filing of the action for the purpose or with the effect of denying or abridging the right to vote on account of race or color: Provided, That no such declaratory judgment shall issue with respect to any plaintiff for a period of five years after the entry of a final judgment of any court of the United States, other than the denial of a declaratory judgment under this section, whether entered prior to or after the enactment of this Act, determining that denials or abridgments of the right to vote on account of race or color through the use of such tests or devices have occurred anywhere in the territory of such plaintiff. An action pursuant to this subsection shall be heard and determined by a court of three judges in accordance with the provisions of Section 2284 of Title 28 of the United States Code and any appeal shall lie to the Supreme Court. The court shall retain jurisdiction of any action pursuant to this subsection for five years after judgment and shall reopen the action upon motion of the Attorney General alleging that a test or device has been used for the purpose or with the effect of denying or abridging the right to vote on account of race or color.

If the Attorney General determines that he has no reason to believe that any such test or device has been used during the five years preceding the filing of the action for the purpose or with the effect of denying or abridging the right to vote on account of race or color, he shall consent to the entry of such judgment.

(b) The provisions of Subsection (a) shall apply in any State or in any political subdivision of a state which (1) the Attorney General determines maintained on November 1, 1964, any test or device, and with respect to which (2) the Director of the Census determines that less than 50 percentum of the persons of voting age residing therein were registered on November 1, 1964, or that less than 50 percentum of such persons voted in the presidential election of November 1964.

A determination or certification of the Attorney General or of the Director of the Census under this section or under Section 6 or Section 13 shall not be reviewable in any court and shall be effective upon publication in the Federal Register.

(c) The phrase "test or device" shall mean any requirement that a person as a prerequisite for voting or registration for voting (1) demonstrate the ability to read, write, understand, or interpret any matter, (2) demonstrate any educational achievement or his knowledge of any particular subject, (3) possess good moral character, or (4) prove his qualifications by the voucher of registered voters or members of any other class.

(d) For purposes of this section no State or political subdivision shall be determined to have engaged in the use of tests or devices for the purpose or with the effect of denying or abridging the right to vote on account of race or color if (1) incidents of such use have been few in number and have been promptly and effectively corrected by State or local action, (2) the continuing effect of such incidents has been eliminated, and (3) there is no reasonable probability of their recurrence in the future.

(e)(1) Congress hereby declares that to secure the rights under the Fourteenth Amendment of persons educated in American-flag schools in which the predominant classroom language was other than English, it is necessary to prohibit the States from conditioning the right to vote of such persons on ability to read, write, understand, or interpret any matter in the English language. (2) No person who demonstrates that he has successfully completed the sixth primary grade in a public school in, or a private school accredited by, any State or territory, the District of Columbia, or the Commonwealth of Puerto Rico in which the predominant classroom language was other than English, shall be denied the right to vote in any Federal, State, or local election because of his inability to read, write, understand, or interpret any matter in the English language, except that, in States in which State law provides that a different level of education is presumptive of literacy, he shall demonstrate that he has successfully completed an equivalent level of education in a public school in, or a private school accredited by, any State or territory, the District of Columbia, or the Commonwealth of Puerto Rico in which the predominant classroom language was other than English.

SEC. 5

Whenever a State or political subdivision with respect to which the prohibitions set forth in Section 4(a) are in effect shall enact or seek to administer any voting qualification or prerequisite to voting, or standard, practice, or procedure with respect to voting different from that in force or effect on November 1, 1964, such State or subdivision may institute an action in the United States District Court for the District of Columbia for a declaratory judgment that such qualification, prerequisite, standard, practice, or procedure does not have the purpose and will not have the effect of denying or abridging the right to vote on account of race or color, and unless and until the court enters such judgment no person shall be denied the right to vote for failure to comply with such qualification, prerequisite, standard, practice, or procedure: Provided, That such qualification, prerequisite, standard, practice, or procedure may be enforced without such proceeding if the qualification, prerequisite, standard, practice, or procedure has been submitted by the chief legal officer or other appropriate official of such State or subdivision to the Attorney General and the Attorney General has not interposed an objection within sixty days after such submission, except that neither the Attorney General's failure to object nor a declaratory judgment entered under this section shall bar a subsequent action to enjoin enforcement of such qualification, prerequisite, standard, practice, or procedure. Any action under this section shall be heard and determined by a court of three judges in accordance with the provisions of Section 2284 of Title 28 of the United States Code and any appeal shall lie to the Supreme Court.

SEC. 6

Whenever (a) a court has authorized the appointment of examiners pursuant to the provisions of Section 3(a), or (b) unless a declaratory judgment has been rendered under Section 4(a), the Attorney General certifies with respect to any political subdivision named in, or included within the scope of, determinations made under Section 4(b) that (1) he has received complaints in writing from twenty or more residents of such political subdivision alleging that they have been denied the right to vote under color of law on account of race or color, and that he believes such complaints to be meritorious, or (2) that, in his judgment (considering, among other factors, whether the ratio of nonwhite persons to white persons registered to vote within such subdivision appears to him to be reasonably attributable to violations of the Fifteenth Amendment or whether substantial evidence exists that bona fide efforts are being made within such subdivision to comply with the Fifteenth Amendment), the appointment of examiners is otherwise necessary to enforce the guarantees of the Fifteenth Amendment, the Civil Service Commission shall appoint as many examiners for such subdivision as it may deem appropriate to prepare and maintain lists of persons eligible to vote in Federal, State, and local elections. Such examiners, hearing officers provided for in Section 9(a), and other persons deemed necessary by the Commission to carry out the provisions and purposes of this Act shall be appointed, compensated, and separated without regard to the provisions of any statute administered by the Civil Service Commission, and service under this Act shall not be considered employment for the purposes of any statute administered by the Civil Service Commission, except the provisions of Section 9 of the Act of August 2, 1939, as amended (5 U.S.C. 118i), prohibiting partisan political activity: Provided, That the Commission is authorized, after consulting the head of the appropriate department or agency, to designate suitable persons in the official service of the United States, with their consent, to serve in these positions. Examiners and hearing officers shall have the power to administer oaths.

SEC. 7

(a) The examiners for each political subdivision shall, at such places as the Civil Service Commission shall by regulation designate, examine applicants concerning their qualifications for voting. An application to an examiner shall be in such form as the Commission may require and shall contain allegations that the applicant is not otherwise registered to vote.

(b) Any person whom the examiner finds, in accordance with instructions received under Section 9(b), to have the qualifications prescribed by State law not inconsistent with the Constitution and laws of the United States shall promptly be placed on a list of eligible voters. A challenge to such listing may be made in accordance with Section 9(a) and shall not be the basis for a prosecution under Section 12 of this Act. The examiner shall certify and transmit such list, and any supplements as appropriate, at least once a month, to the offices of the appropriate election officials, with copies to the Attorney General and the attorney general of the State, and any such lists and supplements thereto transmitted during the month shall be available for public inspection on the last business day of the month and, in any event, not later than the forty-fifth day prior to any election. The appropriate State or local election official shall place such names on the official voting list. Any person whose name appears on the examiner's list shall be entitled and allowed to vote in the election district of his residence unless and until the appropriate election officials shall have been notified that such person has been removed from such list in accordance with Subsection (d): Provided, That no person shall be entitled to vote in any election by virtue of this Act unless his name shall have been certified and transmitted on such a list to the offices of the appropriate election officials at least forty-five days prior to such election.

(c) The examiner shall issue to each person whose name appears on such a list a certificate evidencing his eligibility to vote.

(d) A person whose name appears on such a list shall be removed therefrom by an examiner if (1) such person has been successfully challenged in accordance with the procedure prescribed in Section 9, or (2) he has been determined by an examiner to have lost his eligibility to vote under State law not inconsistent with the Constitution and the laws of the United States.

SEC. 8

Whenever an examiner is serving under this Act in any political subdivision, the Civil Service Commission may assign, at the request of the Attorney General, one or more persons, who may be officers of the United States, (1) to enter and attend at any place for holding an election in such subdivision for the purpose of observing whether persons who are entitled to vote are being permitted to vote, and (2) to enter and attend at any place for tabulating the votes cast at any election held in such subdivision for the purpose of observing whether votes cast by persons entitled to vote are being properly tabulated. Such persons so assigned shall report to an examiner appointed for such political subdivision, to the Attorney General, and if the appointment of examiners has been authorized pursuant to Section 3(a), to the court.

SEC. 9

(a) Any challenge to a listing on an eligibility list prepared by an examiner shall be heard and determined by a hearing officer appointed by and responsible to the Civil Service Commission and under such rules as the Commission shall by regulation prescribe. Such challenge shall be entertained only if filed at such office within the State as the Civil Service Commission shall by regulation designate, and within ten days after the listing of the challenged person is made available for public inspection, and if supported by (1) the affidavits of at least two persons having personal knowledge of the facts constituting grounds for the challenge, and (2) a certification that a copy of the challenge and affidavits have been served by mail or in person upon the person challenged at his place of residence set out in the application. Such challenge shall be determined within fifteen days after it has been filed. A petition for review of the decision of the hearing officer may be filed in the United States court of appeals for the circuit in which the person challenged resides within fifteen days after service of such decision by mail on the person petitioning for review but no decision of a hearing officer shall be reversed unless clearly erroneous. Any person listed shall be entitled and allowed to vote pending final determination by the hearing officer and by the court.

(b) The times, places, procedures, and form for application and listing pursuant to this Act and removals from the eligibility lists shall be prescribed by regulations promulgated by the Civil Service Commission and the Commission shall, after consultation with the Attorney General, instruct examiners concerning applicable State law not inconsistent with the Constitution and laws of the United States with respect to (1) the qualifications required for listing, and (2) loss of eligibility to vote.

(c) Upon the request of the applicant or the challenger or on its own motion the Civil Service Commission shall have the power to require by subpoena the attendance and testimony of witnesses and the production of documentary evidence relating to any matter pending before it under the authority of this section. In case of contumacy or refusal to obey a subpoena, any district court of the United States or the United States court of any territory or possession, or the District Court of the United States for the District of Columbia, within the jurisdiction of which said person guilty of contumacy or refusal to obey is found or resides or is domiciled or transacts business, or has appointed an agent for receipt of service of process, upon application by the Attorney General of the United States shall have jurisdiction to issue to such person an order requiring such person to appear before the Commission or a hearing officer, there to produce pertinent, relevant, and nonprivileged documentary evidence if so ordered, or there to give testimony touching the matter under investigation, and any failure to obey such order of the court may be punished by said court as a contempt thereof.

SEC. 10

(a) The Congress finds that the requirement of the payment of a poll tax as a precondition to voting (i) precludes persons of limited means from voting or imposes unreasonable financial hardship upon such persons as a precondition to their exercise of the franchise, (ii) does not bear a reasonable relationship to any legitimate State interest in the conduct of elections, and (iii) in some areas has the purpose or effect of denying persons the right to vote because of race or color. Upon the basis of these findings, Congress declares that the constitutional right of citizens to vote is denied or abridged in some areas by the requirement of the payment of a poll tax as a precondition to voting.

(b) In the exercise of the powers of Congress under Section 5 of the Fourteenth Amendment and Section 2 of the Fifteenth Amendment, the Attorney General is authorized and directed to institute forthwith in the name of the United States such actions, including actions against States or political subdivisions, for declaratory judgment or injunctive relief against the enforcement of any requirement of the payment of a poll tax as a precondition to voting, or substitute therefor enacted after November 1, 1964, as will be necessary to implement the declaration of Subsection (a) and the purposes of this section.

(c) The district courts of the United States shall have jurisdiction of such actions which shall be heard and determined by a court of three judges in accordance with the provisions of Section 2284 of Title 28 of the United States Code and any appeal shall lie to the Supreme Court. It shall be the duty of the judges designated to hear the case to assign the case for hearing at the earliest practicable date, to participate in the hearing and determination thereof, and to cause the case to be in every way expedited.

(d) During the pendency of such actions, and thereafter if the courts, notwithstanding this action by the Congress, should declare the requirement of the payment of a poll tax to be constitutional, no citizen of the United States who is a resident of a State or political subdivision with respect to which determinations have been made under Subsection 4(b) and a declaratory judgment has not been entered under Subsection 4(a), during the first year he becomes otherwise entitled to vote by reason of registration by State or local officials or listing by an examiner, shall be denied the right to vote for failure to pay a poll tax if he tenders payment of such tax for the current year to an examiner or to the appropriate State or local official at least forty-five days prior to election, whether or not such tender would be timely or adequate under State law. An examiner shall have authority to accept such payment from any person authorized by this Act to make an application for listing, and shall issue a receipt for such payment. The examiner shall transmit promptly any such poll tax payment to the office of the State or local official authorized to receive such payment under State law, together with the name and address of the applicant.

SEC. 11

(a) No person acting under color of law shall fail or refuse to permit any person to vote who is entitled to vote under any provision of this Act or is otherwise qualified to vote, or willfully fail or refuse to tabulate, count, and report such person's vote.

(b) No person, whether acting under color of law or otherwise, shall intimidate, threaten, or coerce, or attempt to intimidate, threaten, or coerce any person for voting or attempting to vote, or intimidate, threaten, or coerce, or attempt to intimidate, threaten, or coerce any person for urging or aiding any person to vote or attempt to vote, or intimidate, threaten, or coerce any person for exercising any powers or duties under Section 3(a), 6, 8, 9, 10, or 12(e).

(c) Whoever knowingly or willfully gives false information as to his name, address, or period of residence in the voting district for the purpose of establishing his eligibility to register or vote, or conspires with another individual for the purpose of encouraging his false registration to vote or illegal voting, or pays or offers to pay or accepts payment either for registration to vote or for voting shall be fined not more than $10,000 or imprisoned not more than five years, or both: Provided, however, That this provision shall be applicable only to general, special, or primary elections held solely or in part for the purpose of selecting or electing any candidate for the office of President, Vice President, presidential elector, Member of the United States Senate, Member of the United States House of Representatives, or Delegates or Commissioners from the territories or possessions, or Resident Commissioner of the Commonwealth of Puerto Rico.

(d) Whoever, in any matter within the jurisdiction of an examiner or hearing officer knowingly and willfully falsifies or conceals a material fact, or makes any false, fictitious, or fraudulent statements or representations, or makes or uses any false writing or document knowing the same to contain any false, fictitious, or fraudulent statement or entry, shall be fined not more than $10,000 or imprisoned not more than five years, or both.

SEC. 12

(a) Whoever shall deprive or attempt to deprive any person of any right secured by Section 2, 3, 4, 5, 7, or 10 or shall violate Section 11(a) or (b), shall be fined not more than $5,000, or imprisoned not more than five years, or both.

(b) Whoever, within a year following an election in a political subdivision in which an examiner has been appointed (1) destroys, defaces, mutilates, or otherwise alters the marking of a paper ballot which has been cast in such election, or (2) alters any official record of voting in such election tabulated from a voting machine or otherwise, shall be fined not more than $5,000, or imprisoned not more than five years, or both.

(c) Whoever conspires to violate the provisions of Subsection (a) or (b) of this section, or interferes with any right secured by Section 2, 3 4, 5, 7, 10, or 11(a) or (b) shall be fined not more than $5,000, or imprisoned not more than five years, or both.

(d) Whenever any person has engaged or there are reasonable grounds to believe that any person is about to engage in any act or practice prohibited by Section 2, 3, 4, 5, 7, 10, 11, or Subsection (b) of this section, the Attorney General may institute for the United States, or in the name of the United States, an action for preventive relief, including an application for a temporary or permanent injunction, restraining order, or other order, and including an order directed to the State and State or local election officials to require them (1) to permit persons listed under this Act to vote and (2) to count such votes.

(e) Whenever in any political subdivision in which there are examiners appointed pursuant to this Act any persons allege to such an examiner within forty-eight hours after the closing of the polls that notwithstanding (1) their listing under this Act or registration by an appropriate election official and (2) their eligibility to vote, they have not been permitted to vote in such election, the examiner shall forthwith notify the Attorney General if such allegations in his opinion appear to be well founded. Upon receipt of such notification, the Attorney General may forthwith file with the district court an application for an order providing for the marking, casting, and counting of the ballots of such persons and requiring the inclusion of their votes in the total vote before the results of such election shall be deemed final and any force or effect given thereto. The district court shall hear and determine such matters immediately after the filing of such application. The remedy provided in this subsection shall not preclude any remedy available under State or Federal law.

(f) The district courts of the United States shall have jurisdiction of proceedings instituted pursuant to this section and shall exercise the same without regard to whether a person asserting rights under the provisions of this Act shall have exhausted any administrative or other remedies that may be provided by law.

SEC. 13

Listing procedures shall be terminated in any political subdivision of any State (a) with respect to examiners appointed pursuant to Clause (b) of Section 6 whenever the Attorney General notifies the Civil Service Commission, or whenever the District Court for the District of Columbia determines in an action for declaratory judgment brought by any political subdivision with respect to which the Director of the Census has determined that more than 50 percentum of the nonwhite persons of voting age residing therein are registered to vote, (1) that all persons listed by an examiner for such subdivision have been placed on the appropriate voting registration roll, and (2) that there is no longer reasonable cause to believe that persons will be deprived of or denied the right to vote on account of race or color in such subdivision, and (b), with respect to examiners appointed pursuant to Section 3(a), upon order of the authorizing court. A political subdivision may petition the Attorney General for the termination of listing procedures under Clause (a) of this section, and may petition the Attorney General to request the Director of the Census to take such survey or census as may be appropriate for the making of the determination provided for in this section. The District Court for the District of Columbia shall have jurisdiction to require such survey or census to be made by the Director of the Census and it shall require him to do so if it deems the Attorney General's refusal to request such survey or census to be arbitrary or unreasonable.

SEC. 14

(a) All cases of criminal contempt arising under the provisions of this Act shall be governed by Section 151 of the Civil Rights Act of 1957 (42 U.S.C.1995).

(b) No court other than the District Court for the District of Columbia or a court of appeals in any proceeding under Section 9 shall have jurisdiction to issue any declaratory judgment pursuant to Section 4 or Section 5 or any restraining order or temporary or permanent injunction against the execution or enforcement of any provision of this

Act or any action of any Federal officer or employee pursuant hereto.

(c)(1) The terms "vote" or "voting" shall include all action necessary to make a vote effective in any primary, special, or general election, including, but not limited to, registration, listing pursuant to this Act, or other action required by law prerequisite to voting, casting a ballot, and having such ballot counted properly and included in the appropriate totals of votes cast with respect to candidates for public or party office and propositions for which votes are received in an election. (2) The term "political subdivision" shall mean any county or parish, except that, where registration for voting is not conducted under the supervision of a county or parish, the term shall include any other subdivision of a State which conducts registration for voting. (d) In any action for a declaratory judgment brought pursuant to Section 4 or Section 5 of this Act, subpoenas for witnesses who are required to attend the District Court for the District of Columbia may be served in any judicial district of the United States: Provided, That no writ of subpoena shall issue for witnesses without the District of Columbia at a greater distance than one hundred miles from the place of holding court without the permission of the District Court for the District of Columbia being first had upon proper application and cause shown.

SEC. 15

Section 2004 of the Revised Statutes (42 U.S.C.1971), as amended by Section 131 of the Civil Rights Act of 1957 (71 Stat. 637), and amended by Section 601 of the Civil Rights Act of 1960 (74 Stat. 90), and as further amended by Section 101 of the Civil Rights Act of 1964 (78 Stat. 241), is further amended as follows:

(a) Delete the word "Federal" wherever it appears in Subsections (a) and (c); (b) Repeal Subsection (f) and designate the present Subsections (g) and (h) as (f) and (g), respectively.

SEC. 16

The Attorney General and the Secretary of Defense, jointly, shall make a full and complete study to determine whether, under the laws or practices of any State or States, there are preconditions to voting, which might tend to result in discrimination against citizens serving in the Armed Forces of the United States seeking to vote. Such officials shall, jointly, make a report to the Congress not later than June 30, 1966, containing the results of such study, together with a list of any States in which such preconditions exist, and shall include in such report such recommendations for legislation as they deem advisable to prevent discrimination in voting against citizens serving in the Armed Forces of the United States.

SEC. 17

Nothing in this Act shall be construed to deny, impair, or otherwise adversely affect the right to vote of any person registered to vote under the law of any State or political subdivision.

SEC. 18

There are hereby authorized to be appropriated such sums as are necessary to carry out the provisions of this Act.

SEC 19

If any provision of this Act or the application thereof to any person or circumstances is held invalid, the remainder of the Act and the application of the provision to other persons not similarly situated or to other circumstances shall not be affected thereby.

Approved: August 6, 1965

Source: An act to enforce the fifteenth amendment to the Constitution of the United States and for other purposes, August 6, 1965; Enrolled Acts and Resolutions of Congress, 1789-; General Records of the United States Government; Record Group 11; National Archives.

National Education Association (NEA), *Invisible Minority: Report of the NEA-Tucson Survey on the Teaching of Spanish to the Spanish Speaking* (1966)

In the 1960s, Mexican Americans continued to live mostly in the five southwestern states and in pockets or enclaves in the Midwest and Northwest. By the mid-1960s, it was obvious that Mexican children were not receiving education equal to those of their Anglo peers. In 1966, the National Education Association (NEA) released an important document titled Invisible Minority: Report of the NEA-Tucson Survey on the Teaching of Spanish to the Spanish Speaking. *The report investigated teaching in the five southwestern states. It discussed the problems of the Mexican American, and identified some of the more promising programs. The report advocated the teaching of identity and pride of heritage as a way to motivate students. The significance of the report is that it set the stage for bilingual education programs, validating what Mexican American educators had been claiming for years—that teaching Spanish-speaking children only in English would never work.*

While a majority of the Spanish-speaking people in the Southwest were born in this country and are citizens of the United States, they tend to be regarded both by themselves and others as Mexicans. The term Mexican American would be more nearly accurate. More important than technicalities, however, is how they feel . . . how they regard themselves.

Me. To begin with, I am a Mexican. That sentence has a scent of bitterness as it is written. I feel that if it weren't for my nationality I would accomplish more. My being a Mexican has brought about my lack of initiative. No matter what I attempt to do, my dark skin always makes me feel that I will fail.

Another thing that "gripes" me is that I am such a coward. I absolutely will not fight for something even if I know I'm right. I do not have the vocabulary that it would take to express myself strongly enough.

Many people, including most of my teachers, have tried to tell me I'm a leader. Well, I know better! Just because I may get better grades than most of my fellow Mexicans doesn't mean a thing. I could no more get an original idea in my head than be President of the United States. I don't know how to think for myself.

I want to go to college, sure, but what do I want to be? Even worse, where do I want to go? These questions are only a few that trouble me. I'd like to prove to my parents that I can do something. Just because I don't have the gumption to go out and get a job doesn't mean that I can't become something they'll be proud of. But if I find that I can't bring myself to go to college, I'll get married and they'll still get rid of me.

After reading this, you'll probably be surprised. This is the way I feel about myself, and nobody can change me. Believe me, many have tried and failed. If God wants me to reach all my goals, I will. No parents, teachers, or priest will change the course that my life is to follow. Don't try.

This was a paper turned in by a 13-year old girl for an English assignment in the eighth grade of a school in one of the Southwestern states. The assignment was to write about "Me." The melancholy tone of the essay would suggest that the youngster was a "loner"—obscure, unattractive, not very popular. But no. She was attractive, articulate, an honor student, member of the band, outstanding in girls' athletics, popular among her fellow students, admired by her teachers. "She never seemed to be a child with a problem," remarked one of the teachers, in some puzzlement, after reading "Me."

The problem can be stated plainly and simply: The young girl who wrote that essay was Mexican

American. If she, with all her advantages, felt that her lot inevitably would be failure, how must thousands of other Mexican American children—many of them less endowed physically and intellectually—view their own prospects?

357 YEARS OF HISTORY

To understand the problem fully, we must understand how it came about. The first white people to migrate into what is now the American Southwest were Spanish-speaking. They came by way of Mexico during the period of Spain's colonial expansion and settled portions of the Southwest even before the founding of the Plymouth Colony. Plymouth was established in 1620, but the first Spaniards settled at Santa Fe, New Mexico, a full 11 years before that—in 1609. By 1680, there were some 2,500 Spanish-speaking settlers in what we now call New Mexico. By 1790, there were an estimated 23,000 Spanish-speaking people in the five Southwestern states covered by this study area. Indeed, the white population of the Southwest—what there was of it—was practically all Spanish. New Mexico had the largest concentration.

But soon after the 13 colonies gained their independence from England, the migration of English-speaking Americans into the Southwest began. Mexico, its own independence newly won from Spain, encouraged such migration. This vast Southwestern area, stretching from the western border of Louisiana to the Pacific, belonged to Mexico. She was anxious to see it settled and developed, and few Mexican colonists were moving there. So the government of Mexico granted large blocks of land to contractors who would bring in colonists. The response was large and prompt. By 1835, there were 25,000 to 35,000 American farmers, planters, and traders in Texas, and more were on the way.

WHAT IS BEING DONE: SOME SPECIFICS

Encouraging and exciting programs directed specifically to a more appropriate educational accommodation of children in bicultural communities have been developed in some places. The following reports are illustrative of the wide variety of innovative practice the NEA-Tucson Survey Committee observed in the schools selected for visitation.

Laredo, Texas

Laredo is a Texas border community of some 65,000 population, located on the Rio Grande, just opposite its Mexican counterpart, Nuevo Laredo. Its economic sustenance derives in good part from the pursuits of agriculture and a busy Air Force base.

Two school districts serve the metropolitan area of Laredo. The larger of the two in population is the Laredo Independent School District, serving the city of Laredo proper. Far larger in area is the United Consolidated Independent School District. It is larger, in fact, than Rhode Island, taking in no less than 2,440 square miles and entirely surrounding the Laredo Independent School District on three sides, with the Rio Grande constituting the fourth side. Located within the far-flung boundaries of the United Consolidated Independent School District are the suburban homes of some of Laredo's Air Force families and ranches and farms where many Mexican American families live.

The district operates three elementary schools and a unique high school, much of which has been built underground. This school was built underground to provide fallout protection in case of a nuclear attack on Laredo Air Force Base, to shut out the disrupting screams of jet planes, and for economy's sake. An underground school uses less land, is more economical to air condition, requires no shades or blinds or window cleaning and offers no tempting midnight target for vandals with air rifles.

The educational program of United Consolidated Independent School District has one strong common denominator: bilingualism. Students, Anglo American as well as Mexican American, are encouraged to become truly bilingual—speaking, reading, and writing fluently in both English and Spanish. English instruction and Spanish instruction go side by side.

One Year at a Time

Federal funds had not yet become available for the Laredo "biliteracy" program (as they were subsequently to become available under the Elementary-Secondary Education Act of 1965). The United Consolidated Independent School District had to finance the program itself. And so it started the first year with only the first grade. The next year it expanded to the second grade. It was bilingualism not merely for the Mexican American child but for both Mexican American and Anglo American—for all children.

Eventually bilingualism will extend through all the grades, including high school. Yet even now the high school reflects the beneficial effects of the bilingual-bicultural revolution taking place. Picturesquely displayed at the high school's main entrance, on equal terms, are the proud symbols of the two neighbor nations—the American eagle and the Mexican eagle. They are vividly colored, stylized cutouts made by students and suspended from wire supports. Student artwork is displayed all through the school, and there is stress throughout on the worthiness of each of the two cultures. An unmistakable esprit de corps prevails among the students. They walk proudly. They dress neatly—all of them.

Bilingualism: A Valid Objective

The Laredo program and other similar programs that we observed in our Survey—plus our own experiences and independent studies—have persuaded us beyond any doubt of the validity of bilingualism. Unhappily, a large majority of Southwestern school districts have no bilingual programs. In a few instances, such programs exist but they are conducted inadequately. Most school districts have yet to discover that bilingualism can be a tool. It can be a tool—indeed the most important tool—with which to educate and motivate the Mexican American child. It can be the means by which he achieves an affirmative self-concept—by which he comes to know who and what he is, takes pride in his heritage and culture, and develops a sense of his own worth. It can be an invaluable asset to him as an adult, economically, intellectually, and socially. One of the proofs of the validity of this approach, it seems to us, is the fact that children born and receiving their early schooling in Mexico or some other Spanish-speaking country generally do better in our schools than Mexican Americans born here.

RECOMMENDATIONS FOR DESIRABLE PROGRAMS

This, then, might be the time to make some recommendations that the NEA-Tucson Survey Committee believes to be basic in the education of native speakers of Spanish:

- Instruction in pre-school and throughout the early grades should be in both Spanish and English.
- English should be taught as a second language.
- Contemporaneously there should be emphasis on the reading, writing, and speaking of good Spanish, since Mexican American children are so often illiterate in it.
- A well-articulated program of instruction in the mother tongue should be continued from pre-school through the high school years.
- All possible measures should be taken to help Mexican American children gain a pride in their ancestral culture and language.
- Schools should recruit Spanish-speaking teachers and teachers' aides. Beyond that, a special effort should be made to encourage promising young Mexican Americans in high school and college to consider education as a career.
- Schools, colleges, and universities should conduct research in bilingual education, train or retrain bilingual teachers, create appropriate materials and, in general, establish a strong tradition of bilingual education.

Source: The Invisible Minority. Report of the NEA-Tucson Survey on the Teaching of Spanish to the Spanish Speaking. Washington, DC: Department of Rural Education, National Education Association, 1966.

Ernesto Galarza, "La Mula No Nacio Arisca" (1966)

Every ethnic or racial group in the United States takes pride in the pioneers who made it in the United States despite overwhelming odds. Ernesto Galarza (1905–1984) was such a pioneer. After earning a doctorate from Columbia University, Galarza quit a well-paying job with the Pan American Union—a group that had organized to promote unity, peace, and economic trade among American nations—to organize farmworkers in the Southwest in the late 1940s. Galarza soon found his work to be impossible because of collusion among federal officials, local authorities, and large growers. He wrote a series of books exposing their abuse of the use of braceros *(guest workers) to break strikes. His career included a crusade for bilingual programs and other policy considerations. He gave the following speech before the Center for the Study of Democratic Institutions in Santa Barbara, California—an institute formed by Robert Maynard Hutchins (1899–1977) to bring about democratic reforms. The English title of the speech is "The mule was not born stubborn—it was made this way." The theme was that Mexicans and blacks were not sullen or resentful because they were born that way but because society made them that way.*

When I am asked to take part in conferences or meetings in which the topic is the Mexican American in California, I ask myself: "Why the Mexican Americans?"

It may be that our liberal conscience demands that we talk publicly about this sick spot in our society. Nevertheless, we should not think that the presumed Mexican American problem can be reduced, by public discussion, to the dimensions of one state, abstracting it from those of the nation and of the world. Nor should we think that it can be understood by using an intellectual tool that is comfortable and disarming but untenable: the concept of the subculture.

My working definition of culture runs like this: A culture is characterized by: a) the uses it makes of its material environment; b) the accepted or tolerated relations between the individuals that compose it; c) the symbols, conventional signs, and utilities of everyday behavior; and d) the values by which the society measures its moral performance.

By this rule-of-thumb I see only one culture in the United States: it is the culture of the American people—all of them.

Thus, I do not think we can legitimately presume that there is a subculture of Mexican Americans which explains their depressed conditions of life, or that there is a subculture of Negroes which explains their economic deprivation these past three hundred years.

What the concept of subculture implies, but does not say in so many words, is that alien cultures of a lower grade somehow intruded themselves into the American super-culture. If the Negro family today, for instance, is too often damaged by the absentee father, the working mother, and the delinquent youth, it is said to be a characteristic of their subculture. The concept shines most brightly when we talk about the discomforts of American society—dilapidated housing, crime, and unemployment. It is upon minorities that these discomforts fall most heavily. It is they, to be sure, who populate the ghettos, but it is our entire society, the American society, that spawns slums and breeds poverty.

I am not attempting to lay blame. I am trying to discover connections and relationships. What I see is that, among Negro and Mexican American minorities, what shows up vividly as local color and dramatic contrast are, in truth, cracks and tears in the seamless fabric of American society.

It is not the subcultures that are in trouble. It is the American culture itself.

And what have been some of the major strikes against Mexican Americans and Negroes?

One is the pattern of land ownership, control, and use that has developed in America during the past half century. Out of this pattern came the tractoring-out of the southern sharecropper, the withering of the family farm, and the massive importation of foreign agricultural laborers.

The resulting flight from the soil took millions to the cities, which were already suffering from urban cramps. We have begun to call these cities "ports of entry." The term has happy connotations: it suggests the migrant minority is on its way to better things—that is has made connections, not broken them.

But, in fact, the minority man finds the port congested with people like himself. They, like him, are becoming obsolete as a result of mechanization, automation, and cybernation—American cultural products that are radically altering job requirements, opportunities, and tenure. He finds that those sections of the big city where he has found transient refuge are also becoming obsolete. Here, another American culture concept, acted out with bulldozers, awaits him: urban redevelopment. As soon as a section shows speculative promise, it attracts speculative capital and entire neighborhoods go under. The Mexican American poor move with their anxieties to another place.

These and other massive social decisions are not for the Mexican American poor to make, or even take part in. These choices, and the complicated devices by which they are applied, are not even understood by the poor. To understand them, they would need an educational system that would deal factually and critically with them. But the Mexican American, on the average, barely gets through eight or nine years of school, so that even if the high schools and colleges were undertaking the task, which by and large they are not, they would not be reaching the minority man.

Mexican Americans in California have made progress since the Forties. They are subject to less ethnic discrimination. They have also begun to climb the lower rungs of the economic ladder. Ninety percent of the people I knew as a boy were farmworkers; now, far more than 10 per cent of us work as professors, journalists, bureaucrats, and so on. This change is only recent, but the process is increasing in scope and pace. With new jobs has come an ability to articulate. Today perhaps we even have too many spokesmen. In any event, the time is past when the Mexican American was not heard from. Now he says what he wants.

So far, we have been testing the mechanics of American democracy.

Those of us who have climbed two or three rungs up the ladder have had opportunities to learn how Anglo Americans do things—how they run political parties; how they caucus; how they lobby; how they manipulate all of those niceties of political contrivance, some clean and some unclean; how they use them, sometimes for personal benefit and sometimes for the good of the commonwealth. And two general kinds of Mexican American leaders have emerged: those who conclude that the American political system doesn't have to be tested with values—it works for 195,000,000 people and what more could anyone ask; and those of us who are trying to see whether it really works in terms of human values.

At the same time, the Mexican American community has lost ground—important ground. Our leadership has been dispersed. Political appointments have sent men of distinction to Sacramento, Washington, and abroad. Distance does something to these men: their values and ideas change; politically and ideologically, not just residentially, they are separated from the community. Individuals are entitled to personal satisfaction in life, but, for the community, political dispersal has meant and means political decapitation.

Strains have also occurred within the community. Mechanization and automation, in industry, agriculture, and trade services, have thrown many thousands of Mexican Americans out of work. In farming, machines now pick tomatoes, grapes, oranges, and so on. Where the packing houses and canneries used to employ 85,000 people at the peak of production, they now employ around

45,000. Large groups of Mexican American families have had a steady income cut away, and have been forced to disperse and be mobile. These nuclei of community have broken down as a result.

Marginal workers have not been helped by the trade union movement. Indeed, the trade union leadership helped destroy the farm labor union we organized in the Forties. We had posed the twin issues of power and exploitation in agriculture, but the union leaders shrank from their responsibility to help farmworkers, leaving thousands to a cruel fate. However, they taught the Mexican American community a lesson: the trade unions cannot be a taproot of our salvation. They are interested only in workers who are continuously employed, even though vast numbers of people are now unemployed and probably always will be. Lose your job, or stop paying union dues, and you are no longer "sir" or "brother."

The disintegration of the Mexican American community is apparent in the numerous "shoestring" and "doughnut" communities in which thousands of Mexican Americans live. The "shoestrings" grow along the banks of irrigation ditches, where water is available and land is cheap; here, displaced migrants have pitched their trailers and shacks, and the profile of their settlements is, a shoestring; the classical example is South Dos Palos. The "doughnut" type is found in the city, in places like La Rana (The Frog) in Torrance. There, as in many other places, Mexican American families settled as farmworkers, but now they are surrounded by progress, and they can only wait to be pushed out by urban redevelopment. This community, one might say, is a hole where poor people live surrounded by people with dough.

Among Mexican Americans, the proportion of wasted, discarded, obsolete, or unneeded workers is growing higher. Personal and family anchorage to work they can do and to people they know is becoming more precarious. For these men and women the closest thing to an economic taproot is seasonal hiring in the fields and cyclical employment in the cities. The prevailing mood in the poverty pockets is thus one of puzzlement, insecurity, and resentment. And as insecurity deepens, puzzlement is giving way to the conviction that there is no way out, and resentment is heightening to the point where life is fulfilled not by making progress toward a goal but by shooting at a target.

The welfare services designed for the Mexican Americans and other minorities, diverse and ingenious as they are, are no answer or substitute, for around them no sense of community can arise, no organization of interests can emerge, and from them no effective action can result. Each social service, gigantic like everything else in America, is institutionalized; and each institution asserts its jurisdiction over a slice of the individual or the family. In the battle of jurisdictions, the human meaning of integration, of integrity, is lost.

Vertical integration no longer means a man standing securely upon and belonging to the earth—free of mind and responsible of spirit. It has come to mean the putting together of economic components into smooth-running financial and technical mechanisms.

The demands of the economy and the palliatives of social welfare are manifestations of the American culture as a whole, not of any supposed subculture within it. They originate in the centers of real power and of effective decision. No program for action with regard to the Mexican American minority, or any other minority, therefore, can be more than a provisional tactic to gain time (if there is much left).

What is this provisional tactic? It is the grouping of the poor through organization, around the resources provided by the federal government in various Acts, notably the Economic Opportunity Act of 1964.

As a result of this Act, the Mexican American minority, to take it as an illustration, has the legal opportunity to participate in the initiation, planning, and administration of social services that have heretofore been of the hand-me-down type. Local residents are now able to create a cluster of activities around which democratic organization can take form, and within which they will be able to maintain responsible relationships. The politics of power, inescapable in any event, can be reduced to more manageable proportions.

But if the federal resources are to be subordinated to local community action, local residents must be provided with organizers responsible to them. I am not talking of organizers who are deft with the gimmickry of community organization, but of those who are skilled in recognizing what the vital interests of poor people really are. These interests will in many respects coincide with the services that the federal government stands ready to finance. When they do, the objective of the local community becomes the preparation of action programs and the organization of the neighborhood around them. Into these programs the Mexican Americans themselves must move. Their training must begin from the moment they take on a role, however modest, in a program.

What is the ultimate goal of such action programs? It is simply the re-creation of a human web of relations that will serve to produce a genuine community. Community is all that man has been able to invent to give him at least an approximation to security in his transit through life. I say re-creation deliberately, for there have been times and places in the American past when such relations did exist and did function. But the web of community, these last fifty years, has been strained and rent. If it is to be patched now and perhaps rewoven later, men must do it by their own efforts. I realize that it is only a patching that I am suggesting. It is only the choice of a road, not the end of a journey. But it may be the only road not beset by anger, despair, and violence.

The war on poverty is, at this stage, a mere skirmish. It cannot become a war until Congress appropriates the money to mount a massive attack on unemployment. The problem is not simply to create jobs but to influence the basic decisions, like the allocation of resources, that society makes. Decisions about where the money is to be invested, for instance, are what creates jobs. And to these decisions, the poor are not a party.

Discrimination must be ended, in employment and in every other phase of social relations.

We must also battle for "anthropomorphic education." This is a terrible phrase, but what I mean is that schools have to teach children, not systems. Experiments in Los Angeles have proven that one teacher with fifteen pupils and one expert assistant can do a much better job than one teacher with forty pupils and no assistant. Remarkable discovery! We have to press to make that teacher-student ratio universal because it will mean that the status and authority of the upper strata of administrators will be downgraded and the greatest prestige and largest salaries will go to kindergarten teachers. We cannot give an inch in this battle.

Private wealth can provide a cutting edge in the reconstruction of communities. It could start projects at those points where the government says "no"—and the government can do this without ever really saying "no." There are a lot of experiments the Congress is not going to finance, and there are areas in which federal funds and services either are a handicap or are useless, anyway. Some indispensable things will never happen if we wait for federal funds.

Does the Mexican American community merely want to catch up with the Anglo American culture? The question is important, and we had better be careful before we say "Yes." My experience—in farm labor, in academic work, in politics—has taught me a lot of things about the Anglo American culture that I do not like. Its economic system, for instance, produces certain values and behavior that I don't want to catch up with! Mexican Americans have an opportunity to discriminate between the different values, behavior, and institutions in the pervading culture, and we had better choose wisely.

All my life I have heard that the trouble with the Mexican American is that he is too apathetic. As a boy, in Mexico, I lived among people who, viewed from the outside, were extremely apathetic. Nobody was interested in knowing who was going to be the next president of Mexico, or who the military commander of our zone was. Nobody cared about the location of the nearest college or high school. They were interested in tomorrow's ration of corn.

When we came to California, Anglo Americans preached to us about our apathy and scolded us. And I thought: Are we really so? Of course we are not. What is mistaken for apathy is simply a system of self-defense inherited by people with a long history of being kicked around. And if they don't inherit it, they learn quickly. They learn that they are surrounded by hostile men and forces that will do them in at every turn. They naturally become indifferent and unresponsive. But it is not apathy: it is self-protection. *La mula no nacio arisca*—the mule isn't born stubborn, he's made stubborn.

In the village where I was born, men carried a money belt tied around their waists, and in it they kept all the money they possessed. They worked with the belt on, and they slept with it; they trusted nobody. As they progressed a little further, they put their money in a sock, which was purchased specially for the purpose; since nobody wore socks. Their circle of confidence had increased, but still they hid the sock under the corn crib in their cottage and left their women to protect it. Still a little further along came the piggy bank, which they usually placed on a shelf. Their circle of confidence had expanded further: all the family was trusted, friends too, even strangers who would drop by. Finally there came the sign of maturity: the bank account. Now, not only men were trusted but also a system, run by men who were not seen or even known.

These four stages of social evolution illustrate the so-called apathy of Mexican Americans. How can anybody accuse that villager who kept his money in a belt tied around his body of being apathetic? Considering the circumstances, he was a pretty smart Mexican.

It is often assumed that Mexican Americans need to be "emancipated"; after all, a lot of us used to live in a different culture in Mexico, and survived a feudal economy and society. The mayor of San Francisco remarked once that his city was going to build such a wonderful cultural center that it would make Los Angeles look "like a little Mexican village." Well, what's so wrong with that village? I have some good memories of Janco, my birthplace. There were no electric lights there, but in the evening, as the sun went down, people would sit in front of their cottages and talk by the twilight. And when it was dark the kids were sent to bed, and later the young men and women. Then the men would talk, not about small things but important ones. Some nights we heard a rumble of voices, lasting far into the morning. When I would awaken I would go to the yard and count the number of slits made by machetes in the hard-baked earth, and I would know how many men had gathered. It was these men who sparked the revolution in my village. And it was villages like these that started one of the most portentous events in the history of the Americas: the Mexican Revolution. In my yard.

I have not really been talking of fundamentals here. Not until the economy provides all men with sufficient incomes; not until mothers can stay home and take care of their children; not until massive investments of money are made in places like Watts; not until urban development becomes a weapon for something other than transferring doughnut communities from one part of the landscape to another, will the job of reconstructing communities have begun.

Are Mexican Americans ready? That I don't know, but some of us intend to find out.

Source: Galarza, Ernesto. "La Mula No Nacio Arisca." Center Diary, September–October 1966, 26–32.

Eugene Nelson Jr., "Huelga: New Goals for Labor" (1967)

If the Chicano movement did not start with César Chávez (1927–1993), he certainly made the cause known throughout the United States. Until the 1960s, few white Americans outside the Southwest knew who Mexican Americans were. Chávez gave them a national forum. He was born into a farmworker family. After a stint in the Navy, he returned to the San Jose barrio of Sal Si Puedes

(Get Out If You Can) and became involved with the Community Service Organization (CSO) that was formed in 1947. The CSO was an offshoot of Saul Alinsky's Industrial Areas Foundation, which trained community organizers. Chávez rose through the ranks and became the CSO president in the late 1950s. In 1962, he left a well-paying job and, along with fellow CSO organizer Dolores Huerta (1930–) began organizing farmworkers. In Delano, California, they founded the National Farm Workers Association (NFWA). On September 8, 1965, Filipino farmworkers initiated the Delano grape strike for higher wages. The NFWA supported the strike. Chávez combined trade union tactics with civil rights tactics, such as the nonviolent strategies of Martin Luther King Jr. and India's Mahatma Gandhi. Chávez went on hunger strikes and launched secondary boycotts of grapes to bring attention to la causa *(the cause). The following excerpts are from an article in* The Nation *by Eugene Nelson Jr., one of the early organizers of the farmworkers' union.*

If the word *huelga* has not yet appeared in an English language dictionary, along with other Spanish words which have come into common usage in English, it surely will soon. As many Americans must know by now, "huelga" means "strike." As fewer know, it refers to a certain type of agricultural strike which is also a social movement, interpreted by different people in different ways, and capable at any time of shooting off in new directions which may significantly affect the lives of all Americans. The potentiality is there, despite the fact that at present only a tiny percentage of the American workforce is involved, that these workers are among the most poorly educated of all, and that eventually their number must decline. Even on the surface, the strike and the movement in California, later in Texas, have been exciting and significant.

The huelga began in September of 1965 as just another agricultural strike. When about 1,000 Filipino American members of the Agricultural Workers Organizing Committee of the AFL-CIO left their jobs in the vineyards of Delano, California, demanding to be paid the $1.40 an hour that was guaranteed to the last of the Mexican braceros who had been allowed to work in the United States. Delano was also the headquarters of the independent National Farm Workers Association [NFWA], a unique union which was a combination of labor and social service organization, administering to all the major needs of its 2,000 Mexican American members. The NFWA, headed by César Chávez, joined the strike against thirty-six grape growers, presenting the uncommon spectacle of an alliance of two unions and two ethnic groups, plus a smattering of Anglos, Negroes, and Puerto Ricans.

In corrupt and poverty-stricken Starr County, Texas, where farmworkers earn as little as 40¢ an hour, the movement also exploded last June when 700 melon pickers went out on strike. A subsequent farmworkers' march to Austin united Mexican American groups throughout the state in the demand for a state minimum wage of $1.25 an hour and union contracts for the striking workers. Gov. John Connally and Atty. Gen. Waggoner Carr refused to meet the marchers at the capitol on Labor Day, and many observers say the rebuff was responsible for Carr's defeat in the United States Senate race against Republican John Tower.

On May 15, the United Farm Workers signed their first recognition agreement with a Texas grower—Virgilio Guerra, who will be employing about sixty men in the cantaloupe harvest. Meanwhile, the strike and boycott, launched with the same nationwide machinery that forced Schenley to negotiate, is gaining momentum as the harvest peak nears.

There has been new organizing activity among farmworkers in Oregon, Washington, Wisconsin, New Mexico, Arizona, and Florida. About one-tenth of America's farmworkers were included for the first time this year under the national minimum wage law, starting at $1 an hour. And it is predicted that this year or next farmworkers will be included by Congress in the collective bargaining rights guaranteed other workers under the National Labor Relations Act, thus eliminating the grave injustice largely responsible for their depressed situation in the first place.

Source: Nelson, Eugene, Jr. "Huelga: New Goals for Labor," 724–725. Reprinted with permission from the June 5, 1967, issue of *The Nation*. http://www.thenation.com.

Rubén Salazar, "State Calls for Probe of Judge in Latin Slurs" (1969)

Rubén Salazar was a muckraking reporter for the Los Angeles Times *who later became the news director for KMEX-TV. He was killed by a Los Angeles sheriff's deputy during an August 29, 1970, anti–Vietnam War demonstration. His voice was heard throughout the 1960s exposing discrimination toward Mexican Americans. The following is part of a blistering attack in a* Los Angeles Times *article on San Jose (California) Superior Court judge Gerald S. Chargin who generalized an attack on all Mexicans during his sentencing of a 17-year-old Mexican American youth who allegedly had sex with his 15-year-old mentally retarded sister. Chargin was censured but allowed to remain on the bench.*

"You are lower than animals and haven't the right to live in organized society—just miserable, lousy rotten people. . . . Maybe Hitler was right. The animals in our society probably ought to be destroyed because the have no right to live among human beings. . . . The judge then went on to say that the girl who is pregnant, "probably will have a half dozen and three or four marriages before she is 18." . . .

Source: Salazar, Rubén. "State Calls for Probe of Judge in Latin Slurs." *Los Angeles Times*, October 3, 1969, 3.

Chicano Coordinating Council on Higher Education, El Plan de Santa Barbara: A Chicano Plan for Higher Education (1969)

El Plan de Santa Barbara: A Chicano Plan for Higher Education was written by the Chicano Coordinating Council on Higher Education (CHE), which was formed in about 1969 to coordinate the establishment of Chicano studies programs. The plan represents the synthesis of a three-day conference of educators, students, and community activists on the campus of the University of California at Santa Barbara. The 155-page document contained proposals for a curriculum in Chicano studies, discussed the role of community control in Chicano education, and emphasized the necessity of Chicano political independence. Written in the form of a manifesto, it called for the implementation of Chicano studies educational programs throughout California and resulted in the founding of M.E.Ch.A. (Movimiento Estudiantil Chicano de AztlánAztlan, or Chicano Student Movement), a Chicano student group. El Plan de Santa Barbara was adopted in 1969.

MANIFESTO

For all peoples, as with individuals, the time comes when they must reckon with their history. For the Chicano the present is a time of renaissance, of renacimiento. Our people and our community, el barrio and la colonia, are expressing a new consciousness and a new resolve. Recognizing the historical tasks confronting our people and fully aware of the cost of human progress, we pledge our will to move. We will move forward toward our destiny as a people. We will move against those forces which have denied us freedom of expression and human dignity. Throughout history, the quest for cultural expression and freedom has taken the form of a struggle. Our struggle, tempered by the lessons of the American past, is an historical reality.

For decades, Mexican people in the United States struggle to realize the "American Dream". And some, a few, have. But the cost, the ultimate cost of assimilation, required turning away from el barrio and la colonia. In the meantime, due to the racist structure of this society, to our essentially different life style, and to the socio-economic functions assigned to our community by Anglo American society—as suppliers of cheap labor and dumping ground for the small-time capitalist entrepreneur—the barrio and colonia remained exploited, impoverished, and marginal.

As a result, the self-determination of our community is now the only acceptable mandate for social and political action; it is the essence of Chicano commitment. Culturally, the word Chicano, in the past a pejorative and class-bound adjective, has now become the root idea of a new cultural identity for our people. It also reveals a growing solidarity and the development of a common social praxis. The widespread use of the term Chicano today signals a rebirth of pride and confidence. Chicanismo simply embodies and ancient truth: that a person is never closer to his/her true self as when he/she is close to his/her community.

Chicanismo draws its faith and strength from two main sources: from the just struggle of our people and from an objective analysis of our community's strategic needs. We recognize that without a strategic use of education, an education that places value on what we value, we will not realize our destiny. Chicanos recognize the central importance of institutions of higher learning to modern progress, in this case, to the development of our community. But we go further: we believe that higher education must contribute to the information of a complete person who truly values life and freedom.

The destiny of our people will be fulfilled. To that end, we pledge our efforts and take as our credo what José Vasconcelos [Mexican philosopher] once said at a time of crisis and hope: "At this moment we do not come to work for the university, but to demand that the university work for our people."

POLITICAL ACTION

Introduction

For the Movement, political action essentially means influencing the decision-making process of those institutions which affect Chicanos, the university, community organizations, and non-community institutions. Political action encompasses the elements which function in a progression: political consciousness, political mobilization, and tactics. Each part breaks down into further subdivisions. Before continuing with specific discussions of these three categories, a brief historical analysis must be formulated.

Historical Perspective

The political activity of the Chicano Movement at colleges and universities to date has been specifically directed toward establishing Chicano student organizations (UMAS, MAYA, MASC, M.E.Ch.A., etc.) and institutionalizing Chicano Studies programs. A variety of organizational forms and tactics have characterized these student organizations.

One of the major factors which led to political awareness in the '60s was the clash between Anglo American educational institutions and Chicanos who maintained their cultural identity. Another factor was the increasing number of Chicano students who became aware of the extent to which colonial conditions characterized their communities. The result of this domestic colonialism is that the barrios and colonias are dependent communities with no institutional power base and significantly influencing decision making. Within the last decade, a limited degree of progress has taken place in securing a base of power within educational institutions.

Other factors which affected the political awareness of the Chicano youth were: the heritage of the Chicano youth movements of the '30s and '40s; the failure of the Chicano political efforts of the

'40s and '50s; the bankruptcy of the Mexican American pseudo-political associations; and the disillusionment of Chicano participants in the Kennedy campaigns. Among the strongest influences of Chicano youth today have been the National Farm Workers Association, the Crusades for Justice, and the Alianza Federal de Pueblos Libres, the civil rights, the Black Power, and the anti-war movements were other influences.

As political consciousness increased, there occurred a simultaneously a renewed cultural awareness which, along with social and economical factors, led to the proliferation of Chicano youth organizations. By the mid 1960s, MASC, MAYA, UMAS, La Vida Nueva, and M.E.Ch.A. appeared on campus, while the Brown Berets, Black Berets, ALMA, and la Junta organized the barrios and colonias. These groups differed from one another depending on local conditions and their varying state of political development. Despite differences in name and organizational experience, a basic unity evolved.

These groups have had a significant impact on the awareness of large numbers of people, both Chicano and non-Chicano. Within the communities, some public agencies have been sensitized, and others have been exposed. On campuses, articulation of demands and related political efforts have dramatized NUESTRA CAUSA. Concrete results are visible in the establishment of corresponding supportive services. The institutionalization of Chicano Studies marks the present stage of activity; the next stage will involve the strategic application of university and college resources to the community. One immediate result will be the elimination of the artificial distinction which exists between the students and the community. Rather than being its victims, the community will benefit from the resources of the institutions of higher learning.

POLITICAL CONSCIOUSNESS

Commitment to the struggle for Chicano liberation is the operative definition of the ideology used here. Chicanismo involves a crucial distinction in political consciousness between a Mexican American (or Hispanic) and a Chicano mentality. The Mexican American or Hispanic is a person who lacks self-respect and pride in one's ethnic and cultural background. Thus, the Chicano acts with confidence and with a range of alternatives in the political world. He is capable of developing an effective ideology through action.

Mexican Americans (or Hispanics) must be viewed as potential Chicanos. Chicanismo is flexible enough to relate to the varying levels of consciousness within La Raza. Regional variations must always be kept in mind as well as the different levels of development, composition, maturity, achievement, and experience in political action. Cultural nationalism is a means of total Chicano liberation.

There are definite advantages to cultural nationalism, but no inherent limitations. A Chicano ideology, especially as it involves cultural nationalism, should be positively phrased in the form of propositions to the Movement. Chicanismo is a concept that integrates self-awareness with cultural identity, a necessary step in developing political consciousness. As such, it serves as a basis for political action, flexible enough to include the possibility of coalitions. The related concept of La Raza provides an internationalist scope of Chicanismo, and La Raza Cosmica furnishes a philosophical precedent. Within this framework, the Third World concept merits consideration.

POLITICAL MOBILIZATION

Political mobilization is directly dependent on political consciousness. As political consciousness develops, the potential for political action increases.

The Chicano student organization in institutions of higher learning is central to all effective political mobilization. Effective mobilization presupposes precise definition of political goals and of the tactical interrelationships of roles. Political goals in any given situations must encompass the totality of Chicano interests in higher education. The differentiations of roles required by a given situation must be defined on the basis of mutual accountability and equal sharing of responsibility. Furthermore, the mobilization of community support not only legitimizes the activities of Chicano student solidarity [but is] axiomatic in all aspects of political action.

Since the movement is definitely of national significance and scope, all student organizations should adopt one identical name throughout the state and eventually the nation to characterize the common struggle of La Raza de Aztlán. The net gain is a step toward greater national unity which enhances the power in mobilizing local campus organizations.

When advantageous, political coalitions and alliances with non-Chicano groups may be considered. A careful analysis must precede the decision to enter into a coalition. One significant factor is the community's attitude toward coalitions. Another factor is the formulation of a mechanism for the distribution of power that ensures maximum participation in decision making: i.e., formulation of demands and planning of tactics. When no longer politically advantageous, Chicano participation in the coalition ends.

CAMPUS ORGANIZING: NOTES ON M.E.CH.A.

Introduction

M.E.Ch.A. is a first step to tying the student groups throughout the Southwest into a vibrant and responsive network of activists who will respond as a unit to oppression and racism and will work in harmony when initiating and carrying out campaigns of liberation for our people.

As of present, wherever one travels throughout the Southwest, one finds that there are different levels of awareness of different campuses. The student movement is, to a large degree, a political movement and as such must not elicit from our people the negative reason. To this end, then we must re-define politics for our people to be a means of liberation. The political sophistication of our Raza must be raised so that they do not fall prey to apologists and vendidos [sellouts] whose whole interest is their personal career of fortune. In addition, the student movement is more than a political movement, it is cultural and social as well. The spirit of M.E.Ch.A. must be one of *hermandad* [brotherhood] and cultural awareness. The ethic of profit and competition, of greed and intolerance, which the Anglo society offers, must be replaced by our ancestral communalism and love for beauty and justice. M.E.Ch.A. must bring to the mind of every young Chicano that the liberations of this people from prejudice and oppression is in his hands and this responsibility is greater than personal achievement and more meaningful than degrees, especially if they are earned at the expense of his identity and cultural integrity.

M.E.Ch.A., then, is more than a name; it is a spirit of unity, of brotherhood, and a resolve to undertake a struggle for liberation in society where justice is but a word. M.E.Ch.A. is a means to an end.

Function of M.E.Ch.A.—To the Student

To socialize and politicize Chicano students of their particular campus to the ideals of the movement. It is important that every Chicano student on campus be made to feel that he has a place on the campus and that he/she has a feeling of familia with his/her Chicano brothers, and sisters. Therefore, the organization in its flurry of activities and projects must not forget or overlook the human factor of friendship, understanding, trust, etc. As well as stimulating hermandad, this approach can also be looked at in more pragmatic terms. If enough trust, friendship, and understanding are generated, then the loyalty and support can be relied upon when a crisis faces the group or community. This attitude must not merely provide a social club atmosphere but the strengths, weaknesses, and talents of each member should be known so that they may be utilized to the greatest advantage. Know one another. Part of the reason that students will come to the organization is in search of self-fulfillment. Give that individual the opportunity to show what he/she can do. Although the Movement stresses collective behavior, it is important that the individual be recognized and given credit for his/her efforts. When people who work in close association know one another well, it is more conductive to self-criticism and reevaluation, and this every M.E.Ch.A. person must be willing to submit to. Periodic self-criticism often eliminates static cycles of unproductive behavior. It is an opportunity for fresh approaches to old problems to be surfaced and aired; it gives new leadership a chance to emerge; and must be recognized as a vital part of M.E.Ch.A. M.E.Ch.A. can be considered a training ground for leadership, and as such no one member or group of members should dominate the leadership positions for long periods of time. This tends to take care of itself considering the transitory nature of students.

Recruitment and Education

Action is the best organizer. During and immediately following direct action of any type—demonstrations, marches, rallies, or even symposiums and speeches—new faces will often surface and this is where much of the recruiting should be done. New members should be made to feel that they are part of the group immediately and not that they have to go through a period of warming up to the old membership. Each new member should be given a responsibility as soon as possible and fitted into the scheme of things according to his or her talents and interests.

Since the college student is constantly faced with the responsibility of raising funds for the movements, whether it be for legal defense, the grape boycott, or whatever reason, this is an excellent opportunity for internal education. Fundraising events should always be educational. If the event is a symposium or speech or debate, [it] is usually an excellent opportunity to spread the Chicano Liberation Movement philosophy. If the event is a *pachanga* [party] or *tardeada* [festival] or *baile* [dance], this provides an excellent opportunity to practice and teach the culture in all its facets. In addition, each M.E.Ch.A. chapter should establish and maintain an extensive library of Chicano materials so that the membership has ready access to material which will help them understand their people and their problems. General meetings should be educational. The last segment of each regular meeting can be used to discuss ideological or philosophical differences, or some event in the Chicanos' history. It should be kept in mind that there will always be different levels of awareness within the group due to the individual's background or exposure of the movement. This must be taken into consideration so as not to alienate members before they have had a chance to listen to the argument for liberation.

The best educational device is being in the barrio as often as possible. More often than not, the members of M.E.Ch.A. will be products of the barrio; but many have lost contact with their former surroundings, and this tie must be reestablished if M.E.Ch.A. is to organize and work for La Raza.

The following things should be kept in mind in order to develop group cohesiveness: 1) know the talents and abilities of each member; 2) every semester, [individuals] must be given a responsibility, and recognition should be given for their efforts; 3) if mistakes are made, they should become learning experiences for the whole group and not merely excuses for ostracizing individual members; 4) since many people come to M.E.Ch.A. seeking self-fulfillment, they must be seized to educate the student to the Chicano philosophy, culture, and history; 5) of great importance is that a personal and human interaction exist between members of the organization so that such things as personality clashes, competition, ego trips, subterfuge, infiltration, provocateurs, cliques, and mistrust do not impede the cohesion and effectiveness of the group. Above all, the feeling of hermandad must prevail so that the organization is more to the members than just a club or a clique. M.E.Ch.A. must be a learning and fulfilling experience that develops dedication and commitment.

A delicate but essential question is discipline. Discipline is important to an organization such as M.E.Ch.A. because many may suffer from the indiscretion of a few. Because of the reaction of the general population to the demands of the Chicano, one can always expect some retribution or retaliation for gains made by the Chicano, be it in the form of legal actions or merely economic sanction on the campus. Therefore, it becomes essential that each member pull his load and that no one be allowed to be dead weight. *Carga floja* is dangerous, and if not brought up to par, it must be cut loose. The best discipline comes from mutual respect, and therefore, the leaders of the group must enjoy and give this respect. The manner of enforcing discipline, however, should be left up to the group and the particular situation.

Planning and Strategy

Actions of the group must be coordinated in such a way that everyone knows exactly what he is supposed to do. This requires that at least rudimentary organizational methods and strategy be taught to the group. Confusion should be avoided, with the different plans and strategies clearly stated to all. The objective must be clear to the group at all times, especially during confrontations and negotiations. There should be alternate plans for reaching the objectives, and these should be explained to the group so that it is not felt that a reversal of position or capitulation has been carried out without their approval. The short- as well as the long-range values and effects of all actions should be considered before actions are taken. This assumes that there is sufficient time to plan and carefully map out actions, which brings up another point: don't be caught off-guard, don't be forced to act out of haste; choose your own battleground and your own time schedule when possible. Know your power base and develop it. A student group is more effective if it can claim the support of the community and support on the campus itself from other sectors than the student population.

The Function of M.E.Ch.A.— To the Campus Community

Other students can be important to M.E.Ch.A. in supportive roles; hence, the question of coalitions. Although it is understood and quite obvious that the viability and amenability of coalition varies from campus to campus, some guidelines might be kept in mind. These questions should be asked before entering into any binding agreement. Is it beneficial to tie oneself to another group in coalition, which will carry one into conflicts for which one is ill-prepared or involve one with issues on which one is ill-advised? Can one sagely go into a coalition where one group is markedly stronger than another? Does M.E.Ch.A. have an equal voice in leadership and planning in the coalition group? Is it perhaps better to enter into a loose alliance for a given issue? How does leadership of each group view coalitions? How does the membership? Can M.E.Ch.A. hold up its end of the bargain? Will M.E.Ch.A. carry dead weight in a coalition? All of these and many more questions must be asked and answered before one can safely say that he/she will benefit from and contribute to a strong coalition effort.

Supportive groups. When moving on campus it is often well advised to have groups who are willing to act in supportive roles. For example, there are usually any number of faculty members who are sympathetic, but limited as to the numbers of activities they will engage in. These faculty members often serve on academic councils and senates and can be instrumental in academic policy. They also provide another channel to the academic power structure and can be used as leverage in negotiation. However, these groups are only as responsive as the ties with them are nurtured. This does not mean, compromise M.E.Ch.A.'s integrity; it merely means laying good groundwork before an issue is brought up, touching bases with your allies before hand.

Sympathetic administrators. This a delicate area, since administrators are most interested in not jeopardizing their positions and often will try to act as buffers or liaison between the administration and the student group. In the case of Chicano administrators, it should not be assumed, he/she must be given the chance to prove his/her allegiance to La Causa. As such, he/she should be the

Chicano's person in the power structure instead of the administration's Mexican American. It is from the administrator that information can be obtained as to the actual feasibility of demands or programs to go beyond the platitudes and pleas of unreasonableness with which the administration usually answers proposals and demands. The words of the administrator should never be the deciding factor in students' actions. The student[s] must, at all times, make their own decisions. It is very human for people to establish self-interest. Therefore, students must constantly remind the Chicano administrators and faculty where their loyalty and allegiance lie. It is very easy for administrators to begin looking for promotions just as it is very natural for faculty members to seek positions of academic prominence.

In short, it is the students who must keep after Chicano and non-Chicano administrators and faculty to see that they do not compromise the position of the student and the community. By the same token, it is the student who must come to the support of these individuals if they are threatened for their support of the student. Students must be careful not to become a political lever for others.

Function of M.E.Ch.A.—Education

It is a fact that the Chicano has not often enough written his/her own history, his/her own anthropology, his/her own sociology, his/her own literature. He/she must do this if he is to survive as a cultural entity in this melting pot society, which seeks to dilute varied cultures into a gray upon gray pseudo-culture of technology and materialism. The Chicano student is doing most of the work in the establishment of study programs, centers, curriculum development, entrance programs to get more Chicanos into college. This is good and must continue, but students must be careful not to be co-opted in their fervor for establishing relevance on the campus. Much of what is being offered by college systems and administrators is too little too late. M.E.Ch.A. must not compromise programs and curriculum which are essential for the total education of the Chicano for the sake of expediency. The students must not become so engrossed in programs and centers created along established academic guidelines that they forget the needs of the people which these institutions are meant to serve. To this end, barrio input must always be given full and open hearing when designing these programs, when creating them, and in running them. The jobs created by these projects must be filled by competent Chicanos, not only the Chicano who has the traditional credentials required for the position, but one who has the credentials of the Raza. Too often in the past, the dedicated pushed for a program only to have a vendido sharp-talker come in and take over and start working for his Anglo administrator. Therefore, students must demand a say in the recruitment and selection of all directors and assistant directors of student-initiated programs. To further insure strong if not complete control of the direction and running of programs, all advisory and steering committees should have both student and community components as well as sympathetic Chicano faculty as member.

Tying the campus to the barrio. The colleges and universities in the past have existed in an aura of omnipotence and infallibility. It is time that they be made responsible and responsive to the communities in which they are located or whose members they serve. As has already been mentioned, community members should serve on all programs related to Chicano interests. In addition to this, all attempts must be made to take the college and university to the barrio, whether it be in the form of classes giving college credit or community centers financed by the school for the use of community organizations and groups. Also, the barrio must be brought to the campus, whether it be for special programs or ongoing services which the school provides for the people of the barrio. The idea must be made clear to the people of the barrio that they own the schools and the schools and all their resources are at their disposal. The student group must utilize the resources open to the school for the benefit of the barrio at every opportunity. This can be done by hiring more Chicanos to work as academic and non-academic personnel on the campus; this often requires exposure of racist hiring practices now in operation in many colleges and universities. When functions, social or otherwise, are held in the barrio under the sponsorship of the college and university, monies should be spent in the barrio. This applies to hiring Chicano contractors to build on campus, etc. Many colleges and universities have publishing operations which could be forced to accept barrio works for publication. Many other things could be considered in using the resources of the school to the barrio. There are possibilities for using the physical plant and facilities not mentioned here, but this is an area which has great potential.

M.E.Ch.A. in the Barrio

Most colleges in the Southwest are located near or in the same town as a barrio. Therefore, it is the responsibility of M.E.Ch.A. members to establish close working relationships with organizations in the barrio. The M.E.Ch.A. people must be able to take the pulse of the barrio and be able to respond to it. However, M.E.Ch.A. must be careful not to overstep its authority or duplicate the efforts of another organization already in the barrio. M.E.Ch.A. must be able to relate to all segments of the barrio, from the middle-class assimilationists to the vatos locos.

Obviously, every barrio has its particular needs, and M.E.Ch.A. people must determine, with the help of those in the barrio, where they can be most effective. There are, however, some general areas which M.E.Ch.A. can involve itself. Some of them are: 1) policing social and governmental agencies to make them more responsive in a humane and dignified way to the people of the barrio; 2) carrying out research on the economic and credit policies of merchants in the barrio and exposing fraudulent and exorbitant establishments; 3) speaking and communicating with junior high and high school students, helping with their projects, teaching them organizational techniques, supporting their actions; 4) spreading the message of the movement by any media available—this means speaking, radio, television, local newspaper, underground paper, poster, art, theaters; in short, spreading propaganda of the Movement; 5) exposing discrimination in hiring and renting practices and many other areas which the student because of his/her mobility, his/her articulation, and his/her vigor should take as his/her responsibility. It may mean at times having to work in conjunction with other organizations. If this is the case and the project is one begun by the other organization, realize that M.E.Ch.A. is there as a supporter and should accept the direction of the group involved. Do not let loyalty to an organization cloud responsibility to a greater force—la Causa.

Working in the barrio is an honor, but is also a right because we come from these people, and as such, mutual respect between the barrio and the college group should be the rule. Understand at the same time, however, that there will initially be mistrust and often envy on the part of some in the barrio for the college student. This mistrust must be broken down by a demonstration of affection for the barrio and La Raza through hard work and dedication. If the approach is one of a dilettante or of a Peace Corps volunteer, the people will know it and act accordingly. If it is merely a cathartic experience to work among the unfortunate in the barrio—stay out.

Of the community, for the community. Por la Raza habla el espiritu.

Source: M.E.Ch.A., Pan American University. http://www.panam.edu/orgs/MEChA/st_barbara.html.

Reies López Tijerina, "A Letter from the Santa Fe Jail," 1969

The activities of Chicano activist Reies López Tijerina (1926–) have to be read in the context of New Mexican history, where the question of land still burns and where many northern villagers say that the United States violated the Treaty of Guadalupe Hidalgo (1848), which set the terms for the incorporation of New Mexico into the United States. The treaty had guaranteed property rights and the legal precedents of Mexican and Spanish laws. At the time of the conquest, the northern part of New Mexico was settled by Pueblo Indians and Mexican villagers who lived on communal lands. Not only did the small farms belong to the villagers but so did the use of communal lands that included forests and grazing lands. The U.S. occupation changed the land tenure system. Communal villages were privatized, and the use of grazing lands and forests was taken from the villagers. Tijerina wrote "A Letter from the Santa Fe Jail" while imprisoned there in 1969. This letter was modeled after Martin Luther King Jr.'s (1929–1968) famous "Letter from the Birmingham Jail."

Tijerina was one of the more militant Chicano activists of the 1960s, leading the struggle to restore Spanish and Mexican land grants guaranteed by the Treaty of Guadalupe Hidalgo to Hispanos and Chicanos. Tijerina founded the Alianza of Pueblos and Pobladores (Alliance of Towns and Settlers) in 1963. A charismatic preacher, he traveled through the land telling how Tío Samuel *(Uncle Sam) had dispossessed New Mexicans by nationalizing the forests and privatizing their communal lands.* Tío Samuel *had reduced a once self-sufficient people to beggars forced to take food stamps. In October 1966, Alianza members occupied part of the Echo Amphitheater Park in the Carson National Forest, which belonged to the San Joaquín del Río de Chama grant. The next year, Tijerina led a raid on the Tierra Amarilla Courthouse. In March 1968, he led the Chicano contingent of the Poor People's March on Washington, DC, one of the final initiatives of black civil rights leader King, who was involved in planning the march but was assassinated before it was held. Tijerina was sentenced to two years in a federal prison in 1970 for charges related to the 1967 Tierra Amarilla Courthouse raid. In 1974, he began serving another sentence. The following letter explains his grievances and why he was in jail.*

From my cell block in this jail I am writing these reflections. I write them to my people, the Indo-Hispanos, to my friends among the Anglos, to the agents of the Federal government, the state of New Mexico, the Southwest, and the entire Indo-Hispano world—"Latin America."

I write to you as one of the dearest victims of the madness and racism in the hearts of our present-day politicians and rulers.

At this time, August 17, I have been in jail for 65 days—since June 11, 1969, when my appeal bond from another case was revoked by a federal judge. I am here today because I resisted an assassination attempt led by an agent of the federal government—an agent of all those who do not want anybody to speak out for the poor, all those who do not want Reies López Tijerina to stand in their way as they continue to rob the poor people, all those many rich people from outside the state with their summer homes and ranches here whose pursuit of happiness depends on thievery, all those who have robbed the people of their land and culture for 120 years. . . .

What is my real crime? As I and the poor people see it, especially the Indo-Hispanos, my only crime is UPHOLDING OUR RIGHTS AS PROTECTED BY THE TREATY OF GUADALUPE HIDALGO, which ended the so-called Mexican-American War of 1846–1848. My only crime is demanding the respect and protection of our property, which has been confiscated illegally by the federal government. Ever since the treaty was signed in 1848, our people have been asking every elected president of the United States for a redress of grievances. Like the Black people, we too have been criminally ignored. Our right to the Spanish land grant pueblos is the real reason why I am in prison at this moment.

Our cause and our claim and our methods are legitimate. Yet even after a jury in a court of law acquitted me last December, they still call me a violent man. But the right to make a citizen's arrest, as I attempted to make that day on Evans, is not a violent right. On the contrary, it is law and order—unless the arrested son resists or flees to avoid prosecution. No honest citizen should avoid a citizen's arrest.

This truth is denied by the conspirators against the poor and by the press, which they control. There are also the Silent Contributors. The Jewish people accused the Pope of Rome for keeping silent while Hitler and his machine persecuted the Jews in Germany and other countries. I support the Jews in their right to accuse those who contributed to Hitler's acts by their Silence. By the same token, I denounce those in New Mexico who have never opened their mouths at any time to defend or support the thousands who have been killed, robbed, raped of their culture. I don't know of any church or Establishment organization or group of elite intellectuals that has stood up for the Treaty of Guadalupe Hidalgo. We condemn the silence of these groups and individuals and I am sure that, like the Jewish people, the poor of New Mexico are keeping a record of the Silence which contributes to the criminal conspiracy against the Indo-Hispano in New Mexico.

As I sit in my jail cell in Santa Fe, capitol of New Mexico, I pray that all the poor people will unite to bring justice to New Mexico. My cell block has no day light, no ventilation of any kind, no light of any kind. After 9 p.m., we are left in a dungeon of total darkness. Visiting rules allow only 15 minutes per week on Thursdays from 1 to 4 p.m. so that parents who work cannot visit their sons in jail. Yesterday, a 22-year-old boy cut his throat. Today, Aug. 17, two young boys cut their wrists with razor blades and were taken unconscious to the hospital. My cell is dirty and there is nothing to clean it with. The whole cell block is hot and suffocating. All my prison mates complain and show a daily state of anger. But these uncomfortable conditions do not bother me, for I have a divine dream to give me strength: the happiness of my people.

I pray to God that all the Indo-Hispano people will awake to the need for unity, and to our heavenly and constitutional responsibility for fighting peacefully to win our rights. Already the rest of the Indo-Hispano world—Latin America—knows of our struggle. It is too late to keep the story of our land struggle from reaching the ears of the Indo-Hispano world. All the universities of Latin America knew about our problems when Rockefeller went there last summer. Will Latin America ignore our cry from here in New Mexico and the Southwest? Times have changed and the spirit of the blood is no longer limited by national or continental boundaries.

The Indo-Hispano world will never trust the United States as long as this government occupies our land illegally. The honest policy of the United States will have to begin at home, before Rockefeller can go to Latin America again to sell good relations and friendship. Our property, freedom, and culture must be respected in New Mexico, in the whole Southwest, before the Anglo can expect to be trusted in South America, Mexico, and Canada.

This government must show its good faith to the Indo-Hispano in respect to the Treaty of Guadalupe Hidalgo and the land question by forming a presidential committee to investigate and hold open hearings on the land question in the northern part of New Mexico. We challenge our own government to bring forth and put all the facts on the conference table. We have the evidence to prove our claims to property as well as to the cultural rights of which we have been deprived. We are Right—and therefore ready and willing to discuss our problems and rights under the Treaty with the Anglo federal government in New Mexico or Washington, D.C., directly or through agents.

This government must also reform the whole educational structure in the Southwest before it is too late. It should begin in the northern part of New Mexico, where 80% of the population is [sic] Indo-Hispanos, as a pilot center. If it works here, then a plan can be developed based on that experience in the rest of the state and wherever the Indo-Hispano population requires it.

Because I know We Are Right, I have no regrets as I sit in my jail cell. I feel very, very proud and happy, to be in jail for the reason that I am. June 8 in Coyote could have been my last day on earth.

My life was spared by God, and to be honored by that miracle at Coyote will keep me happy for many years to come. I am sure that not one of my prison days is lost. Not one day has been in vain. While others are free, building their personal empires, I am in jail for defending and fighting for the rights of my people. Only my Indo-Hispano people have influenced me to be what I am. I am what I am, for my brothers.

Source: Reies López Tijerina Collection, University of New Mexico, Albuquerque.

Remarks of Hon. James G. O'Hara of Michigan about the Proclamation of the Delano Grape Workers for International Boycott Day, House of Representatives

(May 10, 1969)

Charismatic labor activist Dolores Huerta (1930–) was born in New Mexico and grew up in Stockton at the northwest end of California's San Joaquín Valley. Huerta had been an organizer with the Community Service Organization (CSO) and worked as a teacher. She left these secure jobs to join labor activist César Chávez (1927–1993) to organize farmworkers. Huerta became the most prominent Chicana labor leader in the United States. She was a seasoned organizer who lobbied in Sacramento, California; traveled the country organizing boycott committees; and spoke to workers. Speaking for the farmworkers' union, Huerta called for an international grape boycott that eventually became an international cause, with supporters refusing to eat grapes until the growers signed contracts with the union. The following is a resolution by the Hon. James G. O'Hara (1925–1989), a Democrat from Michigan, which includes the call for the Delano Grape Boycott.

Mr. Speaker, last Saturday, May 10, was proclaimed International Boycott Day by the Delano grape workers. Consumers everywhere were called upon to withhold their patronage from stores selling table grapes. When the Congress enacted the National Labor Relations Act over 30 years ago, agriculture workers were excluded from the provisions [of] this act. In effect, the Congress made second-class citizens of farmworkers by refusing to protect their right to form unions and to bargain collectively with their employers. For the past 7 years, efforts on the part of the grape workers to bargain collectively have been largely ignored by the growers. Without the protection of the law, the workers had nowhere to go but to the public.

Two years ago, the farmworkers of California called upon consumers to boycott grapes in an effort to force the growers to recognize the rights of the workers and to bargain collectively with them. The boycott has been more and more effective as the public has become more and more aware of the plight of the farmworkers. By boycotting grapes, consumers tell growers that they will not purchase their product until they know that the workers who harvest it are assured of a just wage, humane working conditions, job security, and other employee benefits taken for granted by most working men and women in America.

Mr. Speaker, I insert the proclamation of the Delano grape workers for International Boycott Day at this point in the Record:

Proclamation of the Delano Grape Workers for International Boycott Day, May 10, 1969. We, the striking grape workers of California, join on this

International Boycott Day with the consumers across the continent in planning the steps that lie ahead on the road to our liberation. As we plan, we recall the footsteps that brought us to this day and the events of this day. The historic road of our pilgrimage to Sacramento later branched out, spreading like the unpruned vines in struck fields, until it led us to willing exile in cities across this land. There, far from the earth we tilled for generations, we have cultivated the strange soil of public understanding, sowing the seed of our truth and our cause in the minds and hearts of men.

We have been farmworkers for hundreds of years and pioneers for seven. Mexicans, Filipinos, Africans, and others, our ancestors were among those who founded this land and tamed its natural wilderness. But we are still pilgrims on this land, and we are pioneers who blaze a trail out of the wilderness of hunger and deprivation that we have suffered even as our ancestors did. We are conscious today of the significance of our present quest. If this road we chart leads to the rights and reforms we demand, if it leads to just wages, humane working conditions, protection from the misuse of pesticides, and to the fundamental right of collective bargaining, if it changes the social order that relegates us to the bottom reaches of society, then in our wake will follow thousands of American farmworkers. Our example will make them free. But if our road does not bring us to victory and social change, it will not be because our direction is mistaken or our resolve too weak, but only because our bodies are mortal and our journey hard. For we are in the midst of a great social movement, and we will not stop struggling 'til we die, or win!

We have been farmworkers for hundreds of years and strikers for four. It was four years ago that we threw down our plowshares and pruning hooks. These Biblical symbols of peace and tranquility to us represent too many lifetimes of unprotesting submission to a degrading social system that allows us no dignity, no comfort, no peace. We mean to have our peace, and to win it without violence, for it is violence we would overcome—the subtle spiritual and mental violence of oppression, the violence subhuman toil does to the human body. So we went and stood tall outside the vineyards where we had stooped for years. But the tailors of national labor legislation had left us naked. Thus exposed, our picket lines were crippled by injunctions and harassed by growers; our strike was broken by imported scabs; our overtures to our employers were ignored. Yet we knew the day must come when they would talk to us, as equals.

We have been farmworkers for hundreds of years and boycotters for two. We did not choose the grape boycott, but we had chosen to leave our peonage, poverty, and despair behind. Though our first bid for freedom, the strike, was weakened, we would not turn back. The boycott was the only way forward the growers left to us. We called upon our fellow men and were answered by consumers who said—as all men of conscience must—that they would no longer allow their tables to be subsidized by our sweat and our sorrow: They shunned the grapes, fruit of our affliction.

We marched alone at the beginning, but today we count men of all creeds, nationalities, and occupations in our number. Between us and the justice we seek now stand the large and powerful grocers who, in continuing to buy table grapes, betray the boycott their own customers have built. These stores treat their patrons' demands to remove the grapes the same way the growers treat our demands for union recognition—by ignoring them. The consumers who rally behind our cause are responding as we do to such treatment—with a boycott! They pledge to withhold their patronage from stores that handle grapes during the boycott, just as we withhold our labor from the growers until our dispute is resolved.

Grapes must remain an unenjoyed luxury for all as long as the barest human needs and basic human rights are still luxuries for farmworkers. The grapes grow sweet and heavy on the vines, but they will have to wait while we reach out first for our freedom. The time is ripe for our liberation.

Source: Congressional Record, 91st Cong., 1st sess. May 17, 1969.

José Angel Gutiérrez, "Mexicanos Need to Control Their Own Destinies" (1970)

The following excerpts are from a speech made on May 4, 1970, in San Antonio, Texas, by José Angel Gutiérrez, (1944–), a founder of the Texas La Raza Unida Party (1970). At the time of the speech, he was the newly elected president of the Crystal City school board. Gutiérrez was a student of politics. A 1962 graduate of Crystal City High School in Crystal City, Texas, he worked on the takeover of the Crystal City Council in 1963. He earned a bachelor's degree from Texas A&M University at Kingsville; a master's degree from St. Mary's University in San Antonio, Texas; a PhD in government from the University of Texas at Austin; and a JD from the University of Houston Law School. Among other organizations, Gutiérrez cofounded the Mexican American Youth Organization in 1967 and the Mexican American Unity Council in 1968. Gutiérrez is a respected scholar and has written numerous books and conducted nearly 100 oral interviews with Tejanos (Mexican Texans) during the 1960s and 1970s. The following speech is important because it explains why Chicanos believed they should have their own political party.

As you know, there is a new political party in Southwest Texas. It's called La Raza Unida Party. The history of this party is rather interesting.

For years the Chicano farmworker has made up the majority of the population in the South Texas counties. But he goes trucking across this country on his summer vacation (laughter), and so he's never there to vote. Yet this is precisely the time the primaries are held—in May. And he is already vacationing in his resort area by the time the run-offs are held in June. So, you see, we are in fact not even able to vote.

We have had other problems which we have known about for a long time. For instance, the fact that the Mexicano can't cope with the culture of the monolingual creatures that abound in South Texas. You see, we're literate in Spanish, so we can't recognize the name of John Waltberger on the ballot, but we sure as hell recognize Juan García. (Laughter.)

Supposedly in this kind of a democratic society the citizenry is encouraged to participate in the political process—but not so in South Texas.

Someone asked me recently whether I thought any type of system other than the American political system could work in South Texas. I thought about it for a minute and suggested that the question be reworded because we ought to try the American system first. (Applause.)

They accuse me and Mexicanos in Cristal [Crystal City], in Cotulla and Carrizo Springs, of being unfair. One gringo lady put it very well. She was being interviewed around April 6, right after the school board elections and before the city council elections. The guy from *Newsweek* asked her to explain the strange phenomena that were occurring in these counties: a tremendous voter turnout and a tremendous amount of bloc voting. She said, "Well, this is just terrible! Horrible! A few days ago we elected a bunch of bum Mexicans to the city council." And the reporter said, "Well, they are 85 percent of this county." And she replied, "That's what I mean! They think they ought to run this place!"

By all these little things you can begin to understand how to define the word "gringo," which seems to be such a problem all the time. It's funny, because the Mexicano knows what a gringo is. It's the gringos themselves that are worried about what the hell it is. (Laughter.) Let me elaborate on it.

I'm not going to give you a one-sentence thing on them; I feel they deserve at least two sentences. (Laughter.) The basic idea in using the word "gringo" is that it means "foreigner." The gringos themselves say, "It's Greek to me." So the Mexicano says, "It's griego [Greek] to me." That is one explanation of its origins, according to Professor Americo Paredes of the University of Texas. Another is, of course, the traditional one about the United States troops coming into Mexico with "green coats." The Mexicanos would say, with our own pronunciation, "Here come the 'green coats.'" And there are other explanations.

The word itself describes an attitude of supremacy, of xenophobia—that means you're afraid of strangers. I pick up a fancy word here and there. This attitude is also found in institutions, such as the Democratic Party. It's in policies like the one that says you can't speak Spanish in school because it's un-American. It's in the values of people who feel that unless Mexican music is played by the Tijuana Brass or the Baja Marimba Band it's no good. You can't eat tacos de chorizo [sausage tacos] around the corner for 20 cents. You've got to go up there to La Fonda [fancy Anglo-owned Mexican restaurant] and eat a $3.50 Mexican plate that gives you indigestion. (Applause and laughter.)

The formation of this party came about because of the critical need for the people to experience justice. It's just like being hungry. You've got to get food in there immediately, otherwise you get nauseous, you get headaches and pains in your stomach.

We were Chicanos who were starved for any kind of meaningful participation in decision making, policy making, and leadership positions. For a long time we have not been satisfied with the type of leadership that has been picked for us. And this is what a political party does, particularly the ones we have here. I shouldn't use the plural because we only have one, and that's the gringo party. It doesn't matter what name it goes by. It can be Kellogg's, All-Bran, or Shredded Wheat, but it's still the same crap.

These parties, or party, have traditionally picked our leadership. They have transformed this leadership into a kind of broker, a real estate guy who deals in the number of votes or precincts he can deliver or the geographical areas he can control. And he is a tape recorder—he puts out what the party says.

A beautiful example of this is Ralph Yarborough [Democratic senator from Texas]. The only thing he does for Chicanos is hire one every six years. He's perfectly content with the bigoted sheriff and Captain Allee [Texas Rangers] and the guys that break the strikes in El Rio Grande City and with (Wayne) Connally [brother of former Texas governor John Connally] and all these other people. Well, he gets beaten, and he knows why. The Republicans, the Birchers, the Wallace-ites and all these people went over to support Bentsen in the primaries. Yet I just read in the paper this afternoon that he said, "As always, I will vote a straight Democratic ticket in November."

There is only one other kind of individual who does that kind of work and that's a prostitute. . . .

Four years ago, when the guy who is now running for commissioner in La Salle County in La Raza Unida Party ran in the Democratic primaries, it cost him one-third of his annual income! That's how much it costs a Chicano with a median income of $1,574 per family per year. With the third party, it didn't cost him a cent.

On top of the excessive filing fees, they have set fixed dates for political activity, knowing that we have to migrate to make a living. We are simply not here for the May primaries. Did you know that in Cotulla, Erasmo Andrade [running in the Democratic primary for state senator in opposition to Wayne Connally] lost by over 300 votes because the migrants weren't there? In the Democratic primaries you're not going to cut it. In May there are only 16 more Chicano votes than gringo votes in La Salle County. But in November the margin is two-and-one-half to one in favor of Chicanos.

So you see that what's happening is not any big miracle. It's just common sense. The trouble is that everybody was always bothered and said, "We can't get out of the Democratic Party. Why bite the hand that feeds you?" Well, you bite it because it feeds you slop. (Laughter and applause.) Others say, "Well, why don't you switch over and join the

Republican Party?" Well, let's not even touch on that one.

Why can't you begin to think very selfishly as a Chicano? I still haven't found a good argument from anyone as to why we should not have a Chicano party. Particularly when you are the majority. If you want to implement and see democracy in action—the will of the majority—you are not going to do it in the Democratic Party. You can only do it through a Chicano party. (Applause.)

But you see there is another, more important, reason, and that is that Mexicanos need to be in control of their destiny. They need to make their own decisions. We need to make the decisions that are going to affect our brothers and maybe our children. We have been complacent for too long.

Did you know that not one of our candidates in La Salle County had a job the whole time they were running, and that they still can't get jobs? The same thing happened in Dimmit County. In Uvalde this is one of the reasons there's a walkout. They refused to renew the teaching contract of José García, who ran for county judge. That's a hell of a price to pay. But that's the kind of treatment that you've gotten.

You've got a median educational level among Mexicanos in Zavala County of 2.3 grades. In La Salle it's just a little worse—about 1.5 grades.

The median family income in La Salle is $1,574 a year. In Zavala it's about $1,754. The ratio of doctors, the number of newspapers, the health, housing, hunger, malnutrition, illiteracy, poverty, lack of political representation—all these things put together spell one word: colonialism. You've got a handful of gringos controlling the lives of muchos Mexicanos. And it's been that way for a long time.

Do you think things are going to get better by putting faith in the Democratic Party and Bentsen? Or that things are going to get better because you've got a few more Chicanos elected to office now within the traditional parties? Do you think that things are going to get better now that the U.S. Commission on Civil Rights has officially claimed that there is discrimination against Mexicanos? They've finally found out it's for real—we're discriminated against! (Laughter.) Do you think that things are going to get better simply because kids are walking out of schools—kids who can't vote, who in many cases can't convince the community to stand behind them?

No, it's not going to get better. We are going to have to devise some pretty ingenious ways of eliminating these gringos. Yet they don't really have to be too ingenious. All you have to do is go out there and look around and have a little common sense.

It stands to reason that if there are two grocery stores in town and we are the ones who buy from them, then if we stop buying from them they are going to go down. If you talk about transferring the wealth, that's how you do it. . . .

In 1960, there were 26 Texas counties in which Chicanos were a majority, yet not one of those counties was in the control of Chicanos. If you want to stand there and take that you can. You can be perfectly content just like your father and your grandfather were, con el sombrero en la mano [with hat in hand].

That's why most of our traditional organizations will sit there and pass resolutions and mouth off at conventions, but they'll never take on the gringo. They'll never stand up to him and say, "Hey, man, things have got to change from now on. *Que pase lo que pase* [Let whatever happens happen]. We've had it long enough!"

This is what we've got to start doing. If you don't go third party, then you've got to go the independent route, because there is no other way you are going to get on the November ballot. And don't try to put in a write-in candidate. That never works. . . .

The recent elections here in April for school board and city council demonstrated something that many people knew was a fact. It was almost like predicting that the sun is going to come up in the morning; if you can count, you know what the results are going to be. But an interesting factor is going to enter in now. We won in an off year in the nonpartisan races, which means that we were able to elect a minority to these positions. So now the establishment has all summer long to figure out how to stop the Mexicano. This is where we get back to the old tricks and lies of the gringo.

They tried the "outside agitator" bit on me but it didn't work because I was born in Crystal City. So they changed gears. Then they tried the "Communist" one for a while—until they found out I was in the U.S. Army Reserves. (Laughter and applause.) Then somewhere they dug up my "kill a gringo" thing of about a year ago when I said that I would kill a gringo in self-defense if I were attacked. . . .

Another lie is the white liberal approach. "I like Mexican food. Oh, I just love it!" And this is the kind of guy who's got the molcajete [Aztec mortar and pestle for cooking] sitting as an ash tray in his living room. (Applause and laughter)

This kind of character is the one that cautions you, be careful. Don't be racist in reverse. It's bad enough that gringos don't like 'Meskins' and 'Meskins' don't like gringos. You have to talk things over. You have to turn the other cheek. You've got to be nice. You've got to be polite. You can't use foul language in public. You have to have a constructive program.

They ask us, "What are you going to do for the schools in Crystal City?" And when we answer, "Bring education," they don't know what the hell we're talking about.

You see, that's another thing about the liberal. They always love to make you feel bad. And oh, my God, we hate to hurt the feelings of a good Anglo liberal, don't we? Well, hell, tell them the truth!

We've been hurting for a long time. They think we've got education, but we know different. How come we have 71 percent dropouts in Crystal City? It's miseducation. We ain't got teachers down there, we've got Neanderthals. These are the kinds of problems we are going to be faced with by the time November comes along. But a lot of people ain't going to buy it. The kids in the schools aren't going to stand for it. They see what this whole gringo thing has done to their parents, what it's done to our community, what it's done to our organizations. And nothing is going to prevent them from getting what is due them.

There's no generation gap in Crystal City. To the old people who are experienced this is nothing new. The older people in Crystal City, who have experienced years and years of humiliation and blows to their dignity, know what's going on. There was a problem for a while with the 25- to 45-year-olds who were trying to be gringos. But that's no longer true. You see, those are the parents of these kids, and these kids got their parents straight very early in the game. (Applause.) . . .

You know, civil rights are not just for those under 21. They're for everybody—for grandma, for daddy and mama, and los *chamaquitos* [children] and *primos* [cousins] and sisters, and so on. We've all got to work together. That means that all of us have to pitch in. And this is why in Crystal City you no longer hear "Viva La Raza" and "Chicano Power" and "La Raza Unida" all over the place. We don't talk about it anymore because it's a reality. You see, there la familia Mexicana esta organizada [the Mexican family is organized]. Aztlán has begun in the southwest part of Texas. (Prolonged applause.)

Our actions have made "La Raza Unida" more than just a slogan. Beginning with the walkout, we began organizing and moving in to counterattack every time the gringo tried to put pressure on the Mexicano. Boycott his store. Point the finger at him. Expose him for the animal that he is. Bring in the newspapers and photographers and the tape recorders. Let the world see it. . . .

So don't let anybody kid you. We are the consumers, we are the majority. We can stop anything and we can make anything in South Texas if we stick together and begin using common sense.

This third party is a very viable kind of alternative. It's a solution. For once you can sit in your own courthouse and you don't have to talk about community control because you are the community. And we are not talking about trying to run for Congress because you are sitting on the school board and then four years from now you're going to run for county judge. That's not the name of the game either.

We are talking about bringing some very basic elements into the lives of Mexicanos—like education and like making urban renewal work for Mexicanos instead of being the new way of stealing land. We got screwed once with the Treaty of Guadalupe Hidalgo and now we're getting it under "Model Cities" and urban renewal. (Applause.)

You can be as imaginative as you want and do almost anything you want once you run units of government. I'll give you an example. Everyone publicizes the fact that the Panthers are feeding kids all over the country. And everybody pours out money at cocktail parties and gets very concerned about little kids eating in the morning.

Well, the gringos in Cristal pulled out another one of their gimmicks and just a few days before the elections they decided to experiment with a pilot program of feeding kids in the morning. It was going to last for six weeks and feed 30 kids. They were going to watch them. They were going to experiment, study, conduct a survey to see if they grew an inch. (Laughter.)

Well, right now in Crystal City any kid who wants to eat can eat. Free breakfast in all the schools. You can do that, you see. You can also be very, very friendly to your opposition. You can rule them out of order when they get out of hand. You can slap them on the hand: "That's a no no!"

They can't hold an illegal meeting like they tried yesterday with the school board while I was out of town. They tried to take advantage of the fact that I was out of town to hold a special meeting. But the law says you must give three days' notice. So the gringos failed in their attempt to hire a principal to their liking. We don't need to be experts in parliamentary procedure. All we have to do is follow the book and tell them, "No, no! You can't do that!" (Laughter and applause.)

Let me be serious for a few minutes, because I think we have laughed enough. Mario was talking about having a third party in Bexar County by 1972. Good luck, Mario. (Applause.)

It doesn't matter if you don't agree with MAYO because this thing is no longer just MAYO. The response that we've had to this third party in all sections of our communities has been overwhelming. You saw the results. You can count votes just as I did.

The third party is not going to get smaller. It's going to get bigger.

You have three choices. First, you can be very active in this thing. For once we are not talking about being anti-Democrat or pro-Republican or pro-Democrat and anti-Republican. We are talking about being for La Raza, the majority of the people in South Texas. So there are a lot of things you can do and be very actively involved in.

If you don't choose that route, you can stay home and watch baseball and just come out and vote. But otherwise stay home. Don't get in the way.

The third thing you can do is lend your support, your general agreement. Often we are too critical of ourselves, and the gringo misunderstands that. He says, "You're disorganized, there's no unity among you." Hell, he can't understand an honest discussion when he hears one.

So, you've got these three roles that you can play. Or you can get very, very defensive and say, "This is wrong, this is un-American because you're bloc voting." But don't forget that the Democrats do it too. You can say that this is racism in reverse, but don't forget that we are the majority. And you can say that this is going to upset the whole situation in the state of Texas because we will never be able to elect a senator, because we're segregating ourselves and cutting ourselves apart and that this is not what we should be trying to do, that we should be trying to integrate, etc., etc. Well, before you go on your warpath or campaign, come down and tell that to my sheriff. Tell him how much you like him. Or, better yet, move on down the road a bit and tell it to Ranger Allee himself.

Build your constituency; build your community—that's how we will be electing three and possibly four congressmen in the very near future. There's going to be another congressman in Bexar County, and there's not room for all of them on the North side [Anglo section of San Antonio]. (Laughter and applause.) So we have some very interesting developments coming up.

To the gringos in the audience, I have one final message to convey: Up yours, baby. You've had it, from now on. (Standing ovation.)

Source: Gutiérrez, José Angel. Speech at UCLA. clnet .ucla.edu/research/docs/razaunida/control.htm.

Enrique Hank López, "Overkill at the Silver Dollar" (1970)

The level of violence perpetrated by Los Angeles Police Department and Sheriff's Department deputies at the Chicano Moratorium on August 29, 1970, shocked many Chicanos and other progressives. The murder of journalist Rubén Salazar enraged Angelinos. Around 30,000 peaceful demonstrators against the war in Vietnam marched through East Los Angeles, gathering for festivities at Laguna Park. With little or no provocation, police attacked men, women, children, young and old, clubbing and tear-gassing the demonstrators. Hundreds were arrested and the police killed three Chicanos—among them, respected journalist Rubén Salazar (1928–1970), who had been covering the moratorium from the Silver Dollar Café in East Los Angeles. The Chicano community called the death of Salazar, the director of news at KMEX, the Spanish-language television station, and a reporter for the Los Angeles Times, *an assassination. They thought Salazar had been targeted by the sheriff's deputies because he had written a series of articles and news reports critical of police abuse. It was too much of a coincidence that Salazar had been ordered to stay in the Silver Dollar while a missile projectile was fired into the establishment, hitting Salazar in the head. Hank López, a well-known attorney and writer who unsuccessfully ran for California's lieutenant governor in 1958, penned the following piece on the death of Salazar for* The Nation. *It was one of the more eloquent tributes.*

It was nearly midnight, and the barrio strangely quiet, quiet with fear. I had just left the Carioca restaurant with a dozen tortillas de maíz in a paper bag. I was spending the night before the funeral at my mother's house, and she'd promised to cook my favorite breakfast of menudo con chile. The tortillas, naturally, were essential.

Suddenly, a police car screeched to a stop at the curb. Two cops jumped out and pushed me against the wall, frisking me from top to bottom with rough insolent hands. They said not a word, and neither did I. I was simply not macho enough to protest. A cop like these had blasted the skull of my friend Rubén Salazar, the Chicano columnist for the Los Angeles Times, in the Silver Dollar Café, and I was frankly afraid to cross them.

They have also arrested about 300 Chicanos since the police riot that erupted during the East Los Angeles peace rally that Rubén was covering on the afternoon he was killed. I didn't want to be "prisoner 301"—and, having flown all the way from New York, I certainly didn't want to miss Rubén's funeral. So I accepted the indignity of their frisk with a gut-souring meekness. This is all familiar stuff to anyone who has lived in a Chicano barrio. And when they yanked off my shoes and shook them upside-down, I clamped my mouth to hold back the sour saliva that I'd like to spit in their faces.

"What do you do?" one of them asked.

"I'm a lawyer and a writer."

"Oh—one of those guys," in a tone suggesting one of those smart-ass spicks.

Suddenly noticing the brown paper bag in my hand, one of these guardians of the peace grabbed it and quickly shuffled through the tortillas in an apparent search for marijuana or heroin. Finding none, he gave them back.

Later on I threw the tortillas into a trash can—they must have had a hundred cop fingerprints on them.

They let me go finally—a tribute to my meekness, to what I would rather call my old barrio wisdom. The pragmatism of fear. And in my confusion and resentment (or was it again a sense of prudent resignation?), I had not noticed their badge numbers. Nor would I be able to recognize their faces again. I'm afraid all cops' faces have begun to look alike to me. And that's tragic, in a way, because two years ago I wrote to Mayor Lindsay and the New York Police Commissioner, commending a police officer who had been extremely kind (fatherly kind) to my 10-year-old daughter when she was injured near our apartment while we were away, the baby sitter having gone astray. He had taken her to a hospital and stayed by her side for five hours. So it's not in me to be a cop hater.

Just below Soto and Brooklyn Avenue, while searching vainly for a cab on those deserted streets, I saw a police helicopter swishing over me like a giant insect, its bright, harsh searchlights probing the dark alleys and back yards of the barrio.

I wondered then if the police regard us Mexican-Americans as a community of barricaded criminals. The phrase came easily at that moment because that very afternoon the *Times* had quoted an expert as saying that the kind of missile that killed Rubén "should be used only against a barricaded criminal." Gene Pember, a consultant for the Peace Officers Standards and Training Commission, had told newsmen that the high-velocity tear-gas projectile that pierced Rubén's skull should never be used for crowd control, that "the thing is like a young cannon, really." Such missiles, he said, could go through a thick stucco wall. "That's what they are for—to penetrate a house or an object behind which a dangerous suspect has barricaded himself. But even then they should never be fired at a person."

The 10-inch missile that killed Salazar was fired by a sheriff's deputy through an open doorway at a point-blank range of 15 feet. The deputy who fired that missile may not have known it was Rubén Salazar he was shooting, but he certainly knew it was a Chicano.

Yet, not once during the entire week following this obvious example of heedless slaughter would Sheriff Pitchess admit that his men might have been even slightly negligent. Sam Houston Johnson once told me that his brother LBJ suffered from a profound inability to say "I'm sorry"—to admit any error, however inconsequential. Certainly, a tragic flaw in a human being, and I wonder if the Los Angeles sheriff shares that affliction. Far from blaming any of his men, he keeps talking about "outside agitators."

Small wonder that my fellow Chicanos are willing to believe almost any accusation against the police. When the *Times* subsequently devoted its entire front page to blown-up photos from a community newspaper called *La Raza*, quoting at length from an article titled "The Murder of Rubén Salazar"—they may have begun to entertain even that suspicion.

Earlier that evening (several hours before the cops frisked me), I had attended a rally of Chicanos at the All Nations Auditorium, where I heard their collective rage and frustration—my own as well—burst from the throats of one speaker after another, the packed listeners periodically stamping their feet and raising clenched fists as a symbol of "Chicano Power." The speeches were mostly in English, but occasionally resorted to a schizolingual amalgam of English and Spanish to stress a vital point. ("Let's show los Pinches placas that we're men—que no bastard cop nos puede chingar!") Tough barrio language, most of it spoken with the bitterness of long years of resentment, some of it with a hushed, melancholy sense of bitter resignation.

When Corky Gonzalez was introduced, a thunder of shoes stomped the floor and a chorus of "viva Chicano power" echoed from the walls, throbbing in my head, sending an expectant chill up my spine. But there was no flaming rhetoric from the much loved leader of the Crusade for Justice—no call to arms, no threat of violence. There was instead an urgent plea for Chicano unity, for a grass-roots drive for political power, for a reclaiming of "the occupied territory of Aztlán," that portion of the United States that once belonged to Mexico. It sounded more like a psychic take-back than a real one. The muted anger in his voice was spiced with humorous irony when he told the crowd, "I was busted at the peace rally and charged with suspicion of robbery because I had $325 in my billfold. To the gabacho cops, I guess it's awful damned suspicious for a Chicano to have that much bread."

Clearly moved by Corky's mesmeric hold on the audience, Rene Anselmo (an Anglo millionaire who owns three TV stations) instantly donated $100 to the bail-bond fund for the 300 Chicanos who had been arrested since the riot. By coincidence, Captain Ernest Medina—defendant in the My Lai massacre case—was in Los Angeles during that same period, seeking donations for his defense from fellow Mexican-Americans. I doubt that he could have raised 2¢; from the people who heard Corky, though I'm told that American Legionnaires in his hometown think him a hero.

After the rally, I went to the Carioca bar-restaurant to eat Mexican food. It was also a sentimental gesture. The last time I had seen Rubén Salazar we had come to this restaurant, mostly to hear the mariachi trio that entertains here. They had played our favorite Adelita and Siete Leguas, songs of the Mexican Revolution that led us into a pleasant nostalgic mood. I had once written that my father was the only private in Pancho Villa's army, and he was now claiming that his father was the only private, smiling in that gentle way he had, his eyes shining with impish enjoyment. What better basis for a deep and abiding friendship than our mutual conviction that each of our fathers was the only private in that famous rebel División del norte?

Our conversation became serious after a while. Rubén was deeply concerned about the laggard pace of bilingual education programs for Chicano children in the early grades. Most educators know that everyone's greatest, most intense period of learning is from birth to the age of 5. For a Chicano, that fast-paced, crucial learning is acquired in Spanish or in a "pocho" combination of Spanish and English. But the day he enters kindergarten—a day of intense anxiety even for a child from the most secure Anglo environment—that learning tool is snatched away. He's not permitted to speak the only language he knows. So he sits in frustration, confusion, and fright as the teacher and the "more advantaged" kids talk in alien sounds, making him feel dumb and lost. The experience is repeated hour after hour, day after day, until he's ultimately defeated. There is no one more fragile than a 5-year-old child on alien turf.

The Chicano brings failure to school with him; he has no chance of success, no possibility of the "reward and reinforcement" that child educators feel is indispensable. The high school dropout rate for Mexican-Americans (58 percent in some Chicano ghettos—higher than the rate for black students) is a belated symptom of the dropping out that begins on the first day of kindergarten.

"Why can't they teach our Chicano kids in both Spanish and English?" asked Rubén, fingering an empty glass. "If they could have genuine bilingual classes—Spanish in the morning and English in the afternoon—there would be some trace of comforting familiarity between school and their home. They could feel successful in Spanish, capable of learning. They wouldn't feel dumb, they wouldn't quit trying as they do now. With a gradual transition in kindergarten and the first two grades, English would be easier."

His convictions were an echo of educational theories developed by Dr. Jerome Bruner, director of Harvard's Center for Cognitive Studies, who has said that ghetto youngsters often face insuperable linguistic and environmental obstacles.

Ordering another round of margaritas that evening, we talked of other problems that bedevil Chicano kids. Thinking of the kid-glove treatment used on the Kennedy-Shriver cousins when they were arrested for possession of marijuana, we were both sure that a Chicano or black teenager would have been summarily convicted and sent to a reformatory for at least six months.

I told Rubén of my first encounter with the juvenile court system as a lawyer (I'd had several as a child). A Mexican-American woman had called my office in a state verging on hysteria. Her 13-year-old son—let's call him Ramón Gómez—had been picked up by the police and whisked off in a squad car, but no one at the local precinct station would tell her where he was. Within half an hour we were at the Hollenbeck Station in East Los Angeles, and were informed that Ramón wasn't there. No record of his arrest. Then we hurried to the Juvenile Detention Home, where the desk captain said there was no booking on a Ramón Gómez. But as we were leaving, a young Chicano trustee told us that a boy answering Ramon's description had been taken from the detention home to the Los Angeles General Hospital. "He had a bloody bandage on his face." Checking the prison ward at the hospital, we learned two hours later that he'd received treatment for a fractured nose and then been returned to the detention home.

When we tried to see him at the so-called home, we were told he couldn't have visitors—nor could I see him in my capacity as his attorney. Angered by this refusal (any adult prisoner can see a lawyer), I went to a bail bondsman, who told me that kids weren't entitled to release on bail. Then I called several judges, who told me that they couldn't order his release on a writ of habeas corpus because children weren't entitled to that constitutional right.

When I finally saw the boy, he told me that he'd been accused of trying to break into a bubble-gum machine. "I put a penny in there and the gum didn't come out, so I was shaking it when the police came by. And when I tried to explain what happened, one of them slapped me. Then when I protested, they got me in the car, and one of them started punching my face with his closed fist, calling me a smart-aleck spick. That's how my nose got busted."

The Kafkaesque nightmare continued the next day at Ramón's hearing in juvenile court. The judge immediately informed me that I couldn't act as his lawyer "because this is not a criminal proceeding."

"Then why are you treating him like a criminal?" I asked. "Why has he been detained in that jail?"

"That's not a jail," he said rather testily, "It's only a detention home."

Paraphrasing Gertrude Stein, I said: "It has barred cells like a jail and barred gates to keep those kids inside, and a jail is a jail is a jail—no matter what name you give it."

But he still wouldn't let me appear as Ramon's lawyer, so his mother and I just sat there watching the nightmare proceedings of that quick-justice cafeteria called a "court." Not only were the juvenile defendants (almost all of them black or Chicano) denied lawyers; they couldn't face their accusers, they couldn't cross-examine witnesses against them, they couldn't object to rank hearsay testimony, they weren't protected by any of the normal rules of evidence. They were, in fact, unable to invoke any of the constitutional safeguards that are available to known gangsters.

And when I asked the judge for a transcript of the hearing after he had sentenced Ramon to six months in a reformatory, his mother pleaded with me not to appeal the case. "If we raise a big fuss," she said, "they'll only make it tougher on Ramón when he gets out. He'll be a marked man. We Chicanos don't have a chance."

Rubén had a film of tears in his eyes when I told him about Ramón. "Como son pinches," he said. "How can they be such bastards with little kids? And think of all the other Ramons who've been in the same bag."

Ramón Gómez must be 20 years old by now. He may have been one of the tight-mouthed militants in the angry crowd at the All Nations Auditorium on the night before Rubén's funeral, listening to one speaker comment on the tear-gassing of children at the peace rally, listening to the bitter irony in Corky Gonzalez's [sic] voice. He's heard, as most Chicanos have, that Corky is a marked man, that the FBI probably shadows him from one state to another as he goes from campus to campus, from barrio to barrio, asking his brown brothers to join in common cause. Ramón knows from personal experience (as do too many Chicanos who have been brutalized by certain cops, by the juvenile court system, by those crime-breeding reformatories), knows with a sickening fear that the police may some day crowd in on Corky, and that tragic violence may result.

But quite aside from his own not likely to be forgotten experience with the law, Ramón knows about inferior ghetto schools with indifferent teachers, about poor substandard housing, about high unemployment in the barrio, about radio and television shows that demean and insult his fellow paisanos. And he must be aware that local and federal government agencies largely ignore the plight of 8 million invisible Mexican-Americans. And he certainly knows that the television networks, national magazines, and news syndicates are generally deaf to the despairing voices of the barrio, although the more strident voices from black ghettos get ample notice.

Those same news media have been outraged by the alarming increase of cop killers—and it is well they should be, for any killing is abhorrent. But they should also know that the phrase is sometimes reversed in the ghetto—that Chicanos and blacks and poor whites often talk about killer cops with equal abhorrence.

Ramón and the rest of us Chicanos have been urged to turn a deaf ear to the dangerous cry of the militant, to listen instead to the voices of reason, to the voices of the people like Rubén Salazar. And though I myself felt slightly less than reasonable when those two cops shoved me against the wall on a dark lonely street, I would certainly agree that our only hope is reason and good will.

One must also hope that the police and other authorities will come to realize that reason flows both ways, that this fragile society can ill afford the frightening consequences of the kind of overkill that silenced the most reasonable voice of Rubén Salazar.

López, Enrique Hank. "Overkill at 'The Silver Dollar,'" 365–368. Reprinted with permission from the October 19, 1970, issue of *The Nation*. http://www.thenation.com.

Statement by Elma Barrera (1971)

In the 1970s, there was considerable debate in the Chicano movement on the gender question. The Chicano movement was Nationalist and often held distorted notions of culture. As the movement progressed, many began to question assumptions made by Chicano leaders and themselves. The dialogue was opened by Chicanas but also by the communist press. The struggle to level gender relations dated back to the influence of socialist and anarchist theory in the 1860s. Many Mexican women did not accept the traditional role assigned to them. The "Woman Question" was raised even within the Partido Liberal Mexicano (Mexican Liberal Party), which led the resistance against Mexican dictator Porfirio Díaz (1830–1915). The issue of gender equality was also raised during the Mexican women's suffrage movement of the 1930s. In the 1960s, there was a confluence of more educated women and civil rights, and Mexican American women began to question their position within the Mexican American and Chicano movements. Influenced by the civil rights and feminist movements, they began to conceptualize the question of equality vis-à-vis Chicanas. With the emergence of Chicanas, gender equality became an overriding demand. These voices were clearest in leftist forums but soon spread to mainstream organizations. In 1970, the Mexican American Political Association formed a women's caucus at its annual convention. With varying degrees of success, women's workshops were formed at most major Chicano conferences. The Chicano Youth Liberation Conferences of 1969, 1970, and 1971 in Denver, Colorado, held women's workshops. The Comisión Feminil Mexicana *(Mexican Feminine Commission) was formed at the Mexican American National Issues Conference in Sacramento, California. Meanwhile, Texano Chicanas played a major role in the formation of the La Raza Unida Party. Elma Barrera, an organizer of a national Chicana conference held in May 1971, in Houston, Texas, made the following statement at a national abortion conference attended by more than 1,000 women in July 1971.*

I have been told that the Chicana's struggle is not the same as the white woman's struggle. I've been told that the problems are different and that . . . the Chicana's energies are needed in the barrio and that being a feminist and fighting for our rights as women and as human beings is anti-Chicano and anti-male.

But let me tell you what being a Chicana means in Houston, Texas. It means learning how to best please the men in the Church and the men at home, not in that order.

You know, it's really funny the way that the Church has . . . grasped onto this "sinful" thing about abortion and birth control. It's really funny how the laws only apply to the woman and not to the man. . . . Chicano men . . . fool around, have mistresses, and yet, when it comes to abortion or birth control with their wives, it's a sin. . . .

I will take just one minute to read the two resolutions which came out of the Sex and the Chicana Workshop: "Free, legal abortions and birth control for the Chicano community, controlled by the Chicanas. As Chicanas, we have the right to control our own bodies."

And then out of the workshop on Marriage—Chicana Style: "We as mujeres de La Raza recognize the Catholic Church as an oppressive institution and do hereby resolve to break away and not to go to them to bless our union. So be it resolved that the national Chicana conference go on record as supporting free and legal abortions for all women who want or need them."

GENDER AND THE CHICANA

We feel that in order to provide an effective measure to correct the many sexual hangups facing the Chicano community the following resolutions should be implemented:

I. Sex is good and healthy for both Chicanos and Chicanas and we must develop this attitude.

II. We should destroy the myth that religion and culture control our sexual lives.

III. We recognize that we have been oppressed by religion and that the religious writing was done by men and interpreted by men. Therefore, for those who desire religion, they should interpret their Bible, or Catholic rulings according to their own feelings, what they think is right, without any guilt complexes.

IV. Mothers should teach their sons to respect women as human beings who are equal in every respect. No double standard.

V. Women should go back to the communities and form discussion and action groups concerning sex education.

VI. Free, legal abortions and birth control for the Chicano community, controlled by Chicanas. As Chicanas we have the right to control our own bodies.

VII. Make use of church centers, neighborhood centers, and any other place available.

"Liberate your mind and the body will follow."

"A quitarnos todos nuestros complejos sexuales para tener una vida mejor y feliz" (Let's cast off all our sexual complexes to have a better and happier life).

MARRIAGE—CHICANA STYLE

Reaffirmation that Chicano marriages are the beginnings of Chicano families which perpetuate our culture and are the foundation of the movement.

Points brought up in the workshop:

Chicano marriages are individual and intimate and solutions to problems must be primarily handled on an individual basis.

A woman must educate and acquaint herself with outside issues and personal problem (sexual hangups, etc.).

It is the responsibility of Chicanas with families to educate their sons and thus change the attitudes of future generations.

Chicanas should understand that Chicanos face oppression and discrimination, but this does not mean that the Chicana should be a scapegoat for the man's frustrations.

With involvement in the movement, marriages must change. Traditional roles for Chicanas are not acceptable or applicable.

RESOLUTIONS

I. We, as mujeres de La Raza, recognize the Catholic Church as an oppressive Institution and do hereby resolve to break away and not go to it to bless our unions.

II. Whereas: Unwanted pregnancies are the basis of many social problems, and

Whereas: The role of Mexican-American women has traditionally been limited to the home, and

Whereas: The need for self-determination and the right to govern their own bodies is a necessity for the freedom of all people, therefore,

BE IT RESOLVED: That the National Chicana Conference go on record as supporting free family planning and free and legal abortions for all women who want or need them.

III. Whereas: Due to socio-economic and cultural conditions, Chicanas are often heads of households, i.e., widows, divorcees, unwed mothers, or deserted mothers, or must work to supplement family income, and

Whereas: Chicana motherhood should not preclude educational, political, social, and economic advancement, and

Whereas: There is a critical need for a 24-hour childcare center in Chicano communities, therefore,

BE IT RESOLVED: That the National Chicana Conference go on record as recommending that every Chicano community promote and set up 24-hour day care facilities, and that it be further resolved that these facilities will reflect the concept of La Raza as the united family, and on the basis of brotherhood (La Raza), so that men, women, young, and old assume the responsibility for the love, care, education, and orientation of all the children of Aztlán.

IV. Whereas: Dr. Goldzieher of SWRF has conducted an experiment on Chicana women of westside San Antonio, Texas, using a new birth control drug, and

Whereas: No human being should be used for experimental purposes, therefore,

BE IT RESOLVED: That this Conference send telegrams to the American Medical Association condemning this act. Let it also be resolved that each Chicana women's group and each Chicana present at the conference begin a letter writing campaign to:

Dr. Joseph Goldzleher, Director

c/o SW Foundation for Research & Education

San Antonio, Texas

RELIGION

I. Recognize the Plan de Aztlán
II. Take over already existing Church resources for community use, i.e., health, Chicano awareness, public information of its resources, etc.
III. Oppose any institutionalized religion.
IV. Revolutionary change of Catholic Church or for it to get out of the way.
V. Establish communication with the barrio and implement programs of awareness to the Chicano movement.

Source: Vidal, Mirta. *Chicanas Speak Out! Women: New Voice of La Raza*. Copyright © 1971 by Pathfinder Press. Reprinted by permission. http://latino.sscnet.ucla.edu/research/docs/chicanas/vidal.htm.

Seattle Civil Rights and Labor History Project (ca. 1971)

Chicano activism was not confined to California or Texas but was prevalent throughout the Midwest, the Pacific Northwest, and Utah. Many of the Chicano activists were children of migrant workers who had come to work in productive agricultural farmlands like those of the Yakima Valley. As students they were inspired by United Farm Workers volunteers who drifted into the valleys and college campuses asking students to support the grape boycott. This activism on the campuses in the Northwest began in the late 1960s with Chicano students making demands similar to those of their counterparts in the Southwest. University of Washington historian Erasmos Gamboa, a former student activist and now a professor, has documented this history and broken the stereotype that Chicano history was solely a Texas and California affair. As with Southwest colleges and universities, the University of Washington became known in the late 1960s for student mobilizations against the war in Vietnam, against militarism on campus, and in favor of civil rights. Activism followed a familiar pattern: Chicano students were recruited by the Special Education Program in the fall of 1968, and soon afterward formed the United Mexican American Students (UMAS). The farmworkers were always a model. The UMAS built links to the Yakima Valley and the local community. In the Seattle community, they helped found El Centro de la Raza *(The Mexican People's Center), a clearinghouse for community organizations. All along, they pressed for the recruitment of more Mexican American students and for Mexican American studies classes.*

The following are personal testimonies of student leaders at the University of Washington. They represent the experiences of most Chicano and Latino students who made the transformation from first-generation workers to students. They had to endure the racism and alienation of college life and looked to each other for a support network.

PEDRO ACEVEZ

Pedro Acevez was born in Wapato, Washington, and grew up in the nearby town of Toppenish. He grew up working on his father's farm, as well as doing farm labor in Oregon and Washington, before attending Yakima Valley College and Central Washington University. He transferred to the University of Washington in 1969, a move partly made possible by combining scholarships for both groups.

Acevez was active in MEChA de UW [Movimiento Estudiantil Chicano de Aztlán at University of Washington], and served as its President for one year. During his first school year, he worked with a number of MEChA students to help channel a spontaneous farmworker walkout in Yakima Valley into a United Farm Workers (UFW) organizing drive. During the 1970–71 school year, he served as a resident advisor on the "Chicano Floor," or 5th floor, of Lander Hall—though fired for returning home during an illness, student protests successfully pushed the UW to reinstate him.

Since graduating from the UW in 1975, Acevez has worked as a high school and community college math and science teacher, and currently works for the UW's Health Sciences Center.

RICARDO S. MARTÍNEZ, MECHA DE UW; JUDGE: SUPERIOR COURT; U.S. DISTRICT COURT

Judge Ricardo Martínez was born in the small town of Mercedes in Southern Texas. While in Texas, his family worked in the fields picking cotton, tomatoes, and other crops. When he was six, Martinez's family moved to Lynden, Washington, another small farming town. His family was one of the first Latino families that decided to stay in this area of Washington instead of living there seasonally as migrant workers.

Ricardo Martínez earned a BA from the University of Washington in 1975, and his JD in 1980. While attending the University of Washington, he was a member of Movimiento Estudiantil Chicano/a de Aztlán (MEChA).

After earning his law degree, Martínez worked for the King County Prosecutor's office. In 1989, Martinez began his career as a judge, serving on the King County Superior Court until 1998, and as a U.S. Magistrate Judge for the Western District of Washington until 2004. He currently serves as a United States District Judge for the Western District of Washington—having been nominated by President Bush in 2003 and confirmed by the Senate in 2004.

Quotes on staying in Washington: "Why not? Let's stay here." His parents decided to stay in Washington because they thought moving between migrant farming camps was not good for the children.

On MEChA: "The central theme was the ongoing struggle." All the Chicano groups on campus shared the same goal.

On the Chicano Floor: "Living on the floor in Lander Hall that was designated for Chicano students."

"All students of color come together for the betterment of everyone." The need for all people of color to work together.

JUAN JOSÉ BOCANEGRA MECHA; EL CENTRO DE LA RAZA, LA RAZA UNIDA PARTY; AMERICAN INDIAN MOVEMENT

Juan José Bocanegra was born in Reynosa, Tamaulipas, Mexico and grew up in Corpus Chisti, Texas. While he was in school in the 1950s and 1960s, Corpus Christi's public school system was being desegregated—"it was like a big war between Mexicanos and Anglos in that part of the country," he recalled.

After attending Texas A&I University [which has since changed its name to Texas A&M University] in Kingsville, TX from 1967–71, Bocanegra moved to Seattle to get a graduate degree in social work from the University of Washington. He has been a prominent Seattle-based activist ever since. During the 1970s, he played an active role in the Chicano movement and broader Third World Peoples' movements. He helped lead a successful campaign to diversify the UW School of Social Work and create its multi-ethnic practice program. He was active with the group that occupied the Beacon Hill School and founded El Centro de la Raza in 1972.

In 1973, Bocanegra moved to Brownsville, Texas for six months to run for City Council for the La Raza Unida Party—but was disqualified because he had not established legal residence there. After returning to Seattle, he assumed leadership over the South Seattle Community College Chicano English as a Second Language (ESL) Program after Roberto Maestas left that position to lead El Centro de la Raza. He was also active in the American Friends

Service Committee's Third World Coalition. During the early to mid-1970s, Bocanegra became involved in solidarity work with local American Indian struggles—including the American Indian Movement (AIM), Frank's Landing demonstrations with the Nisqually Tribe, the Puyallup Tribe's takeover of the Cascadia Center in 1976, and the 1976 Trail of Self-Determination.

REBECCA SALDAÑA PCUN; UFW; SEIU LOCAL 6; STITCH

Rebecca Saldaña's father was a Mexican immigrant, and she was born and raised in Seattle. While attending Seattle University, Saldaña became active in farmworker solidarity campaigns, and after graduating became an organizer with Pineros y Campesinos Unidos del Noroeste (PCUN), a farmworker's union in Oregon. At PCUN, she coordinated its boycott of NORPAC Foods. Afterward, she was hired to be a Community Mobilizer for the Fair Trade Apple Campaign for the United Farmworkers of America (UFW)—a campaign that applied lessons learned in fair trade coffee campaigns to the domestic agricultural sector. She currently organizes janitors for SEIU Local 6, and is a Board Member of STITCH—"a network of women unionists, organizers, and activists that builds connections between Central American and U.S. women organizing for economic justice."

Her father's family immigrated from Mexico to the U.S. where he became a migrant farmworker. He eventually settled in Seattle, where he found a union job.

"I am a product of my parents." Rebecca describes the influence of her father's labor union and her mother's religion on her own political development.

"The Farm Workers of the Urban Area: From organizing farmworkers to organizing janitors."

Source: The Seattle Civil Rights and Labor History Project. http://www.civilrights.washington.edu. Courtesy of Pedro Acevez.

Marjorie Heins, *Strictly Ghetto Property: The Story of Los Siete de La Raza* (1972)

The Mission District of San Francisco has almost always been a multi-Latino barrio where Mexicans have shared the streets with Central, South, and Caribbean Americans. Consequently, the culture of the area has often differed from that of the rest of California. Caribbean musical sounds are usual and its ideas are more what many Chicanos at the time called Third World. In 1969, two plainclothes police officers approached seven young men while they were moving furniture. An altercation followed, and an officer died of a gunshot wound. Swarms of officers went to the building, fired automatic rifles, and flooded the building with tear gas. In Santa Cruz, seven youths were later arrested for murder and attempted murder. All were Central American—four Salvadorans, one Nicaraguan, and one Honduran. They had been involved in the Mission Rebels, a youth group, but had been politicized by the times. At their trial, the defendants insisted that the police had drawn their guns. Because the police officers were in plainclothes, the young Central Americans did not know these men were police officers. The trial lasted a year and a half, and the seven were acquitted. The "Los Siete" Defense Committee helped raise the consciousness of youth while it helped the defendants in their defense. The following is from a book about Los Siete *(the seven). It shows the influence of the Chicano movement in politicizing the Mission District and vice versa.*

A little after 10:20 a.m. on May 1, 1969, a police officer was shot to death in San Francisco's Latin barrio, the Mission District. Newspapers said that the dead cop and his partner had been attacked by members of a "burglary ring" they had staked out; police were seeking an undetermined number of "Latin hippie-types" as suspects. After a week of what the papers called "the largest manhunt in the history of Northern California," six young Latin Americans were arrested for the murder.

About a month later, I got involved in a short-lived underground newspaper called Dock of the Bay. Somebody on the staff mentioned that a new and probably newsworthy radical organization called Los Siete de la Raza had been formed in the Mission District. So on a hot June day I went to a small storefront in the heart of the Mission and spoke to a young man named Ralph Ruiz who was in charge of press relations for the organization.

Los Siete de la Raza, Ralph told me, meant "the seven of the race," or of the Latin American people, and it referred to the seven suspects in the recent cop killing, six of whom had been arrested. The new organization had been formed by friends of the seven, to help in their legal defense.

I asked Ralph what the seven now under arrest were like. He said they were all "bad brothers," a compliment in ghetto or barrio language, meaning they were tough. But, he added, they weren't hoodlums, as the papers had said: several of them had been involved in recruiting other young Latinos for a special Readiness Program. . . . All six were politically radical.

Ralph told me the media had already condemned the six with sensationalist headlines and strict adherence to the police version of the incident. In fact, he said, the two cops involved were a notorious plainclothes. . . . One played the good guy and the other played the motherfucker." It was the "good guy" who had been killed. Ralph said the six were considered heroes in the barrio for having stood up to these two "pigs."

My next stop was the office of the *San Francisco Chronicle*, the larger of the city's two dailies, where I bought copies of all the back issues containing articles about the incident. After studying these articles, I understood what Ralph meant: the *Chronicle* had taken its stories from police announcements and the stories all played on racial stereotypes, leaving little room for doubt that all six Latinos charged with murder were guilty.

From the articles and from my talk with Ralph I wrote my first story on Los Siete for Dock of the Bay. I began to follow the pre-trial hearings in the case, and to get to know other people in the Los Siete organization. One of them, Donna James, had attended San Francisco State College, been active in the recent strike there, and finally quit school to work with Los Siete full time. Like Ralph, Donna had known several of the "brothers," as the six who were arrested came to be called. When, almost a year after the incident, Ramparts Press suggested I write a book on Los Siete, Donna agreed to give me help and advice.

The need for such a book was obvious. The police hoped to convict all six in jail and with the help of the dead policeman's widow had begun a vigorous pro–capital punishment campaign. Mayor Joseph Alioto, conscious of the law-and-order reaction which followed the college strikes of 1968 and '69, had called the suspects "punks" and offered a $5,000 reward for information leading to the capture of each. Responding to these pressures, the city's mass media steered clear of any in-depth reportage about the lives of the six young men, the conditions in the Mission District which produced their confrontation with the two cops, or the political consciousness which led to the formation of the Los Siete defense organization. . . .

Some of the changes Pinky noticed when he got out of jail had to do with rising political consciousness among La Raza people. A brown movement was beginning, which would replace feelings of hopelessness and inferiority among La Raza with pride and determination to change the conditions of their lives. This movement got its start in 1965 with the struggle of Chicano farmworkers in California's San Joaquin Valley. César Chávez, Dolores Huerta, and other organizers had founded the National Farm Workers Association (later the United Farmworkers Organizing Committee) in Delano, California, and in October 1965 joined with a largely Filipino union to strike against Delano grape growers for higher wages and union recognition. The growers refused to recognize the union and pretended there was no strike. They sprayed pesticides near the strikers, got injunctions against bullhorns and rallies, and imported scabs from skid rows, depressed rural areas, and Mexico.

The workers turned to boycotting Delano's second largest grape grower, the Schenley Corporation.

The strike and boycott captured the imaginations of Chicanos and other sympathetic people across the country. In San Francisco, protesters succeeded in stopping grape shipments when longshoremen refused to cross their picket line. The farmworkers' symbol, a stylized eagle derived from an Aztec migration myth, appeared on buttons and, as graffiti, on the walls of Mission High.

In March 1966, the farmworkers held a pilgrimage through three hundred miles of California's San Joaquin Valley, from Delano to Sacramento. They marched behind an image of the Virgin of Guadalupe, Mexico's patron saint, the same saint whose image was carried by Miguel Hidalgo and the Indians of his parish when they began the war for Mexican independence in 1810.

"We are conscious of the historical significance of our pilgrimage," the NFWA (National Farm Workers Association) wrote in its Plan of Delano.

"It is clearly evident that our paths travel through a valley well known to all Mexican farmworkers . . . because along this very same road, in this very same valley, the Mexican race has sacrificed itself for the last hundred years. . . .

"We are sons of the Mexican Revolution, a revolution of the poor seeking bread and justice. . . . Across the San Joaquin Valley, across California, across the entire Southwest of the United States, wherever there are Mexican people, wherever there are farmworkers, our movement is spreading like flames across a dry plain."

When the farmworkers arrived in Sacramento they learned that Schenley had finally agreed to come to the bargaining table. Eventually, all the wine growers accepted the union. A few years later, the huge table-grape-growing corporations began to give in. The struggle spread to other parts of the country, and to other crops.

Among those who marched to Sacramento was a young Chicano from south Texas, Aaron Manganiello. Manganiello was already a veteran of civil rights sit-ins, jazz tours with John Handy's Freedom Band, and Berkeley's Vietnam Day Committee. He would eventually have a strong influence on three of Los Siete—Mario and Tony Martínez and Nelson Rodríguez—and on the political direction of the organization that grew up around their case. (Manganiello was one of the first to emphasize the need for brown radicals to study Marxist literature.) With the growth of the farmworkers' struggle, Manganiello, like many other politically minded brown people, saw the need for some kind of organized movement in the urban barrios.

The Brown Berets were one response to this need. Founded by David Sánchez, who was once elected Los Angeles's "outstanding high school student," the Berets combined paramilitary-type training with a desire to establish cultural and political self-determination for La Raza in the Southwest, the area which the Chicano movement calls Aztlán. In March 1968, the Berets led a massive walkout of Chicano high school students in Los Angeles. They were demanding courses in their cultural history, teachers who lived in their communities, bilingual instruction, an end to corporal punishment, and an end to students doing janitorial work. The walkout spread the name of the Brown Berets across the Southwest, and many young Chicanos began, unofficially, to call themselves Berets.

Aaron Manganiello and a friend, Manuel Gómez, convinced the Los Angeles Berets to let them set up an official Northern California branch in Oakland. Chapters soon spread to barrios in dozens of cities throughout the country. The chapters varied in their political outlook. Many were strongly "cultural nationalist," believing that Raza cultural unity was the best basis for organizing; others disagreed, feeling that this perspective was too narrow and could become damaging if an attachment to cultural traditions were to stand in the way of change. . . .

Los Siete de la Raza began as a group of students and ex-students attempting to organize street youth around issues like police brutality. By the time the clinic and legal defense office were established in the spring of 1970, Los Siete was beginning to represent the interests of working families, the basic social unit in the Mission District. Coming out of a movement which consisted of students, radicals, and some street people, this was an essential transition.

People within Los Siete were trying to develop the historical understanding and self-discipline they considered necessary attributes of true revolutionaries. In developing this understanding and discipline they had to struggle with anti-intellectualism. As with the Young Lords in New York, members of Los Siete were supposed to read each day; the books were then discussed in political education classes. This reading, in addition to work at the clinic or legal defense, writing for and selling *Basta Ya!* (*Enough Is Enough*), raising money, leafleting, public speaking, and, for some, school, jobs, or children to care for, imposed a heavy schedule. As a result, Los Siete remained small, with an increasing number of friends who worked with Los Siete projects but weren't actually members of the organization.

One of the most impressive aspects of Los Siete was the personal changes in many of its members. Although some people left to form new groups, or just to give up politics for a while, those who remained grew more responsible, articulate, dedicated, and mellow. Almost everyone in the group learned to speak convincingly in public, to read carefully and think analytically, and to shoulder responsibility.

The women in Los Siete grew stronger and more independent.

Like the Young Lords, Los Siete fought machismo in political work as well as in personal relations. This was no easy fight, since some young men who were fairly sophisticated radicals and good workers still wanted their wives or girlfriends to stay home and keep out of political work. Stronger women in the organization made a conscious effort to step aside and let other women take the lead.

People in Los Siete were trying to become revolutionaries, which necessarily required defining what "revolutionary" meant for brown people in the United States. Clearly it meant solidarity with wars of liberation such as the war in Indochina; and Los Siete, through *Basta Ya!*, tried to show people in the Mission that they, the Indochinese, and many guerrillas in Latin America had a common enemy: Yankee imperialism.

"Revolutionary" also meant devoted to changing the entire social and economic system. Los Siete members believed—partly because of their experience in poverty programs—that in the long run reforms were not going to improve conditions for the masses of Latin people. But they realized they were at the beginning of a long revolutionary process. Their immediate goal was not to "start the revolution then and there," as Bebe Melendez once put it, but to organize, educate, and learn from the people.

"Revolutionary" for Los Siete also meant "internationalist"; that is, rejecting cultural nationalism in favor of a class struggle which crossed racial and even national boundaries. But despite this opposition to cultural nationalism, Los Siete remained a brown organization. Its precise appeal was its concern for the needs of Latin people in a predominantly Latin area. Its members felt there was no use combining with other groups to form a multiracial organization until a significant number of brown people had been united around revolutionary demands. It was also important to Los Siete to remain within the brown movement which, despite its fragmented nature and the diversity of its political ideologies, held a tremendous appeal for Chicano and Latin youth—an appeal stemming from its proud, assertive new spirit, a spirit so important to people who have been discriminated against and taught they are inferior.

It's hard to say what success Los Siete has had after its first two years. The hostility of the powerful mass media has made its message difficult to spread; Los Siete's available avenues of communication with its people aren't nearly so powerful: a small, street-vended newspaper and day-to-day contacts at the clinic or legal defense office with people who often have little time to get involved in politics. But a few events toward the middle of 1971 indicated that people were beginning to make time.

Meetings, leafleting, and picketing around a threatened eviction of the clinic in the early summer of 1971 mobilized neighborhood people and developed a strong core of Los Siete partisans. The landlord, who owned a pharmacy on the ground floor of the building, wanted to get rid of the clinic and rent to some "real doctors with real patients and real money," as he put it, who would send people downstairs to buy at his store. (El Centro de Salud dispensed free drugs whenever possible and so didn't provide any clients for the drug store.)

When the landlord said he wouldn't renew the lease, Los Siete called meetings with people who had used the clinic, asking them to pass the word and boycott the pharmacy. In the week that followed, the pharmacy lost fifty percent of its business. When the landlord still didn't give in, picketing was begun. Insisting that community people must fight for the clinic or it wasn't worth saving, Los Siete resisted the temptation to use outside pressure from friendly doctors or other, mostly white, health professionals. Enough community people responded—a number of them housewives—to convince the landlord to reconsider after only one day of picketing. The women who had come to the clinic's defense would hopefully remain organized as a pressure group on health care issues in the Mission.

It would seem that after two years, Los Siete was at least moving in the right direction; that more genuine contacts had been made, more trust established, than by radical organizations in the past—especially in the Mission District, where political activity has been dominated either by the Democratic Party and its Mexican American friends, or by Office of Economic Opportunity—funded groups which are often full of opportunists. Los Siete is indigenous; it is not being paid by anyone to exist, and its members work mainly from idealistic motives—as Tony Herrera put it, "dedicated heart and soul to serving the people."

Source: Heins, Marjorie. *Strictly Ghetto Property: The Story of Los Siete de La Raza* Berkeley, CA: Ramparts Press, 1972, 11–12, 49–51, 203–206.

MAYO Document on Student Walkouts, Crystal City, Texas (1973)

In 1967, the Mexican American Youth Organization (MAYO) was formed to fight for the civil rights of Mexican Americans. Founded by José Angel Gutiérrez (1944–), Willie C. Velásquez (1944–1988), Mario Compeán, and others in San Antonio, Texas, the organization was dedicated to the planned transformation of the situation Mexicans faced in Texas. MAYO members were key to the formation of La Raza Unida Party, which was organized because neither Democrats nor Republicans were addressing Chicano issues or running Chicano candidates. Velásquez later founded the Southwest Voter Registration and Education Project (1972), which led national drives in which they registered hundreds of thousands of Latinos. MAYO led at least 18 school walkouts throughout Texas, including those in Crystal City, Kingsville, Edgewood, and Lanier high schools in San Antonio. Gutiérrez and his wife, Luz, moved back to Crystal City specifically to plan a political takeover of the city. The following excerpts are by José Angel Gutiérrez on the walkouts.

The Crystal City, Texas, school walkouts organized by MAYO in 1969–1970 precipitated other Chicano Movement activity in the Winter Garden District, such as the rise of La Raza Unida Party. Below are the demands that MAYO organizers and their local supporters, known as the Ciudadanos Unidos, wanted school administrators to concede before they would call off the strike and return to classes. The detailed set of demands required that the school board allow greater input from the Chicano community in order to insure, among other things, that students would not be discriminated and that course content would reflect the needs of the Mexican American majority in Crystal City.

WALKOUT DEMANDS

Walkout demands were that all elections concerning the school be conducted by the student body. Concerning class representatives, the petition asked that the qualifications such as personality, leadership, and grades be abolished. These factors do not determine whether the student is capable of representing the student body. The students are capable of voting for their own representatives. The representatives are representing the students, not the faculty. All nominating must be done by the student body, and the election should be decided by a majority vote.

The present method of electing the most handsome, beautiful, most popular, and most representative is elected [sic] by the faculty. The method of cumulative voting is unfair.

National Honor Society—the grades of the students eligible must be posted on the bulletin board well in advance of selection. The teachers should not have anything to do with electing the students.

An advisory board of Mexican American citizens should be a part of the school administration in order to advise on the needs and problems of the Mexican American.

No other favorites should be authorized by school administrators or board members unless submitted to the student body in a referendum.

Teachers, administrators, and staff should be educated; they should know our language—Spanish—and understand the history, traditions, and contributions of Mexican culture. How can they expect to teach us if they do not know us? We want more Mexican American teachers for the above reason.

We want immediate steps taken to implement bilingual and bicultural education for Mexican Americans. We also want the schoolbooks revised to reflect the contributions of Mexicans and Mexican Americans to the U.S. society, and to make us aware of the injustices that we, Mexican Americans, as a people have suffered in an "Anglo" dominant society. We want a Mexican American course with the value of one credit.

We want any member of the school system who displays prejudice or fails to recognize, understand, and appreciate us, Mexican Americans, our culture, or our heritage removed from Crystal City's schools. Teachers shall not call students any names.

Our classes should be smaller in size, say about twenty students to one teacher, to insure more effectiveness. We want parents from the community to be trained as teachers' aides. We want assurances that a teacher who may disagree politically or philosophically with administrators will not be dismissed or transferred because of it. Teachers should encourage students to study and should make class more interesting, so that students will look forward to going to class. . . .

There should be a manager in charge of janitorial work and maintenance details, and the performance of such duties should be restricted to employees hired for that purpose. In other words, no more students doing janitorial work.

We want a free speech area plus the right to have speakers of our own.

We would like September 16 as a holiday, but if it is not possible, we would like an assembly with speakers of our own. We feel it is a great day in the history of the world because it is when Mexico had been under the Spanish rule for about three hundred years. The Mexicans were liberated from the harsh rule of Spain. Our ancestors fought in this war, and we owe them tribute because we are Mexicans, too.

Being civic-minded citizens, we want to know what the happenings are in our community. So, we request the right to have access to all types of literature and to be able to bring it on campus. The newspaper in our school does not carry sufficient information. It carries things like the gossip column, which is unnecessary.

The dress code should be abolished. We are entitled to wear what we want. We request the buildings open to students at all times.

We want Mr. Harbin to resign as principal of Fly Jr. High.

We want a Mexican American counselor fully qualified in college opportunities. We need more showers in the boys' and girls' dressing rooms.

Source: "MAYO document, José Angel Gutiérrez files, Crystal City, Texas, 1973" is reprinted with permission of the publisher of *Testimonio: A Documentary History of the Mexican American Struggle for Civil Rights*, edited by F. Arturo Rosales, 387–388. Houston: Arte Público Press–University of Houston © 2000.

Robert Kistler, "Women 'Pushed' into Sterilization, Doctor Charges" (1974)

Sterilization has its roots in the social Darwinism eugenics movement of the early 20th century; American eugenicists believed that people could be categorized according to intelligence and that the United States could genetically engineer its racial composition. The extreme position called for sterilization of those considered undesirable—a notion that was popular through the 1960s. There is evidence that even some members of the Peace Corps, established in 1961, promoted sterilization programs. Domestically, sterilizations were a major problem in the Puerto Rican, Chicano, and Native American communities. The following Los Angeles Times *article documents the existence of sterilization programs at one of the nation's major doctor training hospitals—the County/University of Southern California facility at Los Angeles, a prestigious facility where medical interns practiced on the facility's low-income patients, who were mostly black and Mexican. A large percentage of these patients were minorities, especially Chicanos and Latinos. Physician Bernard Rosenfeld blew the whistle on the hospital when its doctors performed sterilizations on Latino patients without their consent. Often the women were given forms in English granting permission for sterilization at the moment they were in labor. The women victims filed a $6 million lawsuit against the hospital. Rosenfeld was horrified at the attitudes of fellow doctors who performed the sterilizations for racial and* *other reasons, which included the fact that sterilization allowed the physicians to perform more complex surgical procedures. The only doctor who supported Rosenfeld and testified that these procedures were taking place was Juan Nieto. Thousands of women, mostly poor and minority, were pushed into giving permission for sterilization, according to Rosenfeld.*

Thousands of women—most of them from low-income, minority groups—have been victimized by unregulated "voluntary" sterilization programs in some of the nation's most prestigious hospitals, according to evidence compiled by a Los Angeles physician-researcher.

Such abuses, the physician charges, historically have found fertile climates in the nation's giant, core-city teaching complexes such as the Los Angeles County-USC Medical Center, where medicine is high-volume, often impersonal—and practiced on patients who are generally poor, frightened and uneducated.

It is within the halls of these massive, loosely regulated institutions, according to Dr. Bernard Rosenfeld, that women—some while in the throes of childbirth—have been cajoled, pressured and sometimes coerced into consenting to surgical sterilization.

The operation is permanent and the chances of surgically reversing the procedure at some later date are relatively slight (between 20% and 30%, depending upon which study you believe).

[The only physician who would corroborate Rosenfeld was Dr. Juan Nieto, 25.]

Source: Kistler, Robert. "Women 'Pushed' into Sterilization, Doctor Charges." *Los Angeles Times,* December 2, 1974, A1.

Lau v. Nichols (1974)

The demand for bilingual education has been part of the immigrant experience from the beginning. When the Germans arrived en masse they set up German-speaking schools, and Jews and other immigrants also set up schools where children were instructed in their native language. Throughout the early 20th century, Mexicans and other Latinos set up Spanish-speaking classes. It was a proven pedagogical method. In the mid-1960s, President Lyndon B. Johnson (1908–1973) told California congressman Edward Roybal (1916–2005) that when he was a schoolteacher in an all–Mexican American school, he found the students to be intelligent and that the only thing that held them back was lack of knowledge of English. The schools held them back until they learned English. Johnson considered it a waste of time and resources—why not teach them courses such as mathematics and history in Spanish and transition them into English instead of keeping them in the same class dooming them to failure? By the 1970s, many Chinese American students and other immigrant children were falling through the cracks, too, and they also demanded teachers who would address linguistic problems. They built on the Chicano experience and the movement toward bilingual education that had come to a head in the mid-1960s. In the 1970s, bilingual education suffered setbacks when a federal judge in Denver decided in Keyes v. School District Number One, *413 U.S. 189 (1973), litigated by the Mexican American Legal Defense and Education Fund, the premier Mexican American legal defense organization, that placing children in bilingual classes violated antisegregation laws. In 1974, the Supreme Court in* Lau v. Nichols *ordered federally funded school districts to "take affirmative steps" to give special help to students who do not know English and to open special programs for them. The ruling addressed language-based discrimination. The following ruling was made in response to an Asian American suit in San Francisco.*

LAU ET AL v. NICHOLS ET AL.

CERTIORARI TO THE UNITED STATES COURT OF APPEALS FOR THE NINTH CIRCUIT

No. 72-6520. Argued December 10, 1973—Decided January 21, 1974.

The failure of the San Francisco school system to provide English language instruction to approximately 1,800 students of Chinese ancestry who do not speak English, or to provide them with other adequate instructional procedures, denies them a meaningful opportunity to participate in the public educational program and thus violates § 601 of the Civil Rights Act of 1964, which bans discrimination based "on the ground of race, color, or national origin," in "any program or activity receiving Federal financial assistance," and the implementing regulations of the Department of Health, Education, and Welfare. Pp. 565–569. 483 F. 2d 791, reversed and remanded.

Douglas, 1., delivered the opinion of the Court, in which Brennan, Marshall, Powell, and Rehnquist, J.J., joined. Stewart, 1., filed an opinion concurring in the result, in which Burger, C. J., and Blackmun, J., joined, post, p. 569. White, 1., concurred in the result. Blackmun, 1., filed an opinion concurring in the result, in which Burger, C. 1., joined, post, p. 571.

Edward H. Steinman argued the cause for petitioners. With him on the briefs were Kenneth Hecht and David C. Moon.

Thomas M. O'Connor argued the cause for respondents. With him on the brief were George E. Krueger and Burk E. Delventhal.

Assistant Attomey General Pottinger argued the cause for the United States as amicus curiae urging reversal. With him on the brief were Solicitor General Bork, Deputy Solicitor General Wallace, Mark L. Evans, and Brian K. Landsberg.

Mr. Justice Douglas delivered the opinion of the Court.

The San Francisco, California, school system was integrated in 1971 as a result of a federal court decree, 339 F. Supp. 1315. See Lee v. Johnson, 404 U.S. 1215. The District Court found that there are 2,856 students of Chinese ancestry in the school system, 400 who do not speak English. Of those who have that language deficiency, about 1,000 are given supplemental courses in the English language. About 1,800, however, do not receive that instruction.

This class suit brought by non-English-speaking Chinese students against officials responsible for the operation of the San Francisco Unified School District seeks relief against the unequal educational opportunities, which are alleged to violate, inter alia, the Fourteenth Amendment. No specific remedy is urged upon us. Teaching English to the students of Chinese ancestry who do not speak the language is one choice. Giving instructions to this group in Chinese is another. There may be others. Petitioners ask only that the Board of Education be directed to apply its expertise to the problem and rectify the situation.

The District Court denied relief. The Court of Appeals affirmed, holding that there was no violation of the Equal Protection Clause of the Fourteenth Amendment or of § 601 of the Civil Rights Act of 1964, 78 Stat. 252, 42 U.S.C. § 2000d, which exclude from participation in federal financial assistance, recipients of aid which discriminate against racial groups. 483 F. 2d 791. One judge dissented. . . .

We granted the petition for certiorari because of the public importance of the question presented, 412 U.S. 938.

The Court of Appeals reasoned that "[e]very student brings to the starting line of his educational career different advantages and disadvantages caused in part by social, economic, and cultural background, created and continued completely apart from any contribution by the school system," 483 F. 2d, at 797. Yet in our view the case may not be so easily decided. This is a public school system of California and § 71 of the California Education Code states that "English shall be the basic language of instruction in all schools." That section permits a school district to determine "when and under what circumstances instruction may be given bilingually." That section also states as "the policy of the state" to insure "the mastery of English by all pupils in the schools," and bilingual instruction is authorized "to the extent that it does not interfere with the systematic, sequential, and regular instruction of all pupils in the English language."

Moreover, § 8573 of the Education Code provides that no pupil shall receive a diploma of graduation from grade 12 who has not met the standards of proficiency in "English," as well as other prescribed subjects. Moreover, by § 12101 of the Education Code (Supp. 1973) children between the ages of six and 16 years are (with exceptions not material here) "subject to compulsory full-time education."

Under these state-imposed standards there is no equality of treatment merely by providing students with the same facilities, textbooks, teachers, and curriculum, for students who do not understand English are effectively foreclosed from any meaningful education.

Basic English skills are at the very core of what these public schools teach. Imposition of a requirement that, before a child can effectively participate in the educational program, he must already have acquired those basic skills is to make a mockery of public education. We know that those who do not understand English are certain to find their classroom experiences wholly incomprehensible and in no way meaningful.

We do not reach the Equal Protection Clause argument which has been advanced but rely solely on § 601 of the Civil Rights Act of 1964, 42 U.S.C. § 2000d, to reverse the Court of Appeals.

That section bans discrimination based "on the ground of race, color, or national origin," in "any program or activity receiving Federal financial assistance." The school district involved in this litigation receives large amounts of federal financial assistance. The Department of Health, Education, and Welfare (HEW), which has authority to promulgate regulations prohibiting discrimination in federally assisted school systems, 42 U.S.C. § 2000d-l, in 1968 issued one guideline that "School systems are responsible for assuring that students of a particular race, color, or national origin are not denied the opportunity to obtain the education generally obtained by other students in the system." 33 Fed. Reg. 4956. In 1970, HEW made the guidelines more specific, requiring school districts that were federally funded "to rectify the language deficiency in order to open" the instruction to students who had "linguistic deficiencies." 35 Fed. Reg. 11595.

By § 602 of the Act, HEW is authorized to issue rules, regulations, and orders to make sure that recipients of federal aid under its jurisdiction conduct any federally financed projects consistently with § 601. HEW's regulations, 45 CPR § 80.3 (b) (1), specify that the recipients may not . . .

"(ii) Provide any service, financial aid, or other benefit to an individual which is different, or is provided in a different manner, from that provided to others under the program;

"(iv) Restrict an individual in any way in the enjoyment of any advantage or privilege enjoyed by others receiving any service, financial aid, or other benefit under the program."

Discrimination among students on account of race or national origin that is prohibited includes "discrimination . . . in the availability or use of any academic . . . or other facilities of the grantee or other recipient." Id., § 80.5 (b).

Discrimination is barred which has that effect even though no purposeful design is present: a recipient "may not . . . utilize criteria or methods of administration which have the effect of subjecting individuals to discrimination" or have "the effect of defeating or substantially impairing accomplishment of the objectives of the program as respect individuals of a particular race, color, or national origin." Id., § 80.3 (b) (2).

It seems obvious that the Chinese-speaking minority receive fewer benefits than the English-speaking majority from respondents' school system which denies them a meaningful opportunity to participate in the educational program—all earmarks of the discrimination banned by the regulations. In 1970, HEW issued clarifying guidelines, 35 Fed. Reg. 11595, which include the following:

"Where inability to speak and understand the English language excludes national origin-minority group children from effective participation in the educational program offered by a school district, the district must take affirmative steps to rectify the language deficiency in order to open its instructional program to these students."

"Any ability grouping or tracking system employed by the school system to deal with the special language skill needs of national origin-minority group children must be designed to meet such language skill needs as soon as possible and must not operate as an educational deadend or permanent track."

Respondent school district contractually agreed to "comply with title VI of the Civil Rights Act of 1964 . . . and all requirements imposed by or pursuant to the Regulation" of HEW (45 CPR pt. 80) which are "issued pursuant to that title . . ." and also immediately to "take any measures necessary to effectuate this agreement." The Federal Government has power to fix the terms on which its money allotments to the States shall be disbursed. Oklahoma v. CSc, 330 U.S. 127, 142–143. Whatever may be the limits of that power, Steward Machine Co. v. Davis, 301 U.S. 548, 590 et seq., they have not been reached here. Sen. Humphrey, during the floor debates on the Civil Rights Act of 1964, said: "Simple justice requires that public funds, to which all taxpayers of all races contribute, not be spent in any fashion which encourages, entrenches, subsidizes, or results in racial discrimination."

We accordingly reverse the judgment of the Court of Appeals and remand the case for the fashioning of appropriate relief. Reversed and remanded.

Source: Lau v. Nichols, 414 U.S. 563 (1974).

Manuel A. Machado Jr., *Listen Chicano!* (1978)

During the 1960s and 1970s, a break occurred between old-time Mexican American historians and a newer generation of Chicano scholars who challenged what they considered the myths of history. One of the older scholars was Manuel Antonio Machado Jr., a history professor at the University of Montana and a native of Nogales, Arizona. His book Listen Chicano! *was meant to be provocative and a slap at the emerging field of Chicano history. The title was a parody on the C. Wright Mill book* Listen, Yankee *(1960). Machado reduced the history of racism toward people of Mexican origin in the United States to cultural misunderstandings. Machado was of the school that Mexicans should pull themselves up by their bootstraps. He based his chapter on César Chávez on conservative author Ralph de Toledano's* Little Cesar *(1971). The following exerpt is from Manuel Machado's book.*

The Anglo has oppressed you, the Anglo has robbed you, the Anglo has stolen your dignity as a man and as a Mexican. Therefore, rally against the continuation of a system that negates your culture and oppresses your body and overthrow the shackles of Anglo imperialism. Lord save us from the propagandists!

Such calls to battle become more and more strident throughout the Southwest and California. The Mexican American is an awakening minority, becoming aware of its potential as a political and economic force, and the imperative of organization makes necessary a resort to demagoguery of the basest sort. The demagoguery of the Mexican American militant attempts to polarize all Mexican Americans into a single ethnic unit and subsequently organize this group into a viable political force. Such a maneuver bases itself upon a series of assumptions that convert the Mexican American into a homogeneous unit in which all members respond in similar if not identical fashion to a given set of stimuli.

The first of these assumptions, unfortunately, is that of ethnic homogeneity. It is assumed that the Mexican American comprises a single socioeconomic unit. This belief, often held sacrosanct by both Anglos and militant Chicanos, fails to take into account the historical complexity of Mexican American evolution. There exists a patent failure to recognize the vast cultural and economic differences extant within the Mexican American community today.

Moreover, the homogeneity myth is fed by the lack of scholarly investigation about the Mexican American. With the exception of some industrious anthropologists who studied family life in Mexican American communities, very little work has been done to analyze the role of the Mexican American in the life of the United States. No generally accepted historical periods exist, and as a result, difficulties arise in an attempt to place this group in perspective. Scholarly investigators instead bare their bleeding hearts and join the hue and cry for Chicano solidarity and Brown Power while at the same time flagellating themselves with mea culpas.

Divisions within the Mexican American community further destroy ethnic cohesiveness. Mexican Americans often do not like the term Mexican American. If they are descended from the old stock that participated in the initial settlement of the Southwest and California, Mexican denotes a lower class status. Waves of immigration from Mexico since 1848 exacerbated further the divisions between old families and new arrivals.

In addition, as some Mexican Americans progressed up the socioeconomic ladder, they blended more and more with the ultimately dominant Anglo culture. Mexican Americans are represented in all levels of society, and their socioeconomic positions condition their responses more than any sort of amorphous appeal to ethnicity.

As if ethnic solidarity were not enough, the new Chicano militancy declares a racial solidity. Such a declaration negates absolutely the hybridized racial stock that is in fact Mexican. The Mexican American is told that his primary racial stock is Indian and not Spanish. His heroes are Mexico's Indian heroes. Spanish glory and achievement become, for the Mexican American, an ugly story of oppression and subjugation of Mexico's Indian people. Nonsense!

In the last ten years the Mexican American emerged as a power to be reckoned with in the Southwest and in California. In New Mexico, the Mexican American, who comprises approximately 40 percent of the population, received political sops. Dennis Chávez for years served as United States Senator from that state. Upon his death, Joseph Montoya went to Washington. In Texas, Congressman Henry González represents San Antonio. Yet, the last decade has seen the Mexican American organize and become a force at the local level. Mexican Americans now sit on school boards in Los Angeles, in Texas towns, and in communities throughout the Southwest. City councilmen in many areas now have Spanish surnames. All of this adds up to an imperative for consideration.

Into the breach steps the academician and the bleeding heart liberal, terms that occasionally might interchange without loss of meaning. Awareness by liberal spirits of restlessness in the barrios means that programs and agencies must be organized to compensate for the centuries of wrongdoing by the Anglos. An orgy of self-mortification begins. Suddenly the Mexican American becomes a "problem" to be studied but not necessarily understood. We must, proclaim the suddenly interested academics and liberals, care for our little brown brethren of barrio and field. We must give to them the benefits of the American way of life. We must eliminate those things in their existence that keep them from becoming full and active participants in the American way. In short, we must have "gringoized" Mexicans, fitting into some sort of arbitrary cultural mold.

Such ego flagellation becomes, at best, disgusting, for there is no attempt to understand the diverse cultural backgrounds that comprise the somewhat inchoate group called the Mexican American. Instead, the Anglo reformer, like the Chicano militant, grasps at the idea of cultural and racial homogeneity and attempts to force the Mexican American into an arbitrary slot.

Admittedly, the vast majority of the evidence on the Mexican American remains to be unearthed. Yet, it shall stay subsumed in archives and statistical tables until a modicum of rationality is restored and visceral, conditioned responses become aberrations instead of accepted hypotheses.

In all probability, the best approach to the study of the Mexican American lies in the area of comparative history. The vast majority of the Mexican American population inhabits a strip of land approximately two hundred miles north of the Mexican border in the Southwest and California. This political boundary, however, does not divide sharply the cultures that have fused in that region. As a result, the blending of cultures in the Southwest and in California necessitates analyses of those cultural components that have blended as well as conflicted when diverse cultural groups came into contact with each other.

This personalized essay will attempt to suggest some of those elements that need study before the Mexican American can be viewed with any sort of perspective. As a Mexican American, it offends me to receive condescension from Anglo colleagues and associates. Yet, their attitudes are, in a sense, predictable because they have no perspective in which to view the Mexican American. A broadened mind would certainly be more liberal than one that operated on a given set of assumptions.

Source: Machado, Manuel A., Jr. *Listen, Chicano!* Chicago: Nelson-Hall Inc., 1978, xiii–xvi.

University of California Regents v. Bakke (1978)

In 1973, Allan Bakke, a 33-year-old white man, was denied admission to the University of California Medical School at Davis because of his age and a bad interview. His test scores were higher than those of specially admitted minority students. Two years later he applied again. He was again rejected even though his test scores were considerably higher than most of the minorities admitted under a special program that reserved 16 of 100 possible spaces for minorities on the basis that there were not enough black, brown, or Native American physicians. Bakke sued, claiming that his rights under the Equal Protection Clause of the Fourteenth Amendment had been violated. The court ruled in his favor, holding that race could not be a factor in admissions. It said nothing about legacy admissions (i.e., the children of alumni or wealthy donors). The following is an excerpt of the ruling of the U.S. Supreme Court.

The Medical School of the University of California at Davis (hereinafter Davis) had two admissions programs for the entering class of 100 students—the regular admissions program and the special admissions program. Under the regular procedure, candidates whose overall undergraduate grade point averages fell below 2.5 on a scale of 4.0 were summarily rejected. About one out of six applicants was then given an interview, following which he was rated on a scale of 1 to 100 by each of the committee members (five in 1973 and six in 1974), his rating being based on the interviewers' summaries, his overall grade point average, his science courses' grade point average, his Medical College Admissions Test (MCAT) scores, letters of recommendation, extracurricular activities, and other biographical data, all of which resulted in a total "benchmark score." The full admissions committee then made offers of admission on the basis of their review of the applicant's file and his score, considering and acting upon applications as they were received. The committee chairman was responsible for placing names on the waiting list and had discretion to include persons with "special skills." A separate committee, a majority of whom were members of minority groups, operated the special admissions program. The 1973 and 1974 application forms, respectively, asked candidates whether they wished to be considered as "economically and/or educationally disadvantaged" applicants and members of a "minority group" (blacks, Chicanos, Asians, American Indians). If an applicant of a minority group was found to be "disadvantaged," he would be rated in a manner similar to the one employed by the general admissions committee. Special candidates, however, did not have to meet the 2.5 grade point cut-off and were not ranked against candidates in the general admissions process. About one-fifth of the special applicants were invited for interviews in 1973 and 1974, following which they were given benchmark scores, and the top choices were then given to the general admissions committee, which could reject special candidates for failure to meet course requirements or other specific deficiencies. The special committee continued to recommend candidates until 16 special admission selections had been made. During a four-year period, 63 minority [438 U.S. 265, 266] students were admitted to Davis under the special program and 44 under the general program. No disadvantaged whites were admitted under the special program, though many applied. Respondent, a white male, applied to Davis in 1973 and 1974, in both years being considered only under the general admissions program. Though he had a 468 out of 500 score in 1973, he was rejected since no general applicants with scores less than 470 were being accepted after respondent's application, which was filed late in the year, had been processed and completed. At that time, four special admission slots were still unfilled. In 1974, respondent applied early, and though he had a total score of 549 out of 600, he was again rejected. In neither year was his name placed on the discretionary waiting list. In both years, special applicants were admitted with significantly lower scores than respondent's. After his second rejection, respondent filed this action in state court for mandatory, injunctive, and declaratory relief to compel his admission to Davis, alleging that the special admissions program operated to exclude him on the basis of his race in violation of the Equal Protection Clause of the Fourteenth Amendment, a provision of the California Constitution, and 601 of Title VI of the Civil Rights Act of 1964, which provides, inter alia, that no person shall on the ground of race or color be excluded from participating in any program receiving federal financial assistance. Petitioner cross-claimed for a declaration that its special admissions program was lawful. The trial court found that the special program operated as a racial quota, because minority applicants in that program were rated only against one another, and 16 places in the class of 100 were reserved for them. Declaring that petitioner could not take race into account in making admissions decisions, the program was held to violate the Federal and State Constitutions and Title VI. Respondent's admission was not ordered, however, for lack of proof that he would have been admitted but for the special program. The California Supreme Court, applying a strict-scrutiny standard, concluded that the special admissions program was not the least intrusive means of achieving the goals of the admittedly compelling state interests of integrating the medical profession and increasing the number of doctors willing to serve minority patients. Without passing on the state constitutional or federal statutory grounds, the court held that petitioner's special admissions program violated the Equal Protection Clause. Since petitioner could not satisfy its burden of demonstrating that respondent, absent the special program, would not have been admitted, the court ordered his admission to Davis.

Held: The judgment below is affirmed insofar as it orders respondent's admission to Davis and invalidates petitioner's special admissions program [438 U.S. 265, 267], but is reversed insofar as it prohibits petitioner from taking race into account as a factor in its future admissions decisions.

[Dissenting Opinion]

Opinion of Mr. Justice Brennan, Mr. Justice White, Mr. Justice Marshall, and Mr. Justice Blackmun, concurring in the judgment in part and dissenting in part.

The Court today, in reversing in part the judgment of the Supreme Court of California, affirms the constitutional power of Federal and State Governments to act affirmatively to achieve equal opportunity for all. The difficulty of the issue presented—whether government may use race-conscious programs to redress the continuing effects of past discrimination—[438 U.S. 265, 325] and the mature consideration which each of our Brethren has brought to it have resulted in many opinions, no single one speaking for the Court. But this should not and must not mask the central meaning of today's opinions: Government may take race into account when it acts not to demean or insult any racial group, but to remedy disadvantages cast on minorities by past racial prejudice, at least when appropriate findings have been made by judicial, legislative, or administrative bodies with competence to act in this area.

The Chief Justice and our Brothers Stewart, Rehnquist, and Stevens, have concluded that Title VI of the Civil Rights Act of 1964, 78 Stat. 252, as amended, 42 U.S.C. 2000d et seq., prohibits programs such as that at the Davis Medical School. On this statutory theory alone, they would hold that respondent Allan Bakke's rights have been violated and that he must, therefore, be admitted to the [Davis] Medical School. Our Brother Powell, reaching the Constitution, concludes that, although race may be taken into account in university admissions, the particular special admissions program used by petitioner, which resulted in the exclusion of respondent Bakke, was not shown to be necessary to achieve petitioner's stated goals. Accordingly, these Members of the Court form a majority of five affirming the judgment of the Supreme Court of California insofar as it holds that respondent Bakke "is entitled to an order that he be admitted to the University." 18 Cal. 3d 34, 64, 553 P.2d 1152, 1172 (1976).

Our Nation was founded on the principle that "all Men are created equal." Yet candor requires acknowledgment that the Framers of our Constitution, to forge the 13 Colonies into one Nation, openly compromised this principle of equality with its antithesis: slavery. The consequences of this compromise are well known and have aptly been called our "American Dilemma." Still, it is well to recount how recent the time has been, if it has yet come, when the promise of our principles has flowered into the actuality of equal opportunity for all regardless of race or color.

The Fourteenth Amendment, the embodiment in the Constitution of our abiding belief in human equality, has been the law of our land for only slightly more than half its 200 years. And for half of that half, the Equal Protection Clause of the Amendment was largely moribund so that, as late as 1927, Mr. Justice Holmes could sum up the importance of that Clause by remarking that it was the "last resort of constitutional arguments." Buck v. Bell, 274 U.S. 200, 208 (1927). Worse than desuetude, the Clause was early turned against those whom it was intended to set free, condemning them to a "separate but equal" status before the law, a status [438 U.S. 265, 327] always separate but seldom equal. Not until 1954—only 24 years ago—was this odious doctrine interred by our decision in Brown v. Board of Education, 347 U.S. 483 (Brown I), and its progeny, which proclaimed that separate schools and public facilities of all sorts were inherently unequal and forbidden under our Constitution. Even then inequality was not eliminated with "all deliberate speed." Brown v. Board of Education, 349 U.S. 294, 301 (1955). In 1968, and again in 1971, for example, we were forced to remind school boards of their obligation to eliminate racial discrimination root and branch. And a glance at our docket and at dockets of lower courts will show that even today officially sanctioned discrimination is not a thing of the past.

Against this background, claims that law must be "color-blind" or that the datum of race is no longer relevant to public policy must be seen as aspiration rather than as description of reality. This is not to denigrate aspiration; for reality rebukes us that race has too often been used by those who would stigmatize and oppress minorities. Yet we cannot—and, as we shall demonstrate, need not under our Constitution or Title VI, which merely extends the constraints of the Fourteenth Amendment to private parties who receive federal funds—let color blindness become myopia which masks the reality that many "created equal" have been treated within our lifetimes as inferior both by the law and by their fellow citizens. [438 U.S. 265, 328] . . .

The threshold question we must decide is whether Title VI of the Civil Rights Act of 1964 bars recipients of federal funds from giving preferential consideration to disadvantaged members of racial minorities as part of a program designed to enable such individuals to surmount the obstacles imposed by racial discrimination. We join Parts I and V-C of our Brother Powell's opinion and three of us agree with his conclusion in Part II that this case does not require us to resolve the question whether there is a private right of action under Title VI.

In our view, Title VI prohibits only those uses of racial criteria that would violate the Fourteenth Amendment if employed by a State or its agencies; it does not bar the preferential treatment of racial minorities as a means of remedying past societal discrimination to the extent that such action is consistent with the Fourteenth Amendment. The legislative history of Title VI, administrative regulations interpreting the statute, subsequent congressional and executive action, and the prior decisions of this Court compel this conclusion. None of these sources lends support to the proposition that Congress intended to bar all race-conscious efforts to extend the benefits of federally financed programs to minorities who have been historically excluded from the full benefits of American life. . . .

The history of Title VI—from President Kennedy's request that Congress grant executive departments and agencies authority [438 U.S. 265, 329] to cut off federal funds to programs that discriminate against Negroes through final enactment of legislation incorporating his proposals—reveals one fixed purpose: to give the Executive Branch of Government clear authority to terminate federal funding of private programs that use race as a means of disadvantaging minorities in a manner that would be prohibited by the Constitution if engaged in by government.

This purpose was first expressed in President Kennedy's June 19, 1963, message to Congress proposing the legislation that subsequently became the Civil Rights Act of 1964. [438 U.S. 265, 330] Rep. Celler, the Chairman of the House Judiciary Committee, and the floor manager of the legislation in the House, introduced Title VI in words unequivocally expressing the intent to provide the Federal Government with the means of assuring that its funds were not used to subsidize racial discrimination inconsistent with the standards imposed by the Fourteenth and Fifth Amendments upon state and federal action.

"The bill would offer assurance that hospitals financed by Federal money would not deny adequate care to Negroes. It would prevent abuse of food distribution programs whereby Negroes have been known to be denied food surplus supplies when white persons were given such food. It would assure Negroes the benefits now accorded only white students in programs of high[er] education financed by Federal funds. It would, in short, assure the existing right to equal treatment in the enjoyment of Federal funds. It would not destroy any rights of private property or freedom of association." 110 Cong. Rec. 1519 (1964).

It was clear to Rep. Celler that Title VI, apart from the fact that it reached all federally funded activities even in the absence of sufficient state or federal control to invoke the Fourteenth or Fifth Amendments, was not placing new substantive limitations upon the use of racial criteria, but rather was designed to extend to such activities "the existing right to equal treatment" enjoyed by Negroes under those Amendments, and he later specifically defined the purpose of Title VI in this way:

"In general, it seems rather anomalous that the Federal Government should aid and abet discrimination on the basis of race, color, or national origin by granting money [438 U.S. 265, 331] and other kinds of financial aid. It seems rather shocking, moreover, that while we have on the one hand the 14th Amendment, which is supposed to do away with discrimination since it provides for equal protection of the laws, on the other hand, we have the Federal Government aiding and abetting those who persist in practicing racial discrimination.

"It is for these reasons that we bring forth Title VI. The enactment of Title VI will serve to override specific provisions of law which contemplate Federal assistance to racially segregated institutions." Id., at 2467.

Rep. Celler also filed a memorandum setting forth the legal basis for the enactment of Title VI which reiterated the theme of his oral remarks: "In exercising its authority to fix the terms on which Federal funds will be disbursed . . . Congress clearly has power to legislate so as to insure that the Federal Government does not become involved in a violation of the Constitution." Id., at 1528.

Other sponsors of the legislation agreed with Rep. Celler that the function of Title VI was to end the Federal Government's complicity in conduct, particularly the segregation or exclusion of Negroes, inconsistent with the standards to be found in the antidiscrimination provisions of the Constitution. Rep. Lindsay, also a member of the Judiciary Committee, candidly acknowledged, in the course of explaining why Title VI was necessary, that it did not create any new standard of equal treatment beyond that contained in the Constitution:

"Both the Federal Government and the States are under constitutional mandates not to discriminate. Many have raised the question as to whether legislation is required at all. Does not the Executive already have the power in the distribution of Federal funds to apply those conditions which will enable the Federal Government itself to live up to the mandate of the Constitution and to require [438 U.S. 265, 332] States and local government entities to live up to the Constitution, most especially the 5th and 14th amendments?" Id., at 2467.

He then explained that legislation was needed to authorize the termination of funding by the Executive Branch because existing legislation seemed to contemplate the expenditure of funds to support racially segregated institutions. Ibid. The views of Reps. Celler and Lindsay concerning the purpose and function of Title VI were shared by other sponsors and proponents of the legislation in the House. Nowhere is there any suggestion that Title VI was intended to terminate federal funding for any reason other than consideration of race or national origin by the recipient institution in a manner inconsistent with the standards incorporated in the Constitution. The Senate's consideration of Title VI reveals an identical understanding concerning the purpose and scope of the legislation. Sen. Humphrey, the Senate floor manager, opened the Senate debate with a section-by-section analysis of the Civil Rights Act in which he succinctly stated the purpose of Title VI:

"The purpose of title VI is to make sure that funds of the United States are not used to support racial discrimination. In many instances the practices of segregation or discrimination, which title VI seeks to end, are unconstitutional. This is clearly so wherever Federal funds go to a State agency which engages in racial discrimination. It may also be so where Federal funds go to support private, segregated institutions, under the decision in Simkins v. Moses H. Cone Memorial Hospital, 323 F.2d 959 (C. A. 4, 1963) [cert. denied, 376 U.S. 938 (1964)]. In all cases, such discrimination is contrary to national policy, and to the moral sense of the Nation. Thus, Title VI is simply [438 U.S. 265, 333] designed to insure that Federal funds are spent in accordance with the Constitution and the moral sense of the Nation." Id., at 6544.

Sen. Humphrey, in words echoing statements in the House, explained that legislation was needed to accomplish this objective because it was necessary to eliminate uncertainty concerning the power of federal agencies to terminate financial assistance to programs engaging in racial discrimination in the face of various federal statutes which appeared to authorize grants to racially segregated institutions. Ibid. Although Senator Humphrey realized that Title VI reached conduct which, because of insufficient governmental action, might be beyond the reach of the Constitution, it was clear to him that the substantive standard imposed by the statute was that of the Fifth and Fourteenth Amendments.

Senate supporters of Title VI repeatedly expressed agreement with Sen. Humphrey's description of the legislation as providing the explicit authority and obligation to apply the standards of the Constitution to all recipients of federal funds. Sen. Ribicoff described the limited function of Title VI:

"Basically, there is a constitutional restriction against discrimination in the use of Federal funds; and Title VI simply spells out the procedure to be used in enforcing that restriction." Id., at 13333.

Other strong proponents of the legislation in the Senate repeatedly expressed their intent to assure that federal funds would only be spent in accordance with constitutional standards. See remarks of Sen. Pastore, Id., at 7057, 7062; Sen. Clark, Id., at 5243; Sen. Allott, Id., at 12675, 12677 [438 U.S. 265, 334].

Respondent's contention that Congress intended Title VI to bar affirmative-action programs designed to enable minorities disadvantaged by the effects of discrimination to participate in federally financed programs is also refuted by an examination of the type of conduct which Congress thought it was prohibiting by means of Title VI. The debates reveal that the legislation was motivated primarily by a desire to eradicate a very specific evil: federal financial support of programs which disadvantaged Negroes by excluding them from participation or providing them with separate facilities. Again and again supporters of Title VI emphasized that the purpose of the statute was to end segregation in federally funded activities and to end other discriminatory uses of race disadvantaging Negroes. . . .

The conclusion to be drawn from the foregoing is clear. Congress recognized that Negroes, in some cases with congressional acquiescence, were being discriminated against in the administration of programs and denied the full benefits of activities receiving federal financial support. It was aware that there were many federally funded programs and institutions which discriminated against minorities in a manner inconsistent with the standards of the Fifth and Fourteenth Amendments but whose activities might not involve sufficient state or federal action so as to be in violation of these Amendments. Moreover, Congress believed that it was questionable whether the Executive Branch possessed legal authority to terminate the funding of activities on the ground that they discriminated racially against Negroes in a manner violative of the standards contained in the Fourteenth and Fifth [438 U.S. 265, 336] Amendments. Congress' solution was to end the Government's complicity in constitutionally forbidden racial discrimination by providing the Executive Branch with the authority and the obligation to terminate its financial support of any activity which employed racial criteria in a manner condemned by the Constitution.

Of course, it might be argued that the Congress which enacted Title VI understood the Constitution to require strict racial neutrality or color blindness, and then enshrined that concept as a rule of statutory law. Later interpretation and clarification of the Constitution to permit remedial use of race would then not dislodge Title VI's prohibition of race-conscious action. But there are three compelling reasons to reject such a hypothesis.

First, no decision of this Court has ever adopted the proposition that the Constitution must be color blind. See infra, at 355–356.

Second, even if it could be argued in 1964 that the Constitution might conceivably require color blindness, Congress surely would not have chosen to codify such a view unless the Constitution clearly required it. . . . It is inconceivable that Congress intended to encourage voluntary efforts to eliminate the evil of racial discrimination while at the same time forbidding the voluntary use of race-conscious remedies to cure acknowledged or obvious statutory violations. Yet a reading of Title VI as prohibiting all action predicated upon race which adversely [438 U.S. 265, 337] affects any individual would require recipients guilty of discrimination to await the imposition of such remedies by the Executive Branch. Indeed, such an interpretation of Title VI would prevent recipients of federal funds from taking race into account even when necessary to bring their programs into compliance with federal constitutional requirements. This would be a remarkable reading of a statute designed to eliminate constitutional violations, especially in light of judicial decisions holding that under certain circumstances the remedial use of racial criteria is not only permissible but is constitutionally required to eradicate constitutional violations. For example, in Board of Education v. Swann, 402 U.S. 43 (1971), the Court held that a statute forbidding the assignment of students on the basis of race was unconstitutional because it would hinder the implementation of remedies necessary to accomplish the desegregation of a school system: "Just as the race of students must be considered in determining whether a constitutional violation has occurred, so also must race be considered in formulating a remedy." Id., at 46. Surely Congress did not intend to prohibit the use of racial criteria when constitutionally required or to terminate the funding of any entity which implemented such a remedy. It clearly desired to encourage all remedies, including the use of race, necessary to eliminate racial discrimination in violation of the Constitution rather than requiring the recipient to await a judicial adjudication of unconstitutionality and the judicial imposition of a racially oriented remedy.

Third, the legislative history shows that Congress specifically eschewed any static definition of discrimination in favor of broad language that could be shaped by experience, administrative necessity, and evolving judicial doctrine. Although it is clear from the debates that the supporters of Title VI intended to ban uses of race prohibited by the Constitution and, more specifically, the maintenance of segregated [438 U.S. 265, 338] facilities, they never precisely defined the term "discrimination," or what constituted an exclusion from participation or a denial of benefits on the ground of race. This failure was not lost upon its opponents. Sen. Ervin complained:

"The word 'discrimination,' as used in this reference, has no contextual explanation whatever, other than the provision that the discrimination 'is to be against' individuals participating in or benefiting from federally assisted programs and activities on the ground specified. With this context, the discrimination condemned by this reference occurs only when an individual is treated unequally or unfairly because of his race, color, religion, or national origin. What constitutes unequal or unfair treatment? Section 601 and Section 602 of Title VI do not say. They leave the determination of that question to the executive department or agencies administering each program, without any guideline whatever to point out what is the congressional intent." 110 Cong. Rec. 5612 (1964).

See also remarks of Rep. Abernethy (Id., at 1619); Rep. Dowdy (Id., at 1632); Sen. Talmadge (Id., at 5251); Sen. Sparkman (Id., at 6052).

Despite these criticisms, the legislation's supporters refused to include in the statute or even provide in debate a more explicit definition of what Title VI prohibited.

The explanation for this failure is clear. Specific definitions were undesirable, in the views of the legislation's principal backers, because Title VI's standard was that of the Constitution and one that could and should be administratively and judicially applied. See remarks of Sen. Humphrey (Id., at 5253, 6553); Sen. Ribicoff (Id., at 7057, 13333); Sen. Pastore (Id., at 7057); Sen. Javits (Id., at 5606–5607, 6050). Indeed, there was a strong emphasis throughout [438 U.S. 265, 339] Congress' consideration of Title VI on providing the Executive Branch with considerable flexibility in interpreting and applying the prohibition against racial discrimination. Attorney General Robert Kennedy testified that regulations had not been written into the legislation itself because the rules and regulations defining discrimination might differ from one program to another so that the term would assume different meanings in different contexts. This determination to preserve flexibility in the administration of Title VI was shared by the legislation's supporters. When Sen. Johnston offered an amendment that would have expressly authorized federal grantees to take race into account in placing children in adoptive and foster homes, Sen. Pastore opposed the amendment, which was ultimately defeated by a 56–29 vote, on the ground that federal administrators could be trusted to act reasonably and that there was no danger that they would prohibit the use of racial criteria under such circumstances. Id., at 13695.

Congress' resolve not to incorporate a static definition of discrimination into Title VI is not surprising. In 1963 and 1964, when Title VI was drafted and debated, the courts had only recently applied the Equal Protection Clause to strike down public racial discrimination in America, and the scope of that Clause's nondiscrimination principle was in a state of flux and rapid evolution. Many questions, such as whether the Fourteenth Amendment barred only de jure discrimination or in at least some circumstances reached de facto discrimination, had not yet received an authoritative judicial resolution. The congressional debate reflects an awareness of the evolutionary [438 U.S. 265, 340] change that constitutional law in the area of racial discrimination was undergoing in 1964.

In sum, Congress' equating of Title VI's prohibition with the commands of the Fifth and Fourteenth Amendments, its refusal precisely to define that racial discrimination which it intended to prohibit, and its expectation that the statute would be administered in a flexible manner, compel the conclusion that Congress intended the meaning of the statute's prohibition to evolve with the interpretation of the commands of the Constitution. Thus, any claim that the use of racial criteria is barred by the plain language of the statute must fail in light of the remedial purpose of Title VI and its legislative history. The cryptic nature of the language employed in Title VI merely reflects Congress' concern with the then-prevalent use of racial standards as a means of excluding or disadvantaging Negroes and its determination to prohibit absolutely such discrimination. We have recently held that "When aid to construction of the meaning of words, as used in the statute, is available, there certainly can be no 'rule of law' which forbids its use, however clear the words may appear on 'superficial examination.'" Train v. Colorado Public Interest Research Group, 426 U.S. 1, 10 (1976), quoting United States v. American Trucking Assns., 310 U.S. 534, 543–544 (1940). This is especially so when, as is the case here, the literal application of what is believed to be the plain language of the statute, assuming that it is so plain, would lead to results in direct conflict with Congress' unequivocally expressed legislative purpose. [438 U.S. 265, 341] . . .

Properly construed, therefore, our prior cases unequivocally show that a state government may adopt race-conscious programs if the purpose of such programs is to remove the disparate racial impact its actions might otherwise have and if there is reason to believe that the disparate impact is itself the product of past discrimination, whether its own or that of society at large. There is no question that Davis' program is valid under this test. Certainly, on the basis of the undisputed factual submissions before this Court, Davis had a sound basis for believing that the problem of under representation of minorities was substantial and chronic and that the problem was attributable to handicaps imposed on minority applicants by past and present racial discrimination. Until at least 1973, the practice of medicine in this country was, in fact, if not in law, largely the prerogative of whites. In 1950, for example, while Negroes [438 U.S. 265, 370] constituted 10% of the total population, Negro physicians constituted only 2.2% of the total number of physicians. The overwhelming majority of these, moreover, were educated in two predominantly Negro medical schools, Howard and Meharry. By 1970, the gap between the proportion of Negroes in medicine and their proportion in the population had widened: The number of Negroes employed in medicine remained frozen at 2.2% while the Negro population had increased to 11.1%. The number of Negro admittees to predominantly white medical schools, moreover, had declined in absolute numbers during the years 1955 to 1964. Odegaard 19.

Moreover, Davis had very good reason to believe that the national pattern of underrepresentation of minorities in medicine would be perpetuated if it retained a single admissions standard. For example, the entering classes in 1968 and 1969, the years in which such a standard was used, included only 1 Chicano and 2 Negroes out of the 50 admittees for each year. Nor is there any relief from this pattern of underrepresentation in the statistics for the regular admissions program in later years.

Davis clearly could conclude that the serious and persistent underrepresentation of minorities in medicine depicted by these statistics is the result of handicaps under which minority applicants labor as a consequence of a background of deliberate, purposeful discrimination against minorities in education [438 U.S. 265, 371] and in society generally, as well as in the medical profession. From the inception of our national life, Negroes have been subjected to unique legal disabilities impairing access to equal educational opportunity. Under slavery, penal sanctions were imposed upon anyone attempting to educate Negroes. After enactment of the Fourteenth Amendment, the States continued to deny Negroes equal educational opportunity, enforcing a strict policy of segregation that itself stamped Negroes as inferior, Brown I, 347 U.S. 483 (1954), that relegated minorities to inferior educational institutions, and that denied them intercourse in the mainstream of professional life necessary to advancement. See Sweatt v. Painter, 339 U.S. 629 (1950). Segregation was not limited to public facilities, moreover, but was enforced by criminal penalties against private action as well. Thus, as late as 1908, this Court enforced a state criminal conviction against a private college for teaching Negroes together with whites. Berea College v. Kentucky, 211 U.S. 45. See also Plessy v. Ferguson, 163 U.S. 537 (1896).

Green v. County School Board, 391 U.S. 430 (1968), gave explicit recognition to the fact that the habit of discrimination and the cultural tradition of race prejudice cultivated by centuries of legal slavery and segregation were not immediately dissipated when Brown I, supra, announced the constitutional principle that equal educational opportunity and participation in all aspects of American life could not be denied on the basis of race. Rather, massive official and private resistance prevented, and to a lesser extent still prevents, attainment of equal opportunity in education at all levels and in the professions. The generation of minority students applying to Davis Medical School since it opened in 1968—most of whom [438 U.S. 265, 372] were born before or about the time Brown I was decided—clearly have been victims of this discrimination. Judicial decrees recognizing discrimination in public education in California testify to the fact of widespread discrimination suffered by California-born minority applicants; many minority group members living in California, moreover, were born and reared in school districts in Southern States segregated by law. Since separation of schoolchildren by race "generates a feeling of inferiority as to their status in the community that may affect their hearts and minds in a way unlikely ever to be undone," Brown I, supra, at 494, the conclusion is inescapable that applicants to medical school must be few indeed who endured the effects of de jure segregation, the resistance to Brown I, or the equally debilitating pervasive private discrimination fostered by our long history of official discrimination, cf. Reitman v. Mulkey, 387 U.S. 369 (1967), and yet come to the starting line with an education equal to whites.

Moreover, we need not rest solely on our own conclusion that Davis had sound reason to believe that the effects of past discrimination were handicapping minority applicants to the Medical School, because the Department of Health, Education, and Welfare, the expert agency charged by Congress with promulgating regulations enforcing Title VI of the Civil Rights Act of 1964, see supra, at 341–343, has also reached the conclusion that race may be taken into account in situations [438 U.S. 265, 373] where a failure to do so would limit participation by minorities in federally funded programs, and regulations promulgated by the Department expressly contemplate that appropriate race-conscious programs may be adopted by universities to remedy unequal access to university programs caused by their own or by past societal discrimination. See supra, at 344–345, discussing 45 CFR 80.3 (b) (6) (ii) and 80.5 (j) (1977). It cannot be questioned that, in the absence of the special admissions program, access of minority students to the Medical School would be severely limited and, accordingly, race-conscious admissions would be deemed an appropriate response under these federal regulations. Moreover, the Department's regulatory policy is not one that has gone unnoticed by Congress. See supra, at 346–347. Indeed, although an amendment to an appropriations bill was introduced just last year that would have prevented the secretary of Health, Education, and Welfare from mandating race-conscious programs in university admissions, proponents of this measure, significantly, did not question the validity of voluntary implementation of race-conscious admissions criteria. See ibid. In these circumstances, the conclusion implicit in the regulations—that the lingering effects of past discrimination continue to make race-conscious remedial programs appropriate means for ensuring equal educational opportunity in universities—deserves considerable judicial deference. See, e. g., Katzenbach v. Morgan, 384 U.S. 641 (1966); UJO, 430 U.S., at 175–178 (opinion concurring in part). . . .

We disagree with the lower courts' conclusion that the Davis program's use of race was unreasonable in light of its objectives. First, as petitioner argues, there are no practical means by which it could achieve its ends in the foreseeable future without the use of race-conscious measures. With respect to any factor (such as poverty or family educational background) that may be used as a substitute for race as an indicator of past discrimination, whites greatly outnumber racial minorities simply because whites make up a far larger percentage of the total population and therefore far outnumber minorities in absolute terms at every socio-economic level . . . For example, of a class of recent medical school applicants from families with less than $10,000 income, at least 71% were white. . . . Of all 1970 families headed by a [438 U.S. 265, 377] person not a high school graduate which included related children under 18, 80% were white and 20% were racial minorities. Moreover, while race is positively correlated with differences in GPA and MCAT scores, economic disadvantage is not. Thus, it appears that economically disadvantaged whites do not score less well than economically advantaged whites, while economically advantaged blacks score less well than do disadvantaged whites. . . . These statistics graphically illustrate that the University's purpose to integrate its classes by compensating for past discrimination could not be achieved by a general preference for the economically disadvantaged or the children of parents of limited education unless such groups were to make up the entire class.

Source: U.S. Supreme Court, *University of California Regents v. Bakke,* 438 U.S. 265 (1978), 438 U.S. 265, Regents of the University of California v. Bakke, Certiorari to the Supreme Court of California, No. 76–811, Argued October 12, 1977, Decided June 28, 1978.

Interview with Ernie Cortés Jr. (2002)

The Alinsky Institute was founded by Saul Alinsky (1909–1972), a community organizer and founder of the Industrial Areas Foundation (IAF). Alinsky began organizing in Chicago in the 1930s and started an institute to train grassroots organizers. Alinsky was extremely influential in the Mexican American community and helped found the Community Service Organization (CSO) in 1947 in California. The CSO, in turn, trained César Chávez and influenced organizers such as José Angel Gutiérrez. Ernesto Cortés Jr., educated at Texas A&M, dropped out of a graduate program in economics at the University of Texas at Austin to help organize Chicano workers in Texas. Wanting to perfect organizing to a science, Cortés moved to Chicago and studied at the IAF. In 1974, Cortés returned to San Antonio where he helped organize the Communities Organized for Public Service (COPS), a civic organization that lobbied for essential city services like public sewer, drainage, and other public infrastructure for inner-city neighborhoods. COPS was organized through the parish councils of a coalition of interdenominational San Antonio churches. Cortés helped organize 12 IAF groups in Texas and similar groups—such as the United Neighborhood Organizations—in Los Angeles, California. In the interview transcript that follows, Cortés describes his involvement in these and other groups, and his philosophy of organizing people to bring about change.

DT: [Introduction] It's April 12th, year 2002. We're in Austin, Texas, and visiting with Ernie Cortés, who's been involved with organizing and inspiring people to be involved on environmental issues, public health issues, educational fronts, through groups such as COPS [Communities Organized for Public Service], Valley Interfaith, and many others that he's helped build. . . .

EC: Growing up in San Antonio, you saw a lot of things that didn't seem to be quite the way they were supposed to be, so it's hard to say how you develop those kind of interests. The environmental concerns came to me, frankly, out of concern for public health questions, toxicity of water, concern about lack of sewage, impact on health of air quality, and this whole analogy that I like to use, which is not mine originally, but the coal miner's canary, that the environment is like the coal miner's canary. And, so we have to kind of be concerned, about the environment, not only because, for its own sake, but because of its impact on the quality of human life, or even the viability and the sustainability of human life. It comes from me all kinds of places, the Book of Genesis gives us from early on, believing that, that means that we have dominion or responsibility, or stewardship over the Earth and that means we have to, that means quality of life for other, all living creatures, species. So, I don't know where it came from—my parents, my church, my school, my community. . . . I never trained with [Saul] Alinsky, per se, I went to the Industrial Areas Foundation, which is Alinsky's training institute, I met Mr. Alinsky, but I never really worked with him that closely. The guy I worked with at the IAF was Ed Chambers, who was the National Director of Industrial Areas Foundation and worked, built IAF organizations in Chicago and [Rash Shash Shaneer] other places. But long before I went to IAF, I knew . . . [its] concerns about civil rights issues and I learned an incredible amount of, [things about] issues relating to public health, in organizing farmworkers, and working with the farmworkers in organizing Red River Valley and learning about the impact of pesticides. How [pesticides have an impact] on human beings, on farmworkers, in particular. And, also, on us, from eating, thinking about, you know, the impact of eating foods which have been laced with pesticides, and the dangers—of the carcinogenic impact that they have. So, it was not, I mean, it was, there was a lot of other things that were going on, in the sixties when I grew up and was going to school, which affected how I saw the world, so IAF was, was not, didn't shape my interest in those issues. When I went to IAF, it was to learn how to do something about those concerns, not, not to understand those concerns.

DT: Are there some writers . . . people there, alive or dead, people you met or didn't meet, that might've helped influence you.

EC: I can't point to a particular writer who influenced my thinking about environmental questions. . . . I've read enormous numbers of reports about things like impact of chemical . . . petrol chemical products, . . . When, . . . in Houston area, learning about . . . the quality of water in the Rio Grande River and the impact of . . . dumping pollutants from whether it's steel plants, or lead plants, or etc., . . . it's hard to say any particular writer shaped my thinking about issues in environment and public health.

DT: It seems that one of the techniques that you have for organizing people, or at least understanding why people want to organize themselves, is because you listen to them. . . . Can you . . . give some examples of when you went down to the Valley and you helped put together [a] farmworkers community down there, and how you might have learned from them?

EC: In the Valley I was with the Valley Interfaith . . . in organizing that organization . . . I [conducted] . . . hundreds of relational meetings, one-on-one meetings, listening sessions, . . . having conversations with people who are leaders and potential leaders and found out about their concerns, about everything from the burning of toxic waste off the coast of Brownsville, [to] the concerns that people had about the food chain, the impact of burning—there was a chemical waste management corporation . . . [it] was gonna . . . burn toxic waste and they were concerned about that. . . . We began to organize around that particular issue, but then there [was] also the question of a lack of sewers in the colonias, . . . questions of asbestos in the paint in schools, which is making kids sick, molding, . . . which is contributing to absenteeism and enormous visits to doctors. . . . We would meet with people . . . connected with clinics in the Rio Grande Valley . . . [the people] would talk about the impact of Third World diseases, . . . because of the lack of sewers, secondary sewage systems that existed. In El Paso, the same kind of concerns came up, meeting with people with the public health systems and the hospitals. . . . Before I began organizing, . . . I was on the Board of Managers at the Bexar County Hospital District and . . . [I] began to hear about [the] kind of impact that things like lead paints [had, and] through a process of conversations and listening to lots and lots of people, you find out . . . that they really care . . . [and] want to do something about [it]. What they lack is power. And they lack someone to teach them how to act on their concerns. . . . [Their demands are] very specific and concrete so that they can do something about [these concerns]. . . .

DT: Can you give me an example of your work with COPS [Communities Organized for Public Service]? . . .

EC: The organization got heavily involved . . . in the whole question of . . . degradation of the water supply, by trying to limit development over the sensitive areas of the recharge zone . . . it had to do with just zoning questions, and . . . making sure that there were the adequate safeguards. [COPS] got involved in elections, they got involved in fights over the kind and quality of development. . . . unfortunately Texas and San Antonio are notoriously, . . . lax and, and unvigilant, lacking in vigilance and diligence in dealing with . . . these safeguards . . . [mobilizing people] requires an outraged [community which is] effectively organized and mobilized . . . to make sure the public officials do what they're told. . . . The organization . . . got involved in fairly significant fights to clean up the toxicity around Kelly Air Force Base . . . forcing Kelly to do some major cleanups in the areas around the base. . . . The organizations that we build, the IAF organizations are political organizations, . . . they don't pretend to be faith-based organizations . . . However, . . . they operate and they act on their . . . values . . . And their values are shaped by their faith, traditions, whether it be Catholicism, Judaism, Islam, the different forms of . . . different Christian traditions, Baptist, Episcopalian, Methodists, etc. So . . . they bring to the table a commitment and an understanding—and a hope for realization of these two sets of values . . . The values of a free and open society, the political values which come out of understanding the seminal and—and meaningful documents of our tradition: the Constitution and the Declaration of Independence, the Bill of Rights . . . various important statements, the Emancipation Proclamation, Northwest Ordinances, which kind of affirm and—and reaffirm, you know, our commitment to certain things which are real important to us . . . Freedom of expression. So, there is this kind of . . . secular faith, that is part of our tradition and part of what makes us tick and makes us, and . . . animates us, and gives us some energy. This faith in . . . democratic traditions and institutions. At the same time, . . . [there is the] understanding and that commitment and that tradition is also connected to and challenged by and agitated by, hopefully, and shaped by commitment to the values of Judaism and Christianity, particularly those which have to do with concern for the stranger and the Exodus, the stories that come out of the Exodus tradition. A fear of God, as over against the Pharaoh, a fear of God as over against secular authorities, which means a disposition to—to—take the kinds of risks that are, you know, that are, that are, conceptualized, and—and—the stories of the Exodus traditions, whether it be the midwives who refused to yield the Pharaoh's beckon—beckoning, or—or the prophetic tradition, where the prophets go after the muckety-mucks, as I call them, the powerful people, the—the king . . . and the land owners who control the institutions . . . dispossessing people of their land and of their work and of their very lives . . . So, . . . there is a strong, powerful tradition which animates and shapes and motivates people, gives meaning to their lives and we draw heavily upon, and are nourished by, particularly in—in battles which require patience and—and constant vigilance and constant endurance. We draw heavily upon those traditions and the resources of those traditions to sustain us over time. . . .

EC: Justice takes on many different dimensions and many different understandings, . . . there is the kind of justice which comes out of the biblical traditions. The word mishpot comes to mind, which has to do with the concrete realization of certain ideals, in certain municipal institutions, which have to do with the fact that no one should be left out, no one should be deprived of the means to participation in . . . the prosperity of the community, and that's, in the prophetic tradition, this notion of mishpot meant that no matter who you were that you were not to be, no one could take away from you the tools that were necessary [for life]—your house, your . . . farm implements, . . . In order to be able to participate in the shared prosperity of the community. Even so, . . . if you owed money to a money lender, if you owed money to a landlord, and even though that debt was legitimate if it meant, in order to pay the debt, if it meant losing your capacity to have shelter, your capacity to own, to make a livelihood, that justice would not allow that to happen, and so therefore it is incumbent upon the people who ran these municipal courts to not deprive you of that, and to—and to rule in your favor . . . against the powerful interest of people who were . . . the economic power players of that particular lot and community. And so that understanding, that tradition is something which animates us, and frankly, it is reflected in the populace tradition in Texas . . . The Homestead Exemption comes out of that understanding, and the notion of a safety net comes out of that understanding that . . . there's a level below which people should not ever fall and so you may have an enterprise economy with risk taking and dynamism and etc. and winners and losers, but there's a—there's a level below which people never fall. And, so therefore, that we never deprive people of certain basic things, which are important for their humanity. . . . Adam Smith and *TheWealth of Nations* said that . . . a just society is one where a working person can appear in public without shame, without being humiliated, . . . that meant for, in his time, being able to have a decent shirt, pair of shoes. . . . [It] was important for the people who ran that society to understand that everyone should have the access to those things which are necessary to appear in public without feeling humiliated, and so, then the question for us is, . . . in the year 2002, . . . what is necessary for a person to be in public without shame? And I always argue, it's more than just clothes, it's also access to health care, it's access to education, it's access . . . to running water, . . . shelter. In 1949, the Republican controlled Congress, . . . led by Sen. Robert Taft, passed a Housing Act . . . of 1949 [that] said that every American, no matter who he or she is . . . should be given, and should be provided with a decent home and a suitable living environment.

An Israeli scholar by the name of [Avishai] Margalit, wrote a book called *A Decent Society* and he said that there's a difference between a civilized society and a decent society and a just society. A civilized society is where the people of that society are nice to each other and kind and sensitive. . . . But you can have a civilized society which is not a decent society because that civil [and] decent society requires that the institutions of that society do not humiliate adults. So you could have a society where the institutions humiliate adults . . . which treat adults as second-class citizens, even though people are nice to each other. . . . In South Texas . . . with Mexicans, . . . and in San Antonio . . . institutions . . . denied people the right to participate. You had institutions which treated adults as second-class citizens to be seen and not heard. That is not a decent society. . . . So, in order for there to be a decent society, those institutions, whether it be the school, the workplace, the universities, have got to make it possible for people to feel that they are first-class citizens. They have a right to be heard, a right to participate, a right to deliberate. Now, in order for it to be just, it means that they have to have access . . . to the resources of that society which are necessary in order for them to maintain a decent standard of living, health care, education, full employment, which enables them to participate, again, in, we call the shared prosperity, or what the Hebrew community would call the shalom of the community. . . . San Antonio was not a decent society because there were—and it certainly was not a just society because you had whole communities which were left out of access to public facilities, that did not have flood control in their communities. When it rained, . . . people couldn't go out. Their homes were flooded, . . . ipso facto unjust society. . . . It was not a decent society because when they tried to participate, . . . there was a resistance to their participation. And it took the organizing of COPS in order to open up . . . the institutions, whether it be the political institutions, etc. to enable them to participate. The same thing is true in the Rio Grande Valley, when you have people who live in whole colonias and hovels, who don't have water, who don't have access to sewer. . . . Then, clearly, you know, that community is not just. If, when you pay people less than a decent standard of living, when you pay people poverty wages and when you subsidize, you know, and give corporate welfare . . . to developers . . . who sustain poverty wages, then it's clearly [sic] you have an unjust system, and in order to change that unjust system, you're going to have—often times, you have to create or enable institutions to develop capacity, and that means, in the process of making it just, you make it decent as well. . . .

BM: COPS is Communities Organized for Public Service, O.K., which is an IAF organization in San Antonio. COPS Metro Alliance, it's made up of about 60 different institutions, congregations, unions, neighborhood groups. All across San Antonio, particularly, in the beginning stages, in the South and West and East sides, in the older areas. Now, it's much—much more expanded and in a much more metropolitan scope, and so it includes areas all over the city of San Antonio, from Helotes on the Northeast, or the Northwest side, excuse me, to congregations on the Southeast side, and so it's a broad coalition of institutions, an organization of organizations whose purpose is to develop capacity to teach people effectively how to participate in the political, social, and cultural life of the community.

EC: [Cortés describes the IAF network] . . . One of the greatest leaders of the COPS organization was a priest named Albert Benavides [who] unfortunately drowned in 1984. In Valley Interfaith, you have people like Carmen Anaya, Father (inaudible), Estella Sosa-Garza, O.K. In El Paso, in La Pisa organization. You have enormous numbers of people in Dallas Area Interfaith, Rev. Gerald Britt, here in Austin, Regina Rogaolf. You have a whole range of leaders Jewish, from Jewish congregations to Roman Catholic churches, school leaders, school principals like, Claudia Santa Maria, parent leaders like Lourdes Sanmaron, . . . who've been developed and—and they've learned through action and reflection, through research actions, through relational meetings, through house meetings, . . . all across the state of Texas they've developed skills and understanding and wisdom . . . about public and social life. . . . Most of them, all of them, had curiosity and imagination and, but they didn't look like they were smart, they didn't look like they were effective, they didn't look like they were people who could—could be significant. . . . Over the course of a year and out of the thousand, you find . . . 50, 60, 75 [emerge] who's got enough talent, and then they go back and look for people among the other people that you met with and so that you begin to create this kind of collaborative group of leaders . . . who you mentor and you guide and you teach and you develop, and they, in turn, go out and do the same for others. . . .

The challenge of this work is . . . not to organize the community, but to find the people who are going to do the organizing, to find the people who got the energy, the imagination, the curiosity, the talent to do that kind of work, and so that then you then mentor and guide and teach and put them in different situations and develop their capacity to act and develop their capacity to gain recognition and significance. And, so therefore, organizing them becomes really the teaching of these skills and these insights, and—and helping people understand and interpret their experiences, tell their stories in creative and effective ways, tell their stories to news media, tell their stories to political figures, tell their stories to corporate leaders, so that they begin, they begin to create a different kind of conversation. . . . A different understanding of what is essential to the life of that particular community, whether it is about schools, health care, jobs, etc. . . . The role of time horizon for a corporate executive is the quarter. . . . The role of a time horizon for a politician is the next election. The role of a time horizon for—for a hospital, or educational bureaucrat is the budget cycle. But, the role of a time horizon for a grandmother is a generation, because she's concerned about what happens to her grandchildren. So, the difficulty is finding people who understand the role of time horizons. . . . And, when you have, you know, kind of a faddish, kind of instantaneous kind of . . . society where people, again, expect immediate results, . . . it's hard to get people to think about what is the role of a time horizon. . . . [in getting diverse people to work together] If they just want to be comfortable, they feel good, then you just kind of connect to people that you know and feel good about. . . . If you want to have power, then you got to go beyond just your identity, politics. You got to go beyond your comfort zone and take some risks with people that you don't know very well, that you don't feel so comfortable with, that you can't make small talk with. . . . The question then is how to teach people how to engage and how to have a conversation with somebody whose background they don't know anything about or they never went to school with or they don't know what to talk about and they feel awkward at first. . . . And get them over those feelings of awkwardness, or hostility, or fear, or anger, or whatever it is that comes to mind, because people, we're taught, we're taught to be fearful, we're taught to be, to be dismissive, we're taught to—to basically, to be hostile, . . . to be other, whether that otherness is sexuality, whether the otherness is religion, whether the otherness is race, whether the otherness is faith . . . you try to teach people what we call relational power, . . . and the difficulty is that people operate out of . . . unilateral power, which is zero sum "I win, you lose." . . . So, that the gains we get are going to come only at your expense. Well, if you teach people, no, now wait a minute, there is a different way of thinking about this, . . . there is a concept of relational power which means we can both win. . . . But that means, by expanding the pie. We can both win by creating more capacity. . . . If we don't allow . . . other people to play the prisoner's dilemma on us . . . where they isolate us or separate us, [i.e.] the prisoner's dilemma; I do it to you before . . . you do it to me. Rather than . . . teaching people to know about each other's stories, their histories, their backgrounds, their fears, their anxieties. . . . So, on the basis of that, we can act on small things and develop some trust and some understanding of reliability and develop what Hannah Wren . . . calls public friendship, the friendship that emerges among colleagues, or people who fight together, argue, dispute with each other, but always maintain their relationship. And, so to teach people how to do that is the critical thing. Now, we did this in Dallas, . . . where people like Gerald Britt, an African American minister, coalitioned Dallas Area Interfaith and organized and, with Latinos and people from the . . . Anglo community, which is not really accurate. . . . But, you know, Lutherans, and . . . Methodists, and other Protestant denominations on behalf of after school programs and got the Dallas School Board to vote. . . . Latinos and African Americans to come together when they had been divided around these after school programs. So the question is, how . . . can they begin to come together? They were able to recently get bond election passed. . . . [The] process [was] of [holding] individual meetings, house meetings, research actions, teaching people how to negotiate with each other, teaching them that they could get things for their schools, for their communities . . . if they collaborated and worked together, and negotiated. I'll work for you on your issue, but you got to work for me on my issue.

DT: When you're trying to organize people, . . . I hear about the house meetings and the things, yet your [sic] organizing in communities where you have multiple adults having to work multiple jobs to make ends meet and the constraints of . . . the people who need to do and say the most are, by the very institutions that are oppressing them, have the least time of all the commodities to do it. How do you convince them to put in the two hours, four hours, of it's not their own child who's sick, or it's not actually touching them personally, how is [it] made to be worth their time?

EC: It's worth their time because, the ones you start off with, because they want certain kinds of, because they're not satisfied with the life as it is. And so, even though, . . . it may not directly, immediately impact their child, or immediately impact their community, . . . it impacts them and the quality of their life as they see it. . . . You find enormous capacity on the part of people to find dimensions of their lives. . . . I organize ours around a particular problem, . . . cleaning up a ditch, etc. But once that was done, they left. . . . Or, you organize them around getting a new school. And, once they got the school, they were out. The question [or alternative]—to build an organization like COPS, or Metro Alliance, or Valley Interfaith, or Apeaso, [where] you have to find people who want more than that. They want more than just their house fixed, they want more than just a new school, they want more than just a lot, they want those things to be sure, and it has to be about those things, otherwise they won't stay in it. But they also want something else. And those something elses are quite intangible. But they're just as important to them, and they have to do with their ability to understand the world, they have their ability to find meaning in their lives, have to do with their meaning—ability to deal with relationships and to understand relationships and—and to understand what the human condition is all about . . . and all the questions that plague all of us and have plagued all of us from time immemorial . . . .

DT: Sounds like those are special people.

EC: An optimist is somebody who—who looks, who just kind of looks beyond reality, O.K., in my humble opinion. Hanna Wren put it this way, she said that in order for things to change you need anger and humor. She said, hope, unfortunately in her terms, which I'm going to use optimism, jumps over reality. . . . And so, you don't engage reality. Anger teaches you how to engage reality, . . . and humor situates you in a context so that you don't take yourself too seriously and notwithstanding your appropriate anger and so therefore, you can have perspective. . . . So that combination of hope and anger, that synthesization of it . . . forces you to engage the world as it is, at the same time situates you in . . . geological time. So that you don't take yourself too seriously. . . . And, therefore, don't burn yourself out. That gives you hope, and that's what I mean by hope, . . . is that understanding of the world as it is, and not recognizing the challenges and the daunting nature of what we are trying to strive for, we can still recognize the possibilities. . . . The role of the organizer [is to combine] anger and humor and perspective, that maturity to know that anger is not hatred and—and not outrage. . . .

DT: How [do] you keep activists from burning out? Did they come to some sort of mature outrage, some kind of anger that they can sustain, that's a cold anger that doesn't consume them?

EC: Well, I hope it is. I don't know if I can keep anybody from burning out, I mean, I can keep myself from burning out, and if it helps me, I point out to people what sustains me, and what gives me energy and what gives me the capacity to go on. But, they have to figure that out for themselves. Now, I'll be more than happy—I am more than happy to work with people to help them figure that out. But, everybody's different. . . . Not everybody does—enjoys what I enjoy. And so, part of the job that I have is to try help people figure out what is it that makes sense to them? What is it that is meaningful to them; where is the joy in their life. Because you can't do this work if you can't find some joy in it. If you don't find meaning in it, if you don't find significance in it, over time, I mean, because it's not enough, I don't think, O.K., to rectify a situation. It's not enough to, you know, even do things that are important, big, I mean, we—to make it possible for people to have a living wage job, that's very significant, very important. To make it possible for people to have water that didn't have it, that's very important. But after a while, it—you know—that's not enough. And so—but people have to figure out what is—what else is it that will sustain them in this work. . . . We try to teach them these kind of things early on, that a lot of them just would not listen. That you just can't—you can't just exhort and scold people. It doesn't do any good; it just gets their back up. Now I'm not trying to say I don't believe in confrontation, I'm not trying to say I don't believe in tension. I think, unfortunately, that—that's the law of change, you know. That all change comes about either through pressure or threat. . . . That there is no nice way to get change. What I'm talking about is if you're going to get people to act in such a way that they're willing to bring about pressure, if they're willing to create the tension, then they gotta under—they gotta have some sense of power. And if they're always involved in institutions where they're being told, being told what to do by experts, after a awhile, that's not good—they're not gonna sustain themselves in those kinds of organizations. . . . We teach, you gotta be selective. You gotta pick and choose your fights. And you gotta pick and choose fights which help you build an organization. So you gotta ask yourself, how does this fight, how does [*sic*] this issue gonna help us build the organization. And then, the activist will say, Yeah, but you're not dealing with this issue, and this issue, and this issue, and all these things. But they all demand immediate concern, we just can't deal with every single one of them at the same time, it just won't happen. . . . And that's part of the tragedy of life, sometimes the best solution gets in the way of a good enough solution and so sometimes you gotta learn, so that's what I mean by learning how to understand politics. . . . It's really about learning how to negotiate when you don't have that much power, and learning that sometimes you gotta take, you know, victories, and build for the future. And even though all those victories look like big, huge defeats. . . . Or so you're in a situation where, yeah, the other guy wins, . . . we're not gonna stop development over the Aquifer. . . . But, we don't have the power to do it right now. So, what do we do then? Well, we try to build, we try to get some concession, some victories, teach our people that at the same time we won, . . . that there is still a larger issue out there which we haven't dealt with, and haven't addressed, but we gotta be able to organize and build capacity if we're gonna deal with that issue. I don't know if I'm being clear or not. . . . So you don't give up on the fight and you teach it, and you don't pretend that there's not a serious problem out there. But you also recognize that we don't have the power to deal with that problem right now. So we gotta build some more power. This victory we got here today was good, it's significant—it's important and meaningful. But, is it the solution? No. [Does] it solve the problem? No. Is it—do the other side, are they still doing some horrible things? . . . Then, why are we negotiating with these people? Because we gotta live in the world as it is. And we gotta learn, that if we're gonna be successful, O.K., we're gonna have to figure out a couple of things. One is how to build our organization. Two is turn yesterday's adversaries into today's allies, or tomorrow's allies. . . . The way to organize around people with environmental concerns is to teach them how they affect public health. And I think that the more effective way to do this is to talk about questions of health and quality of life and viability . . . Because otherwise you allow those people who don't care about it to kind of paint you in a picture . . . [They] stereotype you as people who are quaint and tree huggers or whatever . . . it appears to become the province of very self-absorbed, very comfortable people, who've gotten theirs and don't want anyone else to share in the bounty. They've got their nice home viewing the ocean and they don't want anyone else to have—you know, to disturb their view. . . . And so you become relegated to people who become self-absorbed and narcissistic. And I think that's the biggest danger. For people who are concerned about the environment, is they gotta figure out a way in which it affects the lives, the quality of lives of people who are in minority communities and low-end communities. The average state, you know, guy who, basically, is just trying to make a buck for his family, O.K. Alright. [End of Interview with Ernie Cortés.]

Source: Ernie Cortes (EC) Interviewers: David Todd (DT) and David Weisman (DW); April 12, 2002; Austin, Texas REELS: 2185 and 2186, LaRed Latina of the Intermountain Southwest. http://www.texaslegacy.org/m/transcripts/cortesernietxt.html.

Elizabeth Martínez, "A View from New Mexico: Recollections of the Movimiento Left"

(2002)

Elizabeth "Betita" Martínez (1925–), Chicana activist, author, and educator, is best known for her 1990 book 500 Años del Pueblo Chicano/500 Years of Chicano History: In Pictures. *She is currently working on a similar volume focusing on Chicanas. Martínez was active in the civil rights movement as a member of the Student Nonviolent Coordinating Committee. She worked as a United Nations researcher on colonialism in Africa. In 1968, she joined the Chicano movement in New Mexico, where she coedited the newspaper* El Grito del Norte (The Call of the North) *from 1968 to 1976 and cofounded the Chicano Communications Center, a barrio-based organization. In 1982, she ran for governor of California on the Peace and Freedom Party ticket. In 1997, she cofounded and still directs the Institute for MultiRacial Justice in San Francisco and is active in the anti–Iraq War movement. Reproduced here are excerpts from her 2002* Monthly Review *article.*

If ever there has been a chapter of the U.S. left with deep cultural roots in every sense, it is the movimiento of New Mexico.

The roots include social relations, economic traditions, political forms, artistic expression, and language—everything that defines peoplehood. They are Native American, Spanish, and Mexican mestizo (mixed), and they go back centuries. Migrant workers of the last 150 years have played a crucial part, but "immigrant" does not describe the totality of those roots.

Unlike any other area except southern Colorado, the movimiento in Nuevo Mexico evolved within the framework of a long, popular struggle against U.S. colonization and for land—that is to say, nothing less than the means of production. Its origins lie in the colonization of First Nation peoples like the Pueblos and the Dine (Navajo) in what became Nuevo (later New) Mexico and their long resistance to occupying forces. In 1680, some of the Indians joined with Mexican workers in Santa Fe and drove out the Spanish for twelve years.

The land struggle that came much later, waged by Spanish-speaking mestizo people and sometimes armed as well as underground, could be called nationalist. But if we do so, we should not equate it with the nationalism of many other U.S. movement groups. It was not primarily cultural, not exclusionary of other peoples, not "mi Raza primero" (my people first). And whether or not we call that land struggle consciously left, it directly or indirectly encouraged militant leftism including Marxism during the movimiento years.

New Mexico had remained a territory for over fifty years after the war on Mexico. It did not become a state until 1912, when its Spanish-speaking, Catholic majority had given way to an Anglo majority that made white easterners much less nervous. Before and after that date, Mexicans carried out underground actions against Anglo landowners, mainly in rural areas of the north. Cutting Anglo fences and burning barns were common forms of protest against the continuing land robbery.

After arriving in 1968, I soon learned to respect names like *Las Gorras Blancas* (White Caps) a long-standing underground resistance group, and *La Mano Negra* (Black Hand), reputed to be headed by a woman at that time. Resistance nourished by historical, cultural, or religious tradition was also strong. Examples could be found in the Penitentes (a semisecret religious organization), dances and plays performed on certain holidays reenacting key moments in the area's colonial history, the curanderos who cured with herbs not usually known to outsiders, along with other expressions of a long isolated, necessarily self-sufficient society—from building with adobe bricks, to cultivating a unique variety of chilies for cooking. A spirit of collectivity and interdependence ran strong in all this.

Politically, northern New Mexico presented an almost classic example of European colonialism. Anglos stood at the top holding economic and political power while "Hispanos" formed a control or buffer class that included teachers, judges, police, and other local officials, leaving the majority of Mexicans at the bottom. That colonial reality defined the anti-imperialist project and its class contradictions.

The Alianza Federal de Mercedes emerged in the 1960s to initiate a new, militant stage in the land struggle, making national news with its 1967 armed takeover of the courthouse in the mountain village of Tierra Amarilla to protest state repression. Alianzistas, led by Reies López Tijerina, organized to win back communally held land that had been distributed to their ancestors in grants by

Spain (which had seized it from indigenous peoples). Their Spanish colonial ancestry, which preceded Mexico's rule, made them probably the only group in the United States today who can call themselves "Hispanic," or Hispano, with some accuracy.

In the 1960s and early 1970s, Alianzistas sympathized with the struggles of other peoples of color, like African Americans (the Alianza welcomed visiting SNCC leaders twice), Puerto Ricans, and Palestinians. Of all the possible alliances with Native Americans at home, the Alianza is best known for supporting the long Taos Pueblo struggle to get back their sacred Blue Lake lands.

The worldview of Alianza's constituency—impoverished, dispossessed, small landowners—could be very conservative. They were not radical in the sense of consciously seeking to restructure the entire society as opposed to achieving justice in one area, recovery of land ownership that the United States had promised to respect under the 1848 Treaty of Guadalupe Hidalgo. At the same time, their goal could hardly be met without that restructuring, any more than the U.S. government was likely to "give it back to the Indians." For some Alianzistas and supporters, who saw that their poverty could not be ended without systemic change, their worldview could certainly be called revolutionary nationalism.

The anticommunist influence of McCarthyism could be found among a few Alianzistas, who equated the word with dictatorship. However, Tijerina himself did not take virulent anticommunist positions. His conservatism in other areas was notable, for example, having an almost entirely male Alianza leadership and expressing male supremacist attitudes. (On the unofficial level, many Alianza women were respected for their wisdom, strength, and leadership in ways similar to what I had found in rural Mississippi in 1964.)

The overall attitude in northern New Mexico toward socialism or communism was not negative. One or two Alianza supporters whom I met had even tried to get to Cuba and join the revolutionary forces there in the late 1950s. A sprinkling of old left members could be found like Vicente Vigil, who became a columnist for the newspaper *El Grito del Norte* (Cry of the North). Organizers in the land grant and other movements received frequent support from a small but sturdy number of Anglo socialists and Communist Party (CP) members or sympathizers in New Mexico.

We can also recall the 1951 Silver City strike against Empire Zinc, inspired by proletarian goals with help from committed CP organizers, and made into the movie *Salt of the Earth.* Years later some of the strike leaders did support work for the Chilean resistance after the 1973 coup, which reflected an ongoing radical tradition.

El Grito del Norte, a newspaper I co-founded with movement attorney Beverly Axelrod, began in 1968 as a vehicle to support the Alianza. It soon expanded to cover the Chicano movement in urban areas, workers' struggles, and Latino political prisoners, along with a broad spectrum that ranged from the black liberation movement to Mexican student protest to radical whites. At the same time, *El Grito* encouraged nationalist consciousness and cultural self-respect among Chicanos as sources of strength in sparking a movement, especially among youth.

The paper never abandoned its focus on the land struggle in New Mexico, and linked it with contemporary land struggles in Hawaii, Japan, and Third World countries, thus internationalizing it. This combination of what could be called liberatory or revolutionary nationalism with internationalism made *El Grito* very unusual among the dozens of more nationalist Chicano movement newspapers that covered the Southwest and inspired activists.

El Grito's favorable coverage of Vietnam, Cuba, and China left no doubt that it was pro-Socialist. It sent reporters to all those countries. We also sent a reporter and photographer, along with a carload of supporters, to Wounded Knee during the long, armed American Indian Movement occupation in 1973. All this did not seem to limit the paper's popularity, at least not in the north. Probably we were helped by the fact that the 1967 Tierra

Amarilla courthouse raiders were our friends and one, Jose Madril, an editor with *El Grito*. Nobody messed with those guys!

We did encounter some harassment from the police in Española, where our office was located, for example when they detained Antonio Cordova who had photographed them tear-gassing people at a demonstration.

With a predominantly female set of regular columnists, writers, artists, photographers, and production workers like Jane Lougee, Tessa Martinez, Adelita Medina, Kathy Montague, Sandra Solis, Rini Templeton, Valentina Valdes, and Enriqueta Vasquez, together with myself as managing editor, the paper made its feminism clear. This continued a cultural tradition in which numerous Mexican women journalists played a major role during national struggles like the 1910 [Mexican] revolution.

El Grito also sought to encourage and train young Chicanas in putting out a paper. One of the main successes here was a series on Vietnam written by grassroots organizer Valentina Valdes, who had to read a book on Vietnam the first time with a dictionary—and then read it again—for background. Another example: Adelita Medina and Sandra Solis started the publication *Tierra y Libertad*, in Las Vegas, New Mexico, after having been trained at *El Grito*.

In Albuquerque, the Black Berets also followed an internationalist approach. They adopted principles and a program sometimes modeled on the Black Panthers, for example, its breakfast program, that made it less strictly nationalist than Brown Beret groups in Texas and California. The Black Berets also founded the Bobby Garcia Memorial Clinic, committed to the idea that health is a human right, not a privilege. Their main leader, Richard Moore, and others went to Cuba on the Venceremos Brigade. The Berets and *El Grito* were partners, sharing news, analysis and sometimes members like reporter Antonio Cordova, who along with Beret Rito Canales, was assassinated by police in 1972.

In the early 1970s, *El Grito* began looking for a new strategy and tactics, both for the newspaper and the movimiento in general. To do this, we ceased publication of the paper in 1973, and some of us moved to Albuquerque. With other local activists we launched the Chicano Communications Center (CCC) as a multimedia, educational barrio project. Soon after, the CCC established a formal alliance called CLARO (Chicano League Against Racism and Oppression) together with the Bobby Garcia Memorial Clinic and the Cafioncito Wood Cooperative based in a land grant area just outside the city. CLARO had a central committee for decisionmaking; it set up a study program on Marxism and contemporary socialism, attended by CLARO people.

In 1974, self-identification with the Socialist vision reached a high point. That was the year Richard Moore went to Cuba with another Beret leader, Joaquín Lujan. Marvin García of Cañoncito went with a group to China. A major meeting took place to discuss strategy in the face of what we saw as heightening repression. Over fifty seasoned activists came from all over the state. In a dialogue about our long-range goals, someone asked what was socialism. I explained some basic points and added it was a stage on the way to communism but not the final goal, communism. At that point a Chicana cried out, "Well, in that case, we're Communists!" and everyone clapped to my and others' amazement.

Also in 1974, another group that wanted to focus on mass organizing started and linked up with CLARO. Its name: MAO (Movement Against Oppression). Happily, this name did not mean CLARO had decided there were two equally destructive imperialisms or spend time on endless battles over that and other lines. This was largely because of New Mexico's relative isolation from the national left mainstream, an isolation that proved both a blessing and, over time, a limitation. The Socialist Workers Party (SWP), did exist but in very small numbers, although some members commanded personal respect. The major, crucial exception to that isolation was travel to Cuba, going back to *El Grito* and now the Venceremos Brigade. Richard Moore served on the Brigade's

National Committee and went to Cuba every year through the 1970s. That experience is why he could say, as he did recently, "we didn't pull any punches about being for socialism then. We might use slightly different language with grassroots folk but the ideas were there. We were not afraid of saying so." It didn't hurt that Richard was a big, tough-talking guy whose politics came more from the street than books.

It also didn't hurt that we had two beloved, world-famous Latino revolutionary heroes. Emiliano Zapata, whose portrait provided the logo for *El Grito*'s masthead, had raised the cries that echoed all over northern New Mexico: "*Tierra y libertad*" and "*Tierra, Pan y Justicia!*" (Land and Liberty; Land, Bread and Justice). The other was Ernesto "Che" Guevara, whose image adorned many public spaces including the waiting room of the Tierra Amarilla clinic started by movimiento activists. Those two icons symbolized the Chicano movement culture all over the Southwest.

If a certain male domination is creeping into this description of our work, then the contributions of various women must be noted. Nita Luna's theatrical genius generated a teatro group for the CCC that rocked Albuquerque, especially with her play about the Watergate scandal. Luci Rios, factory organizer and poet, along with Susana and Cecilia Fuentes, Susan Seymour, Ruth Contreras, and others not only got much of the CCC's work done but were also leading sisters.

It was also in 1974 that some CLARO members, mostly from the CCC, received a series of visitors from national Marxist-Leninist formations to see about possibly affiliating with one of the groups as a way of sharpening our strategy. The only formation to attract serious interest was the August Twenty-Ninth Movement (ATM), founded in 1974 and named after the historic August 29, 1970, Chicano Moratorium against the Vietnam War, in Los Angeles. ATM had emerged from the Labor Committee of the La Raza Unida Party (LRUP) in Los Angeles, which was well to the left of most LRUP chapters. It had a primarily Chicano membership rather than the almost all-white leadership of most other national formations that visited, and it included local activists personally known to the CCC.

What followed was the kind of destructive experience often found on the U.S. left during these party-building years when vanguardism and sectarianism ruled the day. ATM's politics, set forth in such publications as "Fan the Flames: A Revolutionary Position on the Chicano National Question" and its "Unity Statement," followed the tendency of denouncing the Soviet Union as revisionist, hailing the leading role of China and Albania, and pledging to unite with all genuine (that tricky word!) Marxist-Leninists. For the Chicano movement, ATM adopted Stalin's definition of a nation and affirmed Chicanos were a nation—not just a national minority, as other left formations believed.

That position was a major reason, I was told later, why ATM rejected the bilingual book published in 1976 by the CCC, *450 Years of Chicano History in Pictures* (reprinted later as 500 Years of Chicano History). The book did not declare Chicanos to be a nation; the CCC people were not yet convinced of it. That alleged crime and others apparently compelled ATM members, who took over the CCC, to have the entire second printing of the book shredded in 1976.

ATM in New Mexico also severely undermined the struggle of the Cañoncito land grant group, and a labor struggle. Soon after the ATM takeover, the CCC dissolved. Later, members of ATM in northern California expressed concern privately that New Mexico's ATM included one or more government infiltrators. Many activists in New Mexico believe to this day that such infiltration explains the destruction of *500 Years of Chicano History.* That appears to be true.

At the same time, as anyone who participated in the New Communist Movement of the 1970s knows, the cause might have been garden-variety vanguardism, or a power play to eliminate the influence of certain CCC leaders. The CCC itself was not free of vanguardist tendencies, as shown by its Maoist-style "campaign against liberalism" or its attempt to fulfill cadre-type demands that at one point included meeting to discuss whether, given the needs of the revolution, one member could get pregnant (as she wished). Our dogmatic imposition of cadre demands ran against the barrio culture and longtime styles of organizing.

In short, ATM's actions were destructive yet not incomprehensible for the times. In this way, New Mexico's leftism shared qualities with leftism elsewhere. Those qualities, it must be added, included unlimited commitment to La Causa, great personal self-sacrifice, and a spirit of willingness to die if the revolution needed that.

Today, the left tradition can be seen in New Mexico, for example, in the battle against environmental racism where the enemy is so clearly capitalism. The SouthWest Organizing Project of Albuquerque (SWOP) and the Southwest Network for Environmental and Economic Justice (SNEEJ), with headquarters in that city, confront capitalism and imperialism constantly. Richard Moore of the Black Berets was cofounder of SWOP and coordinates SNEEJ. In the homeland of the atomic bomb and crucial military bases, New Mexican radicals also confront militarism firsthand on many levels including environmental racism. Chicanos/as and other Latinos in New Mexico, as elsewhere, have a long way to go to develop a strategy and tactics for social transformation. Learning from the past is our first crucial step, and calls for much more analysis than this brief essay.

A reason to be hopeful for Chicano left politics across the Southwest is that the fear of being labeled Communist has diminished, especially among urban youth, even though people may not be consciously Socialist or even anticapitalist. One example comes to mind. In 1970, I visited North Vietnam as the first Chicana/o organizer to do so. On returning, I tried to talk other antiwar Chicano activists into going, as I had been invited to do by the Vietnamese. With one exception, they were too worried about the effect of such a trip on their grassroots community organizing. They couldn't afford to be labeled red.

I do not think that would happen today. More and more Chicanos, especially youth, are recognizing that the revolution, of which many speak so passionately, has to be won through anti-imperialist struggle, not with an exclusively or primarily nationalist agenda. Also, Latinos who have come here from Central America, and other arenas of long struggles against U.S.-supported repression, understand imperialism only too well. They are less fearful of the Communist label (setting aside the policies of particular, often sectarian groups).

There are also Chicanos/as committed to moving beyond the "Chicanismo" of the movimiento years, which was often culturally nationalist, sexist, lacking in any class analysis, and defined by its worship of Corky Gonzales, José Angel Gutiérrez, César Chávez, and Reies López Tijerina. "Beyond Chicanismo," a project based on community college campuses in Denver, is setting a bold example with their demand for Chicano Studies to be focused differently. If their politics are not overtly Marxist or Socialist, they are radical and internationalist.

Another trend that has grown strong today is indigenismo, embraced by those who identify with the cultures and struggles of the indigenous peoples of the Americas. Its adherents emphasize indigenous expressions of spirituality and respect for all living creatures. At best, they uphold indigenous concepts of communal interdependence and collectivity rather than private property, commodification, and individualism. Philosophically, this puts indigenismo a short distance from communism.

The idea that Marxism is a white philosophy—which somehow prevailed through the years of adoration for Cuba and Che, China and Mao, Vietnam and Ho Chi Minh, and Guinea-Bissau and Cabral, to mention only a few folks of color who found Marxist theory relevant—is not dead. In insisting on an ideology that incorporates a critique of racism, sexism, and heterosexism, as it should, some Latinos reject Marxism because it "ignored" those other -isms. Or, perhaps more often, because of "all those crazies"—sectarian left formations that claim to speak in its name.

Radical Chicano youth today may not embrace the centrality of class or use what they call "old" words like socialism to define the new society. But they still want to go to Cuba, and they do go. They are far less sexist than their predecessors. Their anger is more profound than that of youth forty years ago, their grasp of the fundamental politics of the United States does not take as long to develop. Their rage comes more quickly; it goes from hip to hop.

Source: Martínez, Elizabeth. "A View from New Mexico: Recollections of the Movimiento Left." *Monthly Review*, July–August 2002.

Lorena Oropeza and Dionne Espinoza, eds., *Enriqueta Vásquez and the Chicano Movement* (2006)

Enriqueta Vásquez has lived with the Chicano community and participated in most of its struggles to attain equality. She coedited El Grito del Norte (Call of the North), *a newspaper in New Mexico, where she wrote about social and economic injustice. Vásquez was not limited to Chicano issues and expressed solidarity with the Vietnamese and Cuban people. She also sought to bring about needed change within the Mexican American community by writing about racism, sexism, imperialism, and poverty. She introduced these questions in a logical but firm manner and was respected for her commitment to progressive thought. Reproduced here are excerpts from the book* Enriqueta Vásquez and the Chicano Movement.

LOS POBRES Y LOS RICOS

A while back, I attended a meeting where I heard a man speak about his experience in Washington on the Poor People's March. It was good to hear one of our Raza stand up and speak for the Raza and our life here and the way of the poor.

During the discussion there was a lady present (Raza) that spoke up and said, "I am not poor, I work." Here was a person who has a nice home (mortgaged), two cars (mortgaged) and many beautiful useless things (also mortgaged). If this woman's husband was to become sick and hospitalized for a few months and she was not able to work, you would end up with human beings who would lose all of their material wealth and find themselves quickly changed from "wishfully middle class" to the "poor class." The picture would be changed, but fast. . . . What would they be?

Let us first of all forget the idea that we will never be poor and by all means let us never look down on the poor. For that matter, the poor are often times better people in that, because they do not have money, they know what to do with themselves and their time. Those with money and things are useless and have no real purpose in life. Take away their money and livelihood (I don't wish this on anyone) and you would find them jumping out of windows.

Now we come to the question, just what is it that we want? Do the poor want money? Do we want to be like the Anglo? What do we really value?

Just looking at the different government machines, I believe that probably the Department of Defense has the provisions for life that the poor people need. Do you know that they take care of their armies from cradle to grave? The entire family of a soldier is taken care of. Now, why can't everyone in this country have this? Isn't this an abundant economy? We have food surplus. Anytime they want, they can solve the job problem by cutting the working hours in half. Really, the amount of money spent for the people of this country is very little. A drop in the bucket in comparison with that which we spend in war killing little people in little countries. Asking for a share of the wealth is not asking too much.

We should also unite with our people, all of us. This stuff about "I made it, you can too," does not sound good to me. It sounds too much like the higher-up talking to the down-there. This competitive (playing one human against the other) way of life is what the "Americano" has given us. They build their lives around competition. And if you don't know what I mean, just watch that lousy TV and see what advertising is all about. They can make you want more fancy junk you don't need than you would ever believe. They have a way of making you build your lives around things and this, Hermanos, is what it is all about. The Anglo society is built on a value system of things, not humans. Once you begin to value things more than humans, it is like an alcoholic that craves more and more and there is no end to satisfying the thirst that wants more.

The Raza in the Southwest is not asking for things so much as being ourselves. Being human. We want our history back. We want our language and culture to be our way of life. We refuse to give in and submit to a hypocritical way of life. This Southwest was built on Indian, Spanish, and Mexican history, not English. Our cities, our mountains and rivers were explored and settled by Indians and Spaniards, not pilgrims and wagon masters. The first cattle raisers, cowboys, and farmers were Raza, we weren't waiting here to be saved by the great white fathers. In Mexico, the Indians had big beautiful cities, they had mathematicians and astronomers and they weren't waiting to be "civilized."

We want to be treated with the dignity that is ours. In matters of jobs, law enforcement, and business we are now second-rate citizens.

In 1968, U.S. defense spending constituted 46.0% of federal outlays, or $81.9 billion versus $96.2 billion on non-defense expenditures. See Harold W. Stanley and Richard G. Niemi, eds., *Vital Statistics on American Politics*, 4th ed. (Washington, D.C.: Congressional Quarterly P, 1994), 361.

The only place where we are first-rate citizens is in the draft call and I sure don't consider it a compliment to be part of a useless machine. Let's all stop and look at ourselves for what we are. Let's wake up and help each other. Let's look at the issues, let's look at our country, let's look at our communities, let's look at ourselves and our families, let's look at our law enforcement agencies, and let's look at this thing called justice. Let's not sit back and give up. We need YOU now. The time is NOW. Let's all stand up, beautiful people. Let's all stand up. LA RAZA UNIDA.

Despierten mis hermanos, no nos podemos permitir perdernos en la rueda de la vida hipócrita con precios anglos. Para que triunfe nuestra cultura e historia tenemos que hablar y gritar y cantar nuestra historia. La tierra es de nosotros. Defiendanla, ella no se vende ni se compra. Es de nosotros.

Wake up, my brothers and sisters, we cannot lose ourselves in the hypocritical wheel of life with Anglo prices. In order for our culture and history to triumph, we must speak out, yell, and sing about our history. The land is ours. Defend it, it is not to be sold or bought. It belongs to us.

October 5, 1968

Translated by Herminia S. Reyes.

Bjorn Kumm, "The Loyola Opposition: El Salvador's Rebel Priests" (1978)

Even before the fall of Nicaraguan dictator Anastasio Somoza (1925–1980) in 1979, there were movements within El Salvador for reforms. Many priests, especially the Jesuits, were at the forefront of championing land redistribution and demanding more democracy. A landed oligarchy of 2 percent of the population with links to U.S. businessmen controlled or owned 60 percent of the land. El Salvador was one of the 10 poorest Latin American countries; a third of its population was living in poverty. The oligarchy considered the clergy communists and declared war on them. The excerpts here are from an article in The Nation *that tells of the Church's involvement in reform during the late 1970s, especially the Jesuits and Fr. Rutilio Grande García, S.J. (1928–1977). They were at the forefront of liberation theology, which essentially taught the peasants that their rewards should be in this life; God does not want them to suffer injustices, and they should act as a community to bring about justice. Grande, with two other Salvadorans, was assassinated in 1977. This assassination changed Archbishop Oscar Romero (1917–1980), who began to publicly speak out against injustice and demand an investigation into Grande's murder. Romero was later assassinated in church while distributing communion.*

In El Salvador, there is a head-on collision between the government, controlled by rich coffee planters, and the Catholic Church, which is today the country's only effective legal opposition.

Catholic priests are unlikely revolutionaries—or at least they were in the Latin America of earlier days, when peasants knew their station and the churchmen considered it their main task to provide the sacraments. . . . In those days, too, the Church was a trusted ally of the landlords, the oligarchs. . . .

In the past decade, after Pope John XXIII's "Populorum Progressio," the Second Vatican Council, and the 1968 meeting in Medellin, Colombia, of Latin American bishops, things have changed a great deal . . . in El Salvador. . . . "There are priests in this country who talk as if they were Fidel Castro," says Ernesto Rivas Gallont, secretary general of the Salvadorean Association of Industries (and in his spare time honorary consul of Rhodesia and South Africa). "The priests are telling the peasants that everything should be distributed equally. . . . They side with the peasants. They consider us the bad ones." . . . [The oligarchy] with the help of the army has build up a paramilitary organization, called Orden, in Spanish, means "order". . . . They are given some military training (the government hesitates, however, to give them guns) and told to keep tabs on possible revolutionaries in their areas especially union organizers and Catholic priests.

One of the Salvadorean priests murdered last year . . . Fr. Rutilio, certainly was no Gild-eyed revolutionary. He had spent his formative years at seminaries in Europe and Central America, often in great spiritual anguish, since he did not consider himself a good Christian. . . .

In the early 1970s [Rutilio] . . . found that his task in the area almost amounted to missionary work, preaching the gospel all over again to peasants who had been left on their own by the priests, except that they were regularly squeezed for money. . . . "The peasants around Aguilares are living under medieval conditions," said Fr. Rutilio. "They are serfs under their landlords. The wealthy coffee farmers of El Salvador have ceased being Christian. It is not our Lord they are praising when they get up in the morning. They cross themselves in the name of their lord, Coffee. And when they have prayed to their lord Coffee, then they pray to their lord Sugar." Prophetically, Fr. Rutilio referred to the landowners in the Aguilares area as the "brothers Cain." . . . Six months after he and his colleagues started there in the parish, a major strike hit the sugar plantations, organized by two radical peasant organizations with Catholic links.

[Fr. Rutilio was shot down]. . . . the Jesuits were preaching the need for the peasants to organize. A couple of months after Father Rutilio's death, the army moved in force to occupy Aguilares and expel the remaining Jesuits. Aguilares was kept under occupation for eight, days. . . .

Archbishop [Oscar] Romero is an intensely private man who suffers a great deal from the public stand he has been forced to take during the past two years. He says that he would prefer to make his protest by withdrawal, by keeping absolutely silent. But circumstances do not permit. The death of Fr. Rutilio, his close friend, seems to have been the turning point for the Archbishop, who has literally become the voice of the opposition in El Salvador.

Every Sunday morning at eight o'clock the giant cathedral in the country's capital is so packed that the congregation spills out onto the sidewa1ks. The former cathedral burnt down a few years ago, under mysterious circumstances, and the present structure is hardly impressive, looking like a great unfinished hangar. The government has been contributing toward a new building, but the Archbishop seems uninterested in architecture. "He does not consider it his task to erect buildings," says a Catholic nun in El Salvador. "What the Archbishop is really doing is building the people."

Every Sunday morning, the sermon of the Archbishop, the unwilling leader of El Salvador's opposition, is broadcast from the Catholic University station. . . .

"We are seeing the ugly face of our history," preaches the Archbishop, "It is not the Church which is sowing the seeds of violence. Violence is the fruit of unjust laws. . . . If the Church is trying to change things and at the same time trying to maintain its identity, keeping true to Christ, this is not communism, it is Christian justice. Our Savior taught us that you must lose you.

"But," adds the Archbishop bitterly, "these men who are ruling us do not want to lose anything at all." Archbishop Romero thinks it is likely that the government will intervene and slap ban on his sermons.

However, until he is silenced he will go on preaching and presenting to the public the testimonials of peasants who were evicted from their houses and their bits of land during their clashes between Orden and the peasant organizations. Making their way over the mountains, the roads being blocked by the army, hundreds of peasants and their families reached the Archbishop's office in a seminary in San Salvador. It is doubtful that they will ever be able to go home. They will add themselves to the hundreds of thousands of slum dwellers in the capital.

"The clashes in the countryside, in effect, help the landowners to modernize agriculture, as well as rid themselves of agitators," says an observer. "The coffee men made lot of money during the past few years' coffee boom. They need fewer workers on the land, and the population is increasing steadily. But they might need them in the towns, as cheap labor for their new tax-free industries geared for exports. Our oligarchs have always been able to adapt to new circumstances."

"For a little while, the Salvadorean oligarch was running scared. Many members of the leading families (they are popularly known as "the fourteen," but are in fact somewhat more numerous) moved to Miami where a number of them have bought expensive condominiums. Now they are returning. They still worry about the Church and its revolutionary priests, but heartened by the growing presence of U.S.-financed Protestant missionaries.

"The Protestants are true Christians," says Alfonso Quiñones Mesa, a leading Salvadorean oligarch and once his country's "coffee ambassador" to London. "They do not mix religion with politics."

Source: Kumm, Bjorn. "The Loyola Opposition: El Salvador's Rebel Priests," 738–740. Reprinted with permission from the December 30, 1978, issue of *The Nation*. http://www.thenation.com.

Silvia M. Unzueta, "The Mariel Exodus: A Year in Retrospect" (1981)

From April 15 to October 31, 1980, more than 125,000 Cubans departed from Cuba's Mariel Harbor and landed in southern Florida. The United States had broken diplomatic relations with Cuba in the early 1960s and imposed an economic boycott on the island that prohibited Americans from trading with or visiting Cuba. This boycott created an economic hardship, and Cubans were barely able to buy necessities. They were forced to rely on the Soviet Union for aid. With growing hunger on the island, many Cubans sought to immigrate to the United States. In 1980, about 10,000 Cubans sought asylum in the Peruvian embassy. Cuban leader Fidel Castro announced that anyone who wanted to leave could leave. With the cooperation of Cuban Americans, a boatlift got under way. It caused almost immediate strains with the United States, negatively affecting President Jimmy Carter as thousands of Cuban refugees landed in Florida. There were accidents as some overcrowded boats capsized and 27 migrants died. The following article describes the boatlift.

The massive arrival caused problems for local government agencies. While earlier migrations of Cubans had been largely white and middle class, the Marielitos, as they were called, had a larger proportion of Cubans of African origin. Critics accused Castro of emptying out the prisons and sending a large number of homosexuals and convicts. This said more about the critics since regardless of their color or sexual orientation, most Marielitos were only seeking economic stability. The record below shows efforts of Dade County, Florida officials to incorporate the Marielitos and provide them with medical and social services.

Before their [Marielitos] arrival, the population of Dade County was 35% Hispanic, 16% Black American, and 49% White (Reference: Metro Dade County Planning Department, 1979). The Black Americans are about equally divided between those from the [Caribbean] Islands and those from the Deep South. After their arrival, the Hispanic population increased by a half of a percent. More than most other metropolitan areas, Dade County was a city of descendants of immigrants or immigrants themselves.

The exodus of over 125,000 Cuban men, women, and children started when more than 10,800 Cubans moved into the grounds of the Peruvian Embassy in Havana, on April 4, 1980, after the Cuban Government guards were removed from the Peruvian Embassy. The word quickly spread throughout the island. The removal of the guards was Castro's response to a dispute between the Cuban and the Peruvian Governments, when the previous week a small group broke into the Embassy seeking asylum.

At that time, no one predicted that the removal of the Cuban militia guard from the Embassy was to be interpreted as anything but "teaching a lesson," to Peruvian authorities. Instead, in less than twenty-four hours, over 10,800 Cubans jammed into the Embassy grounds seeking political asylum. Dramatic photographs of crowded men, women, and children in trees, and on the Embassy roof without water, food, and basic necessities hit the world press, creating embarrassment, and pressure for their release. After extensive third country negotiations and humanitarian requests from all over the world, the Cuban Government agreed to allow the departure of Cubans holding the Embassy. Peru, Spain, and Costa Rica, along with the United States, agreed to give refuge to the 10,800 Cubans seeking political asylum. During these negotiations, spontaneous demonstrations of support by Cuban Americans throughout the United States, other countries, and the world press, helped to highlight the incident and eventually helped to achieve the release of approximately 1,500 of the 10,800 originally in the Embassy. Upon the arrival of the initial group in San Jose, Costa Rica, and Madrid, the Cubans shared with the world media, the horrors lived while at the Embassy. This exposure generated a negative opinion for the aging Cuban Revolution. A few days later, in a skillful and talented show of strategy, Fidel Castro announced the opening of the Port of Mariel and invited Cuban Americans to come to Mariel, Cuba, and pick up their relatives who wanted to leave the island. The announcement was well received by the Cuban American community which immediately began what appeared to be an endless flotilla through the Florida Straits.

After a few weeks, it was evident that the Cuban Government had no intention of fulfilling their promise. Instead, some individuals released from jails and mental institutions became part of the human flow that constituted the Mariel exodus. The "human avalanche" reached unprecedented numbers. During the month of May, 88,817 Cubans arrived. This figure constitutes the largest number of Cubans that arrived in any single previous year.

During May, a number of other factors converged to create a very special situation. President Carter stated that: "We will continue to provide an open heart and open arms to refugees seeking freedom from Communist domination." That statement was qualified less than a week later. Decisions surrounding the handling of the Mariel exodus became entangled in the national political scene.

In Dade County, the initial processing and housing of refugees was skillfully handled by a handful of local, state, and federal officials under the coordination of Metropolitan Dade County Government. At Tamiami Park, a twenty-four-hour processing center was set up where more than 1,500 Cubans were scrutinized by Immigration and Naturalization Service, fingerprinted, X-rayed, and released to family, friends, and supportive others. Food, clothing, and shelter were generously donated by individuals, local business, and civic groups. The processing and housing operation involved more than 1,500 volunteers daily, who worked day and night in a unique and heart warming show of care and goodwill. The Tamiami Park opened its doors on Monday, April 21st and operated until the evening of Friday, May 9th, when the process was moved to an old hanger near Opa-locka Airport.

That same month, a state of emergency was declared by the President and the Federal Emergency Management Agency (FEMA) was put into action. FEMA is the arm of the federal government responsible for coping with natural disasters and emergencies. FEMA's efforts were plagued by a lack of staff with knowledge of the language and culture of the people arriving, changes in personnel, policy inconsistencies, lack of clear direction, and clashes among various federal agencies. A Cuban-Haitian Task Force was appointed in an effort to guide federal efforts during the emergency.

Although many errors were committed and several criticisms of the federal management had been voiced throughout this process, many individuals were served because of the work and dedication of workers and volunteers.

FEMA's presence, however, attempted to bring the needed federal dollars and the recognition of the exodus as a national emergency. Meanwhile, the Cuban Government had turned what had been a negative internal situation for them into a serious emergency for some of us in the United States. The masses of humanity continued arriving in Key West and other parts of Florida. In Cuba, one of the results of Mariel was alleviating serious internal administrative and political problems, and exporting a high-risk population to its political rival, the United States. The exodus freed jobs, houses, and prison space for the Cuban establishment, and these were critically needed in the island. The departure of dissidents and other marginal persons relieved Cuba from explosive internal pressure.

At this time, still in May, another phenomenon took place: FEMA opened four refugee camps in Florida, Arkansas, Pennsylvania, and Wisconsin:

> Eglin Air Force Base in Northwest Florida, housing 10,025. This was the first camp, a city of tents.
>
> Indiantown Gap, in Pennsylvania, with a population of 19,094 Cuban refugees.
>
> Ft. McCoy, in Wisconsin, housing 14,243.
>
> Ft. Chaffee in Ft. Smith, Arkansas, with 19,060 refugees. . . .

Life in camp began another chapter in the lives of these new immigrants. Physical and psychological abuse, beatings, and rapes were happening along with riots as the weeks went by and many Cubans remained tangled up in the red tape of federal bureaucratic management. At one point in the month of June, more than 62,000 Cubans were in the four camps. . . . Most of those without relatives and who had broken away from their sponsors or "padrinos", gravitated to areas of high Hispanic populations. California, New York, New Jersey, and Florida became primary targets where homeless Cubans sought refuge.

In the Miami, Dade County area . . . [t]he Orange Bowl was opened by the City of Miami in the second week of June. On June 20th, Metro Dade County obtained a special allocation from Washington to feed refugees breakfast and one hot meal a day. . . . Up to 800 Cubans were housed in Tent City at one time, and more than 4,000 lived there during the two months it was open. Tent City remained open until September 30, 1980. . . .

Although no conclusive figures are available, individuals familiar with the Mariel population place the number of non-Whites as high as 30% to 40%, and males making up approximately 60% to 70% of the population. The average educational level is estimated to be between the 6th and the 9th grade, with few of the arrivals being able to communicate in any language but Spanish.

Perhaps the most serious problem this group faces is a lack of attachment to family and friends outside of Cuba. This lack of a support system has often inhibited effective resettlement efforts. . . .

Dr. Jose Szapocznik, Director of CAMP, Cuban-American Adolescent Management Program, University of Miami, Department of Psychiatry, Spanish Family Guidance Center, which provided services to Cuban unaccompanied minors, reports their total in the camps at 672. Of those, more specific information was obtained on 549 cases; of these . . .

55 or 10% were females;
43% were non-white;
18% have been or were in a marital or paired relationship;
12% reported coming directly from jail;
50% reported having been in jail at some point of their lives; and
59% reported having some relative in U.S., but only about half of these could give any portion of an address.

Parental occupation and education was reported to be:

70% labor/agricultural,
20% skilled labor, and
10% professional.

Szapocznik reports that a large portion of the interviewees appeared to have poor adjustment to school. Sixty-five percent stated that they had stopped going to school. The rough literacy assessment turned up approximately 8% illiteracy rate.

Six of the 55 female minors stated that they thought or knew that they were pregnant at the time of the interview. Fifty-six, or almost 10% of the respondents reported sexual abuse, venereal disease, or multiple sexual problems in their recent or distant past.

Clinical judgments of a series of psychiatric symptoms and conditions reported the following characteristics:

47% had experienced behavioral problems in Cuba,
14% had experienced hallucinations,
8% had experienced delusions,
31% were or had been clinically depressed,
22% had experienced suicidal tendencies, and
14% had made a suicide attempt.

Much has also been said about the percentage of homosexuals in those arriving from Mariel. However, no data is available as to the actual number of homosexuals in the Mariel population. . . .

Legally, the individuals coming in the Mariel Flotilla have been granted the new administrative category of "entrant." This technicality rendered them ineligible for assistance available through the U.S. Refugee Act of 1980. Many experts believe that the denial of refugee status to these people greatly contributed to the many problems encountered at all levels. It was through the Fascell-Stone Amendment to the Refugee Act of 1980, that special funding was authorized, and in the form of cash assistance, reached the entrants during the latter part of February 1981. . . .

CRIMINAL JUSTICE

The increase of criminal activity has been one more item often blamed on the Mariel refugees. As of December 26, 1980, Unzueta reports that of 163 Cubans charged and/or convicted felons housed in Dade County's main jail, 103 or 63.9% are Mariel refugees, 11 or 6.8% are Cuban ex-political prisoners, and 47 or 29.1% are Cuban Americans. Mariel refugees represented 9.8% of individuals in the main jail. In the Women's Detention Center, where females either charged or convicted of felonies or misdemeanors are housed, Unzueta reports 8 or 4.6% Cuban American women along with 8 or 4.6% Mariel Cuban females and 7 homosexual Mariel males. Mariel refugee women represent 4.6% of the total females, while Mariel homosexual men represent 4.0% of the total individuals housed in the Women's Detention Center on December 26, 1980. The increase in criminal activity has impacted heavily on the entire Dade County judicial system.

Source: Document 0033 Cuban Information Archives. http://cuban-exile.com/doc_026-050/doc0033.html.

Chip Berlet, *The Hunt for Red Menace: How Government Intelligence Agencies and Private Rightwing Counter Subversion Groups Forge Ad Hoc Covert Spy Networks That Target Dissidents as Outlaws*

(1987)

In 1979, the Salvadoran military responded to student protests by installing a military junta. The following year saw the rise of extreme right-wing Salvadoran major Roberto D'Aubuission (1944–1992) and the Alianza Republicana Nacionalista (ARENA, or Republican Nationalist Alliance). The military received a boost with the election of Republican Ronald Reagan (1911–2004) as U.S. president in 1980. Reagan gave more than $1 million dollars a day to the Salvadoran military to fight rebels who were demanding democratic elections. Meanwhile, D'Aubuission's death squads (i.e., military units assigned to assassinate dissidents and church people), with the support of the U.S. Central Intelligence Agency, killed thousands. Hundreds of thousands of Salvadorans came to the United States in response to the civil war in their country. The Salvadoran civil war lasted 12 years, from 1980 to 1992, costing El Salvador 75,000 lives. The United States spent between $4 billion and $6 billion in El Salvador alone. The peace accords of 1992 between the Salvadoran government and the rebels gave a place in the nation's politics to both the conservative ARENA party and the Frente Farabundo Martí para la Liberación Nacional (FMLN, or Farabundo Marti National Liberation Front) rebels. While in the United States, many of the exiles helped set up organizations that would bring peace to their country. Because many of these organizations supported the rebels, they came under intense surveillance. The following report discusses government infiltration of the Committee in Solidarity with the People of El Salvador, which was based in New York City. It was a national activist organization with chapters in major cities in the United States. Founded in 1980, it supported the FMLN and the progressive social movement in El Salvador and sought support in the United States for the guerrilla army.

The genesis of the FBI probe of CISPES was a complex network of groups and individuals with a common counter-subversive worldview: The underlying theories which prompted the FBI investigation of CISPES were developed at the start of the Cold War, and reflect the same discredited view of subversion that the American public finally rejected to end the McCarthy period. Individuals and groups who hold this discredited view of subversion played influential roles in shaping the policies of the Reagan Administration in this area, and then in some cases moved on to become consultants and staff members in Administration and Congressional posts.

These same groups and individuals then set out to rebuild a private counter-subversion network among conservative and rightist groups with the goal of assisting the government, and specifically the FBI, in investigating subversion. The results of their investigations were published in a range of newsletters and journals in articles which frequently cross-cited each other and often traced back to unsubstantiated charges of Communist subversion made by persons testifying before congressional witch-hunting committees.

Young conservatives from colleges and universities were recruited and trained to participate in monitoring and analyzing the activities of alleged subversive groups through a network of interlocking conservative institutions based in Washington, D.C. Information and documents collected by private right-wing groups were provided to government law enforcement agencies that would otherwise be prevented from obtaining the information by constitutional and legislative restrictions. This biased and unverified information was then used to justify criminal investigations of dissidents in general and the anti-interventionist CISPES in particular.

Many activists involved in Central American issues became aware of ham-handed snooping by Federal Bureau of Investigation agents in the early 1980s. In 1986, the Center for Investigative Reporting in California used the federal Freedom of Information Act [FOIA] to obtain FBI files which suggested a large-scale probe into CISPES. In 1987, testimony by a former FBI informant, Frank Varelli, also suggested a broad attack on CISPES by the FBI. Varelli later told reporters of the involvement of other governmental and private right-wing groups in targeting CISPES.

Some 1,300 pages of additional FBI files released in 1988 by New York's Center for Constitutional Rights (CCR), on behalf of CISPES, reveal in sharp detail the extent and nature of the FBI probe into CISPES. More importantly, the files show that the FBI, to justify its actions, accepted as fact a right-wing conspiratorial worldview which sees dissent as treason and resistance to oppression as terrorism.

The first FBI investigation of CISPES was launched in September of 1981 to determine if CISPES should be forced to register under the Foreign Agents Registration Act. Among the documents used by the FBI to justify this CISPES probe, according to Congressional testimony by FBI official Oliver "Buck" Revell, was a 1981 article by a former FBI informant and ongoing right-wing private spy—John Rees. The Rees article appeared in *Review of the News* a magazine published by the paranoid ultra-right John Birch Society. This FBI investigation was terminated without indictments in December of 1981.

A second FBI investigation of CISPES began in March of 1983. It was premised on the right-wing conspiracy theory that CISPES was a cover for "terrorist" activity. To justify this view, the FBI relied not only on reports from its informant Varelli, but also in part on a conspiratorial analysis contained in a report written by Michael Boos, a staffer at the right-wing Young Americas Foundation. This FBI "counter-terrorism" investigation was terminated without indictments in 1985.

The FBI relying on the malicious musings of paranoid right-wing ideologues to justify probes of the anti-Administration CISPES is rather like the IRS assigning Jerry Falwell to audit the financial records of the American Civil Liberties Union.

THE TERRORIST-BAITING OF CISPES

The June 1984 report on CISPES by Michael Boos, the staff member at the Young Americas Foundation, was titled: "Group in Nation's Capitol to Aid Left-Wing Terrorists." In the report, Boos wrote that the D.C. Chapter of CISPES would "soon launch a fundraising campaign to provide direct military assistance to the Soviet-supported Marxist terrorists seeking to overthrow the recently elected government in El Salvador." This conclusion was reached when Boos made the Kierkegaardian assumption that the shoe factory CISPES planned to help build in El Salvador would not really benefit civilians, but would secretly make and repair boots for rebel soldiers—and thus constituted military aid for "Soviet-supported Marxist terrorists."

Boos wrote his report after attending a public CISPES meeting in Washington, D.C. According to a spokesperson at the Young Americas Foundation, Boos was apparently engaging in a freelance information-gathering activity not directly connected with his staff position. Boos filed his report with the right-wing newsletter American Sentinel, and sent an unsolicited copy to the FBI. The FBI promptly distributed it to 32 of its field offices and apparently sent it to other federal agencies as well.

It is ironic that the Boos report on CISPES for American Sentinel was revealed in the FBI documents on CISPES since the Young Americas Foundation is only a minor player in the right-wing information network. The [Young Americas] Foundation primarily is involved in recruiting college students into the conservative anti-Communist movement. Boos, while at Young Americas

Foundation, circulated a newsletter reporting on campus activists, but it too is not influential in right-wing circles.

The Young Americas Foundation is a haven for aging former members of the right-wing campus-based Young Americans for Freedom (YAF). While it was started by a former YAF staffer, the [Young Americas] Foundation is not formally tied to that group. They are certainly right-wing ideological soul-mates, however, and they cooperate closely. The [Young Americas] Foundation once sent out a fundraising mailing calling former Sen. George McGovern "anti-American," and claimed "our classrooms are full of teachers and textbooks that tear down our system of republican government and free enterprise while glorifying communism and socialism."

The American Sentinel, the newsletter which published the Boos report on CISPES (without attribution) is, however, one of the core right-wing outlets for red menace diatribes. The Sentinel frequently touts its relationship to law enforcement. The Sentinel raised funds to send its blacklist-style report to "723 FBI offices and local police departments," pledging to keep track of "the liberals, the left-wingers, the radicals and the Communists."

PARANOID THEORIES AND THE FBI PROBE OF CISPES

That the views of the paranoid right wing find safe harbor at the FBI is supported by the documents they released under the FOIA concerning the probe of CISPES. As Alicia Fernandez of the Center for Constitutional Rights explained in an article appearing in the Movement Support Network News:

> In order to justify its investigation, the FBI utilized two rationales: it posited the existence of a covert program and it resurrected a 1950s favorite, the concept of a 'front group.' These two notions were extremely useful. By positing a covert program, FBI headquarters was able to reason away the lack of findings in investigations conducted by the field offices.
>
> When a field office reported that assiduous investigation had revealed that a local CISPES chapter pursued only such projects as teach-ins, slide shows, and pickets, headquarters would remind the field office of the "covert program." This, headquarters explained, was known to only a few CISPES members, but represented CISPES' true intentions and activities. Thus headquarters would caution the field office not to be deceived and urge it to dig deeper. The deeper the field office dug, with no results, then clearly, reasoned the FBI, the deeper they needed to dig.
>
> When field offices cabled headquarters to inform it that they had located no CISPES chapter but had found a Central American solidarity committee, or a Latin American human rights group, or a sanctuary church, headquarters would recommend aggressive investigation and explain that CISPES operated through "fronts," in which respectable people were duped for its "terrorist purposes."

In this way, any group which ever worked with CISPES or shared members became a potential "front." "The very logic of these rationales increased the pressure to expand the hunt for fronts and intensify the search for covert activities," Fernandez points out.

The FBI probe of CISPES involved 52 of the 59 Field Offices of the FBI. Dossiers were compiled on hundreds of other organizations which intersected in some vague way with CISPES during the course of the investigation.

Margaret Ratner of the Center for Constitutional Rights called the FBI probe of CISPES a "sweeping and intrusive investigation . . . the FBI utilized wiretaps, undercover agents, and informants in addition to the type of intensive physical surveillance that is normally reserved for investigation of serious crimes." According to Ratner:

> The investigation, which was begun in 1981 to determine if a violation of the Foreign Agents Registration Act existed, was quickly turned into a "Foreign Intelligence/Terrorism" inquiry, even though no basis for such existed. The new category, however, allowed the FBI to utilize "special

> techniques," that are considered illegal when applied to domestic investigations. It allowed the FBI to avoid strictures developed to remedy the abuses that came to light in the post-Vietnam protest era.

Ratner charges that "the investigation was used as one of the pretexts for the harassment and surveillance" being reported by those who oppose the Reagan administration's foreign policy.

FBI director William Sessions, however, defended the CISPES investigation as a legitimate probe into criminal activity. But one FBI agent assumed a more sinister motive for the CISPES investigation in a memo which warned:

> It is imperative at this time to formulate some plan of action against CISPES and, specifically, against individuals [deletion] who defiantly display their contempt for the U.S. government by making speeches and propagandizing their cause while asking for political asylum.

New Orleans is of the opinion that the Departments of Justice and State should be consulted to explore the possibility of deporting these individuals or at best denying them re-entry after they leave.

Among the many groups named in the CISPES FBI files were: Central American Solidarity Committee, Clergy and Laity Concerned, Church of the Brothers, Chicago Interreligious Task Force, Fellowship of Reconciliation, Friends Religious Society, Maryknoll Sisters, National Education Association, Southern Christian Leadership Conference, United Steel Workers Union, and the United Auto Workers Union. Also named in the files were a number of individual churches, colleges, religious orders, community organizations, women's groups and political groups.

The following excerpt from the Pittsburgh FBI field office file on the local CISPES affiliate, the Central American Mobilization Committee (CAMC), showed the ideological framework which forms the basis of the FBI investigation:

> The membership of the CAMC and its affiliated groups appears generally to be of two type groups: the "core" membership and the "affiliate" membership. The "core" membership consists of individuals with strong Communist or Socialist beliefs who have a history of being active in Communist or Socialist political organizations, some since the Vietnam War era. The "affiliate" membership, on the other hand, consists in large part of local college students relatively new to the political scene. It has at least one female high school student member. Some of these younger "affiliate" members appear to be politically unsophisticated in that they know little of current international events save what they read or hear at their political meetings. Pittsburgh has noted at least two of these members or affiliates both were young females.

The CISPES FOIA revelations came on the heels of charges by former FBI informant Frank Varelli that he was pressured into inventing information to show that CISPES was tied to terrorists. Varelli told a Congressional subcommittee in 1987 that his reports were designed to provide an excuse for the FBI to intimidate critics of Reagan's Central America policies.

According to Varelli,

> The FBI led me to believe that CISPES was a radical "terrorist" organization. . . . Ironically, never once during the next three years of my association with CISPES did I encounter anything even close to the picture painted by the FBI. The CISPES organization was peaceful, nonviolent, and devoted to changing the policies of the United States towards Central America by persuasion and education.

Varelli sued the FBI, alleging they refused to pay him $65,000 in back pay. Varelli was terminated as an informant when the FBI agent controlling him carelessly lost in a car burglary files containing secret information that might have blown Varelli's cover.

Source: Berlet, Chip. *The Hunt for Red Menace: How Government Intelligence Agencies and Private Rightwing Counter Subversion Groups Forge Ad Hoc Covert Spy Networks that Target Dissidents as Outlaws*. Rev. ed. Cambridge, MA: Political Research Associates, 1993. http://www.publiceye.org/huntred/Hunt_For_Red_Menace 12.html.

Brittmarie Janson Pérez, "Political Facets of Salsa" (1987)

What is amazing is that after more than 100 years of colonial rule, Puerto Ricans have maintained their language and traditions, as have most Spanish-speaking Caribbean people. Many people attribute this in part to salsa music and dance, which binds youth together. Salsa is a product of many Latin and Afro-Caribbean dances. For instance, mambo has a pattern of six steps danced over eight counts of music. Whereas mambo moves generally forward and backward, salsa moves more from side to side and creates a mood. There are Cuban, New York, Los Angeles, Dominican, Columbian, and, of course, Puerto Rican styles of salsa. Caribbean music takes 80 percent of its roots from Africa, and it is part of a nightclub life that brings youth together. The following excerpts from an essay in Popular Music *discuss the political aspects of salsa.*

Late at night, in a discotheque in a Latin American country whose political system is dominated by the military and is not particularly known for its respect for human rights, a crowd is dancing salsa, a generic term covering Caribbean dance music. The song is Willie Colón's "El General." It starts with a roll of drum beats and a sarcastic description of the general getting up in the morning to put on his uniform and dictate orders to the president. A thrill of fifes follows and a [stentorian] shout: "To the right!" The verse describes citizens as delighted not to have a free press and a dangerous democratic system with its tricky politicians. The military gazette is very enjoyable and it is reassuring to have a regime which puts men with strange ideas behind bars. In the discotheque, the crowd continues dancing. The next stanza says the general is rumored to be about to retire: What will happen to the country and the people without him? "For a long time I've wanted to thank you," is the refrain, "goodbye and thank you, my general."

By this time, one of the dancers is consciously aware of the lyrics and wondering, "what kind of a song are we dancing to?" It is a long song which thanks the general in the name of those who are no longer there, the *desaparecidos* [disappeared]. A chorus which starts by asserting that there is no censorship in the country cleverly turns the refrain into a denouncement: Censura! This is followed by the sounds of an execution. Someone orders: "Aim . . . Fire!" A spatter of shots is heard followed by a military march and the ominous sound of a siren. Over a megaphone, a male voice with a Chilean accent announces a curfew. The next stanzas are loaded with hypocritical thanks to the jefe supremo for all he has done for the people, for what he did for Pablo Pueblo, who came home from the factory to find his family missing. "In the barrio we all toast the general with rum and cold beer, waiting for the day he can rest," the lyrics add. Addressing the general, the song continues: "Either you retire or they retire you, but what a glorious day that will be. How happy I am that you will go. . . . Goodbye little general, tyrant of my life."

The song is a dramatic composition with bold sound effects and elements in the verse with which people from many parts of Latin America can identify. A proper semiotic analysis is impossible here; only a few examples can be given. A general who dictates orders to the president is compatible with many past and present regimes in Caribbean countries. The missing, the desaparecidos, are a characteristic of dictatorships, but the term is most closely connected with the Argentine and Chilean experiences. The general's early rise and his work routine are reminiscent of Paraguayan radio newscasts which often start with such reports. The apologia for not having a democratic system is a standard one for military regimes in Latin America.

This song, which was brought to my attention by the dancer just referred to, is not unique. There is a trend in many contemporary salsa recordings to include one or two topics, such as poverty and injustice in Latin America or the oppression of Latin Americans living in the United States, and to present them as a product of corrupt regimes, U.S. imperialism, or capitalism. Denouncements of electoral fraud, government censorship and officially sanctioned drug trafficking are among the themes dealt with in salsa by Panamanian composer and singer Pedro Altamiranda. The proclamation of nationalist causes is seen in the work of other composers from the Caribbean region. The range of issues is broad but the one whose social and political implications is rarely addressed is machismo.

The question of why "El General" could be played under the particular circumstances just described is a fascinating one, but because the permissibility of aesthetic protest is heavily dependent on the country and the prevalent political climate, it will not be broached here. Instead, I want to explore two broader questions: why salsa, an eminently danceable genre, is being used as a medium for powerful political messages; and whether commercial, ideological, and technological impingements threaten salsa's survival.

2. THE GENRE

Politics has rarely been absent from Latin American music; Mexico's politicised [politicized] corridos are well known. Puerto Rican composers voiced their independentist concerns in a few boleros, also a Latin American dance genre. The highly committed nueva canción latino americana has been amply documented. Salsa differs from these, however, in that it is a large-scale capitalist commercial production, a consumer product aimed at all of Latin America and Hispanics residing in the United States but which, nevertheless, contains critiques of capitalism from various viewpoints. The salsa of sociopolitical themes is not the type of protest song sung in demonstrations, rallies, or overtly political contexts. It is protest embedded in everyday life: songs heard over the radio or record player, and music danced to at parties and in nightclubs or discos. The public is in a passive, recipient situation in contrast with, for instance, the U.S. blacks of the civil rights movement who sang "We Shall Overcome" in active resistance. This recipient relationship in popular music, between the product and the consumer, should not be overemphasized, however, since in the end it is the individual who, in accepting or rejecting a song, has the last say as far as commercial success is concerned.

The birth of salsa was the product of an eminently political event: the Cuban Revolution of 1959 and the OAS [Organization of American States] boycott of the island which ensued. Until that time, Cuba was the undisputed centre of Caribbean or Afro-Antillean music. Commercial production of popular music in Cuba for export was brought to an end by these events and many prominent Cuban musicians, composers, and singers emigrated to the United States, where New York still had sufficient big bands to be able to assimilate the influx. But the final end of the big band era was in sight by the time the Beatles swept the entire continent in 1964. U.S. recording companies had stopped production of Cuban music several years before. Yet New York was the mecca of Latin American artists as well as the centre of large-scale migration, not only from Puerto Rico but from all Caribbean Basin countries. Marginalized in the new land and consigned to an inferior status not unlike that of U.S. blacks—many of the emigrants were black—the émigrés settled in ghettos of their own, the barrio, adjacent to slums such as Harlem. In New York, the musical outcome was the emergence of barrio music and musicians, of small ensembles which played for their barrio brethren and incorporated into their music the sounds and daily problems, the cacophony and violence of the urban slum. The musical roots of these compositions—which were in part a quest for affirming ethnic identity—were eminently Cuban or Afro-Antillean. The clave, a rhythmic time-line of 312 or 213 over two beats, became the pattern not only for the reinterpretation of already existing Caribbean music, but also for new compositions. The use of traditional instruments such as congas, maracas, güiros, bongos, the piano, plus trumpets and trombones—which were emphasized to translate the sound of the barrio—was retained as an ideological affirmation of the Caribbean heritage. The new music was heavily indebted to the highly syncopated Cuban son [sound or musical style].

In the following years, a most interesting phenomenon occurred: although salsa was still not identified as such, the genre which started in New York was rapidly taken up in the big cities of the Caribbean in a spontaneous process, unconnected with fashion or commercial promotion. Possibly this was because the need for cultural identification felt by the Latins in alien New York was basically the same as that of Caribbean barrio inhabitants; both lacked a musical expression to represent them at a time when radio stations were playing the Rolling Stones and television stations were dominated by canned U.S. serials.

By the early 1970s, salsa reached its first stage of maturity in New York and the recording industry made its influence felt. Barrio music was given a label, salsa, and actively promoted. The salsa boom which followed had its apex in 1974, fuelled by a recording enterprise, Fania, which came to dominate the salsa market.

But the boom was double-edged. It gave employment to many Latin American musicians but the enterprise's efforts at "crossing over" into the broader U.S. and European markets had negative effects. In general terms, "crossing over" means validating an economically, politically, or racially subordinate culture before a hegemonic culture. In this case, the goal was commercial: to invade the lucrative big markets with salsa. For this effort to be successful, however, the enterprise's executives deemed it necessary to modify the genre. For the salsa industry to become really big-time and surpass the confines of the Latin consumers market, Fania's managers felt that they had to change salsa's image radically. From being the music of the barrio, associated with poverty, delinquency, and marginality, it had to be polished and approximated to the overwhelming U.S. pop culture. . . .

The salsa boom would increase sales but eventually it killed the music's feeling and indeed its reason for being. Fania started producing supermarket music which insistently and desperately denied the true essence of salsa and became a Caribbean-type music disguised for "gringo" consumption. An example of such music is Rhythm Machine released by Fania with CBS in 1977. Productions such as these were rejected by the Latin public. The boom was exhausted in New York by 1979, at which time Venezuela and Puerto Rico took up the slack. But the demand for new recordings resulted in very poor quality, overnight productions which did not satisfy the public. Salsa seemed to be on its way out. . . .

However, in keeping with Raymond Williams' theory of the flux of dominant, emergent, and residual elements in the cultural hegemonic process, an emergent trend arose within salsa—itself the product of an emergent, oppositional, and co-opted element—which was to give new life to the genre in the nick of time. The downward slide of commercial salsa was dynamically broken by what I here term sociopolitical salsa. . . .

3. IDEOLOGY

As already noted, from its earliest days, barrio music contained a number of compositions which in sound and themes provided a meta-commentary on poverty, delinquency, oppression, and domination. These themes were, to a large extent, submerged during the salsa boom but once that boom waned they returned to prominence through the contributions of Willie Colón, Catalino Curet Alonso, and Rubén Blades. These, and other figures, each deserve more individual attention than they can be given here. I have chosen to focus on Rubén Blades, who has played a stellar role in the introduction and popularisation of sociopolitical themes in salsa and whose co-production with Colón, Siembra (Planting), became the best selling salsa record in 1979, when the end of the boom was in sight. . . .

A Panamanian composer and singer, lawyer, and film star who emigrated to New York in the early 1970s, Blades appears to have a twofold mission. On the one hand, his musical compositions are directed at Latin America in an effort to give Latin Americans an identity and to raise their political consciousness. Ideologically, he has identified with the left in Latin America and the left has identified with him. On the other hand, Blades seeks to represent Latin America in the non-Latin world, to validate the Hispanic presence and seek its rightful place in the order of things, particularly in entertainment.

He contrasts in these efforts with Pedro Altamiranda, who is also a Panamanian, has a Ph.D. in linguistics from the University of Paris, and whose sociopolitical songs seek to capture the language and lifestyle of his fellow countrymen. Altamiranda is strictly focused on his country. He has described himself politically as "oppositional and anti-militaristic" and has refused offers to enter into the glossy international entertainment world.

This, however, is the world in which Blades is eminently successful. In his quest to give Latin Americans an identity and to unify them ideologically, he has been triumphant and has become the idol of Latin American leftists and the public in general. His songs have dealt with the predicaments of the common man in Hispanic America as well as of Latin Americans living in the United States. His most overtly political album, Buscando America (Searching for America), was released in 1984, after Blades had done a stint with various salsa artists and recording companies in New York, and had become the first Latin American artist to be signed by a U.S. mainstream label, Elektra Asylum. . . . The songs deal with themes such as emigration because of political repression ("Caminos Verdes"—"Green Roads"); the assassination of Salvadoran Archbishop Oscar Arnulfo Romero ("El Padre Antonio y el Monaguillo Andres"—"Father Anthony and the Acolyte, Andres"); his search for unity, identity, and social and economic justice in America ("Buscando America"—"Searching for America"); the secret police ("GBDB"); difficult decisions in everyday life ("Decisiones"—"Decisions"); and missing persons in dictatorships ("Desapariciones"—"Disappearance").

Previously recorded songs which gained him his outstanding position in sociopolitical salsa include "Pablo Pueblo" ("Paul People"), to which Willie Colón referred in "El General," "Pedro Navaja" ("Peter, the Switchblade"), and "Juan Pachanga" ("Juan, the Playboy").

In his second objective, to make the Latin American presence felt in the international entertainment world (or "crossing over," which is the subject of his second film, *Crossover Dreams*, released in 1985), Blades has been no less successful.

He has received extensive media coverage in the U.S., been featured on the cover of New York magazine (19 August 1985) and Current Biography (May 1986), and been written up in other publications too numerous to mention. His U.S. television appearances have included interviews on the Johnny Carson Show and 60 Minutes. He has been on several world tours, appeared as an opening star in a concert given by Joe Jackson in Baltimore in 1984 and at the Olympia Music Hall in Paris in May 1986. As an actor he has appeared in two films and is in two more scheduled to be released in 1987: *Continental Divide,* directed by Michael Apted and co-starring with Richard Pryor, and *The Milagro Beanfield War*, directed by Robert Redford.

His unqualified success in crossing over (he himself dislikes the term and prefers to use "convergence") may ultimately jeopardize his other role, that of addressing Latin America. To be lionized in the heart of capitalism, starring in Hollywood productions, and being selected as one of the ten sexiest men of the year by Playgirl may place him in the situation of playing a discrepant role. . . . That is to say, his loyal Latin American constituents may ask how, if he represents oppositional sectors, can he be so applauded by the culture which dominates them? In the United States he has announced his intentions of putting Colombian Nobel Prize winner Gabriel Garcia Marquez' stories to music and to compose an album entirely in English, singing calypso under a new name, not his own persona but in that of an alter ego, "Panama Blades". . . . In a Panamanian television interview, he announced that he would record a two-album series of songs for Panama and by Panamanians and omitted mention of his plans to make the English-language record. . . .

Blades has explained his cinematographic efforts to his constituents—who may some day become his real constituents as he has announced at various times that he may enter into the Panamanian political arena—in the following terms:

"Right now, I am in the United States helping to end the stereotype of the Latin in the United States and also helping the 20 million Latins who live in that country for many reasons but generally because of the opportunities it affords. [I am in the United States] also for economic reasons, to make my life more possible to maintain once I return to Panama. [The latter] because in situations where you are economically controlled, money is freedom. That will give me an opportunity when I return to Panama not to have to ally myself with discredited groups and to see in what way I can do my work here. . ."

Blades' situation has been discussed here because it is relevant within the framework of Williams' previously cited work. More will be said about this in a moment. Within salsa, the success of Blades' sociopolitical songs has attracted a large number of imitators. Some songs, such as Willie Colón's "El General" are of the same quality as Blades' own best productions, while others, such as the work of Pedro Altamiranda, is [sic] of an entirely different nature and follows different aims. But there are many imitators of a vastly inferior quality, characterised by trite themes and virtually inaudible lyrics. Oscar D'Leon, for example, a Venezuelan salsa star, recently released an album which contains two sociopolitical themes, one on the errant street boy and another on poverty, which are wholly lacking in originality, feeling and clarity. In the end, commercial enterprises and imitators may kill off the authenticity and attractiveness of sociopolitical salsa. In other words, again, what was once a brave ideological and artistic effort may be co-opted by commercialism.

The question which now arises is: What is going to happen to salsa? Such important figures as Willie Colón and Elías López have commented on its current problems. . . . If its themes are played out, are there other resources that can prevent this genre from falling into the musical fossil pit of tangos, boleros, and other past Latin American genres which are heard today only for reasons of romantic nostalgia? If one looks to either ideology or technology to rescue the genre, there is little cause for optimism for the following reason: ideology is constraining technology.

4. TECHNOLOGY

The very affirmation of ethnic identity in the face of a dominant, hegemonic culture led early and later salsa composers and arrangers to eschew electronic music and rely for the most part on traditional instruments with which they were more comfortable. It was believed that the purity of Latin music would be lost to a technology which was essentially capitalistic. But the use of traditional Caribbean instruments and the cautious introduction of electronic music into salsa have resulted in a sound which is anachronistic from the viewpoint of today's stereophonic record players, equipped as they are to transmit sounds which are far beyond the range of these instruments, particularly in the bass. In the opinion of informed individuals whom I have interviewed, salsa simply cannot compete in sound with rock music. The model for those who advocate change is the Miami Sound Machine, a group of musicians of Cuban origin who seem to have been successful in the crossover quest. They were recent guests at the unveiling of the Statue of Liberty, have played for President Reagan in Miami and in festivals in Chile, Peru, Costa Rica, Mexico, and a number of other Latin American countries. . . . Although retaining a Latin beat, the Miami Sound Machine is contemporary in its use of electronic instruments. Its clientele in Latin America is formed by a younger generation more in tune with rock, computers, and arcade games than with the legacies of the past. On the other hand, this musical group is [an] anathema to the nationalist left.

This war of ideology embedded in technology is felt at another level, that of composers. Tille Valderrama, a Panamanian composer and arranger who has a degree from Berklee Music College in Boston, expresses the frustration felt by some contemporary composers in Latin America. He feels that salsa is becoming obsolete because of the strictures of those who dominate its commercial production (as, for example, in their insistence on keeping the clave rhythm for the sake of the dancers who, if the rhythm were changed, might reject it). Additionally, they eschew the richness of what Valderrama calls the American drum set and are extremely hesitant to use electronic music.

The whole issue has become ideological: to use electronic music or to change the rhythm is felt to be as much a betrayal of the culture as what Fania enterprises did to the original salsa. If Blades uses electronic music or changes the rhythm it is accepted. If other composers do it, it is ideological treason.

5. CONCLUSIONS

We can see, therefore, that the history of salsa has been one of fluctuation between emergence and co-optation by capitalism. I have not said "by the dominant culture" because that is what the whole issue of "crossing over" involves. Whether or not salsa or the issues raised in sociopolitical salsa will be accepted by the public who are part of the hegemonic cultures is very open to question. It may depend on the success of the efforts of Blades or someone else, or upon the emergence of yet another saving lifeline. What seems to be clear is that the whole process of the dominant culture's absorption of emerging or oppositional elements is very complex. On the one hand, there are purely commercial efforts to exploit emergent trends. On the other, one sees individuals from emergent trends or subordinate cultures seeking validation through inclusion in the dominant stream. Crossing over may be done with a number of intents and poses a thorny problem. An artist may seek to have his ethnic group represented in the world's entertainment field and be very successful in doing so. On the other hand, he may run the risk of losing his constituency for failing to represent them ideologically. The whole process of the emergent being absorbed by the dominant may thus be seen as an active one on the part of both sides—with certain qualifications and intents on the part of both—rather than as a one-way path in which the dominant makes use of and manipulates the subordinate, emergent, or oppositional.

Another question concerns the use of an eminently danceable genre to transmit powerful political messages. It is here suggested that in the Caribbean and regions influenced by the Caribbean cultures, dance music is a privileged genre. Not only do the cultures which make up this region fall roughly within what one calls oral or residually oral culture . . . but there is a strong African heritage whose musical traditions, e.g., the heavy use of drums and syncopation, may also privilege dance music as an aesthetic communicative genre . . . explains:

As far as the Caribbean is concerned, far from entailing a sacrifice to dance, music always entailed an emphasis on dance. It is not a question of falling into the mediocre classification of making music to dance to; it is simply that music, with all its virtues, innovations, and variations, has dance implicit in it. In this part of the world there is no sense in making music that is not danceable.

As far as salsa is concerned, it is not difficult to conceive of a political message being successfully transmitted when heard at home, over the radio or record-player; it is much more difficult to assess its effectiveness in a social context, when a crowd is enjoying itself drinking and dancing.

There is more than one way to approach this subject. One can draw on Maurice Bloch, who declares "you can't argue with a song," because it involves abandonment of the freedom of natural discourse, and no argument or reasoning can be communicated. . . . In this particular context, the implications might be that the recipients of sociopolitical salsa receive and accept the message without question. Alternatively, a view held by several research assistants and record salesmen is that people go along with the music and either do not listen to the words, or listen to them selectively. The implication here is that the political effect upon listeners is slight.

However, both the dancer who brought "El General" to my attention and the large number of Blades' followers seem to indicate that some individuals do listen to the lyrics and others, being ideologically attuned to a particular trend or identifying with a particular genre, are indeed highly conscious of the lyrics, even when dancing.

Lastly, one may think of the recipients of the messages of sociopolitical salsa in terms of Freudian psychoanalytic theory: In the same way tunes that come into one's head without warning turn out to be determined by and belong to a train of thought which has a right to occupy one's mind though without one's being aware of its activity. It is easy to show then that the relation to the tune is based on its text or origin. . . .

From this perspective one could imagine that there is ideological penetration of the listener who, whether he listens to the lyrics or not, is unwittingly having his consciousness raised.

The answer to this question may include all three of these opinions. It is hard to argue with a song and song therefore has a great deal of force. Many people do not pay attention to the lyrics, but it is possible that the lyrics may penetrate their subconscious. Other people identify with the lyrics or with a particular ideology and for them the song has the greatest force. Additionally, if we are dealing with a culture in which dance is not only a comfortable but indispensable and traditional component, the fact that a political message is embedded in a dancing song should not affect these various conditions of receptiveness just discussed.

Source: Pérez, Brittmarie Janson. "Political Facets of Salsa." *Popular Music* (Latin America) 6, no. 2 (May 1987): 149–159.

Testimony of Peter Kornbluh, "Congressional Inquiry into Alleged Central Intelligence Agency Involvement in the South Central Los Angeles Crack Cocaine Drug Trade"

(October 19, 1996)

The civil wars in Central America created push factors that drove many Central Americans to the United States during the 1980s and 1990s. In the United States, the nation was divided over U.S. involvement in the region: one camp condemned U.S. intervention and the other said it was necessary to stop communism. When Nicaraguans elected Marxist Sandinistas, U.S. Central Intelligence Agency (CIA) involvement was stepped up with CIA funding and aid for the contras—right-wing Nicaraguan counterrevolutionaries who sought to overthrow the Sandinistas. Seeking to limit U.S. involvement, Congress passed the Boland Amendments in 1982 and 1984, which were aimed at limiting U.S. government assistance to the contras. However, this did not stop CIA involvement; they simply switched to covert actions. Congressional investigations revealed that the United States sold arms to Iran in exchange for the release of hostages taken by Iranian militants in 1979. The profits from arms sales went to the contras. Further investigations suggested that the contras received more money through other illegal programs that were coordinated by Colonel Oliver North of the National Security Council. President Ronald Reagan (1911–2004) denied knowledge of the affair—even though it was clear his administration had circumvented the provisions of the Boland Amendments. Vice President George H. W. Bush (1924–) and former director of the CIA William J. Casey (1913–1987; Casey died in the midst of the investigations) were implicated but not charged with violating the Boland Amendments. The following formerly classified redacted document shows that on February 10, 1986, North was informed by his liaison, Robert Owen, that a plane being used to run materials to the contras was previously used to run drugs, thus proving U.S. complicity in trying to overthrow the constitutionally elected Sandinista government. The turmoil throughout Central American was the principal reason for immigration to the United States, and it formed the politics of many of the refugees when in the United States.

Testimony of Peter Kornbluh
Senior Analyst
National Security Archive
October 19, 1996

Congresswoman Juanita Millender-McDonald, members of the Black and Hispanic Caucus, and the Select Committee on Intelligence, I want to thank you for affording me the opportunity to both testify at, and be witness to, this important hearing.

The name of my organization, the National Security Archive, sounds like the type of government agency that might be involved in this scandal. I can assure you that we are not. We are a public interest documentation center, specializing in obtaining the declassification of internal national security documentation and making it available to Congress, to journalists and to concerned citizens to enhance the public debate over foreign policies that are conducted in our name but often without our knowledge.

The Archive—which is nonpartisan and does not take a position on legislation—often deals with documents that are classified TOP SECRET for national security reasons but that, in truth, have no real bearing on the security of our nation. Today, however, I am happy to have the opportunity to share with you declassified White House documents which indeed address a real and present danger to the national security of this country, to the security of our cities, of our households, and to the health, well-being and personal security of each and every citizen in this room—the scourge of drugs.

Let me say at the outset that I cannot speak to, nor provide evidence for, the allegations that are stated and implied in the San Jose *Mercury News* stories. Internal U.S. government documents on the early years of the contra war that might shed light on the issues reported by Gary Webb have not been declassified. Hopefully, public pressure brought on the CIA, the Justice Department, the National Security Council and the Drug Enforcement Agency will result in the release of those documents.

But I can and will address the central premise of the story: that the U.S. government tolerated the trafficking of narcotics into this country by individuals involved in the contra war.

To summarize: there is concrete evidence that U.S. officials—White House, NSC and CIA—not only knew about and condoned drug smuggling in and around the contra war, but in some cases collaborated with, protected, and even paid known drug smugglers who were deemed important players in the Reagan administrations obsessed covert effort to overthrow the Sandinista government in Nicaragua.

Exactly two years ago this weekend, this issue came up during Oliver North's failed run for Virginia's U.S. Senate seat. *The Washington Post* ran an article which I have included in your packet suggesting that North had failed to give important information on the contras and drugs to the DEA. In response, Mr. North called a press conference where he was joined by Duane Clarridge, the CIA official who ran the contra operations from 1981 through mid 1984, and the former attorney general of the United States, Edwin Meese III. Mr. North called it a "cheap political trick . . . to even suggest that I or anyone in the Reagan administration, in any way, shape or form, ever tolerated the trafficking of illegal substances." Mr. Clarridge claimed that it was a "moral outrage" to suggest that a Reagan Administration official "would have countenanced" drug trafficking. And Mr. Meese stated that no "Reagan administration official would have ever looked the other way at such activity."

The documentation, in which Mr. North, Mr. Clarridge and Mr. Meese all appear, suggests the opposite. Let me review it here briefly:

1. KNOWLEDGE OF DRUG SMUGGLING

Oliver North's own diaries, and internal memoranda written to him from his contra contact, reveal explicit reports of drugs trafficking.

On April 1, 1985, Oliver North was informed by his liaison with the contras, Robert Owen, that two of the commanders chosen by the FDN to run the southern front in Costa Rica were probably, or definitively "involved with drug running."

On July 12, 1985, Oliver North was informed that the contras were considering the purchase of arms from a supplier in Honduras. The $14 million that the supplier had used to finance the guns, "came from drugs."

On August 9, 1985, Oliver North was informed that one of the resupply planes being used by Mario Calero, the brother of the head of the largest contra group the FDN, was "probably being used for drug runs into [the] U.S."

On February 10, 1986, North was informed by his liaison Robert Owen that a plane being used to run materials to the contras was previously used to run drugs, and that the CIA had chosen a company whose officials had a criminal record. The company, Vortex Aviation, was run by Michael Palmer, one of the biggest marijuana smugglers in U.S. history, who was under indictment for ten years of trafficking in Detroit at the same time as he was receiving more than $300,000 in U.S. funds from a State Department contract to ferry "humanitarian" aid to the contras.

In not one of these cases, Congresswoman Millander-McDonald, is there any record of Oliver North passing this important intelligence information onto proper law enforcement or DEA officials. Out of the tens of thousands of documents declassified during the Iran-Contra investigations, there is not a telephone message slip, not a memo, not an e-mail, nor a letter.

We also know that Mr. North, who you remember thought it was a "neat idea" to use the Ayatollah Khomeini's money to fund the contras, was predisposed to use drug monies to fund the contras when they ran short of cash. In 1984, during a drug sting the DEA was attempting against leaders of the Medellin Cartel, he asked two DEA agents if $1.5 million in cartel money aboard an informants plane could be turned over to the contras. The DEA officials just said no.

2. PROTECTION FOR DRUG SMUGGLERS

The case of José Bueso Rosa demonstrates the lengths to which high White House and CIA officials were willing to go to protect an individual who fit the classic definition of a "narco-terrorist." General Bueso Rosa was involved in a conspiracy to import 345 kilos of coke into Florida—street value $40 million. Part of the proceeds were to be used to finance the assassination of the president of Honduras. I think most people in this room would agree that a major cocaine smuggler and would-be international terrorist such as General Bueso Rosa should be locked up for life. But because this general had been the CIA's and the Pentagon's key liaison in Honduras in the covert war against Nicaragua, North, Clarridge, and others in the Reagan administration sought leniency for him. As North put it in an e-mail message U.S. officials "cabal[ed] quietly to look at options: pardon, clemency, deportation, reduced sentence." The objective of our national security managers was not to bring the weight of the law down on General Bueso, but to "keep Bueso from . . . spilling the beans." By the way, he ended up serving less than five years in prison—in a white collar "Club Fed" prison in Florida.

3. COLLABORATION WITH DRUG SMUGGLERS

It is the documentation on U.S. relations with another Latin American general, General Manuel Noriega in Panama, that most clearly demonstrates the shameless attitude of the highest U.S. national security officials toward major drug smuggling into our cities. General Noriega is currently serving 40 years in prison for narcotics trafficking. All of us in this room remember that General Noriega's involvement with the Medellín Cartel was so significant that President Bush ordered the U.S. military to invade Panama to arrest him, at the cost of American lives, Panamanian lives and hundreds of millions of dollars.

The 1989 invasion of Panama was code-named Operation Just Cause. But in 1986, when U.S. officials had the same evidence of Noriega's career as the Cartel's man in Panama, the Reagan administration appeared to have another kind of "Just Cause" with Gen. Noriega.

Shortly after the *New York Times* published a front page story titled "Panama Strongman Said to Trade in Drugs, Arms, and Illicit Money," General Noriega contacted Oliver North with a quid pro quo proposal: help him "clean up his image" and he would have his covert agents undertake major sabotage operations against economic targets inside Nicaragua.

Instead of telling Noriega that he should rot in jail—as most everybody in this room would have done—Oliver North supported this quid pro quo proposal; indeed North even wanted to pay General Noriega one million dollars, yes, one million dollars in money diverted from the sale of arms to Iran, to carry out these sabotage operations (which the contras would have then taken credit for). In one of the most striking, and candid, electronic mail messages ever written inside the White House, North wrote to his superior, National Security Adviser John Poindexter that "You will recall that over the years Manuel Noriega and I have developed a fairly good relationship. . . . The proposal sounds good to me and I believe we could make the appropriate arrangements."

And Admiral Poindexter authorized North to jet off to London to meet secretly with Noriega and work out the details on U.S. help to "clean up his image" and collaboration in the covert war. As Poindexter declared in his electronic response: "I have nothing against Noriega other than his illegal activities."

RECOMMENDATIONS

Representative Millender-McDonald and other members of the panel, this is but some of the documented evidence we have of the attitudes and actions of high U.S. officials toward narcotics trafficking and traffickers during the covert war against Nicaragua. While these records do not address the issue of who knew what, when, here in California, they do demonstrate a rather shocking pattern of government behavior that demands an accounting.

The key question, it seems to me, is how that accounting can, and should take place over both the short and long term future. Allow me to conclude with several brief recommendations:

First, members of Congress should call on the President to authorize his Intelligence Oversight Board to conduct a six-month inquiry into the questions of official knowledge, tolerance, and complicity in drug trafficking during the covert operations against Nicaragua during the 1980s. With all due respect to the inspector general of the Justice Department and the CIA, an internal investigation is not likely to result in the public disclosure of information required to lay this scandal to rest. The Intelligence Oversight Board is a far more independent body, and far more likely to conduct a thorough investigation that can be declassified along with supporting documentation for a public accounting.

Second, while you, and other Representatives patiently wait on CIA director John Deutch to complete his internal review, you should demand that the CIA immediately declassify a previous internal investigation and report that the agency completed in 1988. This report is already known to exonerate the CIA of wrongdoing. But declassifying it, and all the files on which it was built, is likely to give us a far greater sense of CIA awareness of contra/drug operations, and the action or inaction of Agency officials in the face of this awareness over the course of many years. If the CIA doesn't have anything to hide, it should have no problem releasing this documentation. Its refusal to do so up till now, I suggest to you, should set off the alarm bells throughout the halls of Congress.

Third, a number of files should be released by the Justice Department immediately. Those include files that were not turned over to the Senate Subcommittee chaired by John Kerry in 1987 and 1988, particularly the files related to the so-called Frogman case in San Francisco. Similarly the Justice Department should release its never-filed indictment against Norwin Meneses and all of the supporting prosecution files that went into drafting that indictment, as well as all records relating to why that indictment was never filed and is now locked away in a vault in San Francisco.

Fourth, all DEA investigative records on Meneses and Danilo Blandón should be declassified immediately. In the case of Blandón, the DEA must also release the files on his informant status, including documentation on the deliberations to make him a high-paid informant. The U.S. intelligence community just devoted considerable resources to addressing the scandal of the CIA paying a known torturer and assassin in Guatemala as an informant. Having a major California drug dealer on the U.S. payroll as an informant strikes me as demanding at least as equal an accounting.

Finally, let me say that although the National Security Archive takes no position on legislation, I would personally hope that the political and social organization and mobilization that has been generated by public concern and the commitment of individuals like Rep. Millender-McDonald, Rep. Maxine Waters, Senator Barbara Boxer and others, will address the broader debate over the future of covert operations and intelligence reform. When you think about it, all of the CIA's major covert wars—in Indochina, in Afghanistan, and in Central America—have had as their byproducts drug trafficking and addiction. As the issue we are addressing here today suggests, all too often, covert operations conducted against some obscure enemy abroad have returned home to haunt the very people whose security they are ostensibly designed to protect.

This scandal provides an opportunity—and a challenge—for the American public to protect themselves from their protectors so that five, ten, or twenty years from now, we will not be sitting again in this gymnasium attempting to redress future crimes of state.

Thank you.

Source: National Security Archive Electronic Briefing Book No. 2, http://www.gwu.edu/nsarchiv/NSAEBB/NSAEBB2/pktstmny.htm.

Regina Aragón, Jennifer Kates, and Liberty Greene, "Latinos' Views of the HIV/AIDS Epidemic at 20 Years: Findings from a National Survey" (2001)

Latinos in the United States are affected by HIV/AIDS in a greater proportion than their representation in the U.S. population. The rates are the second highest in the nation by race/ethnicity. In 2006, there were approximately 1.2 million people living with HIV/AIDS in the United States, including about 200,000 Latinos. As the largest and fastest-growing ethnic minority group in the United States, the problem will increase. Although Latinos represent approximately 14 percent of the U.S. population they accounted for 19 percent of the AIDS cases diagnosed in 2005. The following report is a major study of the devastating epidemic of HIV in the Latino community, which until recently was ignored.

Latinos, who now comprise the largest and fastest growing ethnic minority in the United States, continue to be disproportionately affected by HIV/AIDS. Although they represent approximately 14% of the U.S. population, Latinos accounted for 19% of new AIDS cases reported in 2000. The AIDS case rate (per 100,000) among Latino adults (30.4) was almost four times that for whites (7.9), and AIDS is now the fourth leading cause of death for Latinos between the ages of 25 and 44. The epidemic's effect on different subgroups of Latinos is also striking. For example, the AIDS case rate among adult Latinas is 13.8 per 100,000, more than six times the rate for white women (2.2). And although Latino youth represent approximately 14% of U.S. teenagers, they accounted for 20% of new AIDS cases reported among those ages 13–19 in 2000. In addition, in a recent study of young men who have sex with men (MSM), HIV prevalence (the proportion of people living with HIV in a population) for young Latinos was 6.9, compared to 3.3 for whites. Finally, there is growing evidence that the HIV/AIDS epidemic is increasingly concentrated in low-income communities in which people of color are often disproportionately represented. Such communities generally are faced with multiple other health and social issues and limited resources with which to respond to the epidemic.

UNDERSTANDING THE VIEWS OF LATINOS

The disproportionate impact of HIV on Latinos, as well as the continued growth of the Latino population in the United States, point to the need to understand their views and knowledge of the epidemic. Such views can play an important role in how community leaders, health officials, and other policymakers target educational information and design programs that best meet the needs of this community.

This report, based on a national survey, examines Latinos' views of HIV/AIDS, including differences between Latino subgroups. Where data are available, analyses of changing attitudes over time are also provided. The survey indicates that Latinos are concerned about the epidemic and that attitudes toward HIV/AIDS vary significantly by race and ethnicity, with Latinos expressing more concern and urgency about the epidemic than the public overall. In addition, views within the Latino population vary significantly by income, education, language, and age. Although the sample size in this survey does not allow for comparisons of views by national background (i.e., Mexicans, Puerto Ricans, Cubans, etc.), such distinctions are also important given the role ethnic identity and culture play in individuals' beliefs and attitudes. . . .

More than one-third of Latinos (37%) say AIDS is a more urgent health problem for their local community today than it was a few years ago. While the proportion of Latinos who believe this to be the case decreased since 1997 (52%), it is still significantly greater than the proportion of whites (18%). Moreover, almost seven in ten (69%) Latinos say AIDS is a serious problem for people they know, including 54% who say it is a "very serious" problem. The proportion saying AIDS is a serious problem for people they know has declined from 76% in 1995 and 81% in 1997. Nearly four in ten (38%) Latinos also say they know someone who has HIV/AIDS or has died of AIDS. Latinos (38%) are as likely as whites (42%), but less likely than African Americans (57%) to report knowing someone who is living with HIV/AIDS or has died of AIDS.

Latinos also express concern about the impact of HIV/AIDS in their own lives, with a majority (53%) saying they are either "somewhat" or "very" personally concerned about becoming infected with HIV. Personal concern among Latinos has fluctuated over the past five years from 51% in

1995 and 64% in 1997. Personal concern among Latinos (53%) is much greater than that expressed by whites (33%), as is concern among African Americans (56%). More than four in ten (43%) Latinos say that their concern has grown in the past few years (compared to 18% of whites and 35% of African Americans). . . .

THE FACTS ABOUT HIV/AIDS

Most Latinos understand that a person can become infected with HIV through unprotected intercourse (98%), sharing an IV needle (96%) and having unprotected oral sex (88%); however, as with the general public, misperceptions about the risk of contracting HIV through casual contact persist. For example, 37% of Latinos say that a person can become infected with HIV through kissing; an additional 8% of Latinos do not know whether or not kissing poses a risk of infection. According to the CDC, casual or close-mouth kissing poses no risk of transmission, and even open-mouth kissing in the absence of open wounds or sores in the mouth is considered a very low-risk activity. Nearly three in ten (29%) Latinos incorrectly believe that touching a toilet seat poses a risk for infection or do not know whether this poses a risk. Among Latinos, men (27%) are twice as likely as women (13%) to believe that a person can become infected this way. One in four (24%) Latinos thinks that sharing a drinking glass used by someone with HIV/AIDS poses a risk for infection or do not know whether this activity poses a risk. In general, Latinos, as well as African Americans, are more likely than whites to say that these activities pose a risk for infection.

Source: "Latinos' Views of the HIV/AIDS Epidemic at 20 Years" (#3184), The Henry J. Kaiser Family Foundation, November 2001, 2, 4 and 8. This information was reprinted with permission from the Henry J. Kaiser Family Foundation. The Kaiser Family Foundation, based in Menlo Park, California, is a nonprofit, private operating foundation focusing on the major health care issues facing the nation and is not associated with Kaiser Permanente or Kaiser Industries. http://www.kff.org/hivaids/3184 index.cfm.

John R. Logan, "The New Latinos: Who They Are, Where They Are" (2001)

The Lewis Mumford Center was established at the University of Albany in 1988 to conduct urban research that is both comparative and historical in scope. John R. Logan, a professor at Brown University, has conducted extensive studies of the 2000 U.S. census through the center. The following excerpts from Logan's report focus on new Latino immigrants—those arriving en masse in the United States since 1980. This is one of the first studies to separate out the groups via the 2000 census. As pointed out in the report, differences in the groups delineate obstacles to their receiving equal protection.

As the Hispanic population in America has grown in the last decade (from 22.4 million to 35.3 million), there has also been a shift in its composition. The fastest growth is not in the traditionally largest Hispanic groups, the ones who arrived earliest in the largest numbers (Mexicans, Puerto Ricans, or Cubans), but among New Latinos—people from the Dominican Republic and a diverse set of countries in Central American (such as El Salvador) and South America (such as Colombia). Based on Census 2000 and related sources, the Mumford Center estimates that the number of New Latinos has more than doubled since 1990, from 3.0 million to 6.1 million.

Cubans are still the third largest single Hispanic group in the United States, at 1.3 million. But there are now nearly as many Dominicans (1.1 million) and Salvadorans (also 1.1 million). There are more New Latinos than Puerto Ricans and Cubans combined, and these new groups are growing much more rapidly.

The New Latinos bring a new level of complexity to the rapidly changing complexion of ethnic America. This report reviews what we now know about this important minority: who they are (in comparison to the better known Hispanic groups) and where they live. For those who wish further information about specific metropolitan regions, population counts are now available through the web page of the Lewis Mumford Center.

WHO ARE THE NEW LATINOS?

An outstanding characteristic of the New Latinos is their diversity. Not only do they come from many different countries. More important is that they have a wide range of social and economic backgrounds, some better prepared for the U.S. labor market than any of the older Hispanic groups, and others much less successful. Our best information about their backgrounds is from the Current Population Survey; in order to maximize the size of the sample on which they are based, our figures here are pooled estimates from the CPS conducted in March 1998 and 2000.

Nativity and year of entry. Puerto Ricans are considered by definition to be born in the United States. The majority of Cubans are foreign-born (68%), though relatively few of those entered the country in the last ten years (27%). They mainly represent a pre-1990 immigration stream. In contrast, only about a third of Mexican Americans (36%) were born abroad, but nearly half of their foreign-born members are recent immigrants (49% in the previous ten years).

The New Latino groups are like Cubans in having a majority of foreign-born, ranging from 63% of Dominicans to over 70% for Central and South Americans. But they are like Mexicans in that they represent the most recent wave of immigration—generally 45–50% of their foreign-born arrived in the last ten years.

Education. Mexicans are the least educated of the older Hispanic groups, with an average education of only 10.2 years (for those aged 25 and above). Puerto Ricans average 11.4 years, and Cubans 11.9 years. The New Latino groups range both below the Mexicans and above the Cubans. Salvadorans and Guatemalans have the least education (below 10 years). But Hispanics from most South American origins are better educated than Cubans, averaging 12.6 years.

Income. Compared to Puerto Ricans and Mexicans, Cubans in the United States have always been regarded as economically quite successful. The mean earnings of employed Cubans are above $13,500, compared to about $10,000 for Puerto Ricans and $8,500 for Mexicans. Only 18% of Cubans fall below the poverty line, compared to 26% of Mexicans and 30% of Puerto Ricans.

Among the New Latinos, Dominicans stand out for their very low income: mean earnings below $8,000 and more than a third in poverty (36%). The major Central American groups are roughly equivalent to Puerto Ricans in average earnings, though they are less likely to fall below the poverty line. On the other hand, Hispanics from South America do considerably better, and on average they earn more and have lower poverty rates than do Cubans.

Unemployment and public assistance. Levels of unemployment among Hispanic groups are generally consistent with what we found to be their average earnings. New Latinos from the Dominican Republic have higher than average unemployment and they are the group most likely to be receiving public assistance (above 8%—in both respects they are less successful than Puerto Ricans). Those from South America have the lowest levels of unemployment and are even less likely than Cubans to receive public assistance. . . .

Counting the New Latinos

The New Latinos are hard to count in Census 2000. Up to now a single "Hispanic question" on the census has served reasonably well to distinguish Hispanics from different national origins. In the last two decennial censuses people who identify as Hispanic were asked to check one of three boxes (Mexican, Puerto Rican, or Cuban), or to write in another Hispanic category. In Census 2000, unlike in Census 1990, no examples of other categories were provided to orient respondents. Probably for this reason an unprecedented number of Hispanics in 2000 gave no information or only a vague identification of themselves (such as "Hispanic" or "Spanish"). These people, **6.2 million or 17.6% of all Hispanics,** have been counted in census reports as "Other Hispanics." This is nearly double the share of Other Hispanics in the 1990 census, and a very large portion of them is New Latinos.

The result is a severe underestimate of the number of New Latinos. National studies that rely solely on the Hispanic origin question of the decennial census find only modest growth for such major sources of Hispanic immigration as El Salvador (+16%) and Colombia (+24%). States and metropolitan areas where New Latinos are particularly concentrated are dramatically affected by this problem. In the State of California, for example, the census estimated the number of Salvadorans in 1990 as 339,000; ten years later the estimate is only 273,000. In Miami the census counted 74,000 Nicaraguans a decade ago, but only 69,000 in 2000. It is implausible that these New Latino groups actually fell in this period of intensified immigration. We conclude that their number has been understated as a result of the large Other Hispanic count in Census 2000.

Another reason to be wary of the Census 2000 estimates is that they diverge so widely from the results of other studies conducted by the Bureau of the Census. . . . The estimates of the number of Central and South Americans are very different in these three sources: 3 million in Census 2000 (which classed 17.6% as Other Hispanic), a million more in the Census 2000 Supplemental Survey conducted at the same time (based on a sample of nearly 700,000 and which classed only 9.6% as Other Hispanic), and almost another million in the March 2000 Current Population Survey (with a sample of about 120,000 and only 6.1% Other Hispanic).

In this report we present improved estimates of the size of New Latino groups, compared to relying solely on the Hispanic origin question in Census 2000. Our procedure uses the Current Population Survey, which has the advantage of being conducted in person or by telephone, as the basis for determining what is the percentage of Hispanics who "really" should be classified as Other Hispanic. We then apply this target to Census 2000 data at the level of census tracts. Where the census has an excessive number of Other Hispanics, we allocate them across specific national origin groups according to a pre-established formula. Details of the procedure for 1990 and 2000 are documented in the Appendix to this report.

New Latinos in the United States, 1990 and 2000

[The Table] provides a detailed breakdown of the Hispanic population at the national level (not including Puerto Rico) in 1990 and 2000. There are very large disparities between these and the Census counts from the Hispanic origin question, especially in 2000.

In absolute numbers, the Mexicans are the group most affected by our reallocation of Other Hispanics, increasing by 2.4 million from the Census count. In proportion to their number, however, it is the New Latinos for whom the figures are most changed. Taken together the Mumford estimates show that New Latinos more than doubled their number, compared to an increase of about a

Table Estimates of the Hispanic Population in the United States, 1990 and 2000

	Mumford Estimates			Census Hispanic Question		
	1990	2000	Growth	1990	2000	Growth
Hispanic total	21,900,089	35,305,818	61%	21,900,089	35,305,818	61%
Mexican	13,576,346	23,060,224	70%	13,393,208	20,640,711	54%
Puerto Rican	2,705,979	3,640,460	35%	2,651,815	3,406,178	28%
Cuban	1,067,416	1,315,346	23%	1,053,197	1,241,685	18%
New Latino groups	3,019,780	6,153,989	104%	2,879,583	3,805,444	32%
Dominican	537,120	1,121,257	109%	520,151	764,945	47%
Central American	1,387,331	2,863,063	106%	1,323,830	1,686,937	27%
Costa Rican		115,672			68,588	
Guatemalan	279,360	627,329	125%	268,779	372,487	39%
Honduran	142,481	362,171	154%	131,066	217,569	66%
Nicaraguan	212,481	294,334	39%	202,658	177,684	–12%
Panamanian	100,841	164,371	63%	92,013	91,723	0%
Salvadoran	583,397	1,117,959	92%	565,081	655,165	16%
Other Central American	68,772	181,228		64,233	103,721	
South American	1,095,329	2,169,669	98%	1,035,602	1,353,562	31%
Argentinian		168,991			100,864	
Bolivian		70,545			42,068	
Chilean		117,698			68,849	
Colombian	399,788	742,406	86%	378,726	470,684	24%
Ecuadorian	199,477	396,400	99%	191,198	260,559	36%
Paraguayan		14,492			8,769	
Peruvian	184,712	381,850	107%	175,035	233,926	34%
Uruguayan		30,010			18,804	
Venezuelan		149,309			91,507	
Other South American	311,353	97,969		290,643	57,532	
Other Hispanic	1,530,568	1,135,799	–26%	1,922,286	6,211,800	223%

third reported by the Census Bureau. We calculate more than 350,000 additional Dominicans and Salvadorans, 270,000 additional Colombians, and 250,000 additional Guatemalans.

- By all estimates, Mexicans are by far the largest Hispanic group, about two-thirds of the total and still growing rapidly. The Mumford count is now over 23 million, an increase of 70% in the last decade.
- Puerto Ricans and Cubans remain the next largest Hispanic groups, but their expansion is now much slower, up 35% and 23% respectively since 1990.

- The largest New Latino groups are Dominicans and Salvadorans, both of whom doubled in the last decade and have now reached over 1.1 million.
- There are now over a half million Colombians (nearly 750,000) and Guatemalans (over 600,000) in this country. And three other groups are quickly approaching the half million mark: Ecuadorians, Peruvians, and Hondurans.

States with the Largest New Latino Populations

There are growing numbers of New Latinos in most states, but about three-quarters of them are found in just five states: New York, California, Florida, New Jersey, and Texas. . . . The Mumford Center webpage provides more detailed breakdowns for all 50 states, including both 1990 and 2000 and both Mumford estimates and counts from the Census Bureau.

- **New York State** has the most New Latinos (close to 1.4 million, up from 800,000 in 1990). About half (650,000) are Dominicans, who have had a noticeable presence in New York City since the 1950s. Close to half a million are various South American countries, a much newer immigrant stream. Puerto Ricans were once the predominant source of Hispanic immigration. Now they account for barely more than a third of the state's Hispanics, and they are outnumbered by New Latinos.
- **California** has almost as many New Latinos as New York (also close to 1.4 million), though they are greatly outnumbered by Mexicans. The largest share—over a million—are from Central America, including especially El Salvador, Guatemala, and Nicaragua.
- **Florida's** Hispanic population is well distributed among many national-origin groups. The Cubans are by far the best known of these at a national level (and they are still the largest, with nearly 900,000 residents statewide). Yet their growth has been slower than other groups, and nearly an equal number now are New Latinos (850,000), weighted toward South American origins. There are also over half a million Puerto Ricans and close to 400,000 Mexicans.
- Because of its proximity to New York, **New Jersey's** Hispanic population might be expected to mirror that of its neighbor. It is similar, in that Puerto Ricans still are about a third of them (385,000). And Puerto Ricans are now outnumbered for the first time by New Latinos (over 500,000). The difference is that a much smaller share in New Jersey is Dominican; about half of the state's New Latinos are from South America.
- Finally, **Texas** now has 400,000 New Latinos, more than doubling since 1990. As is true of California, the largest share is from Central America, especially El Salvador. They are barely noticeable statewide, next to 6 million of Mexican origin. But as will be shown below they are most heavily concentrated in Houston, where they are about a sixth of the Hispanic population. . . .

The New Latino population lives almost entirely within metropolitan regions. . . . Some parts of the country deserve special attention:

- The entire region surrounding **New York City**—including the New York, Nassau-Suffolk, Newark, Jersey City, Bergen-Passaic, and Middlesex-Somerset-Hunterdon metro areas—is the most important focal point for New Latino immigration. The New York PMSA alone has over 1.1 million, and the surrounding and largely suburban metro areas add another half million. Dominicans are about half of these in the New York PMSA. Central Americans (especially Salvadorans) are more than half of the New Latinos in suburban Long Island. In Northern New Jersey, many specific groups are present, but a plurality is South American.
- **Los Angeles-Long Beach** is the center for New Latino immigration in Southern California,

where it has a mostly Central American flavor (300,000 Salvadorans, nearly 200,000 Guatemalans). In nearby metro areas (Riverside-San Bernardino and Orange County) New Latinos are also plentiful, but they tend to be dwarfed by the huge and growing Mexican population.

- In **Miami** and neighboring **Fort Lauderdale** there are about 600,000 New Latinos. They are about evenly split between Central and South Americans in Miami, and more tilted toward South Americans in Fort Lauderdale.
- **Washington, DC** is the next great center for New Latino growth (over 300,000). About two-thirds are Central American (130,000 Salvadorans) and one-third South American.
- Finally, **Houston** has 200,000 New Latinos, of whom the largest share is Salvadoran (90,000).

New Latinos: Present and Future

The scale of immigration from less traditional Hispanic sources brings new and less known groups into the United States. Within ten years, we need to become as aware of Dominicans, Salvadorans, and Colombians—people with very different backgrounds and trajectories—as we are of Puerto Ricans and Cubans.

Because they are so highly concentrated in a few regions, and often in a fairly narrow set of neighborhoods within those regions, each group has special local significance in those places. There are two ways in which accurate knowledge about New Latino groups is most critical.

One is in the realm of political representation. Public officials and leaders of political parties need to be aware of changes in their constituencies. Although political redistricting is not required to take into account the internal composition of the Hispanic population, surely some choices about where to draw lines, whom to support for public office, and what issues to highlight in public policy initiatives will depend on whether the constituency remains more Mexican, Puerto Rican, or Cuban, and to what extent it is becoming Dominican, Salvadoran, or Colombian.

The other is in the provision and targeting of public services. Particularly since so many services are now provided through non-profit organization, often seeking to serve specific ethnic populations, it is important for public officials to know who are the clients in a given locale. Again, whether the client base remains more Mexican, Puerto Rican, or Cuban, and to what extent it is shifting toward one or more of the New Latino groups, should reasonably be expected to affect judgments about how to serve the Hispanic community.

The serious inadequacies of the Hispanic origin question in Census 2000 require that alternative estimates be made available. Undercounted can too easily translate into underserved. The Mumford Center offers one approach. Our procedure makes maximum use of publicly available data, it can be replicated, and it offers usable figures at the level of individual census tracts. We encourage others to assess the plausibility of these estimates and to seek better methods of estimation. In particular, we encourage the Bureau of the Census to use the whole range of data that it has on hand for this purpose. Information from the Supplemental Survey or the long form of Census 2000 on country of birth and ancestry, taken together with the Hispanic origin question, would allow the Bureau to create a new composite variable for a large sample of the population. This new composite variable would provide an excellent estimate of Dominican, Central American, and South American populations for the nation and for many states and large metropolitan regions—clearly better than our adjustment procedure.

Such data would also make possible a substantial refinement of our tract-level estimates. We urge the Bureau to begin consideration of these and other ways in which the resources of the decennial census could be more fully applied to understanding the composition of America's Hispanic population.

Source: Excerpt from Logan, John R. "The New Latinos: Who They Are, Where They Are." 2001. Lewis Mumford Center. http://www.s4.brown.edu/cen2000/HispanicPop/HspReport/MumfordReport.pdf.

Roberto Suro and Audrey Singer, "Latino Growth in Metropolitan America: Changing Patterns, New Locations" (2002)

Since the Ford Foundation funded the University of California at Los Angeles 1960 census study of people of Mexican origin, statistics have become an obsession and an important tool in defining the needs of Latino communities. The Pew Foundation, a public interest charitable fund, established a Hispanic Center housed at the University of Southern California, which generates important data. The Pew Research Center is a self-styled "fact tank" based in Washington, DC, that provides reports on issues, public opinion, and trends in the United States and the world. The Pew Hispanic Center has issued the most important studies on Latinos in the past decade. Its 2002 research showed that there were 10 million second-generation Latinos—29 percent of all Latinos. There were 11 million third-generation Latinos—31 percent of all Latinos. The U.S. Census Bureau projects that by the year 2025, the Latino population will jump from 35 million to 61 million and will make up 18 percent of the total U.S. population. The following excerpt from a Pew Hispanic Center report follows this growth in urban centers.

FINDINGS

An analysis of the U.S. Hispanic population across the 100 largest metropolitan areas finds that:

- **The Hispanic population is growing in most metropolitan areas, but the rate and location of increase varies widely. Four distinct patterns of growth can be discerned.** *Established Latino metros* such as New York, Los Angeles, Miami, and Chicago posted the largest absolute increases in Latinos between 1980 and 2000. However, new *Latino destinations* like Atlanta and Orlando charted the fastest growth rates, despite their historically smaller Hispanic bases. Metros with relatively larger Latino bases, such as Houston, Phoenix, and San Diego, meanwhile, became *fast-growing Latino hubs* during the past 20 years, with population growth averaging 235 percent. *Small Latino places*, such as Baton Rouge, posted much lower absolute and relative growth than the other locales.
- **Fifty-four percent of all U.S. Latinos now reside in the suburbs; the Latino suburban population grew 71 percent in the 1990s.** In 1990, the central-city and suburban Hispanic populations in the 100 largest metros were nearly identical, but during the next decade suburban growth so outpaced central-city growth that by 2000 the suburban Hispanic population exceeded the central-city population by 18 percent. New Latino destinations saw the fastest growth of Latino suburbanites.
- **Hispanic men outnumber Hispanic women by 17 percent in new Latino destination metros where the Latino population grew fastest.** By contrast, in slower growing metros with large and well-established Latino communities, more Hispanics live in family households and gender ratios are more balanced.

Source: Suro, Roberto, and Audrey Singer. *Latino Growth in Metropolitan America: Changing Patterns, New Locations*. Center on Urban & Metropolitan Policy and The Pew Hispanic Center, July 2002.

Rodolfo F. Acuña, "The Inquiring Mind and Miguel Estrada" (2002)

There are differences within the Latino community related to class and, consequently, the interests of the group. For example, some of the exiles who have arrived in the United States since 1980 are middle class and do not understand the civil rights history in this country. Their views differ from those of working-class Latinos. The Puerto Rican community, for instance, is five times as large as the Cuban American community and has a lower median age and income. Mexican and Central Americans have large first-generation groups and a median age of around 25, whereas the median age among Cubans is 40. Moreover, the status of Latinos in Los Angeles and New York differs from that of Miami, where there is still a Cuban American political and social hegemony. Not every Latino supports Cuban American anti-Cuban government politics. And not every Latino supports other Latinos' views of their native countries. What binds them culturally should not necessarily be confused with what binds them politically, where class and race interests are more important than art or music or language. The following article deals with attorney Miguel Estrada (1961–), a Honduran American whom President George W. Bush (1946–) sought to appoint to the 4th Circuit Court of Appeals. The appointment met with strong opposition by progressives and many in the Latino community because of his ultraconservative views and history of supporting right-wing organizations.

The hearings on the nomination of Miguel Estrada, 41, to the Circuit U.S. Court of Appeals, District of Columbia, are nearing a close. But despite the high stakes involved in selecting the wrong person to the federal bench, Latino moderates and liberals have remained quiet, seemingly oblivious to its consequences. A bad appointment would rank on a par with the impending war in the Middle East. Right-wing Latino organizations and Republicans have stepped into the void and accused Democratic members of the Judiciary Committee of racism for preventing a vote on the nomination of Miguel Estrada.

If confirmed, Estrada would be in line for the U.S. Supreme Court, something the Latino community considers a barometer of its political influence. It would follow the historical tradition of the appointment of Jewish, African American, and women justices who were expected to represent more than just their own interests. By raising the race card, conservative forces have made race an issue—which is unfortunate.

In a previous article I posited that Estrada, Honduran-born and raised, could not be called a U.S. Latino if we apply the test of the civil rights movement and ask who is an oppressed minority. I would have to agree with African American Harvard sociologist Orlando Patterson that by stretching the definition of Latino and qualifying anyone with a Spanish surname to entitlements, giving affirmative action a bad name.

In the case of Estrada, he has no record that indicates or suggests that he identifies with the working Latino community. This does not make him a bad person nor is he unique. Many Latin Americans from privileged backgrounds come to the United States and do not understand the civil rights histories of Mexican Americans and Puerto Ricans.

The truth be told, Estrada comes from a privileged background. His family in Honduras did not relate to the issues of working-class Latinos there. Instead of addressing the question of what comes under the definition of a definable or disadvantaged minority, I have received angry letters from Hondurans accusing me of being divisive and even anti-Honduran. These critics suggest that because a person is a Honduran American or a Cuban

American, this automatically makes them Latinos and should be supported by members of that fantasy heritage.

What in fact is divisive is supporting Estrada based on his surname and it has opened this Pandora's box. Does it mean that if Mexican billionaire Carlos Slim, the world's third-richest man, were to take up residence in the United States, he would be a Latino entitled to affirmative action?

Let us not play games; there are millions of upper- and middle-class Latinos who immigrate to this country who, like Estrada, have received good educations in their own country and do not relate to poor immigrants or U.S.-born Latinos. It is easy for them to become Republicans and associate with organizations such as the Federalist Society who pursue right-wing policies that are damaging to Latinos.

Reacting to the claims of Estrada's supporters that he is a Latino Horatio Alger, a Latino who turned adversity into opportunity by going from rags-to-riches, I have delved into his background. He came to this country at 15, and two years after immigrating to the United States, Estrada took the SAT in English and was accepted to Columbia University in New York, from which he graduated magna cum laude. A remarkable feat. More amazing since his supporters infer that he knew no English at the time he immigrated to this country.

What contributed to this phenomenal accomplishment?

Well, these questions have not been asked or answered by the media and the Department of Justice or Estrada's supporters. My independent sources reveal: Estrada's father is a lawyer and owns land in the south of Honduras. He is wealthy but does not appear to be a latifundista. His father does not have a notoriously bad reputation such as links to military or conservative politicians.

Estrada is not a working-class Honduran by any means who through hard work made it in this country. According to a fellow Honduran, Estrada "is a middle- to upper-class Honduran, from urban professional background, and probably was already highly educated before he came here." Given this background, Estrada probably grew up learning English in elite private schools.

These facts would not be important if his supporters had been honest and forthcoming. It is a disservice to many poor immigrant children who have to attend ghetto schools and live below the poverty line to use Estrada as a role model.

Class is the defining factor in academic success in America. Hence it is intellectually dishonest to claim that Bush nominated Estrada solely on his qualifications. George Bush would not have nominated Estrada if he were not a Latino and an ultraconservative.

Further, Estrada is not uniquely qualified. There are literally scores of lawyers who have graduated cum laude from Harvard Law School, and who, unlike Estrada, have published. For example, Clinton nominated Jorge Rangel (Harvard Law Review) from Corpus Christi, Texas, for the Court of Appeals. Rangel was not confirmed. Moreover, there are thousands of Latinos who have graduated from premier law schools; Harvard is not the only good law school in the U.S. So, beyond his law school transcript, what makes Estrada so eminently qualified?

The problem is that because Estrada was never a judge, he lacks a paper trail establishing his views, forcing critics to make assumptions based on what could be called circumstantial evidence. Estrada is known to be a conservative, but he has made few public comments expressing his legal views.

Lacking a public record, his associations take on greater importance. For instance, Estrada is a partner at Gibson, Dunn & Crutcher, a Los Angeles–based law firm that represented President George W. Bush before the Supreme Court during the contested 2000 election. Estrada also worked for then-Solicitor General Kenneth Starr during George W. Bush's father's administration and was a law clerk for Supreme Court Justice Anthony Kennedy. As mentioned, Estrada is a member of the Federalist Society, an ultra conservative group formed at the University of Chicago in 1983 with Antonin Scalia, the future Supreme Court justice, and Robert Bork as faculty advisers.

Because of these associations, members of congress want to take a closer look at the record. Estrada could eventually become a Supreme Court Justice.

So the Senate Judiciary Committee has requested internal memos written by Miguel Estrada from 1992 to 1997 while working in the Office of the Solicitor General, a branch of the Justice Department. This branch is charged with arguing cases before the Supreme Court. Disingenuously the Bush administration has claimed executive privilege and prudence, in other words, Bush claims confidentiality, something denied to former President Bill Clinton.

Given the slimness of Estrada's public record, and the testimony of a former supervisor that Estrada advocates extreme positions that aligned with ideological biases more than Constitutional reasoning, raises a "red flag." What is Bush trying to hide? Since Estrada has never served as a judge on a lower court, the memos would offer an opportunity to see how he would analyze cases as a judge.

Although my own superficial findings did not uncover any connection with the Honduran-Bush Family and the funding and support of the Contras [Nicaraguan counter revolutionaries], it is disconcerting that the media ignored the possibility. The confirmation fight of U.N. ambassador John D. Negroponte, who served as ambassador to Honduras from 1981–85, was sent to the senate at the same time as Estrada's nomination. Given Negroponte's secret arming of Nicaragua's Contra rebels, the CIA-backed Honduran death squad, and the Iran-Contra deal, this should have been an area of inquiry.

It is unfair to the nation and Estrada to leave these issues in the limbo of speculation.

What makes all of this so unpleasant is the silence of Latino civil rights organizations. I would have expected Latino Civil Rights organizations and Latino politicos to be proactive, opposing this nomination until more was known about Estrada. The Hispanic Congressional Caucus has rolled over. The truth be told, the only reason that we are entitled, is that large sectors of our community are poor and oppressed. Our entitlements are not based on our surnames.

Source: Acuña, Rodolfo F. Urban Archives, September 2002, California State University at Northridge.

Ramona Hernández and Francisco L. Rivera-Batiz, "Dominicans in the United States: A Socioeconomic Profile"

(2003)

The Dominican Republic shares the island of Hispaniola with Haiti—the Republic makes up the western half of the island. Puerto Rico is its eastern neighbor. The Dominican Republic has a population of approximately 5.5 million people. Of the 169,147 Dominican-born residents in the United States at the time of the 1980 census, only 6.1 percent had come to the United States before 1960. More than a third came during the political instability of the 1960s; 56 percent arrived in the 1970s. During the 1980s, Dominican immigration soared as more than 250,000 Dominicans were legally admitted to the United States. Although Dominicans are relatively small in numbers in relation to other Latin American nationalities, their numbers are growing, and they are active in profiling their community. The following excerpts are from one of the many self-studies done by that community.

SUMMARY OF FINDING

This research report presents the first detailed study of the socioeconomic status of the Dominican population of the United States. Using information recently provided by the 2000 U.S. Census of Population, the study concludes that:

1. The Dominican population in the United States rose from 520,121 in 1990 to 1,041,910 in 2000, making it the fourth-largest Hispanic/Latino group in the United States, after Mexicans, Puerto Ricans, and Cubans. It is estimated that, at current population growth rates, the Dominican population will overtake the Cuban population before the year 2010, making it the third largest Hispanic/Latino population in the country.
2. The major source of Dominican growth continues to be immigration. Between 1990 and 2000, close to 300,000 Dominicans migrated to the United States on a net basis.
3. Besides substantial immigration, the Dominican population born in the United States rose sharply in the 1990s. There were 394,914 Dominicans born in the U.S. residing in the country in 2000. This constitutes one out of every three Dominicans.
4. The largest concentration of Dominicans continues to be located in the state of New York, but there has been a significant spread to other states in the last decade. The state of New York was host to 617,901 Dominicans in 2000; followed by New Jersey, with 136,529; Florida, with 98,410; Massachusetts, with 69,502; Rhode Island, with 24,588; Pennsylvania (13,667); and Connecticut (12,830). There were also budding Dominican communities in almost every region of the country, from Alaska to Hawaii.
5. New York City continues to dominate the location of Dominicans in the United States. The Dominican population of New York rose from 332,713 to 554,638 between 1990 and 2000. Dominicans are currently the second largest Hispanic/Latino population of New York, following Puerto Ricans. But the Puerto Rican population in the City declined substantially in the last decade. If current population growth trends continue, Dominicans will overtake Puerto Ricans as the largest Hispanic/Latino population of the City within the next ten years.
6. The greatest concentration of Dominicans in New York continues to be in Manhattan, where one out of every three Dominicans in the City resided in 2000. But just as the population has spread throughout the country, Dominican New Yorkers have also spread throughout the City. The Dominican population in the Bronx is now almost as large as that in Manhattan, with 32.7 percent of all Dominicans. There has also been substantial growth in Queens, Brooklyn, and Staten Island.
7. The expanding Dominican population outside New York City has reduced the proportion of Dominicans in the City from 73.4 percent in 1980 to 65.1 percent in 1990 and 53.2 percent in 2000. Following New York City, there are major Dominican populations in the City of Lawrence (Massachusetts), where 22,111 Dominicans reside, the City of Paterson (New Jersey), with 19,977 Dominicans, Providence (Rhode Island), with 19,915 Dominicans, and Boston (Massachusetts), with 19,061 Dominicans. The cities of Jersey City, Passaic, Perth Amboy, and Union City in New Jersey also have substantial Dominican populations, as do the City of Yonkers in New York, and Miami in Florida. Many other cities all over the country have smaller, but rapidly growing Dominican populations.
8. The mean annual per-capita household income of the Dominican population in the United States was $11,065 in the year 1999. This was about half the per-capita income of the average household in the country that year. It was also significantly lower than the per-capita income of the Black/African American population and even slightly lower than the income of the average Latino household.
9. There is substantial variability in the socioeconomic status of Dominicans in various parts of the United States. Among the most

populous states, Dominicans in Florida had the highest per-capita household income, equal to $12,886 in the year 1999. By contrast, Dominicans in Rhode Island had the lowest average per-capita income, equal to $8,560 in the year 1999.

10. In New York City, the average per-capita income of Dominicans was below the average for the United States. The poverty rate of 32 percent among Dominican New Yorkers was the highest of the major racial and ethnic groups in New York. The overall poverty rate in New York in 1999 was 19.1 percent, while it was 29.7 percent for the overall Hispanic/Latino population.
11. A high proportion of Dominican families in poverty consist of female-headed families, with no spouse present. In 2000, as much as 38.2 percent of Dominicans in New York lived in this type of family, compared to 22.1 percent for the overall City. Close to half of Dominican female-headed families in New York City were poor, more than twice the poverty rate for other households.
12. Despite the low relative socioeconomic status of Dominicans in New York City, their income displayed significant growth in the 1990s, rising by close to 16 percent in the decade (adjusted for inflation). The overall increase of per-capita income in the City in the decade was 9.2 percent, but both the Black/African American population and the overall Hispanic/Latino population in the City had lower income growth rates. The White population in the City displayed a growth of over 20 percent in per-capita income.
13. The labor force participation rate of Dominicans is lower than that for the rest of the population. In 2000, it was approximately 64 percent for men and 53.1 percent for women. The figures for the overall U.S. workforce are 72.7 percent and 58.5 percent, for men and women, respectively.
14. The unemployment rate of Dominican women and men in 2000 greatly exceeded that of the overall labor force in the United States. In 2000, Dominican men had an unemployment rate of 7.8 percent, compared to an overall unemployment rate of 3.9 percent for men in the country. Among women, the Dominican unemployment rate was 10.7 percent in 2000, compared to 4.1 percent in the country overall.
15. Despite the comparatively high unemployment rates of Dominicans, these rates declined sharply between 1990 and 2000. In New York City, for instance, the male and female unemployment rates among Dominicans were 15.7 percent and 18.4 percent, respectively, in 1990. These dropped to 8.9 percent and 13.1 percent by 2000.
16. The comparatively high unemployment rates of Dominicans in New York City are connected to a painful long-term switch in the employment of the Dominican labor force from manufacturing to other sectors. In 1980, close to half of the Dominican workforce was employed in manufacturing. This declined to 25.7 percent in 1990 and to 12.4 percent in 2000.
17. The Dominican labor force is very young and mostly unskilled. Only 17.3 percent of Dominicans in the United States have managerial, professional, and technical occupations, about half the proportion for the overall United States. As a result, the average earnings of Dominican men and women are substantially lower than those of other workers in the nation.
18. The overall educational attainment of Dominicans in the United States is among the lowest in the country. In 2000, 49 percent of Dominicans 25 years of age or older had not completed high school and only 10.6 percent had completed college. By contrast, less than 20 percent of the American population had not completed high school in 2000, and 24.4 percent had finished college.
19. But the educational situation of Dominicans varies enormously when decomposed by immigrant status. Although the educational attainment of Dominican immigrants is very low, the situation for U.S.-born Dominicans is sharply different.

20. The Dominican second-generation in the United States has educational indicators that suggest a remarkable acquisition of human capital over the last 20 years. This differs from the overall situation of U.S.-born Hispanics/Latinos, whose educational indicators are substantially worse than those for Dominicans. In 2000, close to 60 percent of all Dominicans born in the United States with 25 years of age or older had received some college education, with 21.9 percent completing a college education. By contrast, among U.S.-born Mexicans, only 13.3 percent had completed college, and 12.1 percent of U.S.-born Puerto Ricans had finished college.
21. The explosive increase of the educational attainment of U.S.-born Dominicans is reflected in the experience of Dominican New Yorkers. For U.S.-born Dominicans in New York, the proportion who attained some college education rose from 31.7 percent in 1980 to 42.8 percent in 1990, and to 55.1 percent in 2000.
22. Dominicans have school enrollment rates that are higher than those for other minority groups. In New York City, Dominican high school retention rates are substantially higher than for the overall Hispanic/Latino population, and for women, they approach the average New York City high school retention rate.
23. There were 111,553 Dominican children enrolled in the New York City public school system. This constitutes 10.4 percent of the New York City school student body in 2000. Among public college students in New York City, 8.5 percent are Dominicans, exceeding the proportion among Puerto Ricans, which was 7.7 percent in 2000.

This report presents a mixed picture of the Dominican population of the United States. On the one hand, Dominicans have among the lowest per-capita income in the country, comparatively low labor force participation rates, high unemployment rates, and low earnings. On the other hand, Dominican income and employment indicators did improve significantly in the 1990s, and the Dominican second-generation appears to be accumulating vast amounts of human capital, increasing its educational attainment very rapidly. Therefore, despite facing considerable challenges in its remarkable growth during the last twenty years, the prospects for the future look bright for Dominicans in the U.S.

Source: Hernández, Ramona, and Francisco L. Rivera-Batiz. *Dominicans in the United States: A Socioeconomic Profile 2000.* Dominican Research Monographs, Dominican Studies Institute, City College, City University of New York, November 2003.

Council on Hemispheric Affairs, "Guatemala's Cursed Armed Forces: Washington's Old Friend Is Back in Town"

(March 16, 2006)

Guatemala, a country of 10 million people, is the largest Central American nation. Sixty percent of Guatemala's population is Mayan Indians. From the Spanish colonial period, Guatemala has been a leader in the region. In the 20th century, American corporations, such as the United Fruit Company, invested heavily in the country, and thus Guatemala suffered from U.S. involvement and U.S.

support of military regimes. For the past 30 years, the Guatemalan military has brutally suppressed popular movements among the indigenous people resulting in the deaths of more than 150,000 people. Much of the U.S. support for the Guatemalan military has come under the guise of the war on drugs. The following is a report by the Council on Hemispheric Affairs, an independent, nonprofit, nonpartisan, tax-exempt research and information organization that has been in existence since 1975. The state of Guatemala is important because political instability is a major factor in sending immigrants to the United States. According to the 1990 census, of the 268,779 Guatemalans in the United States, 225,739 were foreign-born. In 2000, there were 463,502 Guatemalans. Migration does not happen by accident.

One can be forgiven for arguing that Defense Secretary Donald Rumsfeld, who demonstrably is losing the war in Iraq, is now trying to achieve an easy win in Latin America, where he is presiding over the rehabilitation of what he sees as the Latin American military's sense of honor. But the murderous reputation of that institution was established not due to invention or superficial judgment, but because of the fact that during the 1970s and 1980s, tens of thousands of innocent civilians were tortured and murdered throughout the region at the hands of local armed forces.

Under such conditions, restoring one's good name is no easy task. But due to Rumsfeld's spirit of generosity, all has been forgiven at the Pentagon. At the cost of tens of millions of dollars, it has been staging periodic ministerial meetings with Rumsfeld's counterparts from throughout the hemisphere since 1995, as well as funding the successor to the infamous School of the Americas at Fort Benning. Furthermore, the Secretary of Defense has made an on-site visit to seemingly obscure Paraguay, ostensibly to thank the local leaders for the possible U.S. usage of the Mariscal Estigarribia airstrip, and for allowing U.S. national guardsmen to rotate into the country. In addition, Rumsfeld has facilitated the sale of F-16 fighter jets to Chile, the major military sale from the U.S. to Chile since the end of the Pinochet era, in a deal first arranged by Lockheed lobbyist Otto Reich, and which could ultimately spark an open arms race between Chile and hostile neighboring countries like Peru, Bolivia, and Argentina.

Guatemala's newly appointed defense minister, General Francisco Bermudez, is currently in Washington D.C., for a four-day visit that began on March 13. On his agenda is an appointment with the Secretary of Defense. In that meeting, Rumsfeld is expected to address the matter of a renewal of U.S. military aid to Guatemala, and possibly the construction of a DEA [Drug Enforcement Administration] base in the Guatemalan rainforest to help combat drug trafficking in Central America. The relatively high visibility of Bermudez' visit is not adventitious, but represents a long-standing Rumsfeld policy of upgrading ties with some of Latin America's most reprehensible and unsavory military establishments, who during the 1970s and 1980s savaged their nations' constitutions and citizenry, including in Chile, Argentina, El Salvador, and, perhaps most of all, Guatemala.

The Guatemalan Military: *Presente*

Bermudez's visit comes as a follow-up to last October's defense conference, "Security and Economic Opportunity," which took place in Key Biscayne, Florida. At that reunion, Rumsfeld met with Central American defense ministers and representatives from different branches of the region's armed forces. It was during this gathering that the then-Guatemalan defense minister, General Carlos Aldana, called for the creation of a Central America peacekeeping force, which putatively would promote political stability, as well as provide emergency relief to civilians after natural disasters such as hurricanes. Secretary Rumsfeld said the talks were a "unique moment in the Americas." But, what Rumsfeld didn't say out loud, was that by attempting to revive the Latin American military, he could be putting to risk the very civil governance whose creation is at the heart of what he says is his Iraq policy.

It was ironic to hear Guatemalan military officers discussing political stability. The armed forces of that Central American nation have long had a reputation for their covert behavior and unqualified brutality, whether they were overthrowing de facto governments almost at will, setting up infamous death squads, staging massacres of indigenous communities in Guatemala's highlands in their "beans and bullets" crusade, and torturing tens of thousands of civilian victims. Dating back to 1960, it is estimated that almost 200,000 civilians have been put to the sword by the Guatemala military, as part of Washington's "Cold War"–abetted national security hemispheric policy. The country's 1960–1996 civil war, which featured unspeakable cruelty, has been sometimes referred to as the "silent Holocaust," for its mindless slaughter. Unfortunately, the end of military rule and civil war did not bring about a new era featuring highly professional, law-abiding, loyal-to-the-nation armed forces. Nor has the Guatemalan government had the temerity to implement some of the most important of the requirements listed by the country's "Truth Commission" in 1999. Despite the Guatemalan military's notorious reputation for drug trafficking, contrabanding, and harsh treatment of the indigenous population, the U.S. is once again involving itself in the internal affairs of the country, extending a growing amount of military aid in exchange for the country's participation in the "war against drugs." In that war, Washington's best friend in Central America is the Guatemalan military, closely followed by the Salvadoran and Honduran armed forces. Ironically, the DEA will remind you that in recent years, the Guatemalan military—particularly its G-2, was the prime drug trafficking cartel in the country.

Washington's Drug Strategy

At the same time, the *Boston Globe*'s Indira Lakshmanan ("Cocaine's New Route," November 30, 2005), cited interviews with senior Guatemalan officials who said that they would ask for stepped-up U.S. military cooperation and a permanent DEA base in the country's dense jungle bordering Mexico. This will not make Mexico City, nor that country's military, particularly happy in having the U.S. as its neighbor, not once, but twice. Such activities could also mark a return to the early 1990s, when the DEA had a fleet of helicopters stationed in Guatemala for purposes of surveillance and interdiction. Since then, "enforcement efforts have shifted to other areas," leaving a dearth of resources for enforcement in Central America. This was revealed by DEA director of operations Michael Braun, in his November 9 testimony before a Congressional subcommittee. The *Boston Globe* article also mentions that Guatemalan convictions of traffickers, whether private citizens or officials, are rare. None of the 16 alleged Guatemalan traffickers wanted in the United States have been extradited in the last dozen years since warrants against them were issued, allegedly because of delays in that country's judicial process, noted Michael P. O'Brien, the DEA's representative in Guatemala.

The most striking example of this new counter-drug relationship occurred last year, when Rumsfeld declared that the U.S. will lift its ban on military aid to that country's armed forces. In March 2005, Washington gave $3.2 million to initiate a modernization process of Guatemala's military capacities. Assistance had been withdrawn in 1990, after it was learned that Guatemalan military forces had been involved in the killing of U.S. citizen Michael Devine. Rumsfeld's repeated expressions of concern for Americans fighting in Iraq apparently doesn't easily transfer to the fate of U.S. nationals Michael Devine in Guatemala or Lori Berenson in Peru. The alleged murderer of Devine, in fact, was Col. Julio Roberto Alpirez, who attended the School of the Americas and was reportedly on the CIA's payroll for many years. While the case remains unsolved, the Bush administration has apparently decided to overlook this, as well as the cold-blooded murder of tens of thousands of Guatemalans during the civil war, in favor of more pressing issues like the war on drugs and Washington's need to erect a thin line of allies to fend off the seepage of the "pink tide" to the north.

Military vs. The World

Washington was very active in creating the monster that is the Guatemalan military and which terrorized the country during the 1960–1996 Guatemalan conflict. It is ironic, but not entirely surprising, that the U.S.—which has always been fully knowledgeable regarding the face of the Guatemalan beast—now praises the country's ersatz democracy and begins anew to pour money into its corrupt leadership, this time with the help of the newly authorized Millennium Account, which is the White House's new slush fund to fund pro-U.S. personalities and projects throughout Latin America. This is a way to tell President [Oscar] Berger (1946–) "thank you" for his support on issues like CAFTA [Central American Free Trade Agreement]-DR.

Guatemalans deserve a military that they can be proud of, but that does not seem likely to be a fact of life in the immediate future. At best, they will have to wait another generation, when a new group of military officers come to power, who might just be disgusted enough with what their predecessors have done to bring the desperately needed positive change to their pariah institution.

Source: Council on Hemispheric Affairs. "Guatemala's Cursed Armed Forces: Washington's Old Friend Is Back in Town." March 16, 2006. http://www.coha.org/2006/03/16/guatemala%e2%80%99s-cursed-armed-forces-washington%e2%80%99s-old-friend-is-back-in-town.

Chicanas/Chicanos and Mexican Americans in Contemporary Society

Summary of the Immigration Reform and Control Act (Simpson-Mazzoli Act) (1986)

The 1965 Immigration and Nationality Act was a defeat for nativists committed to the ideals of national origins, that is, strict quotas for immigrants from—according to restrictionists—the least desirable nationalities. It kept Third World immigrants, with the exception of Latin Americans, out of the country. But the act was only a partial loss for nativists because, for the first time, Latin American immigrants were put on a quota. As nonwhite immigrants poured into the country beginning in the 1970s, nativists sent up an alarm and pressured politicos to pass anti-immigration laws. The most obvious immigrant was the Mexican, as undocumented immigration from Mexico had accelerated in the 1970s. By the mid-1980s, the nativists gathered momentum as right-wing think-tank foundations married this issue with campaigns against bilingual education, English only, and affirmative action. These nativist forces made immigration restriction a political wedge issue. In Congress, legislators such as Republican senator Alan Simpson of Wyoming and Democratic congressman Peter Rodino of New Jersey sponsored nativist bills in their respective chambers. In 1986, Democratic congressman Romano Mazzoli of Kentucky had replaced Rodino in the House of Representative as cosponsor, and the Simpson-Mazzoli Act, also known as the Immigration Reform and Control Act, passed amendments to the Immigration and Nationality Act of 1952. Anti-immigrant forces won: those knowingly employing undocumented workers would face financial and other penalties, and additional funds would be used for border patrol. The law also provided amnesty for undocumented residents who had been in the country for a certain period of time. The following excerpts are from that important law, which gave documents to 2.7 million immigrants.

SUMMARY AS OF:

10/14/1986—Conference report filed in House. (There are 4 other summaries)

(Conference report filed in House, H. Rept. 99–1000)

Immigration Reform and Control Act of 1986

Title I: Control of Illegal Immigration—Part A: Employment—Amends the Immigration and Nationality Act to make it unlawful for a person or other entity to: (1) hire (including through subcontractors), recruit, or refer for a fee for U.S. employment any alien knowing that such person is unauthorized to work, or any person without verifying his or her work status; or (2) continue to employ an alien knowing of such person's unauthorized work status.

Makes verification compliance (including the use of State employment agency documentation) an affirmative defense to any hiring or referral violation.

Establishes an employment verification system. Requires: (1) the employer to attest, on a form developed by the Attorney General, that the employee's work status has been verified by examination of a passport, birth certificate, social security card, alien documentation papers, or other proof; (2) the worker to similarly attest that he or she is a U.S. citizen or national, or authorized alien; and (3) the employer to keep such records for three years in the case of referral or recruitment, or the later of three years or one year after employment termination in the case of hiring.

States that nothing in this Act shall be construed to authorize a national identity card or system.

Directs the President to monitor and evaluate the verification system and implement changes as necessary within 60 days after notifying the appropriate congressional committees (within two years for a major change). Prohibits implementation of a major change unless the Congress provides funds for such purpose. Authorizes related demonstration projects of up to three years.

Limits the use of such verification system or any required identification document to enforcing this Act and not for other law enforcement purposes.

Directs the Attorney General to establish complaint and investigation procedures which shall provide for: (1) individuals and entities to file written, signed complaints regarding potential hiring violations; (2) INS investigations of complaints with substantial probability of validity; (3) Department of Justice–initiated investigations; and (4) designation of a specific INS unit to prosecute such violations.

Sets forth employer sanction provisions. Provides for a six-month period of public education during which no employment violation penalties shall be imposed.

Provides for a subsequent 12-month period during which violators shall be issued warning citations. Defers enforcement for seasonal agricultural services.

Provides, at the end of such citation period, for graduated first- and subsequent-offense civil penalties, injunctive remedies, or criminal penalties (for pattern of practice violations). Subjects violators to graduated civil penalties for related paperwork violations.

Directs the Attorney General to provide notice and, upon request, an administrative hearing in the case of a disputed penalty. States that: (1) judicial review of a final administrative penalty shall be in the U.S. court of appeals; and (2) suits to collect unpaid penalties shall be filed in U.S. district courts.

Makes it unlawful for an employer to require an employee to provide any type of financial guarantee or indemnity against any potential employment liability. Subjects violators, after notice and hearing opportunity, to a civil penalty for each violation and the return of any such amounts received.

States that such employer sanction provisions preempt State and local laws.

Requires the General Accounting Office (GAO) to submit to the Congress and to a specially created task force three annual reports regarding the operation of the employer sanction program, including a determination of whether a pattern of national origin discrimination has resulted. States that if the GAO report makes such a determination: (1) the task force shall so report to the Congress; and (2) the House and the Senate shall hold hearings within 60 days.

Terminates employer sanctions 30 days after receipt of the last GAO report if: (1) GAO finds a widespread pattern of discrimination has resulted from the employer sanctions; and (2) the Congress enacts a joint resolution within such 30-day period approving such findings.

Amends the Migrant and Seasonal Agricultural Worker Protection Act to subject farm labor contractors to the requirements of this Act, beginning seven months after enactment.

Directs the Attorney General, in consultation with the Secretary of Labor and the Secretary of Health and Human Services, to conduct a study of the use of a telephone system to verify the employment status of job applicants. Requires related congressional reports.

Directs the Comptroller General to: (1) investigate ways to reduce counterfeiting of social security account number cards; and (2) report to the appropriate congressional committees within one year.

Directs the Secretary of Health and Human Services, acting through the Social Security Administration and in cooperation with the Attorney General and the Secretary of Labor, to: (1) conduct a study of the feasibility of establishing a social security number validation system; and (2) report to the appropriate congressional committees within two years.

Makes it an unfair immigration-related employment practice for an employer of three or more persons to discriminate against any individual (other than an unauthorized alien) with respect to hiring, recruitment, firing, or referral for fee, because of such individual's origin or citizenship (or intended citizenship) status. States that it is not an unfair immigration-related employment practice to hire a U.S. citizen or national over an equally qualified alien.

Requires that complaints of violations of an immigration-related employment practice be filed with the Special Counsel for Immigration-Related Unfair Employment Practices (established by this Act) within the Department of Justice. Prohibits the overlap of immigration-related discrimination complaints and discrimination complaints filed with the Equal Employment Opportunity Commission.

Authorizes the Special Counsel to: (1) investigate complaints and determine (within 120 days) whether to bring such complaints before a specially trained administrative law judge; and (2) initiate investigations and complaints. Permits private actions if the Special Counsel does not file a complaint within such 120-day period. Sets forth related administrative provisions.

Makes it illegal to fraudulently misuse or manufacture entry or work documents.

Part B: Improvement of Enforcement and Services—States that essential elements of the immigration control and reform program established by this Act are increased enforcement and administrative activities of the Border Patrol, the Immigration and Naturalization Service (INS), and other appropriate Federal agencies.

Authorizes increased FY [fiscal year] 1987 and 1988 appropriations for: (1) INS; and (2) the Executive Office of Immigration Review. Obligates increased funding in FY 1987 and 1988 for the border patrol.

Directs the Attorney General, from funds appropriated to the Department of Justice for INS, to provide for improved immigration and naturalization services and for enhanced community outreach and in-service personnel training.

Authorizes additional appropriations for wage and hour enforcement.

Revises the criminal penalties for the unlawful transportation of unauthorized aliens into the United States.

Authorizes a $35,000,000 immigration emergency fund to be established in the Treasury for necessary enforcement activities and related State and local reimbursements.

Permits the owner or operator of a railroad line, international bridge, or toll road to request the Attorney General to inspect and approve measures taken to prevent aliens from illegally crossing into the United States. States that such approved measures shall be prima facie evidence of compliance with obligations under such Act to prevent illegal entries.

Expresses the sense of the Congress that the immigration laws of the United States should be vigorously enforced, while taking care to protect the rights and safety of U.S. citizens and aliens.

Requires INS to have an owner's consent or a warrant before entering a farm or outdoor operations to interrogate persons to determine if undocumented aliens are present.

Prohibits the adjustment of status to permanent resident for violators of (nonimmigrant) visa terms.

Title II: Legalization—Directs the Attorney General to adjust to temporary resident status those aliens who: (1) apply within 18 months; (2) establish that they entered the United States before January 1, 1982, and have resided here continuously in an unlawful status (including Cuban/Haitian entrants) since such date; and (3) are otherwise admissible.

Authorizes similar status adjustment for specified aliens who entered legally as nonimmigrants but whose period of authorized stay ended before January 1, 1982. (States that in the case of exchange visitors, the two-year foreign residence requirement must have been met or waived.)

Prohibits the legalization of persons: (1) convicted of a felony or three or more misdemeanors in the United States; or (2) who have taken part in political, religious, or racial persecution. Requires an alien applying for temporary resident status to register under the Military Selective Service Act, if such Act so requires.

Directs the Attorney General to adjust the status of temporary resident aliens to permanent resident if the alien: (1) applies during the one-year period beginning with the 19th month following the grant of temporary resident status; (2) has established continuous residence in the United States since the grant of temporary resident status; (3) is otherwise admissible and has not been convicted of a felony or three or more misdemeanors committed in the United States; and (4) either meets the minimum requirements for an understanding of English and a knowledge of American history and government, or demonstrates the satisfactory pursuit of a course of study in these subjects. (Authorizes an exemption from such language and history requirement for individuals 65 years of age or older.)

Specifies circumstances in which the Attorney General may terminate an alien's temporary resident status. Permits travel abroad and employment during such period.

Authorizes the filing of status adjustment applications with the Attorney General or designated voluntary or governmental agencies. Directs the Attorney General to work with such agencies to: (1) disseminate program information; and (2) process aliens. Provides for the confidential treatment of application records. Establishes criminal penalties (fines, imprisonment, or both) for: (1) violations of such confidentiality; and (2) false application statements. Provides for application fees.

Waives numerical limitations, labor certification, and other specified entry violations for such aliens. Permits the Attorney General to waive other grounds for exclusion (except criminal, most drug-related, and security grounds) to assure family unity or when otherwise in the national interest.

Requires the Attorney General to provide an alien otherwise eligible but unregistered who is apprehended before the end of the application period, an opportunity to apply for the legalization program before deportation or exclusion proceedings are begun. States that such alien shall be authorized to work in the United States pending disposition of the case.

Provides for administrative and judicial review of a determination respecting an application for adjustment of status under this Act.

Makes legalized aliens (other than Cuban/Haitian entrants) ineligible for Federal financial assistance, Medicaid (with certain exceptions), or food stamps for five years following a grant of temporary resident status and for five years following a grant of permanent resident status (permits aid to the aged, blind, or disabled). States that programs authorized under the National School Lunch Act, the Child Nutrition Act of 1966, the Vocational Education Act of 1963, chapter 1 of the Education Consolidation and Improvement Act of 1981, the Headstart-Follow Through Act, the Job Training Partnership Act, title IV of the Higher Education

Act of 1965, the Public Health Service Act, and titles V, XVI, and XX of the Social Security Act shall not be construed as prohibited assistance. Continues assistance to aliens under the Refugee Education Assistance Act of 1980 without regard to adjustment of status.

Requires the Attorney General to disseminate information regarding the legalization program.

Establishes procedures for the status adjustment to permanent resident of certain Cuban and Haitian entrants who arrived in the United States before January 1, 1982.

Updates from June 30, 1948, to January 1, 1972, the registry date for permanent entry admissions records.

Authorizes FY 1988 through 1991 appropriations for State legalization impact assistance grants. Permits States to spend unused funds through FY 1994. Prohibits offsets for Medicaid and supplemental security income costs. Bases State amounts on the number of legalized aliens and related expenditures. Permits States to use such funds to reimburse public assistance, health, and education costs. Limits reimbursement to actual costs.

Title III: Reform of Legal Immigration—Part A: Temporary Agricultural Workers—Separates temporary agricultural labor from other temporary labor for purposes of nonimmigrant (H-2A visa) worker provisions.

Requires an employer H-2A visa petition to certify that: (1) there are not enough local U.S. workers for the job; and (2) similarly employed U.S. workers' wages and working conditions will not be adversely affected. Authorizes the Secretary of Labor to charge application fees.

Prohibits the Secretary from approving such petition if: (1) the job is open because of a strike or lock-out; (2) the employer violated temporary worker admissions terms; (3) in a case where such workers are not covered by State workers' compensation laws, the employer has not provided equivalent protection at no cost to such workers; or (4) the employer has not made regional recruitment efforts in the traditional or expected labor supply.

Provides with regard to agricultural worker applications that: (1) the Secretary may not require such an application to be filed more than 60 days before needed; (2) the employer shall be notified in writing within seven days if the application requires perfecting; (3) the Secretary shall approve an acceptable application not later than 20 days before needed; and (4) the employer shall provide or secure housing meeting appropriate Federal, State, or local standards, including making provision for family housing for employees principally engaged in the range production of livestock.

Provides that for three years, labor certifications for specified employers shall require such an employer to hire qualified U.S. workers who apply until the end of 50 percent of the H-2A workers' contract work period. Requires the Secretary, six months before the end of such period, to consider the advisability of continuing such requirement and to issue regulations (in the absence of enacting legislation) three months before the end of such period.

States that employers shall not be liable for specified employment penalties if H-2A workers are dismissed in order to meet such 50 percent requirement.

Permits agricultural producer associations to file H-2A petitions.

Provides for expedited administrative appeals of denied certifications.

Prohibits the entry of an alien as an H-2A worker if he or she has violated a term of admission within the previous five years.

Authorizes permanent appropriations beginning with FY 1987 for the purposes of: (1) recruiting domestic workers for temporary labor and services which might otherwise be performed by nonimmigrants and agricultural transition workers; and (2) monitoring terms and conditions under which such individuals are employed.

Authorizes permanent appropriations beginning in FY 1987 to enable the Secretary to make determinations and certifications.

Expresses the sense of the Congress that the President should establish an advisory commission to consult with Mexico and other appropriate countries and advise the Attorney General regarding the temporary worker program.

Establishes a special agricultural worker adjustment program. Provides for permanent resident adjustment for aliens who: (1) apply during a specified 18-month period; (2) have performed at least 90 man-days of seasonal agricultural work during the 12-month period ending May 1, 1986; and (3) are admissible as immigrants. Sets forth adjustment dates based upon periods of work performed in the United States. Authorizes travel and employment during such temporary residence period.

Authorizes applications to be made inside the United States with the Attorney General or designated entities and outside the United States through consular offices. Provides for confidentiality and limited access to such information. Establishes criminal penalties for false application information, and makes an alien so convicted inadmissible for U.S. entry.

Exempts such admissions from numerical entry limitations.

Permits waiver of exclusion (except for specified criminal, drug offense, public charge, Nazi persecution, and national security grounds) for humanitarian or family purposes, or when in the national interest.

Provides for a temporary stay of exclusion or deportation (and authority to work) for apprehended aliens who are able to establish a nonfrivolous claim for status adjustment.

Provides for a single level of administrative appellate review of such status adjustment applications. Limits such review of the order of exclusion or deportation.

Defines "seasonal agricultural services" as the performance of fieldwork related to growing fruits and vegetables of every kind and other perishable commodities as defined in regulations by the Secretary of Agriculture.

Directs the Secretaries of Agriculture and of Labor, jointly before each fiscal year (beginning in FY 1990 and ending in FY 1993) to determine whether additional special agricultural workers should be admitted because of a shortage of such workers in the United States. Sets forth factors to be considered in making such determinations.

Authorizes associations and groups of employers to request additional admissions due to emergency or unforeseen circumstances. Authorizes groups of special agricultural workers to request decreased admissions due to worker oversupply. Requires the Secretaries to make request determinations within 21 days.

Sets forth numerical limitations for such admissions beginning with FY 1990.

Provides for the deportation of newly admitted special agricultural workers who do not perform 60 man-days of seasonal agricultural work in each of the first two years after entry. Prohibits naturalization of such workers unless they have performed 60 man-days of such work in each of five fiscal years.

Treats temporary agricultural workers and special agricultural workers as "eligible legalized aliens" for purposes of Federal assistance to State and local entities for specified costs associated with such workers during their first five years in the United States.

Establishes a 12-member Commission on Agricultural Workers to review the special agricultural worker provisions, the impact of the legalization and employer sanctions on agricultural labor, and other aspects of agricultural labor. Requires a report to the Congress within five years. Authorizes appropriations. Terminates the Commission at the end of the 63-month period beginning with the month after the month of enactment of this Act.

States that specified agricultural workers shall be eligible for legal assistance under the Legal Service Corporation Act.

Part B: Other Changes in the Immigration Law—Increases the annual colonial quota from 600 visas to 5,000 visas.

Includes within the definition of "special immigrant": (1) unmarried sons and daughters and surviving spouses of employees of certain international organizations; and (2) specified retirees of such organizations ("I" status) and their spouses.

Grants nonimmigrant status to: (1) parents of children receiving "I" status while they are minors; and (2) other children of such parents or a surviving "I" status spouse.

Authorizes the three-year pilot visa waiver program for up to eight countries providing similar benefits to U.S. visitors. Requires such visitors to the United States to: (1) have a nonrefundable roundtrip ticket; and (2) stay in the United States for not more than 90 days.

Authorizes an additional 5,000 nonpreference visas in each of FY 1987 and 1988 with preference being given to nationals of countries who were adversely affected by Public Law 89–236 (1965 immigration amendments).

Includes the relationship between an illegitimate child and its natural father within the definition of "child" for purposes of status, benefits, or privilege under such Act.

States that for suspension of deportation purposes, an alien shall not be considered to have failed to maintain continuous physical presence in the United States if the absence did not meaningfully interrupt the continuous physical presence.

Prohibits for one year the admission of nonimmigrant alien crew members to perform services during a strike against the employer for whom such aliens intend to work.

Title IV: Reports—Directs the President to transmit to the Congress: (1) not later than January 1, 1989, and not later than January 1 of every third year thereafter, a comprehensive immigration-impact report; and (2) annual reports for three years on unauthorized alien employment and the temporary agricultural worker (H-2A) program.

Directs the Attorney General and the Secretary of State to jointly monitor the visa waiver program established by this Act, and report to the Congress within two years.

Directs the President to submit to the Congress an initial and a second report (three years after the first report) on the impact of the legalization program.

Directs the Attorney General to report to the Congress within 90 days regarding necessary improvements for INS.

Expresses the sense of the Congress that the President should consult with the President of Mexico within 90 days regarding the implementation of this Act and its possible effect on the United States or Mexico.

Title V: State Assistance for Incarceration Costs of Illegal Aliens and Certain Cuban Nationals—Directs the Attorney General to reimburse States for the costs incurred in incarcerating certain illegal aliens and Cuban nationals convicted of felonies. Authorizes appropriations.

Title VI: Commission for the Study of International Migration and Cooperative Economic Development—Establishes a 12-member Commission for the Study of International Migration and Cooperative Economic Development to examine, in consultation with Mexico and other Western Hemisphere sending countries, conditions which contribute to unauthorized migration to the United States and trade and investment programs to alleviate such conditions. Requires a report to the President and to the Congress within three years. Terminates the Commission upon filing of such report, except that the Commission may function for up to 30 additional days to conclude its affairs.

Title VII: Federal Responsibility for Deportable and Excludable Aliens Convicted of Crimes—Provides for the expeditious deportation of aliens convicted of crimes.

Provides for the identification of Department of Defense facilities that could be made available to incarcerate deportable or excludable aliens.

Source: Summary of The Immigration Reform and Control Act (IRCA), Pub.L. 99–603, 100 Stat. 3445. Library of Congress. http://thomas.loc.gov/cgi-bin/bdquery/z?d099:SN01200:@@@L&summ2=m&|TOM:/bss/d099query.html.

Memo from John Tanton to WITAN IV Attendees (October 10, 1986)

The major issue for Mexican Americans and other Latinos during the 1980s and into the next century was immigration. Pro-immigrant groups faced a lobby of well-financed foundations. The following memo is from physician John Tanton (1934–), founder of such anti-immigration groups as the Federation of American Immigration Reform and U.S. English and publisher of the Social Contract Press, *a quarterly devoted to anti-immigrant pieces. In 1986, Tanton signed a memo that caused an uproar. He charged that Latino immigrants brought a culture of political corruption to the United States and were unlikely to become good citizens. He stated that the power of whites was being diluted by Latinos. Tanton laid out an agenda for anti-immigrant groups and called for an investigation of the Mexican American Legal Defense and Education Fund. He drew a picture of two Americas—the white property owners and the propertyless blacks and Hispanics. For many, the Tanton memo raised the question of racism within the ranks of anti-immigrant organizations, something that was vehemently denied. Some members of English Only resigned in protest but most tacitly agreed with Tanton.*

TO: WITAN IV Attendees

FROM: John Tanton

DATE: October 10, 1986

Here is a set of questions and statements that I hope will help guide our discussion of the non-economic consequences of immigration to California, and by extension, to the rest of the United States. These are not highly polished; I ask your indulgence.

These notes are based on reading Bouvier's and related papers, on the WITAN III Meeting, and my own thinking over several years on the topic of assimilation and the character of American society. The assignment of subtopics to the main categories is a bit arbitrary; many of them could be moved around.

I. Political Consequences

1. The political power between the states will change, owing to differential migration [in] six immigrant-receiving states. The heartland will lose more political power.
2. Will the newcomers vote Democratic or Republican, liberal or conservative, and what difference does it make? A lot, if you're one or the other.
3. *Gobernar es poblar* translates [to] "to govern is to populate" (Parsons' [Thomas Malthus] paper, p. 10, packet sent May 8). In this society where the majority rules, does this hold? Will the present majority peaceably hand over its political power to a group that is simply more fertile?
4. Does the fact that there will be no ethnic majority, in California, early in the next century mean that we will have minority coalition-type governments, with third parties? Is this good or bad, in view of the European and other experiences?
5. Shall illegal aliens be counted in the census and used to apportion congressional and statehouse seats, thereby granting them political power?
6. Is apartheid in Southern California's future? The demographic picture in South Africa now is startlingly similar to what we'll see in California in 2030. In Southern Africa, a White minority owns the property, has the best jobs and education, has the political power, and speaks one language. A non-White majority has poor education, jobs, and income, owns little property, is on its way to political power and speaks a different language. (The official language policy in South Africa is bilingualism—the Blacks are taught in Zulu and related tongues.)

In California of 2030, the non-Hispanic Whites and Asians will own the property, have the good jobs and education, speak one language and be mostly Protestant and "other." The Blacks and Hispanics will have the poor jobs, will lack education, own little property, speak another language and will be mainly Catholic. Will there be strength in this diversity? Or will this prove a social and political San Andreas Fault?

7. Illegal aliens will pay taxes to the Federal Government; their costs will mostly be local.
8. The politicians are way behind the people on these issues. This brings to mind the story told of Gandhi: he was sitting by the side of the road when a crowd went by. He said, "There go my people. I must get up and follow them, for I am their leader!"
9. Griffin Smith's point from the Federalist Papers: It was argued that the colonies would make a good nation, as they shared a common culture and language. Nineteen eighty-seven is the celebration of the adoption of the Constitution, 1988 its ratification, and 1989 the setting up of the first Federal Government. Can we tie into these discussions?

II. Cultural

1. Will Latin American migrants bring with them the tradition of the mordida (bribe), the lack of involvement in public affairs, etc.? What in fact are the characteristics of Latin American culture, versus that of the United States? See Harrison's *Washington Post* article in the September 3 packet.
2. When does diversity grade over into division?
3. Will Blacks be able to improve (or even maintain) their position in the face of the Latin onslaught?
4. How will we make the transition from a dominant non-Hispanic society with a Spanish influence to a dominant Spanish society with non-Hispanic influence?
5. Do ethnic enclaves (Bouvier, p. 18) constitute resegregation? As Whites see their power and control over their lives declining, will they simply go quietly into the night? Or will there be an explosion? Why don't non-Hispanic Whites have a group identity, as do Blacks, Jews, Hispanics?
6. Note that virtually all the population growth will come from immigrants and their descendants.
7. Is there a difference in the rates of assimilation between Asians and Latins?
8. Should something be said about the competing metaphors of the salad bowl and the melting pot?
9. What exactly is it that holds a diverse society together? Gerda's paper said that in our case, it was a common language.
10. Is assimilation a function of the educational and economic level of immigrants? If so, what are the consequences of having so many ill-educated people coming in to low-paying jobs?
11. We're building in a deadly disunity. All great empires disintegrate, we want stability. (Lamm)
12. Enclaves lead to rigidity. (Hardin)
13. The theory of a moratorium: the pause in immigration between 1930–1950, combined with the assimilating experience of fighting side-by-side in the trenches in World War II, gave us a needed pause so that we could assimilate the mass of people who came in the early years of the century. Do we again need such a pause?
14. Concerning the moratorium, here are some phrases that could be used: "The pause that refreshes." "A seventh inning stretch." "Take a break, catch-up, eliminate a backlog, take a breather."
15. Perhaps mention should be made of Pacific Bell's move to install completely separate Spanish and Chinese language phone systems in California (see May 27 packet).
16. Novak's term "unmeltable ethnics" is probably better than some of the others that have been suggested. Similarly, ethnicity is a more acceptable term than race. It should also be

noted that 50% of all Hispanic surname people on the census forms designate themselves as White. So perhaps we should speak of Hispanic Whites and non-Hispanic Whites, to further diffuse the issue. Is Anglo a better term that White? Language is very important here.

III. Conservation and Demography

1. What will be the effect on the conservation movement, which has drawn its support in the past from other than the minorities, and which has relied on the political power of the majority to pass legislative measures? As the people that groups like the Sierra Club represent go into opposition (minority political status), will many of the things they've worked for be lost because the new majority holds other values?
2 Can homo contraceptivus compete with homo progenitiva if borders aren't controlled? Or is advice to limit one's family simply advice to move over and let someone else with greater reproductive powers occupy the space?
3. What are the consequences to California of the raw population growth that is coming, the ethnic change aside?
4. What is the conservation ethnic [sic] of the Asian and Latin American newcomers? Will they adopt ours or keep theirs?
5. The Sierra Club may not want to touch the immigration issue, but the immigration issue is going to touch the Sierra Club! (To mention just one group.)
6. On the demographic point: perhaps this is the first instance in which those with their pants up are going to get caught by those with their pants down!
7. Do you agree with Teitelbaum's statement, "International migration has now become an important point of intersection between the different demographic profiles of developing and developed countries"? *(Fear of Population Decline*, p. 134—see also pp. 111–115.)

IV. Jurisprudence

1. What are the consequences for affirmative action of the ethnic change coming along? Will the non-Hispanic Whites (NHW) have a limited number of spots in professional schools, etc. proportionate to their numbers? Or will affirmative action go beyond this (as it does now in Malaysia) to cut spots to below their proportionate share, to enable other groups to "catch-up"?
2. Anything to be said about drugs and the border?
3 Will we get more of the Napoleonic Code influence, and does it make a difference?
4. What do we demand of immigrants—or more correctly, what should we demand of them:
   a. Learn our language.
   b. Adopt our political ideals.
   c. Assimilate and add their flavoring to our stew.

V. Education

1. What are the differences in educability between Hispanics (with their 50% dropout rate) and Asiatics (with their excellent school records and long tradition of scholarship)?
2. Where does bussing fit into the picture? Keep in mind that by 1990, over 50% of all the people under 15 years of age will be of minority status. They will also be heavily concentrated in certain geographic areas.
3. The whole bilingual education question needs to be mentioned.

VI. Race/Class Relations

1. What will be the fate of Blacks as their numbers decline in relationship to Hispanics? As they lose political power, will they get along with the Hispanics? Relations are already heavily strained in many places.
2. What happens when we develop a new underclass, or a two-tiered economic system? Especially if the two groups can't speak the same language! (See Bouvier and Martin Chapter 5.)
3. Is resegregation taking place, in the Southern part of the state in particular?
4. Phil Martin's point: In agriculture, the Whites and Asiatics will own and manage, but will not be able to speak to the Hispanic fieldworkers. They will need bilingual foremen. Does this sound like social peace? Or like South Africa?

Keep in mind the poor educational level of the field hands.

VII. The Economy

I don't think we should dwell much on the economy: I think we should try to make our contribution by talking about the non-economic consequences of immigration. Nonetheless:

1. Do high levels of immigration cut back on innovation (Bouvier, p. 27)?
2. Does it reduce the tendency and need of employers to hire current minority teens (Bouvier, p. 27)?
3. Is there a downward pressure on labor standards in general (Bouvier, p. 28)?
4. Phil Martin's point on the colonization of the labor market. (Chapter 5.)

VIII. Retirement

1. Since the majority of the retirees will be NHW, but the workers will be minorities, will the latter be willing to pay for the care of the former? They will also have to provide the direct care: How will they get along, especially through a language barrier (Bouvier, p. 40)?
2. On the other hand, will the older and NHW groups be willing to pay the school taxes necessary to educate the burgeoning minorities?
3. The Federal Government may have to pay for the care of the elderly in schools—will it?

IX. Religious Consequences

This is the most difficult of all to tackle, and perhaps should be left out. Nonetheless:

1. What are the implications of the changes for the separation of church and state? The Catholic Church has never been reticent on this point. If they get a majority of the voters, will they pitch out this concept?
2. Same question for parochial schools versus public schools.
3. Same question for the topic of abortion/choice, birth control, population control.
4. Same question for the role of women.
5. Will Catholicism brought in from Mexico be in the American or the European model? The latter is much more casual.
6. Keep in mind that many of the Vietnamese coming in are also Catholic.
7. Is there anything to be said about the Eastern religions that will come along with the Asiatics?

X. Mexico and Latin America (Chapter 7, Bouvier & Martin)

Perhaps the main thing to be addressed here is whether or not shutting off the escape valve will lead to revolution, or whether keeping it open can avert it.

XI. Additional Demographic Items

Teitelbaum's phrase, "A region of low native fertility combined with high immigration of high-fertility people does not make for compatible trend lines!"

Finally, this is all obviously dangerous territory, but the problem is not going to go away. Who can open it up? The question is analogous to Nixon's opening of China: he could do it, Hubert Humphrey could not have. Similarly, the issues we're touching on here must be broached by liberals. The conservatives simply cannot do it without tainting the whole subject.

I think the answers to many of these questions depend on how well people assimilate. This, in turn, depends heavily on whether the parent society has made up its mind that assimilation is a good thing (we're confused on this point now), whether it works at assimilating newcomers (as Canada and Australia do by following them longitudinally), whether the people coming want to assimilate (not all of them do), and, even if all the factors are favorable, whether the numbers are small enough so as not to overwhelm the assimilative process.

Good luck to us all!

Source: John Tanton to WITAN IV Attendees, October 10, 1986. Intelligence Report, Summer 2002, Southern Poverty Law Center, http://www.splcenter.org/intel/intelreport/article.jsp?sid=125.

"In Memory: Remembering César Chávez" (ca. 1993)

César Chávez (1927–1993) is the best-known Chicano/Mexican American civil rights leader. He is the symbol of David taking on Goliath—a small Chicano man taking on the large and powerful agribusiness. As head of the farmworkers, he earned $5.00 a week—working more than 100 hours a week in an effort to bring social, political, and economic justice to the most underpaid and exploited sector of the U.S. economy. Chávez's death in 1993 was a huge loss for the millions who labor on U.S. farms and vineyards and for working people of all colors. Chávez was more than a labor leader—he was an icon—and immediately after his death there were campaigns to name streets in his honor and to have a national holiday designating his birthday. In 1984, Chávez said, "Once social change begins, it cannot be reversed. You cannot uneducate the person who has learned to read. You cannot humiliate the person who feels pride. You cannot oppress the people who are not afraid anymore. . . . And [as] you cannot do away with an entire people, you cannot stamp out a people's cause. Regardless of what the future holds for our union, regardless of what the future holds for farmworkers, our accomplishments cannot be undone." The following document from the César E. Chávez Foundation provides a compilation of Chávez quotations from throughout his lifetime. Chávez was not only a leader but also a teacher.

"People who have lost their hunger for justice are not ultimately powerful. They are like sick people who have lost their appetite for what is truly nourishing. Such sick people should not frighten or discourage us. They should be prayed for along with the sick people who are in the hospital."

"The love for justice that is in us is not only the best part of our being, but it is also the most true to our nature."

"Preservation of one's own culture does not require contempt or disrespect for other cultures."

"If you are going to organize and ask for commitment, you cannot go to the most desperately poor. They are not likely to take action. If you stand on a man's head and push it into the dirt, he may not even see the heel of your boot. But if his whole face is already above ground, he can see your heel and he can see freedom ahead."

"Years of misguided teaching have resulted in the destruction of the best in our society, in our cultures, and in the environment."

"If you really want to make a friend, go to someone's house and eat with him. . . . The people who give you their food give you their heart."

"Our very lives are dependent, for sustenance, on the sweat and sacrifice of the campesinos [farmworkers]. Children of farmworkers should be as proud of their parents' professions as other children are of theirs."

"What is at stake is human dignity. If a man is not accorded respect, he cannot respect himself, and if he does not respect himself, he cannot demand it."

"Non-violence, which is the quality of the heart, cannot come by an appeal to the brain."

"Non-violence is a very powerful weapon. Most people don't understand the power of non-violence and tend to be amazed by the whole idea. Those who have been involved in bringing about change and see the difference between violence and non-violence are firmly committed to a lifetime of non-violence, not because it is easy or because it is cowardly, but because it is an effective and very powerful way."

"We cannot seek achievement for ourselves and forget about progress and prosperity for our community. . . . Our ambitions must be broad enough to include the aspirations and needs of others, for their sakes and for our own."

Source: César E. Chávez Foundation. "In Memory: Remembering César Chávez." http://multinationalmonitor.org/hyper/issues/1993/05/mm0593_02.html.

Jorge R. Mancillas, "At UCLA, the Power of the Individual—Chicano Studies: The Hunger Strike Was a Morally Justifiable, Politically Reasonable Use of the Tactic"

(1993)

Throughout the 1980s, Chicano and Chicana students at the University of California at Los Angeles (UCLA) sponsored workshops on how to establish a Chicano studies department. They formulated plans and a rationale for having a department rather than a program, which was what UCLA proposed. This campaign intensified under the leadership of Marcos Aguilar, Minnie Fergusson, and Bonnie Díaz. Finally, in 1993, believing that all procedures had been exhausted, nine Chicanas and Chicanos, led by Aguilar and Fergusson, began a two-week hunger strike that was supported by Latino students throughout the Los Angeles Basin. The strike was vehemently opposed by white administrators and faculty members, as well as a number of Chicano and Latino faculty members. When the strike successfully concluded, UCLA historian Robert Dalleck alleged that the university had negotiated with a gun to its head. In the Los Angeles Times, *Dalleck stated that the compromise "happily ends the threat to the protesters' health. But it diminishes UCLA's integrity, inflames social tensions, and contributes to what historian Arthur Schlesinger, Jr., has aptly described as 'the disuniting of America.'" The following* Los Angeles Times *article by Jorge Mancillas, a UCLA biology professor who became part of the hunger strike and was later denied tenure, explains why he joined the hunger strike and the significance of this action.*

When on the misty morning of Tuesday, May 25, a group of students and I began a hunger strike in front of Murphy Hall at UCLA, we announced that ours was not a symbolic act. We knew that we would either succeed or we would die. We did not die, and now people feel free to criticize us.

Our action has been characterized in many ways, from inspiring to irresponsible, from courageous to suicidal, but to us, it was above all an act of faith and an assumption of responsibility. We had faith in the substance and moral force of our argument. An interdepartmental program in Chicano Studies, taught by professors from traditional departments as "community service" could not fill what has become an urgent necessity in light of the racial strife tearing our society apart.

The hunger strike was decided on and led by a large, multiracial group of students; some participated in it, others organized its logistics and support activities, and others who represented us in negotiations. In a city where so many adults focus on the infantile pursuit of "fun," these young people displayed the highest sign of maturity: the willingness to assume responsibility for the solution of our social and educational problems. The young people who led me into that tent displayed more maturity than many of my elders, and I was willing to follow their lead.

In spite of our success, we have been criticized for our use of "too heavy a tactic," the use of maximal action for an issue of smaller magnitude that "was solvable by other means." This reveals a complete ignorance of history and political strategy. Gandhi used the same tactic, but he did not gain India's independence through a hunger strike. He used the tactic at specific moments within the struggle, in a given context and to achieve defined, measurable goals.

Our hunger strike had a successful outcome because we used it in support of a morally sustainable cause, at the crest of a movement and to focus other ongoing efforts, when other methods had been exhausted. Most important, we applied it in the pursuit of an objective achievable within the time frame of the limits for human survival. Ours was a morally justifiable, politically reasonable, intelligent use of the tactic.

It is ironic that our action was compared to "putting a gun to someone's head." At a time when guns are continuously [sic] pointed at heads and triggers pulled in the streets of our cities because of lack of understanding between people of different backgrounds, we resorted to a nonviolent approach.

Our efforts were aimed at enriching the academic curriculum for all UCLA students, regardless of their major. Upon graduation, they must not only have technical expertise in their chosen fields; they also must understand the realities of the world in which they will work.

Our society is being torn apart by tension, confrontation, and violence because of the pursuit of the politics of self-interest. Our message was that we must embrace a different approach, and be willing to give of ourselves, whatever is necessary—our lives if need be—for the collective interest, for the common good. We must pursue life, liberty, and happiness for all of us, not for some of us at the expense of others. We must leave behind the "trickle down" approach to empowerment, the belief that all will benefit in a given community if an individual representative climbs the ladders of economic and political hierarchies. We must give democracy its true meaning and all become participants in the steering of our common economic and political destiny.

The most powerful message of our hunger strike is the illustration of the power of the individual: A small group of individuals with no political power, wealth, or influence was able to play a significant role in influencing the course of events. All it takes is clarity of mind, strength of convictions, and determination.

We may have made many mistakes, and will probably make more. But as Edward R. Murrow once said, "No one makes a bigger mistake than he who did nothing because he could only do a little." Each of us can do more than we realize. Each of us alone, can only do a little. Together, we can make history.

Source: Mancillas, Jorge R. "At UCLA, the Power of the Individual Chicano Studies: The Hunger Strike Was a Morally Justifiable, Politically Reasonable Use of the Tactic." *Los Angeles Times*, June 11, 1993, 7.

"An Interview with Sub-Comandante Marcos of the Zapatista Army of National Liberation"

(1995)

Subcomandante Insurgente Marcos is the pseudonym of the spokesperson for the Ejercito Zapatista de Liberación Nacional *(Zapatista Army of National Liberation" (EZLN), a revolutionary army in Chiapas, Mexico. Marcos wears a mask to conceal his identity. The EZLN has pursued a nonviolent revolution and has garnered the sympathy of the world while it holds Mexican officials at bay. The Zapatistas are fighting for the rights of the Mayan people to preserve their culture and way of life. The 1994 North American Free Trade Agreement, which opened the Mexican economy to U.S. industries and promoted the privatization of the Mexican economy, threatened Mayan villages, prompted the destruction of communal lands, and hastened the commercialization of agriculture. In the following interview, Marcos explains why the Mayans revolted against the Mexican government. This message has been the movement's greatest defense and has attracted worldwide support.*

San Cristobal

Mexico

He is among the few whose face is covered and is armed with a machine gun. He is not indigenous. While he speaks, he pulls a pipe from a pouch, puts it in his mouth through the opening of the Ski mask, but does not light it. He expresses himself with the clarity of the intellectual accustomed to communicating with the poor. He is surely Mexican, but it is not possible to identify the accent. A young woman with Asian eyes in a black mask stands next to him throughout the interview.

Comandante Marcos, you occupied San Cristobal on January 1st, 1994, who are you?

We are part of the Zapatista Army of National Liberation and we demand the resignation of the federal government and the formation of a transitional government which convenes free and democratic elections in August 1994. We want that the major demands of the peasants of Chiapas be met: food, health, education, autonomy, and peace. The indigenous people have always lived in a state of war because war has been waged against them and today the war will be in their favour. Whatever the case, we will have the opportunity to die in battle fighting instead of dying of dysentery, as the indigenous people of Chiapas usually die.

Do you have relationships with some political organisation of peasants?

We have no such relationships with any open organisation. Our organisation is exclusively armed and clandestine.

Were you formed out of nothing? Improvised?

We have been preparing ourselves in the mountains for ten years; we are not an improvised movement. We have matured, thought, learned, and made this decision.

Do you have racial and ethnic demands?

The Committee of Directors is made up of indigenous Tzotziles, Tzeltles, Choles, Tojolabales, Mames, and Zoques, all of the major ethnic groups of Chiapas. They all agree, and apart from democracy and representation, they demand respect, respect which white people have never had for them. Above all, in San Cristobal the residents, insult and discriminate again them as a daily occurrence. Now white people respect the Indians because they see them with guns in their hands.

How do you think the government will respond?

We do not worry about the response of the government. We worry about the response of the Mexican people. We want to know what this event will provoke, what will move the national consciousness. We hope something moves, not only in the form of armed struggle, but in all forms of struggle. We hope this will put an end to this disguised dictatorship.

Don't you have confidence in the PRD as an opposition party in the next elections?

We don't distrust the political parties as much as we do the electoral system. The government of Salinas de Gortari is an illegitimate party, product of fraud, and this illegitimate government can only produce illegitimate elections. We want a transitional government and that the government hold new elections—but with a capacity that is genuinely egalitarian, offering the same opportunities to all political parties. In Chiapas, 15,000 Indians per year die of curable diseases. It is a statistic of the same magnitude that the war produced in El Salvador. If a peasant with cholera comes to a rural hospital, they will throw him out so that no one will say there is cholera in Chiapas. In this movement, the Indians who form part of the Zapatista Army want to first dialogue with their own people. They are the real representatives.

Excuse me, but you are not an Indian.

You must understand our movement is not Chiapaneco. It is national. There are people like me, others who come from other states, and Chiapanecos who fight in other states. We are Mexicans, that unifies us, as well as the demand for liberty and democracy. We want to elect genuine representatives.

But now are you not afraid of heavy repression?

For the Indians, repressions exist for the past 500 years. Maybe you think of repression in terms of the typical South American government. But for the Indians, this kind of repression is their daily bread. Ask those who live in the surrounding communities of San Cristobal.

What development would you consider a movement?

We would like others in the country to join this movement.

An armed movement?

No, we make a broad appeal which we direct towards those who are active in civil, legal, and open popular movements.

Why did you choose January 1st to attack San Cristobal?

It was the Committee of Directors which decided. It is clear the date is related to NAFTA, which for the Indians is a death sentence. Once it goes into effect, it means an international massacre.

What do you believe the international response will be? Are you not afraid the United States will intervene like it has in other parts of Latin America?

The U.S. used to have the Soviet Union as a pretext, they were afraid of Soviet infiltration in our countries. But what can they make of a movement which claims social justice? They cannot continue to think we are being manipulated from the outside, or that we are financed by Moscow gold, since Moscow no longer exists. The people in the U.S. should be aware that we struggle for those things that others struggle for. Did not the people of Germany and Italy rebel against a dictatorship? Does the rebellion of the Mexicans not have the same value? The people in the U.S. have a great deal to do with the reality which you can observe here, with the conditions of misery of the Indians and the great hunger for justice. In Mexico, the entire social system is based upon the injustice in its relations with the Indians. The worst thing that can happen to a human being is to be Indian, with all its burden of humiliation, hunger, and misery.

This is a subversive movement. Our objective is the solution of the principal problems of our country, which necessarily intersect with problems of liberty and democracy. This is why we think that the government of Salinas de Gortari is an illegitimate government which can only convene illegitimate elections. The solution is a call to all citizens and to the House of Deputies and Senators and to comply with their patriotic duty and remove Salinas de Gortari and all his Cabinet and to form a transitional government. And the transitional government should call elections, with equal opportunity for all political parties.

Based on that, the compañeros say other demands can be negotiated: bread, housing, health, education, land, justice, many problems, which within the context of indigenous people, are very serious. But the demands for liberty and democracy are being made as a call to all the Mexican Republic, to all the social sectors to participate, not with guns, but with the means which they have.

We have been isolated all these years, while the rest of the world rebelled against dictatorships or apparent dictatorships and this was viewed with logic. In this country, however, a series of dictatorial measures were being adopted and no one said anything. We believe there is an international consensus that only the Mexicans were missing, who have suffered under an absolute dictatorship by the Party and now by one person, who is Carlos Salinas de Gortari, now through Luis Donaldo Colosio. I think that at the international level they will see that a movement with demands like these is logical.

There is not in the movement of the Zapatista Army of National Liberation an ideology perfectly defined, in the sense of being Communist or Marxist-Leninist. There is a common point of connection with the great national problems, which coincide always, for one or the other sector, in a lack of liberty and democracy.

In this case, this sector has used up any other method of struggle such as the legal struggle, the popular struggle, the economic projects, the struggle for Sedesol [La Secretaria de Desarrollo Social, federal office in charge of local development of indigenous people], and it ends following the only method which remains, the armed struggle. But we are open to other tendencies and to other forms of struggle, in the enthusiasm to generate a genuine national and revolutionary movement which reconciles these two fundamental demands, liberty and democracy. On these grounds a movement can be formed which will create a genuine solution to the economic and social problems of each sector, whether indigenous or peasant, workers, teachers, intellectuals, small business owners of the small and medium-sized industry.

The repression on the indigenous population has been present for many years. The indigenous people of Chiapas suffer 15,000 deaths per year, that no one mourns. The great shame is that they die of curable diseases and this is denied by the Department of Health.

We expect a favourable reaction from Mexican society toward the reasons which give birth to this movement because they are just. You can question the method of struggle, but never its causes.

Source: Revolutionary Democracy I, no. 2 (September 1995). http://www.revolutionarydemocracy.org/rdv1n2/marcos.htm.

Testimony of Commissioner Richard M. Estrada, U.S. Commission on Immigration Reform, "Agricultural Guest Worker Programs" (December 7, 1995)

A notion that has been picking up momentum in the United States is that an immigration reform bill must have a provision for a guest worker program. The fact is that without Mexican and other Latino labor, U.S. agriculture would suffer huge losses. Already the United States is buying vegetables from China to offset the diminishing supply. In 1942, the United States entered a similar contract to bring workers to the United States as temporary guest workers. The program ended in 1964 and was fraught with corruption and abuses. This renewal of the bracero *program of World War II vintage was the cornerstone of President George H. W. Bush's (1924–) immigration policy. The rationale was that, in this way, Mexican workers could be contracted for temporary periods and returned to their country of origin once their labor was no longer needed. The following is the 1995 testimony of ultraconservative columnist Richard M. Estrada (1950–1999), who argued against the* bracero *program because of its abuses and the lack of provisions enabling workers to, in time, become permanent residents. He saw worker conditions as the same as rented slaves. Estrada's testimony seems as relevant today as it did then. Estrada frames his argument against the guest worker program in terms of "unfree" labor. Free labor has the right to organize and gain from the fruits of its labor; unfree labor has no rights.*

FREE VS. UNFREE LABOR

I oppose new or expanded agricultural guest worker programs because they represent "unfree" labor.

Doubtless, some will immediately object to the use of this term because all the workers in question would presumably come to America willingly. Despite uncertainty about the circumstances under which guest laborers in such programs are selected, let us concede for the sake of argument that all guest workers do in fact come willingly.

One must still insist that the absence of slavery does not imply the presence of freedom. As commonly understood, the term free labor also implies that an individual can sell his or her labor on the open market to whomever will contract for it. It is in this regard that guest worker programs are, by definition, unfree labor arrangements or, at the very least, not totally free labor arrangements.

To be specific, the agricultural guest worker is explicitly obligated not to sell his or her labor anywhere else but to the agricultural employer who sponsors entry. Employers tend to prize guest workers for their abilities, true. But they also value them because they have no options and are, therefore, more malleable. (Employers tend to prefer the term "disciplined.")

This basic characteristic is the ugly underbelly of any and all agricultural guest worker programs: the foreign worker is virtually indentured to the agricultural employer, with an important exception. Unlike indentured servitude as practiced in America in the eighteenth century, the guest worker has no expectation based in the legal provisions of his or her entry that he or she will be able to become a free laborer in America.

In addition, guest worker programs tend to have no worker protections. When it comes to housing and health care, uneducated and often illiterate guest workers, who often do not speak English and who have little or no disposable income, are left to fend for themselves. There are thousands of such people roaming the agriculture-based communities of America today. Reasonable and honorable people may disagree about guest worker programs in general, but the specific practice of providing no meaningful worker protections in this manner is unacceptable. It is wrong. It is immoral.

Finally, Congress should consider that the "bracero" guest worker program was implemented in 1942 under extremely unusual conditions. With millions of native-born rural workers suddenly called off to war, turning to foreign labor through a temporary guest worker program was justified. Even so, the fact that it took more than twenty years to end the bracero program, long after the end of the Second World War, should give Congress pause about reintroducing it. Cheap, unskilled foreign labor has proven to be an opiate to agricultural employers. Congress should dispense it sparingly, if at all.

Source: U.S. Commission on Immigration Reform. http://www.utexas.edu/lbj/uscir/120795.html.

Linda Lutton, "Old-Time Chicago Politics Aren't Dead Yet—Just Ask 'Chuy' García"

(1998)

Before entering politics, Cook County commissioner Jesús García was a community activist and prominent member of the Centro de Accion Social Autonoma *(Center for Autonomous Social Action). A native of Durango, Mexico, García, like so many Mexicans in Chicago, had arrived there at an early age. In 1986, he was elected as alderman and committeeman for the 22nd Ward as one of the city's first Mexican American aldermen. He got his first office as a supporter of Chicago reforming mayor Harold Washington (1922–1987). García then became an Illinois state senator in 1992, representing the Pilsen and Little Village districts, which were heavily Mexican American. García lost his state senate seat in 1998, which was a surprise to his supporters. The following article discussing his loss was written at the time of García's state senate defeat. He was elected to the Cook County Board of Commssioners in 2009*

Jesús "Chuy" García looked like a shoo-in. The incumbent Illinois state senator had a long history of work in the Latino neighborhoods he represented; he had 14 years of legislative experience, first on the Chicago City Council and then in the state Senate; he was respected at home and had won a reputation nationally and even internationally as a dedicated progressive and an advocate for the poor, labor, and immigrants. "He's the most admired Mexican American candidate in the entire state," says Cook County Clerk David Orr, a fellow progressive who served with García on the City Council during Mayor Harold Washington's administration in the mid-'80s. "He's been a good organizer, he's never a guy with a big ego, he's always willing to help other people . . . a wonderful record, well liked, well respected—in my mind, he's really one of the most outstanding elected officials in the state." He lost anyway. García and his supporters are still reeling from his defeat by a no-name candidate—Antonio "Tony" Muñoz, a Chicago cop with no legislative or community experience—in the Democratic primary last March. García admits that his campaign made some strategic mistakes, but he's also clear about the biggest factor in his defeat. "There is a machine in this town," he says. "It's a new type of machine . . . but it still does what the old machine was capable of doing." That old machine reached its height under Richard J. Daley, who served as mayor from 1955 until he died in 1976. Daley controlled 40,000 city jobs as well as nearly all 50 aldermen and Democratic committeemen. Gary Rivlin wrote in *Fire on the Prairie* that Daley's Cook County Democratic Party central committee "ran city government just as the Communist Party's politburo ran the Soviet Union. . . . It was no wonder that people outside the city's borders looked on Chicago with awe and horror. It was home to not only the last of the great big-city machines but also the most awesome of them all." Just as ward committeemen and aldermen were beholden to Daley, they had armies of precinct workers beholden to them. It was at the ward level that patronage jobs and favors were passed out: Knocking on doors and bringing out the vote for the machine slate on Election Day could get you a promotion and perks; losing your precinct could mean having to join the unemployment lines. Daley's death and the internal fight over who would succeed him weakened the machine in the late '70s and early '80s, but the organization took its first real hit when Harold Washington won the Democratic mayoral primary in 1983, beating Mayor Jane Byrne and Richard M. Daley, Richard J.'s son, who split the machine vote. Washington was an African American, progressive reformer who promised to be "fairer than fair." A coalition of blacks, Latinos, and progressive whites swept him to victory, and he became Chicago's first black mayor, serving until he died in 1987. Richard M. Daley was waiting in the wings; right after his father's death he had been mentioned as a possible heir to the mayoral throne. Washington's death, and the almost immediate dissolution of his progressive coalition, offered the younger Daley his chance. He was first elected as mayor in 1989. Since then, García says, "We've witnessed probably the most rapid consolidation of power that any large city has experienced within the last 40 or 50 years. The influence that the Daley group exerts is vast: City Hall, County Board, the agencies—CTA, Park District, Board of Education—they control it all. And we've witnessed the evolution of the machine from relying on the precinct captain to deliver, to relying on direct mail and utilization of the electronic media to stay in power. The precinct captains aren't that key anymore, but they still decide races like mine. They can still produce." Daley has paid particular attention to Latinos; who are Chicago's fastest growing and soon-to-be largest ethnic minority. As one *Chicago Tribune* political reporter noted in 1994, "The old line 'regular polls' are grooming some younger talent. These emerging new players are Hispanic, predominantly Mexican-Americans, and the mutual hope is that a white–Latino coalition can maintain hegemony over Chicago." The Latino arm of the Daley machine proved in the García race that old-time machine tactics haven't been shelved quite yet. "Patronage is alive and well in the city of Chicago even though [we] have Shakman," says Miguel del Valle, a progressive state senator from Chicago's Northwest Side and the only other Latino in the Illinois Senate. The Shakman decree is the federal court ruling that prohibits patronage hirings and firings. "Someday people will understand that this administration in many respects functions the way that the old administrations functioned," del Valle says. García gave the machine plenty of reasons to pick him as a target. While the mayor has been able to win over or eliminate nearly all of his opposition—more than a third of the current City Council was originally appointed by Daley—García has been steadfast in pursuing a progressive agenda. He's been consistently critical of Daley's development policies for the city, protesting the upscale development of near-downtown neighborhoods that is displacing long-time and poor residents. His name also has been on the short list of potential challengers to Daley in the upcoming February 1999 mayoral elections. "Chuy is about neighborhoods and he's about people and he's therefore a threat," says Alton Miller, Harold Washington's second-term press secretary and biographer. Miller says García was "absolutely the target of a machine attack. Anytime anybody raises his head a little bit higher, the Daley folk want to knock it down. He was and is a real threat to their long-term aims, because . . . he's a person who's going to be out there blowing the whistle and keeping people mindful of what the real priorities are." But it wasn't just the old Daley machine that took out García. A newly organized Latino wing of the machine, the Hispanic Democratic Organization (HDO), made up of Latino leaders loyal to Daley and an army of Latino patronage workers, joined forces with white ethnic machine bosses to bridge a generation and ethnic gap and bring out the vote for Muñoz. Most HDO members are city workers who got to their positions by politicking and understand that's how they'll get promoted as well. While they may like García, they're fundamentally concerned about getting what's theirs, and they believe that the way to do that is to support those in power and wait for the perks. The combination of new and old that the machine put together for the primary does not bode well for other Latino progressives. Topping the hit list: 22nd Ward alderman and García protégé Rick Muñoz (no relation to Tony) is up for re-election in February. García-mentored state Rep. Sonia Silva won the primary by just 55 votes and in November faces a Republican challenger with Democratic machine ties. U.S. Rep. Luís Gutiérrez is also vulnerable. If these three were replaced with machine Latinos it would almost completely wipe out independent Latino voices in public office. And Daley's Latinos have proven a loyal bunch: In an analysis of key City Council votes, for instance, *Illinois Politics* concluded that "Hispanic aldermen provided near unanimous support for the mayor, with only nine dissenting votes out of 157 cast by the seven Latinos." The First District on Chicago's Southwest Side has a greater number of immigrants than any other district in Illinois. It is an odd mix of old white ethnic neighborhoods—parts of Daley's home ward are in García's district—and the largest, most concentrated Mexican and Mexican American neighborhoods in the Midwest.

March 17 was an Election Day that brought back memories of the way things used to be. Old machine veterans and their well-taught Latino brethren brought out the works for Muñoz: campaigning city workers, job promises and city services galore. Despite a cold rain that fell all Election Day, the streets of the district had the air of a fiesta. There were so many precinct workers out that in some places they stretched from one polling place to another, like part of a long parade snaking through the district. "This was probably the most effective mobilization of the city–county patronage army in a long time," García says. "I don't think I've seen it like this in my 14 years in elected office." Precinct workers were 10 deep. City building inspectors, off-duty cops, and community policing volunteers huddled around polling places. Muñoz campaign workers wore yellow City-issued raincoats and warmed themselves beside portable Streets and Sanitation heaters. City trucks drove slowly down streets with loads of brand-new garbage cans. If it hadn't been for the rain, voters in one precinct would have had to practically step over city workers laying new sidewalks outside the polling place. Weeks before the election, campaign workers went door to door and made phone calls asking residents if they needed a tree cut down, new garbage cans, a street light turned on, and encouraging them to vote for the machine slate. People who had filed applications for employment with the city received anonymous phone calls and were told not to vote for García. City services were so critical to the Munoz campaign that even Muñoz seemed duped by the tactic. When Spanish-language TV news asked him what he planned to do in the Senate, he answered in English—he doesn't speak Spanish—that he'd make sure residents got their city services, sounding more like he'd just clinched an appointment as a ward superintendent rather than the Democratic nomination for the state Senate. Going up against the machine should have been nothing new to García. He came of age at a time when the political consciousness of Latinos and blacks in the city was being jolted awake. By his mid-twenties, he was involved in some of the strongest anti-machine, progressive neighborhood organizing going down in Chicago. In the late '70s and early '80s, García and other progressive Latinos built what would prove to be the most efficient independent political organization in the city and began to form coalitions with their progressive minded African American neighbors, a formula that eventually led to Harold Washington's victory. García spent much of his time before the March primary stumping for two candidates for state representative in his district. "There wasn't really a campaign focusing on my re-election," he admits. García lost by 960 votes out of nearly 13,000 cast, his support dropping in every ward, including two of the most heavily Latino wards. "We took our eye off of the formula that's enabled us to get elected against great odds, to get re-elected, and then to expand," García says. "That was framing the election as a fight between the neighborhood versus power brokers who want control—the machine. That's how we first got elected, that's how we got re-elected, and this last time that wasn't the message that we had out there. As a matter of fact, the message was pretty vague." García's supporters had no reason to think that their candidate would lose. "Our voters were asleep on Election Day, and that's why we lost," says García. "If we had felt threatened, and if we would have communicated that to our volunteers and to our voters, we would have had higher turnout. We didn't. They stayed home." It's hard to fault him for being overconfident. The machine looked almost desperate. No one had heard of Tony Muñoz. He had no legislative experience and didn't speak Spanish. But García ran headlong into a recurring problem for the left: While he was debating immigration and Welfare reform issues, gentrification and neighborhood development, the machine was passing out city services and counting votes. "We see things politically," says Larry González, García's press secretary. "[But] people just say, 'Hey. These guys came and they gave us something.'" García has blamed his defeat on the traditional machine wards, arguing that voter turnout among whites was higher than in previous elections while Latino turnout was lower. Why would whites be any more likely to vote for someone named Muñoz than for someone named García? "They did their precinct captain a favor," says Richard Barnett, who's been involved in independent politics in Chicago's black community for the past 44 years. "Years ago, the precinct captain used to go around and tell the people in his precinct, 'Could you do me a favor?' In 1964, we elected a dead man for Congress, we sure did. Because the people did their precinct captain a favor." As is his custom, Daley never officially endorsed Muñoz. But witnesses say his choice in the race and the importance he put on it was obvious to everyone from Springfield lobbyists to his Latino underlings. "This mayor has a reputation for being hands-off and for staying out of ward races and other kinds of races," del Valle says. "What people don't realize is that there's this roving band of City Hall Latino patronage workers who will go wherever they're assigned. This last time around, they were assigned to concentrate on defeating Sen. García." The "roving band of Latino patronage workers" is the HDO. HDO has been registered as a PAC in Illinois since 1993, with the avowed purpose of promoting "the goals and ideals of the Hispanic Community through the exercise of the right to vote." HDO's top guns have expensive City Hall jobs (head of the Mayor's Office of Inter governmental Affairs, commissioner of Human Services, deputy commissioner of Streets and Sanitation, director of personnel at Human Services, etc.) and refuse to comment on the group's structure or activities. Muñoz was apparently a founding member of the group, but denies it has any political purpose, despite its name. "It's just a bunch of guys who get together, that's all," he says. "We basically talk. We've had picnics and stuff." Insiders paint a picture of a large group of mostly city workers, 85 percent Hispanic. "HDO's 1,500 strong," says one Muñoz campaign worker at the Streets and Sanitation outpost where he's employed. "You're looking at that many city employees from various departments. When issues come up as far as services, we can touch bases on just about every department—Streets and Sanitation, whatever. When I knock on your door you can be sure of one thing: That when I ask you for the vote, 90 percent of the time you're gonna go my way. . . . I got a lady here last night called me, 'Someone dumped a load of tires in my alley, what do I have to do to get 'em out?' First thing I'm gonna do this morning is make sure a truck goes over there. The people won't forget that." HDO's win against García will likely strengthen the organization significantly. The group took a huge bite out of García's base in the Latino community. "The fact that they beat Chuy means more attention is going to be given to them from the administration," says one political consultant who's worked against HDO on the North Side. But he doesn't think García-allied politicians up for re-election in the near future should throw in the towel just yet. "I think you're going to witness a backlash to Chuy's loss," he says.

"There's a growing 'Remember Chuy' type of fever." It's unclear how many voters actually rejected García for his politics. A conservative block of Chicago Latino voters definitely exists: To them it may not be important that a candidate speaks Spanish—they may speak only English themselves. Bilingual education and immigrant rights are not on their list of priorities. They have no intention of allying themselves with blacks and are most concerned with getting what's theirs. As one Latino machine precinct captain puts it, "If you're not supportive of the people that are in power, then you can just about count yourself out as far as getting that piece of the cake." But despite the media talking about "a message from Latino voters," it would seem impossible to deduce voter opinion on García's politics in an election where city services and job promises played a bigger role than what either candidate thought about any given political issue. For del Valle and García, the loss of the Senate seat to a machine candidate is a shot at the heart of the fight for Latino self-determination, political representation, and democracy. "The irony here is that it's the same individuals we went to court to fight to gain Latino political representation when we had nothing," del Valle says. "These days, it's not that they're electing someone who is non-Latino, but they're still around, determining which Latino." "That's what you wind up with in machine politics—control," García says. "The cost that you pay is the ability to control your representatives and to make them work for you. What differences are there between the mayor and his allies? There can't be differences. If there are differences you negotiate through jobs, contracts, things of that sort. It's about keeping total control of elected officials. And it's about eliminating opposition that may get complicated. And I guess that complication is the swing factor. If Latinos aren't under control, it makes governing risky and uncertain. It makes it democratic." Adds David Orr: "Fighting for democracy in a place like Chicago—I'm not gonna compare it to a place like Guatemala—but it's a struggle. It's not like Wisconsin or Minnesota. If people forget that for a moment, that's when these kinds of things can happen."

Source: Lutton, Linda."Old-Time Chicago Politics Aren't Dead Yet—Just Ask 'Chuy' García." *In These Times*, October 4, 1998, 17.

Rodolfo F. Acuña, "Latino Leaders Take a Holiday" (1999)

Relations between the police and Mexican Americans have always been contentious, especially between Los Angeles police and civil rights leaders. Since before the Sleepy Lagoon Case of 1942—when almost two dozen Mexican American youths were rounded up and tried for the murder of José Díaz—Mexican Americans have complained about disparate treatment at the hands of police. Another landmark case was the "Bloody Christmas" case of 1951, when seven young Chicanos were beaten to a bloody pulp by 50 police officers. The pattern continued in the 1950s as Los Angeles police and deputy sheriffs attacked a peaceful crowd of 30,000 protestors on August 29, 1970, and beat the members of the crowd, killing three. The Ramparts case of 1999 deserves equal billing. On September 8, 1999, Los Angeles police officer Rafael Pérez, 32, was caught stealing a million dollars' worth of cocaine from police evidence locker facilities. Pérez made a plea bargain to rat out corruption within the Los Angeles Police Department. He was in a special police unit that was supposed to be combating gangs in the Ramparts Division, just west of downtown Los Angeles. Pérez told a tale of bogus arrests, perjured testimony, and weapons planted on unarmed civilians. In all, Pérez implicated about 70 officers in wrongdoing. The following article criticizes Mexican American elected officials for not displaying moral outrage at the police and raises the question of whether this was because a great many residents in the Ramparts Division were of Salvadoran extraction. Would the elected officials have acted differently if the victims had been Mexican American voters?

The other day, a TV-media reporter asked me why Latino politicians and leaders had been so silent on what was happening in the Ramparts Division. I was at a loss for words, realizing that I myself had said absolutely nothing about this blatant abuse of police power.

In stark contrast to the silence of Latino leaders, the brutal beating of Rodney King by four LAPD officers touched off a torrent of moral outrage that paralyzed the city. As a result, Mayor Tom Bradley convened what became known as the Christopher Commission that, after extensive hearings, produced small reforms. The fallout, however, proved so devastating that Chief of Police Daryl F. Gates was forced to resign and, for the first time in recent history, the city brought in a chief from outside the department.

In testimony before the Christopher Commission, late Asst. Chief Jesse A. Brewer stated, "We know who the bad guys are. Reputations become well known. . . . " Police authorities promised to weed out the bad cops. Yet the election of Richard Riordan as mayor wiped out hard-fought gains of the community. His law-and-order rhetoric energized the police. And, although the police continued knowing who the bad cops were, they kept the bad apples in the barrel.

Given that the Rodney King beatings were outrageous, the events surrounding the Ramparts Division of the Los Angeles Police Department pale it. Indeed, if they had happened in any other community in L.A., Black and white leaders would have been rightfully up in arms. In contrast, Latino leaders have allowed police officers with the power to kill or destroy lives to hide behind a wall of secrecy.

What happened at the Ramparts Division is part of "L.A.'s Dirty Little War on Gangs." Its particulars became known in September 1999 when LAPD officer Rafael A. Pérez spilled the beans after being caught stealing eight pounds of cocaine from police evidence lockers. He turned whistleblower: In return for a plea bargain agreement, Pérez implicated fellow officers. What unfolded was a story of police brutality, perjury, planted evidence, drug corruption, and attempted murder.

Much of the narrative revolves around the anti-gang unit, known as CRASH (Community Resources Against Street Hoodlums). In July 1996, CRASH raided an apartment house on Shatto Place in the heart of the MacArthur Park district of Los Angeles, near the old headquarters of the American Civil Liberties Union. Its target was the notorious 18th Street Gang, L.A.'s biggest and admittedly most violent gang. LAPD's finest assaulted the building in warlike fashion, killing one gang member and wounding another.

Although the LAPD's own report showed that police fired all the shots, the cops who staged the raid claimed the gang bangers were armed. Two pistols, believed to have been throw downs, were found on the scene. A survivor, José Perez initially denied having a gun. He later pleaded guilty to assault. José Pérez [no relation to Rafael Pérez] later explained that he pleaded guilty to avoid a long prison sentence; he had no gun at the time of the raid. As usual, a department investigation found nothing wrong.

The story did not end there. Officer Rafael Pérez, labeled a rogue cop by the media, triggered an internal investigation and the FBI looked for civil rights violations. So far, over a dozen Ramparts Division police have been fired or relieved of duty.

In another case, in 1996, Pérez and his partner Nino Durden, shot Javier Ovando, leaving him paralyzed and in a wheelchair for life. Ovando was allegedly unarmed when he was shot. The officers then planted a semiautomatic rifle on the unconscious suspect and claimed that Ovando had tried to shoot them during a stakeout. Their testimony put Ovando away for 23 years for assault. Because of what has come out, Ovando has been freed from prison. He has filed notice of a $20 million suit against the city, Pérez and other cops. He was allegedly the dealer through whom Pérez and Durden sold their drugs.

After spending more than two years behind bars, Rubén Rojas, 30, is expected to have his drug conviction overturned because authorities now believe it was based on fabricated evidence and false testimony by Pérez. They arrested Rojas on March 5, 1997, after Pérez and Durden allegedly watched him sell rock cocaine to two men near Marathon and Dillon streets. They allegedly saw Rojas make two sales before calling for backup. After the arrest, Pérez planted powder cocaine in Rojas' front pants pockets.

Rojas pleaded no contest. He said: "I was informed that I was facing 25 years to life by my defense counsel and that there was no way I could have won my case because I was up against a police officer . . ." Rojas claimed the police officers framed him after he told the officers that he did not know the whereabouts of a gang member. (The real motive appears to have been that Rojas was seeing a girlfriend of Officer Pérez.)

Because of Pérez's whistle-blowing, Los Angeles District Attorney Gil Garcetti has been forced to release at least three prison inmates jailed by the Ramparts Division. The DA admits that another forty cases could be reversed because of false testimony by police. Investigators are looking into allegations involving the Ramparts Division, ranging from illegal shootings and drug dealing to excessive use of force and "code of silence" offenses.

The reaction of Los Angeles Mayor Richard Riordan is predictable. His spokespersons said that the mayor had complete confidence that LAPD Chief Bernard Parks would implement the reforms passed after the 1991 King beating. There is no need for an oversight commission. Just a couple of rotten apples. Ironically, it was this mayor who called for an entire reshuffling of the Los Angeles Unified School District and instigated the crude coup of Superintendent Rubén Zacarías because the "code of silence" was too imbedded within the culture of the school system. Apparently, there is one standard for teachers and another for police officers.

One only has to look at Los Angeles' media coverage and compare it with its treatment of the Rodney King uprisings to realize the disparate treatment of the incidents. All of this is, however, predictable. What is not, is the reaction of Latino politicians and leaders who are mute in the face of this gross violation of L.A.'s civil rights. From a historical perspective, Ramparts ranks with the Sleepy Lagoon case of 1942 and is more heinous than the Blood Christmas beatings of the early 1950s.

While I know that term limits have forced Latino políticos constantly to play musical chairs, and I realize that the community itself is so anti gangsters as to intimidate políticos, we cannot afford to be silent. The políticos' silence is almost sanctioning a situation like that which occurred in Brazil a few years back. In 1993, a death squad of off-duty Rio de Janeiro police officers executed eight children as they slept on the steps of the Candelaria Church in downtown Rio. Three years later, they were still shooting children in Brazil. On Rio's Ipanema Beach, an 11-year-old street kid was found dead, hanging by the neck, a sign around his neck that read: "I had to be killed because I didn't go to school. I was worthless to society and my only expectation as a grown up was to be a criminal." Some 85 percent of Brazilians polled supported the police even after a police officer shot an apprehended youth three times, point-blank, in the back of a head at a shopping center.

I guess that I naively believed that Chicanos, having experienced the civil rights struggle of the sixties, would be different. Most of us have experienced injustice and know its meaning. We are also bright enough to know that the problem is more systemic than a couple of bad apples. Perhaps we should inspect the barrel. For us to remain silent is so much worse than for others; more is expected of us.

Source: Acuña, Rodolfo F. "Latino Leaders Take a Holiday." December 12, 1999. In Urban Archives, California State University, Northridge.

David Bacon, "Crossing L.A.'s Racial Divide: City Could Elect Its First Latino Mayor in More Than a Century" (2001)

Like so many of his contemporaries, Los Angeles mayor Antonio Villaraigosa (1953–) was active in MEChA (el Movimiento Estudiantil Chicano/a de Aztlán), *a nationwide Chicano student organization fighting for equal treatment on college and university campuses. He was later a member of the* Centro de Acción Social Autónoma *(Center for Autonomous Social Action), which defended the rights of undocumented immigrants. He worked as an organizer for United Teachers Los Angeles, a teachers' union, and was elected to the California Assembly, where he became Speaker. Villaraigosa was elected mayor of Los Angeles in 2005. The following article describes Villaraigosa's unsuccessful run for mayor of Los Angeles in 2001.*

Fifty years ago, Bert Corona had a dream. Latinos in California—the field workers and factory hands, the kids in school forbidden to speak Spanish—could win real political power. Transforming the excluded and marginalized into power brokers in the state with the largest population in the country seemed a task so gargantuan that only a visionary like Corona—social radical, labor militant, Chicano activist, and father of the modern Latino political movement—could consider it achievable.

Yet on June 5, Antonio Villaraigosa, one of Corona's disciples from the heady days of the '60s, may be elected mayor of Los Angeles. Villaraigosa learned politics in that era, becoming a community activist in an early left-wing immigrant rights organization founded by Corona, the Centro de Accion Social Autonóma [Center for Autonomous Social Action] (CASA). From those radical roots, Villaraigosa went on to get a law degree at Los Angeles' People's College of the Law, a unique project creating community lawyers from community activists. He worked as an organizer for the city's huge teachers' union, United Teachers Los Angeles. And he began running for office. Villaraigosa eventually became speaker of the State Assembly, one of California's most powerful political positions.

June 5 election is a runoff, pitting Villaraigosa against James Hahn. Both are Democrats, itself a notable change in a city governed for eight years by Republican Richard Riordan. If Villaraigosa is elected mayor, he'll be the first Latino in that position in more than a century.

The election is partly the story of changing demographics. Los Angeles has the largest urban population of Mexicans outside of Mexico City, and racial minorities in California now make up a majority of the state's population. Most of this demographic shift is due to immigration, and the state is home to as many as half of the nation's undocumented residents.

But the changing population only provides a base. And in California, it took former Gov. Pete Wilson to transform it into a formidable voting force. In 1994, Wilson won re-election by betting his political future on Proposition 187, which sought to exclude the undocumented from schools and medical care.

It was a Pyrrhic victory. Proposition 187 passed, but in the election's wake, thousands of immigrants became citizens with the express intention of never again being excluded from the political process. They then set out to administer a punishment to the Republican Party from which it's still reeling. Democrats today control both houses of the state legislature, and a Democrat sits in the governor's mansion. The new immigrant vote has become the decider in race after race, especially in Los Angeles.

But having a Spanish surname alone isn't enough to get elected in Los Angeles. Although minorities make up 60 percent of city residents, they account for only 39 percent of its voters—14 percent are African American, 20 percent are Latino, and 5 percent are Asian American. Class issues are increasingly the glue holding together a new progressive coalition, bringing together progressive whites with a new generation of leaders in minority communities. "I think the big issues are economic," says Kent Wong, director of UCLA's Labor Center. "People are voting for things like a living wage, affirmative action, and an economic development policy that promotes growth based on good jobs, and which pays attention to underserved communities."

The city has become a hotbed of labor activity. In the past five years, Los Angeles has seen major strikes and organizing drives by immigrant janitors and hotel workers. While immigrants have been the most visible part of that upsurge, African American and Asian American union members have been very much a part of labor's rise.

The Los Angeles County Federation of Labor, which elected its first Latino secretary, Miguel Contreras, five years ago, has put these issues on the political agenda. In a series of bruising electoral fights, it has built up a core of precinct walkers and phone callers, and used them effectively to win upset victories for pro-labor Latinos against more conservative ones, like Hilda Solis, who beat longtime Congressman Marty Martinez last November. The Villaraigosa campaign is the biggest test yet for the federation because it has to be won citywide, involving a larger labor turnout than ever before. "It was a very big risk for the labor movement to step out front and endorse Villaraigosa in the primary," Wong says. "But it has a lot of boldness and daring, and it has built up an incredible ground operation involving hundreds and hundreds of people each weekend."

Unlike Villaraigosa, who has been a high-profile community activist and legislator, Hahn has been a quiet member of an old guard his father helped build. He has been an elected official for 16 years, first as controller and then as city attorney.

Hahn's father, Kenny, was a county supervisor for 40 years, during the era when Mayor Sam Yorty was notorious for racist scare attacks directed at white voters. Hahn was a leading white liberal who stood up for the African American community in South Central Los Angeles. People definitely remember Kenny Hahn, but few voters can point out initiatives taken by his son.

In the local press, the Villaraigosa–Hahn battle is being portrayed as a conflict between blacks and Latinos. "But there's a whole political realignment taking place here," says Anthony Thigpenn, chairman of Agenda, a South Central community organization, and a leading activist in the Villaraigosa campaign. "It's happening in the African American community, like everywhere else, and many of us are looking to be part of it."

Karen Bass, executive director of South Central's Community Coalition, says that Latinos and African Americans have more issues in common than ones that divide them. "Ninety percent of the kids in the criminal justice system and in foster care are African American and Latino," she says. "The most important factor here is that we're neighbors."

In the first election, while Hahn got a majority of black votes, Bass says Villaraigosa still won 26 percent in South Central precincts, while rolling up big majorities in heavily Latino neighborhoods. She predicts the African American vote for Villaraigosa will go higher in the runoff as people become more familiar with him.

"Villaraigosa has a long record, not just supporting the issues important to all of Los Angeles' locked-out communities, but leading many of the efforts to put them into practice," Wong adds. "If he becomes mayor, those communities will have access to power. The ability to turn our issues into real policy will increase dramatically."

Source: Bacon, David. "Crossing L.A.'s Racial Divide: City Could Elect Its First Latino Mayor in More Than a Century." *In These Times*, June 11, 2001, 5.

Dane Schiller, "Castro Upholds Family's Involvement Tradition" (2001)

In Los Angeles there is a link between MEChA (el Movimiento Estudiantil Chicano/a De de AztlánAztlan), *a national Chicano student organization;* Centro de Accion Social Autónoma *or Center for Autonomous Social Action, a pro-immigrant rights organization; and the League of Revolutionary Struggle, a national Marxist organization. All of these organizations were active since the early 1970s. A high proportion of their membership became union organizers, civic leaders, and politicians. The same can be said of the La Raza Unida Party of Texas, the Chicano political party of the 1970s that ran statewide candidates in Texas. Many of today's heads of old-time Mexican American organizations, school board members, judges, and politicos were once members of La Raza Unida. The following article from the* San Antonio Express-News *tells the story of Rosie Castro, who in the 1970s ran unsuccessfully for a seat on the San Antonio, Texas, City Council. Conceding defeat, she told everyone that she would be back, and 30 years later she was—to witness one son sworn in as state senator and the other as a member of the city council.*

A recent Harvard Law School graduate was sweeping a crowded field Saturday to take the reins of City Council District 7. Julian Castro, 26, who watched election returns from his West Side home, appeared to be easily defeating five other candidates, garnering about 60 percent of the vote. Although the post would be his first elected office, Castro has long been groomed for politics by his mother, a well-known grassroots activist. She unsuccessfully ran for a council post 30 years ago but has remained active in politics. "My victory is the product of hard work of many people," said Castro, who was born and raised in the district, which covers the West and Northwest sides. "We had an excellent early vote return and even better Election Day results," he said. Castro was trailed by Fred Rangel, a business consultant, and John Coleman, a retired Air Force officer. Others in the race were Raul Quiroga Jr., Michael Gonzales, and John García. Surrounded by about 80 supporters, Castro vowed to bring a bold brand of leadership to the district and carry on the style of Ed Garza, who has served two terms. Castro ran on a platform of preserving the character of neighborhoods, enhancing accountability at City Hall and bringing more aviation and technology jobs to San Antonio. "I'd be ready for a mini-vacation, but I'll be back at the law office Monday," said Castro, a business litigation attorney with the Akin, Gump, Strauss, Hauer & Feld law firm. Rosie Castro, his mother and unofficial campaign manager, said her son will carry on the family's tradition of political involvement. "I'm excited," she said. "That was 30 years ago we lost, but today, my son has won City Councilman District 7" "I'm real confident he will be an excellent representative," she said. She said her son, who spent about $30,000 on the race, has the tools to find innovative solutions to problems. She pointed to his coast-to-coast experience, including graduating from Harvard in 2000 and earning a bachelor's degree from Stanford University. Castro, whose twin brother Joaquín served as his treasurer, was a White House intern in 1994. Coleman, who planned to call and congratulate Castro, said he got in the race too late. His contributions of less than $800 were no match for Castro's war chest, he said.

"It is unfortunate I didn't start earlier," Coleman said. "I think I could have won this thing."

Source: Schiller, Dane. "Castro Upholds Family's Involvement Tradition." *San Antonio Express-News* (Texas), May 6, 2001, 18A.

Suzanne López, "The Dense, Impenetrable Adobe Ceiling" (2003)

In 2004, in the United States, white women earned 73 cents for every dollar earned by a white man; Asian women, 68 cents; African American women, 64 cents, Native American women, 58 cents, and Latina women 51 cents. Latina girls left high school at a much higher rate than any other group. The major factor was teenage pregnancy but close seconds were marriage, gender roles, stereotyping, family demands, economic status, and attitudes of teachers. These stereotypes continued even after many had made it through college. This article from The Hispanic Outlook in Higher Education *talks to leading Chicana professionals about the "adobe ceiling" that has limited their upward mobility. The article features Cecilia Burciaga, a university administrator who experienced discrimination at various universities.*

While White women are said to encounter a glass ceiling that prevents them from progressing in their careers, Latinas face a more formidable barrier—an adobe ceiling—an obstacle far more challenging to overcome because a glass ceiling at least provides a vision of what lies ahead, said a higher education leader in California.

"With a glass ceiling, you are allowed to see the next level," said Cecilia Preciado Burciaga, former associate vice president for student affairs at California State University at Monterey Bay (CSUMB). "At least you can see through it and practice for the promotion. But an adobe ceiling is dense, impenetrable, and it doesn't allow you to see to the next level. I would like that luxury to see what's next. Once Latinas do break through it, they are often surprised by the personal and professional costs."

Burciaga, who has a master's degree in sociology policy studies from the University of California at Riverside, has spent the last few years developing her theory about the adobe ceiling and has spoken about the subject at public forums. This summer, during a speech at Pima County Community College District in Tucson, Ariz, she shared her thoughts on the ceiling and what it takes to break through it. The event had many cosponsors: the International Women's Film and Speaker Series of the Dean's Interdisciplinary Education Grant, the Crossing Border Speaker Series of the Dean's Minority Education Grant—both funded through the community college, the Arizona Association of Chicanos for Higher Education, Desert Vista Campus, the CSUMB foundation, and its Equal Employment Opportunity Affirmative Action Office.

Burciaga, 57, has 28 years of administrative experience in higher education. She served on the White House Commission on Educational Excellence for Hispanic Americans (1994–2001) and has been named one of the "Top 100 Most Influential Latinas of the Century" by Latina magazine.

She speaks of the adobe ceiling from personal experience. Burciaga recently won a discrimination lawsuit she'd filed against CSUMB with two other Latinas. As part of the settlement, she agreed to leave the University early this year, but CSUMB paid $1 million in damages shared among the defendants and an additional $1.5 million for scholarships to Salinas County area students. University officials said they could not comment, as part of the settlement terms of the lawsuit.

"Our population deserves more respect," said Burciaga, adding that she was surprised to have encountered the adobe ceiling at Monterey Bay because more than half of the population in the area is Latino.

Burciaga said she worked for 20 years at Stanford University where she also encountered the adobe ceiling. She climbed through the ranks and held a variety of positions while at Stanford, including director of the Office of Chicano Affairs, associate dean, and director of development in the Office of the Vice President for Student Resources. When she joined Stanford in 1974, the student body was just 2 percent Mexican American, and there were few Chicano faculty or staff. She worked diligently to increase the numbers of Latinos on the campus so she "wouldn't be the only one there." By 1992, the student body had grown to 11 percent Chicano, and the faculty was increasingly diverse, for which Burciaga said she feels she could take some credit. When she was at Stanford, her staff recruited more women and minorities into the University's PhD programs.

In an interview with the *Christian Science Monitor*, Burciaga said that she did not find open resistance to affirmative action at Stanford, but she did have to fight against apathy.

"It is the faculty that hire faculty," she said in that interview. "They know best how to find their own animals. That means faculty members have got to want it."

In the 1970s, she worked for the U.S. Civil Rights Commission and was named by then President Jimmy Carter to a National Advisory Committee for Women and on the International Commission on the Observance of International Women's Year.

"Cecilia is one of the people I look up to," said Mickie Solorio Luna, California state president of LULAC [League of United Latin American Citizens]. "She's always in the trenches."

While Latinas and White women face different types of ceilings in the workplace, their home lives widen the gap between the two even further. Anglo women can escape the glass ceiling once they leave their workplace at the end of the day because their spouses, parents, and siblings often enjoy the benefits of being part of the "elite culture," said Burciaga. Latinas, on the other hand, have families who are all generally part of the "non-power" group.

Burciaga said she believes that the personal and social connections Anglo women enjoy through marriage or through their parents and siblings help them get through the glass ceiling but Latinas lack those familial connections, making the adobe ceiling virtually impenetrable.

Another aspect of the glass ceiling analogy is the saying that Anglo women also encounter a sticky floor in their efforts to advance their careers, but Burciaga said the sticky floor provides traction. Latinas encounter a dirt floor under their adobe ceiling, a floor that she said allows Latinas to be swept away.

"It's so true what she said," said Luna. "We're on a slippery floor. We're pushed aside, pushed out the door. Latinas always fight for equality for everybody else. We don't get recognition. Latinas are very humble, and we don't ask for recognition."

Burciaga's theory is backed by numbers. A recent study on corporate America by the Hispanic Association on Corporate Responsibility (HACR) found that Hispanic women are grossly underrepresented. They hold only 0.3 percent of all board seats and represent 0.08 percent of all executive officer positions in Fortune 1,000 companies. Of 141 Hispanic board members at Fortune 1,000 companies, only 21 are women, and of 110 Hispanic executive officers, only eight are women.

"Hispanic women, in particular, have encountered a 'concrete ceiling' in corporate America," said HACR President and CEO Anna Escobedo Cabral. "Even though there are more Hispanic women professionals and the number of businesses owned by Hispanic women is one of the fastest growing sectors, Hispanic women continue to be excluded from contributing as board members and executive officers of the largest companies in the nation."

Burciaga said she feels that Latinas not only encounter the adobe ceiling and dirt floor in corporate America but also in higher education. Anglo women are making strides in becoming college presidents and vice presidents, and she said it is important they not forget their Latina hermanas as they create leadership teams for their institutions of higher education.

"This is an opportunity for them to manifest deeper change in the women's movement," said Burciaga. "The question is 'are they diversifying their leadership teams any more than Anglo males?'"

Burciaga expressed concern that the women's movement in general failed to clearly convey the message to women that their advancement carried a responsibility to bring about positive change for all women in the workplace. All women have a responsibility to younger women to help them move forward because any progress that has been made by the women's movement is always at risk and those freedoms can be lost, she said.

But, Burciaga said Latinas must also be more proactive in advancing their own careers, in highlighting their professional successes, a skill that traditionally has been difficult for many Latinas to carry out.

"I tell Latinas not to believe in the good tooth fairy, that if we're good, someone will put a promotion under our pillows," said Burciaga. "Part of our culture is not to be boastful. We're not comfortable with self-promotion. It is important to learn to talk about your accomplishments in a way that is not offensive. To not talk about your accomplishments is deadly."

Amalia Mesa-Bains, director of the Institute for Visual and Public Arts at CSUMB, said she is optimistic about the future for young Latinas. Older Latinas have been striving to develop a model that provides a balance between the family demands of Latino culture and the demands of professional career. Younger Latinas struggle with the Anglo version of having to choose between family and professional aspirations to be successful and the model evolving among Latinas brings the two aspects together.

"I think the young girls are going to kick in the ceiling," said Mesa-Bains. "They are very connected to the goals of the [Latino] community. The unique model we have created for them springs from our family-based and community-based experience. I see us at the adobe ceiling, and I see us finding an opening. We want to open the adobe ceiling, but we do not want to forget the adobe itself."

Burciaga said she feels she is making a contribution, chipping away the adobe ceiling Latinas encounter by filing her lawsuit, mentoring young women, speaking out about the adobe ceiling, and pushing her career forward.

"Cecilia stood her ground for what she believes in, and she never felt sorry for herself," said Luna. "She made a difference and gained the respect from everybody around her. I hope other women will learn from this and stand up for younger women."

Mesa-Bains, co-chair of the Chicano-Latino Faculty and Staff Association at CSUMB, praised Burciaga for her heroic efforts to bring about change at the University.

"We need to recognize the heroism of someone who is willing to sacrifice her own career to force a university to live up to the vision it espouses and to commit the resources necessary to realize that vision."

Burciaga hopes other Latinas are working with her on drilling through the adobe ceiling. Having a network of Latinas to rely on helps make the process of breaking through the adobe ceiling easier, she said. She praises the network of Latinas she relies on and has befriended over the years, saying that they show her that there is a peephole of light and hope through the adobe ceiling.

"Too often we work alone, but we must come together to conquer," Burciaga said. "I have made a commitment to keep chipping away."

Luna said she too believes that if Latinas keep chipping away, eventually the walls will come down.

Burciaga is a first-generation Chicana of parents who were natives of Jalisco, Mexico. She and her late husband, Jose Antonio Burciaga, a poet and artist, have two children, María Rebeca and José Antonio.

Source: López, Suzanne. "The Dense, Impenetrable Adobe Ceiling," *The Hispanic Outlook in Higher Education* 13, no. 10 (February 24, 2003–March 9, 2003): 16, 17.

Erica Frankenberg, Chungmei Lee, and Gary Orfield, "A Multiracial Society with Segregated Schools: Are We Losing the Dream?" (2003)

The Harvard Civil Rights Project originally produced the following report. Since then, Professor Gary Orfield has moved this project on segregated schools to the University of California at Los Angeles. This project brings with it countless reports on the state of Latino education and the progress, or lack thereof, that it has been made since Brown v. the Board of Education

(1954), which did not end segregation in the United States. In 2005, Latino students were more segregated than in 1954. And segregation was worsening. The effects of segregation are devastating in that schools in minority areas are invariably inferior to those in white middle-class areas. The school buildings are older and not maintained with the same care, and the teachers are less experienced and less qualified. The following original Harvard study is on the state of Latino education in the 21st century. It is important because without this and similar data it would be difficult to change education for the better. The report establishes needed guideposts. The following is an extract from the report.

The growth in the Latino student population is happening throughout the country. Although the four primary states in Table 6 with Latino enrollments greater than 150,000 in 2000 are in the West, there are also two states in the South, two in the Northeast, and one in the Midwest. Florida, for example, has had the highest rate of growth in Latino student enrollment in the last thirty years with an unparalleled increase of 614%; Illinois shot up 304% during the same time period. With an increase of almost 2 million since 1970, California has had the largest absolute change in Latino enrollment, a 270% increase.

Unlike black students who have been the focus of hundreds of desegregation orders and Office for Civil Rights enforcement efforts, Latinos have remained increasingly segregated, due, in part, to demographic changes in the population and limited legal and policy efforts targeted to increasing desegregation for Latinos. Latinos were not included in most desegregation court orders due to their small presence in most Southern districts during the 1960s. As a result, Latino students have, until recently, consistently been more isolated from white students than the average black student [See Table 7]. Currently, the average Latino student goes to school where less than 30 percent of the school population is white.

The percentage of Latino students in predominantly minority schools has steadily increased since the 1960s and actually exceeded that of blacks in the 1980s. In the last decade, with the dismantling of desegregation orders and the resegregation of blacks, the level of black segregation is now comparable to that of Latinos: seven out of ten black and Latino students attend predominantly minority schools. The percentage of Latinos in

Table 6 Growth of Latino Enrollments, 1970–2000*

States	1970	2000	Enrollment Change 1970–2000	Percent Change 1970–2000
California	706,900	2,613,480	1,906,580	269.7
Texas	565,900	1,646,508	1,080,608	190.9
New York	316,600	533,631	217,031	68.6
Florida	65,700	469,362	403,662	614.4
Illinois	78,100	315,446	237,346	303.9
Arizona	85,500	297,703	212,203	248.2
New Jersey	59,100	201,509	142,409	240.9
New Mexico	109,300	160,708	51,408	47.0
Colorado	84,281	159,547	75,226	89.3

Source: DBS Corp. 1982; 1987; 2000–2001 NCES Common Core of Data Public School Universe.

*Table includes states with more than 150,000 Latino students in 2000.

Table 7 Most Segregated States for Latino Students, 2000–2001

Rank	% of Latinos in Majority White Schools		Rank	% of Latinos in 90–100% Minority Schools		Rank	% Whites in School of Typical Latino	
1	New York	13.3	1	New York	58.7	1	New York	18.4
2	California	13.3	2	Texas	46.9	2	California	21.0
3	Texas	16.6	3	California	44.0	3	Texas	22.5
4	New Mexico	17.4	4	New Jersey	40.7	4	New Mexico	27.5
5	Rhode Island	20.0	5	Illinois	40.0	5	Illinois	28.7
6	Illinois	25.5	6	Florida	30.0	6	New Jersey	28.8
7	New Jersey	25.8	7	Pennsylvania	27.6	7	Rhode Island	30.5
8	Arizona	28.2	8	Connecticut	27.1	8	Arizona	32.6
9	Florida	29.3	9	Arizona	25.6	9	Florida	32.7
10	Connecticut	29.6	10	Rhode Island	25.4	10	Connecticut	35.7
11	Maryland	31.1	11	New Mexico	24.8	11	Maryland	36.0
12	Massachusetts	35.2	12	Maryland	21.1	12	Massachusetts	39.6
13	Pennsylvania	35.3	13	Massachusetts	18.8	13	Pennsylvania	40.3
14	Nevada	39.1	14	Wisconsin	16.7	14	Nevada	41.9
15	Georgia	44.5	15	Colorado	15.2	15	Georgia	45.8
16	Colorado	46.0	16	Georgia	12.6	16	Colorado	46.3
17	Louisiana	47.8	17	Indiana	11.2	17	Louisiana	48.8
18	Virginia	49.6	18	Louisiana	10.3	18	Virginia	49.5
19	Kansas	52.7	19	Michigan	10.3	19	Delaware	52.4
20	Washington	55.3	20	Nevada	8.3	20	North Carolina	52.7

Source: 2000–2001 NCES Common Core of Data Public School Universe.

predominantly minority schools is slightly higher than that of blacks (76% for Latinos, 72% for blacks).

More Latinos than ever before are also now in intensely segregated schools (90–100% minority), rising from 462,000 in 1968 to 2.86 million in 2000, an increase of 520% in a little over 30 years. After a low of 23% in the late 1960s, the percentage of Latinos attending these schools has consistently increased to reach an unprecedented 37% in 2000.

Source: Frankenberg, Erica, Chungmei Lee, and Gary Orfield, "A Multiracial Society with Segregated Schools: Are We Losing the Dream?" The Civil Rights Project, University of California at Los Angeles, January 2003, 32–33, 44, 52. http://www.civilrightsproject.ucla.edu/research/reseg03/resegregation03.php.

Chip Jacobs, "Return of the Native" (2005)

The person probably most responsible for the California Latino Political Revolution, the election of a critical number of Chicanos to the California State Legislature and the Los Angeles City Council, was Richard Alatorre (1943–). Alatorre was elected to the California Assembly and Los Angeles City Council during a time in the early 1980s when there were no Mexicans on those bodies. He served on reapportionment committees in the state legislature, made deals, and was always controversial. However, he always kept East Los Angeles in his heart, and although the deals were often in his interests, they rarely went against the interests of the area. Alatorre, along with state senator Richard Polanco (1951–), who was chair of the legislature's Latino caucus for a 12 years and tripled its membership, molded a new generation of Latino politicos who became a force in California politics. The following article from Los Angeles *City Beat is based on an interview with Alatorre. The article explains the process whereby Latinos became a third of the Los Angeles City Council and a majority of the Democratic Party caucus in the California Assembly.*

The 200 folks squished into the VIP lounge of the Henry Fonda Music Box Theater were grinning and yipping as the early poll results blinked on the big screens. It was primary night, March 3, and the Antonio-Villaraigosa-for-Mayor bandwagon resembled a Winnebago. A Motown band crooned, the liquor went fast, and if you noticed it, off to the side of the victory buzz, a gaggle of small-town mayors, party operatives, and various believers were embracing a dark-eyed legend many were afraid to be seen with a few years ago. Richard Alatorre was touchable again.

"He was getting hearty hugs, unsolicited, and people wanted their picture with him," recalls Don Justin Jones, a Democratic activist from Pasadena who has known Alatorre since the 1960s. "There's a saying, 'You don't shake hands with a dead man or he'll pull you down with him,' and the establishment was treating Richard like the long-lost prince of the city. You know he was happy when he was calling people, 'Babe.'"

Had a few things gone differently, it might've been Richard José Alatorre taking the oath as Los Angeles' first Latino mayor in modern times, not the slick, cherubic-faced Villaraigosa (should he unseat Jim Hahn May 17). Had Alatorre not tried to house a little girl who lost her mother nine years ago, some grand building might now bear his name.

Destiny, however, had other ideas. His storybook ascent from barrio kid to Hispanic political royalty collapsed in soap-operatic disgrace in 2001 with a graft conviction and drug allegations. He was banished to the Siberia of house arrest, his legacy tarnished no matter the heartfelt tributes from senators and do-gooders.

Should Villaraigosa need a primer on toughness, the man who has been his unofficial campaign consigliere can go one better. He knows history can be viciously ironic.

In 1992, in a recession-flattened, riot-torn Los Angeles, it was Alatorre, the mainstream Democrat, whom the conservative Richard Riordan most feared as his opponent in the mayor's race. It was Alatorre who masterminded the district reapportionment that enabled Villaraigosa to win Alatorre's old seat that he has used to challenge Hahn. And it was Alatorre, along with County Supervisor Gloria Molina, his longtime nemesis, who hoed the path for a fresh crop of Mexican American politicians. One of them was Richard Alarcón, the defeated mayoral candidate and Valley Councilman who liked stressing he was no Alatorre (read: corrupt).

Having jogged through hell and back, Alatorre is in his salad days now—happier, healthier, and holier, those close to him say. The impatient snarls that seemed to bubble from a tormented soul—what writer Hunter S. Thompson once called a politician's inner werewolf—surface less often. At 63, he is a family guy and elder statesman, both felon and community icon, living sorry for the shame he caused yet convinced that he was hunted.

"I don't condone what I did, but I did it out of desperation," Alatorre explains, slitting his eyes at Camilo's Bistro, one of his Eagle Rock hangouts. "I made a mistake and paid for it. It was a very humiliating experience for my family and friends and the institutions that I was part of. It made me assess the role I'd played in things.

"For five years, I had to wake up wondering what the next story was coming up," he adds. "Because of what happened, I'm the sum of the end of my career, when things were bad. I've got that asterisk on my resume that overshadowed 28 years of work."

That episode now seems like yesterday and never-happened. Peers don't worry anymore if they're being taped when they call him. A grayer, chubbier Alatorre gets warm smiles at City Hall. Politicians frequently call him for advice, or to help settle feuds. He's also not skating fast over the thin ice of insolvency anymore. Working quietly, tooling around in his steel-gray Jaguar, he consults for the Affordable Housing Development Corp., the Los Angeles Port Police, the city of Alhambra, and others. Clients chase him, though he refuses to lobby because of disclosure rules that once got him in hot water as a politician.

"I'm making more money than I ever have," Alatorre confirms. "But I'm not trying to chase the buck. All I want is to support my family and live as privately as humanly possible."

Alatorre, unlike the impeached Bill Clinton or a defrocked televangelist, took his lumps old school: he suffered quietly. Sequestered at home, calling in to his probation officer, he didn't court votes or campaign dough. He's learned to make beds, empty the garbage, and enjoy the peace of not having to attend endless meetings. There was no image-revival campaign, no weepy appearance on Oprah, even if he believed that the media had unfairly portrayed him as a sleazebag.

"I wasn't going to let reporters know I had little respect for them driving me out of town," he says.

The Natural

Before he died, José Alatorre left his son with a nugget: Use your head to make a living, because "you aren't any good with your hands." Young Richard embraced that advice, becoming student body president at Garfield High and part-time collection agent for a Whittier Boulevard jewelry store—a job that taught him when to intimidate people and when to back off.

He was an outgoing teenager, slightly rebellious, sure to attend Mass to check out the girls or pray that his jump shot fell during basketball season.

"I was the typical Catholic hypocrite," Alatorre chuckles. (Today, he's hard-core devout.)

At Cal State Los Angeles, Alatorre majored in sociology and then got his master's in public administration from USC, no small feat. While teaching college courses, he happened one day to run into East L.A. Assemblyman Walter Karabian, who knew potential when he saw it. He gave the kid a staff job.

Itching to be the man, Alatorre soon ran and won the assembly seat vacated by David Roberti. His timing sparkled, and he nuzzled in with a fun-loving set of heavy-hitters led by Speaker Willie Brown and his lieutenant, Mike Roos. Brown so liked Alatorre's preternatural cunning that he gave him the committee chairmanship overseeing juiced gambling and liquor interests. Picketing with Chávez, as Alatorre did in 1966 to protest farmworkers' conditions, fed the soul. Working at the state capital during the Chicano era on pesticide regulation and rent control fed his conviction that the little guy needed protection.

But it wasn't heaven. Being in Sacramento meant he saw little of his two sons, who were living in Alhambra with his divorced first wife, Stella. He was terrified of flying, and distances required he do it constantly. He had a few harrowing experiences, including one occasion when the plane's nose cone blew off. To soothe his nerves, he drank.

Tired of flying and jonesing to put his stamp on local politics, he ran for L.A. City Council in 1985. He won, oiled by special interest money, joining the flamboyant Nate Holden, the stately John Ferraro, and erudite Zev Yaroslavsky at the Council horseshoe. In a portentous act, he paid a record $142,000 settlement to the City Attorney's office for failing to disclose contributors.

Alatorre savored the pothole politics that Brown had laughingly warned him he'd come to despise. He was the king of a fiefdom that ran from Boyle Heights to the Glendale border. In that district's volatile immigrant neighborhoods and yuppified hills, everybody recognized his swarthy, rutted complexion and sandpaper voice.

Mayor Tom Bradley also found his Council point man in Alatorre, even if the two couldn't be any different personality-wise. Alatorre proved to be masterful at three-dimensional thinking and lining up votes—without an excess of silky oratory.

Yaroslavsky, now a Westside supervisor, felt a kinship with Alatorre because they both grew up in the same destitute area and understood tough personalities. Their similarities made for some electric combat.

"I judge people in politics by whether their word was good and whether you can depend on them hunkered down in battle, and yeah, I could trust him," Yaroslavsky said. "The thing about him that I always appreciated, even though we don't always agree . . . he always was the real deal. He cares about people on the margins. . . . I'm not going to defend what he did, [but] when I was up against him, I knew I was in the fight of my life."

By the 1990s, Yaroslavsky's portrait was the general impression of Alatorre: a fighter and even a bully. He'd holler at building officials who weren't moving fast enough to get repairs done. He'd sometimes unload on his own staff, exploding like a volcano while aides were left quivering.

Alhambra Mayor Daniel Arguello was part of Alatorre's assembly staff from 1977 to 1982. He remembers him for his odd mix of tenderness, agile thinking, and combustibility.

"As a boss, he was the most fun I've ever had, and there were other times when I wanted to kick in the door," Arguello remembered. "I'd worked for Tom Bradley, and his control was his presence. When Richard Alatorre was angry, everybody knew it."

This explosiveness, Alatorre now believes, was evidence of buried emotions. He was a "dry drunk" who missed his dad terribly. He couldn't uncork his feelings. He regretted what kind of father he'd been. Here he was out at ribbon-cuttings, defending the LAPD, shepherding a budget deal, and yet lost inside.

"People had this impression that I was ruthless, or had no blood in my veins," Alatorre said. "I gave nothing up about my emotions, so they said I was mean, cutthroat, backstabbing. You hear that time in, time out, and you become hardened. You become isolated if you've never taken stock of yourself. I didn't realize that I was bleeding internally."

Little House in Eagle Rock

The world would find out about his hemorrhaging maybe before he did.

In 1997, this reporter wrote a lengthy story in the *L.A. Weekly* about Alatorre's connections to Samuel Mevorach, an Arcadia-based real estate operator who'd bedeviled L.A. housing officials with his dilapidated properties. Among Mevorach's holdings was the Wyvernwood Apartments, a sprawling, once-tidy Boyle Heights complex that had degenerated into blistered, crime-infested units coated with dangerous flaking lead paint; a number of children were poisoned from it. Feeling the heat from inspectors, Mevorach needed Alatorre's sway to grease a $91-million, city-subsidized sale of the property.

Alatorre unluckily needed Mevorach just as much as the slumlord needed him.

The previous year, Belinda Ramos, the sister of Alatorre's third and current wife, Angie, had died of colon cancer. Ramos left behind an adorable, seven-year-old girl whose father was named Henry Lozano. An older man, Lozano was chief of staff to a Democratic congressman and staunchly aligned with Gloria Molina's political machine.

Ramos' dying wish was for Melinda to live with the Alatorres. Melinda loved them, and they loved her back. Two months later, the Alatorres decided to sell their Monterey Hills condo and relocate to an Eagle Rock house with a yard and floor plan roomier for a child.

About this same time, Lozano, who hadn't had much involvement with Melinda, got upset when the little girl didn't want to spend time with him. Lozano's next move was to initiate a custody fight. It exposed a lot more than parenting techniques.

Soon, the *Los Angeles Times* began writing about how the Alatorres had financed their move into the Spanish-style house. The paper found that Mevorach had given Alatorre tens of thousands of dollars under the table and arranged a sham lease on the condo. Stories about money exchanges at greasy restaurants, bagmen, and mysterious new roofs tied to one of Alatorre's political contributors had a Raymond Chandler feel. When those articles subsided, Alatorre's alleged coke use snatched *Times* headlines.

By 1998, it was unclear whether Alatorre would survive the onslaught. The judge overseeing the ongoing custody fight ordered a surprise drug test, and Alatorre was found to have coke in his system despite his proclamation he was clean. The same judge who'd once praised the Alatorres for their care of Melinda ordered her out of their presence. Alatorre's credibility, the judge scolded, had been "totally shredded."

He'd ignited the biggest ethics scandal to hit L.A. since the final term of the Bradley administration. Bradley's plunge began when it was revealed that he was a paid adviser to a bank doing business with the city. Alatorre's crisis, by comparison, gave the public an excruciating glimpse into his narcotics use and personal relationships.

Alatorre had once vowed he wouldn't wind up like Bradley had—a broken man sadly walking away from a job after overstaying his welcome—but suddenly Alatorre was lunch meat in a media feeding frenzy. So many television news crews clogged his new front porch that a fence had to be installed. FBI agents pried into his affairs, with the District Attorney's office not far behind. Supposed friends shunned him, unaware of his sinking health or tattered finances. Family members were sucked into the chaos, as well.

For Angie Alatorre, who'd stood by her husband during the squall, having Melinda removed was the low point. She'd felt guilty that it was her side of the family that had caused her husband's spiral. The drugs, however, were his doing.

"The only time I" got angry "was when we lost Melinda because of Richard's really dumb behavior and the judge sent her to go to my mother's for a week," she recalls. "I told (Richard) that if we didn't get her back, 'I'll never forgive you for this.' I didn't have to say anything else for him to know things had to change."

The next year, Alatorre stunned his backers when he announced he would not seek re-election. He knew that while he'd probably win the election, it'd be a nasty contest that'd cut deeper into his kin. The fact that Melinda was too young to understand the fireworks above her was a blessing they didn't want to exploit.

Ridden to the Ground

Today, private-citizen Alatorre looks healthier than the public one, who often slouched enigmatically at meetings in his fine suits.

Darrell Alatorre, Richard's youngest son, said many people disbelieve him when he says how vibrant his dad has become. With the pressure off, he has time for chatty lunches, USC football games, walks around the Rose Bowl, and doting on Melinda, now a high school junior. Just don't give his dad a home fix-it project because he is all thumbs, Darrell Alatorre laughs.

The late-1990s, conversely, was a wagon-circling time the Alatorre clan would rather forget. The grand jury hauled lots of frightened people before it. Darrell Alatorre lost business clients worried about the stigma. His older brother, Derrick, relocated his family out of the area to relieve the pressure. Alatorre tried reassuring his family he was okay, but he wasn't sleeping well or looking good. The stress contributed to a ruptured diaphragm requiring surgery in 1997 and 1998. Two years later he got prostate cancer. Today he's healthy.

"I didn't worry about his sanity. I worried about his health!" Darrell Alatorre says. "Did I see fear in his eyes? Did he ever break down? Yeah, a couple times. Is that a picture a son wants to see in his father? No! The whole ordeal he went through was bullshit, though there was some truth to his past addiction. I remember asking him during the custody battle why he was doing all this, and he said, 'Mijo, Melinda has nowhere else to go.'"

Meanwhile, as the subpoenas and the stories about him flew, his friends and colleagues were puzzled. Why wasn't he fighting back? His inner circle was baffled that he wasn't holding a press conference to defend himself or announce a libel suit from accusations that many of them believed were untrue or sensationalized. Alatorre was a lot of things, but passive wasn't part of the package.

The *Times,* among other charges, had accused Alatorre's cronies of paying him off through his wife's event-planning business and charities. Where was the context about why they'd wanted the house, his backers asked. Where were the questions about why Richard was abusing? And where was the lowdown on Mevorach, who'd copped a deal with the feds, telling them that Alatorre had "extorted" him for cash when Mevorach had been currying Alatorre's favor for years?

Darrell Alatorre says he was ready to take on the *Times* when a writer friend at the paper tipped him off that it'd budgeted $500,000 for stories about the family and had hired private investigators to dig up dirt. A reporter who worked on the stories says there was no such budget item for these stories and no investigators were retained.

"I couldn't believe it," Darrell Alatorre said. "It seemed such an astronomical amount of money. Later, I'd never seen the paper so demonize somebody."

Angie Alatorre says she and her husband's longtime confidante Lou Moret didn't always agree on tactics, but they thought their man should counterpunch. Moret, though, found that Alatorre just wanted out, and didn't believe blood-smelling reporters with preconceptions about ethnic politicians would listen to him.

"He didn't think he took money for anything more improper than anyone else had," says Moret, who ran Alatorre's 1972 and 1974 Assembly campaigns. "He knew he'd been treated differently, and partly that's because he's Mexican and partly because of his reluctance to sell his viewpoint, philosophically. That's how the cookie crumbles. . . . Richard wasn't forced out. He wasn't defeated. He wasn't recalled. . . . But for the L.A. Times, he was an easy target."

For his part, Alatorre says it wasn't until he left office and reflected back that he realized his spin into coke, self-doubt, and silence had been building for 30-odd years.

Early on April 15, 1964, Alatorre's first son, Derrick, was born at a Boyle Heights hospital. Ten hours later, the ecstasy crumbled when Richard's father suffered a heart attack while painting a crib for his infant grandson and died. For José's boy, the loss was ironic, wrenching, and most of all, lasting.

José Alatorre, stove repairman and seventh-grade dropout, had always preached hard work and keeping personal problems private. While stoic, he prized ideals. If the national anthem were [sic] playing on TV, he'd make young Richard stand, though he didn't always.

In passing away so abruptly, José never saw his string-bean son, then 21, mature from a student leader with a 60-hour-a-week job to one of the nimblest minds in a mostly white state legislature. Nor was he around to dispense wisdom when Richard's weaknesses roared.

"I never knew how much I blamed my dad for dying," Alatorre confides. "It forced me to become something I wasn't ready to be. I had to become head of a household, but I was still a kid. I had no constructive outlet for being hurt later in life. You don't stuff things down in your soul and expect be happy."

Alcoholics Anonymous helped open his eyes, and he accepted that his addictive personality had shown even at age 14, when he chug-a-lugged some wine. By his 20s, liquor quieted his rage. He finally quit in 1988 after getting treatment, not allowing himself to lapse when the graft investigations revved up.

It was the drug all over L.A.—cocaine—that he sought. (Drugs, it's worth noting, are the one subject Alatorre refuses to detail except to say stories about him snorting at City Hall or with a buddy looking for city contracts were mostly false.)

"Through AA, I now understand I am a grateful alcoholic," he says. "We're not normal. A normal person can have one drink and not 10 to 15. I know that if I took one drink, the run would be on. . . . I had so much happening in my life then, when the [stories hit], I didn't know I was powerless."

Nor, some say, did he realize his baggage was slowly entombing him.

"He started locking out friends who would've told him, 'Don't do that! What the f—— is wrong with you?'" Moret adds. "He became a refugee. He wasn't making the right decisions. He got in trouble because he's an addict. Even when he was drinking, it wasn't because he liked it. It wasn't wine or fine Scotch he used. It was Seven-and-Seven. Who drinks that?"

The Al Capone Treatment

Thick pride may have also contributed to his troubles. By 1996, Alatorre's machinations to funnel government work to Hispanic-run ventures struck many as heavy-handed, as did his connections to the East Los Angeles Community Union, Corboda Corp., and various MTA contractors seeking a piece of a $1-billion rail line through his district. Newly elected Council members didn't fear him as others once had. In what turned out to be his last campaign, a political novice forced him into a runoff.

"He didn't want to give his detractors the pleasure of seeing the mighty stag taken down," says Jones, the Pasadena activist. "He didn't want to let folks in on the pain, and maybe that got him into trouble. Fidel Castro said in his famous speech: 'You can find me guilty, but history will absolve me.' When you look back at this period, people will appreciate that Richard didn't cry when his enemies kicked him in the ass, but I guarantee you that his boots were full of blood."

Even after he left office, the bloodletting continued. When Alatorre was lined up with consulting work typical for ex-politicians with the L.A. Department of Water and Power and the Compton Community College District, the *Times* wrote about it, and officials nixed what could have been $70,000-a-year in income. A $114,000-a-year post with a state unemployment insurance board ended, too, when Alatorre settled with the Justice Department.

His legal-defense bills topped $100,000, and to pay them he had to bust open his IRA and pay a $100,000 penalty for early withdrawal. This somewhat undercuts the notion he'd been stashing away money as a guy-on-the-take, as detractors suspected; there were no secret bank accounts. Because he'd always spent what he made, Alatorre says he "didn't have the luxury of not working" and launched his consulting business.

Dine with him and you glean four things: His cell phone never stops jangling, he wolfs bacon like air, and he can spice cuss words into the most delicate topic. The other f-word—"felon"—he doesn't use. The idea that he is one scalds him. It just doesn't seem to obsess him.

If he has any satisfaction about his demise, it's that a four-year, federal-led investigation of his links to people trying to buy his influence did not result in a major corruption charge. Instead, he pled to not disclosing $42,000 in illicit income on his ethics commission and tax filings. Some call this the "Al Capone" treatment: nailing a high-profile figure on a relatively incidental charge. No other big fish was nabbed, either.

"By prosecuting me, I was making somebody's career," Alatorre says. "We ran the city—me, Zev [Yaroslavsky], and John Ferraro—when Bradley was in trouble. Even the *Times* said that. But certain people did not feel like I was the kind of guy who should be mayor, and what's ironic is that I never wanted that."

Maybe not, but that doesn't mean he's short on ideas about how to get it. Still very much on his game, Alatorre will unleash a torrent of expletive-laden opinion about this year's race. And if he's really talking to Villaraigosa as much as he says he is, current Mayor Jim Hahn's ears are burning.

"Jimmy is like the T-ball mayor. I go back to when Jimmy first ran for City Controller, and I had the distinct impression he fell into politics. It's not where his gut is," Alatorre says. "Jimmy is a very honest guy. It's just that he's always around the edges on issues. If you asked his ex-aides, they'd say he's lazy. He doesn't live and breathe politics like his sister [Councilwoman Janice Hahn] does. [Former Gov.] Gray Davis was evil. He was driven. Jimmy isn't driven. He's just blah."

Alatorre does sees promise in Villaraigosa, saying, "I recognize Antonio's shortcomings, but he has the best chance of getting done what L.A. needs," adding: "We need someone who will work well with the City Council and Sacramento, someone who will get L.A. the goodies."

For instance, he notes that Hahn hasn't even taken advantage of L.A.'s respected police chief, William Bratton, to get more cops or anti-terrorism money. "Bratton likes the notoriety here, but he's so far up Jimmy Hahn's butt, and Jimmy is so far up his, neither of them can see. . . . If I were mayor, I'd go put my arm around President Bush and say how much I liked his dad if it got us resources."

That is the kind of thinking that got results, and both the residents who recognize him strolling down Garfield Avenue and the powerful remember. Sympathy is another thing.

"Richard Alatorre was clearly the smartest guy on the City Council when I was there; I admire and love him, but I don't feel sorry for him," says former Mayor Richard Riordan, now California's Secretary of Education. "Judge him as he is today. [After all], we forgive murderers."

The family's saga has ended better than any of them could have imagined four years ago—happily. Alatorre has work aplenty and time with his family. Melinda, now a spunky teenager, worships "pops," as protective of him as he is of her. Henry Lozano is a non-factor in their lives. The family even reads the *Times*.

There probably won't be a beach house he had dreamed about as a young man, but c'est la vie.

"I wake up in the morning," he adds, "happy to be alive."

Source: Jacobs, Chip. "Return of the Native." *Los Angeles City Beat*, April 7, 2005. http://www.lacitybeat.com/article.php?id=1887&IssueNum=96. Courtesy of Chip Jacobs, http://chipjacobs.com/a_returnof.html.

Rakesh Kochhar, Roberto Suro, and Sonya Tafoya, "Report: The New Latino South: The Context and Consequences of Rapid Population Growth" (2005)

Although the overwhelming majority of Mexican immigrants have been concentrated in the Southwest, by the 1990s, Mexican and other Latino immigrants were moving heavily into the American South. This migration was encouraged by the modernizing of the southern economy and a labor shortage that had reached crisis proportions. This encouraged Latino immigrants, both documented and undocumented, to fill the gap. The 1990s saw the Latino population in the South increase more than 200 percent, and some counties experienced more than 1,000 percent growth. It has been estimated that some 80 percent of those immigrants are undocumented.

The following excerpts from Pew Hispanic Center report concern the growth of the Latino immigrant population in the South.

The Hispanic population is growing faster in much of the South than anywhere else in the United States. Across a broad swath of the region stretching westward from North Carolina on the Atlantic seaboard to Arkansas across the Mississippi River and south to Alabama on the Gulf of Mexico, sizeable Hispanic populations have emerged suddenly in communities where Latinos were a sparse presence just a decade or two ago. Examined both individually and collectively, these communities display attributes that set them apart from the nation as a whole and from areas of the country where Latinos have traditionally settled. In the South, the white and black populations are also increasing and the local economies are growing robustly, even as some undergo dramatic restructuring. Such conditions have acted as a magnet to young, male, foreign-born Latinos migrating in search of economic opportunities. While these trends are not unique to the South, they are playing out in that region with a greater intensity and across a larger variety of communities—rural, small towns, suburbs, and big cities—than in any other part of the country. Understanding the interplay of Hispanic population growth and the conditions that attended it helps illuminate a broad process of demographic and economic change in the South and in other new settlement areas as well. To varying degrees, communities scattered from New England to the Pacific Northwest are also seeing surging Hispanic populations. The South, different in so many ways for so much of its history, now offers lessons to the rest of the country. Most of the Latinos added to the population of the new settlement areas of the South are foreign born, and their migration is the product of a great many different policies and circumstances in the United States and their home countries. But there is a local context as well, and it is different in the new settlement areas of the South than it is in states such as California and New York, where migrants join large, well-established Latino communities. Given its distinctive character, Hispanic population growth in these parts of the South will also have distinctive impacts on public policy, and those impacts have only just begun to be felt. This report focuses on six Southern states—Arkansas, Alabama, Georgia, North Carolina, South Carolina, and Tennessee—that registered very fast rates of Hispanic population growth between the censuses of 1990 and 2000 and continue to outpace the national average in the most recent census estimates. . . . This report also examines 36 counties in the South that are experiencing especially rapid Hispanic growth. Some of these counties contain metropolitan areas such as Atlanta, Georgia; Birmingham, Alabama; and Charlotte, North Carolina; that registered huge increases in their Hispanic populations—for example, Mecklenburg County, North Carolina, which includes Charlotte, was up 500 percent. But other counties are predominately rural or contain smaller cities. Their total population in 2000 ranged from fewer than 37,000 (Murray County, a carpet manufacturing community in northwest Georgia) to almost 900,000 (Shelby County, Tennessee, home to Memphis). Thirty-six of these counties, all with an increase in their Hispanic population of 200 percent or more, had enough statistical information available to be studied in detail for this report. And in every case, the Hispanic population was relatively small before it surged. Fewer than 7,000 Hispanics were counted in Mecklenburg in 1990, but by 2000 there were nearly 45,000. Gordon County, Georgia, had just 200 Latinos in 1990 and saw its Hispanic population soar to more than 3,200 by the 2000 census. . . .

Several features distinguish the kind of Hispanic population growth taking place in the new settlement areas of the South: its speed, its relation to the growth of other population groups and the characteristics of the Latinos settling there. In the six southern states with the fastest Latino growth, the Hispanic population quadrupled between 1990 and 2000. That rapid growth reflects the fact that the Latino numbers started quite small, but it represents an extraordinarily quick demographic change nonetheless. And Latinos are not the only group that is growing. In most areas of the South experiencing very rapid Latino growth from a very small base, the numbers of whites and blacks are also increasing, albeit at slower rates. That is not the case in many other parts of the country, where the non-Hispanic populations are static or declining. Finally, the Latino population added to the new settlement areas of the South is younger, more immigrant, and more male than the Hispanic population overall. This has all the characteristics of labor migration in its early stages. . . .

Aside from its speed, Hispanic population growth in these six states is distinctive because it occurred against a backdrop of simultaneous growth in the rest of the population. In other words, although Latinos are a rapidly growing presence in these six states, they are only one factor in an overall pattern of population growth, and in fact they are a relatively small factor in the broader picture. Both whites and blacks contributed greater numbers to the total population increase in these six Southern states, and this trend has held steady since at least 1990. These states are drawing not just Latinos but others as well, and very fast Hispanic population growth is for the most part happening in places where the whole population is growing robustly.

The total population of these six southern states grew by nearly 5.2 million between 1990 and 2000, and Hispanics made up only about 900,000 or 17 percent of that increase. Meanwhile, growth in the white population (2.3 million) accounted for 45 percent of the total increase and added numbers of blacks (1.3 million) accounted for 26 percent. Thus, even if not one Latino had been added to the population of this region, it still would have experienced notable growth.

This picture of rapid Latino growth amid overall growth distinguishes these southern states both from the nation as a whole and from California, New York, New Jersey, and Illinois, states that have large, well-established Latino populations. . . .

Mexico is the country of origin for more Hispanic immigrants in the United States than all other nations put together, accounting for 64 percent of all Latino immigrants. That dominance is even stronger in the six new settlement states in this study, where those born in Mexico make up 73 percent of foreign-born Latinos. . . . Recent data also suggest that some new settlements in the South may be drawing a relatively larger share of migrants from regions of Mexico that have only recently begun sending large numbers of immigrants when compared with the traditional settlement states of California, Illinois, New Jersey, and New York. . . .

The growth in the employment of Hispanic and non-Hispanic workers in the new settlement states and counties was well in excess of the nationwide rate. Data from the decennial censuses show that total employment in the U.S. for Hispanic workers increased by 48.6 percent between 1990 and 2000. However, the increase in employment of Latinos in the six new settlement states was much higher than the nationwide rate. The smallest increase was in Alabama, but even so, the employment of Latino workers there increased by 244 percent. The largest increase, 495 percent, occurred in North Carolina. In the six new settlement states combined, Latino employment was 349 percent higher in 2000 than in 1990. The employment of non-Hispanic workers increased by 14.9 percent in the six Southern states. This was well above the national average growth of 9.1 percent for non-Hispanics in the 1990s. Georgia led the way for non-Hispanic workers as their employment increased by 19.8 percent in that state. However, the new South was more critical to the growth in jobs for non-Hispanic than for Hispanic workers. While the percentage increases in the employment of Latinos are astounding, the absolute increases in number are more modest. In the six southern states combined, the total increase in Hispanic employment was just over 404,000, and that accounted for less than 10 percent of the nationwide increase of 4.4 million in Latino employment. All together, these six states added jobs for 1.9 million non-Hispanic workers between 1990 and 2000. That amounted to 20 percent of the nationwide increase of 9.7 million in non-Latino employment. Overall, more than 80 percent of the new jobs created in these states in the 1990s were filled by non-Hispanic workers and fewer than 20 percent by Hispanics. The Hispanic share of new jobs was much higher on a nationwide basis as Latinos captured 31 percent of the 14 million new jobs created nationally between 1990 and 2000. . . .

Hispanic workers in diverse counties are also likely to be found in management, professional, and related occupations but their representation in these occupations (13.2%) in diverse counties was below their national average (16.1%) in 2000. Similarly, Latinos were far less likely (6.9%) than the national norm (13.7%) to be found in office and administrative-support occupations in diverse counties. These tendencies are, no doubt, a reflection of the fact that Latinos in the new South are far more likely to be foreign born than in the rest of the country.

White and black workers are also far more likely to be found in white-collar occupations in diverse counties in comparison with other counties. In fact, 40.1% of whites could be found in management, professional, and related occupations alone in the diverse counties, well above their national average of 31.6% in 2000. Conversely, white workers were less likely than the national average to be employed as construction or production workers in diverse counties. . . .

Nationally, Latinos were earning 61 percent as much as whites in 2000. The situation was approximately the same in manufacturing oriented counties, as Latinos earned 64 percent as much as whites in manufacturing counties and 58 percent as much in transition counties. But the median income of whites in diverse counties is significantly higher than in the other counties—$34,100 versus $26,000 or less in the other county groups. This reflects the far greater opportunities in white-collar occupations for white workers in diverse counties. Consequently, Hispanic workers earned only 47 percent as much as white workers in diverse counties in 2000.

Source: © 2005 Pew Hispanic Center, a Pew Research Center project, www.pewhispanic.org. Prepared by the Pew Hispanic Center for presentation at "Immigration to New Settlement Areas," July 26, 2005, i–ii, 1, 6, 13, 25, 33–34.

Stuart Silverstein, "Racial Issues Lose Urgency, Study Finds; UCLA Survey Shows That a Record High Percentage of College Freshmen Believe Discrimination Is No Longer a Major Problem in the U.S." (2005)

In a 2005 University of California at Los Angeles (UCLA) survey, freshman Karina Hernández said she did not recall ever having been discriminated against as a Latina; she was not particularly concerned with the issue of race and ethnic relations. The UCLA survey found that 22.7 percent of freshmen believed racial discrimination is no longer a major problem. Race did not seem to matter as much as in the previous generation. This was reflected in other national surveys. The following excerpts summarize the UCLA survey, which is interesting because it raises the questions of whether racism exists in present-day society or if people just don't recognize it. Racism is not as blatant as in the 1940s, when Mexicans were called greasers and were not allowed to use public facilities, or in the 1960s, when greater numbers of Mexicans were drafted into the army and fewer attended institutions of higher learning. What form does racism take today?

In other national results, the survey found that:

- Freshmen were more polarized politically. Students describing themselves as "middle of the road" remained the biggest group, at 46.4%, but that percentage was the smallest in more than 30 years and was down from 50.3% in 2003. Liberals accounted for 26.1% and conservatives 21.9%. Students describing themselves as "far left" climbed to 3.4%, and those as "far right" rose to 2.2%—both record highs.

- A record high 47.2% of freshmen said there was a very good chance that they would have to get a job during the year to pay for college expenses, versus a low of 35.3% in 1989.
- Students who reported frequently being bored in class during their last year of high school climbed to a record 42.8%, up from 40.1% a year earlier and from a low of 29.3% in 1985.

The survey—titled "The American Freshman: National Forms for Fall 2004"—was conducted by the Cooperative Institutional Research Program, a unit of UCLA's Higher Education Research Institute.

The findings were based on responses to a four-page questionnaire filled out last summer and fall by 289,452 entering freshmen at 440 four-year colleges around the country. The margin for error is 0.1% for the national results and 0.3% for the California results.

Source: Silverstein, Stuart. "Racial Issues Lose Urgency, Study Finds; UCLA survey shows that a record high percentage of college freshmen believe discrimination is no longer a major problem in the U.S." *Los Angeles Times*, January 31, 2005, 3.

Enrique C. Ochoa and Gilda L. Ochoa, "Governor's Comments Reveal the Depth of Sexism and Racism" (2006)

Mexican Americans and Latinas had, like almost everything else in society, been commoditized at the turn of the 21st century. As a "product," they were categorized and stereotyped. The following Los Angeles Daily News *article by professors Enrique C. Ochoa and Gilda L. Ochoa from California State University–Pomona and Pomona College, respectively, was written in response to a 2006 remark by California governor Arnold Schwarzenegger (1947–) that Latinas were sexually "hot."*

There is nothing new about Gov. Arnold Schwarzenegger's description of state Assemblywoman Bonnie García as "very hot" because of her "black blood" and "Latino blood." Even García's claims—that the governor's comments are just an inside joke and that she is "a hot-blooded Latina"—are not surprising.

It was just two years ago that Mexican President Vicente Fox made similar offensive comments about African Americans. These "jokes" or "slips of the tongue" are part of the enduring legacy of gendered racism that is woven into the fabric of society. And their ramifications are real.

Schwarzenegger's comments are reminiscent of beliefs that were rampant through the early 1900s. These beliefs equated status in society with genetic, innate differences between groups. Northern Europeans were assumed to be biologically superior to all other groups—including Southern and Eastern Europeans, blacks, Native Americans, Asian Americans and Latin Americans.

Such genetic determinism helped to justify 250 years of enslavement of African Americans, attempts at cultural genocide against Native Americans, and segregation and U.S. imperial expansion.

Schwarzenegger's remarks also echo dominant thinking throughout the nineteenth century where the "mixing of blood" was negatively perceived. The first Anglo Americans who came to what is now the Southwest perpetuated the belief that Mexicans in the region were inferior to Anglos precisely because of their mixed heritage. Such biological thought fueled attempts to maintain "white racial purity," and with the exception of Vermont, all U.S. states introduced legislation banning interracial unions.

Not only should Schwarzenegger's comments be seen in the context of this enduring history of racism, but they also suggest the specific ways that most perceptions have interacted with sexism to justify the denigration, sexualization, and exploitation of women of color. During the period of U.S. invasion and domination of Mexico and Central America, popular music and travel literature written by Anglos stereotypically cast Latinas as sexually promiscuous, available, or "hot blooded." At this time, Asian women were similarly depicted as sexually immoral. As with African Americans during slavery, these characterizations of women of color had significant ramifications. They justified kidnapping and rape, and for Chinese women, they resulted in the Page Law in 1875, where women were excluded from immigrating to the United States until 1943.

Despite attempts to forget this history, its manifestations run deep, and Schwarzenegger's comments reveal the insidious ways that such beliefs continue to shape public consciousness and institutional practices. Central to the anti-immigrant movement today is the mistaken belief that Latinas' sexuality leads to too many children and an overuse of public services. In the current War on Terror, Middle Eastern women are often viewed as repressed victims of a backward culture that need to be saved by a superior U.S. culture.

Communities of color have long challenged these discriminatory attitudes and actions. History is replete with examples, from African American resistance to slavery, Asian American struggles for citizenship, to the civil rights movements of the 1960s and 1970s. By teaching their children counter-histories, maintaining their cultures and languages, and fostering solidarity within their communities, women of color have engaged in multiple forms of resistance. The recent immigrant rights marches are part of the contemporary ways that Latinas/os are countering anti-immigrant movements and white supremacist ideologies.

We should not let this moment pass as an isolated slip. Political leaders should be held accountable for their statements.

Source: Ochoa, Enrique C., and Gilda L. Ochoa. "Arnold's Latina Slip Must Spark Dialogues." *Los Angeles Daily News* (Valley edition), September 12, 2006. N13.

Pew Hispanic Center, "Fact Sheet: Latinos and the War in Iraq" (January 4, 2007)

The Pew Hispanic Center at the University of Southern California continues to be the premier think tank on Latino-related studies. The following study examines the attitude of Latinos toward the war in Iraq. This study shows that two out of three Latinos believe U.S. armed forces should be brought home. Unlike in other wars, the Latino population has been critical, and disapproval of the war is higher among the Latino population than the general population. It is significant because in past wars Latinos, especially Mexicans and Puerto Ricans, believed they had to pay society with their blood. The report is important because it memorializes why Latinos were against the war.

Two out of every three Latinos now believe that U.S. troops should be brought home from Iraq as soon as possible and only one in four thinks the U.S. made the right decision in using military force, according to a new survey by the Pew Hispanic Center.

Hispanics have generally expressed more negative views toward the war compared with the rest of the population. The latest survey, however, shows an even stronger opposition on the part of Latinos, especially when it comes to keeping troops in Iraq.

Two-thirds of Hispanics (66%) now favor bringing troops home as soon as possible, up from 51% in January 2005. Conversely, the share of Latinos who favored keeping troops in Iraq until the situation there has stabilized has declined from 37% to 19%.

Native-born Hispanics are generally more supportive of the war than their foreign-born counterparts. But in the latest survey, the native born are almost as adamant about bringing troops home as the foreign born (62% vs. 68% respectively).

The general public also is more inclined to bring the troops home, but not to the same extent as Hispanics. A survey of the general population by the Pew Research Center for the People & the Press in December found that one in two Americans (50%) favored bringing troops home as soon as possible, up from 41% in January 2005.

The changing attitude toward the war is also evident in the answer to a basic question: Do you think the U.S. made the right decision or the wrong decision in using military force against Iraq? Since 2004, a third or more of Latinos responded that using military force was the right decision. In the latest survey, only 24% of Latinos agreed with that assessment. That is down from 39% in April/June 2004 and from 31% in August/October 2006.

By comparison, 42% of the general public believes the U.S. made the right decision in using military force, according to the survey by the Pew Research Center.

The Pew Hispanic Center survey was conducted by telephone from December 5 to 20, 2006, among a nationally representative sample of 1,006 Hispanics age 18 and older. The sample was drawn using a stratified Random Digit Dialing methodology. Interviews were conducted by bilingual interviewers in English or Spanish, according to the respondents' preferences. The results for the full sample have a margin of error of +/– 3.1%. All fieldwork was conducted for the Center by International Communications Research of Media, PA.

Latino Attitudes on the War in Iraq

The Pew Hispanic Center has regularly tracked Latino public opinion on the war in Iraq since February 2003. As with the rest of the American public, Hispanic views on the war have shifted over time, often in direct response to developments in Iraq. The quick end to the first phase of combat produced a spike, for example, but the subsequent violence and the mounting casualties in 2003 eroded support among Hispanics. The capture of Saddam Hussein in mid-December 2003 rallied Hispanic public opinion, but not to the levels seen shortly after the war started. Since then, Latino views on the war have been marked by increased pessimism.

Table 1 Do You Think the U.S. Should Keep Military Troops in Iraq until the Situation Has Stabilized, or Do You Think the U.S. Should Bring Its Troops Home As Soon As Possible?

	January 2005			December 2006		
	Total Latino	U.S. Born	Foreign Born	Total Latino	U.S. Born	Foreign Born
Keep troops in Iraq	37	47	29	19	28	15
Bring troops home	51	46	55	66	62	68
Don't know/no answer	12	6	15	15	10	17

This fact sheet uses three questions that have been asked in surveys to track how the perception of the war in Iraq has changed among Latinos in the U.S.

While support for keeping troops in Iraq has eroded across the board, the decline has been especially steep among Latinos.

In January 2005, a majority of Hispanics (51%) were in favor of bringing troops home, compared with 41% among the general population. In the latest survey, two-thirds of Latinos (66%) were in favor compared with half (50%) among the general population.

Fewer than one in five (19%) of Hispanics now favor keeping troops in Iraq, a decrease from 37% in January 2005 and 50% in January 2004, when the question was asked in a slightly different way. The Pew Research Center survey in December 2006 found that among the general population 44% were in favor, down from 54% in January 2005.

Described another way, the share of Latinos who favored keeping troops in Iraq declined by 18 percentage points between January 2005 and December 2006. Among the general population, the drop was 10 percentage points.

Even among Latinos who said the U.S. made the right decision in using military force against Iraq, 43% still supported bringing troops home as soon as possible.

Native-born Latinos were roughly split on this question in 2005. However, in the latest survey, the native-born have significantly swung in favor of bringing troops home. Almost two in three (62%) are now in favor of withdrawal, up from 46%. A solid majority of foreign-born Hispanics (55%) were in favor of bringing troops home in 2005 and that share has now increased to more than two-thirds (68%).

Support for bringing the troops home is stronger among those with lower incomes and lower levels of education. Three out of four (75%) Latinos with household incomes of $25,000 or less favored this option, as did 72% of those with a high school education or less. By comparison, among those with household incomes of $75,000 or more, 42% supported bringing troops home. And among Hispanics with college degrees or higher, 57% favored this option.

Perceptions of the war in Iraq vary depending on nativity, with foreign-born Hispanics in general more disapproving. In 2004 and 2005, for example, a plurality among native-born Latinos believed the U.S. had made the right decision in using military force. Even as attitudes toward the war turned negative, 40% of native-born Latinos still felt this way in the two surveys taken in 2006. Among foreign-born Hispanics, however, a majority has said using military force was the wrong decision and that number has pretty much held steady since 2004.

The latest survey also shows an increase in the number of Latinos who express uncertainty on this question. About one in four said they did not know whether the U.S. had made the right decision or the wrong decision or they simply refused to answer, an increase from 12% in the survey conducted between August and October 2006. The uncertainty is more prevalent among foreign-born Hispanics.

Table 2 Do You Think the U.S. Made the Right Decision or the Wrong Decision in Using Military Force Against Iraq?

	April–June 2004			January 2005			August–October 2006			December 2006		
	Total Latino	U.S. Born	Foreign Born	Total Latino	U.S. Born	Foreign Born	Total Latino	U.S. Born	Foreign Born	Total Latino	U.S. Born	Foreign Born
Right decision	39	50	32	37	48	28	31	40	26	24	40	15
Wrong decision	48	42	51	51	46	54	56	52	59	50	42	55
NK/NA	13	8	17	12	5	18	12	7	16	26	18	30

Table 3 How Well Do You Think the U.S. Military Effort in Iraq Is Going?

	December 2003			January 2004			December 2006		
	Total Latino	U.S. Born	Foreign Born	Total Latino	U.S. Born	Foreign Born	Total Latino	U.S. Born	Foreign Born
Very well	16	15	17	30	25	33	8	11	6
Fairly well	26	33	21	32	46	23	11	17	7
Not too well	32	35	30	24	21	25	26	33	23
Not well at all	17	14	19	9	6	11	42	34	46
DK/NA	9	4	13	5	2	8	13	5	17

Hispanics by a wide margin believe that the U.S. military effort is faring poorly in Iraq. More than two-thirds (68%) said it was either going not too well or not well at all.

Latinos are generally of a mind with the American public in this negative assessment of the military effort in Iraq. In the December 2006 Pew Research Center poll of the general population, 64% of Americans agreed that the military effort was going not too well or not well at all. But while relatively few Hispanics (19%) said the military effort was going either very well or fairly well, in the general population almost a third (32%) cast the military effort in a positive light.

This question was asked of Latinos in December 2003, after a period when American casualties were high and the war was not going well and then again a month later, in January of 2004, shortly after the capture of Iraqi leader Saddam Hussein. As with the rest of the American public, the capture produced a significant spike in support among Latinos. A majority (52%) said in January 2004 that the U.S. military effort was going either very well or fairly well, up from 42% just a month earlier. Today, two years later, only about one in five Hispanics agree with this assessment.

Source: Fact Sheet: Latinos and the War in Iraq. Pew Hispanic Center, January 4, 2007. www.pewhispanic.org. http://www.pewhispanic.org/2007/01/04/latinos-and the-war-in-iraq/

The Fight to Save Ethnic Studies in Tucson (2011)

In response to pressure from such right-wing groups as the Tea Party and the American Legislative Exchange Council, Tom Horne (1945–), then Arizona superintendent of public instruction, sponsored Arizona HB 2281, which banned the study of other cultures, specifically Mexican American studies, in kindergarten through the 12th grade on the grounds that such studies were racially divisive and subversive and led to intense confrontations and moral outrage. The issue is still in the courts, but it led to the dismantling of the Tucson Unified School District's highly successful Mexican American studies program, which had dramatically stemmed the dropout of Latino students. As a result, certain books were banned from the classroom, students were arrested for protesting, and teachers lost their jobs. Reproduced here is a Huffington Post *article on the Tucson controversy.*

In one of the most disturbing developments in the long-brewing Ethnic Studies debacle, a broad alliance of Mexican American Studies supporters is charging that Tucson Unified School District (TUSD) administrators have taken several covert measures to intentionally undermine the nationally acclaimed program and gut its enrollment numbers.

Citing a campaign of misinformation, sudden administrative policies that ban teachers from student and parent outreach, increasing obstacles to program enrollment, changing staff decisions, and the reversal of a highly praised ten-year policy of supervision, Tucson education advocates are wondering if the TUSD administration led by Oro Valley-based Superintendent John Pedicone, whose orchestration of excessive police force and the arrest of elderly Latino leaders last May shattered trust among Tucson's diverse communities, has placed the largely unfounded demands of the Tea Party-driven state politicians over the needs of his own students, teachers and district.

Like a public relations train wreck in the making, faced with the renewal of an embarrassing desegregation order, the increasingly isolated TUSD administrators seem to be teetering on the edge of their own appeal of Tea Party state superintendent John Huppenthal's Ethnic Studies ban and a backdoor downsizing effort to dismantle the Mexican American Studies (MAS) program without any public discussion or school board approval.

"There is no doubt in my mind that since registration began for this year's classes," Save Ethnic Studies attorney Richard Martinez said, "there were internal efforts made to discourage enrollment. It is now made much broader the fact that supervision and control of MAS is now being done by Dr. Lupita Cavazos-Garcia per Dr. Pedicone's instruction. The MAS class load has been reduced drastically and it is clear that TUSD under Dr. Pedicone's instruction is systematically dismantling the MAS program. Other factors that are meant to discourage students from taking the classes include Dr. Stegeman's efforts to make the classes electives. This discourages students from taking the courses if they need the credits to graduate."

Background: Despite a state-commissioned audit released in June that found the MAS program to be fully in compliance with Arizona's controversial Ethnic Studies ban, lauded the Mexican American Studies program for its extraordinary success rate and recommended that the program be maintained as part of the core curriculum for high school courses, the extremist Tea Party State Superintendent of Public Instruction John Huppenthal has threatened to withhold $15 million of state funding from TUSD if it fails to adhere to his Orwellian demands.

The end game in this school lesson on dirty politics?

Over the past several months, Pedicone and his administrators have clearly demoralized and disenfranchised the Mexican American Studies program and refused to attend three public forums in Tucson, which drew large crowds and featured panels of distinguished education experts on the program's decade-long mandate and documented success in alleviating the achievement gap for district students. The blatant rejection of any community engagement by TUSD administrators appeared to confirm the concerns of MAS supporters and teachers, who called for Pedicone's resignation at a press conference in June, citing his failure to respond to nine letters seeking dialogue and clarification and his lack of honesty, genuineness, connection to community, leadership and overall performance.

Without any public discussion or school board approval, in fact, Dr. Cavazos-Garcia recently reassigned MAS teachers—including Tucson High School history teacher Jose Gonzales, who was featured in the award-winning film documentary Precious Knowledge—to traditional courses and reversed a nearly 10-year policy of MAS program supervision over the MAS teachers.

Such a drastic move of stripping MAS supervision and teaching responsibilities flies in the face of the recent Cambium Learning audit, which concluded:

"The auditors observed well-orchestrated lessons as evidenced by indicators within the Arizona Department of Education's document of Standards and Rubics for School Improvement and the Closing the Achievement Gap (CTAG) protocol created by Cambium Learning.

Teachers and MASD curriculum specialists created lessons where learning experiences were aligned with the state standards and incorporated targeted performance objectives within multidisciplinary units for real life applications. The curriculum auditors observed teachers using researched-based instructional strategies that were developmentally appropriate and provided students with assignments that required the use of higher-order and critical thinking skills. Every classroom demonstrated all students actively engaged, and when asked to work together, they all worked collaboratively with each other across various sociocultural backgrounds and academic abilities."

In an email statement, Cavazos-Garcia cited declining MAS enrollment ranks for the shift of teaching duties, and noted that she made the unilateral decision of changing supervision on the basis that "MAS teachers have now been brought in line with all other staff members and evaluated by campus principals as required by board policy."

The Assistant Superintendent failed to explain, however, why MAS teachers reassigned to traditional courses would still be paid under the MAS budget.

Cavazos-Garcia also dismissed accusations that MAS teachers had been prevented from taking part in any education outreach and information sharing with new students and parents. She noted: "All TUSD employees are strongly encouraged to do outreach for each other, the community and their students. Every campus has a learning supports coordinator to help remove barriers to learning for students and barriers to teaching for all teachers."

According to Tucson High School MAS literature teacher Curtis Acosta, however, a number of obstacles accounted for this year's lower enrollment, including an explicit mandate to deny MAS teachers a long-time opportunity to contact any students or parents about available classes and course changes. Acosta said that the year's unusually early registration process, along with unmade staffing decisions, and a shift to automated and computerized registration instead of the traditional student-to-teacher registrations in the school arena also contributed to declining MAS enrollment.

Last May, aware of the mounting problems, Acosta requested permission to send a letter to students and parents.

"The letter home was to inform parents and students of key staffing changes that were not known until later in the spring, months after the registration process," he said. "It's not something I ever had to do before when we were able to get information to students. However, regular communication with parents is something that we have always done and have been encouraged to do. This resistance was a massive change."

Despite the need for the update, Acosta was denied permission.

"We had always been encouraged to create bonds with our students and parents," said Acosta, a long-time teacher in the district. "This marked a change in policy and the denial clearly had come from the administration."

Cavazos-Garcia also denied accounts from numerous students across the district that school counselors had openly discouraged students from enrolling in MAS courses, citing staffing and program uncertainties. This sort of confusion, according to MAS supporters, is also compounded by the conflicting messages from TUSD school board president Mark Stegemen over the program's future.

"I oversee the counseling program and counselors have never been told to discourage students from taking these classes," Cavazos-Garcia said in an email statement. "Students enroll in their classes every spring through a computer based master schedule program. All students are advised to make choices that will best prepare them to be college and career ready."

A number of high school students and alumni, however, all of whom preferred to remain unnamed, have cited a common experience among counselors, who informed them that the uncertain and volatile future of the MAS program was cause for enrollment in other courses.

One thing is certain: As state school superintendent Huppenthal throws his support to notorious "Tea Party President" Russell Pearce, the first state senate president in American history to be recalled, the political leadership in the state continues to oversee draconian cuts and the dismantling of effective education programs like the Mexican American Studies program. Huppenthal recently offered this endorsement of Pearce in the upcoming recall election: "Russell has consistently supported accountability in the classroom and school choice. He is a great supporter of education and making sure each child receives a quality education."

Last month, a columnist in Tucson's *Arizona Daily Star* declared: "Audit of TUSD program never mattered—game is rigged."

Last April and May, however, MAS students and community supporters reminded the Tucson school board in a series of dramatic protests that this sort of political corruption has no place in education.

As students and teachers return next week for the new school year, the nation will be watching TUSD administrators and their district students and parents to see if such a lesson in dirty politics will pass or fail.

Source: Biggers, Jeff. "Arizona's Dirty Lessons: Is Tucson School District Dismantling Ethnic Studies to Appease Tea Party?" August 8, 2011. http://www.huffingtonpost.com/jeff-biggers/arizonas-dirty-lessons-is_b_921670.html.

Pew Hispanic Center, "Latino Voters in the 2012 Election" (2012)

By 2012, the Latino population in the United States numbered more than 55 million, at least two-thirds of whom were of Mexican origin. The numbers and their strong presence in large electoral states such as California, Illinois, Texas, and Florida made Latinos a political force. Pundits suddenly came to the realization that no presidential candidate could win election without substantial support from that community. The following excerpt is from the Pew Hispanic Center's report on the 2012 election.

Latinos voted for President Barack Obama over Republican Mitt Romney by 71% to 27%, according to an analysis of exit polls by the Pew Hispanic Center, a Project of the Pew Research Center.[1]

Obama's national vote share among Hispanic voters is the highest seen by a Democratic candidate since 1996, when President Bill Clinton won 72% of the Hispanic vote.

The Center's analysis finds that Latinos made up 10% of the electorate, as indicated by the national exit poll, up from 9% in 2008 and 8% in 2004.[2] The analysis also shows that as a group, non-white voters made up 28% of the nation's electorate, up from 26% in 2008.[3]

Battleground States

Hispanics made up a growing share of voters in three of the key battleground states in yesterday's election—Florida, Nevada and Colorado.

Obama carried Florida's Hispanic vote 60% to 39%, an improvement over his 57% to 42% showing in 2008. Also, Hispanics made up 17% of the Florida electorate this year, up from 14% in 2008.

The state's growing non-Cuban population—especially growth in the Puerto Rican population in central Florida—contributed to the president's improved showing among Hispanic voters. This year, according to the Florida exit poll, 34% of Hispanic voters were Cuban while 57% were non-Cuban. Among Cuban voters, the vote was split—49% supported Obama while 47% supported Romney. Among the state's non-Cuban voters, Obama won 66% versus 34% for Romney.

In Colorado, Obama carried the Latino vote by a wide margin—75% to 23%. The president's performance among Latino voters in Colorado was better than in 2008, when Obama won the Latino vote 61% to 38%. Hispanics made up 14% of Colorado voters this year, up from 13% in 2008.

In Nevada, Obama won the Hispanic vote 70% to 25%. However, the president's Hispanic vote was down from the 76% share he won in 2008. Among voters in Nevada, the Hispanic share was 18%, up from 15% in 2008.

In other states, the president also carried large shares of the Hispanic vote. Among other battlegrounds, Obama won 68% of the Hispanic vote in North Carolina, 65% in Wisconsin, 64% in Virginia and 53% in Ohio.

Top Issues for Hispanic Voters in 2012

For Hispanic voters, according to the national exit poll, 60% identified the economy as the most important issue (of four listed) facing the country today, virtually the same as the share (59%) of the general electorate that identified the economy as the nation's most important issue. On the other three issues asked about, for Hispanic voters, the economy was followed by health care (18%), the federal budget deficit (11%) and foreign policy (6%).

Throughout this election cycle, the issue of immigration has been an important issue for Hispanics. In the national exit poll, voters were asked about what should happen to unauthorized immigrants working in the U.S. According to the national exit poll, 77% of Hispanic voters said these immigrants should be offered a chance to apply for legal status while 18% said these immigrants should be deported. Among all voters, fewer than two-thirds (65%) said these immigrants should be offered a chance to apply for legal status while 28% say they should be deported.

Demographics of the Latino Vote

Among Latino voters, support for Obama was strong among all major demographic sub-groups. Yet some differences were evident. According to the national exit poll, Hispanic women supported Obama more than Hispanic males—76% versus 65%.

Latino youth, just as all youth nationwide, supported Obama over Romney, but did so by a wider margin—74% versus 23% for Latino youth compared with 60% versus 37% among all youth. Obama won other Latino age groups by nearly as large a margin.

Among Hispanic college graduates, 62% voted for Obama while 35% supported Romney. By contrast, 75% of Hispanics without a college degree voted for Obama while 24% voted for Romney.

Another gap was evident among Latino voters when viewed by income. Among Latino voters whose total family income is below $50,000, 82% voted for Obama while 17% voted for Romney. Among Latino voters with family incomes of $50,000 or more, 59% voted for Obama while 39% voted for Romney.

About this Report

Exit poll results for this report were obtained from CNN's Election 2012 website and are based on National Election Pool national and state exit poll surveys of voters as reported on November 6, 2012. In addition to an analysis of the national Latino vote, 12 states were examined. These states are Arizona, California, Colorado, Florida, Illinois, Nevada, New Mexico, North Carolina, Ohio, Pennsylvania, Virginia and Wisconsin.

A Note on Terminology

The terms "Latino" and "Hispanic" are used interchangeably in this report.

While Latino voters were a larger share of the electorate in 2012 than in 2008, the number of Latinos who cast a vote in yesterday's election will not be known until sometime in the spring of 2013, when data from the U.S. Census Bureau's Current Population Survey becomes available. In this year's election, according to Pew Hispanic Center estimates, 23.7 million Latinos were eligible to vote, up from 19.5 million in 2008 (Lopez, Motel and Patten, 2012). Latinos also represent a growing share of all eligible voters and growing shares of eligible voters in many states. Nationally, 11.0% of all eligible voters in the U.S. are Hispanic, up from 9.5% in 2008. . . .

NOTES

1. The analysis in this report is limited to 12 states. These states are Arizona, California, Colorado, Florida, Illinois, Nevada, New Mexico, North Carolina, Ohio, Pennsylvania, Virginia and Wisconsin. Voter survey results from the National Election Pool national exit poll and state exit polls were obtained from CNN's Election 2012 website.
2. Utilizing the National Exit Poll to estimate the share of the electorate that is Hispanic generally produces an estimate that is higher than that observed in the Census Bureau's November voting supplement of the Current Population Survey (CPS). In 2008, according to the National Exit Poll, 9% of voters were of Hispanic origin (Lopez, 2008). However, according to the 2008 November CPS, 7.4% of voters were Hispanic (Lopez and Taylor, 2009). Estimates of the Hispanic share of the electorate for 2012 from the 2012 November CPS will not be available until 2013. For more details on the issues associated with using these data sources to estimate the share of the electorate that is Hispanic, see "Hispanics and the 2004 Election: Population, Electorate and Voters" by Roberto Suro, Richard Fry and Jeffrey Passel.

Source: Lopez, Mark Hugo, and Paul Taylor. "Latino Voters in the 2012 Election." November 7, 2012. http://www.pewhispanic.org/2012/11/07/latino-voters-in-the-2012-election/.

Arizona and Mexican Immigration (2013)

Draconian laws passed in Arizona in 2010 targeted Latino immigrants and led to a series of copycat laws in other Republican states. This movement was part of an effort to privatize state industries such as the prisons and education. The key battleground was Arizona, but progressives throughout the country mobilized against what they perceived as extremism and the racial targeting of brown-skinned people. Reproduced here is a 2013 article on the impact of the immigration controversy in Arizona.

Arizona became synonymous with hardline immigration policy in 2010, when legislators passed SB 1070, a groundbreaking law that deputized local police to investigate and report suspected immigration violators—a job previously reserved for the federal government. The bill was popular with Arizonans and national Republicans at the time, but the resulting backlash from Latino voters around the country helped spark the current national conversation over immigration reform. Now, as Congress considers whether to pursue Arizona's hawkish path or the "Gang of Eight's" legalization plan, the state could once again prove a bellwether for where the debate in Congress is headed.

Politically, while the bill ignited a firestorm, the GOP's hold on the red-leaning state was largely unchanged. Governor Jan Brewer, who took over after her predecessor Janet Napolitano left to become Secretary of Homeland Secretary, rode SB 1070's popularity on the right to dominate the Republican primary field in 2010 and cruise to her first election victory. Republicans still hold solid majorities in both the Senate and House of Representatives, although they lost some ground in the last election from their post-SB 1070 peak. And despite boasts from Democratic strategists that Arizona's Latino voters could turn the state blue in 2012, the presidential race never became truly competitive; Mitt Romney won the state 53%–44%.

But the relative stability of the state's partisan balance masks a sea change within the GOP itself. In the wake of SB 1070, major Republican constituencies grew uncomfortable with the direction the state was heading on immigration.

Among the business crowd, CEOs and investors became concerned that Arizona's reputation as a harsh place for Latinos was affecting their bottom line. Groups opposed to the state's immigration laws led successful boycott efforts against products, tourism, and conferences. In Phoenix, bookings for the local convention center plummeted, costing the economy as much as $132 million by one city estimate.

"Elected officials became Fox News superstars because they offered a lot of red meat," Phoenix Mayor Greg Stanton told MSNBC in an interview. "But instead of looking at the overall impact for the economy, bills were passed to reinforce a point."

Alarmed by the trend, businesses organized to push back. In 2011, SB 1070 champion and Senate president Russell Pearce introduced a new slate of legislation aimed at cracking down on immigration, including a bill that would require hospitals to report undocumented patients and another calling for an end to birthright citizenship. Fearing a new wave of embarrassing publicity from his agenda, 60 business leaders from Arizona's largest companies signed a letter demanding Pearce back away from the issue due to the "undeniable fact that each of our companies and our employees were impacted by the boycotts and the coincident negative image."

The Senate responded, voting down five immigration bills. But it didn't stop there—a group called Citizens for a Better Arizona led a successful petition to organize a recall election against Pearce. Moderate Republicans united behind a Republican rival, Jerry Lewis, and defeated Pearce in an open primary. Pearce's weakness wasn't only business opposition—the local Mormon community, of which Pearce is a member, raised concerns that Arizona's laws had made missionary outreach in Latin America more difficult. Pearce lost again in a 2012 comeback attempt to another Republican rival, Bob Worsley. Many of the state's most prominent anti-immigration figures have faded into the background along with him.

As Pearce's power dissipated, so did the popularity of his signature law, which was also severely limited by the Supreme Court. An October 2012 poll by Arizona State's Morrison Institute found only 32% of residents believed the bill had benefited them, versus 41% who thought it had damaged the state. The political climate has become relaxed enough that Arizona's two Republican Senators, John McCain and Jeff Flake, feel comfortable taking lead roles on the bipartisan "Gang of Eight" bill that would provide a path to citizenship for undocumented immigrants.

Robert Graham, chair of the Arizona Republican party (Pearce is a vice-chair), told MSNBC that "immigration is still a very hot topic" in the state and residents were especially concerned about border security. But he thought that the GOP had improved its "tone" in reaching out to Latino voters and that state lawmakers were more focused on pressuring the federal government to fix immigration.

"It's possible other things could arise within our state legislature, but right now we're keeping an eye on what's happening with Congress," he said.

But the GOP-led Congress is starting to sound more like the Arizona legislature in 2010, causing alarm among some immigration reform supporters. Recently Republicans overwhelmingly voted to oppose President Obama's decision to halt deportations for young unauthorized immigrants, and the House Judiciary Committee is working on a bill that would encourage states to follow Arizona's lead in enforcing federal immigration law.

It's possible they could face similar consequences if they continue down Arizona's path. The Chamber of Commerce is heavily backing the immigration bill, as are a raft of industries from hotels to agriculture to high-tech firms, in the hopes that it will help provide a steady source of labor and talent for hard-to-fill jobs. Religious leaders, including a variety of evangelical groups, are publicly lobbying for it as well. Republican donors and strategists are backing efforts to support immigration reform with radio and TV advertising designed to give political cover to wavering lawmakers. If the House goes the other direction, they could face a backlash from these constituencies akin to Arizona's.

"We're probably five years ahead of the rest of the country on immigration," Nathan Sproul, a Republican strategist in Arizona who supported efforts to unseat Pearce, told MSNBC. "Now the wave is going out here, but not yet nationally."

Part of the reason Republicans are so concerned about getting it right—in Arizona and around the country—is that the political consequences are likely to be more severe the longer they wait. In Arizona, Republicans were able to weather the Latino surge better than nearby blue-tilting states like Nevada, New Mexico, and Colorado. Similarly, Latino voters—while a factor in President Obama's 2012 win—were not on their own responsible for his healthy margin, nor did they make much of a dent in the House, where Republicans are insulated in safe districts.

But both Arizona and the national GOP are unlikely to be able to keep that feat up forever. That's because the Latino population is not only growing, but disproportionately young, meaning it will take up a larger portion of the electorate over time as more residents turn 18. In Arizona, the median age for Latino residents is 25 while the median age for white residents, the GOP's backbone, is 44.

"That population is going to disappear rather quickly and be replaced by a young Latino cohort being socialized in an environment that is telling them the Republican party does not want them," Rodolfo Espino, an associate professor of political science at Arizona State University, told MSNBC.

The combination of factors means that Republicans might easily be misled by short-term success into thinking they dodged a bullet. Arizona Republicans are starting to wake up to the threat to their future viability. Will the House GOP?

Source: Sarlin, Benjy. "What Arizona can teach Republicans about immigration." June 22, 2013. http://tv.msnbc.com/2013/06/22/what-arizona-can-teach-republicans-about-immigration/.

It's Immigration Stupid! (2013)

The consensus of immigration studies concludes that immigration to the United States has historically benefited the country and that providing legal status to undocumented immigrants would boost the American economy. However, nativist groups have fanned the public hysteria that more foreigners will lead to polarization. Despite this, sentiment for immigration reform has increased as the nation and the electorate grows younger. Support for comprehensive immigration reform is divided along ideological grounds: Democratic states tend to support it and Republican states oppose it. The opposition appears to base its opposition along racial grounds and has opposed President Barack Obama's moderate proposals. Reproduced here is an article from the PolicyMic Web site on immigration reform in 2013.

President Barack Obama on Tuesday will lay out a major immigration overhaul, highlighting the need to fix the broken immigration system so that it is "fairer for and helps grow the middle class by ensuring everyone plays by the same rules."

The White House's immigration reform plan expands on a blueprint it released in 2011, but

Obama will stop short of offering his own piece of legislation because of the progress made by the Senate "Gang of Eight."

That Senate plan, titled "A Bipartisan Framework for Immigration Reform," was unveiled on Monday. The senators' proposal confronts the most controversial issue—how to handle the millions of undocumented immigrants in the country—by setting up a system under which immigrants illegally residing in the United States can register with the government, pay a fine, and be given probationary legal residency including the right to work.

What's at Stake?

An estimated 11 million undocumented immigrants reside in the United States, as well as a huge line of persons waiting to get visas or full citizenship. These residents' unclear legal status has led to them being treated as second-class citizens, exploited and discriminated against. America could use this pool of workers to shore up the economy and keep the population growing, but border security concerns, citizenship requirements, lack of legislative action, and xenophobia have combined to prevent real action on the immigration question.

What's Changed?

Most importantly: many Republicans now support a path to citizenship for undocumented immigrants, a position previously deplored by many House GOP members as "amnesty." That position switch removed the last major barrier to a bipartisan solution; it was very likely influenced by the November general election in which GOP presidential candidate Mitt Romney was able to gather less than a quarter of the Latino vote, contributing to his loss.

What Has Congress proposed?

Four Democratic and four Republican senators have recently proposed a plan titled "A Bipartisan Framework for Immigration Reform," which includes the path to citizenship. Undocumented immigrants would be able to register for a work visa and would be granted "end of the line" status for full citizenship. Their proposal requires the federal government to work with a commission of border state law enforcement authorities, governors, and other officials to certify the U.S.-Mexico border is secure before taking any action on immigration reform. Undocumented immigrants would be given "probationary legal status" and remain ineligible for citizenship or a green card until that certification is made.

The bipartisan group is led by Republican Senator Marco Rubio, a Cuban-American legislator from Miami, who has spoken on the need for immigration reform for years.

What Will Obama Propose Today?

The White House has sent indications it approves of the bipartisan group's proposal, but its previous blueprints for immigration reform were more liberal. Obama will likely propose a more direct path to citizenship that skips "probationary legal status" on the belief that the Senate proposal creates an uncertain legal grey area for persons in the program. He will also likely skip the border security certification phase and include language supporting the view that same-sex bi-national couples should have the same rights as heterosexual couples.

What Do Democrats Get?

Democrats will be able to claim leadership on immigration reform and play off accusations that they are weak on border security. The much coveted path to citizenship will become a reality, with the caveat that undocumented immigrants will need to get background checks, pay federal back taxes and a fine, as well as learn the English language and civics.

Those 11 million potential citizens? Most of them will vote for Democrats.

WHAT DO REPUBLICANS GET?

Republicans get a guarantee that the federal government will be required to certify the border is secure, as well as loosen their image. The xenophobic wing of the Tea Party will likely look foolish to the country in any debates or hearings (though not necessarily to their constituents), weakening anti-establishment Republicans on the national stage. Many moderate Republicans will get a shot at trying to capture Latino votes with a message of free enterprise and the American Dream, though it remains doubtful that they can beat the Democratic Party on that front.

What Do Latinos Get?

They'll get to live legally in the United States, and will be granted the desired path to citizenship. Border security certification and bipartisan reform on immigration will likely neutralize some of the more conservative laws either in place or being proposed in many southwestern states—such as Arizona's SB 1070, which authorized law enforcement officers to check immigration status during routine stops. That law was widely seen among Latinos as racial profiling.

Likely, it will also mean that undocumented immigrants will be given a leg up in the job market—without the threat of exposure and deportation, fewer employers will be able to offer exploitative sub-minimum-wage jobs to immigrants.

A more flexible immigration system will also benefit the millions of Latinos who currently reside legally in the United States, by removing the constant stress of immigration enforcement against their communities and families.

Is There a Catch?

There is no catch. However, there are concerns regarding the new proposal's implementation.

Immigration controls—in particular, security benchmarks—will be designed by southwestern border state officials, which could result in unfavorable conditions for the Latino community.

It is currently unclear whether the bipartisan proposal will increase the number of green cards (which allow the holder to live freely in the US and be employed) in circulation; if not, the bill would generate an even greater backlog in the immigration system.

There is no guarantee that either measure will become law. House Republicans in particular tend to treat proposals from the White House as anathema; regardless of whether the Senate reaches an agreement, GOP representatives in the lower chamber may vote to block the legislation on both ideological grounds (accusations of amnesty) or political ones (defeating the president).

Source: McKay, Tom. "Immigration Reform 2013 Will See Historic Changes For 11 Million Undocumented People in the U.S." Policymic, 2013, http://www.policymic.com/articles/24398/immigration-reform-2013-will-see-historic-changes-for-11-million-undocumented-people-in-the-u-s.

Immigration Policy Center, "Who and Where the DREAMers Are" (2013)

Efforts to pass a bill that would provide conditional permanent residency to select immigrants of good moral character began at the turn of the century. The Development, Relief, and Education for Alien Minors (DREAM) Act was first proposed in Congress in 2001. The guidelines were that people had graduated from U.S. high schools, had come here as minors, and had lived here continuously for at least five years before the bill's enactment. If applicants had completed two years in the military or two years at a four-year institution of higher learning, they would obtain temporary residency for a six-year period. Within six years, they would be eligible for permanent residency. This movement grew among young Latinos and Asians as their numbers grew and pro-immigrant marches mushroomed in size, reaching a million protesters in Los Angeles, Chicago, and Dallas. Many Latino youth had been educated in U.S. high schools and held the civil rights movement as a model and were well versed in Martin Luther King Jr.'s "I Have a Dream" speech of 1963. As their organization grew into a national movement, President Barack Obama (1961–) in the heat of the 2012 presidential campaign, issued an executive order "Deferred Action for Childhood Arrivals (DACA)" that gave the "DREAMers" relief. Since then many DREAMers have become impatient as deportations have increased. In the summer of 2013, they challenged the lack of progress in immigration reform with acts act of civil disobedience and sought to force more movement on DACA. Reproduced here is an article from the Immigration Policy Center Web site detailing just who the DREAMers are.

WHO AND WHERE THE DREAMERS ARE

A Demographic Profile of Immigrants Who Might Benefit from the Obama Administration's Deferred Action For Childhood Arrivals (DACA) Initiative.

A new analysis casts some much-needed light on the question of exactly who might be eligible for the Obama Administration's "deferred action" initiative for unauthorized youth who were brought to this country as children. This initiative, announced by Homeland Security Secretary Janet Napolitano on June 15, offers a two-year, renewable reprieve from deportation to unauthorized immigrants who are under the age of 31; entered the United States before age 16; have lived continuously in the country for at least five years; have not been convicted of a felony, a "significant" misdemeanor, or three other misdemeanors; and are currently in school, graduated from high school, earned a GED, or served in the military. Immigrants who meet these criteria are commonly referred to as "DREAMers" because they comprise most (though not all) of the individuals who meet the general requirements of the Development, Relief, and Education for Alien Minors (DREAM) Act.

Other analyses have produced national and state-level estimates of how many immigrants could benefit from the deferred action initiative. However, the analysis by the IPC, together with Rob Paral & Associates, provides a new level of detail, breaking down the DREAMer population by nationality and age at the national and state level (as well as the congressional district level). Not surprisingly, most DREAMers are Mexican and are found in big immigrant-receiving states with large unauthorized populations, such as California and Texas. Yet DREAMers are also found in virtually every state, and significant numbers are non-Mexicans who hail from all corners of the globe. The majority of DREAMers are 15 or older and are therefore eligible to apply for deferred action right now. However, there are also large numbers who are 14 or younger and are not yet eligible to apply, but who will be eligible at some point in the future if the deferred action initiative remains in place. These sorts of demographic details are important as the federal government gears up to implement the deferred action initiative, and as community groups prepare to assist the populations they serve in taking advantage of this opportunity.

There are approximately 1.4 million immigrants currently in the United States who might meet the requirements of the deferred action initiative, either now or when they are older.

- Roughly 936,930 immigrants between the ages of 15 and 30 might immediately meet the requirements of the deferred action initiative.

They comprise 69 percent of all potential beneficiaries. . . .

- Approximately 426,330 immigrants between the ages of 5 and 14 might meet the requirements of the deferred action initiative at some point in the future if the initiative remains in place. They comprise 31 percent of all potential beneficiaries.

Source: "Who and Where the DREAMers Are." Immigration Policy Center. http://www.immigrationpolicy.org/just-facts/who-and-where-dreamers-are-revised-estimates.

Selected Bibliography

Arts, Music, and Popular Culture

Beltrán, Mary. *Latina/o Stars in U.S. Eyes: The Making and Meanings of Film and TV Stardom*. Urbana: University of Illinois Press, 2009.

Benavídez, Max. *Gronk*. A Ver: Revisioning Art History. Los Angeles: UCLA Chicano Studies Research Center, 2007

Berg, Charles Ramírez. *Latino Images in Film: Stereotypes, Subversion, & Resistance*. Austin: University of Texas Press, 2002.

Berumen-Garcia, Frank Javier. *The Chicano/Hispanic Image in American Film*. New York: Vantage Press, 1995.

Candelaria, Cordelia Chavez, Arturo J. Aldama, Peter J. Garcia, and Alma Alvarez-Smith. *Encyclopedia of Latino Popular Culture*. Santa Barbara, CA: Greenwood, 2004.

Carrillo, Charles M. A. *Century of Retablos: The Janis and Dennis Lyon Collection of New Mexican Santos, 1780–1880*. Phoenix: Phoenix Art Museum, 2007.

Chastanet, Francois. *Cholo Writing: Latino Gang Graffiti in Los Angeles*. Arsta, Sweden: Dokument Press, 2009.

Dávalos, Karen Mary. *Exhibiting Mestizaje: Mexican (American) Museums in the Diaspora*. Albuquerque: University of New Mexico Press, 2001.

Gaspar de Alba, Alicia. *Chicano Art Inside/Outside the Master's House: Cultural Politics and the CARA Exhibition*. Austin: University of Texas Press, 1998.

Hinds, Harold, Jr., and Charles Tatum. *Not Just for Children: The Mexican Comic Book in the Late 1960s and 1970s*. Westport, CT: Greenwood Press, 1992.

Latorre, Guisela. *Walls of Empowerment: Chicana/o Indigenist Murals of California*. Austin: University of Texas Press, 2008.

Montaño, Mary. *Tradiciones Nuevomexicanas: Hispano Arts and Culture of New Mexico*. Albuquerque: University of New Mexico Press, 2001.

Noriega, Chon. *Shot in America: Television, the State and the Rise of Chicano Cinema*. Minneapolis: University of Minnesota Press, 2000.

Nyberg, Amy Kiste. *Seal of Approval: The History of the Comics Code*. Jackson: University of Mississippi Press, 1998.

Ochoa, María. *Creative Collectives: Chicana Painters Working in the Community*. Albuquerque: University of New Mexico Press, 2003.

Parson, Jack, Carmella Padilla, and Juan Estevan Arellano Juan Estevan. *Low 'n Slow: Lowriding in New Mexico*. Santa Fe: Museum of New Mexico Press, 1999.

Ramírez Berg, Charles. *Latino Images in Film: Stereotypes, Subversions, Resistance*. Austin: University of Texas Press, 2002.

Ramírez, Yasmin, and Henry C. Estrada. *Parallel Expressions in the Graphic Arts of the Chicano and Puerto Rican Movements*. New York: El Museo del Barrio, 1999.

Rubenstein, Anne. *Bad Language, Naked Ladies, and Other Threats to the Nation: A Political History of Comic Books in México*. Durham, NC: Duke University Press, 1998.

Sabin, Roger. *Comics, Comix, & Graphic Novels: A History of Comic Art*. London: Phaidon, 1996.

Tatum, Charles, M. *Chicano Popular Culture: Que Hable El Pueblo*. Tucson: University of Arizona Press, 2001.

Tatum, Charles, M . *Encyclopedia of Latino Culture: From Calaveras to Quinceañeras*. Santa Barbara, CA: Greenwood, 2013.

Turner, Kay. *Beautiful Necessity: The Art and Meaning of Women's Altars*. New York: Thames & Hudson, 1999.

Valdez, Luis. *Zoot Suit and Other Plays*. Houston: Arte Publico Press, 1992.

Vigil, Angel. *Una linda raza: Cultural and Artistic Traditions of the Hispanic Southwest*. Golden, CO: Fulcrum, 1998.

Wright, Bradford. *Comic Book Nation: The Transformation of Youth Culture in America*. Baltimore, MD: Johns Hopkins University Press, 2001.

Civil Rights, Politics, and Activism

Acuña, Rodolfo F. *Occupied America: A History of Chicanos*. New York: Pearson, 2015.

Acuña, Rodolfo F. *Anything But Mexican: Chicanos in Contemporary Los Angeles*. London: Verso Press, 1996.

Acuña, Rodolfo F. *The Making of Chicana/o Studies: In the Trenches of Academe*. New Brunswick: Rutgers University press, 2011.

Acuña, Rodolfo F. *A Community Under Siege*. Los Angeles: UCLA, 1984.

Bardacke, Frank. *Trampling Out the Vintage: Cesar Chavez and the Two Souls of the United Farm Workers*. New York: Verso, 2011.

Bender, Steven W. *One Night in America: Robert Kennedy, Cesar Chavez, and the Dream of Dignity*. Boulder, CO: Paradigm Publishers, 2008.

Carroll, Patrick. *Felix Longoria's Wake: Bereavement, Racism, and the Rise of Mexican American Activism.* Austin: University of Texas Press, 2003.

Chavez, Leo R. *Covering Immigration: Popular Images and the Politics of the Nation.* Berkeley: University of California Press, 2001.

Cruz, Jose E. *Identity and Power: Puerto Rican Politics and the Challenge of Ethnicity*. Philadelphia: Temple University Press, 1998.

Day, Mark. *Forty Acres: Cesar Chavez and the Farm Workers*. New York: Praeger Publishers, 1971.

Dunne, John Gregory. *Delano: The Story of the California Grape Strike*. New York: Farrar, Straus & Giroux, 1967. Reprint, Berkeley: University of California Press, 2007.

Ferriss, Susan, and Ricardo Sandoval. *The Fight in the Fields: Cesar Chavez and the Farm Workers Movement*. New York: Harcourt Brace, 1997.

Ganz, Marshall. *Why David Sometimes Wins: Leadership, Organization, and Strategy in the California Farm Worker Movement*. New York: Oxford University Press, 2009.

Garcia, Ignacio. *The Forging of a Militant Ethos among Mexican Americans.* Tucson: University of Arizona Press, 1997.

García, Ignacio M. *Hector P. García: In Relentless Pursuit of Justice.* Houston: Arte Público Press, 2002.

Gómez Quiñones, Juan. *Mexican Students for La Raza: The Chicano Student Movement in California, 1967–1977*. Santa Barbara, CA: Editorial La Causa, 1978.

Goodwin, David. *César Chávez: Hope for the People*. New York: Fawcett Columbine, 1991.

Griswold del Castillo, Richard, and Richard Garcia. *César Chávez: A Triumph of Spirit*. Norman: University of Oklahoma Press, 1995.

Hammerback, John, and Richard Jensen. *The Rhetorical Career of Cesar Chavez.* College Station: Texas A&M University Press, 2003.

Jacobson, Robin Dale. *The New Nativism: Proposition 187 and the Debate Over Immigration.* Minneapolis: University of Minnesota Press, 2008.

Jordane, Maurice "Mo." *The Struggle for the Health and Legal Protection of Farm Workers: El Cortito*. Houston: Arte Publico Press, 2005.

Junn, Jane, and Kerry L. Hanie, eds. *New Race Politics: Understanding Minority and Immigrant Politics.* New York: Cambridge University Press, 2008.

Levy, Jacques E. *César Chávez: Autobiography of La Causa*. New York: W. W. Norton, 1974.

London, Joan, and Henry Anderson. *So Shall Ye Reap: The Story of César Chávez and the Farmworkers Movement*. New York: Thomas Y. Crowell Co., 1971.

Matthiessen, Peter. *Sal Si Puedes: Cesar Chavez and the New American Revolution.* Berkeley: University of California Press, 2000.

McWilliams, Carey, and Douglas C. Sackman. *Factories in the Fields: The Story of Migratory Farm Labor in California*. Berkeley: University of California Press, 2000.

Meléndez, Miguel, and José Torres. *We Took the Streets: Fighting for Latino Rights with the Young Lords*. New Brunswick, NJ: Rutgers University Press, 2005.

Munoz, Carlos. *Youth, Identity, Power: The Chicano Movement*. New York: Verso, 1989.

Navarro, Armando. *La Raza Unida Party: A Chicano Challenge to the U.S. Two Party Dictatorship*. Philadelphia: Temple University Press, 2000.

Newton, Lina. *Illegal, Alien or Immigrant: The Politics of Immigration Reform.* New York: New York University Press, 2008.

Orchowski, Margaret Sands. *Immigration and the American Dream. Battling the Political Hype and Hysteria.* New York: Rowman and Littlefield, 2008.

Orosco, Jose-Antonio. *Cesar Chavez and the Common Sense of Nonviolence*. Albuquerque: University of New Mexico Press, 2008.

Pawell, Miriam. *The Union of Their Dreams: Power, Hope, and Struggle in Cesar Chavez's Farm Worker Movement*. New York: Bloomsbury Press, 2009.

Pitrone, Jean M. *Chávez: Man of the Migrants*. New York: Pyramid Communications, 1972.

Prouty, Marco. *Cesar Chavez, the Catholic Bishops, and the Farmworkers' Struggle for Social Justice*. Tucson: University of Arizona Press, 2008.

Ramos, Henry A. J. *The American GI Forum: In Pursuit of the Dream, 1948–1983.* Houston: Arte Público Press, 1998.

Ramos, Henry A. J. *A People Forgotten, a Dream Pursued: The History of the American G.I. Forum, 1948–1972*. Denver, CO: American G.I. Forum of the United States, 1983.

Richardson, Chad, and Rosalva Resendiz. *On the Edge of the Law: Culture, Labor, and Deviance on the South Texas Border.* Austin: University of Texas Press, 2006.

Rosales, Francisco Arturo, ed. *Chicano! The History of the Mexican American Civil Rights Movement.* Houston: Arte Publico Press, 1997.

Rosales, Francisco Arturo, ed. *Testimonio: A Documentary History of the Mexican American Struggle for Civil Rights*. Houston: Arte Publico Press, 2000.

Ross, Fred. *Conquering Goliath: Cesar Chavez at the Beginning*. Keene, CA: El Taller Grafico Press/United Farm Workers, 1989.

Scharlin, Craig, and Lilia V. Villanueva. *Philip Vera Cruz: A Personal History of Filipino Immigrants and the Farmworkers Movement*. Seattle: University of Washington Press, 2000.

Shaw, Randy. *Cesar Chavez, the UFW, and the Struggle for Justice in the 21st Century*. Berkeley: University of California Press, 2008.

Vigil, Ernesto B. *The Crusade for Justice: Chicano Militancy and the Government War on Dissent*. Madison: University of Wisconsin Press, 1999.

Weitz, Mark. *The Sleepy Lagoon Murder Case: Race Discrimination and Mexican-American Rights.* Lawrence: University Press of Kansas, 2010.

Zavella, Patricia. "The Tables Are Turned: Immigration, Poverty, and Social Conflict in California Communities." In *Immigrants Out: The New Nativism and the Anti-Immigrant Impulse in the United States*, edited by Juan F. Perea, 131–161. New York: New York University Press, 1996.

Economics, Work, and Education

Borjas, George J. *Heaven's Door: Immigration Policy and the American Economy.* Princeton, NJ: Princeton University Press, 1999.

Catanzarite, Lisa, and Lindsey Trimble. *The Latino Workforce at Mid-Decade.* ERIC Clearinghouse, 2007.

Crawford, James. *At War with Diversity: U.S. Language Policy in an Age of Anxiety.* Denton: University of North Texas Press, 2004.

Crawford, James. *Language and Loyalties: A Sourcebook on the Official English Controversy.* Chicago: University of Chicago Press, 1992.

Darder, Antonia, and Rodolfo D. Torres. *Latinos and Education: A Critical Reader.* New York: Routledge, 2013.

Deutsch, Sarah. *No Separate Refuge: Culture, Class, and Gender on an Anglo-Hispanic Frontier in the American Southwest*. New York: Oxford University Press, 1987.

Feliciano, Cynthia. *Unequal Origins: Immigrant Selection and the Education of the Second Generation.* New York: LFB Scholarly Publishing, 2006.

Gándara, Patricia, and Frances Contreras. *The Latino Education Crisis: The Consequences of Failed Social Policies.* Cambridge, MA: Harvard University, 2010.

Leal, David L., and Stephen J. Trejo, eds. *Latinos and the Economy: Integration and Impact in Schools, Labor Markets, and Beyond.* New York: Springer, 2010.

Montero-Sieburth, Martha, and Edwin Meléndez, eds. *Latinos in a Changing Society.* Westport, CT: Praeger, 2007.

Murillo, Enrique G. *Handbook of Latinos and Education: Theory, Research, and Practice.* New York: Routledge, 2010.

Ong, Paul, and Anastasia Loukaitou-Sideris. *Jobs and Economic Development in Minority Communities*. Philadelphia: Temple University Press, 2006.

Orner, Peter, ed. *Underground America: Narratives of Undocumented Lives*. San Francisco: McSweeneys, 2008.

Reisler, Mark. *By the Sweat of Their Brow: Mexican Immigrant Labor in the United States, 1900–1940*. Reprint ed. Westport, CT: Greenwood Press, 1976.

Rivera-Batiz, Francisco L. *Education Inequality and the Latino Population of the United States*. ERIC Clearinghouse, 2008.

San Miguel Guadalupe, Jr. *Contested Policy: The Rise and Fall of Federal Bilingual Education in the United States, 1960–2001*. Denton: University of North Texas Press, 2004.

Sikkink, David, and Edwin I. Hernández, eds. *Religion Matters: Predicting Schooling Success among Latino Youth*. Notre Dame, IN: Institute for Latino Studies, University of Notre Dame, 2003.

Silva-Corvalán, Carmen. *Language Contact and Change: Spanish in Los Angeles*. Oxford: Oxford University Press, 1994.

Waldinger, Roger, and Michel J. Litchter. *How the Other Half Works: Immigration and the Social Organization of Labor.* Berkeley: University of California Press, 2003.

History

Acuña, Rodolfo. *Anything But Mexican: Chicanos in Contemporary Los Angeles*. London: Verso, 1996.

Acuña, Rodolfo. *Corridors of Migration: The Odyssey of Mexican Laborers, 1600–1933*. Tucson: University of Arizona Press, 2007.

Acuña, Rodolfo. *Corridors of Migration: The Odyssey of Mexican Laborers, 1600–1933*. Tucson: University of Arizona, Press, 2008.

Acuña, Rodolfo. *The Making of Chicana/o Studies: In the Trenches of Academe*. New Brunswick, NJ: Rutgers University Press, 2011

Acuña, Rodolfo. *Occupied America: A History of Chicanos*. 8th ed. New York: Pearson, 2014.

Acuña, Rodolfo. *Sometimes There Is No Other Side: Chicanos and the Myth of Equality*. Notre Dame, IN: University of Notre Dame Press, 1998.

Daniels, Roger. *Coming to America: A History of Immigration and Ethnicity in American Life*. 2nd ed. New York: Harper Collins, 2006.

Duany, Jorge. *The Puerto Rican Nation on the Move*. Chapel Hill: University of North Carolina Press, 2002.

Garcia, Juan G. *Mexicans in the Midwest, 1900–1932*. Tucson: University of Arizona Press, 1996.

González, Juan. *Harvest of Empire: A History of Latinos in America*. New York: Penguin, 2001.

González, Miguel G. *Mexicanos: A History of Mexicans in the United States*. Bloomington: Indiana University Press, 2000.

Gutiérrez, David G., ed. *The Columbia History of Latinos in the United States since 1960*. New York: Columbia University Press, 2004.

Haas, Lisbeth. *Conquests and Historical Identities in California, 1769–1936*. Berkeley: University of California Press, 1995.

Levine, Robert M. *Secret Missions to Cuba: Fidel Castro, Bernardo Benes, and Cuban Miami*. New York: Palgrave Press, 2001.

May, Robert E. *Manifest Destiny's Underworld: Filibustering in Antebellum America*. Chapel Hill: University of North Carolina Press, 2004.

Menchaca, Martha. *Recovering History, Constructing Race: The Indian, Black, and White Roots of Mexican Americans*. Austin: University of Texas Press, 2001.

Montejano, David. *Anglos and Mexicans in the Making of Texas, 1836–1986*. Austin: University of Texas Press, 1987.

Moya Pons, Frank. *The Dominican Republic: A National History*. 2nd rev. ed. Princeton, NJ: Markus Wiener Publishers, 1998.

Oboler, Suzanne, and Deena J. Gonzalez, eds. *The Oxford Encyclopedia of Latinos and Latinas in the United States*. New York: Oxford University Press, 2005.

Romo, David Dorado. *Ringside Seat to a Revolution: An Underground Cultural History of El Paso and Juarez, 1893–1923*. El Paso, TX: Cinco Puntos Press, 2005.

Shorris, Earl. *Latinos: A Biography of the People*. New York: W. W. Norton, 2001.

Thelen, David, ed. Rethinking History and the Nation State: Mexico and the United States. A special online issue of the *Journal of American History,* September 1999. http://www.indiana.edu/~jah/mexico.

Tijerina, Andres. *Tejanos under the Mexican Flag, 1821–1836*. College Station: Texas A&M University Press, 1994.

Wagenheim, Olga Jiménez de, and Kal Wagenheim, eds. *The Puerto Ricans: A Documentary History*. Princeton, NJ: Markus Wiener Publishers, 2002.

Zavella, Patricia. *Women's Work and Chicano Families: Cannery Workers of the Santa Clara Valley*. Ithaca, NY: Cornell University Press, 1987.

Identity, Culture, and Community

Acuña, Rodolfo. *Anything but Mexican: Chicanos in Contemporary Los Angeles*. New York: Verso, 1996.

Acuña, Rodolfo. *Community under Siege: Chicanos East of the Los Angeles River*. Los Angeles: Mexican American Studies Resource Center, UCLA, 1984.

Bayless, Rick. *Mexico One Plate at a Time.* New York: Scribner, 2000.

Cafferty, Pastora San Juan, and David W. Engstrom, eds. *Hispanics in the United States: An Agenda for the Twenty-First Century.* New Brunswick, NJ: Transaction, 2002.

Castro, Rafaela G. *Chicano Folklore: A Guide to the Folktales, Traditions, Rituals, and Religious Practices of Mexican-Americans.* Santa Barbara, CA: ABC-CLIO, 2001.

Escobar, Edward. *Race, Police, and the Making of a Political Identity: Mexican Americans and the Los Angeles Police Department.* Berkeley, University of California Press, 1999.

Greenbaum, Susan D. *More Than Black: Afro-Cubans in Tampa*. Gainesville: University Press of Florida, 2002.

Jiménez, Tomás R. *Replenished Ethnicity: Mexican Americans, Immigration, and Identity.* Berkeley: University of California Press, 2010.

Macias, Thomas. *Mestizo in America: Generations of Mexican Ethnicity in the Suburban Southwest*. Tucson: University of Arizona Press, 2006.

Mason, Michael Atwood. *Living Santería: Rituals and Experiences in an Afro-Cuban Religion*. Washington, DC: Smithsonian Institution Press, 2002.

Montero, Jose Maria. *Latinos and the U.S. South.* Westport, CT: Praeger, 2008.

Paredes, Américo. *Folklore and Culture on the Texas-Mexican Border*. Edited by Richard Bauman. Austin: University of Texas Press, 1995.

Portes, Alejandro, and Ruben G. Rumbaut. *Legacies: The Story of the Immigrant Second Generation.* Berkeley: University of California Press, 2001.

Quiroga, José. *Tropics of Desire: Interventions from Queer Latin America*. New York: New York University Press, 2000.

Ramirez, Catherine. *The Woman in the Zoot Suit: Gender, Nationalism, and the Cultural Politics of Memory.* Durham, NC: Duke University Press, 2009.

Rivera, Oswald. *Puerto Rican Cuisine in America: Nuyorican and Bodega Recipes*. New York: Four Walls Eight Windows, 2002.

Rodríguez, Clara E. *Changing Race: Latinos, the Census, and the History of Ethnicity in the United States*. New York: New York University Press, 2000.

Rodríguez, Havidán, Rogelio Sáenz, and Cecilia Menjívar, eds. *Latina/os in the United States: Changing the Face of América.* New York: Springer, 2008.

Rodríguez, Sylvia. *The Matachines Dance: Ritual Symbolism and Interethnic Relations in the Upper Rio Grande Valley.* Albuquerque: University of New Mexico Press, 1996.

Salcedo, Michele. *Quinceañera! The Essential Guide to Planning the Perfect Sweet Fifteen Celebration.* New York: Holt, 1997.

Sánchez, George J. *Becoming Mexican American: Ethnicity, Culture, and Identity in Chicano Los Angeles, 1900–1945*. New York: Oxford University Press, 1995.

Thernstrom, Stephan, ed. *Harvard Encyclopedia of American Ethnic Groups.* Cambridge, MA: Belknap Press of Harvard University, 1980.

Vélez-Ibañez, Carlos G. *Border Visions: Mexican Cultures of the Southwest United States*. Tucson: University of Arizona Press, 1996.

Immigration and Migration

Alba, Richard, and Victor Nee. *Remaking the American Mainstream: Assimilation and Contemporary Immigration.* Cambridge, MA: Harvard University Press, 2003.

Andreas, Peter. *Border Games: Policing the U.S.-Mexico Divide.* Ithaca, NY: Cornell University Press, 2001.

Barkan, Elliot R., Hasia Diner, and Alan M. Kraut. *From Arrival to Incorporation: Migrants to the U.S. in a Global Era.* New York: New York University Press, 2008.

Brotherton, David C., and Philip Kretsedemas. *Keeping Out the Other: A Critical Introduction to Immigration Enforcement Today.* New York: New York University Press, 2008.

Buff, Rachel. *Immigrant Rights in the Shadow of Citizenship.* New York: New York University Press, 2008.

Chavez, Leo R. *The Latino Threat: Constructing Immigrants, Citizens and the Nation.* Stanford, CA: Stanford University Press, 2008.

Chavez, Linda. *Strangers Among Us: Turning Today's Immigrants into the Americans of Tomorrow.* New York: Basic Books, 2008.

Delaet, Debra L. *U.S. Immigration Policy in an Age of Rights.* Westport, CT: Praeger, 2000.

Dow, Mark. *American Gulag: Inside U.S. Immigration Prisons.* Berkeley: University of California Press, 2004.

Flores, John, ed. *Divided Arrival: Narratives of the Puerto Rican Migration, 1920–1950.* 2nd ed. New York: Centro Estudios Puertotiqueños, Hunter College, City University of New York, 1998.

Galarza, Ernesto. *Merchants of Labor: The Mexican Bracero Story, an Account of the Managed Migration of Mexican Farm Workers in California, 1942–1962.* Charlotte, NC: McNally & Loftin, 1964.

Gamio, Manuel. *The Life Story of the Mexican Immigrant: Autobiographic Documents*. New York: Dover Publications, 1972.

Gamio, Manuel. *Mexican Immigration to the United States: A Study of Human Migration and Adjustment.* New York: Dover Publications, 1971.

Guerette, Rob T. *Migrant Death: Border Safety and Situational Crime Prevention.* New York: LFB Scholarly Publishing, 2007.

Hing, Bill Ong. *Defining America through Immigration Policy.* Philadelphia: Temple University Press, 2004.

Hing, Bill Ong. *Deporting Our Souls: Values, Morality and Immigration Policy.* Boston: Cambridge University Press, 2006.

Johnson, Kevin. *Opening the Floodgates: Why America Needs to Rethink Its Borders and Immigration Law.* New York: New York University Press, 2007.

Kanstroom, Daniel. *Deportation Nation: Outsiders in American History.* Cambridge, MA: Harvard University Press, 2007.

Kirkorian, Mark. *The New Case Against Immigration: Both Legal and Illegal.* New York: Sentinel, 2008.

Loucky, James, Jeanne Armstrong, and Larry J. Estrada. *Immigration in America Today: An Encyclopedia.* Westport, CT: Greenwood Press, 2006.

Maril, Robert Lee. *Patrolling Chaos: The U.S. Border Patrol in Deep South Texas.* Lubbock: Texas Tech University Press, 2006.

Martinez, Ruben. *Crossing Over: A Mexican Migrant Family on the Migrant Trail.* New York: Metropoiltan Books, 2001.

Massey, Douglas S. *Beyond Smoke and Mirrors: Mexican Immigration in an Era of Economic Integration.* New York: Russell Sage, 2003.

Nevins, Joseph. *Operation Gatekeeper: The Rise of the "Illegal Alien" and the Remaking of the U.S.-Mexico Boundary.* London: Routledge, 2001.

Nevins, Joseph, and Mizue Aizeki. *Dying to Live: A Story of Global Migration in an Age of Apartheid.* New York: City Lights Books, 2008.

Payan, Tony. *The Three U.S.-Mexico Border Wars: Drugs, Immigration and Homeland Security*. Westport, CT: Praeger Security International, 2006.

Portes, Alejandro, and Ruben Rumbaut. *Immigrant America: A Portrait.* 3rd ed. Berkeley: University of California Press, 2006.

Reimers, David. *Other Immigrants: The Global Origins of the American People.* New York: New York University Press, 2005.

Richardson, Chad, and Rosalva Resendez. *On the Edge of the Law: Culture, Labor and Deviance on the South Texas Border.* Austin: University of Texas Press, 2006.

Rumbaut, Ruben, and Alejandro Portes. *Ethnicities: Children of Immigrants in America.* Berkeley: University of California Press, 2001.

Ueda, Reed. *A Companion to American Immigration.* New York: Blackwell, 2006.

Waters, Mary, and Reed Ueda, eds. *The New Americans: A Guide to Immigration Since 1965.* Cambridge, MA: Harvard University Press, 2007.

Literature, Narratives, and Language

Aranda, José, Jr., ed. *Recovering the U.S. Hispanic Literary Heritage*. Vol. 4. Houston: Arte Público Press, 2002.

Artéaga, Alfred. *Chicano Poetics: Heterotexts and Hybridities*. Cambridge: Cambridge University Press, 1997.

Brogan, Jacqueline V., and Cordelia Candelaria. *Women Poets of the Americas: Toward a Pan-American Gathering*. Notre Dame, IN: University of Notre Dame Press, 1999.

Castillo, Ana. *Massacre of the Dreamers: Essays on Xicanisma*. New York: Penguin, 1995.

Elgin, Suzette Haden. *The Language Imperative*. Cambridge, MA: Perseus Books, 2000.

Foster, David. *Mexican Literature: A Bibliography of Secondary Sources*. Metuchen, NJ: Scarecrow Press, 1992.

Foster, David. *Mexican Literature: A History*. Austin: University of Texas Press, 1994.

Gaspar de Alba, Alicia. *The Mystery of Survival and Other Stories*. Tempe: University of Arizona Press, 1993.

Foster, David. *Sor Juana's Second Dream*. Albuquerque: University of New Mexico Press, 1999.

Harrison, Brady. *Agent of Empire: William Walker and the Imperial Self in American Literature*. Athens: University of Georgia Press, 2004.

Kevane, Bridget A. *Latino Literature in America*. Westport CT; London: Greenwood Press, 2003.

Martí, José. *Our America*. New York: Monthly Review Press, 1981.

Moreas, Marcia. *Bilingual Education: A Dialogue with the Bakhtin Circle*. Albany: State University of New York Press, 1996.

Nilsen, Alleen Pace. *Living Language: Reading, Thinking, and Writing*. Needham Heights, MA: Allyn and Bacon, 1999.

Obejas, Achy. *Memory Mambo*. Pittsburgh: Cleis Press, 1996.

Obejas, Achy. *We Came All the Way from Cuba So You Could Dress Like This?* Pittsburgh: Cleis Press, 1994.

Pérez, Domino Renee. "Caminando con la Llorona: Traditional and Contemporary Narratives." In *Chicana Traditions: Continuity and Change*, edited by Norma E. Cantú and Olga Nájera Ramírez, 100–113. Champaign: University of Illinois Press, 2002.

Pérez-Torres, Rafael. *Movements in Chicano Poetry: Against Myths, Against Margins*. Cambridge: Cambridge University Press, 1995.

Rebolledo, Tey Diana. *Women Singing in the Snow: A Cultural Analysis of Chicana Literature*. Tucson: University of Arizona Press, 1995.

Ronowicz, Eddie, and Colin Yallop. *English: One Language, Different Cultures*. New York: Cassell, 1999.

Scollon, Ron, and Suzanne Wong Scollon. *Intercultural Communication: A Discourse Approach*. 2nd ed. Oxford: Blackwell, 2001.

Stephens, Thomas M. *Dictionary of Latin American Racial and Ethnic Terminology*. 2nd ed. Gainesville: University Press of Florida, 1999.

Villanueva, Alma Luz. *Weeping Woman: La Llorona and Other Stories*. Tempe, AZ: Bilingual Press, 1994.

War and Conflict

Alvarez, Luis. *The Power of the Zoot: Youth Culture and Resistance during World War II*. Berkeley: University of California Press, 2009.

Balderrama, Francisco E., and Raymund Rodríguez. *Decade of Betrayal: Mexican Repatriation in the 1930s*. Albuquerque: University of New Mexico Press, 2006.

Castillo, Richard Griswold del, and Arnold De León. *North to Aztlán: A History of Mexican Americans in the United States*. New York: Twayne Publishers, 1996.

Eisenhower. John S. D. *So Far from God: The U.S. War with Mexico, 1846–1848*. Norman: University of Oklahoma Press, 2000.

Ferrer, Ada. *Insurgent Cuba: Race, Nation, and Revolution, 1868–1898*. Chapel Hill: University of North Carolina Press, 1999.

Fraizier, Donald S., ed. *The United States and Mexico at War: Nineteenth Century Expansionism and Conflict*. New York: Macmillan Reference USA, 1998.

Griswold Del Castillo, Richard. *The Treaty of Guadalupe Hidalgo: A Legacy of Conflict*. Norman: University of Oklahoma Press, 1992.

Griswold Del Castillo, Richard. *World War II and Mexican American Civil Rights*. Austin: University of Texas Press, 2008.

Hernández, José M. "Cuba in 1898." The World of 1898: The Spanish-American War. Hispanic Division, Library of Congress. http://www.loc.gov/rr/hispanic/1898/hernandez.html.

Keller, Gary D., and Cordelia Candelaria, eds. *The Legacy of the Mexican and Spanish-American Wars: Legal, Literary, and Historical Perspectives*. Tempe, AZ: Bilingual Review Press, 2000.

Lafeber, Walter. *Inevitable Revolutions: The United States in Central America*. New York: W.W. Norton, 1993.

Leonard, Kevin. *The Battle for Los Angeles: Racial Ideology and World War II*. Albuquerque: University of New Mexico Press. 2006.

Long, Jeff. *Duel of Eagles: The Mexican and U.S. Fight for the Alamo*. New York: William Morrow, 1990.

López, Ian Haney. *Racism on Trial: The Chicano Fight for Justice*. Cambridge, MA: Belknap Press of Harvard University Press, 2004.

Mazón, Mauricio. *The Zoot-Suit Riots: The Psychology of Symbolic Annihilation*. Austin: University of Texas Press, 1984.

McWilliams, Carey. *North From Mexico: The Spanish-Speaking People of the United States*. New York: Praeger; 1990.

Pagán, Edwardo Obregón. *Murder at the Sleepy Lagoon: Zoot Suits, Race, and Riot in Wartime L.A.* Chapel Hill: University of North Carolina Press, 2003.

Peiss, Kathy. *Zoot Suit: The Enigmatic Career of an Extreme Style*. Philadelphia: University of Pennsylvania Press, 2011.

Poniatowska, Elena, and David Dorado Romo. *Las Soldaderas: Women of the Mexican Revolution*. El Paso, TX: Cinco Puntos Press, 2006.

Rivas-Rodríguez, Maggie. *Mexican Americans and World War II*. Austin: University of Texas Press, 2005.

Singletary, Otis. *The Mexican War*. New York: Oxford University Press, 1960.

Zinn, Howard. *A People's History of the United States: 1492–Present*. New York: HarperCollins, 2001.

Web Resources

Arlington National Cemetery Web site. Felix Z. Longoria, Private, United States Army. http://www.arlingtoncemetery.net/longoria.htm.

El Boricua
http://www.elboricua.com/index.html

El Cenro de la Raza
http://www.elcentrodelaraza.com/

Cuban Information Archives. Mariel Boatlift Photographs
http://cuban-exile.com/doc_326–350/doc0332.html

Hispanic Association on Corporate Responsibility
http://www.hacr.org/

Hispanic Business
http://www.hispanicbusiness.com/

Hispanic Genealogical Society
http://www.hispanicgs.com/

Hispanic Network Magazine
http://www.hnmagazine.com/

Hispanic Origin. United States Census Bureau
http://www.census.gov/population/hispanic/

The Hispanic Outlook in Higher Education Magazine
http://www.hispanicoutlook.com/about.htm

Hispanic Scholarship Fund
http://www.hsf.net/default.aspx

Inter-University Program for Latino Research
http://www.nd.edu/~iuplr/

Latin American Network Information Center
http://lanic.utexas.edu/

Latina
http://www.latina.com/

Latino
http://www.latinopolicy.org/lp/introduction.html

Latino Museum
http://www.thelatinomuseum.com/about.htm

Latino Organizations/Organizaciones Latinas
http://www.fundsnetservices.com/latorg.htm

Latino Perspectives Magazine
http://latinopm.com/

League of United Latin American Citizens
http://lulac.org/

Library of Congress, Hispanic Reading Room
http://www.loc.gov/rr/hispanic/

Mauricio Gastón Institute for Latino Community Development and Public Policy
http://www.gaston.umb.edu/

Mexican American Writers
http://www.worldlingo.com/ma/enwiki/en/List_of_Mexican_American_writers

MiamiHerald.com, El Mariel Boat and Passenger Records
http://www.miamiherald.com/cgi-bin/mariel/index

MiamiHerald.com and elNuevoHeraldo.com

Museum of Latin American Art
http://www.molaa.com/

National Institute for Latino Policy
http://www.latinopolicy.org/lp/introduction.html

The Network for Operation Pedro Pan
http://www.miamiherald.com/cgi-bin/pedropan/index

Pew Hispanic Center
http://pewhispanic.org/

Saludos
http://www.saludos.com/

Smithsonian Education, Heritage Teaching Resources, Hispanic Heritage
http://www.smithsonianeducation.org/educators/resource_library/hispanic_resources.html

Smithsonian Latino Center
http://latino.si.edu/

Tomas Rivera Policy Institute
http://www.trpi.org/

United States Hispanic Chamber of Commerce
http://ushcc.com/

University of Texas at Arlington Center for Mexican American Studies Oral History Project, *Tejano Voices Interviewees*
http://library.uta.edu/tejanovoices/gallery.jsp

University of Texas at Brownsville and Texas Southmost College, *Los Del Valle* [The Ones from the Valley].
http://www.utb.edu/its/media/ldv/pages/index.aspx.

Urban Latino Magazine
http://www.urbanlatino.com/

U.S. Census Bureau, Hispanic Population of the United States
http://www.census.gov/population/www/socdemo/hispanic/hispanic.html

U.S. Department of Health and Human Services, Office of Minority Health, *Hispanic/Latino Profile*
http://minorityhealth.hhs.gov/templates/browse.aspx?lvl=3&lvlid=31

Index

About the Editors

Gary Y. Okihiro is a professor of international and public affairs at Columbia University. He is the author of *Pineapple Culture: A History of the Tropical and Temperate Zones,* and *Island World: A History of Hawai'i and the United States*, as well as the *Encyclopedia of Japanese American Internment* (Greenwood, 2013).

Guadalupe Compeán is an independent scholar and co-editor of *Voices of the U.S. Latino Experience* (Greenwood, 2008).